Social Movements

Blackwell Readers in Anthropology

As anthropology moves beyond the limits of so-called area studies, there is an increasing need for texts that do the work of synthesizing the literature while challenging more traditional or subdisciplinary approaches to anthropology. This is the object of this exciting new series, *Blackwell Readers in Anthropology*.

Each volume in the series offers seminal readings on a chosen theme and provides the finest, most thought-provoking recent works in the given thematic area. Many of these volumes bring together for the first time a body of literature on a certain topic. The series thus both presents definitive collections and investigates the very ways in which anthropological inquiry has evolved and is evolving.

Social Movements

An Anthropological Reader

Edited by
June Nash

Blackwell Publishing

BLACKWELL PUBLISHING

350 Main Street, Malden, MA 02148-5020, USA
9600 Garsington Road, Oxford OX4 2DQ, UK
550 Swanston Street, Carlton, Victoria 3053, Australia

The right of June Nash to be identified as the Author of the Editorial Material in this Work has been
asserted in accordance with the UK Copyright, Designs, and Patents Act 1988.

First published 2005 by Blackwell Publishing Ltd

4   2008

Library of Congress Cataloging-in-Publication Data

Social movements : an anthropological reader / edited by June Nash.
   p. cm.
Includes bibliographical references and index.
ISBN 978-1-4051-0108-0 (hardcover: alk. paper)—ISBN 978-1-4051-0109-7 (alk. paper)
1. Social movements. I. Nash, June C., 1927— II. Series.

HM881.S627 2005.
303.48′4—dc22

                                                                 2004003994

A catalogue record for this title is available from the British Library.

Set in 10/12.5 pt Sabon
by Kolam Information Services Pvt. Ltd, Pondicherry, India
Printed and bound in Malaysia
by KHL Printing Co Sdn Bhd

The publisher's policy is to use permanent paper from mills that operate a sustainable forestry policy, and which
has been manufactured from pulp processed using acid-free and elementary chlorine-free practices. Furthermore,
the publisher ensures that the text paper and cover board used have met acceptable environmental accreditation
standards.

For further information on
Blackwell Publishing, visit our website:
www.blackwellpublishing.com

Contents

As contemporary social movements network with one another, form coalitions, and
seek to establish claims to constitute part of national and global civil society, new,
hybrid organizational forms emerge. Analyzing the rise of transnational Central
America-wide civil society initiatives in the 1990s (and their decline and reemergence), Marc Edelman suggests that the new prominence of "networks,"
whether as political claims or as linked computers or social movements, exacerbates
a problem with profound methodological, political, ethical, and representational
dimensions that is acknowledged only occasionally in the social movements
literature – the appearance of "fictitious" or "shell" organizations and, more
recently, "dot causes" or internet-based advocacy organizations with minuscule or
indeterminate constituencies.

The concept of a state-sponsored social movement, particularly a right-wing
movement, contradicts assumptions identifying civil society as counter to the state
and of social movements as ideologically left-wing. Katherine Bowie's study of the
"Village Scouts," a state-sponsored social movement created in Thailand in 1971 to
counter the simultaneous growth of communist insurgency and the pro-democracy

Rutherford explores the prehistory of Papuan nationalist appropriations of
Christianity by examining the practices of Biak islanders, who long have
emphasized the inscrutable character of Christian meaning. In the Dutch colonial
period, Biak adventurers presented the words and objects they acquired from the
Protestant mission as proof of their mastery of distant worlds. At the same time,
Biak prophets periodically initiated millennial uprisings by claiming to know the
truth behind the missionaries' foreign words. This makes the case that Biak visions
of divine potency have implications for today's Papuan nationalists, whose
performances make Christianity central to the quest for global recognition and
the transformation of local spaces and selves.

The Sarvodaya Movement, which began as a grassroots development in Sri Lanka
in the 1950s, has become, since the mid-1990s, the major advocate for a peaceful
solution to that country's lengthy ethnic conflict. This chapter examines the
Gandhian and Buddhist sources of Sarvodaya's vision of both peace and the
construction of a civil society. Employing spiritual resources, Sarvodaya has sought
to bring peace by fostering a non-violent grassroots revolution that would change
both the economic and the political structures of the country.

Evoking the issues that global change has wrought on peripheral populations –
deterritorialization caused by land seizure, environmental degradation, forced
migration in search of wage work, contamination of the environment, and
cultural hybridization – the author asserts that far from losing their commitment
to place and culture, identification to place becomes increasingly important as
people are drawn into global circuits. People overcome distance by reasserting
their claims to place with remittances, by recurrent return visits to their
homelands, and by support of rituals in these homelands they have been forced to
leave. She concludes that global issues of deterritorialization, hybridization, and
fragmentation have to be rethought in ethnographic terms, relating this to her
fieldwork in Chiapas, Mexico and Guatemalan Ixcan settlements, where Mayan
colonizers resisted the encroachment of the army on both sides of the Mexico–
Guatemala border.

This analysis contextualizes the social movement in the Isthmus of Tehuantepec,
Oaxaca, that emerged in 1996 in response to the "Megaproject" development

planned by the Mexican government, within contemporaneous protests against neoliberalism in Mexico. Like other post-1968 movements, the social movement against the Megaproject emphasizes identity politics and local autonomy rather than broad-based rights reflecting changes in the decentralized form of the state. Contrary to theoretical expectations, nationalism remains an important organizing ideology for both state and non-state actors in the global age.

identity," a collaborative politics of recognition draws on an expanded cultural idiom of "citizenship" in blocking the government's sale of Bolivia's shrinking public commons to a transnational corporation.

This chapter addresses the issues of HIV/AIDs in southern Africa from the perspective of women who are at risk for HIV infection through their male partners. Focusing on the ongoing patterns of inequality, from the global to the interpersonal, with respect to the treatment and prevention of HIV/AIDS for women, Susser documents one case in which women's long-term efforts from the personal, through the local community and the national government, to the global have contributed to increasing the strategies available to women to protect themselves from HIV infection.

Indigenous women of Roraima State in the Brazilian Amazon have overcome the opposition of male kinsmen and community leaders in organizing social movements, leading to formal associations, unions, and even political parties. Even though women's empowerment through organizational strategies is in some cases supported by regional male indigenous leadership, the Catholic Church, the state administrations and, eventually, by NGOs, problems persist. By unifying their political organization at a supralocal level through the Association for the Development of Indigenous Women of Roraima, they have been able to surmount difficulties that attend their many successes.

Deepa Reddy traces the processes by which women's issues come to be reframed in the context of post-independence agrarian, civil liberties, and other people's movements. This emergent Indian feminism develops a stringent critique of the state, especially through its analysis of custodial rape and dowry-related violence. As religious nationalism became a defining feature of the late twentieth century, however, both in India and elsewhere in the world, feminists also began to distance themselves from their own prior liberalism, fashioning instead a broader, multiculturalist politics. Reddy shows Indian feminist activism to be resolutely focused on the needs of local communities, ever cognizant of the pitfalls of globalization, while also increasingly capable of drawing upon global networks and resources to facilitate grassroots initiatives for social change.

Acknowledgments

The editor and publishers wish to thank the following for permission to use copyright material:

Lynn Stephen, "Gender, Citizenship, and the Politics of Identity," *Latin American Perspectives* Issue 121, 28(6): 54–69. Reprinted by permission of the author and publisher.

Sharryn Kasmir, "Activism and Class Identity: The Saturn Auto Factory Case." Printed for the first time in this volume with permission of the author.

David B. Edwards, "Print Islam: Media and Religious Revolution in Afghanistan," *Anthropological Quarterly* 68(3): 171–84, 1995. Reprinted by permission of the publisher.

Renée Sylvain, "'Land, Water, and Truth': San Identity and Global Indigenism," *American Anthropologist* 10(4): 1074–85, 2002. Reprinted by permission of the publisher.

June Nash, "Globalization and the Cultivation of Peripheral Vision," *Anthropology Today* 17(4): 5–20. Reprinted by permission of Blackwell Publishing and the author.

Ligia T. Simonian, "Political Organization among Indigenous Women of the Brazilian State of Roraima: Constraints and Prospects" (Portuguese version), in *Mulheres da floresta amazônica: entre o trabalho e a cultura*, Belém: NAEA/UFPA, 2001, pp. 71–101.

Every effort has been made to trace copyright holders and to obtain their permission for the use of copyright material. The authors and publishers will gladly receive any information enabling them to rectify any error or omission in subsequent editions.

Notes on Contributors

Robert Albro is currently visiting Professor of Anthropology and International Affairs at George Washington University, Washington, D.C., as well as a fellow at the Carnegie Council on Ethics and International Affairs. He received his Ph.D. in sociocultural anthropology from the University of Chicago in 1999, and has worked for over ten years on the characteristics of popular identity, the emergence of new social subjects, and the ongoing effects of neoliberal democratization in Bolivia and in Latin America.

George D. Bond is a Professor of Religion at Northwestern University, Evanston, Illinois. His research focuses on Theravada Buddhism in South and Southeast Asia and he did fieldwork in Sri Lanka in 2002 while writing this article. He is the author of several books on Buddhism, including *The Word of the Buddha* (1980) and *The Buddhist Revival in Sri Lanka* (1988), and a forthcoming book on the Sarvodaya Movement.

Katherine A. Bowie (Ph.D., University of Chicago, 1988) is Professor of Anthropology and Director of the Center for Southeast Asian Studies at the University of Wisconsin-Madison. She first traveled to Thailand in 1974 where she initially worked as a freelance journalist. Interested in agrarian politics, she has lived a total of over eight years in Thailand. Her publications include *Voices from the Thai Countryside: The Necklace and Other Short Stories of Samruam Singh* (1991; revised edition 1998) and *Ritual of National Loyalty: An Anthropology of the State and the Village Scout Movement in Thailand* (1997).

Molly Doane is Assistant Professor at Marquette University. She received her Ph.D. from the Graduate Center, City University of New York in 2001. Her publications include "A Distant Jaguar: The Civil Society Project in Chimalapas," *Critique of Anthropology* 21(4), 2001. She is currently working on a book based on her research in Chimalapas, Oaxaca, related to the Plan Puebla-Panama and the mobilization of peasants to retain their lands.

Marc Edelman (B.A. and Ph.D., Columbia University) is Professor of Anthropology at Hunter College and the Graduate Center of the City University of New York. He has done research on agrarian history, rural development, social movements, and the nineteenth- and twentieth-century roots of nationalism and contemporary politics in Latin America. In recent years he has been involved in research on transnational peasant and small-farmer networks in Latin America, North America, and Europe. His books include *The Logic of the Latifundio* (1992), *Peasants Against Globalization* (1999), and a forthcoming anthology on the anthropology of development (Blackwell). Edelman has written two autobiographical reflections on his work as an anthropologist: "Devil, Not-Quite-White, Rootless Cosmopolitan: *Tsuris* in Latin America, the Bronx, and the USSR" (in Carolyn Ellis and Arthur P. Bochner, eds., *Composing Ethnography: Alternative Forms of Qualitative Writing*, 1996) and "De la fría Nueva York al cálido Guanacaste" (in Marc Edelman, Fabrice Lehoucq, Iván Molina, and Steven Palmer, eds., *Ciencia social en Costa Rica: experiencias de vida e investigación*, 1998).

David B. Edwards is Professor of Anthropology at Williams College and Director of the Williams Afghan Media Project. He is also the author of *Before Taliban: Genealogies of the Afghan Jihad* (2002) and *Heroes of the Age: Moral Fault Lines on the Afghan Frontier* (1996).

Kimberly M. Grimes teaches at the University of Delaware in Georgetown and is the Executive Director of Made By Hand International Cooperative, a fair trade organization in Delaware. She is the author of *Crossing Borders: Changing Social Identities in Southern Mexico* (1998) and *Handbook for Fair Trade Retailing* (forthcoming) and coeditor of *Artisans and Cooperatives: Developing Alternative Trade for the Global Economy* (2000). Her research in communities with much outmigration led her to examine sustainable alternatives for impoverished people who do not wish to leave their local communities. She also serves as a Board of Director for the Fair Trade Resource Network, an international organization which educates the public on current trade issues and policies and alternative equitable solutions.

Sharryn Kasmir is Associate Professor of Anthropology at Hofstra University. She researches and writes on issues of class, nationalism, and post-Fordism in the United States and the Basque Region of Spain. She is the author of *The Myth of Mondragón: Cooperatives, Politics and Working-Class Life in a Basque Town* (1996). Currently she is writing a monograph on the Tennessee-based Saturn Automobile Corporation.

Max Kirsch (Ph.D. City University of New York, 1989) is UNESCO Chair in Human and Cultural Rights and Director of the Ph.D. Program in Comparative Studies: The Public Intellectuals Program at Florida Atlantic University. His works include *In the Wake of the Giant: Multinational Restructuring and Uneven Development in a New England Community* (1998) and *Queer Theory and Social Change* (2001). His current research concerns community, labor, and industry in the Florida Everglades.

June Nash is Distinguished Professor Emerita, City University of New York. She has carried out research on semi-subsistence cultivators in Chiapas, with the publication of *In the Eyes of the Ancestors: Belief and Behavior in a Mayan Community* (1970); and on the impact of industrial extraction in Bolivia with *We Eat the Mines and the Mines Eat Us* (new edition, 1993), and *I Spent My Life in the Mines* (1992). She has written essays on feminist movements in Latin America and globalization, publishing three anthologies: *Sex and Class in Latin America*, *Women and Change in Latin America* (coedited with Helen Safa, new edition, 1980), and *Women, Men, and the International Division of Labor* (with M. Patricia Fernández-Kelly, 1983). She has also published on artisan production and the fair trade movement, editing *Crafts in the World Market, Artisan Production in State Formation* (1983), and on cooperatives and collectives, editing the anthology *Popular Participation in Change* (with Jorge Dandler and Nicholas Hopkins, 1976). She is currently researching and writing on human rights and militarization. Her return to research with Myas of Chiapas from 1990 to 2001 resulted in the publication *Mayan Visions: The Quest for Autonomy in an Age of Globalization* (2001).

Deepa S. Reddy is Assistant Professor of Anthropology and Convener of the Women's Studies Program at the University of Houston-Clear Lake. She is the author of *"Hindutva" in the Culture of Ethnicism* (forthcoming), an analysis of Hindu religious nationalism as it is interpreted, inflected, and produced in various activist sites, including those of the Indian women's movement. Her current research interests range from the internationalization/glob-alization of "caste" though the discourses of race and human rights, to the role of genetic research in reconstituting cultural identity among Indian-Americans. She has also written an autoethnographic essay on affect in Indian kinship entitled "Kousi oda ponnu (Kousi's Daughter)" (in James Faubion, ed., *The Ethics of Kinship: Ethnographic Inquiries*, 2001).

Danilyn Rutherford is Assistant Professor of Anthropology at the University of Chicago and author of *Raiding the Land of the Foreigners: The Limits of the Nation on an Indonesian Frontier* (2003).

Ligia T. L. Simonian received her Ph.D. in anthropology at City University of New York in 1993. In addition to teaching and advising Master's and doctoral students, she conducts research at the Nucleus for Higher Amazonian Studies (NAEA), affiliated with the Federal University of Pará (UFPA), where she has a tenured position. She has published on women and violence, women in general, work relations and development, and on women and culture, in addition to other research areas. Her book *Mulheres da floresta amazônica: entre o trabalho e a cultura* was published in 2001. In 2002 she organized an International Conference on *Women, Gender and Development on the Pan-Amazon*, and is editing the proceedings of this event which are scheduled to be published in 2004. She also has acted as consultant to indigenous peoples and extractivist communities from the Brazilian Amazon, in regard to land, gender, and development issues.

Lynn Stephen is professor and chair of the Department of Anthropology at the University of Oregon. She is the author of *Zapotec Women* (1991), *Hear My Testimony: María Teresa Tula, Human Rights Activist of El Salvador* (1994), *Women and Social Movements in Latin America: Power From Below* (1997), and *Zapata Lives!: Histories and Cultural Politics in Southern Mexico* (2002). She is the coeditor, with James Dow, of *Class, Politics, and Popular Religion in Mexico and Central America* (1990), and with Matt Gutmann, Felix Matos Rodríguez, and Pat Zavella of *Perspectives on Las Américas: A Reader in Culture, History, and Representation* (Blackwell, 2003). Her research focuses on gender, ethnicity, political economy, social movements, migration, human rights, and nationalism in Latin America. Her current project explores how two populations of indigenous Mexican migrants are using their multilayered identities and binational labor and living experiences to organize for economic and political change.

Ida Susser is Professor of Anthropology at Hunter College and a member of the Doctoral Faculty in Anthropology at the Graduate Center of the City University of New York. Her publications include *Norman Street: Poverty and Politics in an Urban Neighborhood* (1982) and numerous articles, and she has guest-edited special issues of *Medical Anthropology Quarterly*; the *Journal of Women and Health* and *Critique of Anthropology*. Her most recent research has focused on a women's cooperative in a squatter settlement in South Africa, HIV prevention among rural and township women in South Africa, and HIV prevention in rural Puerto Rico.

Renée Sylvain is a Canadian anthropologist teaching at the University of Guelph, Ontario, Canada. She received her Ph.D. from the University of Toronto in 1999. Her early research was conducted among the San (Bushmen) who work on the white-owned farms in the Omaheke Region of Namibia and focused on gender, race, and class inequalities. Her recent work, largely carried out on resettlement camps and in squatters' villages, focuses on San tourism, indigenous identity politics, and human rights in southern Africa. Her areas of specialization also include hunter-gather studies, anthropological theory, and the history of anthropology. She has worked closely with the Working Group of Indigenous Minorities in Southern Africa, and with the Omaheke San Trust. Her recent work has been published in *Anthropologica*, the *Journal of Southern African Studies*, *Cultural Survival*, and *American Anthropologist*.

James Toth has spent over twelve years in the Middle East, primarily in Egypt, working as a student, teacher, manager, and scholar. His initial study of Egyptian migrant farmworkers appeared in his *Rural Labor Movements in Egypt and Their Impact on the State, 1961–1992* (1999). His research shifted, however, once these laborers, out of necessity, relocated to Egypt's cities and became embroiled in the growing Islamic movement. From 1994 to 2000 he taught anthropology at the American University in Cairo. Currently he is on the faculty of the Sociology–Anthropology Department at Northeastern University in Boston.

Introduction: Social Movements and Global Processes

June Nash

Globalization processes related to the expansion and integration of capitalist invest-ments, production, and markets in new areas have generated social movements of people mobilizing to protect their lands, their cultural identities, and their auton-omy. At the same time, improved communication systems and the development of a global civil society acting through grassroots movements and United Nations and nongovernmental organizations (NGOs) are promoting a growing awareness of inequities in the distribution of wealth and of misfortune related to human rights violations. News of political imprisonment and of impoverishment is disseminated in global circuits alongside the promotion of consumer goods and luxury products.

Populations that feel most threatened by these changes respond by seeking retri-bution or promoting reintegration in new global alignments. There is a resurgence of fundamentalist religious groups seeking redemption, through militant action, against those who promote what they see as godlessness. Summit meetings of global financial and commercial institutions are accompanied by protest demonstrations staged by a motley array of groups from all over the world. In the wake of these movements we find counter-movements designed to repress protest in the interest of ensuring the power of global elites. The worldwide diffusion of arms through transnational networks that promote, and are promoted by, paramilitary and terror-ist groups adds an increasingly lethal dimension to global processes. These networks often recruit youth who are alienated from their communities and families, unable to find employment, and no longer able to claim the prerogatives of males in a world where production is in the hands of an increasingly feminized workforce.

Social movements in a global ecumene[1] show themselves in a diversity of cultural ways as new social actors invent novel expressions for their causes. They necessarily develop "transnational activist networks" (Edelman 2001) that cast the goals of

movements in ever more universal terms. Issues of social justice are more frequently
voiced in global arenas today than in decades preceding global integration. In the
1970s major development institutions such as the World Bank and the International
Monetary Fund (IMF) were in denial about the threats of global trade and direct
foreign investment overseas, resulting in the "deindustrialization" of core industrial
regions and double-digit unemployment. In the 1980s the annual reports of the
World Bank still failed to register the negative effects of their policies, even when
the IMF conditions for debt payments forced whole nations into bankruptcy.

But after the 1997/8 crisis in financial markets this changed. George Stiglitz,
President of the World Bank, introduced his millennial report with the statement,
"The experience of the past year has underscored how financial volatility can
increase poverty significantly in the short to medium term," and concluded that
"in order to maximize the positive effects of growth that can come with openness,
the international community must find ways to reduce the frequency and severity of
economic crises" (Stiglitz 2000). The burden imposed by recurrent crises is borne by
working people, who are often required to work harder; migrate to find jobs far
from home, thus abandoning family and community; accept wage cuts; and/or learn
new skills. This is the "flexibility" of labor markets in developing countries that
Stiglitz, summarizing the lessons to be learned from the 1997–8 crisis in Thailand,
Indonesia, and Malaysia (2000:xi), indicated had helped absorb the shocks. The
turn away from neoliberal rhetoric advocating free and untrammeled markets can
also be seen in the Nobel Prize selection in 2002 of Amartya Sen, an economist
known for his work on the moral implications of global development.

As yet, regulation of global capital investment practices is lacking, and the
"openness" (the World Bank's code word for neoliberal free markets) in commodity
markets required of developing countries is not imposed on Western powers. The
conditions set for "recovery" by the IMF that precipitated political crises in Southeast Asia in 1997–8 devastated Argentina at the turn of the millennium, although the
country was considered the best pupil of the IMF. Yet the lesson of each crisis, that
recovery cannot be achieved internally so long as anti-inflationary financial policies
and "openness" are the unique goals, did not lead to changes in the policies of global
institutions. The United States and Europe can flout free trade and debt limits
without penalties. The fact that their governments persist in dumping their subsidized crops in Third World countries, underselling crops raised by subsistence
farmers, precipitated the end of negotiations at the 2003 Cancun World Trade
Organization summit.

Those who advocate a "moral economy" will only succeed with the massive
mobilizations of the people who now suffer from unconditional free-trade policies.
These are the workers and peasants, the small-scale entrepreneurs, and the professionals, who are forced to bear the "external shocks" of a global system in crisis.
They embody the breakdown in education and health services, both as clients and
providers of diminished public welfare provisions; the generation they produce has
dim prospects for survival or status in a world that requires high technical and
communicative skills. Even as their visions of a better future within the global
system as it is now structured recede, they are the ones who signal "Enough!"

Within the past half-century notions of human rights, environmental conservation, and pluricultural autonomy developed along with and in response to the changes brought about by global integration. Anthropologists have been documenting the impact of global integration and subsistence insecurity for decades (Nash 1994). The difference in the post-millennium period lies in the tripling of the world population in the past half-century and the depletion of unutilized territories and resources. The "flexibility" that Stiglitz refers to is based on the reverse flow of workers from urban to rural areas and from formal to informal employment when urban and industrial employment collapsed in 1997/8.[2]

The locus of working-class struggle in the workplace that emerged with industrial capitalism in the nineteenth century now takes place elsewhere. Shopping mall boycotts, protests against neoliberal policies of the World Trade Organization at summit meeting headquarters, and highway blockades by small-scale commodity producers of Third World countries have become symbolic grounds for protest by the dispossessed and impoverished. Just as the global production and distribution sites demand maximum flexibility in their organizational charts, so do the social movements that respond to them require flexibility in their strategies and agendas. Antonio Gramsci and Rosa Luxemburg, who looked beyond the vanguard of industrial workers favored by Karl Marx or Friedrich Engels, are more important reference points in current social movements. Luxemburg's revival came with feminist scholarship and the recognition of the subsistence sector or "non-capitalist sector" in providing a reserve market for exporting surplus value generated in the industrialized sector (Bennholdt-Thomsen 1981). Bakunin's (1848, 1873) advocacy of multi-ethnic rights that caused him to break with rank-and-file Communists in the nineteenth century draws praise from activists in anti-global protests today. Indeed, just as the dissidents led by these advocates of grassroots and ethnically discriminated groups in earlier revolts were branded anarchists, so are these new cohorts of resistance, protest, and transformative change. With the acceleration of capitalist penetration in today's global markets and the growing threat to the survival of the subsistence sector, we can appreciate other contributions of the non-capitalist sector that were taken for granted. These are the reproduction of the labor force made available at low wages to the capitalist sector, and the care for the aging population once addressed with social security provisions of nation-states and now rejected by neoliberal regimes (Nash 1990, 1994).[3]

In Mexico, Zapatistas tapped the new energy erupting in the countryside of the states of Oaxaca, Chiapas, and Guerrero during and after the celebration of Five Hundred Years of Resistance to the Conquest and Colonization. I learned this when I participated in the national and international conventions following the 1994 uprising. Italian and French socialists, and Spanish anarchists still engaged in their opposition to Spanish central authority, rubbed shoulders with indigenous peoples from Canada and the United States in the Lacandón rainforest. Basques, who are still engaged in their opposition to the Spanish state, were helping the Zapatista support groups to organize peace brigades to the Lacandón rainforest throughout the period of counterinsurgency warfare in the years following the military invasion of the Lacandón.

Zapatistas also understood the futility of old-style guerrilla action. Rather than yield to the cohort of student activists who joined them in the Lacandón rainforest in the 1980s, they persisted in using indigenous strategies that had maintained resistance to assimilation for over five hundred years. In their uprising on New Year's Eve 1994, some of them carried wooden rifles and fought alongside their comrades who had acquired high-powered automatic rifles from narcotic "control" forces operating along Mexico's southern border. Whenever their "army" went on display during their national and international demonstrations, the women and children carried hand-fashioned wooden rifles that dramatized their determination in the face of the heavily armed government troops occupying their communities.

In their departure from the typical behavior of the revolutionary left, Zapatistas symbolize the changed global environment. For them, weapons are an accessory, not the means, to gain power. Their symbolic armaments underline the weakness of their arms at the same time as showing the strength of their determination. The goals of their struggle also differ from traditional rebellions; they do not seek to take over power, but to ensure the democratic participation of all citizens in their own government. The enthusiasm with which this message was received by large sectors of Mexican civil society and people from all over the globe resonates with a formative global civil society.

My main preoccupation in organizing this anthology is to document, through case studies of social movements, their ongoing task of building the institutional networks needed to transform the policies required to ensure social justice in the globalization process. Activists in this agenda are recruited from the discontented but not disconnected feminists, indigenes, cultivators, working class, and petty entrepreneurs. Their weapons are provided by intellectuals and creative artists who are generating a new vocabulary for engaging with, documenting, and analyzing such movements. Avoiding political parties that are considered to be corrupted or co-opted, they find common ground in civil-society mobilizations of morally committed pacifist, leftist political, and religious groups. These are related to central values phrased as human rights, environmental conservation, public as well as personal autonomy, and justice. The meanings assigned to these values are spelled out, in universalizing as well as local contexts, below.

Human Rights

When the United Nations first promoted the Declaration of Human Rights in 1948, the American Anthropological Association rejected the document on the score that it violated the principle of cultural relativity as it lacked input from member nations that would address distinct understandings as to what was universally acceptable as a code of human rights. Since then the civil rights movement in the United States has begun to establish certain inalienable rights of race and gender groups that were excluded from civil society. For the second time in human history, the World Court in Brussels is seeking to determine whether a leader of a nation, Slobodan Milošović, committed acts of genocide against Bosnian and Kosovan Muslims. Another historic advance took place on February 8, 2003 when the African Women's Congress resolved to end genital mutilation in the many nations of Africa where it is still practiced, and the US Immigration Service is now trying to determine whether girls seeking asylum from countries with such practices are indeed victims of human rights violations. The decisions made in these contexts will provide a matrix of precedents with which to define justice and rights in a global context.

Anthropological case studies on multicultural understandings of human rights are beginning to expand the meanings associated with the Western concept. Kay Warren (1993) and Carol Nagengast (1994) are among those who examined the increasing incidence of violence and terror in cross-cultural contexts during the 1980s and 1990s. These studies attune us to cultural and historical differences in the manipulation of state force and how it is countered by those engaged in civil wars. We can see this in the case of Mayan populations divided by the border between Guatemala and Mexico who are engaged in a civil war to change their relations with the state. While the Guatemalan army has killed over 200,000 Indians in their 30-year war, those killed in Mexico number only in the thousands. Structural differences related to the demographic balance of Indians to the *ladino*, or non-Indian, population in each country affect the degree of racism expressed in intercultural relations. The *ladinos'* fear of Indians in Guatemala, where they constitute a majority, heightens the tendency to ethnocidal attacks with any threat to the status quo. The degree to which racial violence is expressed is also related to the greater democracy in Mexico, and the more effective mobilization of civil society in defense of indigenous people (Nash, this volume).

The notion of human rights as addressed by human rights workers throughout the globe includes more than formal political rights. It now extends to the right to adequate nutrition, health care, and the exercise of cultural prerogatives of distinct ethnic groups. For example, in Comitán, Chiapas, the human rights commission investigated a hospital where high percentages of infant mortality suggested a pattern of violation in February, 2003. Investigators concluded that the problem lay in insufficient personnel and funding owing to the military budgetary commitments of the Mexican government in the unresolved "ethnic" conflict in that state. Those whose rights are under attack may have a distinct conception of what the premises for human rights consist of from that of the West, as Christine Kovic's study of a Chiapas Mayan indigenous community in exile reveals. Unlike those in the West, they see rights as reciprocal obligations that must be fulfilled on each side (Kovic 1997). Thus human rights acquire broadened and enriched understandings as more diverse populations are embraced within their orbit.

Environmental Conservation

At the turn of the third millennium the green movements in Europe and the United States have promoted strong advocacy groups for sustainable development programs that measure progress in relation to advances in human welfare. Indigenous Americans are becoming recognized as key protagonists of conservation. Their mobilizations during the 1992 celebration of Five Hundred Years of Resistance promoted an awareness of their commitment to the land and their relationship to it. This led to the 1992 global forum in Rio de Janeiro, where indigenous peoples played a prominent role along with supporters of their programs for sustainable practices of cultivation and extraction. Their distinctive voices are remarkable for the poetry of their expression and the message it conveys of the need for balance in the cosmos and at home. Since then, indigenous women have emerged in national and hemispheric congresses as central protagonists defining the values of their people. At the Beijing Women's Tribunal in 1995 indigenous women defined their relation to global change in these terms: "The Earth is our Mother. From her we get our life, and our ability to live. It is our responsibility to care for our Mother and in caring for our Mother, we care for ourselves. Women, all females, are manifestations of Mother Earth in human form" (cited in Vinding 1998).

Comparative studies of the tropical rainforests bring out remarkably similar trends in development programs and their critics in widely separated regions. Ronald Nigh and Nemesio J. Rodriguez (1995) show the power of comparative analysis of rainforests in the Lacandón in Chiapas and the Amazon in Brazil and Colombia. In both areas, development projects based on planning from above that did not take into account the concerns of indigenous communities have contributed to, rather than alleviated, the devastation of the environment. The programs claiming to restore the forests often resulted in clearing huge areas of variegated tropical forests, replacing them with fast-growing varieties that used quantities of ground water, and destroying precious medicinal trees in the process.

State violence and paramilitary attacks often accompany the implementation of large-scale projects. This was particularly marked in the 1980s in Brazil when the forced movement of indigenous communities and the burning of large areas of the rainforest opened up Amazonia to cattle breeders. They were followed by oil explorers and gold-mining and forestry enterprises that lured men from their communities. Ligia Simonian's chapter in this volume addresses the ways in which women left behind in communities from which men are forced to migrate are organizing collective projects to maintain their families in desperate economic situations. As the political climate changed, a more enlightened state policy acknowledged the need for development programs to consider the deleterious effects on human populations, as well as the fauna and flora.[4]

Along with the invasions of such predators into the rainforest are military and paramilitary forces bent on quelling the protests and rebellions. In the Colombian rainforests indigenous leaders declared in 1996 that "the guerrillas, military, and paramilitaries are killing all of us" (Jackson 2002). As a result of the growing unity among indigenous communities, the government signed two decrees, one establishing a human rights commission and the other a national commission of lands (established on August 8, 1996). But while government policies speak the language of pluralistic national identity, its practice remains vague and generalized (Jackson 2002).

Jean Jackson illustrates the changing discourse as indigenous people criticize Western practices through evoking the law of ancestors, quoting the spiritual leader of the Colombian rainforest, Kancha Vavinquma, who hails from a sacred site in the Sierra Nevada:

> Oil explorations tap the lifeblood of the land. Mother Earth is given by the Eternal Father. Thus oil explorations gives food to every living being, but to not eat too much, because then everything will be finished; to take care of our environment and not maltreat it. For us it is forbidden to kill with a knife, machete, or bullet; our arms are thought and words, our power is wisdom; we prefer death before seeing our sacred elders profaned.

Indigenous people of Colombia who are turning to their traditional leaders as they reject the agents of government raise new questions as to who are the legitimate leaders and who has the rights to the land (Jackson 2002).

Autonomy

The desire for autonomy, or self-governance in accord with their own cultural values, has been central to indigenous societies throughout the colonial and independence periods. The increase in violence attendant upon the invasion of capitalist enterprises in new territories has promoted an awareness among many indigenous populations of the need for control over their lives and territories for their very survival. As women enter into struggles to dismantle the structures of domination, they become acutely aware of their own discrimination as women within their communities and families. Their drive for autonomy often takes the form of gaining control over their bodies in reproductive issues, sexuality, and obtaining mobility and representation in public spheres. As women gain awareness in feminist movements of the way in which their history, creativity, and mental and physical aspirations are suppressed or co-opted in patriarchal society, they are forging the networks whereby they can regain status as independent adults. Women are seeking autonomy not only in their community and region, but also in the home, where they seek relief from patriarchal oppression. This is the demand of the Namibian women as they confront the scourge of AIDs (Susser, this volume), and it is a recurring theme among women of Mexico (Stephen, this volume).

A similar development process is occurring among ethnically different and indigenous people as they assert the right to live their own lives in accordance with their culturally constituted values. In the past, they were able to retain some control over their lives owing to their remoteness from the centers of modernity. The desire for the oil, precious metals, and biogenetic DNA of people, plants, and animals in their territories threatens whatever resource base they retained that allowed them to exercise autonomy. In their present quest for autonomy within the nations in which they reside they seek not the autonomy limited to local community that was part of the colonial accommodation, but regional self-government in areas where they constitute a majority with direct representation in national arenas. This is seen as a means to subvert the corruption of native intermediaries called *caciques* and retain self-rule through consensual governance.

Justice

Justice embraces the many aspects of what revolutionaries of the eighteenth and nineteenth centuries referred to as equality. The class struggle has not been abandoned as an arena of conflict and mobilization for change,[5] so much as it has become encapsulated in multi-stranded institutions that are indirectly related to the accumulation of and power over capital. The invisibility of women's labor in the domestic arena that enabled men to enter public life properly clothed, fed, and sexually maintained in earlier decades (Smith 1987) now becomes part of global assembly lines where women produce and dispense at extremely low prices the goods and services that circulate in international circuits. Their precarious niche in the labor market was, until recently, hardly recognized by trade unions. Lacking entry into national power circuits that, until recently, favored male union leaders, women found that their wage demands and strikes were either ignored or reinserted as paternalistic benefits responding to the dependency status of women in family units. Some breakthroughs have occurred, as in the case of South Korean factory women who achieved labor victories not only for themselves, but for workers throughout the country in the late 1980s, and in Nicaragua, where women in garment-assembly factories sustained a strike in their shops for several weeks.

The encapsulation of labor's struggles in multi-stranded organizations has diverted attention from the fact that the central conflict between the producers of surplus value created in production and those who expropriate and determine its function in society still exists. As a result of labor struggles in the first half of the nineteenth century, employees at every level of the labor hierarchy gained entitlements through government intervention in health and retirement provisions. These publicly based welfare provisions are now threatened by neoliberal policies that dominate global markets, threatening even well-established social democracies of Europe. If capitalist class interests prevail in world markets, there may well be a return to the direct confrontations that characterized labor struggles until the early decades of the twentieth century.

Among the new forms of labor struggles are those seeking fair-market practices in both regional and global markets. The movement for fair trade includes justice on both sides: producers are committed to allowing inspections and certification guaranteeing an organic product of quality with the added value that it take into account environmentally sound practices. Consumers, for their part, are responsible for paying a just price as "citizens of conscience." The movement includes five million people integrated in agricultural cooperatives in eighteen countries with $64 billion sales a year.[6]

The marketplace has itself become the site of labor demonstrations, with student and middle-class protests against sweatshop labor spreading onto the malls and the sales outlets of Gap, Nike, and other internationally known brands. College students and community activists join the movement promoted by progressive unions such as UNITE, and the AFL/CIO textile workers' union. By capturing an audience of potential consumers at the very moment when they are about to express their power of consumption, UNITE has been able to succeed in major strikes for organizing shops in the United States (Nash 1998).

These steps toward developing a moral and juridical framework for global society through human rights commissions, environmental conservation, personal and political autonomy, fair labor, and trade associations are fostered in the context of social movements. The institutional bases for human rights, for a sustainable economy, and for the exercise of autonomy are developing within the framework of the United Nations and in the daily practice of a regenerated civil society. The labor movement may be losing its parochial and gender-biased base with the waning of national state commitments to fair labor laws, but it is gaining strength in these extended networks. Some of the most vigorous labor action occurs in the newly industrialized states, and these organizers often turn to human rights and United Nations organizations such as the ILO (International Labor Organization) for legal and advisory support.

The construction of the spaces for representation changes with each cohort of claimants. Some of these movements were initiated in advanced industrialized countries, such as the women's movement and the civil rights movements of the 1960s, ultimately spreading throughout Latin America and Asia where they acquired new directions among unexpected cohorts. The civil rights movement addressing ethnic and racial discrimination undoubtedly grew out of anti-colonial movements instigated by Gandhi in India and influencing a new generation of nonviolent protest. The reverberations in the American South have found support for long-delayed reforms throughout the North, eventually igniting movements to overcome segregation in Africa and other formerly colonized states. Civil-society mobilizations against corruption in despotic Asian societies such as Indonesia and the Philippines expanded the range and variety of people's mobilizations. Inequities in the labor scene are now addressed through free-trade associations as well as the revitalized trade union movement. Labor unions seek covenants affirming human rights and democratic negotiations in regional trade pacts such as NAFTA (the North American Free Trade Agreement), and the European Community, as well as in bilateral agreements such as that between the United States and China. Small businesses seek entry into trade negotiations along with producer cooperatives that object to unilateral control exercised by multinational corporations. Religious sodalities are becoming increasingly involved in economic discussions as they witness the growing gap correlated with globalization.

I shall now review the models developed for the study of social movements, and then summarize current trends in globalization as they affect social movements.

Theory and Practice in Social Movements

Theoretical models for the study of social movements derived from nineteenth- and twentieth-century political economists are being modified in response to new directions in global processes. The focus on exclusively economic issues in specific sites of labor is diverted with the emergence of civil rights, feminist, and "post-industrialist" identities. Identity-focused and multi-sited case studies responding to the volatile political and economic activism in the 1960s and 1970s demonstrated the need for multiplex analyses of contemporary movements.

The "new social movements" theorists who began to address these issues, such as Alain Touraine (1971), Ernesto Laclau and Chantal Mouffe (1985), and Alberto Melucci (1989) incorporated cultural issues as central to the motivating logic of society. Their rejection of base/superstructure dichotomy was presaged in the challenge made by feminist scholars who rejected Cartesian dichotomies of nature/culture and female/male that precluded agency and intellect in the feminine spheres, and by cultural studies spearheaded by Raymond Williams. By drawing attention to the ethnic, gender, and racial composition of movements that were suppressed by those that gave priority to class position, new social movements theorists opened the stage of history to many new actors. The faceless masses and the suppression of difference in the interest of promoting unity were no longer viable strategies.[7] The new leaders embodied the muted demands of diverse groups as women, ethnic, and religious groups contested repressive conditions. In the course of their struggles, they expanded the cultural potential for symbolizing their objectives and embodying their concerns.[8]

The advances made by proponents of what is sometimes associated with postmodernist theory tapped the bodily and psychic energies of the people as they were affected by change. However, the tendency to emphasize the individual as actor and protagonist of social change in "new" social movements theory often minimized the collective base that inspires many such movements. The resurgence of ethnic identification among populations marginalized in the course of conquest challenged the indigenist ideologies shaped by dominant elites of mixed origins, and brought to the fore collective practices and aspirations that had long been buried.

Indigenism is the ideological ground in which ethnic elites set the parameters for interethnic discourse. Mexican anthropologists engaged in a critical view of the prevalent indigenist ideology as a unilineal lens that extolled the past glories of indigenous civilizations while denying them a position in contemporary society (Warman et al. 1970). As Brazilian anthropologist Alcida Rita Ramos (1998:6) defines it, indigenism is the mirror by which the *mestizos* of the Western hemisphere see themselves in relation to the Indian, just as Orientalism serves the Western European observer. It is a distortion for both ethnic groups, one that exaggerates an essential core of elements while disregarding other characteristics. The claims for autonomy and the right to cultural diversity pose the ultimate challenge to nations that conceptualize their populations as homogeneous, or at least en route toward expunging difference. The governments of both Mexico and Brazil promoted indigenist ideologies that praised cultural diversity even as they promoted policies that contributed to the extinction of cultural difference.

Kay Warren's study (1998) of the Guatemalan pan-Mayan movement is unusual in placing the cultural revindication of Mayan traditions in the context of an intellectual formation. This challenges the tendency to relate ethnicity to subordination and marginalization, repeating the transgressions of the conquerors that destroyed manifestations of the high civilizations that they invaded and sought to conquer. We are also reminded of these still vital cultural expressions in the recuperation of a literature carried in the memory and sometimes transcribed by early Catholic missionaries (Tedlock 1984, 1993). These resources for social mobilizations are a storehouse for future generations.

The conjugated bases for social movements deriving from race, gender, and ethnicity have been explored in studies by feminist anthropologists and sociologists. Transformative change in society must combat the barriers based on race, class, and gender in order to achieve success precisely because of the reinforcement of hierarchy that occurs in each category (Mullings 1997). This conjugation is clarified in the global arena when the distractions of parochial cultural elements are removed and repression prevails in its crudest forms.

The tendency toward using reductionist categories in caricaturing other people is often countered by the subordinate group uniting under one banner bearing what was the term of opprobrium. I have heard indigenous people of Guatemala argue that the term *Indio*, or Indian, should be accepted as their own designation since it reflects their history of opposition to the dominant *ladino*. Women have often found common cause with others related to their role as mothers. Ironically, postmodern deconstructive critiques tend to denounce this kind of discourse as "essentialist," whether used by dominant sectors in denigrating the ethnic sectors they wish to exploit or by activists seeking to unite with other indigenous peoples in self-defense. Yet essentializing is an aspect of all intellectual processes. Michael Herzfeld (1997:36, cited in Ramos 1998) recognizes how essentializing gives shape "to ideas and impressions as they collide with skepticism." It is particularly prevalent among new cohorts of activists in the early stages of mobilization, as they use what some consider to be essentializing language to unite distinct groups around common elements of group consciousness. These constructed emblems of identity enable them to counter negative stereotypes used to denigrate the excluded groups as they seek dignity and respect in the world from which they feel excluded. Lynn Stephen addresses these concerns in her chapter about the CO-MADRES, exiled women who found common cause during the 30-year civil war in Guatemala, and the Zapatista women, who combine their commitment to the rebellion against public subordination with patriarchal domination at home.

Touraine (1988) demonstrated the emergence of ever present but unsuspected premises for political expression in his study of the May 1968 riots in Paris and the Polish solidarity movement. His analysis obviously impressed "Marcos," the *subcomandante* of the Zapatista rebellion, who invited him to the 1996 International Convention Against Neoliberalism and for Humanity in the Lacandón rainforest. In an interview with a reporter for *La Jornada* after the event, Touraine summed up what he saw as the global process in the making:

> Now it is a question of going from revolutionary to something that does not have a name yet, but that ties democracy to the defense of cultural rights, the capacity of communication to the defense of diversity. The union of identity is that of specificity with the universal. I believe that international opinion appreciates a great deal of what Indian communities of Chiapas are, as a people located in a particular space, a time, a culture, who speak a universal language. In some way, the ski masks signify "we are

you," the universality. I am at the same time a member of my community but with the voice of my mountain I speak with the phrase *I am you,* that, along with the phrase, *to command while obeying* is one of the greatest definitions of what is democracy (August 10, 1996:11; emphasis in original, translated from Spanish by June Nash)

Touraine's sense of the potential for universalizing the message of pluricultural coexistence in a global setting is not shared by all scholars of global processes. Hardt and Negri (2000) reject the "new forms of struggle" such as the uprising in Chiapas, along with the Tiananmen Square events of 1989, the Intifada against Israeli authority, the May 1992 revolt in Los Angeles, the strikes in France in December 1995, and those in South Korea in 1996 as failed struggles, "because the desires and needs they expressed could not be translated into different contexts." Yet, as those who have studied the preexisting and subsequent conditions of these movements have pointed out (Nash, this volume,), and as current news emanating from the Middle East confirms, momentous changes are being made in these areas. Korean capitalism has entered a new phase of state-supported enterprise in which the workers have attained rights that exceed those of the export-processing zones of other Asian and Latin American countries. In Mexico, indigenous peoples have gained many supporters for their San Andres Agreement on autonomy, and though it has not yet been implemented by Congress, the indigenous peoples have gained ground in civil society. Although China redrew the line against political freedom in Tiananmen Square, the site remains a signpost for resistance to tyranny in the global arena. As for the other social movements in Los Angeles and Paris, these truly local struggles that do not rank with the other-world struggles have had incremental improvements in the local level.

Indigenous movements are consistently underestimated, except by a few anthropologists and political scientists[9] who are studying them. Yet some believe that they provide one of the few alternative visions of a future in which multicultural coexistence challenges the hierarchies of sovereign nations and empires.[10]

Globalization Processes and Their Opponents

In this anthology I have taken the frequently reiterated themes in the anthropological literature that characterize globalization, and grouped the chapters to show how social movements are engendered in order to oppose what people perceive as threats to central values enunciated above. These processes and the responses they may trigger include (1) the fragmentation and recomposition of society; (2) secularization and fundamentalist reactions; (3) deterritorialization and the politics of space; and (4) privatization, individualization, and global cosmopolitanism. The assumption that global integration would lead to a faceless, borderless, homogenized, and universalized world that exists only to consume the products that are endlessly reproduced in a global assembly line is not realized in ethnographic case studies. What careful study reveals is that social movements often subvert or transform the thrust of these processes in accord with central values related to human rights, environmental conservation, autonomy, and social justice that I refer to above. These values provide an ever-changing frame of reference that animate social movements and serve to validate the changes they institute or the revitalization of an imagined past without conflict.

Contributors to this volume show how the conjugation of differences in race, religion, and gender brought together in spaces where they were never before seen may promote a recomposition of civil society transmitted through NGOs and other transnational networks to a global society.[11] The implicit assumption that the processes designated by analysts of globalization are inevitable concomitants of the new world order is contested by those who are subjected to them. Their reactions may have the power to subvert even the most formidable military force.

I have also avoided the tendency to organize social movements according to specific populations – women, indigenous peoples, etc. – or focused issues that preoccupy social movements. Feminism is a movement against sexism that has expanded to include men and gays as well as women. The goals of many feminist groups are the liberation of society from behaviors that constrict the humanity of any one group. The same is true for indigenous movements that, in seeking the right to express their own cultural values, may also work for the liberation of all people from arbitrarily imposed behaviors.

As the chapters are grouped in sections according to the tensions created by globalization processes, the reader can perceive and compare how the populations affected by them re-envision their positions as they respond to global tendencies in culturally and historically distinct ways recounted in the cases analyzed in each chapter. The fragmentation of family and community is countered by civil-society movements that unite diverse actors around the values enumerated above. Secularization is opposed in fundamentalist religions as well as New Age spirituality. Deterritorialization and forced migrations are the basis for indigenous protests against neoliberal invasions of people's lands and expropriation of their resources. Privatization and the decimation of the social welfare state are opposed by revitalized union movements and the civil-society actions that expand their base. For activists in global civil society, engaged in these many sites for protest and revindication, democracy is no longer limited to electoral politics imposed by foreign superpowers, but is, rather, a participatory practice in the governance of everyday decisions.

Fragmentation and the Recomposition of Civil Society

Fragmentation of society has been characterized by the breaking up of communities and the institutional premises of traditional ways of life through deindustrialization, the forced migration of people to new production sites, or the intrusion of Western beliefs and institutions into native territories. Exclusionary factors that limit the ability of certain members of society to gain access to health services, political power, and economic opportunities often become precipitating causes for class, gender, and ethnic mobilizations directed toward removing the barriers.

In order to emphasize the ephemeral quality of social groupings in a global setting, some of the analysts in this volume have followed the trend visible in social movements to relate to civil society and networks rather than party politics or revolutionary cadres. Organized parties are often criticized as a site for co-optation and social movements, and guerrilla operations seem destined to escalate militarism without addressing the social needs they espouse. Marc Edelman cautions readers of his chapter, "When Networks Don't Work: The Rise and Fall and Rise of Civil Society Initiatives in Central America," to recognize both the multiple usages and interpretations of the terms "civil society" and "networks" by transnational NGOs and national interest groups. Networks linking associations in several countries may also fail to overcome the turmoil that they generate, but in the process they launch many leaders that voice *campesino* issues in transnational arenas.

The reconstitution of society in modernizing nations may also be expressed through state-sponsored movements that are the antithesis to civil-society arbitration in liberal democracy. Katherine Bowie found a distinct manifestation of this when the right-wing Thai government sponsored a scout movement in the 1970s in which young males became the agents for promoting solidarity. The scouts became a distinct embodiment of nationalism and right-wing militaristic surveillance squads at work. For the masses of impoverished youths, the scout movement, with its elaborate initiation rites, gave young men a stake in the government. Bowie's analysis shows that civil society is not just a cohort of fair-minded citizens seeking justice, but may also include those who align themselves with powerful military and statist interests to achieve control over the citizenry.

Women's increasing emergence in public roles adds a volatile dimension in societies where men have dominated civil society. Lynn Stephen shows how Latin American women extend their identities as mothers through the nomenclature of their organizations. Specifically she addresses this issue in the case of El Salvador's CO-MADRES ("godmothers"), who follow the lead of the Mothers of the Plaza de Mayo in Argentina, who were instrumental in bringing down the military regime that killed many of their children. The identification with maternal roles has a strategic as well as spiritual worth, since it evokes the most revered social sentiments in society and endows the nurturing quality that is at the heart of the relationship with enhanced value. The same spirit imbues Zapatista women who oppose the military in Chiapas as mothers who act out of the necessity of fulfilling their maternal roles by shaming young soldiers for their war against their own people. In countering the charge of "essentializing" their status as women as they try to gain positions in the public arenas from which they have been excluded, it is important to recognize that only through self-realization is it possible to overcome their own distancing from public life.

The once unifying basis of class relations that coalesced in industrial society when a workforce, united as a mass of exploited workers confronting industrial capitalists, has diminished as many different forms of labor compete in the global assembly line. The trend away from business unionism in US industry and toward more fluid categories of work such as "co-partnership" or "quality circles" that denied class boundaries was on the increase in the 1980s. In her chapter, "Activism and Class Identity: The Saturn Auto Factory Case," Sharryn Kasmir finds the resurgence of trade union consciousness among Saturn Automobile factory workers when they realized that their immersion in the details of production left them out of policy-making regarding issues that fundamentally affected their work lives, such as wages and hours. By 1999 workers expressed their disaffection from the touted "partnership" to vote in favor of the United Automobile Workers (UAW) as their bargaining agent. Kasmir rejects the thesis of new social movements theorists that class-consciousness is no longer vital for social identity and collective action.

The chapters in this part of the book illustrate the multi-stranded nature of social relations and the way in which this serves to reconstitute social relations that become fragmented. During extreme instances of social breakdown, society tends to resort to extreme role models such as the nationalistic scout movement in Thailand or the Mothers of the Plaza de Mayo in confronting the Argentinian generals. The essentialized forms of such appeals in periods of extreme stress evoke primordial sentiments that may have both positive and negative outcomes, depending on how the energy they release is directed. These essentialized categories, often reviled because of their association with chauvinistic or romanticized sentiments and behaviors, are powerful reminders of our atavistic responses to social breakdown and the attempts to reconstitute society.

Secularization and Fundamentalist Reactions

The alienation from spiritual communities of faith, incipient in eighteenth- and nineteenth-century society, is magnified incrementally with global commoditized exchanges in ever increasing domains of life. In the past twenty years we find that health services, which were once controlled by religious and public institutions, are now rendered only on payment for higher and higher fees in privatized, for-profit hospitals. Biotechnological strategies for achieving reproduction reduce the affective basis for heterosexual and homosexual mating. Just as the Christian world has seen fundamentalist sects reasserting some of the verities that seem threatened by the breakup of established social relations, so has the Muslim world found new and often more militant expressions of Islamic faith. Privatization of what were once publicly available services and goods, combined with secularization of institutions that were based on charity, reduce the basis for renewing communal life.

Islamic resurgence in the face of traumatic political and economic events was furthered by the development of print media that helped diffuse the political ideology of radical Islamic ideology in Afghanistan, as David Edwards shows in his chapter, "Print Islam: Media and Religious Revolution in Afghanistan." Just as national newspapers helped form a sense of the nation in other countries of the West, and spurred revolution in Russia, so did various forms of the media allow the diffusion of new ideologies in Islamic countries. Edwards explores the effectiveness of various forms of the media in promoting a new political culture in pamphlets, magazines, newspapers, and political tracts that were more vibrant than official media.

In his chapter "Local Islam Gone Global: The Roots of Religious Militancy in Egypt and its Transnational Transformation," James Toth reflects on such a passage among Islamic youths of Egypt who have been forced to migrate to other Arabic countries in search of wage work. The demoralization of the youths after the Egyptian defeat in the Six Day War with Israel in June 1967 and the disenchantment with state-led development were precipitating causes for them to reject the secular Arab nationalism and to seek alternatives. The resurgence of *jihad* activism throughout the Muslim world provided the kind of assertive form of Islam that was to attract these youths in the following decades.

Preoccupation with the problem of conversion to the dominant colonial religion, the reaction of indigenous peoples to secular trends in colonial society is rarely analyzed. Yet because of this, some of the more interesting sidelines to the colonial encounter are forgotten. Danilyn Rutherford's chapter, "Nationalism and Millenarianism in West Papua: Institutional Power, Interpretive Practice, and the Pursuit of Christian Truth," shows a variant of "Orientalizing" practice by Papuan Christian leaders as they confront global intrusions. Just as the Christianized leaders sought the hidden passages of the Bible that gave Christian missionaries their divine power in World War II, so do Papuan nationalists seek global recognition in Christian practice. Rutherford's remarkable portrayal of Papuan New Guinea responses to Christian conversion reveals the essentializing tendencies that underlie the encounter between East and West on both sides, a view that destroys the image of the encounter as uniquely Western-biased essentialism.

The Sarvodaya Movement in Sri Lanka sought to unite conflicting Tamil and Buddhist factions in Sri Lanka by turning to Gandhian and Buddhist sources of conflict resolution. Envisioning the traditional values of Sri Lankan village society as an exemplary model for harnessing the energies of pluricultural society in postindependence Sri Lanka, the Sarvodaya movement provides a model for conflict resolution in other countries of Southeast Asia.

The globalizing encounter of oppositional religious and cultural groups more often leads to hostilities than to acceptance of the common human denominator. This requires a dialogic encounter that overcomes the impasse of antagonistic opponents.

Deterritorialization and the Politics of Place

The worldwide deployment of capital demands flexibility in the disbursements of wages and other costs of production. Labor is the principal component of flexibility in the production system. The "deterritorialization" of people, communities, and industries is taken to be axiomatic in global flows (Appadurai 1996, Gupta and Ferguson 1997). But in the postmodern vein of inquiry, the terms of discourse – deterritorialization, creolization, hybridization, or fragmentation – often become reified as processes. This naturalizing of the phenomenon may result in the underestimation of the social movements born in the resistance of local populations to disperse.

In my chapter, "Defying Deterritorialization: Autonomy Movements against Globalization," I analyze this process of resistance to the privatization of land in Chiapas caused by the Salinas administration's "reform" of the Agrarian Reform Act in 1992, and to NAFTA by the Zapatistas, who chose New Year's morning of 1994 as the advent of their uprising to signalize their distress. With these two acts the indigenous people, who migrated to the Lacandón jungle with the promise of gaining title to national territories, were effectively disinherited, and the markets for their commercial crops were lost to competition from the United States. They found support for their mobilization against the neoliberal programs of the Mexican government in Christian Base Communities in highland villages. The fusion of ethnic resurgence and religious faith reinforces their demand for autonomy to pursue collective forms of life and is now directing their opposition to the government program for change called the Plan Puebla Panama.

This development scheme to integrate communication, production sites, and markets in the southern states of Chiapas with the Central American countries is shaking the solidarity of Mayan communities mobilized in the Zapatista uprising. In the early spring of 2003 each day brought news of confrontations in the Lacandón rainforest as those who remained loyal to the Zapatistas opposed megaprojects such as the building of hydroelectric power dams and tourist facilities. But many of the people living in the autonomous communities had begun to accept government dispensations of medicines and to send their children to public schools.

Whether the Mexican Maya's claims to the land as indigenous peoples whose title to collective lands will supersede their affinities with landless peasants is an open question. As yet they have not joined forces with Maya across the Guatemala border where the indigenous people constitute a majority of the population. If this should occur, the nightmare of Guatemalan *ladinos* that has driven the government to massive violations of human rights might be realized. The geopolitical reality for autonomy within Mexico cannot be realized without the strong and continued support of Mexican civil society. But the expansion of an economic zone created by the Plan Pueblo Panama might provide the basis for broader associations of class and ethnicity to oppose capitalist invasions.

The indigenous people of Oaxaca are also seeking alternative development enterprises to those of the assembly plants and exploitation of energy sources proposed by the Plan Puebla Panama for the Isthmus of Tehuantepec. As Molly Doane shows in her chapter, "The Resilience of Nationalism in a Global Era: Megaprojects in Mexico's South," Mexico's left-wing leaders appeal to a rescaled nationalism to reinforce pluralism and local autonomy in their attack on global projects. Indigenous people of Chimalapas, Oaxaca turn to international NGOs to bolster their attempt to define their spaces for autonomy in the area of the Oaxaca rainforest where transportation routes projected by the Plan Puebla Panama threaten to remove them from the territories they have colonized, or engage them as cheap labor for assembly manufacture.

There are also parallels in Max Kirsch's review of the effort on the part of community-based organizations to engage Florida Everglades residents in legislative policies. Their concerns about the environment in which they live provoke a distinct solution to that of technocrats and bureaucrats. An anthropological inquiry into the mix of government agents, NGOs, and local inhabitants provides a comparative basis for analyzing the points of conflict and of coordination. Hopefully this will become integrated at a level where local interests can successfully challenge the top-down approach that still characterizes global environmental planning.

The question of identity becomes a crucial issue in state relations with indigenous peoples at a time when indigenous rights to traditional territories are contested. In her chapter, Renée Sylvain discusses the issues of how the Omaheke San of South Africa negotiate their identity in the current dilemma of diminished hunting and gathering territories and encroachment on their lands. This identity is, the author maintains, shaped by the assumptions of apartheid racist premises. In order to convince a still racist government of the authenticity of their claims, they are forced to conform to identity expectations thrust upon them by the state and the international donor community. Whether the San can escape the reductionist position of promoting a stereotypical primordial identity based on an archaic lifestyle will depend on their ability to make alliances with other marginalized and oppressed classes.

The San seem to encompass the full trajectory of human life as isolated bands "living a stone-age culture" – as the media depicts them – to becoming a part of global circuits. For some analysts, like Richard Lee (1988, cited in Sylvain, this volume), the San exemplify a cultural survival of a way of life that is "communally based, that speaks of spirituality, non-capitalist values . . . harmony with nature" and with a strong "sense of place." Sylvain rejects this characterization, which she claims emerged only after independence allowed them the opportunity to make land claims. She envisions a future that would restrict them to playacting a traditional foraging life for eco-tourists seeking the thrills of a true-life safari if they choose the route of cultural survival. If they choose to rethink their ethnicity in all of its "reciprocal accommodations of culture to class oppression" as they live it, they may achieve a cosmopolitan opposition to globalization processes.

In a setting in which tribal people's encirclement by invasive agents of global enterprises, women's embodiment of the needs and spirit of the people they represent can become an impressive assertion of their value as citizens. Ligia Simonian, who worked with the Amazonian indigenous women of Brazil during their most difficult years in the 1980s and 1990s, shows a similar development to that of Namibian women when they emerged as political figures. Their situation as indigenous peoples, often abandoned when their husbands were forced to seek wage work in the gold mines and elsewhere, merits attention since their role as primary food providers and as mothers reinforced their leadership role in their communities. Among their greatest problems are the alcoholism of their men and the subsequent abuse they suffer from them. They must therefore fight a battle on two fronts, at home and in public, against predatory invaders of their jungle habitat. They have, through their own initiatives and the assistance of NGOs, been able to extend their networks to a wide area occupied not only by their tribespeople but also by other language groups. Despite the opposition they face at home, where their husbands object to their political activities, but also in the wider world where white invaders see them as objects of rape and forced servitude, they are achieving some success in their struggles for land, credit, and markets. With the help of NGO promoters, they have extended the range of income-earning potential with their jungle products – body oils, medicines, and handicrafts.

In their struggles to secure their place in national and international settings, Zapatista cultivators of the Lacandón rainforest, indigenous peoples of Chimalapas, Mexico, settlers of the Florida Everglades, women of the Amazonian forest, and the San of South Africa are all asserting their place in their home environment. Max Kirsch's account of the contested conservation of the Florida wetlands can be seen in tandem with Renée Sylvain's concerns with the San's attempt to retain a presence in the Kalahari desert terrain where they once hunted and gathered wild grains. Or either chapter can be illuminated by Ligia Simonian's portrayal of Amazonian women as they attempt to ensure their survival in habitats that are being invaded by gold miners, ranchers, and biodiversity DNA poachers as they engage in community-based political action. Molly Doane's analysis of the defense of Chimalapas's smallholder *campesinos* against highway development is linked to my discussion of the Zapatista uprising triggered by NAFTA, that is now protesting the same megaprojects sponsored by the Plan Puebla Panama in Chiapas. By embodying the many forms of consciousness and practice in specific cultural contexts, the authors elucidate the processes in formation throughout the world.

The current trend toward privatizing the most basic rights to water, land, and the resources by which they ensure their survival heightens the struggle to retain rights that were once taken for granted by virtue of being there. This "environmentalism of the poor" (Guha 1997), encompassing protests by hill villagers against logging companies, by forest tribals against dam builders, and by fisherfolk against multinational corporations deploying trawlers, can mobilize massive protests, and often brings about transformative change without guerrilla action. The recourse to cultural politics of social protests often brings local leaders to the forefront. In the following part of the book, we shall examine how people are reasserting the moral issues in exchange through a global cosmopolitanism that achieves links without the loss of local identity, and reasserts the moral component of national and international trade in the marketplace.

Privatization, Individualization, and Global Cosmopolitanism

Privatization and the individualization of human responsibilities, duties, and claims on society are aspects of modernity that are intensified with globalization. From the perspective of global capitalist enterprises, the private rights to control property and resources are the *sine qua non* of expansion and growth, without which the motivation of profits vanishes. The freeing up of social relations through money exchange, referred to in political economy as the commoditization of all social relations, was seen as a threat to humanistic values. This was particularly marked in the nineteenth century when monetary exchange accelerated in all sectors of life. Marx discusses it in the *Grundrisse*, written in 1857–8, suggesting that as cash exchanges increasingly enter into and mediate social relations, they become emptied of institutional and affective content (Marx 1971:156–8). He envisioned a future in which commoditization progressively would come to dominate all social exchanges, negating their social relational content. As Marx comments (1971:157, original emphasis): "as money expands . . . the social character of the relationship diminishes."

The common characteristic of those living in the global metropolises is the growing privatization and individualization of activities that were once the domain of publicly funded welfare or charitable institutions. Money exchange becomes a substitute for reciprocity and redistributive traditions. Capitalist expansion does not occur without the assurance that private property rights will be respected. Migration of peasants and tribal people from rural and forest areas necessitates a transformation in personal self-presentation as migrants attempt to mask their rustic origins or tribal membership. When the people of the Amazon appear in capital cities wearing feathers (as they did when protesting the burning of the forests by cattle ranchers), or when settlers of the Lacandón appear carrying bows and arrows (as they did in the Quincentennial March Celebrating Five Hundred Years of Survival of Colonial Rule), they are usually there on a political mission.

For others, the isolation effect – or alienation of individuals in society, as Marxists called it – is considered to be rooted in monetary exchange as the products of human labor become commodities. Money not only stands for the value of the product, as Marx pointed out, but releases the seller and the buyer from further obligation. In the *Grundrisse* Marx (1971:59) explores how money takes on a "material existence, apart from the product" that also denies the moral relation between the producer and the consumer. This is dramatically illustrated in the case of prostitution, but lingers in the medical profession in some countries that are not completely commoditized.

Fair-trade organizations provide a counterpoint to the privatization and individualization of global exchanges, introducing a strong moral component that challenges the alienation implied by commoditization. Driven by the desire to render fair prices for the producers, products produced in environmentally sustainable production cooperatives are now an important part of global trade, as Kimberly Grimes shows in her chapter, "Changing the Rules of Trade and Global Partnership: The Fair Trade Movement." For over a decade, student movements have used the boycott to penalize rogue nations for human rights abuses. This moral component in market exchange is expanding as the inequities in global trade become ever more apparent.

Secular institutions are beginning to intervene in the politics of commoditized food markets in the form of fair-trade associations. Mark Ritchie, President of the Institute of the Politics of Agriculture and Trade (IATP) based in Minneapolis, Minnesota, warns that the United States is promoting the dumping of subsidized crops at below market prices. Mexico has been hard hit by these policies, especially since NAFTA opened up the Mexican market for the sale of subsidized US crops. The World Organization of Commerce is fighting the policies of dumping goods because of the destruction of the subsistence production sector. Resources such as water and air are now threatened with commoditization.[12]

Robert Albro's discussion of a social movement triggered by the privatization of water by a multinational corporation is central to understanding the consequences of, and subsequent protests against, privatizing resources considered to be "the gifts of nature." Robert Albro shows how one such water-privatization plan put into operation in Bolivia mobilized massive protests by cultivators led by Oscar Olivera, a labor union leader and urban activist in the Bolivian state of Cochabamba who has become a world-renowned figure in environmental circles. What Robert Albro calls the Water War began when the government allowed a multinational corporation to control and sell water to *campesinos* and urban residents of the region; the people rose up in protest. This extraordinary violation of what is considered the most basic resource of the people became a celebrated international issue caught up in anti-globalization activism. Albro's analysis of the discourse and the cultural symbols utilized by local protest movements can, with the help of NGO strategists, mobilize global support.

Communicable diseases are the most cosmopolitan of world problems, transgressing class, race, and geographical boundaries, and linking the local and personal to global processes. Ida Susser addresses the local definitions of HIV as Africans categorize the patient population and allocate resources for treating it in accord with local priorities. The women's movement in Namibia challenged these priorities, that excluded women from scarce medical treatment as they were becoming the majority of the population affected by HIV. The inequity in the disbursements by male-dominated institutions is so persistent that women's grassroots organizations are proliferating to contest the failure to address women's as well as their children's health problems. Susser's work with Richard Lee in assessing the success of the female condom in limiting the spread of the disease in Namibia is a tribute to the successful cooperation of international agencies and grassroots organizations of Namibian women. It also galvanized women to address other aspects of discrimination in the groups that they formed to combat the threat of HIV.

Women in India have embraced feminist cosmopolitanism in their attempt to escape some of the most extreme forms of gender subordination. As the country became enmeshed in global processes of change, women began to perceive their condition from external perspectives. Yet, as women became engaged in local civil-liberties activism, they went beyond the gender-based injustices that were part of global feminism to mount a critique of state involvement in such practices as gang rape by police custodians and dowry killings. As Deepa Reddy shows in her chapter, women simultaneously entered into public spaces from which they had felt excluded as they strove to reform corrupt state policies. Gender oppression, they reasoned, was not just an outcome of traditional practice, but a product of patriarchal exercise of power to maintain class, gender, and ethnic hierarchies. The broad scope of the women's activism allowed them to challenge oppression in all of its manifestations as they engaged in fundamental social change.

These movements for fair trade, the right to utilize freely the basic resources of the community, and to engage in public life without restrictions based on gender are reactions to the increasing individuation. Michel-Rolph Trouillot refers to the cosmopolitan transfers of human rights and other homogenizing value systems carried in global circuits as "the isolation effect" of globalization (2001:126, 132). This has two dimensions. For some, the antidote to spiritual malaise brought about by the decline of public life is a global cosmopolitanism evoking a unifying vision for democracy. But for others, this promotes a specious vision, since it occurs in a world dominated by globalizing capitalism (Harvey 2001:271).

Conclusions

The authors of the chapters in this anthology retrieve the macro-political and macroeconomic context that is often obscured by those who emphasize identity or single-issue social movements. All have achieved the holistic analysis of social movements that is the hallmark of anthropological studies. They reveal the interlinked effect of gender–class–race–ethnicity in the context of growing wealth gaps and concentration of political power. The inclusion of cases dealing with universal issues confronting diverse societies as they respond to the impact of globalization processes reestablishes the basis for comparative studies that can assist policy makers and international NGO activists. Anthropologists who once ignored the intrusion of national and international in their field site are now among the principal observers of social movements, particularly those of indigenous people, women, and the disinherited, as they seek a new relationship with the states in which they are included. Although the potential of these movements is often underestimated, it is in these circuits once considered marginal to global processes that the major transforming changes are occurring. Because of their cultivated peripheral vision, anthropologists are in a position to assess new directions.

The globalization processes that cultivators and fisherfolk, former hunters, artisans, wage workers, and pastoralists confront relate to the predatory advance of capitalist enterprises in areas that once provided reserves for subsistence-oriented producers and its retreat from areas where the return on capital has diminished. Specifically, the rising demand for energy sources brings about increasing integration of people throughout the world at the same time that it exacerbates the contest for control over these assets. Competition for the most basic resources of water, air, and land raises the price of these increasingly privatized necessities and adds to the precarious conditions of marginalized populations in the global economy. Collective sharing of the social good in conditions of scarcity becomes the bitterly contested redistribution for the impoverished.

If there is a single theme that unites the many social movements in this book, it is the growing autonomy sought by the participants. Women, ethnic minorities, semi-subsistence producers, wage workers, immigrants, are in one way or another seeking a voice and a space of their own. If the predominant theme in the twentieth century was to select a unifying model for action, predicated on dichotomized interests that minimized the expression of difference, the theme running through social movements of the twenty-first century is the right of participants to be themselves. This enhances the plasticity of human responses to our social and physical environment, which was our unique advantage over other species at the dawn of civilization. This remains our best option for survival in a world of diminishing resources where we have become our own worst enemy.

NOTES

1   Ulf Hannerz (1996) defines the global ecumene as the "interconnectedness of the world by way of interactions, exchanges and related development, affecting not least the organization of culture." I have found it useful in analyzing ethnic resurgence to relate the ecumene in which interactions and exchanges unfold to the concept of habitus. This links "the space through which we learn who or what we are in society" (Bourdieu and Wacquant 1992:126–7) with the expanded significance given it by David Harvey (1989:219–21) as the site for relating "generative principles of regulated improvisations" to practices that "reproduce the objective conditions which produce the generative principles" (Nash 2001:32–3, 220–1). The novel sites in which these interactions and communications occur vary from concrete, geographically situated communities to cyberspace.

2   The King of Thailand urged a restructuring of capital, setting aside one-third of land and investments to restore subsistence production. In contrast, the failure of Prime Minister Suharto to respond to the crisis in Indonesia led to his downfall (*New York Times*, May 24, 1999).

3   Veronika Bennholdt-Thomsen et al. (2001) have brought together case studies asserting the importance of retaining subsistence economies as alternatives to the global integration. I address some of these protests against global control in Nash (1993).

4   In an extraordinary conference organized by Dr. Ligia Simonian at the University of Para in Belem in May, 2002 studies carried out in the Amazonian area of Brazil, French Guiana, Colombia, Venezuela, and Bolivia demonstrated the importance of collaborative research with a strong participatory and practical application of knowledge. Papers on the AIDs epidemic, violence against women, drug addiction, and other prevalent health and behavioral problems showed the similar difficulties faced by culturally differentiated groups who share a common environment.

5   In rejecting the "privileging" of class conflict, postmodernist critiques have sometimes gone so far as to deny the existence of any class conflict.

6   Nico Roozen and Francisco Van der Hoff, who founded the Union of Indigenous Communities of the Isthmus Region of Oaxaca, have written a book called *The Fair Trade Adventure: An Alternative to Globalization* (Mexico, 2004), that adds to the growing literature on organic farming traded in just circuits.

7   Leacock and Nash (1977).

8   See Escobar and Alvarez (1992) and Alvarez et al. (1998).

9   Collier and Quaratiello (1994), Gray (1997), Warren (1998), and Warren and Jackson (2002).

10 Andrew Gray (1997) makes a strong case for indigenous autonomy movements as alternative coexisting paths of development, and I have argued the case for the Mayas of Chiapas (Nash 2001).

11 Appadurai (1996), Comaroff and Comaroff (2001), and Gupta and Ferguson (1997) have characterized the devastating impact of global processes in their essays and anthologies.

12 Mark Ritchie announced at a press conference in Mexico that it is planned to privatize the water of New Orleans, Stockton, and Atlanta (*La Jornada*, February 21, 2003:23).

REFERENCES

Alvarez, Sonia E., Evelina Dagnino, and Arturo Escobar
   1998   Cultures of Politics, Politics of Cultures. Boulder, CO: Westview Press.

Appadurai, Arjun
  1996   Modernity at Large: Cultural Dimensions of Globalization. Minneapolis: University
     of Minnesota Press.
Bakunin, Mikhail Alexandrovich
  1848   "An Appeal to the Slavs."
——— 1873   Staat en Anarchie. *Both in* Bakunin on Anarchy: Selected Works by the Activist-
  Founder of World Anarchism. Sam Dolgoff, ed., trans., and intro. New York: Knopf, 1972.
Bennholdt-Thomsen, Veronika
  1981   Subsistence Production and Extended Reproduction. *In* Of Marriage and the
     Market: Women's Subordination in International Perspectives. Kate Young et al., eds.
     Pp. 41–54. London: CSE Books.
Bennholdt-Thomsen, Veronika, Nicholas Faraclas, and Claudia Von Werlhof
  2001   There is an Alternative: Subsistence and World-wide Resistance to Corporate Glob-
     alization. London: Zed.
Bourdieu, Pierre, and Loic J. D. Wacquant
  1992   An Invitation to Reflexive Sociology. Chicago: University of Chicago Press.
Collier, George, with Elizabeth Lowery Quaratiello
  1994   Basta! Land and the Zapatista Rebellion in Chiapas. Oakland, CA: Institute for
     Food and Development Policy.
Comaroff, Jean, and John L. Comaroff
  2001   Millennial Capitalism: First Thoughts on a Second Coming. Durham, NC: Duke
     University Press.
Edelman, Marc
  2001   Social Movements: Changing Paradigms and Forms of Politics, Annual Review of
     Anthropology 30:285–317.
Escobar, Arturo, and Sonia Alvarez
  1992   Social Movements: Theory and Research. Boulder, CO: Westview Press. New
     Brunswick, NJ: Rutgers University Press.
Gray, Andrew
  1997   Indigenous Rights and Development: Self-Determination in an Amazon Commu-
     nity. Providence, RI: Berghahn Books.
Guha, Ramachandra
  1997   The Environmentalism of the Poor. *In* Between Resistance and Revolution: Cultural
     Politics and Social Protest. R. G. Fox and O. Starn, eds. Pp. 17–39. New Brunswick, NJ.
     Rutgers University Press.
Gupta, Ahkil, and James Ferguson
  1997   Beyond "Culture," Space, Identity, and the Politics of Difference. *In* Culture, Power,
     Place: Ethnography at the End of an Era. Pp. 6–23. Durham, NC: Duke University Press.
Hannerz, Ulf
  1991   Scenarios for Peripheral Cultures. *In* Culture, Globalization and the World System:
     Current Debates in Art History 3. Arthur D. King, ed. Pp. 107–128. Minneapolis:
     University of Minnesota Press.
——— 1996   Transnational Connections: Culture, People, Place. London: Routledge.
Hardt, Michael, and Antonio Negri
  2000   Empire. Cambridge, MA and London: Harvard University Press.
Harvey, David
  1989   The Condition of Postmodernity: An Enquiry into the Origins of Cultural Change.
     Cambridge, MA and Oxford: Blackwell.
——— 2001   Cosmopolitanism and the Banality of Geographical Evils. In Millennial Capital-
     ism, and the Culture of Neoliberalism. Jean Comaroff and John L. Comaroff, eds.
     Pp. 271–301. Durham, NC: Duke University Press.

Herzfeld, Michael
  1997 Cultural Intimacy: Social Poetics in the Nation and State. New York and London: Routledge.
Jackson, Jean
  2002 Discourses of Authority in Colombian National Indigenous Politics: The 1996 Summer Takeovers. In Indigenous Movements, Self-Representation and the State in Latin America. Kay B. Warren and Jean E. Jackson, eds. Austin: University of Texas Press.
Kovic, Christine
  1997 Walking with One Heart: Human Relations and the Catholic Church among the Maya of Highland Chiapas. Ph.D. thesis, City University of New York, Graduate School, Department of Anthropology.
Laclau, Ernesto, and Chantal Mouffe
  1985 Hegemony and Socialist Strategy: Towards a Radical Democratic Politics. London: Verso.
Leacock, Eleanor Burke, and June Nash
  1977 The Ideologies of Sex: Archetypes and Stereotypes. Annals of the New York Academy of Science, 285:618–645.
Luxemburg, Rosa
  1950 The Accumulation of Capital. New York and London: Routledge & Kegan Paul and Monthly Review Press. Trans. Agnes Schwarzschild, intro. Joan Robinson. First published 1913. Also republished 1971, Monthly Review Press, with introduction by Tarbuck.
Marx, Karl
  1971 The Grundrisse. New York: Monthly Review Press.
Melucci, Alberto, ed. John Keane and Paul Mier
  1989 Nomads of the Present: Social Movements and Individual Needs in Contemporary Society. Philadelphia, PA: Temple University Press.
Mullings, Leith
  1997 On Our Own Terms. New York: Routledge.
Nagengast, Carol
  1994 Violence, Terror, and the Crisis of the State. Annual Reviews of Anthropology 23: 109–136.
Nash, June
  1990 Latin American Women in the World Capitalist Crisis. Gender and Society 4(3): 338–353.
——1994 Global Integration and Subsistence Insecurity. American Anthropologist 96(1): 7–30.
——1998 Diversity and the Labor Movement. In Anthropology of Diversity. Ida Susser, ed. Baltimore, MD: American Anthropological Association.
  2001 Mayan Visions: The Quest for Autonomy in an Age of Globalization. New York and London: Routledge.
Nigh, Ronald, and Nemesio J. Rodriguez
  1995 Territorios Violados: Indios, Medio Ambiente y Desarrollo en America Latina. México, DF: Dirección General de Publicaciones del Consejo Nacional para la Cultura y las Artes.
Ramos, Alcida
  1998 Indigenism: Ethnic Politics in Brazil. Madison: University of Wisconsin Press.
Roozen, Nico, and Frans van der Hoff
  2004 The Fair Trade Adventure of Just Commerce: An Alternative to Globalization. México. D.F.

Simonian, Ligia, ed.
  n.d. Proceedings of Conference: Women, Gender, and Development in the Trans Amazon,
     26–29 May, 2002. University of Pará, Belém, Brazil.
Simonian, Ligia, and Jean Jackson, eds.
  2002 Indigenous Movements, Self-representation, and the State in Latin America. Austin:
     University of Texas Press.
Smith, Dorothy
  1987 [1972] Peculiar Eclipsing: Women's Exclusion from Man's Culture. *In* The Everyday
     World as Problematic: A Feminist Sociology. Pp. 27–43. Boston: Northeastern University
     Press.
Stiglitz, Joseph E.
  2000 Global Economic Prospects and the Developing Countries. International Bank for
     Reconstruction and Development/World Bank: Washington, DC.
Tedlock, Dennis
  1984 Popol Vuh: The Mayan Book of the Dawn of Life. New York: Simon & Schuster.
  —— 1993 Breath on the Mirror: Mythic Voices and Visions of the Living Maya. San
     Francisco: Harper.
Touraine, Alain
  1971 The Post-Industrial Society: Tomorrow's Social History: Classes, Conflicts and
     Culture in the Programmed Society. New York: Random House.
  —— 1988 Return of the Actor. Minneapolis: University of Minnesota Press.
Trouillot, Michel-Rolph
  2001 The Anthropology of the State in the Age of Globalization: Close Encounters of the
     Deceptive Kind. Current Anthropology 42(1):125–138.
Vinding, Diana
  1998 Tribal Women in Uttar Pradesh. *In* Indigenous Women: The Right to a Vote.
     D. Vinding, ed. Copenhagen: IWGIA.
Warman, Arturo, Bonfil Batalla, and Nolasco Armas, eds.
  1970 De eso lo que se llaman antropología mexicana. México, DF: Editorial Nuestro
     Tiempo.
Warren, Kay B.
  1993 Death Squads and Wider Complicities: Dilemmas for the Anthropology of Violence.
     In The Violence Within: Cultural and Political Opposition in Divided Nations. Kay B.
     Warren, ed. Pp. 226–247. Philadelphia: University of Pennsylvania Press.
  —— 1998 Indigenous Movements and their Critics. Princeton, NJ: Princeton University
     Press.

Part I

Fragmentation and the Recomposition of Civil Society

1

When Networks Don't Work: The Rise and Fall and Rise of Civil Society Initiatives in Central America

Marc Edelman

Introduction

"Civil society," "network," and "social movement" are imprecise, frequently contested terms. Many social-scientific discussions of collective action are characterized by considerable slippage in the use of these and other, similar concepts. To a large extent, this reflects the emergence of new, hybrid organizational forms, as contemporary social movements network with one another, form coalitions, and seek to establish claims to constitute part of national and global civil society. While this chapter indicates that it may be heuristically helpful to refine distinctions between these categories, it argues that it is probably more useful to integrate insights from the too often separate streams of scholarship that focus respectively on civil society, networks, and social movements. In particular, the rise in the 1990s of transnational Central America-wide civil society initiatives (and their decline and reemergence) suggests that: (1) contested notions of civil society have a real-world impact on the shape and activities of diverse social movements and NGOs; (2) that "networks" – far from being durable and potent

organizational forms, as scholars of the right and left have forcefully maintained – are at times quite fragile and ephemeral and are characterized by periodic cycles like those of social movements (Arquilla and Ronfeldt 2001a, Castells 1996, Tarrow 1998); and (3) the new prominence of "networks," whether as political claims or as linked computers or social movements, exacerbates a problem with profound methodological, political, ethical, and representational dimensions that is acknowledged only occasionally in the social movements literature – the appearance of "fictitious" or "shell" organizations and, more recently, "dot causes" or Internet-based advocacy organizations with minuscule or indeterminate constituencies (Tilly 1984:311, Anheier and Themudo 2002:209–10).

Real-World Impacts of Civil Society and Network Debates

It has become commonplace to refer to the 1980s in Latin America as "the lost decade." With the hindsight of today, it is clear that in many respects the "lost" maxim was not hyperbolic. Despite occasional and scattered signs of progress, the continent is still reeling from the impact of the debt crisis (the result, in part, of overvalued currencies and the "exhaustion" of "statist" models of development, but also of soaring interest rates in the 1970s, falling commodity prices, and anemic taxation systems) and an increasingly volatile globalized economy, the intractable poverty that continues to affect more than a third of the population (and which, in most countries, has changed little in relative terms since 1980) (CEPAL 2002:64–65), and continuing instability in Argentina, Ecuador, Colombia, Venezuela, and elsewhere. The end of the military regimes and the democratization processes of the early 1980s generated tremendous hopes and opened up political space, but two decades later Latin Americans express very low levels of satisfaction with how "democracy" works in their countries (Latinobarómetro 2002).

In the small nations of Central America, the 1980s were doubly "lost." Impacted like the rest of the hemisphere by economic crises and restructuring, these countries also became a locus of superpower competition and massive social struggles, suffering levels of violence and destruction that beggar the imagination.

The crisis of the 1980s, however, also gave rise to an unprecedented mobilization of diverse sectors of civil society, particularly in the latter part of the decade, when the civil wars ended or ebbed, and in the decade that followed. There were several sources of this political effervescence. The reduction of civil conflict and the democratization of the political systems opened up "space" for new kinds of actors to express demands from sectors of society that had been on the defensive during the wars, but which also felt empowered as a result of their participation in a decade or more of arduous struggle. The accords which settled the wars included specific provisions for resettling refugees, incorporating ex-combatants into institutional life, and involving civil society in processes of building peace and strengthening national

reconciliation. Throughout the region, new notions of rights had taken hold among highly politicized populations, and politicians across the spectrum articulated a new discourse of *concertación* (consensus and reconciliation). Intellectuals who had been downsized as part of public-sector retrenchment, as well as those who returned from exile or from the mountains, flocked to a growing number of nongovernmental organizations (NGOs). Finally, external actors which had been active in the region throughout the 1980s – notably the United States and the European Community (EC) – intensified their support for what were, broadly speaking, two competing civil society projects.

"Civil society" is, of course, a contested notion, with a complex genealogy that is beyond the scope of this chapter. For our purposes, it is worth noting that contrasting theoretical conceptions about how to bound the "civil society" category are often tied to distinct political-economic agendas and views of democratization. Different perspectives generally agree that "civil society" is the associational realm between the household or family and the state. Beyond that, however, at the risk of oversimplifying too much, it is possible to distinguish two polar positions, separated by opposing views on whether to include markets and firms within "civil society." Those who argue for considering markets and corporations as part of the category typically back a conservative agenda (something ironic, given this position's roots in Hegel and Marx) which sees "civil society" as a domain outside of and morally superior to the state. They posit choice and freedom of association as fundamental characteristics of both the market and "civil society," making support for economic liberalization and "civil society" institutions not only entirely compatible, but complementary strategies for checking state power. In contrast, theorists who exclude the market and firms from "civil society" usually consider it a domain of associational life that attempts to defend autonomous collective institutions from the encroachments of *both* the market and the state. Frequently they invoke Gramsci, while conveniently ignoring or downplaying his suggestion that achieving working-class hegemony within "civil society" could be a prelude to seizing state power. In comparison with conservative theorists, they tend to accord much greater analytical importance to how social inequality and power differentials structure or limit political representation (Cohen 1995, Cohen and Arato 1992, Hearn 2001, Keane 1998, 2001, Macdonald 1997, Nielsen 1995).

This theoretical polarization between differing visions of "civil society" was reflected in Central America in two political projects promoted by the two key external actors, the United States and the European Community (after 1993, the European Union, or EU). Each project – and here, for heuristic purposes, I am again ignoring some complexities – had a contrasting understanding of the underlying causes of the conflicts and a corresponding conception of democratization. In essence, Washington, and particularly the Reagan and Bush administrations, saw the region's revolutionary movements, wars, and related unrest as rooted fundamentally and almost exclusively in communist subversion and Soviet–Cuban interference. European policy-makers – especially (but not only) the Spanish, Scandinavian, and German social democrats – emphasized inequality, poverty, systematic human rights violations, and authoritarian rule as central causes of the upheavals. The US approach was overwhelmingly military until the late 1980s, although it also involved encouraging free elections, legal reforms, privatization of public-sector entities, and rapid economic liberalization. Its civil society component involved strong backing for private-sector lobbies and export promotion organizations, many of which received large subsidies from USAID (the United States Agency for International Development) (Cuenca 1992, Echeverría 1993, Escoto and Marroquín 1992, Rosa 1993, Sojo 1992).

European governments, apprehensive about the possibility of a major Central American war that might eventually compromise their own region's security, actively promoted diplomatic efforts (first Contadora, and then Costa Rican President Oscar Arias's initiative that culminated in the 1987 Esquipulas Accords). From 1984, they sponsored annual European–Central American ministerial-level meetings (called the San José Dialogue) to hammer out "cooperation" or aid agreements. Most of the sudden increase in flows of European cooperation, however, was channeled through donor NGOs rather than bilateral or official EU agencies. These European NGOs frequently received most of their funding from their respective governments (Ibis-Denmark or Novib-Holland, for example). They nonetheless placed great emphasis on establishing "horizontal" relations with grass-roots "counterparts" that permitted medium- and long-term, rather than project-specific, funding. The European vision of democratization aimed at reining in the excesses of the market and at empowering historically powerless sectors of the population (the poor, indigenous and minority groups, women) so that they could participate effectively in political institutions and combat structural inequalities, poverty, and environmental destruction (Biekart 1999, Freres 1998, Fundación Arias para la Paz y el Progreso Humano 1998, Grabendorff 1984, Hansen 1996, Macdonald 1997, Reuben Soto 1991, Roy 1992, Sanahuja 1996, Schori 1981).

Increasingly over the course of the 1990s, efforts to theorize "civil society" – and "global" or "transnational" civil society in particular – employed the notion of "network" as an analytical category, a metaphor for a social condition, and a description of emerging organizational and institutional forms, communications technologies, and knowledge practices. "Network" has come to have diverse meanings (again, beyond the scope of this chapter), though its genealogy is nowhere near as lengthy as that of the similarly complicated "civil society." As in the "civil society" literature, with which it overlaps, the new "network" scholarship is characterized by a pronounced left–right split. Here, though, the division is less about how to bound the object of study than over the emancipatory potential versus the danger that network organization implies. In the former camp, one study of "new social movements" is optimistically titled "Networks that Give Liberty" – *Redes que dan libertad* (Riechmann and Fernández Buey 1994). Two key works on transnational activism conclude that "dense" networks, with many nodes, are most likely to be effective (Keck and Sikkink 1998:206, Smith 1997:54–55). Castells's ambitious examination of this "new social morphology" – which includes case studies of diverse social movements, as well as organized crime – suggests that "networks are open structures, able to expand without limits, integrating new nodes as long as they are able to communicate within the network" (Castells 1996:470). While acknowledging intellectual debts to Castells, the RAND Corporation's Arquilla and Ronfeldt argue that "nimble bad guys" – terrorists, criminals, and "militants" – have become more adept than "good guys" at deploying "network" forms and waging "netwar" (Arquilla and Ronfeldt 2001b). Concerned primarily with elaborating new counterinsurgency or "counter-netwar" military doctrine, at times these authors have a troubling tendency to conflate international human rights activists with al-Qae'da or Colombian drug cartels: "They know how to penetrate and disrupt, as well as elude and evade. All feature network forms of organization, doctrine, strategy, and technology attuned to the information age....They are proving very hard to beat; some may actually be winning" (Arquilla and Ronfeldt 2001b:v).[1] Across the spectrum, from "Networks that Give Liberty" to "Networks and Netwars," a strong consensus exists about the potency and durability of network forms. As in the broader collective action literature, where the study of unsuccessful social movements is distinctly undertheorized (Edelman 1999, 2001), only a few lone

voices – notably Annelise Riles in her ethnographic tour de force, *The Network Inside Out* – row against the current and call attention to the possibility that the "network" may be "a form that supersedes analysis and reality" and that its "'failure' is endemic, indeed, ...[an] effect of the Network form" (2001:174, 6).[2] While perhaps not applicable to all networks in all times and places (as Riles seems to claim), this latter perspective deserves consideration when analyzing the rise and decline of certain civil society networks in Central America in the 1990s. I will return to it in my conclusion.

Regional Civil Society in Central America

This chapter examines these issues primarily in relation to the recent history of Central American peasant and small-farmer organizations. It looks, in particular, at the meteoric rise and subsequent decline of a regional network of *campesino* groups, the Association of Central American Peasant Organizations for Cooperation and Development (*Asociación de Organizaciones Campesinas de Centroamérica para la Cooperación y el Desarrollo*, or ASOCODE), which briefly enjoyed an extraordinarily high profile in isthmian politics, attending, for example, numerous presidential and ministerial summit meetings and generating a number of related networks that included both non-agrarian and non-Central American organizations. Founded in 1991 as an outgrowth of a European-sponsored food-security education program, ASOCODE rapidly took on a life of its own and garnered growing legitimacy with its elite interlocutors and foreign funders, as well as with *campesino* activists from different countries, who recognized increasingly that their counterparts elsewhere confronted similar problems and shared the same concerns. The Association was, nonetheless, beset from the beginning by a variety of tensions that ultimately contributed to its undoing. These included differences of nationality and political orientation, entrenched patriarchal traditions, and leadership styles (Edelman 1998). Dependence on foreign donors also created unexpected vulnerabilities. Finally, the meager gains from transnational activism and the continuing salience of national political struggles eventually led some peasant organizations to question their earlier commitment to globalization from below and regional-level struggles.

The charismatic and energetic leadership of Wilson Campos, a young Costa Rican activist, helped to maintain tensions within manageable limits and to cement relations with foreign cooperation institutions during ASOCODE's first five years. Campos moved easily in a range of milieux, from rural farmsteads to presidential summits to UN agencies in New York and foundation offices in Europe. Adept at making those with whom he came in contact feel heard and appreciated, he attracted considerable sympathy in policymaking and donor circles. This role, however, entailed serious costs in greatly reduced attention to the local and national organizations in Costa Rica in which he had previously been a key player, and in the growing centralization in a single person of duties relating to ASOCODE's international and internal organizational relations. Other leaders, often distrustful of Costa Ricans to begin with, also resented this concentration of affective attachments and organizational responsibilities.

One way to gain a sense of ASOCODE's rise and fall is through outlining its funding strategy, which clearly responded to a shift in European cooperation strategies in the late 1980s and early 1990s when multilateral, bilateral, and NGO donors let it be known that they preferred to support projects that had a Central American regional, as opposed to a national or local, focus (Biekart 1999:204–206). In 1992 and 1993, three ASOCODE delegations toured Europe, meeting with NGO, EC, and European Parliament officials and representatives of the governments of Holland, Denmark, Norway,

Germany, Belgium, and France. By 1993, the organization had an annual budget of over US$300,000, almost entirely from European (and a few Canadian and US) donor groups. A monthly subsidy of US$1,000 per month was paid to each of the seven national coalitions that made up the Association. The general coordinator's salary was US$13,000 per year (handsome compensation for a mid-level professional in Central America, especially when other perquisites were included, such as the *aguinaldo* or "thirteenth month" year-end bonus, the use of vehicles, and free housing in Managua). By 1995 the subvention to each national organization had risen to four or five thousand dollars per month for each coalition, most of which was spent as salary for the two representatives that each country assigned to part-time work in ASOCODE's coordinating council (Edelman 1998). In 1996 the Association's budget rose to US$1.5 million (Biekart 1999:280).

The sudden abundance of resources created a heady atmosphere. Indeed, in the 1994–97 period, according to an internal organizational report, "cooperation resources were so abundant that they exceeded the capacity of the headquarters" to administer them (ASOCODE 1999:24). Perhaps not surprisingly, success in fundraising, together with an intense round of activities, could easily be mistaken for political impact and influence. It also accentuated the top-down character of the Association, lessening its accountability to its national components, and simultaneously created "new needs" that essentially responded to donor offers and priorities (Biekart 1999:286–293).

In the competition for European funding, claiming to be a "popular organization" that "represented" a historically marginalized sector of the population came to be increasingly important. In ASOCODE's case, the degree of "representativity" could be established by summing the impressive, though not always unexaggerated, membership figures of its constituent organizations. A certain hubris or even grandiosity tended to accompany claims of this sort. By 1997, for example, ASOCODE leaders asserted confidently that within a short time they would have expanded the "Campesino a Campesino" extension program – which had only a modest presence outside of Nicaragua – to all of Central America.[3]

Given the historical antagonism in Central America between "popular organizations" and NGOs, it is striking how much the two forms converged. Analyzing Latin American feminist movements, Sonia Alvarez (1998) calls this a process of "NGO-ization" of popular organizations. ASOCODE, headed by some of the most belligerent anti-NGO activists in the region, resembled nothing so much as a large NGO (a 1999 internal retrospective evaluation indicates candidly that by 1994, the Association had institutionalized its "function as a cooperation agency"). Headquartered in a spacious house in an upper-middle-class neighborhood of Managua, the Association had all of the typical NGO trappings: computers, photocopiers, fax machines, secretaries, maids, a driver, technicians who generated a never-ending stream of project proposals and "strategic plans," and foreign "cooperators," first from Denmark and later Canada. It published a glossy bimonthly newsletter in Spanish and English (the latter, some said, was for the Belizeans, although others conceded that it was primarily for foreign consumption). ASOCODE leaders and technical staff from outside Nicaragua would often dash home (sometimes in Association vehicles) to Honduras or Costa Rica for the weekend. Many became fluent in the banal and repetitive "NGO-speak" ("sustainability," "transparency," "participation," "accountability," etc.) devastatingly lampooned in Argentine human rights activist Gino Lofredo's (1991) parody, "Get rich in the 1990s. You still don't have an NGO?"[4]

Part of the sense that ASOCODE was in the ascendant derived from its very real access to presidential and ministerial summit meetings and from its membership in the Consultative Council of the SICA (Sistema de Integración Centroamericana), Central America's main supranational regional governance institution. Several of the national coalitions participating in ASOCODE used their newfound access to funds to carry out rural development programs and to support struggles for land rights, credit, and technical assistance. At regional level, however, the principal activity continued to be summit-hopping lobbying, organizational meetings, and training workshops and seminars.

In the early to mid-1990s ASOCODE also initiated or encouraged the formation of several new networks: the Indigenous and Peasant Community Agroforestry Coordinating Group (Coordinadora Indígena y Campesina de Agroforestería Comunitaria, CICAFOC); the Central American Indigenous Council (Consejo Indígena Centroamericano, CICA); the Civil Initiative for Central American Integration (Iniciativa Civil para la Integración Centroamericana, ICIC); the Latin American Coordination of Rural Organizations (Coordinadora Latinoamericana de Organizaciones del Campo, CLOC); and the Vía Campesina/Peasant Road, which eventually included representatives of farmers' organizations from some fifty countries (Desmarais 2002, Edelman 2003). Following the massive devastation by Hurricane Mitch in October 1998, ASOCODE, together with CICAFOC and a regional network of small coffee producers, set up a new Central American Rural Coordinating Group (Coordinadora Centroamericana del Campo) to join a broader Central America Solidarity Coordinating Group (Coordinación Centroamérica Solidaria) at the Stockholm meeting of European cooperation organizations involved in the reconstruction effort. The proliferation of networks meant a sharp rise in the number of regional meetings, many of which were attended by the same individuals. Some of the more enterprising activists reportedly received full-time salaries simultaneously from more than one network (similar to what Riles 2001:47 reports in the Pacific).

Decomposition and Recomposition: "Crisis," "Rupture," and "Transition"

Networks beget networks. The phenomenon is noteworthy, since new organizational structures were assumed or claimed to correspond to new political or economic functions or objectives. Ironically, the most intense period of ASOCODE involvement in creating new networks occurred just before its own decomposition. This section describes an organizational decline that some viewed as a demise and that others euphemistically called a "transition." The following, concluding section of the chapter suggests why processes of network genesis and decomposition are not coincidental, but rather integrally related to each other.

In 1997 and 1998, ASOCODE entered a period that its own internal evaluation characterizes as "crisis and rupture" (ASOCODE 1999:25). First the English and then the Spanish edition of the newsletter ceased publication. Organizational divisions involved more and more energy, and the Association diminished its lobbying at regional and international meetings. Much of the discord manifested itself in a factional split – present from the Association's beginnings – between the Panamanian and Salvadoran "verticalists" (with orthodox Leninist proclivities), on the one hand, and the five other countries' representatives on the other. Additional controversies divided the coordinating council along different lines, for example, whether the Association should be a regional *campesino* lobby or attempt to resolve immediate on-the-ground problems in the member countries. The diversity of the constituent organizations and their social bases – agricultural workers, indigenous groups, independent peasants, cooperative members – once seen as a strength, became a further source of polarization as some countries' representatives (Nicaraguans and Costa Ricans, in particular) argued for a narrower orientation toward smallholding producers. Worsening

disputes between the headquarters and the different national coalitions over control of resources also led some significant organizations to withdraw and others to be expelled from the national coalitions. Sometimes this occurred because national organizations saw the coalitions which represented them at regional level as too involved in ASOCODE to attend to pressing issues at home.

In 1999, the Association abandoned all efforts at lobbying international, regional, and national institutions. When donor organizations became aware of the turmoil and withdrew their support, the downward spiral accelerated. Some agencies indicated that henceforth they would reverse their previous practice of funding regional initiatives and channel support earmarked for ASOCODE to its constituent national organizations. The coalition which had represented Guatemala in ASOCODE dissolved, decimated by the loss of cooperation funds and eclipsed by the rise of other more dynamic alliances of Guatemalan peasant organizations (in which it had briefly participated). The lavish headquarters in Managua – an example of what one prescient critique termed network "macrocephaly" (Morales and Cranshaw 1997:55) – closed its doors. "Since March 2000," an internal report commented in April 2001, "we have not had any financial support from any cooperation agency or organization...the different activities have been carried out with the support provided by their organizers. Operating expenses until December 2000...were obtained through the sale of equipment from the headquarters" (ASOCODE 2001:1).

In April 2001, 25 delegates (15 of them women) from 5 countries met in Tegucigalpa (representatives from Belize and Guatemala were invited and confirmed their participation, but never arrived). Their agenda was to consolidate what some described as a "transition." Instead of a costly headquarters and a regional coordinating committee, ASOCODE decided to divide into issue-specific working groups that would communicate virtually or meet physically on an ad hoc basis.

The Honduran member coalition, already host to the global Vía Campesina network, agreed to serve as ASOCODE's office as well and to initiate the paperwork needed to establish its legal personality in Honduras (and to obtain a Honduran email account). Despite the near demise of the Association, the transition commission's report pointed to a wide range of activities over the previous year: regional "encounters" on agrarian problems and the landless in Honduras, El Salvador, and Nicaragua, on rural women in Nicaragua, and on preparing proposals for the civil society Consultative Council of the Central American Integration System (SICA) in El Salvador, as well as participation in forums in Montreal, Madrid, Bangalore, and Nairobi.

Nor did the Tegucigalpa "transition" meeting neglect public relations. The ASOCODE brochure was updated, a press conference scheduled at the end of the event, and plans were made to announce the new organizational structure on the Association's web page. The Panamanians (in a move consonant with Riles's [2001:32, 89] observations about how networks fetishize their own reports) urged the rest of the delegates "to reaffirm the presence of ASOCODE in Central America, taking advantage of all the documents on the letterhead of the different national coalitions [mesas], adding the name of ASOCODE [to each, for] example APEMEP-ASOCODE, ADC-ASOCODE, COCOCH-ASOCODE" (ASOCODE 2001:8).[5]

Conclusion: Some Reasons Why Networks Don't Always Work

It would be tempting to explain the decline of ASOCODE, its lowered profile in Central American regional politics, and the demise of some of its spinoff networks as the result of bitter factional infighting, a macrocephalic organizational structure, battles over money, or an exaggerated dependence on foreign donors. This would not be wrong. But behind the conflicts between "verticalists" and their opponents, the often opportunistic pursuit of individual or organizational economic security, the currying favor with European cooperation agencies, and the propagation of donor-driven agendas lie some lessons that speak to the role of nation-states in the globalized economy and to the broader limitations of transnational civil society projects.

Networks are typically represented by social scientists and by their participants as two-dimensional linkages between nodes or focal points of equal weight or significance. This portrayal – whether of "chain," "star and hub," or "all channel" network forms (Arquilla and Ronfeldt 2001a:8) – often fails to capture how networks are experienced by those who participate in them (Riles 2001). Network activists, like other overworked professionals, feel the tug of disparate demands emanating from the regional, national, and local organizations in which they take part. The network diagrams that show ties between national coalitions (which are very much the same in Central America and in the Pacific) fail to indicate the existence of this third dimension that links national coalitions to their very diverse constituent member groups. Concretely, the same individuals who mobilize delegates for international network conferences may also have to put together a legal team to defend disputed property titles, follow up on late orders for a cooperative's rubber boots, or harvest a field of cabbages. Unlike electrical engineering diagrams, which typically indicate resistance to flows, formal network organograms imply agile and unobstructed movement of information between nodes or focal points. The network's representation of itself erases political, historical, and personal forces that might, in practice, impede the networking process.

The two-dimensional representation of networks – in part an artifact of commonly used graphics software – effaces not just this third dimension of linkages between a "hub" and its components, but also the fourth dimension of how time and periodicity affect civil society initiatives. Social movements everywhere rise and fall, often as part of broader "cycles of protest" (Tarrow 1998, Tilly 1984). US, European, and autochthonous civil society projects of the late 1980s and early 1990s in Central America shared an urgency born out of a decade or more of severe crisis and inconceivable violence. Over the course of the 1990s, these imperatives receded in importance. Donors experienced "fatigue," became enamored of new fashions, and shifted their attention to other regions – notably eastern Europe and southern Africa – where needs seemed more immediate and political hopes appeared to have greater possibilities of realization. In Europe, in particular, the rightward shift in several key countries led to diminished official support for grass-roots organizations in the Third World. And in several countries in Central America, as democratization advanced, traditional political forms – parties, unions, and lobbies – assumed as their own many of the demands initially articulated through civil society initiatives.

Analysts of transnational politics increasingly question the pundits' facile vision of contemporary globalization as a zero-sum game in which states lose as markets and supranational governance institutions gain. Sassen, for example, points out that while states everywhere are forfeiting their historical role as regulators of financial markets, they continue to play a major role in extending the interstate consensus in favor of globalization, if for no other reason than that national legal systems remain the principal means through which the contracts and property rights so essential in the world economy are enforced (Sassen 2000:61, Helleiner 1994). Tarrow, similarly, emphasizes "that states remain dominant in most areas of policy," such as domestic security, border control and exercising legal dominion with their territories. "Citizens," he says,

> can travel more easily than before and can form networks beyond borders . . . , but they still live in states and, in democratic ones at least, they have the opportunities, the net-

works, and the well-known repertoires of national politics. . . . Those are incentives to operate on native ground that the hypothetical attractions of "global civil society" cannot easily match. (2001:2–3)

The tensions within ASOCODE between the possibilities of regional, transnational organizing and the imperatives of national politics need to be seen in this light, even though for many global networkers (and especially for rural ones) the "attractions" of international travel and a more cosmopolitan lifestyle might be greater than Tarrow indicates. Jorge Hernández, a long-time *campesino* organizer in Costa Rica, had been a founder in the early 1980s of the politically centrist National Union of Small and Medium Agricultural Producers (Unión Nacional de Pequeños y Medianos Productores Agropecuarios, UPA-NACIONAL), still by far the country's largest peasant organization. Later, he had a leading role in the creation of the ASOCODE and the Vía Campesina networks and saw UPANA-CIONAL, his "base organization," marginalized from both. An astute, committed activist who was present as part of a Vía Campesina delegation at the "Battle of Seattle," Hernández Cascante explained in 2001 why he and his organization had decided to eschew regional politics and concentrate on national-level struggles:

> From UPANACIONAL's point of view, we discerned two serious problems in ASO-CODE. One was the social composition of the movement. There were some groups clearly made up of small and medium-size agriculturalists and others which had labor and other sorts of demands. At the same time that movements like UPANACIONAL were interested in the right to make the land produce – because we live from the land – there were others who were concerned about rural wages, the [cost of] the "basic market basket" [i.e., cost of living]. This began to divide the movement. The other question concerned representation. We valued highly representative organizations, not so much purely in terms of numbers of members,

which is important, but also in terms of actions in practice, in real struggle. These exist in all of Central America. But we also saw that there were organizations whose support base wasn't very clear.... They had a great name, but at the moment when pressure tactics were needed, to block a highway or stage a demonstration, their supporters didn't appear and the leaders still talked about how they had "X" quantity of members.... This was notorious and even the cooperation agencies began to talk about organizations that were like shells.... We considered that it wasn't worth being in a process where the concepts of representation were so thin.... The organization that has an agenda of very intense internal, national work prefers to leave aside that type of problems and not get involved in that type of dispute.... It's very exhausting. Moreover, the national agenda doesn't wait. The government's policies don't wait, nor the free trade treaties nor the pressure that has to be brought on the Legislative Assembly. If one doesn't do it now, they pass a law or a tax or a new free trade treaty and they put us there without any protection for grain producers, or potatoes, or onions. So the organization has concentrated more on this agenda, which is our responsibility as representatives of the small and medium-size Costa Rican agriculturalists and, much to our regret, it has had to leave aside that regional, more Latin American, world level. In that whirlwind of events and seminars, which often were just images to project to the outside, there was a lot of discussion, a lot of politics, but very little advance in plans that might effectively aid the region's producers. (Hernández Cascante 2001)

The conflict was not simply one of global or regional versus national politics. The tension between politics and the agricultural production that was so central to the Association's claimed identity also became a source of contention and disputed legitimacy. Sinforiano Cáceres, a long-time leader of Nicaragua's National Cooperative Federation (Federación Nacional de Cooperativas, FENACOOP), served as ASOCODE's

general coordinator from 1996 to 1998. Somewhat later, factional disputes led FENACOOP to withdraw from the UNAG. Since the national coalitions – UNAG in this case – were the conduits for participating in ASOCODE and had to vouch for their own member groups that sought participation in the regional Association, FENACOOP (and Cáceres) found itself excluded. "A *campesino* organization," Cáceres Baca remarked,

> can't be directed by people who aren't *campesinos*.... In ASOCODE – in confidence, through friendship and all that – we realized that there were people who weren't agriculturalists, who didn't understand. If I'm not an agriculturalist and to understand the problem of production I have to read a document, that puts me at a disadvantage. Because, in addition to reading it, I have to commit myself, to take it to heart [*asumirlo*]. But if I'm an agriculturalist, I definitely understand the crisis of maize – that's my production, maize, cassava, citrus. I understand it because I live it and, moreover, I've committed my family's economic base and my intellect to it. There's a combination of the personal, the social, the interest group [*gremio*], and the political.... We're not outside, nor on top. We're on the inside. The critical thing is that [the leader] be a producer. He can be an old-timer or someone who recently got involved, or who inherited the farm, not necessarily just a *campesino* from the countryside, but someone who is a producer. When we talk about leaders, when we get together among ourselves, we say that we need an embrace that encourages us and not an embrace that strangles. (Cáceres Baca 2001)

The depictions of ASOCODE as a "whirlwind of events and seminars" or "an embrace that strangles" unknowingly echo Annelise Riles's assertion that a key distinctive characteristic of network activity is "its dual quality as both a means to an end and an end in itself" (2001:51). While the Fijian and Pacific women's organizations Riles studied might not seem the most obvious point of comparison for analyzing a male-dominated peasant association in Central America, the organizational forms and knowledge practices of each are strikingly similar and suggestive of patterns that are likely ubiquitous in global civil society. These include (1) the constitution of networks that appear, formally, to link organizations, but which also, informally, are based significantly on personal ties between activists (and between activists and funders) and on processes of exclusion which, despite a pervasive rhetoric of inclusion and consensus, reflect an unwillingness to accommodate political differences (or a tendency to explain them as personal in nature), even when these do not exceed the statutory or self-defined mission of the network; (2) an aesthetics that manifests itself in network "artifacts," such as glossy newsletters for external consumption and "agendas," directories, "platforms for action," and funding proposals for internal and donor consumption; and (3) a proclivity for demonstrating the effectiveness of the network with reference to its own self-description and activities. Network practices of representation – submitting proposals, organizing meetings, collecting data, drafting documents – are, Riles argues, all too familiar to academics, which is perhaps one reason why scholars of social movements and civil society have often been unable to establish analytical distance from their objects of study. "In its parody of social-scientific analysis ...," she writes, "the Network plays on academic sentimentality about finally having found a 'people' who speak our language, who answer our questions on our own terms. It appeals to our collective fantasy about linking up with our subjects and finding in the 'data' exactly what we set out to find" (2001:174).

Why are processes of network genesis and decomposition so integrally related, as I suggested earlier in this chapter? This becomes clearer if we accept as a working hypothesis Riles's position that network activity has a "dual quality as both a means to an end and an end in itself." In the case of ASOCODE, the formation of new networks was osten-sibly intended to broaden common struggles by incorporating new constituencies. The Central American Indigenous Council (CICA), for example, founded at a 1994 ASOCODE meeting in Panama, sought to involve native peoples alongside non-native peasants in a wide range of campaigns. It also served, however, as a new institutional vehicle for approaching donors and attracting funds. Unable to shake off its image as a creation of EU cooperation agencies, its impact was minimal (Tilley 2002:542–550). As ASOCODE entered into decline, the other regional and extra-regional networks it generated took on increasing importance for some of its leaders as sources of employment and outlets for continued activism. This activism, however, remained largely confined to the existing network modes – seminars, workshops, and congresses, each with its corresponding declaration, poster, and funding agency report.

As if to make this dynamic even clearer, in 2001 two new transnational peasant networks emerged in the Central American region. A decade earlier the most salient elite-led regional free-market project was the Central American Integration System (SICA), and peasant efforts to "globalize from below" took place within the Central American region and in explicit opposition to the vision of the dominant groups. Now, however, anxieties about the SICA had shifted and political space was reconfigured as a result of Mexican President Vicente Fox's proposed Plan Puebla-Panamá (PPP), a new regional integration project, funded primarily by the Inter-American Development Bank, that sought to link southern Mexico and the Central American isthmus in a single free-trade and development zone. One network – the Mesoamerican Peasant Platform or Meeting (Plataforma Campesina Mesoamericana or Encuentro Campesino Mesoamericano, ECM) – arose to oppose the PPP, fueled in part by Guatemala's CONIC (National Indigenous and Peasant Coordination, Coordinadora Nacional Indígena y Campesina) and by the Latin

American Coordination of Rural Organizations (Coordinadora Latinoamericana de Organizaciones del Campo, CLOC), another network which had recently moved its headquarters to Guatemala. While Central America (without Mexico) was the key regional reference point for regional cross-border peasant organizing in the 1990s, the PPP has expanded the relevant space to Mesoamerica, which is usually understood to include Mexico and most of Central America. In 2002 the president of an almost moribund ASOCODE joined Mexican organizations in convening the meetings and remarked that the new ECM network "was betting on Mesoamerica as a space of convergence" (CCS-Chiapas 2002, Bartra 2002). The group's Action Plan called for gaining the ECM "public recognition as Regional Coordinator" of the organized peasantry in Mexico and Central America, a status previously claimed, in the latter zone at least, by ASOCODE. Thus the ECM's declarations made no mention of earlier networks in the region that had raised similarly militant opposition to free trade (and that still existed, or claimed to), or of the implications of the redundancies of old and new networks operating in largely the same terrain, made up of many of the same organizations, and advancing similar demands (ECM 2002a, 2002b).

The second network to emerge in 2001 had a more ambivalent position regarding PPP and was concerned primarily with influencing the impending free-trade treaty between the Central American countries and the United States and, secondarily, the proposed Free Trade Area of the Americas. The Mesoamerican Initiative on Trade, Integration and Sustainable Development (Iniciativa Mesoamericana de Comercio, Integración y Desarrollo Sostenible or Iniciativa, CID) brought together organizations excluded from ASOCODE and the Vía Campesina as well as other peasant organizations (such as Honduras's COCOCH) that were key players in both. It also included a range of research and action-oriented NGOs from Mexico and

Central America, suggesting that the geographical scope of network activity was broadening irrespective of political orientation. Ironically, both of the activists quoted above as eschewing transnational networking in favor of national politics, Jorge Hernández and Sinforiano Cáceres, have been participants in this new Initiative, along with their respective organizations in Costa Rica and Nicaragua (Iniciativa CID 2002). Supported in part by Oxfam International and the AFL-CIO, this group sought to dialogue with the Inter-American Development Bank and to identify possible "opportunities" that might exist for grass-roots organizations in the proposed free-trade treaties. This orientation, as well as the funding sources, is suggestive of an emerging fissure in the peasant networks between pragmatic elements who, along with Oxfam, call for making trade fair, and what might be called "rejectionists" who, like Food First, demand that agriculture be taken out of the World Trade Organization (WTO) and who favor strengthening localized rather than global markets for small agriculturalists' output (curiously invoking new interpretations of concepts such as "subsidiarity," that is, the EU governing principle – articulated first in the Maastricht Treaty – that decision making should be as close to the community level as possible).

It would probably overstate the case to suggest that networks don't ever work or that they simply propagate endlessly with no measurable impact. The development in Central America of a significant sector of highly sophisticated peasant activists could be viewed as one indicator of impressive success (and of the inadequacy of Gramsci's concept of "organic intellectuals," whom he assumed would never emerge from the peasantry; 1971:6). Of the several networks ASOCODE helped to initiate, several are moribund (or virtually so), but others – like those just mentioned that were born in 2001 – maintain intense programs of activity. Those that survive seemed to have learned different lessons from the experience of the

1990s. The Vía Campesina, headquartered in Honduras, has a lean organizational structure which suggests that the dangers of network macrocephaly have been taken into account. It has also achieved a high profile in global justice movements, singled out by *Newsweek* following the 2001 G-8 summit in Genoa as one of eight "kinder, gentler globalist" groups behind the anti-G-8 protests (Newsweek 2001:17). Ironically, though, its presence in Honduras is entirely due to the erstwhile strength of ASOCODE, which was once perceived as the most dynamic of the regional units of Vía Campesina. The diversity of rural interests that became a source of conflict in ASOCODE and the strong influence of organizations with pronounced "verticalist" tendencies (such as the Brazilian Landless Rural Workers Movement, Movimento dos Trabalhadores Rurais sem Terra, MST) have, however, contributed to processes of exclusion from the Vía Campesina. The Indigenous and Peasant Community Agroforestry network (CICAFOC) has shown itself to be similarly vital, in large part by keeping overheads low and by prioritizing the on-the-ground needs of its local base organizations.

"On-the-ground" is an inescapable dimension of successful social movements, though not necessarily of the kind of networks that incorporate social movements or that – like the "dot causes," Internet-based advocacy groups with immeasurable constituencies (Anheier and Themudo 2002) – describe themselves unproblematically as social movements. The appearance of "dot causes" and "shell" organizations and networks clearly complicates social scientists' (as well as donors' and policymakers') efforts to evaluate activists' claims. Some suggest that research focus not on organizations, which tends to privilege their claims and obscure less formal processes of political and cultural change, but on the broader "social fields" in which organizations operate (Burdick 1998). This, however, is more easily done with place-based social movements than with

transnational networks. The phenomenon of virtual or fictitious organizations also raises thorny questions of accountability, democracy, and representation. Part of the potential power of virtual organizations is that their representational claims are difficult or impossible to evaluate and they may have an impact out of proportion to their real numbers – including, at times, impacts that contravene or obstruct the decisions of democratically elected, genuinely representative institutions. While global civil society groups have rightly sought to hold supranational governance institutions, such as the World Bank, responsible for their actions, the nature of the accountability that ought to be expected of NGOs, social movement organizations, and networks is far from clear. As if the emergence of hybrid organizational forms were not enough, responsibilities to elected and appointed leadership bodies, dues-paying members and affiliated organizations, donors and beneficiaries, real and imagined constituencies, and broader publics can become hopelessly confused and a source of considerable contention.

Tellingly, even before the decline of the ASOCODE network, the images peasant activists used to describe its shortcomings were rich in metaphors of flight and distance from the ground (and some of my richest interviews for this project have occurred – or been arranged – at airports and in the planes that shuttle between Central America's capital cities). Some activists in the mid-1990s grumbled about the leadership as a "*jet-set campesino*," while others noted the network's seeming inability to "land" or bring its ambitious "action platforms" to the ground (*aterrizar*). In a moment of self-critical, retrospective candor, ASOCODE's first general coordinator recognized that "when a leader originates at the base [and then] becomes bureaucratized and distant from the base, the people say that he's become like a kite [*se papaloteó*], that he goes up and up into the sky, and then suddenly the string breaks and he's lost" (Campos Cerdas 2001).

NOTES

The author is grateful to the US National Science Foundation for fieldwork support.

1 Arquilla and Ronfeldt played a key role in codifying the US military's strategy against the Taliban regime in Afghanistan and al-Qae'da (Pisani 2002).
2 Comaroff and Comaroff (1999:33) also call attention to how "Euro-modernist forms" of civil society "may be emptied of substance,...turned into a hollow fetish...[or] a dangerous burlesque." At the same time, they acknowledge, as Riles rarely does, that "civil society" nonetheless serves as a vessel for utopian visions and for opening up democratic spaces.
3 On the Campesino a Campesino Program, see Bunch (1982), Enlace Sur–Sur (1998), Holt-Giménez (1996), and Núñez, Cardenal, and Morales (1998).
4 For a less jocular approach to the same problem, see Stirrat (1996).
5 APEMEP (Asociación de Pequeños y Medianos Productores de Panamá), ADC (Alianza Democrática Campesina [El Salvador]), COCOCH (Concejo Coordinador de Organizaciones Campesinas de Honduras).

REFERENCES

Alvarez, Sonia E.
  1998 Latin American Feminisms "Go Global": Trends of the 1990s and Challenges for the New Millennium. In Cultures of Politics/Politics of Cultures: Re-Visioning Latin American Social Movements. Evelina Dagnino Sonia E. Alvarez, and Arturo Escobar, eds. Pp. 293–324. Boulder, CO: Westview Press.
Anheier, Helmut, and Nuno Themudo
  2002 Organisational Forms of Global Civil Society: Implications of Going Global. In Global Civil Society 2002. Marlies Glasius, Helmut Anheier, and Mary Kaldor, eds. Pp. 191–216. Oxford: Oxford University Press.
Arquilla, John, and David Ronfeldt
  2001a The Advent of Netwar (Revisited). In Networks and Netwars: The Future of Terror, Crime, and Militancy. John Arquilla and David Rondfeldt, eds. Pp. 1–25. Santa Monica, CA: RAND.
  ——2001b Preface. In Networks and Netwars: The Future of Terror, Crime, and Militancy. John Arquilla and David Rondfeldt, eds. Pp. v–vi. Santa Monica, CA: RAND.
ASOCODE [Asociación de Organizaciones Campesinas de Centroamérica para la Cooperación y el Desarrollo]
  1999 Documento para la discusión sobre el "Proceso de reorganización y reorientación de ASOCODE." Managua, January.
  ——2001 Memoria: Encuentro regional de dirigentes campesinos centroamericanos, Tegucigalpa, 4 and 5 April.
Bartra, Armando
  2002 Sobre la realización del Encuentro Campesino Mesoamericano. La Jornada Virtual, May 2. <http://www.jornada.unam.mx/2002/may02/0200502/correo.php>. Accessed January 3, 2003.
Biekart, Kees
  1999 The Politics of Civil Society Building: European Private Aid Agencies and Democratic Transitions in Central America. Amsterdam: International Books and the Transnational Institute.
Bunch, Roland
  1982 Two Ears of Corn: A Guide to People-Centered Agricultural Improvement. Oklahoma City: World Neighbors.
Burdick, John
  1998 Blessed Anastácia: Women, Race, and Popular Christianity in Brazil. New York: Routledge.
Cáceres Baca, Sinforiano.
  2001. Author's interview with Sinforiano Cáceres Baca, FENACOOP [Federación Nacional de Cooperativas], Managua, Nicaragua, July 31.
Campos Cerdas, Wilson
  2001 Author's interview with Wilson Campos Cerdas, Mesa Nacional Campesina, San José, Costa Rica, July 27.
Castells, Manuel
  1996 The Rise of the Network Society. The Information Age: Economy, Society and Culture, vol. I. Oxford: Blackwell.

CCS–Chiapas [Coordinación de Comunicación Social, Gobierno del Estado de Chiapas]
    2002   Comunicado de Prensa – Con la participación de la CNPA, UNORCA, CIOAC y CLOC en Tapachula, May 5. <http://www.ccschiapas.gob.mx/pagina_ anterior/boletines/2002/mayo/bol1115. htm> Accessed January 3, 2003.

CEPAL
    2002   Anuario estadístico de América Latina y el Caribe 2001. Santiago, Chile: Comisión Económica Para América Latina y el Caribe–Naciones Unidas.

Cohen, Jean
    1995   Interpreting the Notion of Civil Society. *In* Toward a Global Civil Society. Michael Walzer, ed. Pp. 35–40. Providence, RI: Berghahn Books.

Cohen, Jean, and Andrew Arato
    1992   Civil Society and Political Theory. Cambridge, MA: MIT Press.

Comaroff, John L., and Jean Comaroff
    1999   Introduction. *In* Civil Society and the Political Imagination in Africa: Critical Perspectives. John L. Comaroff and Jean Comaroff, eds. Pp. 1–33. Chicago: University of Chicago Press.

Cuenca, Breny
    1992   El poder intangible: La AID y el estado salvadoreño en los años ochenta. Managua: CRIES/PREIS.

Desmarais, Annette-Aurélie
    2002   The Vía Campesina: Consolidating an International Peasant and Farm Movement. Journal of Peasant Studies 29(2):91–124.

Echeverría, Carlos Manuel
    1993   La integración centroamericana y las relaciones extrarregionales fundamentales: La visión de FEDEPRICAP. Presencia 5(19):100–105.

ECM
    2002a   07/15. Declaración Campesina de Nicaragua II Encuentro Campesino Mesoamericano <http://movimientos.org/cloc/show_text.hp3?key = 1041 Managua>. Accessed August 8, 2002.
    ——2002b   07/15. Plan de Acción II Encuentro Campesino Mesoamericano. <http://movimientos.org/cloc/ show_text.hp3?key = 1040 Managua>. Accessed February 10, 2002.

Edelman, Marc
    1998   Transnational Peasant Politics in Central America. Latin American Research Review 33(3):49–86.
    ——1999   Peasants Against Globalization: Rural Social Movements in Costa Rica. Stanford, CA: Stanford University Press.
    ——2001   Social Movements: Changing Paradigms and Forms of Politics. Annual Review of Anthropology 30:285–317.
    ——2003   Transnational Peasant and Farmer Networks. *In* Global Civil Society 2003. Marlies Glasius, Helmut Anheier, and Mary Kaldor, eds. Oxford: Oxford University Press.

Enlace Sur–Sur
    1998   ¿Qué es Campesino a Campesino? <http://www.laneta.apc. org/mexsursur/ quiensom.htm Mexico>. Accessed July 16, 2001.

Escoto, Jorge, and Manfredo Marroquín
    1992   La AID en Guatemala: Poder y sector empresarial. Managua: CRIES/ AVANCSO.

Freres, Christian
    1998   La cooperación de las sociedades civiles de la Unión Europea con América Latina. Madrid: AIETI.

Fundación Arias para la Paz y el Progreso Humano
    1998   Elementos para el debate sobre la cooperación y las ONG en Centroamérica <http://www.arias.or.cr/documentos/nmmr/onceenf/part11.htm>. Accessed June 16, 1998.

Grabendorff, Wolf
    1984   The Internationalization of the Central American Crisis. *In* Political Change in Central America: Internal and External Dimensions. Heinrich-W. Krumwiede, Wolf Grabendorff, and Jörg Todt, eds. Pp. 155–171. Boulder, CO: Westview Press.

Gramsci, Antonio
    1971   Selections from the Prison Notebooks. Trans. Quintin Hoare and Geoffrey Nowell Smith. New York: International Publishers.

Hansen, Finn
  1996 Relaciones Europa–Centroamérica: Ayuda externa y comercio desfavor-
  able. Managua: CRIES.
Hearn, Jonathan
  2001 Taking Liberties: Contesting Visions
  of the Civil Society Project. Critique of
  Anthropology 21(4): 339–360.
Helleiner, Eric
  1994 From Bretton Woods to global
  finance: A world turned upside down.
  In Political Economy and the Changing
  Global Order. Richard Stubbs and Geoffrey R.D. Underhill, eds. Pp. 163–175.
  New York: St. Martin's Press.
Hernández Cascante, Jorge
  2001 Author's interview with Jorge Her-
  nández Cascante, UPANACIONAL
  [Unión Nacional de Pequeños y Media-
  nos Productores Agropecuarios], Tibás,
  Costa Rica, July 27.
Holt-Giménez, Eric
  1996 The Campesino a Campesino Move-
  ment: Farmer-Led, Sustainable Agricul-
  ture in Central America and Mexico.
  Development Report, vol. 10. Oakland,
  CA: Institute for Food and Development
  Policy.
Iniciativa CID [Iniciativa Mesoamericana de
  Comercio, Integración y Desarrollo]
  2002 Campaña Regional en Torno al
  Tratado de Libre Comercio entre los
  Estados Unidos y Centro América.
  Document provided by the Federación
  Nacional de Cooperativas, Nicaragua.
Keane, John
  1998 Civil Society: Old Images, New
  Visions. Stanford, CA: Stanford Univer-
  sity Press.
——2001 Global Civil Society? *In* Global
  Civil Society 2001. Marlies Glasius
  Helmut Anheier, and Mary Kaldor, eds.
  Pp. 23–47. Oxford: Oxford University
  Press.
Keck, Margaret E., and Kathryn Sikkink
  1998 Activists Beyond Borders: Advo-
  cacy Networks in International Politics.
  Ithaca, NY: Cornell University Press.
Latinobarómetro
  2002 Latinobarómetro: Opinión Pública
  Latinoamericana <http://www.latinobar-

ometro.org/English/iniconst-i.htm>.
  Accessed April 10, 2002.
Lofredo, Gino
  1991 Hágase rico en los 90. (Usted toda-
  vía no tiene su ONG? Chasqui 39:15–
  18.
Macdonald, Laura
  1997 Supporting Civil Society: The Political Role of Non-Governmental Organizations in Central America. New York:
  St. Martin's Press.
Morales, G. Abelardo, and Martha Isabel
  Cranshaw
  1997 Regionalismo Emergente: Redes de la
  sociedad civil e integración centroamericana. San José: FLACSO and Ibis–
  Dinamarca.
Newsweek
  2001 The New Face of Protest: A Who's
  Who. July 30:17.
Nielsen, Kai
  1995 Reconceptualizing Civil Society for
  Now: Some Somewhat Gramscian Turn-
  ings. *In* Toward a Global Civil Society.
  Michael Walzer, ed. Pp. 41–67. Provi-
  dence, RI: Berghahn Books.
Núñez, Orlando, Gloria Cardenal, and Juan
  Morales
  1998 Desarrollo agroecológico y asocia-
  tividad campesina. 2nd edition. Managua: Centro para la Investigación, la
  Promoción y el Desarrollo Rural y
  Social.
Pisani, Francis
  2002 "Best Story, Not the Biggest
  Bomb": How to Fight the Terror Networks. Le Monde Diplomatique, June.
  60http://mondediplo.com/2002/06/
  02networks> Accessed June 11, 2002.
Reuben Soto, William
  1991 El papel de las ONG en la cooperación europea hacia Centroamérica.
  In Más allá del ajuste: La contribución
  europea al desarrollo democrático y
  duradero de las economías centro-
  americanas. Raúl Ruben and Govert
  Van Oord, eds. Pp. 337–369. San José:
  Departamento Ecuménico de Investiga-
  ciones.
Riechmann, Jorge and Francisco Fernández
  Buey

1994 Redes que dan libertad: Introducción a los nuevos movimientos sociales. Barcelona: Ediciones Paidós.

Riles, Annelise
2001 The Network Inside Out. Ann Arbor: University of Michigan Press.

Rosa, Herman
1993 AID y las transformaciones globales en El Salvador: El papel de la política de asistencia económica de los Estados Unidos desde 1980. Managua: CRIES.

Roy, Joaquín, ed.
1992 The Reconstruction of Central America: The Role of the European Community. Miami, FL: University of Miami.

Sanahuja, José Antonio
1996 América Central y la Unión Europea: En busca de nuevas formas de cooperación. *In* Unión Europea Centroamérica: Cambio de scenarios. Abelardo Morales, ed. Pp. 117–158. San José: FLACSO and Comisión Europea.

Sassen, Saskia
2000 The State and the New Geography of Power. *In* The Ends of Globalization: Bringing Society Back. Marco van der Land, Don Kalb, and Richard Staring, eds. Pp. 49–65. Lanham, MD: Rowman & Littlefield.

Schori, Pierre
1981 El desafío europeo en Centroamérica. San José: EDUCA.

Smith, Jackie
1997 Characteristics of the Modern Transnational Social Movement Sector. *In* Transnational Social Movements and Global Politics: Solidarity Beyond the State. Jackie Smith, Charles Chatfield, and Ron Pagnucco, eds. Pp. 42–58. Syracuse, NY: Syracuse University Press.

Sojo, Carlos
1992 La mano visible del mercado: La asistencia de Estados Unidos al sector privado costarricense en la década de los ochenta. Managua: CRIES.

Stirrat, R. L.
1996 The New Orthodoxy and Old Truths: Participation, Empowerment and Other Buzz Words. *In* Assessing Participation: A Debate from South Asia. S. Bastian and N. Bastian, eds. Pp. 67–92. New Delhi: Konark Publishers.

Tarrow, Sidney
1998 Power in Movement: Social Movements and Contentious Politics. 2nd edition. Cambridge: Cambridge University Press.
——2001 Transnational Politics: Contention and Institutions in International Politics. Annual Review of Political Science 4:1–20.

Tilley, Virginia Q.
2002 New Help or New Hegemony? The Transnational Indigenous Peoples' Movement and "Being Indian" in El Salvador. Journal of Latin American Studies 34:525–554.

Tilly, Charles
1984 Social Movements and National Politics. *In* Statemaking and Social Movements: Essays in History and Theory. Charles Bright and Susan Harding, eds. Pp. 297–317. Ann Arbor: University of Michigan Press.

2

The State and the Right Wing: The Village Scout Movement in Thailand

Katherine A. Bowie

In much of the contemporary literature on social movements, civil society and the state appear as opposing forces. As David Slater writes, "social movements have tended to be interpreted as part of civil society, which in turn has been distinguished as separate from the political affairs of the modern state" (1998:384; see also Hann 1996). Although the state is included in analyses of "contentious politics," the focus has been on the oppositional movements generated by historical processes of nation-state formation (McAdam et al. 2001, Tarrow 1998, Tilly 1986:6). In general, the theoretical focus tends to be on the ways "a movement can coopt a segment of the state" (McCarthy and Wolfson 1992:274). As Zald writes, the role of states "as determinants and constraints on social movement mobilization and outcomes" has not been sufficiently studied (1992:327; see also Carley 1997:153, Gale 1986:202). However, in an older literature, the state was imbricated in civil society, with the ruling classes seeking to establish their hegemony by constructing "an organic passage from the other classes into their own" (Gramsci 1971:260). While a current gener-

ation of social movement theorists have given agency to the subaltern, they have paid less attention to the role of the state in seeking the "active consent of those over whom it rules" (Gramsci 1971:244). So heavily has the contemporary scholarly literature favored mobilization from below, one might wonder if a state-sponsored social movement is not a definitional contradiction in terms.[1]

Because "civil society" has been interpreted as a "language in which to talk about the utopian ideals of democracy and moral community" (Comaroff and Comaroff 1999:viii), academics have focused on leftwing social movements resistance (Escobar and Alvarez 1992:2, Melucci 1996:31). Only more recently are scholars recognizing that "social movements may be socially conservative" (Castells 1997:70; see also Alvarez et al. 1998:8, Cohen and Arato 1992:24, Melucci 1996:31) and that rightwing movements should receive more attention (see especially Pichardo 1997 and Edelman 2001).[2] As Edelman suggests, "conservative responses are also an outcome of proliferating social tensions, rapid cultural change, the advance of democratization, and the progressive movements themselves" (2001:293–4). If left-wing movements are characteristically in opposition to the state, right-wing movements are more ambiguous. As Diamond argues, "To be right-wing means to support the state in its capacity as enforcer of order and to oppose the state as distributor of wealth and power downward and more equitably in society" (1995:9). However, as Berlet and Lyons note, some rightist movements have advocated downward distribution of wealth and power, and yet others have rejected the state entirely (2000:5–6).

This chapter reinserts the state into the contested domain of civil society by presenting an extreme case of right-wing social movement deliberately created by the Thai state.[3] The Village Scouts (also called Wild Tiger Cubs) was the largest right-wing movement in Thai history, reaching its zenith in the mid-1970s. Founded in 1971 under the auspices of the Ministry of the Interior's powerful Border Patrol Police and given royal patronage in 1972, the state-sponsored Village Scout movement was intended to counter the threat of "communism." War was raging in Thailand's neighbor countries – in Vietnam, Cambodia, and Laos. Simultaneously, Thailand's long-entrenched military dictators found themselves facing a rapidly growing domestic communist guerrilla campaign and an even more rapidly growing popular movement calling for democratic reforms. At its peak in 1976, over 2,387 initiation sessions were held and some two million adult Thais became members. All told, some five million people have been initiated into its ranks, or approximately one-fifth of Thailand's adult population.

In addition to military suppression, the Thai state responded to its internal opposition with a surreal anthropology of magical state lore. Rumors were generated of communist potions which shrank penises, of blood-sucking vampires in search of blood for wounded guerrillas, and of spirit mediums able to communicate with the repentant spirit of Karl Marx. Thousands of amulets and white *phaa yan* cloths imprinted with mystical designs were blessed by high-ranking monks and distributed by military officers to protect soldiers from communist guerrillas. Amongst its seemingly surreal responses to the growing popular demands for reform was the inauguration of a nationwide Village Scout movement. At first glance, the Village Scout movement seemed an unlikely candidate to succeed in the serious business of combating communist insurgency. And yet, remarkably, the Village Scout movement became the largest right-wing popular organization ever fabricated in Thai history.

Dedicating themselves to "King, Nation and Religion," the primary criterion for membership in the Village Scouts was participation in a five-day initiation ritual. Initiation to Village Scouthood involved five days and four nights of singing light-hearted songs specially written for the movement such as "Holiday in America" and "Smile! Smile," dancing the duck-waddle dance, a dance intended to be ridiculous; performing skits; holding evening campfires; and listening to a few didactic lessons in the midst of the entertainment. Although the initiation was designed to be entertaining for its participants, it was in fact quite sophisticated and had entailed considerable planning, testing, and refinement (see Bowie 1997, Muecke 1980 for initiation details). Sleep deprivation – participants only received a total of about thirteen hours' sleep over the five-day period – and the course of this initiation ritual wrought its magic on the minds of its participants. On the final day, the initiates received a maroon kerchief, a gift from the king and a symbol of their new identity as Village Scouts. So effective was the initiation that its grand finale became a predictable and repetitive sight: initiates being carried off on stretchers sobbing hysterically and feeling themselves overwhelmed by an intense love of the Thai nation and royal family. As one elderly village woman recalled, "I had always loved the king but never as intensely as I did at that moment. That moment I felt it through the core of my being [*saabsyyng*]."

The Village Scout movement had a two-fold approach. Viewed broadly, the movement sought to inoculate the Thai body politic against communism by injecting its citizenry with a dose of nationalism. Viewed more immediately, the movement served to intimidate anyone critical of the government into silence and to inform on those who refused to be intimidated. Upon initiation, Village Scouts throughout the country were encouraged to become "eyes and ears" (*pèn huu pen taa*) for the government and "to inform local officials about any strangers entering their village" (McNabb 1978:142). As one Village Scout song, "News," explains:

> What is he doing?
> Where is he doing it?
> When is he doing it?
> Whom is he doing it with?
> Who is he?
> And how is he doing it?
> Just tell us! (MacNabb 1978:142)

The vast majority of Village Scout activities appeared innocuous. Members spent their time visiting the evening campfire sessions of scout troops undergoing initiation, receiving troop flags, or celebrating the annual anniversaries of their own initiations. Scouts also swept the streets in their neighborhoods or cleaned up canals, parks, and other public areas. They participated in local temple festivals and gave donations to scouts or others whose homes had burnt down or had experienced similar disasters. Yet other activities were highly politicized. They visited government soldiers wounded in combat with communist guerrillas. Very often, apparently innocent street-cleaning projects were timed to coincide with progressive rallies being organized by workers, peasants, or students. In the course of my own work as a freelance journalist, I received a death threat ostensibly from village-based scout organizations. If initially there had been those who dismissed the Village Scouts as a harmless, even naive, attempt at counterinsurgency, by the mid-1970s, everyone took the Village Scouts seri-

ously. By far the most terrifying moment of the Village Scout movement was their frenzied participation in the bloody and gruesome attack on Thammasat University on October 6, 1976. On this day Village Scouts enthusiastically assisted in the beating and killing of scores of university students; some students were shot, others garroted, and yet others doused with gasoline and set ablaze. The day ended with abrogation of parliament and the return of military rule.[4]

This chapter summarizes the role of the Thai state in the creation and spread of the Village Scout movement. Although the role of the state was fundamental, the movement's spread can be best understood by exploring the intersection between the crisis facing the Thai state and the varying hopes and fears of its citizenry. The chapter is divided into three main sections. In the first section, corresponding with the years 1970–1, I describe the role of the state in the origin of the movement, noting the particular role of the Border Patrol Police and the king. In the second section, corresponding with the years 1972–6, I describe the factors underlying the dramatic expansion of civilian participation, highlighting the complex symbolic role played by the king in catalyzing both hopes for progressive reform and a conservative backlash. In the third section, corresponding with the period after the return to military rule on October 6, 1976 up to the present, I describe the irony of the state clamping down on its own creation. The Thai state did not open its Pandora's box of right-wing conservatism lightly; as soon as its crisis of legitimacy eased, it sought to replace the lid.

The State: Of Communism and Counterinsurgency

The Founder and the Border Patrol Police

Major-General Somkhuan Harikhul was the official founder of the Village Scout movement in Thailand.[5] At the time he began the Village Scouts, he was a commanding officer of the Border Patrol Police (BPP) base in northeastern Thailand. The BPP, under the Ministry of the Interior, is one of Thailand's premier counterinsurgency agencies. In line with prevailing theories of counterinsurgency of the day, which emphasized police over military forces, the BPP was founded in cooperation with American CIA advisors in the 1950s (see Blaufarb 1977, Lobe 1977). Unlike many other high-ranking government officials, Somkhuan did not come from a wealthy urban family. He was born in the southern province of Krabi, the son of a low-ranking government official. With five children in the family, his father wondered how he would be able to receive an advanced education. Fortunately, Somkhuan's grandfather was a temple abbot and so he was able to live free of charge at the temple while attending elementary school. Because he was a good student and because of his father's connections, he received a partial scholarship enabling him to receive his secondary schooling. He earned additional funds for school by hiring himself out for manual labor. Ironically, because of the low regard in which ordinary people held police, Somkhuan did not want to become a police officer, but a schoolteacher. However, because of the push to swell the ranks of the Thai police, Somkhuan was able to receive a scholarship to study to become a police officer. His awareness of poverty, the abuse of power by police and other corrupt government officials, and other such rural grievances was reinforced in the course of his work, most notably during his years as a paratrooper when he lived and traveled extensively among villages in remote parts of the country. These early life experiences gave him a greater awareness of the difficulties of poor people in Thai society. As Somkhuan advanced through the ranks, he also received special training in military intelligence and psychological warfare.

Major-General Somkhuan attributes the genesis of his idea to develop the Village Scouts to a major battle between government troops and communist guerrillas which occurred in December, 1968. At the time of this battle Somkhuan was serving as superintendent of Border Patrol Police Region 4, headquartered in Udorn Thani province in Thailand's impoverished northeastern region. As part of a strategy to encourage villagers living in remote areas to trust government officials and share information about local political developments, the BPP were often assigned to remote villages to serve as teachers. On this occasion, communist guerrillas burnt to the ground a BPP school in a village in the remote mountainous region where Petchabun, Phitsanulok, and Loei provinces meet. As soon as he was notified of the attack, he sent BPP and provincial police forces to the scene. For 17 days there was intense fighting. His men were pinned down and unable to retreat. Additional forces were called in, both police and military. In the course of the fighting, over a hundred men were killed or wounded. This battle marked the most serious military encounter between guerrillas and government forces to date; it also represented the spread of guerrilla insurgency into the interior of the country.[6]

After one of the days of battle, while returning to BPP headquarters, Somkhuan was forced to ride in a helicopter carrying the bodies of his dead men. The helicopter was so full he had nowhere to sit except upon the corpses of these men. As he explained to me, he could not sleep that night. He wondered why Thailand was turning into a battlefield with Thais killing each other instead of living in peace and harmony. He stayed up all night thinking and ended up writing eight pages reflecting on the causes of this collapse of civil society.

That night marked the beginning of serious efforts by Somkhuan to find a solution to what he himself described as the beginnings of a civil war. His personal knowledge of poverty and village life together with his training in psychological warfare reinforced his tendency to seek a political rather than military solution. Shortly after this battle, Somkhuan participated in a week-long Wood Badge training camp. Border Patrol officers routinely promoted Boy Scout activities as part of their work with village youth in sensitive areas. As part of his Boy Scout activities, he decided to undertake a Wood Badge leadership-training program in 1969. Somkhuan was struck by the way in which the training brought together complete strangers who, by the end of the week, came to experience deep bonds of love and friendship. He began to encourage his fellow police officers to receive Wood Badge training, even arranging some sessions himself. Somkhuan was convinced that drawing upon Wood Badge techniques would enable him to develop a program fostering bonds not just among youth, but adults.[7]

However, his initial proposals were rejected by his superiors, who were concerned that this movement would politicize villagers and get out of control. The Thai government had long had laws prohibiting villagers from joining associations organized at a supra-village level; even agricultural associations were only legal if they were organized under the auspices of the state. Successions of military governments had gone so far as to ban the gathering of more than five individuals at a time to discuss politics. As George Tanham, a Thai counterinsurgency expert, explains the ethos of the time: "Inciting the masses to political action, trying to organize them in large groups, and developing a greater popular awareness have not been part of Thai politics. Rather the leaders have tried to keep the people away from political matters and have them concentrate on their own mundane affairs" (1974:37).

Meanwhile, government security was deteriorating. Conflict in the area where the school had been burnt down continued, as did communist infiltration. Somkhuan increased the number of BPP village teachers and sent more troops into the area. Yet these increases did not ease the situation. When his superior officer was transferred, Somkhuan

again proposed his idea for an adult version of the Wood Badge program. The new superior officer gave Somkhuan permission to develop a pilot initiation session in Loei province. Somkhuan's position as a commanding officer placed the necessary personnel and budget resources at his discretion. Scores of planners from Somkhuan's BPP staff and the local district office spent months developing the music and lyrics for the scout songs, conceiving skits and lessons, and handling the logistics.

Despite some initial difficulties when villagers wanted compensation for their participation, the pilot session proved to be largely successful. Some 120 villagers, 30 from each of four villages, attended.[8] According to Somkhuan, instructors and participants alike wept when it became time to separate. With the basic design tested, the first official Village Scout initiation session was held on August 9, 1971. In the first few years, the number of initiations increased slowly. Sessions followed in villages along the Thai-Lao border, in Udorn Thani, Nong Khaaj, Sakon Nakhorn, and Nakhon Phanom provinces. According to Somkhuan, wherever initiation rites had been held, villagers began to cooperate with officials and it became possible to withdraw many of the additional BPP troops.

That the Village Scout movement would have originated within the ranks of the BPP can be attributed to three aspects of its relative position in the Thai state. First, while anticommunist rhetoric served a useful purpose in intra-bureaucratic competition, the military and other key political players were generally more concerned with maintaining national power in the capital than with the growth of communism upcountry. The actual hands-on responsibility of coping with "border" problems was relegated to the Border Patrol Police. Secondly, because of this hands-on involvement, the BPP had the most incentive to minimize the need for combat and the resulting likely casualties. As Somkhuan explained in his interview, the Thai border was far too long to patrol effectively without village cooperation. Because the BPP worked closely with villagers, it was aware of the importance of gaining villagers' trust, cooperation, and loyalty. Thirdly, the BPP was the agency in the best position within the structure of the Thai state to be free to innovate because of its relative autonomy and its close relations to the palace. Although formally located in the Ministry of Interior, Lobe and Morell suggest that the BPP had no authority over it other than the palace (1978:169), and thus "had the freedom to be different, to devise innovative relationships between an armed component of the government and the Thai people" (1978:171).

Royal Patronage and Multiple Government Agencies

However, Somkhuan's success with his initial scout initiation sessions formed only a small part of what the Village Scout movement was to become. At the time, his jurisdiction was limited to the northeastern region of the country, in the remote border regions in which the BPP operated. Nationwide, the BPP only operated in specific, generally remote, mountainous regions of the country. However, the Village Scouts became a multi-agency government operation of remarkable scale. At its peak in 1976, some 2,387 initiation sessions were held, involving 1,897,540 new initiates. Not including the personnel needed to take care of administrative matters before and after the initiations, each initiation session involved, at a minimum, some 40 people.[9] Since each of these 40 people spent at least 5 days in each initiation, approximately 477,400 labor days were involved in simply staffing the initiation sessions. This figure represents an annual staff of 1,836 people working around the clock (instructors were on duty for 24 hours a day throughout the course of the 5-day initiation). Were the labor days recalculated on the basis of a normal work week, an annual staff of 5,508 people would be involved – just for the actual ritual itself.

Not only did the Village Scout movement represent a tremendous commitment of personnel, it also required considerable inter-agency cooperation. The staffing needs alone far surpassed the capabilities of a single government agency. From the beginning, the Village Scout movement had involved the inter-agency collaboration; however, these connections were ad hoc and localized. Formalized cooperation with other government agencies was also essential. As more and more different departments within the Ministries of the Interior, Education, and Public Health became increasingly involved with various aspects of the Village Scout administration and oversight, the opportunities for bureaucratic conflict increased. The larger the movement became, the more remarkable the level of cooperation which the Village Scouts movement demanded of the bureaucracy.

Royal patronage played a critical role in facilitating intra-bureaucratic cooperation. The royal family had long-standing relations with the BPP since its officers served as royal bodyguards and accompanied members of the royal family on their upcountry visits (Lobe and Morell 1978:157, 172). In November 1971, the king's mother, who had long worked with the BPP to improve public welfare and border security, visited the ninth Village Scout initiation held in a village in the northeastern province of Nakhon Phanom. King Bhumiphol and Queen Sirikhit then attended the 30th Village Scout initiation held on March 19, 1972.[10] Favorably impressed, the king invited Somkhuan and his commanding officer to an audience at Chitrlada Palace. At this meeting the king formally offered the movement his patronage and made an initial donation of 100,000 baht. The king's motivation in giving his patronage to the movement can be understood both as a way of supporting government counterinsurgency efforts and as a way of establishing a popular base from which to counter certain factions in the Thai state. By building an antimilitary, anticorruption, pro-development, and pro-grass-roots popular organization, the king may also have hoped to develop an alternative mechanism for redressing village grievances.[11] Thereafter, King Bhumiphol and other members of the royal family became closely identified with the Village Scout movement. In addition to providing the distinctive maroon scarves for initiates, members of the royal family began attending many scout functions in person.

Royal patronage provided the political pressure to facilitate intra-bureaucratic cooperation. On October 25, 1972 the Royal Secretary sent a letter to the Deputy Minister of the Interior asking that all provincial governors be encouraged to cooperate with the BPP in holding Village Scout initiation sessions (*Daily News*, June 2, 1976). Notably, the Royal Secretary's brother, Praphat Charusathien, was then Minister of the Interior. The royal directive provided the political incentive to establish a working relationship across different nationwide government agencies and provided the Village Scout movement with the tremendous personnel resources of the Ministry of the Interior. Of all the various agencies involved in the Village Scout movement, the Ministry of Interior was the most significant; the elementary schoolteachers who provided most of the staffing for initiation sessions were under its administration. On October 8, 1973, the working relationship between the BPP and the Ministry of the Interior as a whole was formalized in an official directive which ordered every provincial governor to become personally involved in organizing Village Scouts in their respective provinces (*Daily Times*, June 14, 1976).

However, bureaucratic support for staffing was only one hurdle to be overcome by scout organizers; defraying the financial costs of the movement was another. The initiation rites were expensive. Depending on the lavishness of the stage props and the quality of the food provided to the staff, an average session cost between 15,000 and 40,000 baht. This sum did not include the hidden staff salaries, food costs, or the expenses borne by the individual initiates.[12] Accord-

ingly, the 2,387 sessions held in 1976 alone represented a cost of some 35–95 million baht (US$1.8–4.8 million). Thailand's first countrywide wage law, only passed in October 1974, established 10 baht a day (50 cents) as the minimum wage.[13] Using the official minimum wage as an indication, the minimum costs of these initiation rites represented the entire annual income of over 13,000–26,000 people working 365 days per year. Should the hidden salary costs for staffing be included, the figure would be even higher. For a country with only a meager social welfare program, the Village Scout movement entailed a considerable financial commitment.

Royal involvement not only stimulated intra-governmental cooperation, it also facilitated fundraising. Although government funds were spent in salaries paid to government officials involved in staffing scout activities, the king placed pressure on the Village Scout movement not to use government funds for scout events. The mainstay of Thai businesses are in the hands of Sino-Thai. Because the Sino-Thai have from time to time been the victims of xenophobic persecution, the king and these businessmen had developed a mutually advantageous relationship. Sino-Thai businessmen have often donated generously to royally sponsored charities, and since the king often rewarded their generosity with awards and titles, they, in turn, have received a kind of royal protection which helped to vouchsafe public goodwill (Girling 1981:142). Royal patronage played a crucial role in facilitating both inter-agency cooperation and fundraising efforts as the scout movement was launched.

The People: Of Village Hopes and Urban Fears

The King, the Progressives, and the Hopes of the Agrarian Poor

The Thai state has supported scores of programs and, despite government support, many programs still fail. Since 1950, government counterinsurgency efforts generated no less than 120 development projects, 12 security projects, and at least 20 initiatives for different types of paramilitary forces; none caught on like the Village Scout movement.[14] At the time of the Scout movement's inception, the king's standing was rising rapidly and his patronage played a critical role in facilitating popular participation. Royal involvement enabled the movement to spin its emotional magic by drawing on the aura of the Thai monarchy, giving currency to a rumor that Naresuan, a famous sixteenth-century king, had appeared in a dream to Queen Sirikhit, telling her that "Thailand would fall unless the people were united, and that the Village Scouts was the means to unite them" (Muecke 1980:413n.). In explaining the power of the Thai monarchy, there are those who would appeal to notions of "divine kingship"; such accounts undermine our understanding of the extent of which King Bhumiphol's position was achieved and not ascribed.

Throughout much of the twentieth century, the institution of monarchy was weak. When King Bhumiphol ascended the throne in 1946, he was very young and kept removed from politics (see Bowie 1997: 87–91, Chaloemtiarana 1979:309–34, Girling 1981:140, Keyes 1987:80). However, during the 1960s, the king became more active. He held private meetings with military leaders and businessmen, and traveled more frequently to rural areas. He became increasingly concerned with the failure of the army suppression campaign in the border regions and also with the growing corruption of this regime. By 1968–9, he began making public statements insinuating his sentiments. In 1968, he told Thammasat University students that it would be the last year they would meet without a constitution. In March, 1969, he gave an address at Chulalongkorn University in which he expressed his concern over the government's interaction with villagers. Having developed considerable knowledge of hill-tribe issues, he shared

the concerns of those who felt that the military's policies of bombing hill-tribe villages and relocating hill-tribe populations to refugee centers were counterproductive. Speaking in September, 1971 at Chulalongkorn University, the king encouraged students to continue protesting corruption so that in the next 20 years there would be no corruption in Thailand (Morell and Samudavanija 1981:66–7).

The demand for constitutional government grew amongst all strata of Thai society, leading ultimately to a popular uprising that ousted the hated military government on October 14, 1973. Mismanagement of rice supplies led to rice shortages in urban centers. Inflation contributed to a spate of labor unrest and strikes. Student organizations across the country began to organize protests on a variety of issues, ranging from campus concerns to national concerns such as Japanese involvement in the Thai economy, American military presence, government corruption, and rice shortages (for details see Darling 1974, Heinze 1974, Reynolds 1978). The king indicated his support for the pro-democracy movement in a variety of ways. During one massive student protest in June, 1973, he instructed the police not to use violence against students and had tents and food prepared for the demonstrators in the palace grounds (Heinze 1974:494). In a speech given in late September at Chulalongkorn University, the king stated that the public was ready to support the students any time they saw that student activities were beneficial to society. A prominent newspaper editor, himself a member of the royal family, began publishing editorials calling for the government's resignation (Reynolds 1978:146). So great was the tension between the government and the monarchy that rumors proliferated that the regime was even planning to establish a republic and eliminate the monarchy.

Events came to a head in October 1973. On October 13, the largest demonstration in Thai history was held, as a crowd of some 400,000 marched from Thammasat

University to Democracy Monument. The demonstrators bore Thai national and Buddhist flags, and carried large pictures of the king and queen. In the early hours of the morning of October 14, shooting broke out. As word spread, the popular uprising spread (for detailed accounts, see Heinze 1974, Punyodhayana 1975, Reynolds 1978). During the course of the day some seventy demonstrators were killed and about a thousand injured. As the military opened fire, many of the fleeing students sought refuge in the palace grounds. By throwing open the palace gates to the fleeing demonstrators, the king won himself a firm place in the students' hearts. At 7:15 PM that Sunday evening King Bhumiphol appeared on national television and, after expressing his sorrow at the violence, announced the resignation of the military government and his interim appointment of a widely respected university rector as prime minister. At the official request of the king himself, the military dictators were forced into exile. In well-publicized visits, the king and queen met hospitalized students (Marks 1977:54). The king also appointed to a national convention 2,436 members who were charged with selecting an interim National Assembly. Unlike previous Assemblies, the convention members included many rural leaders and few military or police officers (Keyes 1987:87). Thus, in the days following these dramatic events, the king set in motion the crucial machinery to institute a constitutional democracy and begin the healing process. The king's reputation could not have been higher.

The Village Scout movement combined the emotional rhetoric of family and village with the ideology of monarchy and nation. Scout instructors portrayed the king and queen as parental figures and all scouts as their children. Villagers were encouraged to believe that by joining the Scout movement they were becoming part of a national extended family of mutual assistance. Instructors cited examples of Scouts helping one another with funerals, rebuilding homes destroyed by floods or fires, and providing generous con-

tributions to local temples. Rumors were rife that Village Scouts received free or cheaper medical care and other benefits from the state. In this appeal to family, the Scout movement drew upon villagers' warm associations with their immediate extended families and the longstanding practices of mutual cooperation in which the village as a whole served as a large family or support network.[15] The king's high standing facilitated deployment of the symbols of the nation as a loving family in which the king and queen were national parents.

Furthermore, the king's gift of a maroon kerchief – blessed by the nation's most revered monks – allowed the movement to tap into a vast lore of amulets and sacred powers which exists in Thai popular culture (see Reynolds 1977, Tambiah 1984). Protective amulets are a favorite topic of conversation amongst urban folk and villagers alike. Most Thais traveling any distance – and many as part of their daily attire – wear one or more amulets around their neck. An object may be sacred in its own right (as a relic of the Buddha or famous monk) or by having been blessed by someone with considerable sacrality. Combining royal majesty with village beliefs in sacred amulets, the Village Scout designers developed a mystical folklore drawing on the magical protective power of the scout kerchiefs. The king's high stature at the time contributed significantly to the belief that the royal Village Scout kerchiefs were sacred.[16]

Many villagers hoped that by joining what they saw as a royal organization they would gain direct access to the king or members of his entourage for assistance with their problems. At the very least, because of the threat of lèse-majesté, it would be difficult for villagers to avoid joining the movement.[17] Some villagers joined under duress, fearing that if they did not join they would be labeled as communist sympathizers. Some villagers joined because they had heard the five-day initiation was a lot of fun, with plenty of opportunity for flirtation, since both men and women participated. Some joined

because they had heard of the magical properties of the royal kerchief and wanted to
obtain one. Still others joined because they
hoped that they would become part of a
broader network of mutual support, developing closer ties with wealthier villagers and
townspeople for assistance in times of need.
Some hoped to develop connections with
government officials in order to facilitate requests for licenses or to ward off harassment
otherwise made likely by inevitable minor
violations of bureaucratic regulations. Yet
others joined in the general hope that, should
overwhelming problems arise, they might
have a better chance of having their letter
read by His Majesty the King and thus receive special assistance.

The King, Conservatives, and the Fears of Urban Elites

While royal support clearly contributed to
the initial expansion of the Village Scout
movement, the movement experienced dramatic growth only after 1975. In 1971, only
eight sessions were held. In 1972, 113 sessions were held involving 16,137 initiates. By
the end of 1974, there were still under
100,000 members. Membership began to
expand significantly in 1975; the year 1976
alone saw almost two million members initiated. To understand the rapid expansion of
the Village Scout movement, it is necessary to
understand the changing significance of royal
patronage in the context of a volatile political
economy. The fledgling civilian government
was facing growing economic difficulties,
which in turn intensified the political polarization between left and right. The domestic
tension was heightened by the fall of the
regimes in Vietnam, Laos, and Cambodia in
1975, and by the withdrawal of US troops
from Thailand in 1976. As the peasantry and
workers increasingly moved to the left,
sectors of the middle class and the elite
moved to the right.[18] The polarization of
Thai society, together with the rightward
shift of the king, combined to fuel the phase
in which the Village Scouts underwent a

spectacular period of growth. Terrified by
the domestic upheavals and the events in
Indochina, conservatives loosened their
purse strings. Money poured into the Village
Scout movement.

The king found both the changes in Indochina and the growing internal discord of
concern. As Shawcross noted at the time,
the king "is said to have been personally
horrified" by the deposition of the king of
Laos and Prince Sihanouk's "retirement" in
Cambodia (1976:60; see also Anderson
1977:23–4; Morell and Morell 1977:338–9).
Furthermore, the king was worried
about "the steady drift to the left of student
and labor groups" (Marks 1977:55). Increasingly, the king and his followers came to feel
that "student violence, firebombing, labor
violence, unbridled corruption, rocketing inflation and crime rates" were undermining
faith in parliamentary forms (Marks
1977:55). As Morell and Morell summarize,
the king was "becoming increasingly convinced that the results of an open political
system threatened the very foundations of
the monarchy, that student, labor, and farmer
leaders were 'communist agitators' themselves or were influenced by such elements,
and that the demise of the Chakri Dynasty
was a distinct, foreseeable possibility"
(1977:338).

With the king increasingly sharing their
views, the Village Scouts presented conservatives with a perfect option. The Village Scout
movement's evocation of family imagery
allowed different meanings for the elite who
espoused it and the peasantry who embraced
it. For the poor, the familial ideology represented an ideal of a caring government protecting and nurturing its dependents. For the
elite, the authoritarian structure of the family
provided a perfect paradigm to justify the
continuation of the status quo from which
they benefited. In appropriating the family
motif, the initiation ritual encouraged a hierarchical view of the state. As parents have a
moral obligation to care for their children, so
children have an obligation to be obedient to
their parents; thus citizens should obey the

authorities.[19] For some conservatives, the simplicity of the Village Scouts' appeal to all Thais to unite and love each other was an attractive antidote to the escalating divisiveness of Thai society. Yet others saw the movement as a potential power base from which to affect future developments in the country.

With this intensifying involvement of a conservative elite, the Village Scout movement underwent a significant change in the character of its membership. During the early years, the initiation rites were held in upcountry provinces and hence had a rural, counterinsurgency orientation. However, as the movement grew, Village Scout initiation sessions began to be held in provincial towns across the country. From January 1976, Village Scout initiations were even held in Bangkok itself, with the active support of the Bangkok metropolitan government. By September, 1976 the Bangkok government had held 36 training sessions, enrolling 19,828 members (Morell and Samudavanija 1981:244). With the growth of the urban scout movement in the capital, more initiates were drawn from the higher echelons of Thai society, including wives of army generals, business leaders, bankers, and members of the royal family (Morell and Samudavanija 1981:244). Increasingly, the public activities of the Scouts became more overtly political. The scout movement was transforming into a vehicle linking urban right-wing politicians with the countryside. Despite the royal admonition that scouts were to refrain from overt political involvement, local and national candidates for political offices were increasingly seeking to sponsor and participate in scout activities as a way to expand the power bases of their political parties or their election campaigns.

During the elections of 1975 and 1976, the Village Scouts campaigned heavily for right-wing and military candidates. In October, 1976, various Scout chapters were mobilized for a mass protest when the civilian government excluded two right-wing politicians from its reshuffled cabinet. The ultimate demonstration of the might of the new

urban-based Village Scout movement came on the fateful morning of October 6.[20] That morning the movement reached its zenith; it helped topple the civilian government and usher back military rule. The urban-based Village Scout movement was losing sight of its goal of winning the hearts and minds of villagers in the border areas, and was beginning to be used as a political base for various politicians seeking national-level positions of power in the capital.

Government Clampdown

Yet just when the movement seemed all-powerful, the new post-coup government called a halt to further initiations. Ironically, the factions which successfully staged the coup on October 6, 1976 were not the factions which had mobilized scout participation on that day. The movement's popularity had created a host of political complications. Although many of these problems were already beginning to surface during the civilian period, they became particularly acute for the new post-coup government. Tensions were increasing within the ranks of the bureaucracy; for example, while some schoolteachers were helping to staff the scout initiations and receiving special recognition for their efforts, other schoolteachers were having to teach additional classes without any special compensation. Scout troops were increasingly coming into conflict with local government officials; sometimes Scout chapters were seeking to oust corrupt officials, but sometimes they sought to oust honest officials trying to enforce laws that thwarted the business interests of local elites who were often the heads of Scout chapters. Such local elites were often involved in extralegal activities such as illegal teak-logging or illegal gambling operations. Furthermore, the perception that the king had given a green light to the coup plotters of October 6, 1976 served to undermine his previously high political standing. The Village Scouts were now increasingly seen not merely as patriotic nationalists, but as the acolytes of specific right-wing political factions. As Somkhuan Harikhul explained in a newspaper interview at the time, "The matter that is of grave concern at present is that there are members of certain groups who disguise themselves as scouts but are waiting for their chance to damage the movement by using the movement for their personal ends" (*Chaw Thai*, January 8, 1977).

The moratorium was used to institute structural changes in the Village Scout movement. After a series of regional meetings which included civilian businessmen, the Ministry of Interior announced new strictures on all future scout initiations on April 7, 1977. Among the new guidelines was a rule that sessions were not to be held in the same location more than twice. In the early years, initiation sites were selected on the basis of counterinsurgency considerations; however, during the civilian period, initiations were being held in urban centers where the funding and popular enthusiasm were strongest. This new guideline shifted the initiation locations away from urban centers and back to the countryside. The new guidelines also provided a central budget to Ministry of Interior district officers to cover half of the basic costs of initiations; the other half was to be raised among the local villagers being initiated. Such underwriting made it possible to hold sessions in poorer areas where villagers were less likely to have the financial means to sponsor an initiation. In the civilian period, initiations were held at popular request; the new guidelines targeted villages and subdistricts suspected of having leftist sympathies. Furthermore, scout chapters were now to come under the direct control of their respective district officers and provincial governors.

With the ending of the moratorium in May, 1977, a wave of upcountry scout initiations followed. Although the scout movement was now under tighter government control, this new phase of the movement generated new complications. Local government officials had to assume more responsibility for scout activities. District officers and district police chiefs were expected to serve as guests of honor for at least one or two segments of each initiation; evening campfires often lasted until 3 AM. The district education officers were responsible for staffing the rural sessions and also processing all the paperwork for each of the hundreds of participants in each initiation. With so many rural schoolteachers required to serve as staff in the scout initiations, the quality of teaching in village schools suffered. Other local government functions also suffered.

The new guidelines also placed new pressures on the village elite. Not only were they expected to contribute to the initial costs of the initiation sessions, but also to subsequent costs. The Village Scout ideology, drawing upon Buddhist beliefs about merit-making, placed considerable moral pressure on the rural elite to be generous. Elected to scout leadership positions, the village elite I knew felt euphoric in the wake of an initiation. In their evening chats, the village scout elite vowed that they would visit their junior scout chapters on every possible occasion and help their less fortunate members. However, it did not take long for this enthusiasm to pall. When scouts made merit at any one of the dozens of temples in the district, the organizers always contacted the local village elite for contributions. When scouts met to clean up the district office grounds, to clear the canals of weeds, to make merit at another temple, to visit a junior scout troop, or to engage in any other of the myriad scout activities, the village elite were invariably asked to provide transportation and other expenses. Furthermore, since the poor outnumbered the rich, it is not surprising that even the most charitable of rich villagers felt hard-pressed when asked repeatedly for loans of money and rice. Nor did their loans necessarily meet with gratitude; borrowers often resented having to pay the going interest rates of 5–10 percent per month. Thus, although the village elite cooperated with the Village Scout movement initially and justified their sacrifice of time, money, and effort in patriotic terms, over time, the village elite came to resent this financial burden. A matter of a few months separated the euphoria of the initiation from the ensuing apathy.

As wealthier scouts became less and less willing to assist their less fortunate neighbors, the hopes of the poorer and middle-class villagers, ironically aroused by the Village Scout movement itself, were increasingly disappointed.[21] As time went by, villagers became less and less circumspect in their criticism of the Village Scout movement and of the government. As one jaded scout remarked to me:

> The government makes all this big to-do about the scouts. It thinks that this way it will keep us from becoming communists. But really it is like tiger balm on a wound [i.e., aspirin for a headache] – it doesn't cure it, but it makes the hurt go away for a short time. All that you really get from the scouts is the scarf. And what good is that? – you can't eat it and you can't sell it.

Albeit for different reasons, the various classes and class factions within the village began to drift away. Thus, underlying the national pattern was a micro-trajectory of ebbing enthusiasm within the ranks of the older members.

After the moratorium, membership in the Village Scouts continued to increase in 1977 and 1978. However, by 1979, it was clear that the number of new initiates was falling and by 1981, new initiations tapered off to about 200 per year. In part, the decline in the movement can also be attributed to internal splits occurring within the Communist Party of Thailand (CPT)[22] and a series of reforms instituted by the Thai government. In 1980, with the government's offer of a general amnesty, former guerrillas began surrendering and returning to civilian life; the arrest of key members of the central committee marked the end of the CPT as a coherent political force. Nonetheless, the decline in the Village Scout movement was not entirely

inevitable. Had the CPT continued to provide a meaningful challenge to the government, the national Thai elite would have been more motivated to continue to pour money into the movement. With the provision of funds to aid the rural poor, participation in the Village Scout movement would have appeared more attractive for a longer period of time.

Although the Village Scouts continue to initiate new members at a rate of about 200 sessions a year, the movement is no longer the political force it was during the mid-1970s. Nonetheless, the Village Scouts continue to surface at various points.[23] The most recent occasion was during the uprising against the military government in May, 1992, when Somkhuan Harikhul himself intervened to prohibit scout mobilization by the government.[24] What the movement's political potential is or might be in the future is unclear. For some observers the movement has become moribund; for others it is a sleeping giant which can awaken when summoned. Some attribute the low initiation figures to lack of interest; others suggest that everyone who wanted to become a scout already has and consequently the nation is in a state of constant preparedness. Thus, some scouts I interviewed made comments such as, "The scouts are in the past. People just lost interest in it. After all, what was there in it except a scarf?" Yet others hold a different view. As one scout leader said, "The movement lives on. We are all trained and in readiness. Should the need ever arise, we could be mobilized in a flash." At present, the Village Scout movement has little political vitality. However, it is possible that in a certain conjuncture of structure and event the Village Scout movement could become revitalized. The ambiguity remains.[25]

Conclusion

States rely on a variety of means to establish their hegemony, including social and cultural institutions such as schools, the media, religion, or the arts. The Thai state, like many other Third World governments, could not rely on such institutions to affect the political consciousness of its citizenry. At the time of the creation of the Village Scout movement, the Thai educational system only required villagers to attend four years of school (see Keyes 1991). Although most villagers had access to a radio, few villagers had access to television or newspapers. Buddhism has proven to be an uncertain instrument for the consolidation of the state, having nurtured as many revolts against the state as it has discouraged (see Jackson 1989, Keyes 1977, Nartsupha 1984, Reynolds 1977, Tambiah 1984). Few villagers ever saw the inside of a movie theater. Thus the Thai state needed a vehicle to shape the political consciousness of its citizens at a time when its rule had little popular legitimacy and the state lacked alternative avenues to reach "the hearts and minds" of its citizenry. The Village Scout movement became that vehicle. Maurice Bloch, in his book on the use of rituals by the state in Madagascar, ridicules the idea that rituals could be "created as a plot by cynical rulers who deliberately invent subtle and totally convincing mystifying devices for the domination of others" (1986:6). Yet the Village Scout movement is a clear-cut case of a state-sponsored initiation ritual deliberately designed to manipulate its participants. As Somkhuan Harikhul explained forthrightly, "We used processes of mass psychology to create a group sense of unity" (interview, 1991). By combining the hopes of the poor with the fears of the rich, the Village Scout movement drew upon the mystique of monarchy and family to forge a temporary cross-class alliance. Cloaking reality in a veil of maroon kerchiefs, the Village Scout movement succeeded in masking its inherent contradiction: the generation of mass support for the perpetuation of elite advantage. By taking an anthropological perspective to states as actors actively seeking the consent of the governed (Evans et al.1985, Skocpol 1979), the concept of a state-sponsored social movement is not a

definitional contradiction in terms. Only by imbricating the state can civil society become the "true source and theater of all history" (Marx and Engels 1970:57).

NOTES

This chapter draws on my fieldwork in Thailand in 1974–9, my personal observations of a Village Scout initiation ritual in 1977, and subsequent interviews in 1990 and 1991, as well as Village Scout publications, newspaper accounts, and material published in Bowie 1997. The author would also like to acknowledge the assistance of Kate Bjork-Guneratne, June Nash, and Gay Seidman.

1 As Sidney Tarrow explains, social movements are "those sequences of contentious politics that are based on underlying social networks and resonant collective action frames, and which develop the capacity to maintain sustained challenges against powerful opponents" (1998:2). While this description leaves the definition of "powerful opponents" open, Tarrow continues: "Much of the history of movement-state interaction can be read as a duet of strategy and counterstrategy between movement activists and power holders" (1998:3). My essay presents a case of power holders creating a movement. Attention to the state as an active agent in the creation of social movements is further diverted by the current wave of literature exploring the role of globalization; this literature often sees states as losing influence in the contexts of neoliberal democracies and global forces.
2 Bacchetta and Power (2002), Berlet and Lyons (2000), Blee (1991), Cardoza (1982), Diamond (1995), Ginsburg (1998 [1989]), Hall (1988), Larsen (2001), Lo (1982), Mosse (1975), Payne (2000), Schneider (1986), and Tilton (1975) are among a growing body of scholarship on right-wing movements.

3   By left-wing I mean social movements seeking to change the overall structure of society on behalf of the majority, and by right-wing I mean efforts to maintain a status quo benefiting the interests of an elite minority.

4   In response to military radio broadcasts, thousands of scouts massed outside Thammasat University and two other designated locations in the city (see Morell and Samudavanija 1981, Shawcross 1976, and Ungphakorn 1977). As the surviving students were being arrested, Village Scouts helped rip Buddhist amulets from their necks.

5   The information about Somkhuan Harikhul's life history is based on interviews with me (1991, 1992) and an official Village Scout publication (SH Mss 1984:16).

6   The growth of the Communist Party of Thailand was related to Thai government foreign policies, the increased militarization of the counterinsurgency effort in Thailand, and the failure of Thai government development policies in the countryside (see Bowie 1997:60–70, Kerdphol 1986, Race 1974, Tanham 1974, Turton et al. 1978, Wongtrangan 1983).

7   The Wood Badge training course is an eight-day course in leadership skills for adults involved in the Boy Scout organization (for details, see Bowie 1997:306).

8   Only two or three days into the pilot session, the participants refused to cooperate any longer, threatening to return home unless they received a per diem, free meals, uniforms, weapons, ammunition, and elephants, the last to be used to transport goods. Somkhuan negotiated with villagers for hours, countering that they received benefits such as roads and schools. For more details, see Bowie 1997:86, 306n.7).

9   This is the minimum number of staff required for a ritual initiating some 250–300 people. In 1976, the average number of initiates per ritual was 795 (see Bowie 1997:289–98).

10 The initiation was held at the BPP Region IV headquarters in Udorn Thani province. The invitation to the king and queen was arranged through Somkhuan's superior officer, Police Major General Charoenrit Chamrasromran, who had attended an earlier initiation session as master of ceremonies and later became head of the Village Scout Operation Center of Thailand; and Police Lieutenant General Suraphon Chulabrahm, then the deputy commanding general of the BPP and later director of the BPP (interview, 1991, Morell and Samudavanija 1981:242). The king's mother may have also played a role.

11 As Kershaw explains, "a monarchy which was identified with corrupt, military regimes would simply have guaranteed its own early extinction. Bhumiphol therefore set himself the task of fostering...a 'constituency'" (1979:257; see also Reynolds 1977:279). The king established 12 guidelines for the administration of the scout movement which included admonitions to remain apolitical, to "avoid abuse of status and power by stressing democratic methods" and "avoid involvement with money, as it easily leads to bribery" (Muecke 1980:423). To encourage unity, scouts were also forbidden to wear uniforms to minimize status or class differences.

12 The session I observed had a budget of 15,000 baht, which proved insufficient. In Bangkok in 1976, the average session apparently cost 30,000–40,000 baht for an initiation of 400–500 people (see Kriangsak Lohachaala 2519/1976:67). The more expensive initiations had very lavish stage props such as huge papier-mâché tiger-heads as portals through which initiates passed to enter the camp. The staff – not the initiates – were given meals and a small per diem for their participation.

13 This law was rarely enforced and most villagers working as agricultural laborers earned even less. For more details, see Morell and Samudavanija (1981:206–13) and Turton (1978: 113).

14 See Kerdphol (1986:82). Such village-oriented projects included: the Village Defense Corps, the Village Security Officers, the Peoples' Assistance Teams, the Census Aspiration Teams, the Village Security Force, the Border Security Volunteer Teams, and even the Hunter-Killer Teams.

15 Villagers traditionally have pooled labor resources for house building and agricultural work. Most have funeral societies in which all villagers contribute toward the costs of funerals.

16 Royal patronage facilitated the generation of magical stories about the royal scout kerchief and hence facilitated popular interest among ordinary people in acquiring such a scarf. Stories were told of villagers who had lost their kerchiefs and gone insane. I was told of one man who had left his royal kerchief on the dashboard of his car. While he was driving, the scarf slipped to the floor near his feet. Instantly he went berserk. He stopped his car, got out, and ran up and down the road, beside himself, until some passing villagers discovered his scout scarf on the car floor. As soon as they picked up his scarf, he recovered his sanity. Scouts also told of fires in which villagers lost all their possessions and their homes, but from which the sacred scout kerchief was retrieved completely unharmed from the burning ashes. So engulfing was this realm of ritual magic the Thai state had created that the very first night I attended a Village Scout event, a participant committed suicide because he had lost his kerchief. The generation of these stories was deliberately encouraged by the scout instructors. Throughout the five-day ritual, the instructors themselves told incredible stories of the magical power of the royal kerchiefs.

17 Charges of *lèse-majesté* have invariably been brought by the government, not by a representative of the monarchy directly. The charge of *lèse-majesté* has proven useful at various times for governments seeking to hide their activities from public comment by associating them with the monarchy. See Anderson (1977:23–4) and Streckfuss (1995) for further discussion.

18 Anderson portrays the entire Thai bourgeoisie as moving to the right. I believe the Thai bourgeoisie split, with some moving right and others moving left. After all, the university students leading many of the demonstrations were themselves members of bourgeois families. The CPT itself drew many of its members of the Thai middle classes.

19 The seventh scout law specifically states: "A good scout respects and listens to the wishes [literally, "orders," *chyafang khamsang*] of his parents and superiors."

20 Many scholars have speculated about what provoked the villagers' turn toward the Right on October 6. I, in contrast, believe that few ordinary villagers were in fact involved in October 6. Instead the Village Scouts who participated in these events were more likely to have come from the district towns near Bangkok, as well as Bangkok itself. Somkhuan himself, in an interview with me, indicated that the BPP trucks picked up Village Scouts from the provincial centers at fairly short notice, further supporting my view that few villagers would have been involved.

21 The poorest of villagers, those most likely to be sympathetic to socialist rhetoric, were, ironically, often too poor to be able to afford the time or money involved in becoming a scout.

22 The death of Chairman Mao in China in 1976, China's conflicts with Vietnam, Vietnam's invasion of Pol Pot's Cambodia, and China's reconciliation with the Thai state placed considerable stress on the Communist Party of Thailand (see Girling 1981, Keyes 1987:107–11, Marks 1994, Morell and Samudavanija 1981:303–7, Ongsuragz 1982, Wongtrangan 1984).

23 In 1984, Village Scouts, apparently opposed to the amnesty policy, participated in an effort to topple the Prem

government. Some 1,000 Village Scouts rallied in front of Government House to demand the prosecution of a famous intellectual, Sulak Sivaraksa, on charges of *lèse-majesté*. Scouts submitted a letter signed on behalf of 24 Village Scout districts representing 100,000 members in Bangkok urging that legal action be taken (Sivaraksa 1985:337–8). Another incident occurred in August, 1986 when a small group of Village Scouts rallied in support of the Crown Prince after an incident with the Japanese government; this rally was short-lived and uneventful.

24 Somkhuan confirmed his intervention (interview, 1994). Although the Village Scouts remained dormant, the Red Gaurs participated in defense of the military government.

25 The Thai government is not the only government to attempt to create popular-based conservative organizations to buttress its position. Similar organizations have been created in South Vietnam, the Philippines, Indonesia, Japan, and Nationalist China. Ultimately, comparisons can be made with fascist organizations which developed in Germany, Italy, and elsewhere. Even the original Boy Scout organization developed in the context of an insecure England fearing German expansionism (see Rosenthal 1986 for a fascinating discussion). Far more research needs to be done on conservative, anti-reform movements in general.

REFERENCES

THAI SOURCES

Chaw Thai
Daily Times
Daily News
Interviews with Somkhuan Harikul. February 4, 1991 and January 1992. In Bangkok, Thailand. Interview by telephone, September 1994.
Kriangsak Lohachaala "Luuksyachawbaan Krungthepmahaanaakorn" (Village Scouts in Bangkok). Nithetsarn (Journal of Communication Arts) 5/3 (December 2519 [1976]) 65-70.
SH Mss. Phontamruat Trii Somkhuan Harikhun. Sixtieth Birthday Volume. n.p. December 13, 1984.

ENGLISH-LANGUAGE REFERENCES

Alvarez, Sonia E., Evelina Dagnino, and Arturo Escobar
1998 Cultures of Politics, Politics of Cultures: Re-visioning Latin American Social Movements. Boulder, CO: Westview Press.
Anderson, Benedict
1977 Withdrawal Symptoms: Social and Cultural Aspects of the October 6 Coup. *In* special issue. Bulletin of Concerned Asian Scholars 9(3):13–30.
Bacchetta, Paola, and Margaret Power
2002 Right-Wing Women: From Conservatives to Extremists Around the World. New York: Routledge.
Berlet, Chip, and Matthew N. Lyons
2000 Right-Wing Populism in America: Too Close for Comfort. New York: Guilford.
Blaufarb, Douglas S.
1977 The Counterinsurgency Era: U.S. Doctrine and Performance 1950 to the Present. London: Free Press.
Blee, Kathleen M.
1991 Women of the Clan: Racism and Gender in the 1920s. Berkeley: University of California Press.
Bloch, Maurice
1986 From Blessing to Violence: History and Ideology in the Circumcision Ritual of the Merina of Madagascar. Cambridge: Cambridge University Press.
Bowie, Katherine
1997 Rituals of National Loyalty: An Anthropology of the State and the Village Scout Movement in Thailand. New York: Columbia University Press.
Cardoza, Anthony L.
1982 Agrarian Elites and Italian Fascism. Princeton, NJ: Princeton University Press.

Carley, M.
  1997 Defining forms of successful state repression of social movement organizations: A case study of the FBI's COINTELPRO and the American Indian Movement. Research in Social Movements, Conflict and Change 20:151–176.
Castells, Manuel
  1997 The Information Age: Economy, Society and Culture. Vol. 2. The Power of Identity. Oxford: Blackwell.
Chaloemtiarana, Thak
  1979 Thailand: The Politics of Despotic Paternalism. Bangkok: Social Science Association of Thailand and Thai Khadi Institute, Thammasat University.
Cohen, Jean L., and Andrew Arato
  1992 Civil Society and Political Theory. Cambridge: MIT Press.
Comaroff, John L., and Jean Comaroff
  1999 Civil Society and the Political Imagination in Africa: Critical Perspectives. Chicago: University of Chicago Press.
Darling, Frank
  1974 Student Protest and Political Change in Thailand. Pacific Affairs 47(1):5–19.
Diamond. S.
  1995 Roads to Dominion: Right-Wing Movements and Political Power in the United States. New York: Guilford.
Edelman, Marc
  2001 Social Movements: Changing Paradigms and Forms of Politics. Annual Review of Anthropology 30:285–317.
Escobar, Arturo, and Sonia E. Alvarez, eds.
  1992 The Making of Social Movements in Latin America: Identity, Strategy and Democracy. Boulder, CO: Westview Press.
Evans, Peter B., Dietrich Rueschemeyer, and Theda Skocpol, eds.
  1985 Bringing the State Back In. Cambridge: Cambridge University Press.
Gale, Richard
  1986 Social Movements and the State: The Environmental Movement, Counter-Movement and Governmental Agencies. Sociological Perspectives 29(April): 202–240.
Ginsburg, F. D.
  1998 [1989] Contested Lives: The Abortion Debate in an American Community.

2nd edition. Berkeley: University of California Press.
Girling, John L. S.
  1981 Thailand: Society and Politics. Ithaca, NY: Cornell University Press.
Gramsci, Antonio
  1971 Selections from the Prison Notebooks. Quintin Hoare and Geoffrey Nowell Smith, trans. New York: International Publishers.
Hall, Stuart
  1988 The Toad in the Garden: Thatcherism Among the Theorists. In Marxism and the Interpretation of Culture. Cary Nelson and Lawrence Grossberg, eds. Pp. 35–57. Chicago: University of Illinois Press.
Hann, Chris
  1996 Introduction: Political Society and Civil Anthropology. In Civil Society: Challenging Western Models. Chris Hann and Elizabeth Dunn, eds. Pp. 1–26. London: Routledge.
Heinze, Ruth-Inge
  1974 Ten Days in October – Students Vs. the Military: An Account of the Student Uprising in Thailand. Asian Survey 14(6):491–508.
Jackson, Peter A.
  1989 Buddhism, Legitimation, and Conflict: The Political Functions of Urban Thai Buddhism. Singapore: Institute of Southeast Asian Studies.
Kerdphol, General Saiyud
  —— 1986 The Struggle for Thailand: Counter-Insurgency 1965–1985. Bangkok: S. Research Center Co., Ltd.
Kershaw, Roger
  1979 Three Kings of Orient: The Changing Face of Monarchy in Southeast Asia (Part 1, 2, and 3). Contemporary Review 234:200–206, 256–265, 299–304.
Keyes, Charles
  1977 Millennialism, Theravada Buddhism and Thai Society. Journal of Asian Studies 36(2):283–302.
  —— 1987 Thailand: Buddhist Kingdom as Modern Nation-State. Boulder, CO: Westview Press.
  —— 1991 Reshaping Local Worlds: Formal Education and Cultural Change in

Rural Southeast Asia. Monograph No. 36. New Haven, CT: Yale University Southeast Asian Studies.

Larsen, Stein U., ed.
2001 Fascism Outside Europe: The European Impulse against Domestic Conditions in the Diffusion of Global Fascism. Boulder Social Science Monographs. New York: Columbia University Press.

Lo, Clarence
1982 Counter-Movements and Conservative Movements in the Contemporary US. Annual Review of Sociology 8:107–134.

Lobe, Thomas
1977 United States National Security Police and Aid to the Thailand Police. Monograph Series in World Affairs 14(2): n.p.

Lobe, Thomas, and David Morell
1978 Thailand's Border Patrol Police: Paramilitary Political Power. Part 4. *In* Supplementary Military Forces: Reserves, Militias, Auxiliaries. Louis Zurcher and Gwyn Harries-Jenkins, eds. Pp. 153–178. Beverly Hills, CA: Sage.

Marks, Thomas A.
1977 The Status of the Monarchy in Thailand. Issues and Studies 13(11):51–70.
—— 1994 Making Revolution: The Insurgency of the Communist Party of Thailand in Structural Perspective. Bangkok: White Lotus.

Marx, Karl, and Friedrich Engels
1970 The German Ideology. New York: International Publishers.

McAdam, Doug, Sidney Tarrow, and Charles Tilly
2001 Dynamics of Contention. Cambridge: Cambridge University Press.

McCarthy, John D., and Mark Wolfson
1992 Consensus Movements, Conflict Movements, and the Cooptation of Civic and State Infrastructures. *In* Frontiers in Social Movement Theory. Aldon Morris and Carol McClurg Mueller, eds. Pp. 273–297. New Haven, CT: Yale University Press.

McNabb, Scott F.
1978 Study Service in Thailand: The Case of the Maeklong Integrated Rural Development Project. Ph.D. Dissertation, Department of Education, University of Virginia.

Melucci, Alberto
1996 Challenging Codes: Collective Action in the Information Age. Cambridge: Cambridge University Press.

Morell, David, and Samudavanija Chai-anan
1981 Political Conflict in Thailand. Cambridge, MA: Oelgeschlager, Gunn & Hain.

Morell, David, and Susan Morell
1977 Thailand: The Costs of Political Conflict. Pacific Community 8(2):327–340.

Mosse, George
1975 The Nationalization of the Masses: Political Symbolism and Mass Movements in Germany from the Napoleonic Wars through the Third Reich. Ithaca, NY: Cornell University Press.

Muecke, Marjorie A.
1980 The Village Scouts of Thailand. Asian Survey 20:407–427.

Nartsupha, Chattip
1984 The Ideology of Holy Men Revolts in North East Thailand. *In* History and Peasant Consciousness in Southeast Asia. A. Turton and S. Tanabe, eds. Pp. 111–134. Osaka, Japan: National Museum of Ethnology.

Ongsuragz, Chantima
1982 The Communist Party of Thailand: Consolidation of Decline. *In* Southeast Asian Affairs. Pp. 362–374. Singapore: Heinemann Educational Books (Asia) Ltd.

Payne, Leigh
2000 Uncivil Movements: The Armed Right Wing and Democracy in Latin America. Baltimore, MD: Johns Hopkins University Press.

Pichardo, Nelson A.
1997 New Social Movements: A Critical Review. Annual Review of Sociology 23:411–430.

Punyodhyana, Boonsanong
1975 The Revolutionary Situation in Thailand. *In* Southeast Asian Affairs. Pp. 187–195. Singapore: Institute of Southeast Asian Studies.

Race, Jeffrey
1974 The War in Northern Thailand. Modern Asian Studies 8(1):85–112.

Reynolds, Frank E.
1977 Civic Religion and National Community in Thailand. Journal of Asian Studies 36(2):267–282.
——1978 Legitimation and Rebellion: Thailand's Civic Religion and the Student Uprising of October, 1973. *In* Religion and Legitimation of Power in Thailand, Laos, and Burma. Bardwell, L. Smith, ed. Pp. 134–146. Chambersburg, PA: AMIMA Books.
Rosenthal, Michael
1986 The Character Factory: Baden-Powell and the Origins of the Boy Scout Movement. London: Collins.
Schneider, Peter
1986 Rural Artisans and Peasant Mobilisation in the Socialist International: The Fasci Siciliani. Journal of Peasant Studies 13(3):63–81.
Shawcross, William
1976 How Tyranny Returned to Thailand. New York Review of Books, 9 December:59–62.
Sivaraksa, Sulak
1985 Siamese Resurgence. Bangkok: Asian Cultural Forum on Development.
Skocpol, Theda
1979 States and Social Revolutions. Cambridge: Cambridge University Press.
Slater, David
1998 Rethinking the Spatialities of Social Movements: Questions of (B)orders, Culture, and Politics in Global Times. *In* Cultures of Politics, Politics of Cultures: Re-visioning Latin American Social Movements. Sonia E. Alvarez, Evelina Dagnino, and Arturo Escobar, eds. Pp. 380–401. Boulder, CO: Westview Press.
Streckfuss, David
1995 Kings in the Age of Nations: The Paradox of Lèse-Majesté as a Crime in Thailand. Comparative Studies in Society and History 7(3):445–475.
Tambiah, Stanley Jeyaraja
1984 The Buddhist Saints of the Forest and the Cult of Amulets. Cambridge: Cambridge University Press.

Tanham, George K.
1974 Trial in Thailand. New York: Crane, Russak.
Tarrow, Sidney
1998 Power in Movement: Social Movements and Contentious Politics. 2nd edition. Cambridge: Cambridge University Press.
Tilly, Charles
1986 The Contentious French. Cambridge, MA: Harvard University Press.
Tilton, Timothy Alan
1975 Nazism, Neo-Nazism, and the Peasantry. Bloomington: Indiana University Press.
Turton, Andrew
1978 The Current Situation in the Thai Countryside. *In* Thailand: Roots of Conflict. Andrew Turton, Jonathan Fast, and Malcolm Caldwell, eds. Pp. 104–142. Nottingham: Russell Press.
Turton, Andrew, Jonathan Fast, and Malcolm Caldwell, eds.
1978 Thailand: Roots of Conflict. Nottingham: Russell Press.
Ungphakorn, Puey
1977 Violence and the Military Coup in Thailand. Bulletin of Concerned Asian Scholars, special issue 9(3):4–12.
Wongtrangan, Kanok
1983 Change and Persistence in Thai Counter-Insurgency Policy. Bangkok: Institute of Security and International Studies, Faculty of Political Science, Chulalongkorn University. ISIS Occasional Paper, no. 1.
——1984 The Revolutionary Strategy of the Communist Party of Thailand: Change and Persistence. *In* Armed Communist Movements in Southeast Asia. Lim Joo-Jock, and S. Vani, eds. Pp. 133–182. Aldershot: Gower.
Zald, Mayer N.
1992 Looking Backward to Look Forward: Reflections on the Past and Future of the Resource Mobilization Program. *In* Frontiers in Social Movement Theory. Aldon D. Morris and Carol McClurg Mueller, eds. Pp. 326–348. New Haven, CT: Yale University Press.

3

Gender, Citizenship, and the Politics of Identity

Lynn Stephen

Many antiessentialist critiques have been made of ethnic, gender, racial, and national conceptions of identity. In fact, some of the most dynamic areas of feminist theorizing have interrogated concepts such as "women," "men," "the feminine," "masculine subjectivity," and "sex" as falsely unifying heterogeneous groups of people (Butler, 1990; 1993; Fausto-Sterling, 1997; Garber, 1993). What, then, is the need for a further debate about "identity"? The concept of identity, however flawed, is nevertheless, obviously still useful to those engaged in grassroots social movements. Rather than abandon the concept of identity, Stuart Hall proposes that we continue to think with it in a detotalized and deconstructed form. He also proposes that we focus on the process of identification, which he sees as a construction, a process never completed. In the end, identification is "conditional, lodged in contingency. Once secured, it does not obliterate difference.... Identification is, then, a process of articulation, a suturing, an over-determination not a subsumption.... And since as a process it operates across difference, it entails discursive work, the binding and marking of symbolic boundaries, the production of 'frontier-effects'" (Hall, 1996a: 2–3).

While it is clear to women in grassroots movements that participation is a constant process of negotiating difference, the need to create unitary names, symbols, and goals can result in the essentialization of women as "mothers," as in the case of El Salvador's CO-MADRES, or as "Indians," as in the case of indigenous women participating in and supporting the struggle of the Ejército Zapatista de Liberación Nacional (Zapatista Army of National Liberation – EZLN), and more broadly, Mexico's national movement for indigenous autonomy. Organizing requires the projection of "sameness" to outsiders. Strategically, demands must stem from a coherent social location understandable to those who are the audience for them – often institutions of the state. The political necessity of projecting "sameness" does not, however, explain how a movement operates, what it means to those involved, or what it is able to accomplish. It is also not evidence of shared consciousness or identity. My objective, then, is to compare the process internal to a social movement with its presentation of "self" to outsiders. We need to examine the tension between political identity formation as the constant and contingent negotiation of difference within organizations and the need to project unitary identities that usually result in essentialization.

Here I will focus specifically on the process of identification in two discursive fields bound to grassroots movements. First, with regard to the Comité de Madres y Familiares de Presos, Desaparecidos y Asesinados de El Salvador "Monseñor Romero" (Committee Of Mothers and Relatives of Political Prisoners, Disappeared and Assassinated of El Salvador, Monseñor Romero – CO-MADRES) I will explore the construction of "motherhood" by those within the movement and contrast it with the way they have been read by outsiders. Second, I will explore construction of the concept of "indigenous autonomy" within the national movement for indigenous rights in Mexico and its simultaneous endorsement and challenge by indigenous women and their advisers.

After discussing these cases, I will draw some comparative conclusions suggesting ways to deal with the contradictory aspects of identity found in women's grassroots organizing. Earlier analyses of women's participation in grassroots movements have relied on dichotomous paradigms such as "feminine" versus "feminist" or a continuum of "practical" versus "strategic" demands (see Molyneux, 1985). Focusing on the contradictory aspects of identity and the process of identification, I believe we can better get at the complexities and contradictions which emerge in the process of women's collective action rather than resorting to binary categories of explanation. Theoretical analyses of earlier movements as "feminine" or "feminist," have given way to recognition that many women's movements in Latin America beginning in the 1980s, combined a commitment to basic survival for women and their children with a challenge to the subordination of women to men.

The CO-MADRES of El Salvador: What Does Motherhood Mean?[1]

Founded in 1977, CO-MADRES was one of the first groups in El Salvador to denounce the atrocities of the government and the military. It was formally established as a committee on Christmas Eve 1977 under the auspices of Monseñor Oscar Romero (Schirmer, 1993: 32). By the mid-1980s, the initial group numbering approximately nine, had grown to several hundred. The membership was from the beginning quite heterogeneous in terms of class and occupation, including teachers, workers, peasants, students, lawyers, market women, housewives, and small shop keepers.

The work of the CO-MADRES initially consisted of trying to locate the bodies of the victims of the repression by the Salvadoran security forces directed against activists in labor unions, Christian base communities, independent peasant organizations, student groups, human rights organizations, and the outlawed political parties that made up the Frente Farabundo Martí de Liberación Nacional (Farabundo Martí National Liberation Front–FMLN). The CO-MADRES also defended the rights of political prisoners and the families of victims of human rights abuses. Their tactics ranged from public demonstrations to taking over buildings such as cathedrals and the headquarters of the Salvadoran Red Cross. They also made daily visits to body dumps, clandestine cemeteries, and morgues to search for new victims of repression. Once found, they attempted to identify them and locate their families. The fate of such victims was also publicized to the outside world to publicize the ongoing violation of human rights in El Salvador.

Beginning in 1979 they began to take their message overseas, traveling in Latin America, Europe, and Australia, Canada, and the United States. They were the first recipients of the Robert F. Kennedy Human Rights Award in 1984. Their trademark tool for political organizing was testimony. Women told their personal stories of losing loved ones and of what happened to them in their search. These stories included Salvadoran history and a message about the need for change in the economic and political conditions in the country (see Stephen, 1994; 1997a). The CO-MADRES participated in a wide range of national and international forums on human rights as well as participating in the Federación Latinoamericana de Familiares de Detenidos y Desaparecidos (Federation of the Relatives of the Disappeared and Detained in Latin America – FEDEFAM), which includes organizations from 17 Latin American countries. In such forums and in the press coverage of them the CO-MADRES projected an image of mothers but also became more and more identified as human rights activists who operated in an ever-widening theater, local, national, and international.

The CO-MADRES themselves became the victims of government repression. Their first office was bombed in 1980, and since then their offices have been bombed at least four more times. The majority of the most active CO-MADRES have been detained, tortured, and raped. Between 1977 and 1993, forty-eight members were detained, 5 have been assassinated for their activism, and 3 have been "disappeared" (Stephen, 1994; Schirmer, 1993). Even after the Salvadoran peace accords were signed in December, 1991, harassment and disappearances continued. In February 1993 the son and nephew of one of the founders of CO-MADRES were assassinated in Usulután. This woman had already lived through her own detention, the detention and gang rape of her daughter, and the disappearance and assassination of other family members. For many, the human rights abuses committed against them fortified their determination and resulted in a difficult confrontation with their own treatment as women at the hands of national security forces.

While the formal agenda of the CO-MADRES remained focused on confronting the sources of human rights abuses in El Salvador, in their private conversations, some members began a serious questioning of female gender roles. Many women activists received no support from their husbands or were beaten. When detained CO-MADRES were raped as part of their torture, they faced rejection by their husbands and families as damaged goods. Internal discussions about what kinds of rights they had as women, as workers, and as mothers slowly became part of their public agenda at the end of the 1980s. Support for a questioning of oppressive gender roles for women came in part from El Salvador's small feminist movement (see Stephen 1997a, 56–107; Ready, 1999). As women's sections of other popular organizations began to question their subordinate positions in their own organizations and homes, other Salvadoran women were beginning to take a public stand on issues often identified with feminism – rape, unequal work burdens in the home, the political marginalization of women, and women's lack of control over their own sexuality and bodies.

After the signing of the peace accords in late 1991, the political situation changed significantly in El Salvador. Human rights abuses continued but at a slower pace. Much energy was devoted to the United Nations Truth Commission's investigation of human rights abuses. The CO-MADRES worked with the Commission and also became involved in broader Salvadoran politics as the FMLN became a legal political party and a wide range of women's groups came together to develop a women's political platform. By the mid-1990s all of the women's groups that had associated with the five political parties of the FMLN were autonomous – some more than others.

Internationally, solidarity organizations began to lose members in the 1990s, and by 1995 many international committees supportive of the CO-MADRES and other grassroots organizations had disappeared or been severely reduced. The CO-MADRES continue their work in El Salvador with fewer activists, many having gone into other kinds of political work. Nevertheless, they maintain their office and presence and continue to press for human rights and to develop internally, focusing on human rights, domestic violence, women's health, and the economic problems of marginalized women.

A majority of women in CO-MADRES are mothers. While these women share the experience of giving birth and/or adoption and a general notion of what it means to be a Salvadoran mother, this does not mean that they joined CO-MADRES with uniform views. The diversity of class and occupational sectors represented and women's varied political experiences ensured a variety of perspectives on motherhood.

A significant number of women in CO-MADRES had suffered repression in their families for their participation in Christian base communities, and leaders such as Alicia Panameño de García were already questioning their roles as wives and mothers responsible for all housework, child care, and general reproductive maintenance. Others, however, were not. Sofía Aves Escamillas, for example, identified herself as a mother who had a legitimate right to know the whereabouts of her children. She was from a peasant background, and her sons were disappeared for their participation in an independent peasant cooperative. As she stayed with CO-MADRES over a 15-year period, she began to explore other issues such as female sexuality and the overall oppression of women, but her thinking on these issues remained distinct from that of other women such as Alicia Panameño. Sofía was never comfortable discussing issues of sexuality, and, while she listened, she did not actively participate or approve of this type of discussion. Sofía and Alicia thus came to the CO-MADRES with different ideas about what motherhood meant, how it defined them as persons, and what kinds of political actions would stem from it. Each was also profoundly changed by her experience in the CO-MADRES.

Being a "mother" and "motherhood" were constantly changing concepts which were expansive in the sense that being a mother came to represent a wide range of issues within the organization – bearing and rearing children, defending them and oneself against state repression, having the right to free speech and being heard as a full citizen, having control over one's body and its physical integrity within marriage, within families, in prison, and in any state institution, and recognizing and controlling one's sexuality. This range of meanings of motherhood was not equally experienced or shared by all women in the CO-MADRES but was the discursive field within which motherhood came to be represented and contested.

People outside of the CO-MADRES and other "mothers'" movements have sometimes reduced the meaning of "mother" to a very narrow one. In the 1980s, these movements were generally seen as using "traditional" expectations of what mothers do to conduct political demonstrations in times and places where no one else could. Capitalizing on Marianismo, the cult of the Virgin Mary, women such as the Mothers of the Plaza de Mayo were portrayed as making an appeal based on "the most conservative aspects of feminine identity" (Feijóo 1989: 88). The response of mothers to the kidnaping of their children was described as being based on the simple fact of their motherhood. While many mothers were no doubt strongly affected by the loss of their children and extremely militant in their efforts to find them, we cannot conclude that their motherhood somehow imbued them with a uniform identity or interpretation of what they were doing. As Diana Taylor (1997: 194) argues in her analysis of the performance of motherhood by the Mothers of the Plaza de Mayo in Argentina,

> The mother's movement did not begin when the individual mothers became acquainted in their search for their children; it originated when the women consciously decided to protest and agitate *as* mothers. That *as* marks the conceptual distance between the essentialist notion of motherhood attributed to the Madres and the self-conscious manipulation of the maternal role – understood as performative – that makes the movement the powerful and intensely dramatic spectacle that it is.

Hegemonic gender constructions in Argentina, El Salvador, and elsewhere no doubt did allow women to tread on political terrain where others dared not to go under repressive times such as the Proceso in Argentina and the repression during the civil war in El Salvador. But such hegemonic constructions of motherhood also have contradictions within them, and the meaning of motherhood has always varied with age, class, ethnic, and racial affiliation. The process of identification in terms of motherhood involves contestation terrain for both individuals and groups. Unity based on identity (gendered and otherwise) is not natural or inevitable but the result of the continual construction of artificial closure against the constant grain of difference (Hall, 1996a: 5).

In the case of the CO-MADRES, the contingent process of identification with motherhood was constantly negotiated both by individuals within their homes, where they struggled daily against static definitions of their "proper" roles, and collectively in their public actions as they pushed against larger cultural expectations of motherhood. What facilitated the CO-MADRES' dramatic public actions and ongoing confrontations with the repressive state and military forces of El Salvador in the 1980s was, I believe, the fact that motherhood in Latin America has always been multidimensional and both public and private. As observed among the women of the CO-MADRES, for example, mothering can mean bringing your four children with you to a stall in a public marketplace, staying there all day, walking home with them after dark, and stopping to visit relatives on the way. It can also mean bringing your children to church, to cemeteries, and to jails as you confront government officials in search for your family. Alternative cultural discourses of motherhood are constantly being spun out of the different daily lives of women in Latin America. The existence of these varied discourses on motherhood not only facilitated the "public" actions of the CO-MADRES but allowed them to develop and remain resilient in the face of severe repression and harassment in all arenas of their lives.

As Taylor (1997: 196–7) notes for the Mothers of the Plaza de Mayo and I have noted elsewhere for the CO-MADRES (Stephen, 1997a: 35–7), group demonstrations of public motherhood engender a contradiction that allows those performing motherhood to be reclassified as whores or madwomen. The public performance of mothering in El Salvador worked best as an initial strategy for obtaining political space and connecting with international solidarity organizations such as the support chapters that were formed in the 1980s in the United States, Europe, and Australia. Deliberate essentializing can only be taken so far before the behavior of women like the CO-MADRES is as subversive. Subversives become subject to treatment on the part of security forces that is not considered appropriate for "good" human beings and proper mothers. Such reclassification demonstrates the permeability of the identity boundaries.

Engendering Indigenous Rights and Culture in Mexico

The two and a half years of negotiations between the EZLN and the Mexican government between 1994 and 1996 produced the first document on indigenous rights signed by the state that included the participation of indigenous peoples. The San Andrés Accords on Indigenous Rights and Culture were formally signed by the Mexican government and the EZLN in February of 1996. After more than five years of intransigence, and a continued pressure by indigenous organizations and a national tour of 23 Zapatista comandantes, the Mexican Congress and Senate passed a watered-down version of the San Andrés Accords in April of 2001 that differ substantially from the document signed in 1996. The 2001 Law of Indigenous Rights and culture is much weaker in terms of indigenous self-determination, in terms of recognition of collective rights to land, territory, and natural resources, and in terms of the right of indigenous communities to regional affiliation, among other points. In April, 2001 the Zapatistas denounced the new law and broke off contacts with the government and pulled out of yet-to-begin new peace talks. What follows is the story of how indigenous women attempted to influence these accords and in the process built a national network.

In the preparation of the accords and in National Indigenous Congresses held in Mexico City in 1996 and 1997, indigenous women helped to broaden the notion of indigenous autonomy and made it clear what kind of political culture they understand it to include. In the process they have expressed their sense of themselves as citizens in a variety of arenas – family, community, organization, and nation. The National Indigenous Congress, a coalition of hundreds of indigenous organizations and communities representing more than 20 ethnic groups, has loosely defined indigenous autonomy as respect for the internal practices and decision-making modes of indigenous communities and nations. It has also demanded that indigenous communities have the opportunity to participate in the various levels of economic, political, cultural, and legal decision-making associated with the state (see Stephen 1997b; Regino Montes 1996).

Women who have participated in the National Indigenous Congress and in the preparation of the 1996 Accords on Indigenous Rights and Culture have attempted to influence several arenas of citizenship at once and to integrate concerns of ethnicity and gender with nationalism. The notion of autonomy articulated by indigenous women and their advisers through almost three years of meetings and workshops in Chiapas and elsewhere is expansive. They refer to economic autonomy, access to and control over means of production; political autonomy, basic political rights; physical autonomy, the right to make decisions concerning their own bodies and the right to a life without violence; and sociocultural autonomy, the right to assert their specific identities as indigenous women (Hernández Castillo, 1997: 112). The

women's resolutions from the 1996 National Indigenous Congress (Meneses 1996) are as follows:

The women demand recognition of their right to equality in homes, community, and in all of the spaces of the nation.... They demand that their citizenship rights be recognized; their right to equal political participation with men, their right to property and land, and to participate in decision-making in their communities. Because of these rights they demand legislation which equalizes the position of indigenous women and guarantees their right against being violated physically, psychologically, sexually or economically. In terms of the undeclared war.... they demand an end to the rape of indigenous women: women cannot continue to be war booty. We demand an immediate and careful investigation of all of the acts of violence against indigenous women and exemplary punishment for those responsible.

In documents produced by women in the National Indigenous Congress, the physical and psychological integrity of women's bodies and reproductive decisionmaking are linked to the right to land, property, and participation in political decisionmaking in all arenas. This integrated vision makes visible the systematic marginalization of indigenous women and suggests specific ways to correct it. This vision has its origins in the Chiapas Women's Convention held in preparation for the EZLN's 1994 National Democratic Convention which drew 8,000 participants from throughout Mexico to the Lacandon jungle (see Stephen, 1995). The Chiapas Women's Convention asked that women make up 50 percent of the delegates to the proposed Constitutional Convention and envisioned a model of government that was democratic and participatory rather than patriarchal, vertical, discriminatory, or corporativist (Rojas 1994: 190–5). While the summary document of the Chiapas Women's Convention mentions the need for laws to guarantee women's equal participation with men in a wide range of arenas, the most detailed proposals fall under the heading of "Family Life." Some of the points highlighted include the following (Rojas, 1994:194–5):

[We want] men to change, to respect us and to learn that we have rights and that they should help us so that everyone respects our rights.

[We want] to be respected for our choice of marriage partner, and we want those who sell women [into marriage] to be punished.

[We want] mothers and fathers to teach their sons and daughters how to do domestic work at a young age and that the work of women matters as much as that of men.

[We want] both parents to decide together how many children to have, and we want men to help women with the responsibility of family planning.

[We want] men who don't respect women, who rape and mistreat women, and don't fulfil their responsibilities to be punished.

[We want] women's rights to inherit property to be recognized and their rights to land respected whether or not they are widows.[2]

Here the notion of participatory citizenship at the level of the home is clearly expressed. While the document is the outcome of the participation not only of indigenous women, but also of mestiza advisers from a variety of organizations, it contains the seeds of ideas that are followed through in the discussions of the meaning of indigenous autonomy for women.

In two subsequent forums, in October 1995 and January 1996 to prepare the Accords on Indigenous Rights and Culture, the most contentious issue for women was the meaning of *usos y costumbres* – roughly, the customs and traditions of indigenous culture. While one of the central points of proposals for autonomy was respect for indigenous systems of justice and political decisionmaking, some of the "traditions" included under *usos y costumbres* did not promote gender equity – quite the opposite. For example, while the inclusion of men, women, and even children in community assemblies is

the practice in some Zapatista base communities, this is uncommon in many parts of Chiapas and in other indigenous communities in Mexico. "Traditional" political decisionmaking in many Zapotec communities in Oaxaca, for example, involves community assemblies attended by men between the ages of 18 and 70. In such assemblies, the majority of men present generally do not speak, but listen and simply vote silently with their hands if a resolution is put forward (see Stephen, 1991). (In ejidos with a significant number of women ejidatarios this pattern may be changing somewhat [Stephen, 1994]). Thus for many indigenous women "traditional" community decision-making processes exclude them. Other such "traditions" may include the beating of women by men, the negotiation of marriages by parents without respecting their children's wishes, and divisions of labor in which women work many more hours than men – patterns that I found to be common in a significant number of households in rural Oaxaca, Nayarit, and Chiapas.

In the forum of October 1995, indigenous women from the states of Chiapas, Oaxaca, Puebla, Querétero, Mexico, Hidalgo, and Mexico City and their advisers put forward a key modification of the term *usos y costumbres*: "We demand that our customs and traditions be respected if and when they do not violate women's rights" (Ce-Acatl, 1995: 22). This wording was more or less adopted in the 1996 accords. In October 1996, the EZLN and the Comisión de Concordia y Pacificación (National Commission of Concord and Pacification – COCOPA), composed of representatives from Mexico's three leading political parties, announced that a joint commission had been formed to monitor the implementation of the Accords. The COCOPA developed a legislative proposal endorsed by the EZLN, in which women's rights were stated as follows: "[Indigenous peoples] have the right... to apply their own normative systems in the regulation and solution of internal conflict, respecting individual rights, human rights, and the

dignity and integrity of women." The proposal recognizes the right of indigenous
peoples "to elect their authorities and exercise their own forms of internal government
in accordance with their norms ... guaranteeing the equal participation of women" (*La
Jornada*, January 13, 1997). The words
"customs" and "traditions" have been replaced in the COCOPA draft with "normative systems," indicating the volatility of the
notion of "customs and traditions" from a
gendered point of view. The draft thus subtly
addresses the political participation of
women where "traditionally" they have
often been absent and also discourages
internal forms of conflict resolution that do
not respect women's rights.

Other issues highlighted in these preparatory meetings, including women's right to
land, unequal divisions of labor in households, domestic violence, and rape were,
however, absent in the 1996 accords and
legislative proposal. The accords omitted all
the demands concerning the democratization
of the home and sexual violence and
addressed women only at the level of the
community, stating that they should participate in all legislative processes and be involved in choosing local leaders. The Law
on Indigenous Rights and Culture approved
by the Mexican Senate and Congress in April
2001 similarly omitted most of the demands
made by women in the preparatory meetings,
only focusing on women's right to political
participation in their communities. Nevertheless, the demands of indigenous women have
been inserted permanently into national politics in Mexico and an ongoing dialogue between indigenous women from different
regions of Mexico has been established.

For many women who participated in the
process leading up to the signing of the 1996
accords, coming together with other people
from throughout the nation – in this case
other indigenous women – has created networks that have lives of their own. Ultimately these networks may prove to be more
important than the accords themselves or the
2001 law. Women in the national movement

for indigenous autonomy have begun to
carve out a space and a political vision that
links home, community, and nation to a new
framework for being indigenous in Mexico –
autonomous in economic, cultural, and political decisionmaking but part of the Mexican nation. This vision and the political
culture it represents have the potential to
open up new political spaces not only for
indigenous women but for other women in
Mexico as well. In order to do this, indigenous women from different regions of the
country, with distinct regional histories and
ethnic relations and different languages, had
to essentialize themselves as "women" within
the National Indigenous Congress and in relation to the state. At the same time, however,
they had to recognize and mediate their differences.

This involved bridging the difference between, for example, María Elena Pérez, a
Yaqui indigenous leader who works with
the Frente Independiente de Pueblos Indios
(Independent Front of Indian Peoples – FIPI)
from the state of Sonora and Lorenza Gon-
zalez Xochil, a Tzotzil woman from Chiapas.
The Yaqui consider themselves to be a nation
within a nation and have a territory of
490,000 hectares divided into eight autonomous communities. Lorenza comes from a
small community that is politically divided,
with some members having allegiances to the
PRI and others being aligned with the Zapatistas or with parties of political opposition.
María Elena spends a lot of time in Mexico
City in the larger circles of national indigenous coalitions, and Lorenza works on a local
level with a women's weaving cooperative.
What indigenous autonomy means for each
of these women and the circumstances under
which they conduct their politics are vastly
different.

Indigenous women's unity against some of
the men who wished to silence them no
doubt helped to facilitate this process. The
women's internal dialogue around a wide
range of issues speaks to their multiple identities as primarily rural, indigenous, and
female. This process did not create a

homogeneous identity out of many, but provided a discursive field within which women participated from different positions.

During 1998, Mexico hosted two continental meetings of indigenous women that included representatives from Colombia, Guatemala, Peru, Ecuador, Chile, Canada, the United States, Panama, and El Salvador. In these meetings indigenous women from Mexico shared their problems with many others and thus moved into an even more heterogeneous organizing context. This dual process of organizing first, as ethnically distinct indigenous women within a national indigenous movement, and secondly, as Mexican indigenous women in the context of a larger grouping of indigenous women from the Americas, both reinforces and works against women's different senses of distinct ethnic identities and sense of Mexican nationalism. Such interlinked national and transnational organizing produces embedded layers of what Gayatri Spivak (1989; 1990; 1993) has called strategic essentialism – the need to project "sameness" to outsiders.

Conclusions: Identity, Strategy, and Citizenship

These two examples illustrate the contested nature of identification. What it means to be a mother in the CO-MADRES is differentially constituted for each woman upon entering the group and continues to be contested as women join together in strategic actions. The discursive context of these actions – going to clandestine cemeteries with peasants, occupying the headquarters of the International Red Cross, a radio station, church, talking to a touring German feminist organization, discussing domestic violence and rape under torture – continually shape and change the meaning of "mothering" for women in the CO-MADRES. This contested sense of "mothering" has a counterpart in their projections of themselves as "mothers" – providing a unified label for who they are.

For women who are participating in the National Indigenous Congress and the movement for indigenous autonomy in Mexico, "autonomy" is a contested discursive field that frames the internal process of participation in a coalition by women from many different locations. In Mexico the paradox of being indigenous in a country that has built its nationalism out of a "proud Indian past," but relegates its indigenous citizens to the bottom of the heap in the present has provided an ideological opening for women from different locations to question their marginality within indigenous organizations, communities, and families as well as in "the Mexican nation." A diverse group of indigenous women has engaged in forums on autonomy and questioned the unexamined notion of "tradition" in what have been largely male discussions of indigenous autonomy. They have questioned the invented tradition of "Indian communities" and the assumption of democracy within these communities.

By insisting that discussions on autonomy address the multiple arenas of home, community, and nation, indigenous women have simultaneously fractured the image of "Indian autonomy" projected by the National Indigenous Congress and deliberately essentialized themselves externally by projecting the demands of "indigenous women". Internal debates have highlighted significant regional differences between women in terms of the particular models of community autonomy they embrace – depending on whether they live in multiethnic communities, communities that are mono-ethnic but subordinate to non-Indian communities, or monoethnic hamlets politically subordinated by another indigenous ethnic group. Despite the mediated regional, ethnic, and even class differences that come to light in discussions and planning, their demands for "indigenous women's right to inherit property," "to be respected for our choice of marriage partner," "to have fathers teach their sons that the work of women matters as much as that of men," result in the creation of a homogeneous identity as read externally. This does not, however, erase their internal differences.

Identities are constructed through difference – through the relation to what is not, to what is lacking, to what has been called "the other" or the "constitutive outside." Identities "can function as points of identification and attachment only *because* of their capacity to exclude, to leave out, to render 'outside,' abjected" (Hall, 1996a: 5; see also Butler, 1993, Laclau, 1990). The form of unity, of closure that they exhibit is constructed and discursive. Another way of stating this is that identities involve discursive processes of essentialization and homogenization.

This is true also of politics and the exercise of citizenship by women in Latin America. Grassroots political organizing that interfaces regularly with the state in Mexico and El Salvador requires a homogeneous identity, a strategic essentialism, a constituency that is visible and capable of being counted. The 1996 accords signed by the EZLN and the Mexican Government on indigenous rights and the 2001 Law on Indigenous Rights and Culture are framed in terms of "indigenous" peoples and deal marginally with "indigenous women." Many nongovernmental and other organizations supporting the National Indigenous Congress and the Zapatista movement also have programs targeting "indigenous women". Bargaining with the state and holding it accountable requires the deployment of essentialist identities and categories.

In El Salvador, the CO-MADRES maintained a constant struggle to be recognized as any category other than "subversive" throughout their existence. Their projection of "mothers" as an organizational identity was part of a strategy for achieving recognition and protection from repression. As we have seen, the strategy had much better results internationally then in El Salvador, where they were often victims of repression. Once the peace accords were signed in 1992, however, their identity as mothers and family members of the disappeared gave them a basis for political participation in the United Nations Truth Commission and in national politics.

The double-edged sword of identity is nowhere clearer than in women's grassroots organizing. The fact that political recognition of women and other marginalized sectors of nations such as indigenous peoples requires political action on the basis of essentialized identity categories points to at least an initial strategy based on affirmative action rather than on abstract notions of universal citizenship. The difference between politics and cultural analysis is that while we can deconstruct essentialist categories and show the contingency, temporality, and incompleteness of identity formation, essentialist categories are alive and well in the political arenas of Latin America. While universal citizenship may be appealing in a poststructural world where all hierarchies of power and oppression have been deconstructed, in the real world such hierarchies persist. Thus women in organizations such as the CO-MADRES and the National Indigenous Congress are bound to exercise their citizenship rights – at least for now – through the imagined unity of identities that in everyday life are never experienced as a stable core of self, unchanging through time. That "essentialism has been deconstructed theoretically, does not mean it has been displaced politically" (Hall, 1996b: 249).

NOTES

1 Portions of this section draw upon Stephen 1994:2–4.
2 While under Mexican law women can have landholding rights while married and as single mothers, in many communities, women receive land rights only when they are widowed.

REFERENCES

Butler, Judith
    1990 Gender Trouble: Feminism and the Subversion of Identity. New York: Routledge.

—— 1993 Bodies that Matter: On the Discursive Limits of "Sex." New York: Routledge.

Ce-Acatl
1995 Grupo de Trabajo 4, Situación, derechos y cultura de la mujer indígena: Declaración de asesores e invitadas del EZLN. Ce-Acatl 73:21–27.

Fausto-Sterling, Anne
1997 How to Build a Man. *In* The Gender, Sexuality Reader: Culture, History, Political Economy. Roger Lancaster and Micaela di Leonardo, eds. Pp. 244–248. New York: Routledge.

Feijóo, María del Carmen
1989 The Challenge of Constructing Civilian Peace: Women and Democracy in Argentina. *In* The Women's Movement in Latin America: Feminism and the Transition to Democracy. Jane Jaquette, ed. Pp. 72–93. Boston: Unwin Hyman.

Garber, Marjorie
1993 Spare Parts. *In* The Lesbian and Gay Studies Reader. H. Abelove, Michele Aina Barale, and David M. Halperin, eds. Pp. 321–335. New York: Routledge.

Hall, Stuart
1996a Introduction: Who Needs "Identity"? *In* Questions of Cultural Identity. Stuart Hall and Paul du Gay, eds. Pp. 1–17. London: Sage.
—— 1996b When Was the "Post-colonial"? Thinking at the Limit. *In* The Post-Colonial Question: Common Skies, Divided Horizons. Iain Chambers and Lidia Curti, eds. Pp. 242–269. New York: Routledge.

Hernández-Castillo, Rosalva Aída
1997 Between Hope and Adversity: The Struggle of Organized Women in Chiapas since the Zapatista Rebellion. Journal of Latin American Anthropology 3(1):102–120.

Laclau, Ernesto
1990 New Reflections on the Revolution of our Time. London: Verso.

Meneses, Juan Anzaldo
1996 Nunca más un México sin nosotros. Resolutivos del Congreso Nacional Indigena. <http://www.laneta.apc.org/cni/>

Molyneux, Maxine
1985 Mobilization without Emancipation? Women's Interests, the State and Revolution in Nicaragua. Feminist Studies 11(2):227–254.

Ready, Carol A.
1999 Between Transnational Feminism, Political Parties and Popular Movement: Mujeres por la Dignidad y la Vida in Postwar El Salvador. Ph.D. thesis, Graduate Faculty of Anthropology, City University of New York.

Regino Montes, Adelfo
1996 Los derechos indígenas, en serio. La Jornada, October 22.

Rojas, Rosa
1994 Chiapas:(y las mujeres qué? México, DF: Ediciones la Correa Feminista, Centro de Investigación de la Mujer, AC.

Schirmer, Jennifer
1993 The Seeking of Truth and the Gendering of Consciousness: The CO-MADRES of El Salvador and the CON-AVIGUA Widows of Guatemala. *In* "Viva": Women and Popular Protest in Latin America. Sarah A. Radcliffe and Sallie Westwood, eds. Pp. 30–63. London: Routledge.

Spivak, Gayatri C.
1989 In a Word: An Interview. Differences 1:124–156.
—— 1990 Postcolonial Critic: Interviews, Strategies, Dialogues. New York: Routledge.
—— 1993 Inside the Teaching Machine. New York: Routledge.

Stephen, Lynn
1991 Zapotec Women. Austin University of Texas Press.
—— 1994 Hear my testimony: María Teresa Tula, Human Rights Activist of El Salvador. Boston: South End Press.
—— 1995 The Zapatista Army of National Liberation and the National Democratic Convention. Latin American Perspectives 22(4):88–99.
—— 1997a Women and Social Movements in Latin America: Power from Below. Austin University of Texas Press.

—— 1997b Redefined Nationalism in Building a Movement for Indigenous Autonomy in Mexico: Oaxaca and Chiapas. Journal of Latin American Anthropology 3(1):72–101.

Taylor, Diana
1997 Disappearing Acts: Spectacles of Gender and Nationalism in Argentina's "Dirty War." Durham, NC: Duke University Press.

4

Activism and Class Identity:
The Saturn Auto Factory Case

Sharryn Kasmir

In February 1999, union elections were held at the Saturn automobile factory in Spring Hill, Tennessee. Mike Bennett and other members of the Vision Caucus headed Local 1853 of the United Automobile Workers (UAW) since 1986, when they were appointed to direct the new local. This caucus took the optimistic name "Vision" because it worked with corporate chiefs to implement a labor-management partnership that is singular in US automobile history: At Saturn the union is represented on management councils, all managers have union-side partners, production is carried out by self-directed teams, and workers' pay is adjusted according to performance. Running against the Vision slate were representatives of Members for a Democratic Union. Despite growing friction in the months before the election – when union members considered jettisoning the Saturn accord, voted to authorize a strike, and saw their paychecks decline with the slump in the small car market – there was little expectation that the Vision candidates would lose. The Vision Caucus appeared to have solid control over the plant. Indeed, Mike Bennett called early elections so that his leadership would be secure as he prepared to negotiate with management

to get a new product for the plant. It therefore came as a great surprise when all thirteen Vision officers were ousted from their posts.

This election was momentous beyond its impact at Saturn, for what it suggested about the project of labor-management cooperation, as well as for what it said about shop-floor activism in post-Fordist plants. I conducted anthropological research at Saturn during this eventful time (1998–9). This chapter examines how class identities were mobilized at Saturn in this period. I found that workers were substantially committed to the project of labor-management cooperation, which involved them in becoming self-actualizing, aspiring subjects. Nevertheless, shop-floor activists and union dissidents drew out an oppositional consciousness that was critical of the union for collaborating with management and that called for a more assertive worker identification. In this chapter, I discuss the range of class identities at Saturn, and I consider how they affect the labor movement.

An exploration of class identity is important for a consideration of social movements because, as June Nash notes in the introduction to this volume, when academics and critics rejected class as a privileged site of struggle, they often cast aside the fundamental premises of class analysis – that labor and capital have opposing and different interests stemming from unequal control over the means of production and the labor process. Following World War II, "end of ideology pundits" argued that in advanced industrial countries, the Fordist compact between labor and management, which granted managerial control over the work process in exchange for higher wages and job security, brought a decline in class consciousness. Frankfurt-school critics similarly maintained that the relative prosperity of US and European workers signaled their integration into the capitalist apparatus. After French workers failed to join student protests in 1968, new-social-movement theorists proposed that class categories had shifted, and the once-central opposition of workers and managers had given way to the ascendance of knowledge workers and an alliance of students and technicians. Broadly, scholars writing about social movements argued that historical agency was no longer to be found in a workers' movement but instead in feminist politics, ethnic groups, and environmental and anti-nuclear coalitions that mobilized around non-class identities.[1]

This critique has motivated scholars who study workers in Fordist and post-Fordist regimes to revisit their assumptions about consciousness and identity. For anthropologists engaged in this debate, the writings of E. P. Thompson (1966) and Antonio Gramsci (1971) have been particularly influential. Thompson elaborated the distinction made by Karl Marx between a "class-in-itself," formed by the objective conditions of collective, alienated labor, and a "class-for-itself," cognizant of its mutual interests, poised for solidaric action, and strengthened in this struggle by shared culture and ritual. He argued that working classes must be made in both of these incarnations, the first by property relations and the capitalist labor process, the second by individuals, labor unions, and mass movements. The central

message for anthropologists is that we need "to study the production of interest, identification, grievance and aspiration" (Jones 1983:22) within the domain of social action – that is, class identity is neither primordial nor automatic, but must be brought into being by social actors.

Gramsci's concept of hegemony has likewise been key for our understanding of the establishment, and recent unraveling, of the industrial and cultural regime of Fordism. An early observer of corporate welfarism and the "American Plan," Gramsci showed how workers were disciplined by force (union-busting, company-hired thugs, regressive labor laws), as well as by consent (family wage, corporate paternalism, company unionism). Workers' very subjectivity was crafted by a new mode of life that reformed work discipline, housing, nutrition, gender and sexual relations, parental roles, and recreation. Gerald Sider (1996) has suggested that anthropologists are especially well poised to interpret the related phenomena of class consciousness and hegemony since we listen over long periods of time to what people say about capitalism and class relations, and to their shifting biases against and sympathies with other culturally constituted racial, ethnic, and gender segments of the working-class. We are thus privy to the "actually existing" (75) ideas of working people in specific social and historical contexts as they are shaped by the power relations of factory, community, and state.

Corporate hegemony molds workers' expectations, aspirations, and daily habits and it can condition their protest, as June Nash (1989) illustrates in her ethnography of Pittsfield, Massachusetts. Nash studied the community response to economic decline after General Electric (GE) downsized in the 1970s–80s, leaving thousands unemployed or in low-paying service jobs. When GE announced that it would close a major division of the Pittsfield plant and would open a factory in Canada jointly with Westinghouse, a union delegate declared "GE is climbing into bed with the competition and leaving us bareassed in the cold!" Nash explains, "workers objected not so much to the arbitrary control of investments by corporations that were not held accountable to the community, as to the failure to live up to their own code of competitive free enterprise within national boundaries" (6). Workers' outrage was framed in the very language of corporate hegemony, as they charged that GE foreclosed on the social pact by which labor and corporation were to work together to produce economic opportunity and stability. Nash makes the important point that workers were also agents of this corporate ideology, since the unions they built fought for the compromises that constituted the Fordist compact.

Workers' identity is itself an artifact of hegemony, as August Carbonella (1998) demonstrates in his study of the paper-mill town of Jay, Maine. Carbonella finds that Fordism narrowed workers' allegiances, political networks, and senses of self to focus on community and factory. He argues that an alternative consciousness in Jay was ignited during a long and bitter strike at International Paper (IP), when the predominantly white workers not only stood against IP at the factory gates but extended the terrain of their struggle, making connections with African- and Native-American communities as striking workers set out on caravans and speaking tours to bring their story to other towns and cities. Thus their resistance involved a new geography of identity and politics. Rather than claiming that either the Fordist, localist identity or the geographically broadened political identity was primordial, Carbonella instead describes how both were created by material conditions, ideology, and social actors.

The role of social activism in forging class identities is also developed in Geraldine Casey's (2002) study of women secretaries at the University of Puerto Rico. Secretaries are represented by two distinct organizations: a professional association which galvanizes members to develop themselves and to become middle class, and a trade union

which views secretarial work through a more working-class lens. A strike against University administration transformed secretaries' consciousness, pushing them to take an oppositional stance and to use class rhetoric; even those who were members of the professional association rather than the union were thus rallied. Casey shows that gender identity can be used to either foster or suppress class-based action, and she documents how trade unionism and the independentist Puerto Rican Socialist Party have mutually constituted a politically conscious Puerto Rican working class. Class identity, like gender and nation, has to be "named, claimed and mobilized in the arena of social action" (6).

In the case of university secretaries, the particularities of white-collar work, performed in close proximity to a professional boss, created conditions which favor a professional or middle-class identification, but anthropologists studying elsewhere have discovered similarly contradictory identities among assembly-line workers. In my own study of the Basque town of Mondragón (Kasmir 1996), I found that workers in distinct factory regimes expressed different class identities. Workers in cooperative factories were more likely than their peers in privately owned companies to describe themselves as middle class, and they were less likely to be members of unions and to attend labor demonstrations.

My research corroborates Mona Rosendahl's (1985) ethnographic account of factory workers in a small, ethnically homogeneous Swedish town that in her words contained "a whole spectrum of ideas about class . . . and sometimes this can be found within the same individual in different situations" (143). This "mixed" consciousness pertained even though in Sweden the socialist-influenced trade union movement and the labor party, with access to state power, provided a ready "language of class."[2]

Rick Fantasia (a sociologist sympathetic to an ethnographic perspective) advises us to be skeptical of conclusions about the failure of working-class consciousness that are drawn from the results of sociological surveys and questionnaires (1988). He argues that consciousness is better seen in what workers do than in what they say, and he uses the Marxist concept of "praxis" – the dialectical interplay between thought and action – to see consciousness in "cultures of solidarity" or the "embodiment of oppositional practices and meanings" (17). Fantasia reevaluates the history of US workers in late twentieth century from this perspective and finds instances of solidaric praxis; for example, "rank-and-file insurgent groups within unions can be transformative activities that create and express solidarity, embodying consciousness" (11).

These studies provide several insights that guide my interpretation of Saturn employees: Workers' expression and identity are molded by the hegemonic accord regarding the conditions of work and obtain until those premises are abrogated. This break can come during a strike or other action, including the activities of rank-and-file dissidents, when a new consciousness of collective goals may be formed. This new class identity (like the one it supplants) is uneven and contradictory, often combining oppositional meanings and aspirations with those derived from the hegemonic, corporate project. Class consciousness is, thus, not a given, and the anthropologists' job is to document the mutable character of workers' identifications and to determine the conditions in which different identities are made. I use these ideas in the following sections to examine class identities at Saturn.

I found that Saturn workers have multiple and contradictory identities that are forged by different social forces and actors. Workers' ideas about work, class relations, and themselves are often in line with Saturn's corporate mission. I explore the operation of hegemony on the shop floor to show how Saturn's version of post-Fordism organizes identity and consciousness to create self-actualizing employees. However, workers' senses of self also tack back and forth between this self-actualizing subjectivity and a defiant working-class self. I also examine workers' oppositional consciousness, and I consider how shop-floor dissidents summon this identification to upset the post-Fordist status quo.

Mobilizing Aspiring Selves at Saturn

"Make the most of your day."
(outgoing voicemail message, elected union official, Vision Caucus, 1998)

This quote introduces a central dilemma of class identity at Saturn: The factory is permeated by messages from both union and management that encourage workers to think of themselves as aspiring, self-actualizing, risk-taking subjects, who achieve more than the successful completion of their assembly or off-line task but who work to "continuously improve" themselves and the corporation (Kasmir 2001).[3] When a Saturn worker hears the phone message "Make the most of your day," s/he is entreated by a union officer to do as the corporation asks: to realize her/himself. This promotion of identity is at the center of Saturn's project.

Like many major corporations, General Motors (GM) responded to increased global competition in the late twentieth century by experimenting with new, post-Fordist management strategies.[4] Saturn is the most developed of these experiments. Saturn was formed in 1985 as an autonomous unit of GM. Saturn and the UAW forewent the standard labor contract in favor of a short (some thirty pages), continuously bargainable Memorandum of Agreement. Saturn's Memorandum breaks with pattern bargaining in the auto industry and was not fully supported by the international UAW. Indeed, there was strong opposition to the Saturn arrangement because it exchanged longstanding domains of union strength, such as job classification and seniority, for participation in management. Though a significant part of the UAW promotes "jointness" (combined labor-management projects) and quality-of-work-life programs, Saturn was seen by many as going too far. The Memorandum of Agreement is interpreted by some in the UAW as a give-back, a bad precedent, and a forfeiture of union power and solidarity (see Parker and Slaughter 1994, 1997, Rinehart, Huxley, and Robertson 1997). As such, Saturn's local has been somewhat alienated from the international union. For years, leaders of Local 1853 turned this estrangement into a badge of pride, proof that they were mavericks whose "vision" was leading the way forward from entrenched and outmoded labor relations.

Saturn's Memorandum devolves aspects of managerial prerogative to the union. The union is represented on all management councils, including those that deal with sales and advertising, as well as the highest-level Strategic and Manufacturing Advisory Council. Companies in the US are not legally required to bargain over sales, capital allocation, and production, and most labor contracts have a management-rights clause that further secures this domain as the exclusive prerogative of management; the Saturn agreement is path-breaking in the decision-making role it assigns to union representatives. Car production is carried out by self-directed teams of workers who rotate assembly and off-line jobs, as well as budgeting and maintenance responsibilities. Several teams are arranged by task and plant geography into a module. At this and all higher levels of governance, there are partnered union and management leaders who jointly arrange work schedules, monitor production goals, solve personnel problems, and "coach and counsel" errant workers. Saturn also has special teams, which function outside of the usual bureaucratic structure to coordinate all aspects of a project, such as the launch of a new car model. These teams include both managers and workers; as such, they cut across lines of class solidarity and create a commonality of purpose between managers and workers.

In keeping with its emphasis on worker self-motivation and responsibility, Saturn pays workers their base compensation as salary rather than the fixed hourly wage established by the standard UAW contract. The salary is a percentage of the national UAW/GM rate, and the remainder (as much as twelve percent) is "put at risk" through the "risk/reward" system. The company pays risk money and reward bonuses if the workforce achieves production, quality, and training standards that are set in consultation with the union (Rubinstein and Kochan 2001:24–5).[5]

Saturn's shop floor is saturated by a corporate culture in which employees are to be made anew, overcoming the history of supposedly class-rigid Detroit. As other scholars of post-Fordist plants show, language is an important aspect of corporate ideology (e.g., Casey 1995, Graham 1995).[6] At Saturn, words and phrases are invented and borrowed from management gurus[7] to create a corporate language that marks this workplace as "different" from other auto factories.[8] In Saturn parlance, Detroit is the "Old World." To partake of the new world (Saturn) "team members" (as employees are called) should discard "personal baggage." In particular, they should shed an "us/them" attitude; such an outlook is disparaged as having created the inflexible conditions in which union and management see themselves as adversaries. An early print advertisement for Saturn cars publicized this corporate vocabulary of class. The ad boasted, "The very first thing we did was get rid of labels like 'management.' And 'labor.'" Instead, "rep," a shortened form of "represented," refers to a union member and "non-rep" to a manager. While the words "labor" and "management" convey the class position of the person taking on this role, "rep" and "non-rep" point to a circumstance rather than an identity. A team member who is "rep" is entitled to union backing, but he or she is not designated as "belonging" to that collective, being a "union member," or embodying the status of "worker."

Saturn culture sets out to refashion factory-based class relations, as well as what it means to be a worker. One way in which Saturn workers are meant to reshape themselves is that they are supposed to be willing to take risks to reach a goal. "Risk" is a key word in Saturn discourse. Saturn researchers and proponents Saul Rubinstein and Tom Kochan assert, "employees became, in the technical terms, 'residual risk bearers' – they risked their human capital in the same way GM investors and retailers and suppliers risked their financial capital" (2001: 37). As sometime co-authors with Mike Bennett, Rubinstein and Kochan can be said to articulate a Vision perspective on Saturn culture.

When Saturn's Tennessee facility began a second wave of hiring in the late 1980s, the GM/UAW agreement required that it preferentially employ laid-off union members. Consequently the majority of Saturn's 7,000 union workers were originally from the Detroit-Flint area where GM cut thousands of jobs. Other workers left relatively secure jobs and most broke long-standing family and community ties to move to Tennessee. Since Saturn was incorporated as an autonomous unit of GM, workers gave up their GM seniority when they accepted their new jobs. While Saturn's Memorandum affirms the Corporation's commitment to job security, it does not guarantee seniority rights should there be layoffs, transfer rights should the plant close, or supplemental unemployment benefits, all of which are provided in the national contract (Rubinstein and Kochan 2001: 25). These facts are central to Saturn's brand image, "A Different Kind of Company. A Different Kind of Car," which deploys themes of starting over, even at personal and collective risk.

"Risk-taking" is built into the deep structure of the Saturn "origin myth," or its corporate telling of its own history. In my interviews, Saturn workers also feature "risk" in their personal accounts of transferring to Saturn. Tom is a UAW member who came to Saturn after he learned that his plant was going to close.

[O]ne day they announced the plant closing. ... So I took at a look at it, and I made a personal decision first. I said I don't want to go traditional anymore. If I'm going to go anywhere, I'm going to go to Saturn.

And so this is how strong I believed in that. I went to my wife and I sat her down and I said, "Here's the deal. I've got twenty years, and I'm sick of the traditional baloney. I'm going to apply one place and one place only. I'm going to apply for Saturn. And if they don't take me, I'm going to find something else. I'm done with the auto industry." And to my surprise she said "Okay." I really, you know, because of job security and all of that and three kids. But that's how much I believe in this stuff.

Tom portrays his decision to work at Saturn as a heroic act. The dramatic climax of the story is the moment when he gambles security and exercises choice: "I'm going to apply one place and one place only. I'm going to apply for Saturn." Significantly, Tom's story follows the structure of the cultural myth of the American entrepreneur, but it is unusual for a blue-collar worker to tell a story about choosing to work in a factory as evidence of an enterprising impulse. The more familiar worker-as-hero tale begins in the shadow of the factory. Perhaps the central figure's father and grandfather have worked there. Ultimately, the hero's individualism and willingness to forego security spare him the fate of being "trapped" in the factory, and he breaks out of the confines of small town and factory to "make it." Through directing his aspiration toward Saturn, Tom merges the trope of fleeing with the decision to move to Saturn. The act of choosing Saturn stands in for escaping the factory, and the fact that Saturn is different from other auto factories stands in for "making it."

Beth monitors the computer system that contains data on production and labor requirements for the entire plant. This information is used to set or revise production schedules. In a standard auto plant, this job would be supervisory, but Beth is union-side.

She is a long-time UAW member from a working-class family. She told me about her decision to come to Saturn:

> When I was eleven years old, I had a dream that I wanted to work for this company that treated their people right and treated their customers right. Eleven years old. That was my goal in life....
>
> So you know, I went on through life and college and met my husband. And so that all kind of got back-burnered. Then all of a sudden this thing called Saturn came along. And what was Saturn all about, it was about people, and it was about treating customers right. And so here was this dream that I had put on the back burner, that here it was, right in front of me again, you know. Wow, what an opportunity, you know.
>
> So I put in an application. Didn't hear anything from them for a couple of years. I said, well, whatever they want I guess I just don't have. So we bought a new house in May, and in November they called. And I said, I don't think I can come now because we just bought this new house, you know. And I was so miserable that weekend, my husband said, "Call them back." He said, "We can sell the house, we can move." He says, "I just can't live with you like this." Because I was just depressed, you know, here was my dream again.
>
> So anyway I got on a plane came down for the interview. And they said, you know, "Can you be here in January." Well, yeah. I had four kids, and a house, but we did it. I mean, because this is what we wanted to do in life....

In this story, dramatic tension centers on how close Beth comes to not taking a risk and therefore to letting her dream pass her by (for the second time.) Her concern not to uproot her children and husband might have prevented her from taking the job at Saturn. Gender figures into Beth's and Tom's stories differently. Tom makes his decision alone and then tells his wife; his is a manly tale of boldly setting out to "make it." Beth is instead ready to forgo her opportunity; she does not allow

that "her dream" has an independent urgency but is conditioned on the needs of her family. Though their risk follows distinct, gendered routes, both Tom and Beth propose that the outcome of taking a chance is fulfillment. Saturn will allow Beth to realize her childhood wish of working for a company that "treat[s] their people right."

Both Tom and Beth use Saturn language to tell their personal stories. Tom's phrase "valuing people as our greatest asset" and Beth's references to "this thing called Saturn" and "it was all about people" are borrowed from advertisements, corporate recruiting videos, and in-house newsletters and television programs. This commingling of corporate discourse and self-narration suggests that their subjectivity is stirred by the corporate version of Saturn as a place where they can realize their dreams.

The theme of self-actualization also appears in Tom's and Beth's interviews and is likewise dominant in corporate discourse. Jeff is a UAW member in his mid-30s. His story of transferring to Saturn contrasts his despair on the assembly line with his hope that Saturn will offer fulfillment.

> There's a poem which you need to find and read, it's called "50,000 Ashtrays and 100,000 Screws." You need to read that because you cannot understand an autoworker until you do. When you read that poem, I've seen it reduce grown men to tears, autoworkers.... It's somebody basically saying "I've been reduced to a machine, Oh, my God, this is my life."
>
> And Saturn was this bright shining light. It was going to be a way out of this. It was going to be a way to get involved, to manage our own affairs, to get through it.

Saturn holds out the possibility that Jeff would no longer be a "machine," and it heralds a new agency rooted in positive action: "a way to get involved, manage our own affairs, to get through it."

Bob came to Saturn after being laid off by GM. When he arrived in 1990, Saturn was not yet running a full manufacturing schedule.

> [W]e really weren't building that many cars. So [we did] team building exercises.... I left from working strictly on the car [in his previous plant] to working on people skills.... You had to kind of channel everything, and get rid of all of your personal baggage in order to get to the common [goal]....
>
> You were never physically tired. One thing that I did learn very quickly, was that from a blue-collar world, you're always physically exhausted from the labor, but you never, ever thought of meetings, and sitting all day as being physically draining, mentally. And you begin to experience some of that at a meeting here and a meeting here. And your mind is really moving trying to find better ways of doing this, and this, and this. And you realize that it's physically taxing on you also. So you begin to get a feel for both sides. What it was really like looking from a blue-collar as to a white-collar position.

The training Bob attended modeled the self-actualizing subject: one who puzzled over a problem, extended this effort to after-work hours, and felt a sense of achievement in figuring it out. In doing this work, he sympathized with management.[9] He not only came to respect managerial work (meeting, thinking, people skills), he became a kind of person who undertook such work.

The above passages exemplify an ethos in which the application of effort, self-regulation, and responsibility are intrinsically rewarding. They also exhibit a valorization of a subject who takes risks and realizes her/himself on the job. However as the following section shows, workers' involvement in management also rouses class solidarity and resistance.

Solidarity and Resistance

At Saturn, workers are responsible for many administrative, personnel and oversight matters that are the exclusive domain of supervisors and managers in traditional plants. As I showed above, participation in management spurs workers to be aspiring, self-actualizing subjects, but it can also unleash other forms of consciousness. When Saturn began hiring in the mid-1980s, "charter team members" (the first hired) had the autonomy to select their own team members. For Cindy, reviewing applications brought out gender and class solidarity.

> There was a lady that had had probably twenty sick leaves. Her file kept going around and around the table. And they wanted to put it in the "no go" file, and that means that they would never have a job at Saturn. And I just couldn't stand that, especially if you're a woman....
>
> For a woman, when you would go out to have your child, you do go on sick leave and you are out for a while. But your file doesn't tell you that. And the men would just toss them, would just toss them. But this lady kept going around and around, I couldn't let go of her. They finally agreed to let me call her, because I just begged them....
>
> I called her and we talked. And once that started the bond was there. And come to find out, she had had three children and... had taken a lot of time for having her kids. And it ended up that she had had so many sick leaves because she was in a bad relationship where she was beat up with broken bones, her husband beat her up so much....
>
> I got her down here, and she ended up being one of the best. She divorced her husband, brought her kids, and is one of the best workers.

Cindy's stance emerged from her own experience as a woman worker in an auto plant. Her work history was punctuated by pregnancies and arranging for child care for her new babies. She approached the job of evaluating applicants with a sureness that the file did not provide the whole picture of a worker's efforts and promise. She was very proud of her accomplishment in hiring this woman, not only because she realized her own potential in pursuing the matter and persuading others to see things her way, but also because she used her authority to demonstrate sympathy for a fellow woman worker. The organizational structure of Saturn gave her the power to act out of gender and class solidarity.

In the development stage of Saturn, teams also had the responsibility to find suppliers for parts and machines. Teams did not automatically select union shops, thus team members met with and visited non-union suppliers, sometimes where labor conditions were highly exploitative. This experience in a management role deepened a sense of working-class sympathy in Jerry, a worker in general assembly.

> Early on when the teams were still involved in picking suppliers, my team decided that we would all go down to Mississippi to visit our supplier, that we would make a day of it. We got a van from Saturn and packed a picnic lunch and headed down Natchez Trace. When we got to the Mississippi plant, we got out of an air-conditioned van into the plant. They make tubing. It was a hot plant. I saw how hard they work. Most were women. They were welding. It was so hot you almost fainted. And they probably earn very little, and they need every penny they make.

Jerry was emotional as he compared his circumstances – he spent the day with his team on an outing; they traveled in an air-conditioned van; they planned a picnic – to that of the women working for very little money in the hot plant. He reflected on his own good fortune. "Going back to a regular job would blow my mind, I got used to a good job." This is a powerful story of the segmentation of the US working class, what it means for the Mississippi factory women to be excluded from the Fordist compact, and what it means for Jerry to be part of a privileged segment of the working class. Nevertheless, Jerry did not recall his privilege in a gesture of superiority or smugness, rather he was

moved by the workers' exploitation, and he recounted the events with a tone of solidarity. In this instance, Jerry's participation in management had the effect of deepening working-class critique.

A different dialectic of class subjectivity was provoked in other workers. While Bob (quoted above) learned how difficult mental work could be, and he gained sympathy for managers, he was nonetheless aware of the costs to the individual (including increased stress and problems at home) of being an aspiring subject. Reflecting on the mental strain associated with Saturn's post-Fordist regime, Bob commented,

> I think it costs you more this way than the old way. The old way, you go in and you do your eight hours, and you give as much as you have to give. And here, if you give more than you probably intended to, sometimes. I think here they get so much more out of you than in the Old World. In the Old World you could pretty much hit it, and do what you had to do, and ship it. Here you, if this is not right, you're working, you're working, you're working. You've got so many other things going on, and you're just doing so much more.

Bob told me that he preferred Saturn to a traditional auto plant, but he was simultaneously conscious that this mode of work extracted more value, as workers' emotions and aspirations were mined for profit. At Saturn, continuous improvement and the insertion of quality control into the assembly process (two techniques of post-Fordism) mean that workers are counted on to solve problems as they manifest themselves on the line; they are likewise expected to be part of a "highly functioning team" and to resolve any personal conflicts that impede this goal. Bob's recognized the human cost of self-actualization and its value to the corporation.

John was similarly conscious of his exploitation at Saturn. He believed that the team concept was implemented in a class-interested way,

What I think they did with the team concept is that management took all the things, jobs they did not like to do, all the crap jobs, and put them on the teams, like taking care of attendance problems, attitude problems, scheduling work. Those are the things that supervisors did not like to do. They put that on teams.

Bob and John expressed the kind of grievances that we would expect from factory workers: They complained of abuse, manipulation, and exploitation at the hands of management. Remarkably, however, workers' anger at their exploitation was less often directed at management than it was at Local 1853's Vision Caucus. Mike Bennett, long-time union president and advisor to the Manufacturing Action Council, was the target of considerable criticism.

One worker I interviewed remarked that Saturn's local was weak in comparison to his old local. "I think I'm very pro-union. I've never had – well, you see, it'll never be like we had back in [my old plant.]" In this equation, the worker was "pro-union," and his old union was a "real" union. His statement inverted the corporate-invented dichotomy between the "Old World" and Saturn; in this alternative formulation, Saturn would never measure up to the old, pro-union environment. Throughout my interviews, numerous workers equated their old local with solid unionism and strong worker identity, and they characterized Local 1853 with exhibiting weak unionism and identifying with the corporation and management. Other researchers quoted a Saturn worker's lament that "It feels like we don't have a union here" (Parker and Slaughter 1997:217). In essence, workers took up a class critique of labor-management cooperation by criticizing union leadership.

Many charged that the Vision Caucus was so involved in the business side of things that it did not adequately represent workers. One disgruntled member of an assembly team exclaimed, "talking to Mike Bennett is like talking to [the company president]. He is not in bed with management, he *is* management" (quoted in Parker and Slaughter 1997:217). Union leaders' role in strategic planning and manufacturing decisions branded them as "management." Shop-floor dissidents rallied workers to name Vision leaders as "them" and to reclaim an oppositional, working-class "us." By this logic, in voting against Bennett and the other Vision officers, workers could take a stand against management.

Mobilizing Working-Class Identity

This feeling that the Vision team was "them" in contradistinction to a solidaric and working-class "us" underwrote the events of 1998–9, when the terms of class relations and identity shifted at Saturn. In the winter of 1998, a small group of shop-floor dissidents who named themselves Concerned Brothers and Sisters began to meet to discuss their grievances. Union-side leaders were appointed rather than elected, giving the Vision team too much power and making leaders unresponsive to members. Paychecks were smaller since a slump in the small car market reduced overtime and reward bonuses. Saturn's fixed rather than rotating shifts created sleep problems and disrupted family schedules. Over several weeks, dissidents garnered support, until they were able to hold a meeting of 600–700 (by their own estimates) rank-and-file workers at the local high school. The group decided to call a motion at the next union meeting for a referendum to scrap the Saturn Memorandum of Agreement and go back to the national UAW contract. The national contract would not only get rid of rotating shifts and guarantee the GM wage (about $20 per hour for most job categories), but it would effectively end the labor-management partnership.

This level of rank-and-file activism was unprecedented at Saturn. Dissidents told me that there had been individual voices of protest before, but those had been few and marginal. The referendum was defeated two to one, but by their own account, dissidents succeeded in opening a dialogue of solidarity and resistance. Significantly, organizers did not so much urge workers to oppose management as they made the Vision Caucus the object of their protest. They defined the local union's steadfast commitment to the partnership, its control over the plant, and its closeness to management as major grievances.

In challenging the partnership, Concerned Brothers and Sisters echoed the position of New Directions and Labor Notes, two national groups that publicly oppose labor-management cooperation in the auto industry. New Directions is a dissident Caucus in the UAW that condemns the concessionary stance of the union, particularly with regard to labor-management cooperation schemes, and it advocates a return to the militant tactics of the 1930s, when Flint autoworkers took over their plants and battled corporation and police to establish their union (Dandaneau 1996:7–33). Labor Notes publishes a journal and books that criticize the team concept, quality circles and other post-Fordist management techniques (Parker and Slaughter 1985, 1988, 1994). One Saturn dissident attended a Labor Notes conference and others are familiar with these national groups, giving Concerned Brothers and Sisters a broader network and perspective.

Concerned Brothers and Sisters began a second round of organizing in the summer of 1998 during a strike that began at GM Delta over outsourcing. The strike quickly spread throughout GM, and the concerted action of the locals began to look like a solidarity strike. Saturn workers did not walk out with the rest of the UAW. This situation recalled Saturn's isolation during the 1992 strike at GM Lordstown, when Mike Bennett complained to the press that the international union should allow Lordstown workers making Saturn parts to cross the picket line (Parker and Slaughter 1997). That is, Bennett argued that rather than expecting Saturn to show solidarity with other union locals, the UAW should respect Saturn's "difference"

and support its maverick experiment. In 1998, it looked as if Saturn workers would once again stand apart from their fellow autoworkers. Shop-floor dissidents began to act:

> We were the only GM facility working. Bowling Green was still working, but for the only reason that they had parts, and they were at a slower production than most. So we were still working with the local union, with management to outsource the parts. And we were getting parts from Nip and Denso and Japanese suppliers for the spark plug, and we were also getting parts from Red China, to keep the Saturn lines going. . . .
>
> So it made the workers just feel like shit. Here we were building cars with convicts and child labor. And that really made the people think, even the pro-partnership people. That really made them think, what in the hell is going on with our union, that they would agree to this with management. And that really opened a lot of the eyes. So we called ourselves "scabs," that's what we were.

In uttering "scab," dissidents spoke a powerful word of class betrayal. "Scab" evoked class anger turned towards other, less class-conscious factions of the working class; it also envisioned a solidaric collective that stood opposed to the strike breakers. It was a word taken from outside of the Saturn vocabulary of "team members" and "partnership," a language that erased class differences. To call themselves "scabs" was to charge that the corporation had claimed their identities.

Local 1853's poor record of solidarity with the International made this formulation more potent. Saturn workers did not support the Lordstown strike, and their Memorandum of Agreement broke ranks with the national contract, paralleling the condemned practice of "whipsawing" by which unions negotiated concessionary contracts in order to compete with other locals for jobs. Many workers I interviewed told me that back home in

Detroit, Flint, or the northeast, their friends and neighbors were under the mistaken impression that Saturn was non-union. This disturbed workers' senses of self in relation to their fellow union members. Jerry told me that after working several years at Saturn, "I went back to my plant...I brought the union card because people told me Saturn didn't have a union." Jerry was upset and embarrassed that his one-time co-workers thought he had gone south to a non-union facility.

Concerned Brothers and Sisters organized in this environment:

> Our campaign on the shop floor, we kept the membership informed of what was going on. We'd get our news off the internet, and we'd put it out on the floor and keep them informed. And also we started a write a letter campaign....And then addresses of the UAW, Solidarity House, AFL/CIO, the UAW Website. And we encouraged the workers to write letters in opposition to what was going on in Saturn, the outsourcing of the parts.

This shop-floor militancy, combined with pressure from the International on Local 1853, led Saturn to vote to authorize a strike. It was the first time that Saturn workers took such a vote and the first time they acted in concert with the international union. It was a significant moment in US labor. The strikes were already a month-and-a-half old when the Saturn vote was taken. Twenty-five assembly plants and scores of parts facilities were closed, and 186,000 workers were affected in the biggest labor stoppage in GM since the 1970s. When Saturn authorized the strike it was one of only three North American assembly plants still running (Nauss and Fulmer 1998). Saturn's decision to join them was also momentous: The purported model of post-Fordist labor-management cooperation threatened to strike. Dozens of national and foreign newspapers covered the momentous Saturn vote, carrying headlines such as, "Labor's peace with G.M.

unraveling at Saturn," and "Elite car workers ready to strike."[10]

Though the dimension of solidarity was unmistakable, in accordance with the Taft–Hartley amendment to the National Labor Relations Act, the walkouts at GM locals were not sympathy strikes but each was called over local issues.[11] The grievances at Saturn were about job security and pay; declining sales jeopardized both. The Vision Caucus used the threat of a strike to push GM to give the Spring Hill facility a new product in addition to its small-car line, and management settled by promising a high-profit Sports Utility Vehicle. Saturn workers never walked out, but in authorizing the strike, union leaders ruptured the discourse of Saturn "difference" and unleashed a language of solidarity with other GM plants.

When union elections were called several months later, Concerned Brothers and Sisters worked for Members for a Democratic Union (MDU) candidates. The opposition slate ran on a platform to reform of the Memorandum. MDU promised to bring Saturn closer to the national contract and called for stronger unionism. This sentiment had been marginal at Saturn, eclipsed by the corporate project of self-actualization and aspiration, but shop-floor activists used the language of solidarity and class to transform "interest, identification, grievance and aspiration" (Jones 1983:22). Indeed the name "Concerned Brothers and Sisters" evoked the fraternal/sororal language of labor that stood in opposition to the corporate "Saturn family." Moreover, while the designation "Saturn family" obscured class difference, Concerned Brothers and Sisters was shorthand for the labor appellation "union brothers and sisters" that excluded management, as such it redrew the lines of collectivity.

The opposition slate won an overwhelmingly victory. Jeep Williams replaced Mike Bennett as Manufacturing Action Council advisor (the vote was 55.5 percent to 38.6 percent), Ron Hankins became the new union president, and the rest of the Vision Caucus was defeated. In December of 1999, the new officers negotiated a change in the Memorandum of Agreement to reduce the portion of salary at "risk" to three percent (down from twelve percent in the previous agreement), bringing Saturn more in line with standard wage formulas and suggesting that workers' pay should not hinge on "risk."

Discussion

Most Saturn workers I interviewed were at least partly engaged in a project of remaking themselves as aspiring, self-actualizing subjects. Even workers who were cognizant of the particularities of their exploitation (for example, the strain of problem solving and learning people skills) were simultaneously motivated to extend their effort and to achieve more than they had at their old plants. Many like Jeff were pained at having been a "machine" in their previous jobs and wanted to more fully utilize their human capacities to think, plan and decide. It is essential not to minimize the dehumanization in the Taylorist auto factories they left behind, where conception and execution were divorced, and the task division of labor made manual jobs routine and monotonous (Braverman 1974, Chinoy 1992 [1995], Hamper 1986, Linhart 1981). Jeff voiced despair at having himself experienced the equivalent of the poet's "50,000 Ashtrays and 100,000 Screws," and Bob recalled the mindlessness of "hit it, and do what you had to do, and ship it." These are understandable and even expected responses to assembly-line work. As Ely Chinoy (1992 [1955]) showed in his 1950s study of an auto factory, alienation and lack of opportunity led workers to dream of owning farms or small businesses. When the GM plant studied by Ruth Milkman (1997) closed, many workers accepted a buyout and opened small businesses; they earned less than they did in the plant, but they derived more personal satisfaction from their labor. Dreams of fulfillment have a long history in the lives and identities of

auto workers. When Tom, Beth, and others moved to Saturn, they hoped to realize more of their potentials, and they saw "risk" as a rite of passage in remaking themselves in a more enterprising and successful mold.

While these desires are compelling, we must not take for granted their particular configuration at Saturn. A major conclusion of this chapter is that it is not a given that workers would be roused by the project of self-actualization, frame their personal histories in the language of corporate discourse, or channel their energies toward profitability and the Saturn brand image. This self-motivated subjectivity had to be summoned. Saturn workers authored narratives of risk and fulfillment because this was sanctioned discourse – the ideal Saturn subject longed for a more satisfying job and had the guts to transfer to Spring Hill in pursuit of that dream. It is easy to assume that US workers would naturally gravitate to an identity molded by middle-class attributes, since the larger cultural environment prizes upward mobility and achievement, yet this subjectivity was, in fact, constructed by specific social forces and actors.

Corporate ideology, the organization of work, management, and the Vision Caucus together promoted this identity. The Vision officer's voice-mail message "Make the most of your day," spoke of the union's role in urging workers to self-actualize. Notwithstanding, Vision leaders' goals were not the same as the corporation's profit motives. Vision activists saw themselves as waging a battle to limit managerial prerogative. They were responding to the decades-long UAW concern with job enrichment; and they were tackling the problems of dehumanization and anomie experienced by Jeff and others. This has been seen as a progressive agenda to develop a more robust unionism for the twenty-first century (Bluestone and Bluestone 1992, Heckscher 1988, Rubinstein and Kochan 2001). In an interview, Mike Bennett told me:

I was, you know, in an adversarial system in Flint, Michigan. I was raised and brought up in that whole environment in terms of my career. But I still had these other basic beliefs that I think management is too important to leave the managers alone. And so I thought the union as an institution could be a very, very important competitive vantage if given the opportunity. And Saturn was the opportunity in terms of empowering that took place....

Bennett believes that unions are fettered in their effort to secure jobs and a decent standard of living for workers when they are kept out of key business decisions. He worked hard to get GM to give the Spring Hill plant a Sports Utility model (involving significant financial investment) because he was convinced that he represented workers best not when focusing on shop-floor grievances but when participating in the more consequential business decisions that determine the company's future. A fuller telling of the Saturn story will necessarily recount the details of this activism and its impact on the labor movement.

In this chapter, I have argued the Vision team's version of union activism was a re-making of class selves. While this self-actualizing subjectivity was persuasive, it was neither uniformly embraced nor fully formed in individual employees. Some Saturn workers like Cindy and Jerry subscribed to this philosophy, but they also expressed solidarity with fellow workers in their plant, as well in more brutal workplaces; others like John and Bob were conscious that their emotions and aspirations were the objects of profit. But their oppositional consciousness was no more primordial than the aspiring subjectivity it displaced. It too had to be claimed and mobilized.

Shop-floor dissidents' rallies of "us" versus "them," the solidaric naming of "brothers and sisters," and the charge of "scabs" – all taken from labor's language class – were weapons in this struggle over identity. In challenging the premise that enterprise

"risk" should be shouldered by workers, the MDU Caucus also resisted the corporate and Vision production of selves. By negotiating a reduction in the risk portion of pay, the new leaders are presently crafting a subjectivity in which individual effort does not determine pay, union members are wage earners rather than "risk bearers," and Saturn workers are more like other UAW members. Finally then, the contest over union leadership and the terms of the labor contract at Saturn is also a struggle over class-consciousness and identity.

NOTES

1 See Bell (1960), Marcuse (1964), and Touraine (1985). For useful reviews of these debates see Fantasia (1988) and Phillion (1998). Historian Gareth Stedman Jones reminds us that an early round of "end-of-class" theory – Weber, Durkheim and Parsons – followed the post-1850s labor peace in England (1983, 6).

2 I borrow the concept of "language of class" from Jones (1983) who argues that such a language of opposition is essential for the production of working-class identity and grievance.

3 In conceptualizing Saturn's project of subjectivity, I draw on the work of Paul du Gay (1996) and Katherine Casey (1995) who study employees in post-Fordist firms. Like Saturn, the corporations they investigate idealize the self-directed, self-motivated, problem-solving worker, and managerial discourse and work organization are geared toward producing this type of employee. Du Gay (1996) uses the term "enterprise regime" to characterize this kind of workplace: "Enterprise culture is one in which certain enterprising qualities – such as self reliance, personal responsibility, boldness and a willingness to take risks in the pursuit of goals – are regarded as human virtues and promoted as such" (56). My

approach is also informed by Dorinne Kondo's (1990) ethnography of urban Japan in which she conceptualizes work as a domain in which selves are "crafted" by company ritual and discourse.

See Barchiesi (1998) for a discussion of how the post-Fordist strategy of flexibility impacts subjectivity in a South African auto plant. For a related point of view on how the Saturn corporation uses the techniques of education and culture change to impose a set of values on workers see Yanarella (1996).

4 The term "post-Fordism" is often used in human-relations literature to mark a putatively new and better industrial epoch, in which the assembly line has been replaced by job enrichment and multiple tasks, workers engage in conception as well as execution, organizational bureaucracy is superseded by flexibility, and power is decentralized. (For the classic Marxist critique of how the Taylorist labor process dehumanizes workers through the separation of conception and execution and the task division of labor see Braverman [1974]).

I do not use the term in this way, rather I use it to denote a widespread reorganization of Taylorist/Fordist labor process and management practices that occurred in the US beginning in the 1970s. I am persuaded by scholars and labor activists who argue that although they appear in the guise of human relations, post-Fordist management techniques often bring speedups, increase stress, and threaten union power (e.g. Graham 1995, Grenier 1988, Moody 1997, 85-113, Parker and Slaughter 1988, 1994, 1997, Rinehart, Huxley and Robertson 1997, Yanarella and Green 1994, 1996). My own writing on the Mondragón cooperatives contributes to this point of view (Kasmir 1996,1999). As these studies show, factories using post-Fordist methods still use time studies to increase job load (the number of seconds per minute that the worker is engaged in tasks that "add value" to the product). Post-Fordism also relies on just-in-time production, in which stock is kept at a minimum and workers "pull" parts to line as they need them. Mike Parker and Jane Slaughter (1988), long-time critics of workplace reengineering, term this system "management by stress" for the speed-up it brings to the shop floor.

For a helpful and concise overview of workplace reengineering, see Nissen (1997). As Nissen notes, the US government (both Republican and Democratic administrations) promotes workplace reorganization, including labor-management partnership and worker involvement. Several commissions, reports and even awards lend government sanction to this management strategy, thereby giving corporations the backing of the state in these endeavors. Workplace reorganization as it appears at Saturn and other factories is a hegemonic project, involving both capital and the state.

5 On the organizational structure of Saturn see Rubinstein (1996) and Rubinstein and Kochan (2001).

6 Sociologist Katherine Casey (1995) has written a particularly useful study of the production of self in a post-Fordist corporation. Like Saturn, the corporation she researched developed an in-house language to name new relationships and identities, including "teams" and "family," branding employees as a solidaric group without class divisions. She uses the term "language practices" (92) to designate this "technology" of the workplace. In her study of the Subaru-Isuzu plant, Laurie Graham noted a similar invention of words and phrases, such as "associate" to replace "worker" and the corporate principle of "driving out fear" (1995, 107).

7 For an interesting, though less than critical, portrait of one management guru, see Newfield (1998).

8 "Difference" is central to Saturn's brand image: "A Different Kind of Company. A Different Kind of Car." In this public relations slogan, Saturn's difference hinges in large measure on its labor relations. Saturn cultivated a public image, through

media campaigns and showroom tactics, as a "caring," "human" and "post-class" company. This image is carried inside the plant through workplace slogans, management practices, and in-house television, which broadcasts Saturn commercials as well as corporate- and union-produced programs (Rogers 1999). For a discussion of brand image from a business point of view see Aaker (1994).

9 Emily's Martin's work (1994) on the cultural metaphor of flexibility offers an interesting example of this kind of training. She writes about a corporate retreat in which employees are asked to climb high, swaying poles in order to experience the constant movement and groundlessness that purportedly characterize the requirements of the competitive, global market in which the corporation operates. That is, employees are asked to experience risk as a personal embodiment of corporate flexibility.

10 These headlines appeared respectively in *The New York Times*, July 22, 1998, P.A1 and *The Independent* [London], July 21, 1998, p.13.

11 This is one example of the way in which the legal structure of Fordism narrowed the reach of the US labor movement and created localist working-class politics and identity (cf. Carbonella 1998)

REFERENCES

Aaker, David
1994 Building a Brand: The Saturn Story. California Management Review 36(2):114–133.
Barchiesi, Franco
1998 Restructuring, Flexibility, and the Politics of Workplace Subjectivity. A Worker Inquiry in the South African Car Industry. Rethinking Marxism 10(4): 105–133.
Bell, Daniel
1960 The End of Ideology. Glencoe, IL: Free Press.
Bluestone, Barry, and Irving Bluestone
1992 Negotiating the Future: A Labor Perspective on American Business. New York: Basic Books.
Braverman, Harry
1974 Labor and Monopoly Capital. New York: Monthly Review Press.
Carbonella, August
1998 The Reimagined Community: The Making and Unmaking of a Local Working-Class in Jay/Livermore Falls, Maine 1900–1988. Ph.D. Dissertation, Graduate Center of the City University of New York.
Casey, Geraldine
2002 From Bootstrap to Shoulderstrap: Women Secretaries and Class, Culture, and Voice in Contemporary Puerto Rico. Ph.D. Dissertation, Graduate Center of the City University of New York.
Casey, Katherine
1995 Work, Self, and Society After Industrialism. London and New York: Routledge.
Chinoy, Ely
1992 [1955] Automobile Workers and the American Dream. Urbana, IL: University of Chicago Press.
Dandaneau, Steven P.
1996 A Town Abandoned: Flint, Michigan Confronts Deindustrialization. Albany: State University of New York Press.
du Gay, Paul
1996 Consumption and Identity at Work. London: Sage.
Fantasia, Rick
1988 Cultures of Solidarity: Consciousness, Action and Contemporary American Workers. Berkeley: University of California Press.
Graham, Laurie
1995 On the Line at Subaru-Isuzu: The Japanese Model and the American Worker. Ithaca and London: Cornell University Press and International Labour Review.
Gramsci, A.
1971 Americanism and Fordism. *In*: Selections from the Prison Notebooks. Pp. 277–318. New York: International Publishers.

Grenier, Guillermo
  1988   Inhuman Relations: Quality Circles
    and Anti-Unionism in American Indus-
    try. Philadelphia, PA: Temple University
    Press.
Hamper, Ben
  1986   Rivethead: Tales from the Assem-
    bly Line. New York: Warner.
Heckscher, Charles
  1988   The New Unionism: Employee In-
    volvement in the Changing Corporation.
    New York: Basic Books.
Jones, Gareth Stedman
  1983   Languages of Class: Studies in Eng-
    lish Working Class History 1832–1982.
    Cambridge: Cambridge University Press.
Kasmir, Sharryn
  1996   The Myth of Mondragón. Co-
    operatives, Politics, and Working-Class
    Life in a Basque Town. Albany: State
    University of New York Press.
——— 1999   The Mondragón Model as Post-
    Fordist Discourse: Considerations on the
    Production of Post-Fordism. Critique of
    Anthropology 19(4):379–400.
——— 2001   Corporation, Self, and Enterprise
    at the Saturn Automobile Plant. Anthropol-
    ogy of Work Review, 22(4):n.p.
Kondo, Dorrinne K.
  1990   Crafting Selves: Power, Gender,
    and Discourses of Identity in a Japanese
    Workplace. Chicago and London: Uni-
    versity of Chicago Press.
Linhart, Robert
  1981   The Assembly Line. Amherst: Uni-
    versity of Massachusetts Press.
Marcuse, Herbert
  1964   One Dimensional Man. Studies in
    the Ideology of Advanced Industrial So-
    ciety. Boston: Beacon Press.
Martin, Emily
  1994   Flexible Bodies: Tracking Immun-
    ity in American Culture – From the
    Days of Polio to the Age of Aids. Boston:
    Beacon Press.
Milkman, Ruth
  1997   Farewell to the Factory. Auto-
    Workers in the Late Twentieth Century.
    Berkeley: University of California
    Press.

Moody, Kim
  1997   Workers in a Lean World: Unions
    in the International Economy. London
    and New York: Verso.
Nash, June
  1989   From Tank Town to High Tech:
    The Clash of Community and Industrial
    Cycles. Albany: State University of New
    York Press.
Nauss, Don, and Melinda Fulmer
  1998   Saturn Strike Vote Deals GM An-
    other Blow. Los Angeles Times, July 20,
    A1.
Newfield, Christopher
  1998   Corporate Culture Wars. In: Cor-
    porate Futures: The Diffusion of the
    Culturally Sensitive Corporate Form.
    George E. Marcus, ed. Pp. 23–63. Chi-
    cago: University of Chicago Press.
Nissen, Bruce
  1997   Unions and Workplace Reorgan-
    ization. In: Unions and Workplace Re-
    organization. Bruce Nissen, ed. Pp.
    9–37. Detroit: Wayne State University
    Press.
Parker, Mike, and Jane Slaughter
  1985   Inside the Circle: A Union Guide to
    QWL. Detroit: Labor Notes.
——— 1988   Choosing Sides: Unions and the
    Team Concept. Detroit: Labor Notes.
——— 1994   Working Smart: A Union Guide
    to Participation Programs and Reengineer-
    ing. Detroit: Labor Notes.
——— 1997   Advancing Unionism on the New
    Terrain. In: Unions and Workplace Re-
    organization, Bruce Nissen, ed. Pp. 208–
    227. Detroit: Wayne State University Press.
Phillion, Stephen
  1998   Bridging the Gap between New
    Social Movement Theory and Class. Re-
    thinking Marxism 10(4):79–104.
Rinehart, James, Christopher Huxley, and
    David Robertson
  1997   Just Another Car Factory? Lean
    Production and Its Discontents. Ithaca
    and London: Cornell University Press
    and International Labour Review.
Rogers, Brishen
  1999   The New Myth of the Happy
    Worker. The Baffler 12:41–50.

Rosendahl, Mona
  1985 Conflict and Compliance: Class Consciousness among Swedish Workers. Stockholm Studies in Anthropology.
Rubinstein, Saul
  1996 Saturn, The GM/UAW Partnership: Impact of Co-Management and Joint Governance on Firm and Local Union Performance. Ph.D. Thesis, Sloan School of Management, Massachusetts Institute of Technology.
Rubinstein, Saul, and Thomas Kochan
  2001 Learning from Saturn. A Look at the Boldest Experiment in Corporate Governance and Employee Relations. Ithaca, NY and London: Cornell University Press and International Labour Review.
Sider, Gerald
  1996 Cleansing History: Lawrence, Massachusetts, the Strike for Four Loaves of Bread and No Roses, and the Anthropology of Working-Class Consciousness. Radical History Review, Spring, 65:98–84.

Thompson, E. P.
  1966 The Making of the English Working Class. New York: Random House.
Touraine, Alain
  1985 An Introduction to the Study of Social Movements. Social Research 54(4):749–787.
Yanarella, Ernest J.
  1996 Worker Training at Toyota and Saturn: Hegemony Begins in the Training Center Classroom. In: North American Auto Unions in Crisis: Lean Production as Contested Terrain. E. J. Yanarella and W. C. Green, eds. Pp. 125–157. Albany: State University of New York Press.
Yanarella, Ernest J., and William C. Green, eds.
  1994 The UAW and CAW Confront Lean Production at Saturn, CAMI, and the Japanese Automobile Plants. Labor Studies Journal 18(4):52–75.
—— 1996 North American Auto Unions in Crisis: Lean Production as Contested Terrain. Albany: State University of New York Press.

Part II

Secularization and Fundamentalist Reactions

5

Print Islam: Media and Religious Revolution in Afghanistan

David B. Edwards

Introduction

In a series of articles written in 1901 and 1902 Lenin put forward the proposition that the Communist Party needed "an all-Russian newspaper" for its organizing efforts to be successful. Attacked as an "armchair" theorist for this suggestion, Lenin responded angrily to his critics by insisting that

> we can *start* establishing *real* contacts only with the aid of a common newspaper, as the only regular, All-Russian enterprise, one which will summarize the results of the most diverse forms of activity and thereby *stimulate* people to march forward untiringly along *all* the innumerable paths leading to revolution, in the same way as all roads lead to Rome (Lenin 1969: 163–164).

Far from being a funnel for airy abstractions, the newspaper of his imaginings would act as

> an enormous pair of smith's bellows that would fan every spark of class struggle and of popular indignation into a general con-

flagration. Around what is in itself still a very innocuous and very small, but regular and *common*, effort, in the full sense of the word, a regular army of tried fighters would systematically gather and receive their training (p. 166).

In this essay I want to extend Lenin's comments on the relationship of print and politics in two directions. First, I will argue that newspapers are not alone among print forms in achieving revolutionary political effects. Pamphlets, magazines, leaflets, and other print genres are all capable of playing a vital role in the development of revolutionary movements, and all have been employed by revolutionary political parties at different times and places. At the same time, however, it is important to recognize that while different print forms are capable of bringing about revolutionary effects, the nature of those effects is likely to be different in every case since each print form has its own unique features and utilities. Each has also tended to be especially effective in particular settings, and we must therefore be sensitive both to the objective features of particular print forms and to context and circumstance in which they are produced.

The second avenue I pursue in this essay concerns the dialectical nature of print's impact – which is to say, print affects not only those who read texts but also those who produce them. The process of employing and deploying forms of print transforms those engaged in the process, and it does so in ways that may not be at all self-evident to those who are thus transformed.[1] It is thus my contention that print's impact is not limited simply to that effect noted by Lenin of fanning the flames of revolution. Print can, in fact, produce subtler, though equally far-reaching, effects such as advancing the process of internal hierarchization within the party structure, routinizing the adoption of covert procedures, and facilitating the acceptance of personal subordination on the part of party members and supporters.

Lenin's primary interest was in the uses to which newspapers could be put to achieve power. The concern in this essay is to ascertain the role of print in one particular historical context. That context is Afghanistan, and the focus of my comments is on a political party that Lenin would undoubtedly have branded as reactionary rather than revolutionary. The party is Hizb-i Islami Afghanistan [the Islamic Party of Afghanistan] which has been at the forefront of efforts to establish an Islamic government on Afghan soil for the last twenty-five years. Up until the collapse of the Soviet-backed government of Dr. Najibullah in 1989, Hizb-i Islami's chief *casus belli* was the ascendence of atheistic communism in Afghanistan and the foreign domination of the Soviet Union over the Afghan people. Since 1989 Hizb-i Islami's explicit goal has been the establishment of an Islamic government in Afghanistan and the advance of Islamic revolution worldwide.

In pursuing both of these objectives, Hizb-i Islami has consistently opposed the Marxist plan of revolution, but it has been equally insistent on pursuing its own revolutionary program, a program that is as radical in its

implications for Afghan society (and potentially for other Muslim states as well) as the Marxist plan. Indeed, the Islamic revolutionary program put forward by Hizb-i Islami owes a great deal to the indigenous Afghan Marxist parties it has long opposed, beginning with its stated goal of achieving greater social and economic justice for the peasant and landless classes.[2] Likewise, from its earliest years Hizb-i Islami emulated the leftist parties in establishing an authoritarian party structure and network of covert cells in various schools, offices, and military units which were to strive for the violent overthrow of the existing Afghan regime. Finally, and most importantly for this essay, the Hizb-i Islami party followed the Afghan Marxist parties in their employment of print texts to advance the cause of revolution.

In investigating this latter aspect of Hizb-i Islami's history, I will examine three print forms – newspapers, pamphlets, and magazines – that were particularly significant in the party's development. The impact which each of these print forms had on the party was different, and I will try to outline some of these differences, beginning with newspapers with which the party [known then as the Muslim Youth Organization, or Sazman-i Jawanan-i Musulman] had only an indirect association until the late 1970s. Despite this fact, however, it is crucial to begin with newspapers because it was through them that the traditional way in which Afghans conducted their political business received its most decisive shock.

Thus, even though the Muslim Youth Organization from which Hizb-i Islami arose did not publish any newspapers itself during the first formative political period, its leaders and the organization itself were transformed by the ones that were produced, especially the leftist papers. In a fundamental way leftist newspapers laid the foundations of the political culture that the Islamic political parties later adopted, and it is thus necessary that we begin this examination of print and the politics of Islamic revolution with a discussion of the leftist papers and their transformative effect on Afghan political culture in the era of "democratic reform."

Newspapers and the Culture of Confrontation

While it is said that the first newspaper in Afghanistan was founded in the late nineteenth century by the renowned Islamic reformer Sayyid Jamaluddin al-Afghani, it is the case that newspapers in Afghanistan have more often been dominated by forces associated with the left than those sympathetic to Islam.[3] This was especially apparent during the democratic era initiated in 1965 when the government of King Zahir Shah passed a law allowing the publication of independent newspapers. The first groups to seize the opportunity thus afforded were principally leftist political parties which, from the start, set out to use newspapers as much to establish a new political culture as to communicate specific messages to its actual and potential supporters.

Newspapers could facilitate the process of establishing a new political culture, in the first place, because of the kind of objects they were. Because of their ubiquity in our society, newspapers are relatively invisible to us, and it is not as easy to focus on their essential attributes as one might initially suppose. Newspapers are absorbed in the everydayness of their consumption; more often than not, they are read hurriedly and passingly, often at breakfast against a backdrop of children, food, and television. In Kabul during the late 1960s newspapers – or, at least, the independent ones with something new to say – were a novelty, and the educated public, small as it was, was eager for the stimulation they provided. No one was better aware of this situation than the publishers of the leftist papers such as *Khalq* [Masses] and *Parcham* [Banner] who emblazoned their mastheads with bright print and large banner headlines, thus pushing themselves into public consciousness as much through visual aspects as their written rhetoric.

Newspapers tend to be large and floppy to begin with, and as such they draw attention to themselves, particularly when they are sold or handed out openly on the street. Lenin realized this public and visible quality of the newspaper when he referred to them as the "smith's bellows" of revolution. Newspapers have the potential to create a unity of readers by their presence in public and the fact that their essential message can be readily grasped by a large number of people in the same place. The spatial unity engendered by newspapers has a temporal component as well, for unlike books, or even pamphlets and magazines, newspapers are not meant to be saved, or even pondered especially long. They are of the moment; their contents are by definition "new" and meant to be consumed quickly.

Government newspapers, in their repetitive dullness, their emphasis on official statistics and reports, deadened this quality of temporal immediacy, but the independent papers of the left did not. To the contrary, they reveled in it, and in the process constituted in one segment of the Afghan public the novel notion of "news" as a phenomenon in and of itself. Through newspapers, events themselves took on an urgency and pace that they had not had before. The left instilled this sense of urgency, of time passing and opportunities lost, of the synchronicity of events at home and abroad (protests on the streets in all the world capitals), and the larger synchronicity inherent in the ideal of world revolution.

In a similar manner the papers published by the left also helped to constitute another novel ingredient in the emerging political culture of the time, and that had to do with the constitution of a sense of there being a "public-at-large" that was the audience to which the newspapers of the time addressed themselves. The very title of the dominant leftist paper – *Khalq*, or "Masses" – speaks to the left's attempt to create a sense of a more general public with shared interests in common. The idea of "the public" is, of course, an old one in the West, but it must be recognized that it was not an established one in Afghanistan, at least not in the sense that it is in industrialized, urban-centered societies like our own. Afghanistan's public culture – even among the elite classes – has traditionally been centered on such traditional (male) gathering places as restaurants, guesthouses, and tea shops. It also reflects a continuing valorization of ancient concerns for personal reputation, family name, and female honor.

The public, to the extent that it existed, constituted itself as the collective aggregate of those with whom honor was shared and who one recognized as capable and entitled to judge one's own claims to social status and esteem. The notion of the public that the Marxist parties advanced was very different than this one, however. It was constituted as all those who shared the state of being oppressed. It was a public that manifested itself not in its honor but in its suffering. It was a public that could only come into its own through joint political action in defense of its rights and in opposition to those who would keep it from acquiring those rights. In their constitution of this new notion of the public and of public interest, the Marxists demonstrated their intention to reconfigure both the mode of debate and the substance. No longer would men interact in traditional ways according to established interactional structures. Nor, for that matter, would it simply be men who engaged in the debates. From this point on, the parties would struggle not only to shape the hearts and minds of the Afghan public, but also to create a new sense of what that public consisted of, who belonged to it, and what its shared interests might be.

The leftist parties introduced (or at least popularized) another innovation to Afghan political culture that has become perhaps the most characteristic and persistent feature. That innovation was the use of provocation as a form of political action. The most consistent focus of leftist provocations was Islam, and the most dramatic example of this sort of attack occurred in 1970 when the *Parcham* newspaper published a poem entitled "The Bugle of Revolution" written by its editor, Bariq Shafi'i. A panegyric honoring Lenin's contribution to world revolution, the poem incited the wrath of Muslim leaders less for its praise of Lenin (loathsome as that might have been to them) than for its use of a eulogistic invocation [dorud] that was traditionally reserved for the Prophet Muhammad.[4]

Where earlier provocations by the left against Islam had resulted in scattered street protests, outraged mosque sermons, and delegations demanding audiences with the king, *Parcham*'s publication of "The Bugle of Revolution" created a nationwide furor. Given the limited literacy of the Afghan population and the small circulation of newspapers, it is certain that few of those who protested the poem actually saw it, but news of the outrage nevertheless spread throughout the country and inspired an organized protest involving several hundred Muslim clerics from all over Afghanistan who congregated in the Pul-i Khishti mosque in central Kabul to protest the poem and give vent to their larger concern for the expansion of leftist influence in the country.

The so-called Pul-i Khishti demonstration lasted for more than a month during the spring of 1970 and can be seen as an important turning point in Afghan politics, first, because it established the fact that the single most important line of division within the Afghan body politic was that between Islam and Marxism and, second, because it also demonstrated the essentially subordinate role of the government itself. This was a period in which the government was trying to channel political activity within such institutionalized fora as the parliament and a few well-behaved newspapers that were supposed to play by the rules the government established. The Pul-i Khishti protests showed, however, that the approved institutions could not hold the energies that were then being unleashed and that the principal lines of division through which these energies would be expressed were ideological.

At the same time, however, the fact that the demonstration ultimately failed to effect any change in government policy or in the visible presence of leftist parties in the country also helped to engender in the leaders of the Muslim Youth Organization a determination to follow a different strategic path. The older generation of Muslim activists had taken a public route to express their grievances, and they had even chosen to cooperate with the government, agreeing to various stipulations that the government asked of them and meeting continuously with government representatives in an effort to work out a compromise agreement. When the government then turned on the protesters, invading the mosque and summarily dispatching the venerable collection of clerics assembled there, it became clear to the younger generation of activists that a different path would have to be followed, one that emphasized secrecy, covert action, and the insulation of party members from outside subversion.

The failure of the Pul-i Khishti demonstration also underscored to younger Muslims the general unpreparedness of traditional Islamic leaders to respond to the changing political climate in Afghanistan. Older forms of action and organization were outmoded given contemporary political realities, and this fact was nowhere better exemplified than in the arena of propaganda.[5] Thus, while parties on the left managed to get three or four papers into print within a few months of the government's liberalization of press restrictions, only one independent religious newspaper emerged during this period, and it had a much more limited impact than the leftist papers.

The one Islamic paper was the weekly *Gahiz* [Dawn], edited by Menhajuddin Gahiz, which commenced publication in 1968, two years after the passage of the Press Law, and continued until Gahiz's suspicious, though still unexplained, murder in 1972. Despite the relative brevity of its run, *Gahiz* did make a significant contribution to the Islamic movement by reprinting articles by leading Muslim political thinkers such as al-Afghani, Maulana Maududi, and Sayyid Qutb. It also provided a forum for the writings of indigenous authors, including several Islamically-inclined professors at Kabul University and a few leaders of the Muslim Youth Organization.[6] Finally, and perhaps most important of all, *Gahiz* played a significant role during this pivotal period by providing Muslims, especially Muslim students, with the intellectual ammunition they needed to fend off the broadsides that were being aimed at them by leftists who accused Islam of being backward and inimical to modernization and reform. *Gahiz*'s articles and essays countered this reproach by demonstrating that Islamic thinkers were equally concerned with social and economic justice and that they too could formulate programs that addressed Afghanistan's problems.

At the same time that *Gahiz* helped to advance the ideological position of Islam in Afghan political discourse, however, it also demonstrated the organizational weakness of Islamic politics in Afghanistan, for unlike the leftist newspapers, *Gahiz* had no direct organizational component through which to implement in practice the ideas it was laying down in print. Menhajuddin Gahiz himself had close relations with the leaders of various Muslim political "parties," but according to the testimony of various informants, these relations were informal and the "parties" themselves were little more than networks of like-minded individuals who met and talked together from time to time.

The absence of an organizational structure to help actualize the ideological propositions that *Gahiz* was publishing essentially meant that the student readers of *Gahiz* were left to their own devices. Lacking a public organ of their own with which to try to establish a popular base (as the Marxist parties were doing), the Muslim Youth Organization increasingly turned away from public strategies and concentrated on developing its position within the student population itself. Though Muslim Youth Organization candidates ran for office in university student elections and participated in campus and citywide protest demonstrations, most of the group's activities focused on the formation of study groups within the university and later in various schools in Kabul and the provincial capitals. These study groups became the nuclei of the covert cells that would eventually seek to implement the party's plan of violent revolution. At the center of these study groups and essential to their transformation was another kind of text, the pamphlet, which was less public than the newspapers considered so far but equally important – particularly in the next stage of political development when covert action and party loyalty would be the essential requirements for success.

Pamphlets and the Politics of Covert Action

If newspapers were the primary vehicle by which political radicals succeeded in creating a climate of confrontation and polarization in Afghanistan, pamphlets were one of the principal means by which the evanescent emotions and energies generated by newspapers and demonstrations were translated into coherent political ideologies and concrete organizational structures.[7] In considering the role of pamphlets in the development of Islamic politics in Afghanistan, there are several political organizations that one could focus on, but none is more pertinent or exemplary of this stage of political action and organization than the Muslim Youth Organization itself. Probably more than any other contemporary Afghan political party, the Muslim Youth recognized the potential utility of political pamphlets as an ideological tool and harnessed them to their purposes. The Muslim Youth Organization also figured out that the utility of pamphlets was not simply for conveying ideas. They were also invaluable for articulating new modes of political relationship based on obedience to authority, organizational secrecy, and the relentless pursuit of party objectives.

These new kinds of political relationship were not the invention of the Muslim Youth, of course. The Marxist parties, guided by their Soviet sponsors, were responsible for introducing the principles and techniques of party organization years earlier, just as they pioneered the use of newspapers and pamphlets as a vehicle of revolutionary praxis. However, the Muslim Youth Organization's adoption of the same principles and techniques within an Islamic framework helped to overcome the weaknesses that had plagued the Islamic political protests organized by the older generation of Muslim leaders and, concomitantly, set the stage for the underground political struggle that climaxed in the overthrow of the Afghan government in 1978 and that subsequently developed into the civil war that has consumed Afghanistan since that time.

Accounts of the origins of the Muslim Youth Organization differ, depending on the present political affiliation of the speaker, but it is generally agreed that Muslim students began to meet on the campus of Kabul University in 1966 or 1967 and that a group of students representing different faculties within the university formally established the party in 1969. The founding members of the Muslim Youth were initially inspired by a group of professors in the Faculty of Islamic Law who had studied in Cairo in the 1950s and come in contact with members of the radical Muslim Brotherhood (al-Ikhwan al-Muslimun) during their stay there. Although these professors did not take a direct role in student activities, they informed them of movements going on in other parts of the Muslim world and provided them with a sense of how Islam could be made relevant to the social and political transformations of the late twentieth century. More immediately, the professors gave their Muslim students an ideological foundation to counter Marxist students whose strident attacks against traditionalists on campus provided the primary spur to Muslim organizing efforts.[8]

In response to these challenges, Muslim students began to distribute excerpts from works by writers like al-Afghani and Sayyid Qutb which professors and students in the Faculty of Islamic Law had translated into the local languages of Persian and Pashtu. In addition, there were also speeches and statements made by leaders of the Muslim Youth Organization that directly addressed issues relevant to Afghanistan's situation. Few of the works that were distributed in this period were very long. For the most part, they were only a few pages in length and were hand-copied by the students themselves. In local vernacular, these texts were referred to as *nothâ* (Persian) or *notuna* (Pashtu), cognate terms which are derived from the English word "note" and which reflect the source of these works in the university student population (a population which had become accustomed to "taking notes" on the lectures given by their instructors, some of whom were from Europe and America). Members of the Muslim Youth distributed these writings by hand to those they judged sympathetic to Islam, and each recipient was then expected to make ten to twenty copies of the original and pass them on to others.

Initially these samizdat works were distributed within the university community; however, the Muslim Youth Organization gradually expanded to include informal networks of sympathetic students attending the medical college in Ningrahar, various teacher training institutes, and secondary schools in Kabul and the outlying provinces. Over time, recruitment procedures by which new members were incorporated into the group became increasingly formalized, particularly as tensions between Muslim and Marxist students rose and as the government stepped up its efforts to suppress dissident political movements. These efforts at greater secrecy and protection were initiated under the regime of King Zahir Shah, but became increasingly strict after the coup d'état of Muhammad Daud, a cousin of the king and a former prime minister, who took power in July 1973.

Given the longstanding animosity between the Muslim students and their leftist counterparts, the sudden emergence of an avowedly pro-Soviet government whose leader was thought to be especially hostile to Islam increased the vulnerability of all those who had aligned themselves with Muslim parties. Consequently, in the months following Daud's coup, Muslim activists, including members of the Muslim Youth party, began planning their own violent coup d'état in conjunction with members of other covert Islamic organizations operating primarily in the military officer corps. These plans were uncovered, however, and a number of important Muslim leaders, including some of the principal figures in the Muslim Youth Organization, were arrested in Kabul while still others were forced to flee to Pakistan.

These early setbacks did not end the party's commitment to overthrowing the government, however. New plans were formulated that culminated in 1975 when the Muslim Youth Organization launched attacks against a number of provincial centers. Timed to occur simultaneously, these attacks were intended to draw troops away from the capital, at which time loyal Muslim units within the military would strike against the president and his chief supporters in Kabul. Instead, the attacks fizzled as the local Muslim Youth cadres failed to generate any popular support for their endeavor, and the government succeeded in capturing not only the majority of the participants in the abortive attacks but also most of the remaining Muslim Youth Organization leaders who were still in Kabul.[9]

In considering the significance of different kinds of texts to Hizb-i Islami during this stage of its development, it is important to note that most of the students that joined radical Islamic political parties gained their first exposure to radical Islamist political ideology from hand-produced pamphlets rather than from the more formal channel of books or newspapers. Reading Afghani or Sayyid Qutb, even in abridged versions, students saw for the first time the possibility of addressing social questions from an Islamic perspective, and they also came to realize that the issues that were of concern to them were of concern to Muslims in other parts of the world as well. The significance of these early Islamic texts, however, is not simply that they provided needed ideas to a receptive audience; rather, the vehicle by which the ideas were transmitted itself helped to create that audience and to shape the need which the audience felt for the ideas being presented.

To clarify what is meant by this assertion, one must begin by considering pamphlets in relation to that which they displaced as the primary vehicle of religious instruction and indoctrination, which is to say, the Qur'an itself. The idea that a political tract, however enlightened, could in any sense replace the Qur'an, the revealed word of God, might be construed as a heretical notion, but the fact remains that for many Afghans who came of age in the 1960s and 1970s, their first serious immersion in Islamic ideas came not through the Qur'an but through pamphlets and "notes." Thus, even if an individual had spent part of his early education in an Islamic madrasa, in all likelihood he would have spent little of his time being exposed to Islamic ideas. Rather, he would have spent most of his school day memorizing Qur'anic phrases whose meaning he would not have understood or been expected to understand since in Afghanistan, as elsewhere in the Muslim world, understanding was considered a later stage in the educational process. In this regard Eickelman's comments on Morocco are equally applicable to Afghanistan:

"Understanding" (*fahm*) in the context of such concepts of learning was not measured by any ability explicitly to "explain" particular verses. Explicit explanation was considered blasphemy and simply did not occur. Instead, the measure of understanding was implicit and consisted of the ability to use particular Qur'anic verses in appropriate contexts (1978: 494).

Given the centrality of the sacred text to religious education, Afghan students suffered under even greater handicaps than their peers in North Africa and the Middle East. Because of their lack of familiarity with Arabic, they had to learn the grammatical rules of a language which they could not even begin to speak.[10] This process was described by Sayyid Bahuddin Majrooh, the grandson of a prominent sufi-scholar and himself the dean of the Faculty of Literature of Kabul University, as follows:

The student would learn by heart all the grammatical rules, but was never taught how to apply them; he would recite the conjugation of [a] large number of Arabic verbs in all tenses, always starting with the verb "zaraba" (to beat: I beat, you beat, he beats, I have beaten, etc); but he was never able to make an Arabic sentence or understand an Arabic text. Grammar was considered as a sacred knowledge having its value in itself (Majrooh 1986: n.p.).[11]

The introduction and distribution of pamphlets (and the related nothâ) fundamentally altered the character and scope of Islamic political activity. The presentation of the ideas of men such as Sayyid Qutb and Maulana Maududi in a vernacular language accessible to those without years of religious study indicated not only that Islam was applicable to the modern world, but also that Islam as an ideology could be understood and activated by individuals who had not served an extensive apprenticeship in Islamic madrasas. In this sense pamphlets brought Islam out of the culture of the madrasa and out from under the domination of a system of instruction that emphasized memorization over meaning and respect for authority over the articulation of relevance. With the spread of political pamphlets, Muslims could talk about current events and challenge the assertions of leftists who denigrated the role of religion in the modern world, and they could do so with a degree of sophistication that was never before possible.

At the same time, however, while pamphlets introduced new ways of thinking about and engaging in politics for Afghan Muslims, it would be misleading to romanticize the impact of pamphlets, for while they no doubt opened up Islamic political discourse in one respect, they also played a role in making the new direction of Islamic political activity increasingly authoritarian in practice and ideologically intolerant in its attitude to other parties and ideological perspectives (even – or especially – other Islamic ones). In analyzing the role of pamphlets and particularly handmade "notes" in this evolution, it is important to pay attention to their basic physical properties and the way in which they were produced and disseminated.

On the face of it, there would not appear to be much to discuss in this regard. Individually produced "notes," after all, would appear to be the humblest of texts: a few pages of writing on notepaper fastened at the corner. The only technology involved in producing this text is a pen and paper or, when available, a typewriter and mimeograph. Likewise, the process of dissemination is equally simple: a producer of texts passes his production onto the next set of readers who duplicate the procedure, producing copies of the original work and delivering them to other members or potential members in turn.

All very straightforward, even banal. However, the mundaneness of the object and the simplicity of the process should not lead us to overlook the significance of what was going on, for in the act of repeatedly copying the same text over and over again and then passing it from hand-to-hand, the members of the Muslim Youth were not simply engaging in an exchange of ideas. Rather, they were implicating an ever-widening network of students in what amounted to a political conspiracy, and they were not only establishing pathways through which ideas could pass; they were also creating lines for the transmission of instructions and commands: lines which would prove invaluable when the party made the decision to attempt the violent overthrow of the government. In this sense the process of copying and

transmitting "notes" can be considered the foundational act through which the Muslim Youth transformed itself from a more or less egalitarian study circle into a hierarchically organized political party bent on the violent overthrow of the Afghan government. More than anything else, it was the act of producing and transmitting this simple text that enabled the party to establish its chain of command and to instill in the membership the requisite attitude of obedience for the authority of the words emanating from the party leadership.

Magazines and the Popularization of Authority

After the Marxist coup of April, 1978, the Muslim Youth Organization, which began calling itself Hizb-i Islami Afghanistan sometime after the failed uprising in 1975, developed a small publishing industry centered in Peshawar, Pakistan. Among the publications produced by the party are newspapers (in half a dozen languages intended for outsiders as well as party members), school books, doctrinal pamphlets, manuals on the use of small arms, Islamic law handbooks to be used by mujahidin units to solve disputes in the field, and revisionist history books. Of all of the various publications produced in exile, however, magazines (*mojale*) have perhaps been the most significant means by which the party has articulated its own ideological direction and through which it has sought to define in an authoritative and incontestable manner the meaning of the war.

To the best of my knowledge, the party began magazine production in 1980, shortly after the Soviet invasion. Since that time, Hizb-i Islami has published a number of magazines under different titles and in a variety of languages. (Persian, Pakhtu, Arabic, Urdu, and English are the languages of magazines I have personally examined.) For the purposes of this essay, I will discuss two of these magazines: *Shafaq* [Dawn] which ran monthly for twelve issues from June 1980 until February 1981; and *Sima-yi Shahid* [Image of the Martyr] which was initially published from November 1980 until March 1982. Both magazines were put out by the Cultural Affairs Department of Hizb-i Islami and were terminated when Hizb-i Islami agreed to join The Islamic Alliance of Afghan Mujahidin [ettihad-i islami mujahidin afghanistan] and merge its publication apparatus with the other parties in the alliance.[12] Although *Shafaq* and *Sima-yi Shahid* were similar in layout and style, they were fundamentally different in content since *Shafaq*'s articles dealt with a wide variety of topics from party policy to scriptural interpretation (*tafsîr*), while *Sima-yi Shahid* was confined largely to biographies of martyrs and articles dealing with the subject of martyrdom. Despite this difference, however, the two publications clearly comprise two aspects of the same ideological assemblage and need to be discussed together.

Shafaq

Looking first at *Shafaq* – especially the magazine's contents – several features stand out, among them the prominent place given to interviews with representatives of other Muslim countries. Thus, in virtually every issue of the magazine, there was at least one interview included with an ambassador or other government official. The most frequent country represented in these interviews was Iran (six interviews), followed by Pakistan (two interviews), Indonesia (one interview), Egypt (one interview with an associate of Hasan al-Bana, the founder of the Muslim Brothers), and Sudan (one interview). These interviews were supplemented by frequent editorials and commentaries concerning political affairs in the world, not uncommonly political affairs unrelated to the Afghan conflict. One typical issue (no. 16–17 published in September/October 1980), for example, contained the following articles:

- "How the Zionists captured Jerusalem"
- "The undercover conspiracy of the Camp David Accords will ultimately be revealed"
- "The opposition of Sadat to the Ikhwan is like fighting with fire"
- Interview with Ayatollah Shirazi
- "Your struggling brothers in Egypt"
- "Message of condolence to Imam Khomeini from Engineer Hekmatyar" (after the bombing of the parliament in Teheran)

A second feature of *Shafaq* was the use of works by renowned Islamic writers, including al-Afghani, Sayyid Qutb, Maulana Maududi, and Imam Ghazali (who was featured in a continuing column, "Advice of Imam al-Ghazali"). These selections from the most prominent Islamic writers were supplemented by anonymously-authored articles on what constitutes right thinking and action in Islam. Some sense of the range of concerns covered in these anonymous articles can be gained by considering the titles included in one issue of *Shafaq* (the same issue cited above):

- "The position of mankind on the border between materialism and idealism"
- "The ways of Islamic invitation"
- "What is Islam?"
- "The natural frontiers of God's party"
- "The views of Imam Abu Yusuf on conversion"
- "To follow your inner wishes when it leads to polytheism"
- Discussion of belief (*aqayed*)
- "The time when heroic women lived" [on the pious conduct of the daughter of Abu Bakr Sidiq]

A third distinctive feature of *Shafaq* was its portrayal of history. Generally, *Shafaq* contained few, if any, references to Mahmud of Ghazni (the founder of the Ghaznavi dynasty), Khushhal Khan Khattak (the poet-warrior who fought the Mughal empire), Ahmad Shah Durrani (the eighteenth-century

founder of the Kingdom of Kabul long referred to as "the father of Afghanistan"), or
any of the other standard figures associated
with Afghan national history. Instead, the
history authored by Hizb-i Islami concerned
itself principally with sacred history, particularly that centered around the life of the
Prophet Muhammad and the first four
caliphs (of whom, Umar, whose government
was represented as the model toward which
all Islamic states should strive, is the one
most commonly featured). After Umar, little
attention was paid to the intervening centuries prior to the late nineteenth century when
Sayyid Jamaluddin al-Afghani appeared to
signal the reawakening of Muslim political
consciousness.

Thereafter, pride of place in the magazine's
historical view was given to other radical
political theorists and earlier revolutionary
parties, such as the Muslim Brotherhood in
Egypt and Maududi's Jama'at-i Islami in
Pakistan. These organizations were praised
for their vanguard role in the Islamic movement, but not surprisingly the magazine was
far less concerned with the specifics of their
history than it was with that of Hizb-i Islami
itself. In particular, Shafaq highlighted the
role of the Muslim Youth Organization
from which Hizb-i Islami was born, and the
sense one gets from reading Shafaq is that all
of history can be seen as a prelude to the
establishment of this student group. In keeping with this view of history, a large percentage of the magazine's contents was devoted
to commemorating the Muslim Youth Organization's achievements through the inclusion of finely calligraphed quotations of
deceased leaders, "I-was-there" interviews
with surviving members, and hagiographic
biographies of those martyred in the party's
early days.

A final feature of Shafaq that must be
mentioned is the central place given to the
party leader, Engineer Gulbuddin Hekmatyar. In any given issue the first article was
usually a commentary written by Hekmatyar.
Throughout the magazine one sees many
photographs of Hekmatyar – addressing a

meeting of refugees, visiting wounded mujahidin in the hospital, greeting a visiting delegation of foreign dignitaries – and one also
encounters the texts of many of his political
speeches, along with interviews given to
friendly reporters from other Islamic countries, and various of his aphorisms and
slogans that are displayed in finely wrought
colophons throughout the magazine. Hekmatyar also contributed one other notable
feature to Shafaq, which was a regular
column on Qur'anic tafsîr (interpretation).
In this column Hekmatyar used passages
from the Qur'an and the Traditions [hadith]
of the Prophet Muhammad to address current political issues and defend the leadership
role of his party in the jihad. A typical
example of this sort of political exegesis can
be seen in his use of the Qur'anic passage on
the Prophet Noah (surah 71) to illustrate the
point that a right-minded leader (such as
himself) will frequently face protracted resistance and limited popular success before
finally accomplishing his mission:

> Hazrat Noah issued his summons [dawat] to
> the people for 950 years, but in his long
> career of militancy [mobareza] the total
> number of his followers still only filled one
> boat. Nevertheless, in the end, since he
> was on the right path, he and his few sup-
> porters were saved, and all those who didn't
> believe him were drowned (Shafaq, vol. 1,
> nos. 7–8: 7).

Sima-yi Shahid

A second magazine published by Hizb-i
Islami in the early 1980s was Sima-yi Shahid
which was principally devoted to preserving
the memory of those who had died in the
jihad. In the ideology of Hizb-i Islami martyrdom played a prominent role, and magazines like this one signalled the party's
intention that those who had supported the
party and died in its cause would not be
forgotten. In keeping with its general theme,
each issue of Simayi Shahid was largely given
over to obituaries and other pieces related to

martyrs and martyrdom, including panegyric poems on particular individuals and theological commentaries and pronouncements on what constitutes martyrdom in Islam and the reward that those who meet the criteria can hope to gain in the next world. Another feature of the magazine was the inclusion of numerous photographs, the most dramatic of which were always the front and back cover illustrations. Usually studio portraits of young men in coats and ties, these photographs have been blown up, airbrushed, and color-tinted to foreground blushing pink cheeks and piercing eyes that are usually set against luridly colored backdrops.

On opening the magazine, one finds that the lead article was always the obituaries of the individuals whose pictures appeared on the front and back covers. These obituaries were always eulogistic in tone, relating the earlier formative events of the individual's life to the ultimate meaning contained in his final sacrifice. Each of the obituaries that followed the cover story was progressively less detailed, with ordinary martyrs (those with no particular position in the party) being displayed together toward the back of the magazine under collective headings such as "Meet the Martyrs of the Path of Truth," "Sacrifices on the Path of God," and "Rose-Colored Shrouds from the Trench of Truth."

In each of these sections one finds photographs accompanied by short paragraphs that usually contain the individual's name, father's name, place of residence, some brief details of his life and the circumstances of his death, and finally a more or less formulaic denigration of the enemy and a slogan in praise of Islam. At the very back of the magazine, a final section of obituaries was dedicated to those individuals killed in the conflict for whom no photograph could be found. There are relatively few of the faceless dead, however, since most Afghans have had photographs taken of themselves for use on their Afghan and/or refugee identity cards, and it is these photographs that the magazine most often published.

The implicit organizing principle of these memorials was that one's status was determined by seniority and position in the party. Consequently, those honored with a cover photograph were invariably young student leaders who were imprisoned by the government back in the early 1970s and who died in prison before the formal onset of fighting in 1978. Front commanders generally received the second place in the hierarchy of *Sima-yi Shahid*, and, finally, those ordinary mujahidin who died in the fighting were attended to at the back of the magazine with a few formulaic sentences. Throughout, what mattered most was not battlefield accomplishments per se, but service to the party, the earlier the better. Thus, an individual might have fought devotedly for five years at the front before his death, but his place in the line of martyrs would still be after that of a secondary school student who had joined the Muslim Youth Organization for a few months, got himself arrested under President Daud, and then disappeared in prison when the Marxists seized power.

In evaluating the organization of *Sima-yi Shahid*, it is important to emphasize that the organization of obituaries was not an abstract issue. Rather, it had immediate political significance for how the party presented itself to the people and how it attempted to control the ultimate meaning which Afghans imparted to the events of the war and the manner in which they thought about Afghanistan's future, especially its political future. For Afghans, very little good has come out of the conflict. Little of value can be gleaned to ease the suffering they have endured. At least a million people have died. Hundreds of thousands more have been crippled for life, and untold thousands of villages have been utterly destroyed.

The only solace that many can salvage from the abyss they have been living in is the belief that those who have died will be rewarded for their faith. The Qur'an promises this, and so too does the party. Indeed, the party decided early on to publicly acknowledge the sacrifice of party members who had died in the conflict, and in doing so it seems to have recognized that martyrdom was an effective occasion for cementing its political authority. Who, after all, would want to challenge the party's authority when it was the party that determined who was and who was not a proper martyr? Further, what surviving family member of a dead mujahidin would want to question the authority of the party that had honored its family member (and assured his status as divine martyr) by publishing his photograph in its magazine?

A final point to consider with regard to the commemoration of martyrs in the pages of *Sima-yi Shahid* concerns the use of photographs. In this regard it is important to keep in mind that the vast majority of Afghans are illiterate and therefore largely impervious to the propagandistic effects of print. In the absence of words photographs become especially important tools for the party in its efforts to expand its membership beyond the limited base of educated young people (which has been its primary source of support from its founding in the late 1960s) to the far larger body of uneducated rural villagers who are generally suspicious of political parties in general, be they of the right or left.

Photographs of the war dead are especially effective in this regard, for they are not "about" ideology. Rather, they are "about" relatives and/or friends who have died in the fighting, and they confirm to the viewer what they desire most to know: that those loved ones who have died in the fighting, the loved ones memorialized in magazines like *Sima-yi Shahid*, are in fact martyrs. They have died in the service of God, they will be granted the eternal rewards of paradise, and if anyone doubts this fact, they have only to consult the pages of the magazine to realize the truth.[13] The payoff – directly conceived of as such or not – to the party in thus memorializing the dead is that the dead also confirm the status of the living: specifically, legitimacy of the party as the temporal arbiter of God's judgement. In essence, the faces of the martyrs become the emblems of the party's

authority, for in looking out at the reader, neatly arrayed in formation (as they might be arrayed before God on the Judgment Day), they become conspirators in advancing the party's pursuit of political power.

In assessing the significance of magazines as vehicles of political discourse and organization, it is important to note that Hizb-i Islami was hardly the first organization (nor certainly the last) to utilize this technology for the attainment of political ends. To the contrary, Hizb-i Islami merely adopted a practice that the Afghan government had been involved in since the mid-1920s when it first got into the business of publishing literary and ministerial magazines. For the government, one of the practical advantages in publishing these magazines was that they provided a source of employment for graduates of secular and religious schools. This same point can be made for Hizb-i Islami as well, for since 1978 over three million refugees have fled to Pakistan. Most of these refugees lived in camps and found what employment they could as day-laborers. However, tens of thousands of literate refugees, including former teachers, students, and government officials, looked to the resistance parties to provide employment, and the large number of magazines, newspapers, and other publications which Hizb-i Islami and other resistance parties have been publishing consistently since 1980 has been one answer to this problem.

An additional factor to consider in evaluating the significance of magazines is their role in making Hizb-i Islami (and its rival parties) appear substantial, and substantially like the government it seeks to become. Magazines could help political parties achieve this goal of appearing significant in part because they have a solidity to them that newspapers and pamphlets lack. Their covers are shiny, their paper is slick, their photographs are clear: the whole package has a heft to it missing in other publications. In a similar fashion a magazine's contents also convey an impression of concreteness absent in other forms of media. This can be seen in any given issue which covered a large variety of topics and always in a manner that conveyed the party's determinant authority. The publication of interviews with foreign leaders also increased one's sense that the party was a respected actor in world affairs, even if it did not yet have a country to govern. Finally, it can be argued that magazines gain additional solidity from the fact that they are published serially. The knowledge that the text he is reading is one in a series assures the reader that the publication has some permanence, that it has existed in the past and will appear again and again in the future.

Conclusion

In this article I have tried to chart some of the political implications of print in recent Afghan history. Beginning with a discussion of the role of newspapers in creating the political climate of confrontation in Afghanistan, I have gone on to examine the use of pamphlets by the Muslim Youth Organization and the way in which pamphlets enabled this nascent political party to mobilize a segment of the population – traditionally oriented young people alienated both by the leftist extreme and conservative religious leaders – that no other political groups had yet succeeded in reaching. Relying heavily on ideological positions developed in Egypt and Pakistan, the Muslim Youth recycled these ideas in their pamphlets and other less formal publications to university and secondary students in Kabul and most of the provincial capitals. In so doing, they succeeded not only in informing young people of an alternative way to develop their country, but also in making those young people co-conspirators in their political plans for Islamic revolution.

The final stage of the evolution that I have charted involves the use of magazines which have proven to be an important instrument of the exiled political parties in their search for political control and legitimacy. Magazines have provided parties such as Hizb-i Islami with an important forum for projecting an image of the party as a government-in-exile and of its leaders as statesmen and world leaders. Unlike the small-format pamphlets which could easily be tucked away in a pocket and covertly passed from hand to hand, magazines are very much an above-ground form of political propaganda designed to draw attention to themselves through the use of bright graphics and florid calligraphy. Through their use of photographs, particularly photographs of martyrs, magazines have also attempted to broaden the party's reach to the illiterate masses that had previously been immune to the blandishments and persuasions of their written publications.

The next stage of the media revolution in Afghanistan involves the use of electronic media. Until the last decade, electronic media (principally radio and television) have been dominated by the Afghan government, but since the beginning of the war Islamic resistance parties have also ventured into this field, first through the distribution of anti-government speeches recorded on tape cassette, later through the broadcast of radio programs into Afghanistan, and more recently through the use of video cameras which have allowed the parties to show their side of the war to foreign television audiences, particularly in the Muslim world. These are historical developments that deserve scholarly attention, as do the changes that will no doubt come about as the Islamic forces attempting to form a government in Kabul begin to take advantage of the newspaper, television, and radio resources that become available to them. As the impact of these changes becomes apparent, it will be useful to recall that Afghanistan has moved from manuscript culture to video culture in little more than two generations. In essence, the print revolution that began to transform European society 500 years ago only commenced in Afghanistan seventy-five years ago and has not yet fully been absorbed by the still mostly illiterate population of the country.

The war that has devastated Afghanistan for almost two decades has partially impeded the print revolution by destroying the educational system producing the nation's future readers, but once the war has ended the print revolution will undoubtedly be overtaken by the electronic one. Regardless of this fact, however, the leaders of the resistance parties that now control the country have come to recognize the importance of print to their cause. During the course of the war, all of the Afghan political parties – even those led by traditional mullahs – have come to depend upon the vehicles of newspapers, pamphlets, and magazines (as well as other kinds of printed materials, particularly school books). All of these leaders realize the significance of texts, and no matter who comes out on top in the ongoing political struggle, the victors will undoubtedly seek to secure their hold on the reins of print power.

What is less certain, however, is the extent to which securing control of electronic media will be as easy for Afghanistan's leaders as dominating print media has been. As the schools reopen, the Islamic leadership will most certainly assert control of which texts are used in the classroom, and they will exert a tight control over the publication of newspapers, magazines, and books. But, as the conflict in the country settles down in the next few years, will they have an equal ability to control which audio cassettes are listened to or which VCR tapes? As computers gradually enter the scene (as they already have in the party offices in Peshawar) can the anarchic world of computer networks be far behind? And what of satellite dishes that have already become prevalent in neighboring countries – can the government of Kabul compete head-to-head with CNN? The answers to these questions are unknowable at present, but it can be stated with certainty that while countries like Afghanistan lagged far behind in assimilating the changes brought by print, they will not trail so far behind in responding to the ongoing media revolution. The distance that insulated Afghanistan from western technologies in the past has shrunk to nothing, and each new generation of leaders – whether they be of an Islamic or secular orientation – will have to keep up with the radical transformations in media communication if they are to successfully win the battle for the hearts and minds of the people they seek to rule.

NOTES

1   This point has been developed by a number of scholars in a range of disciplines, including Anderson 1983; Bourdieu 1977; Goody and Watt 1962–1963; Havelock 1963; Ong 1982; and Williams 1977.

2   For a more inclusive overview of Hizb-i Islami's history and the development of its ideology, see Roy 1986.

3   al-Afghani is said to have briefly published a newspaper in Afghanistan in 1867. al-Afghani's newspaper was reportedly called *Kabul*, but no copy of this newspaper is known to exist (Reshtiya 1948: 72).

4   The poem written "to the glory of the land of Lenin and the miracles of the life-bearing revolution" ended with the following lines:

For this matchless achievement
We send DORUD to that pioneer party,
And to the heroic people.
We send DORUD to that great leader,
The Great Lenin (Dupree 1971: 23).

A similar example of this kind of incitement occurred a year earlier in 1969 when the newspaper *Islah* [Reform] published a cartoon that depicted a character obviously intended to represent the Prophet Muhammad who was accompanied by a cluster of veiled women. In the cartoon the man and his wives are turned away by the hotel manager, who tells him: "Here there is no room for a man with nine wives." During an earlier period of political liberalization in the late 1940s, there was another incident of this sort which centered around the publication by the left-of-center *Watan* newspaper of a letter to the editor that criticized the government for supporting the construction of a shrine in eastern Afghanistan intended to house a beard hair purportedly belonging to the Prophet Muhammad. This incident also struck a nerve among devout Muslims and led to several days of protests.

5   Within a year after the passage of the liberal press law allowing publication of independent newspapers in July 1965, three openly Marxist papers had been launched, including *Khalq* and *Parcham*, the organs of the Khalq and Parcham branches of the nascent People's Democratic Party of Afghanistan, and *Shu'la-yi Jawed* [Eternal Flame], the principal mouthpiece of the Maoist party of the same name. Though it was banned after only six issues (published in April and May 1966), *Khalq* received wide distribution within the capital (20,000 copies of the first issue; 10,000 copies of subsequent issues) and succeeded in generating massive public debate because of its explicit use of Marxist rhetoric and its advocacy of radical policies such as land redistribution. *Parcham*, which came to be associated with Babrak Karmal's faction of the PDPA, was published from March 14, 1968, until its banning on July 15, 1969. *Shu'la-yi Jawed*, the organ of the Maoist *Jamiyat-i Democrati Nawin* (New Democratic Party), was published from April 1968 until it too was banned during the 1969 election campaign. Dupree lists a total of twenty-four independent newspapers launched between January 1966 and October 1969 (Dupree 1973: 602).

6   Although Menhajuddin Gahiz does not appear to have been actively involved with the more important Afghan Muslim political parties that were beginning to form during this period, there is evidence that he visited Pakistan in order to establish links between the Islamic forces of his

country and the Jama'at-i Islami Pakistan party of Maulana Maududi. The paper was also a significant training ground for a number of religious scholars who had taken employment in the government, including Maulawi Yunis Khales, who was then an employee in the Ministry of Information and Culture and who later became the leader of one of the two Hizb-i Islami Afghanistan parties (personal interview with Maulawi Khales, April 22, 1984). See also Roy (1986: 70); Hyman (1982: 60–61); Rahman and Qureshi (1981: 76).

7   For an extended analysis of the role of pamphlets in Afghanistan and an overview of their ideological content, see Edwards 1993. For an analysis of the very different role played by pamphlets during the Iranian Revolution, see Bakhash 1984.

8   According to a number of informants, leftist insults and provocations were constant at the university. Like the Marxist newspapers, leftist students also used provocations as a way to isolate and ridicule their Muslim opponents. This tactic is discussed in the following quote from a speech made by Engineer Gulbuddin Hekmatyar, the leader of Hizb-i Islami:

In the university, which was a great center of knowledge and where the future rulers of the country were trained, nobody could use the name of religion. Nobody there could wear national clothes.... Nobody could keep the fast. The students openly asked for food from the president and dean of the university during the month of Ramazan.... When those from the College of Islamic Law and other colleges came into the dining halls, from one side and the other, students would ball up food and throw it at them and insult them. In the [provincial] high schools, the communists would ridicule anyone who had the feeling of Islam, [saying] that they were "backward sheep" who would progress as soon as they got to the university.... When they got to the center of knowledge and civilization, they would recognize their path. There they wouldn't care anymore about praying, fasting, and '*musulmani*' [Muslim practice].

[The author was given a tape cassette of this speech, but was unable to ascertain the date or location of the speech.]

9 For additional information on this operation, see Roy (1986: 75).

10 After reading a draft of this essay, Dale Eickelman reminded me that Arabic is a second language for many in Morocco and that even when it is not, the distance between Qur'anic Arabic and colloquial Arabic is considerable and represents a major obstacle to mastery of scriptural texts. While this is undoubtedly the case, Afghan students still had a more difficult time of it since they never had the opportunity to hear Arabic spoken outside the confines of the madrasa classroom itself.

11 This quotation is taken from a manuscript on the "Sovietization of Afghanistan" given to me by Professor Majrooh in 1986. The manuscript was later published in Peshawar, but I have been unable to obtain a copy of it since his assassination in 1988. The quotation therefore might differ from that in the published version of the same text.

12 *Shafaq* was first put out under the name of *Shahid*, then renamed. *Sima-yi Shahid* was originally launched as a newspaper, then changed to a magazine-style format. While both magazines ceased publication when the Islamic Alliance of Afghan Mujahidin was formed, informants have indicated that they were later revived.

13 In *Camera lucida* Roland Barthes makes the following observation concerning a photograph of young Lewis Payne who had tried to assassinate Secretary of State William Seward in 1865:

The photograph is handsome, as is the boy: that is the *studium*. But the *punctum* is: *he is going to die*. I read at the same time: *This will be* and *this has been*; I observe with horror an anterior future of which death is

the stake. By giving me the absolute past of the pose (aorist), the photograph tells me death in the future (1981: 96).

REFERENCES

Anderson, Benedict. 1983. *Imagined communities: Reflections on the origin and spread of nationalism*. London: Verso Editions.

Bakhash, Shaul. 1984. Sermons, revolutionary pamphleteering and mobilisation: Iran, 1978. In *From nationalism to revolutionary Islam*, ed. Said Amir Arjomand. Albany: State University of New York Press.

Barthes, Roland. 1981. *Camera lucida*. New York: Hill and Wang.

Bourdieu, Pierre. 1977. *Outline of a theory of practice*. Cambridge: Cambridge University Press.

Dupree, Louis. 1971. A note on Afghanistan, 1970. American University Field Staff Reports.

—— 1973. *Afghanistan*. Princeton: Princeton University Press.

Edwards, David. 1993. Summoning Muslims: Print, politics, and religious ideology in Afghanistan. *Journal of Asian Studies* 52(3): 609–628.

Eickelman, Dale. 1978. The art of memory: Islamic education and its social reproduction. *Comparative Studies in Society and History* 20(4): 485–516.

—— 1989. National identity and religious discourse in contemporary Oman. *International Journal of Islamic and Arabic Studies* 6(1): 1–20.

Goody, Jack and Ian Watt. 1962–1963. The consequences of literacy. In *Literacy in traditional societies*, ed. Jack Goody. Cambridge: Cambridge University Press.

Havelock, Eric A. 1963. *Preface to Plato*. Cambridge MA: Harvard University Press.

Hyman, Anthony 1982. *Afghanistan under Soviet domination, 1964–81*. New York: St. Martin's Press.

Lenin, V.I. 1969. *What is to be done?* New York: International Publishers.

Majrooh, S. Bahuddin. 1986. The sovietization of Afghanistan (manuscript).

Ong, Walter J. 1982. *Orality and literacy: The technologizing of the word*. New York: Methuen and Co.

Rahman, Fath-ur and Bashir A. Qureshi. 1981. *Afghans meet Soviet challenge*. Peshawar: Institute of Regional Studies.

Reshtiya, Qasim. 1948. Journalism in Afghanistan: A brief historical sketch. *Afghanistan* (Journal of the Historical Society of Afghanistan) April–June: 72–77.

Roy, Olivier. 1986. *Islam and resistance in Afghanistan*. Cambridge: Cambridge University Press.

Williams, Raymond, 1977. *Marxism and literature*. Oxford: Oxford University Press.

6

Local Islam Gone Global: The Roots of Religious Militancy in Egypt and its Transnational Transformation

James Toth

Very often, it is hard to actually imagine a social movement that spans the entire spectrum from the very local and microscopic to the grand, global, and macroscopic. However, the Islamic movement is an exception. Since 1967 – the month of June, to be exact, when Israel won the Six Day War – radical and militant Islamic movements have appeared in country after country throughout the Middle East and South Asia. Yet they have remained essentially remote, localized affairs, as so many books and articles have testified. Then on September 11, 2001, this detachment suddenly dissolved as so many Americans came to realize the full global extent of Islamic militancy. This chapter chronicles the emergence of local Islamic militancy in southern Egypt, concluding that its genesis in the grassroots of the Egyptian Sa'id is critically important to understanding its subsequent transnational transformation. Only once its parochialism is well established and understood can we then begin to conceptualize how such a local oppositional movement transmogrified into the worldwide al-Qa'eda network headed by one man, Osama bin Laden. From a small but important insurrection in one region of one Arab country, Egypt, to an Afghani-based, but globally connected web of holy warriors – this is the movement that I document here.

What follows, then, is one case study of one portion of the Islamic movement as it emerged in southern Egypt and as it was revealed through anthropological fieldwork conducted in one of this region's major cities. In and by itself, it did not simply become transformed into al-Qa'eda, which is, after all, a river fed by multiple tributaries from many different sources. Nor can this one case study be justifiably generalized to include *all* Islamic movements, which vary from militant to radical to moderate, from political to cultural, from pragmatic activism to doctrinaire orations. It does, however, pinpoint the political economy, the social and community base, the theological and ideological justification, and the government actions and deeds that, duly multiplied and amplified, fed into the formation of the group that eventually attacked New York City and Washington, DC.

So many have argued that what has been called "terrorism" is born of poverty and resentment. However, this begs the question why such religious militancy is not pandemic throughout the Third World, or at least among the Islamic nations. Poverty and domination, in and of themselves, do not breed violence, for just as often, they produce the opposite – work or laziness, and submission. In this case, however, it is the perceived injustice of the distribution of wealth and power, not the actual allocation per se. Poverty and political impotence have been around for quite some time, yet seldom do they generate the resentment and anger that are provoked when individuals believe these were begotten in illegal or immoral ways. Accusations of corruption are not merely economic or financial indictments; they are first and foremost moral criticisms. Allegations of arrogance are not simply political grievances; they are also principled arguments against the misuse of authoritarian power. Participants say these ethics and principles derive directly from the Qu'ran and the universal theory of Islam. In Muslim societies where secularists are still a minority and the secular separation of religion and politics a colonially imposed doctrine, Islam still strongly colors the beliefs, actions, and perceptions of movement activists, as we shall see. Thus this focus on poverty and power, on corruption and arrogance, gives the Islamic movement its peculiar sense of frustration but also its uncommon appeal and strength. As with so many social movements, then, a political economy and sociology, while necessary, are not sufficient analyses. The doctrines and cultural beliefs, too, must be examined to more fully understand how local movements erupt into global crusades, and why.

Egypt's Underdevelopment: Midwife to Contemporary Islamism

The rise of the current Islamic movement in Egypt took place at a conjuncture of three different trends in the global economy and regional politics which critically shaped Egypt's growing underdevelopment and the outbreak of violence that emerged as a militant attempt to repair it.

First, there was a 20-year worldwide recession induced by the higher energy costs from the 1974 and 1979 oil price hikes. Within the Third World, these trends were exacerbated still further by the declines in petrodollar investments after the 1985 oil price collapse. This then generated a realignment in the international division of labor whereby businesses in the First World, in order to reverse the profit squeeze generated by costly oil and labor power, deindustrialized their production facilities and relocated them to more favorable cheap-labor sites within the Third World.

After the economic recession of 1967 and the oil price shock of 1974, industrial investment declined in the First World but increased throughout the Third World. These areas became the Newly Industrializing Countries, or NICs, that now include Singapore, Taiwan, South Korea, and Hong Kong. Financing such investments came from oil revenues recycled through multinational corporations and offshore banks. Their principal markets lie in trading with other Third World countries and in re-exporting to the West.[1]

However, the result of this development polarized the new economic order. While some countries benefited from the transfers of First World capital, other countries, like Egypt, were further impoverished. Egypt is not an NIC, and has only sporadically benefited from transfers of First World capital. Like many Third World countries, Egypt suffered a debt crisis in the 1970s owing to energy costs, worldwide inflation, overvalued currency, stagnant public-sector industrialization, and a deteriorating agricultural sector.[2] Farming was squeezed of crops, capital, and labor, but agricultural exports which could earn hard currency were low, and government-appropriated profits from crop sales subsidized a growing urban labor force instead of financing industrialization.[3] Import substitution industrialization (ISI) failed owing to lack of investment, especially in new technology. Despite attempts throughout the 1970s to privatize, new capital-intensive competition from foreign markets, rigid government regulations, and outmoded production facilities kept Egypt's public sector moribund.[4] Moreover, what little investment entered the country was overwhelmed by the doubling of Egypt's population from 19 million in 1947 to 37 million in 1976, and specifically among the 15–45 age group, that most in need of jobs and social services.[5]

Then finally, a third, more specific direction emerged from Egypt's humiliating defeat in the Six Day War of June, 1967. This led to a subsequent disenchantment with centralized, state-led development and a popular rejection of 'Abd al-Nassir's secular Arab nationalism and radical modernization program.[6] The first meant depending increasingly on private investors, and the latter suggested a turn toward religion.

Thus the global development of capitalism since the 1970s proved oddly paradoxical, for at the same time that First World economies contracted and "deindustrialized," many Third World countries in Asia and Latin America actually experienced rapid economic growth. How, then, could Egypt be so unfortunate as to see such development pass it by and watch its society emerge on the brink of religious insurrection?

Unable to accumulate foreign currency from agricultural or industrial exports, Cairo increasingly turned to international finance. At first Egypt attempted unsuccessfully to attract foreign investment by relying principally on its ties to neighboring Arab petroleum exporters. But its efforts were stymied as petrodollars moved first to regional rivals like Lebanon, later into First World banks, and then on to more profitable peripheral economies elsewhere. The 1979 Camp David treaty further advanced Egypt's estrangement. Until a regional reconciliation could be achieved, Egypt relied, instead, on revenues from domestic oil production, declining cotton exports, canal fees, and tourism.[7]

Throughout the 1970s and early 1980s, these conditions were insufficient by themselves to fuel economic growth. Instead, Egypt depended on US assistance and foreign aid, international bank loans, and remittances from emigrant workers. In particular, it capitalized on its large labor force such that labor remittances became a potential source of foreign currency for the state, and emigration abroad became a new major source of income and ambition for Egyptian workers. High incomes earned abroad were converted into consumer purchases, real estate, and housing; later, returning emigrants established small informal businesses. Many also sought to finance pious deeds and charitable acts as ways of demonstrating their momentary success and eternal gratitude.

Yet despite this increase in capital, the government was unable to access it. Rather than financing employment-generating industrial projects, much of the private hard currency fueled "soft" investments in commerce, banking, real estate, and tourism.[8] Therefore, in order to expand and generate the jobs needed for a growing population, the government was forced to borrow. But because of its unsatisfactory credit rating, Cairo's only recourse was the International Monetary Fund (IMF), whose austere lending conditions included raising consumer prices, devaluing the Egyptian pound, raising domestic interest rates, reducing national budget deficits by eliminating subsidies and raising taxes, and privatizing the public sector. These requirements, in turn, aggravated the impoverished circumstances of thousands of individual workers and consumers.

Soon, many urbanites and their families became more vocal in demanding higher incomes and more employment as their already precarious standard of living became further eroded by the steep rise in consumer costs and the added burden of unemployed dependants. As a result, their anger became more intense and their opposition more prominent.

By the early 1990s, economic disorder came to overwhelm more and more of

Egypt's consuming public, including the rural and urban working classes, and even the heretofore comfortable middle class as well. Unable to legitimately influence government policy, many of the disaffected turned to other outlets for recourse. The secular Left, already neutralized by two decades of marginalization, was unable to provide the leadership to shape and transform such disaffection. Instead, such guidance came from middle-class radicals who joined the Islamist movement and who galvanized mass discontent into a serious challenge to the state. The proletarian core of their support came not so much from the organized labor located in large urban factories, but from the unorganized multitudes who had flocked into the small district towns, provincial capitals, and urban interstices where they had found a variety of jobs in small construction crews, unregistered workshops, and informal service activities.

Religious Insurrection

The rise of the current Islamic movement builds on a hundred-year history that began with Muhammad Abduh, head of al-Azhar in the late nineteenth century. Abduh called for purifying Islam from centuries of *sufi* and superstitious accretions, rejecting the intermediaries between worshipers and God (no polytheism or idolatry) that had crept into *sufi* Islam, and returning to the practices and beliefs of a Golden Age Islam of the *salaf*, or ancestors.

The ideas of this "grandfather" of the Islamic movement were among those adopted by Hasan al-Banna when he established the Muslim Brotherhood in 1928 which thereafter (in the 1930s and 1940s) became the prototype for later Islamist organizations. Under Abduh, *salafiya* Islam had paralleled the growth of nationalism and evolved gradually into what most Muslims in Egypt today practice and believe. Under al-Banna, however, *salafiya* Islam was radically reinterpreted in defense against attacks by modernists and secularists.

One major intellectual in the Brotherhood, Sayyid Qutb, who was jailed and martyred by Jamal 'Abd al-Nassir, wrote what I would call the "Islamic Manifesto" while he was in prison from 1954 to 1966. Qutb radicalized this defensive rhetoric to a far greater extent and preached an interpretation of Islam that became the intellectual foundation of contemporary Islamist associations.

These organizations proliferated after the Six Day War, principally among college students on campuses throughout Egypt. At first they were encouraged by the government until Anwar al-Sadat's visit to Jerusalem in November, 1977 turned them against a state that would forgive and make peace with its enemies. Thereafter, the government became the principal target as these associations raised an ethical campaign against what they saw as official corruption and injustice.[9]

Since its inception in the late nineteenth century, the social base of the Islamic movement in Egypt has changed, becoming less elitist and more populist.[10] That is, the horizontal line that separated "genuine" Muslims from Westernized Muslims descended down the class hierarchy. The social pattern began as two equivalent groups – Egyptians on one side, non-Egyptians on the other – and then, after the 1920s, the elites, along with the palace, were included in the opposition, in contrast to the middle and lower classes who were considered genuine participants. By the 1970s and 1980s, the line had fallen even further, with the middle class itself split between "authentic" Egyptians (labeled as *ibn al-balad*) vs. Westernized Egyptians (or *ibn al-zawwat*).[11]

Those who considered themselves genuine and authentic but who had become strongly disaffected from their secular and Westernized counterparts joined a movement that was difficult to distinguish so clearly from the actual religion itself. Islam is a radically monotheistic religion which requires both correct belief (orthodoxy) and correct practice (orthopraxy)[12] – believing in one single God and practicing the code of conduct revealed in the Qur'an. Its profession of faith, the *shahada* – "There is no god but God, and Muhammad is His Messenger" – includes and unites these two aspects. The first clause professes a strict monotheism and anti-polytheism; the second clause declares its compliance to the words God commanded Muhammad to recite. When carried to its logical conclusion – some would say, to its extreme – the *shahada* presents a program for revolutionary action in today's modern world: reject as polytheism all authority that is elevated to the level of God, and reject as unbelief all codes but those contained in the Qur'an.[13]

Activists in the Islamic movement see the world as a society in crisis, a crisis arising from a deterioration in traditional religious values, beliefs, and practices.[14] But more than experiencing mere decline, these traditional doctrines are also under vigorous attack, both from outside society by foreign elements (principally Western), but also (and perhaps more importantly) from within, by "agents" of those foreigners (consciously compradors or otherwise) who have become secular under their influence. Consequently, corruption, dishonesty, impropriety, poverty, injustice, and personality cults appear not only pervasive, but successful. The degeneration of religion that produced this crisis is similar to the ignorance, or *jahiliya*, that prevailed before the rise of Islam and that disappeared with the acceptance of monotheism and the Qur'an.

The Islamic movement's explanation for the general cause of this crisis rests on the accusation that Muslim society has deviated from the *shahada*, bringing about the elevation of false gods to God's level and the replacement of His words and precepts with man-made laws. But what specifically causes this degeneration varies with time: first, the colonial domination of Christian Britain, then the secularist abolition of the caliphate and Islamic law and the adoption of French legal codes, then, later, nationalism and its elevation ("worshiping") of leaders to a god-like status, and, more recently, the assaults by crusaderism, Zionism, communism, and others hostile to Islam.

Based on this interpretation, Islamist leaders concluded that in order to overcome this crisis of ignorance and deviation from the Right Path, the movement must strive to reestablish both God's sovereignty over Muslim practices and the fierce unity and monotheism of Muslim belief. This means, primarily, to reinstitute divine *shari'a* law as the law of society and to abolish all that is (or who are) worshiped beside God. Exactly *how* these goals are to be achieved varies, however, and herein lie a number of different approaches that lead, in turn, to organizational distinctions within the Islamic movement. These different approaches can all be grouped under the rubric of *jihad*, but then it is no longer possible to define *jihad* just as "holy struggle," as most popular translations would have it. *Jihad* is not just the violent or militant implementation of correct Islamic practice and belief, although it is certainly one important approach. Instead I prefer to define *jihad* as "activism" and then to distinguish three types: *jihad bi al-qalb*, or activism of the heart; *jihad bi al-kilma*, or activism of words; and, finally, *jihad bi al-haraka*, or a *jihad* of action, of proper deeds and achievements as well as violence and militancy.[15]

Thus the Islamic movement as such includes a wide range of participants and activists, based on which tactics they choose to implement these goals. Not all Muslims are even in the movement, and instead may follow modern, secularized understandings of Islam or else pursue the more mystical teachings of *sufism*.[16] Of those who identify with the movement, the vast majority advocate a *jihad* of the heart where their own personal practices, beliefs, and identity are subjectively but privately reoriented in order to conform to the movement's definition of what is correct.

A much smaller number go further and advocate *da'wa*, or preaching in missionary fashion, implementing a *jihad bi al-kilma* as their approach to achieving the movement's aims. In essence, this follows an educational approach in changing society. Those who follow a *jihad bi al-kilma* are the moderates who advocate a gradual realization of correct practice and belief. They may also insist on performing good deeds and pious acts that provide a "demonstration effect" of what a proper Muslim should be like.

The radicals, on the other hand, call for more immediate and speedy tactics. The difference between *kilma* and *haraka* is similar to the one between reform and revolution. When *jihad* by action involves violence and armed struggle, then radicals become militants, often discouraged by the slow pace of establishing God's sovereignty through *da'wa*, or else disillusioned when religious deeds and projects are destroyed by police action.

The Islamic Crusade in Southern Egypt

The recent growth of the Islamic movement has been particularly intense in Egypt's southern region, known as the *Sa'id*. From 1994 to 2000, I conducted anthropological fieldwork in one of the area's major cities[17] which had become a notorious hotbed of Islamic radicalism and militancy. Actual field research into radical and militant Islam is rare, for obvious security reasons.[18] Here I capitalized on an informal network of old friends acquired while managing an international program of community development in the mid-1980s. Because of tight state security, the research remained somewhat restricted. Nevertheless, I was able to delineate the contours of this religious movement and the government's response to it. I should add "*movements*" plural, for here, as elsewhere, the Islamic crusade was not one consistent, homogenous movement but rather contained a profusion of small, local, uncoordinated autonomous associations. In the process of interviews and informal discussions, certain patterns emerged that cast a new light on the shape and substance of this well-known but not well-understood religious campaign.

The *Sa'id* is less developed than the rest of Egypt – not only compared with Cairo and the urban provinces, of course, but also even when measured against the Delta, the country's other rural region north of Cairo.[19] It has a simpler division of labor. For example, while the *Sa'id* is more urban than the Delta, with a higher proportion of its population in cities and towns, it has fewer of them actually engaged in industrial production. Its urban areas, then, become centers for commerce and services (construction and transportation) – value-added, but not value-creation – as villagers migrate from what was more estate and large-plot farming than found in the rest of Egypt. (The Delta, on the other hand, had been carved up into smaller plots much earlier and much more thoroughly because of the combined action of commercial banks, debt, and dispossession.[20]) At the same time, for those *Sa'idis* remaining in the countryside, a far greater proportion work just in agriculture rather than engaging in the wider variety of non-farm occupations operating within the village that is displayed in the Delta.[21]

Of course, the Delta benefits from having the major cities of Cairo and Alexandria, and the Canal Zone just over its borders, although the proportion of industrial workers in the Delta *per se* still exceeds that of the *Sa'id*. Meanwhile, the *Sa'idi* population is more distant from these (or any other) major metropolitan areas and is more dependent on the smaller cities and towns within its boundaries. In fact, many Egyptians from the Delta actually commute daily or weekly to their urban worksites while still living in their villages. *Sa'idis*, on the other hand, are forced to move permanently in order to access urban employment in these faraway locales. Much, of course, depends on the specific transportation topography. There is, though, just one bottleneck channel coming into Cairo from the south, whereas routes going north into the Delta fan out spoke-like from their southern convergence.

Sa'idi mythology claims that this region has long remained outside of Cairo's purview, whereas the Delta has been subdued for a longer time. The state had come to dominate and penetrate the north in ways that never occurred in the south, which retained a fierce autonomy. When the Ottoman Turks conquered Cairo in 1517, the Delta came easily under their sway, but those Mamluks discontented with their new rulers sought safe refuge and free sanctuary further south. During Muhammad Ali's time, the *Sa'id* still remained wild and distant, and Mamluks continued to threaten Egypt's new independent Pasha. The perennial irrigation known for some centuries in the Delta came more slowly to the *Sa'id*. The *Sa'id* remained more tribal and more clannish, whereas the nuclear family appeared as the norm much earlier in the north.[22]

The *Sa'id* also displays a pattern of sectarian distribution that is different from the rest of the country and which goes back, so I was told, to this "wild autonomy" of yesteryear. In the *Sa'id*, the Coptic population is much larger and more rural than in the Delta.[23] It is said that when the Muslim general, Amr ibn al-'As, conquered Egypt in 640, he ordered the Copts into the cities. This command was, by and large, implemented in the Delta, but was never executed to the same degree in the south due to its political and social distance from Cairo. The result is that in the *Sa'id*, the Copts, because of their larger numbers and rural background, represent a more visible but more conservative community.

Thus the *Sa'id* is largely rural, with small towns and cities that serve as commercial entrepôts rather than industrial centers, which remain relatively undeveloped. It is socially and politically remote, if not downright isolated, from the rest of the country. As in many emerging economies, the south has developed at a slower pace than the countryside in the northern Delta and the urban areas of Cairo and Alexandria. But it is also *seen* as slower, a southern drawl if you will, that pinpoints the *Sa'idi* as intellectually and culturally backward as well. Pejorative *Sa'idi* jokes (the purpose of which, in the United States, is performed by Polish jokes, or whatever minority we wish to laugh at) fill the repertoire of most Cairene comedians. Most

of the *Sa'idi* jokes I know were told me by *Sa'idis* themselves. They point to both the stigma and the pride that *Sa'idi* identity endures.[24]

Since the rise of the regional petro-economy after 1974, skilled workers and white-collar employees in towns and cities up and down the southern Nile valley had emigrated abroad much sooner and in much greater proportion than the rest of the country. But the larger share of *Sa'idis* working in Libya, Saudi Arabia, the Gulf, and Iraq made their return after the 1985 oil-price drop even more problematic. Those laborers bumped out by repatriates did not return to their village and its agriculture, but neither did they easily find new jobs in the city. This further expanded the quantity of those experiencing urban economic hardship.[25] Thus poverty became much more acute in the south than in the rest of the country. In the early 1990s, the number of those *Sa'idis* living below the poverty line reached as high as 40 percent according to one Parliament council report.[26]

State budgets and investments had consistently neglected the *Sa'id*. As the overall amount of government spending contracted under IMF pressure, the south received even less as a proportion. Then, as reports of government corruption and dishonesty multiplied, many *Sa'idis* saw this depleting what little was left for services and development. Endemic poverty combined with smaller budgets, discrimination, and improbity generated an outrage against injustice that pauperism alone could not provoke.

Thus the *Sa'id* remained much more underdeveloped than other parts of Egypt and so social discontent became much more pronounced. The south's greater emphasis on extended kinship relations beyond the nuclear family also meant literally a more clannish, conservative culture. Moreover, the central *Sa'idi* provinces of Suhag, Asyut, and al-Minya included a larger portion of Copts, which ensured that communalism was not likely to be ignored. All these factors combined to generate a higher incidence of social turmoil in the south in the 1980s. Even so, by the early 1990s, this unrest had begun to spread to the rest of Egypt as well.

The Islamic associations found throughout the *Sa'id* were outgrowths of the campus organizations that had arisen in the 1970s. They first grew out of the requirement, I was told, to practice a more devout and pious Islam by providing development, charity, and guidance to those in need. But their popular appeal and success seriously alarmed Egypt's government and threatened the routine way the state operated. Unwilling or unable to change, the administration instead sought to eliminate this challenge. As state persecution increased and government corruption deepened, the battle intensified to establish a moral crusade based on Islam.

Those who found these radical Islamist associations appealing and inspiring fell into two social classes[27] that had both experienced the dislocation of rural-to-urban migration:[28] middle-class professionals and working-class indigents.

The middle-class Islamists I met were, for the most part, university students from the countryside who had first come from village farm families. They had benefited from the new free education policies implemented by the 'Abd al-Nassir administration in the 1960s and had since graduated into an uncertain urban job market. These included well-educated but nonetheless frustrated white-collar professionals such as doctors, engineers, lawyers, teachers, accountants, and bureaucrats.[29] They were highly motivated and accomplished; among the best and brightest students in their class. Bereft of the family connections and parlor mannerisms of upper-class urban Egyptians, they achieved their brilliance through hard, diligent work, and demonstrated merit. Many had participated in the state-supported campus Islamic associations of the 1970s.

On graduation, however, these students, coming as they did from the stigmatized south, discovered that despite their costly education – dearly paid for not only in money but also in the personal sacrifice of

their families – the road to gaining better professional employment and achieving higher class status that leads inevitably to the capital was essentially blocked by the ascriptive wall of Cairene elite society. Frustrated when wealthy family connections took precedence over merit, they instead migrated to Libya, Iraq, and the Gulf to acquire the better incomes unavailable at home.

However, from 1985, when regional oil revenues began to decline, these professionals returned home to the *Sa'id* to stay. They reactivated the piety and spirituality learned during their college days and reinforced while working abroad. They chose to emulate the life of the Prophet Muhammad, to grow beards and dress in white robes, and to perform charitable acts and good deeds that would bring them closer to their religion. But they also remained thwarted in their quest for upward mobility, and therefore they channeled their frustration into mobilizing an equally discontented ex-rural working class. The tone was one of moral outrage. The adversary became those corrupted by opportunism and contact with Western authorities.[30]

Those who followed these middle-class leaders included disgruntled members of the working class[31] who labored in construction crews, service-sector activities, or small informal-sector businesses (when they were employed at all, which was rarely constant). As ex-rural workers coming from a depressed agricultural sector, they had had to migrate from the village to the city but were still unable to change the misfortunes and hardship caused by Egypt's faltering economy.[32] Constrained by high prices, low wages, and unemployed kin, they came to rely heavily on the largesse of private benefactors to get them through tight times.

Proletarianization and rural-to-urban migration had been taking place in Egypt for decades, if not longer. But in the 1970s, this process accelerated rapidly after the seven years of economic stagnation following the Six Day War of June 1967.[33] This exodus was not so much a torrent of rural workers and ex-peasants moving abroad as an immense flow into urban communities to replace those who did emigrate outside Egypt. Yet after 1985, fewer skilled urban workers traveled abroad, and those who did so came home sooner. Back in the *Sa'id*, so I learned, they mixed with their unskilled colleagues who had never emigrated, and together both groups sought work in an informal sector whose investments already were in decline.

Together, these ex-rural workers and ex-rural technocrats became strongly linked through the pervasive mutuality of paternalism.[34] I refer here to the favors and privileges from employers that are exchanged for services and commitments from workers. These reciprocal, personalized relations were first forged in the countryside, and later, when employment shifted to the city, they enabled patrons to maintain a readily available workforce and allowed clients to guarantee future employment opportunities.[35] These loyalties were then readily transferred to other benefactors even when they appeared outside the actual labor process, so that critical services from middle-class professional patrons were exchanged for faithful support from working-class client beneficiaries.

They both joined religious association that re-created and reinforced the intimacy of an imagined but bygone village community. Middle-class village students attending urban universities for the first time in the history of their families were unfamiliar with the impersonality of large campuses, crowded classrooms, and indifferent professors. Rural workers moving into the city and finding employment in construction crews, workshops, and services were unaccustomed to the detached bureaucracy of government offices and large companies and the rapid transactions of commercial exchange. This shared sentiment and uncertainty drove both groups into the more familiar, intimate surroundings of the Islamic associations. This contrasted sharply with urban organizations such as professional syndicates, labor unions, and political parties in which the

anonymity and coldness alienated these potential members. Instead, these impersonal – and secular – organizations attracted more the urban-born activist.[36]

Yet ironically, the doctrines of these religious associations were not the same as those which these villagers had left behind. Village Islam had been textured by the passive and tolerant quietism of *sufism*, saint shrines, and miracles. Urban Islamist associations rejected such "superstition," as they called it, and instead exhibited the indignant political activism of *salafiyism*, legalism, and self-righteousness.[37] The shift from rural to urban had been paralleled by a transformation from "traditional" to "modern." However, it was not a secular modernity based on the European Enlightenment, but rather a religious one inherited from the doctrines of Muhammad Abduh, Hasan al-Banna, and Sayyid Qutb.

Very few of these associations ever reached the violent intensity practiced by such well-known organizations as *al-Jihad* or *al-Jama'a al-Islamiya*,[38] although many members did switch associations once government persecution increased. Instead, most enthusiasts embraced a non-militant religiosity which advocated performing good deeds and pious acts on the one hand, and bestowing devout blessings and grateful loyalty on the other. Their militance, if and when it came, would arise later.

Since the start of skilled labor emigration abroad after 1971, especially to such conservative Muslim countries as Saudi Arabia and those in the Gulf, many devout, university-trained professionals remitted their ample salaries home and allocated a significant portion toward performing Islamic good deeds, pious acts, and funding community development and charity projects. In the early 1980s, such financing increased even further with the profit-sharing and monetary transactions routed through Islamic investment companies. Moreover, the supervision by like-minded colleagues over the religious *zakat* donations to local private mosques guaranteed that the bulk of these contributions would reach the surrounding communities and those in need.

Islamic investment companies appealed to devout Egyptian Muslims because they applied the principles of Islamic finance. They were also attractive because they earned high rates of return that exceeded those of regular banks. Islamic companies operated on the basis of Islamic commercial law that is similar to the profit-sharing of a small private stock exchange or mutual fund. Depositors did not receive interest, which is forbidden in Islam, but instead shared the profit or loss incurred on money-making activities.[39] Since dividends, when paid, were not technically a form of interest, they were not subject to strict state regulation. In the mid-1980s, depositors were receiving shares that, when computed as rates of return, earned dividends as high as 25 percent annually – twice what the public banks offered.[40]

Zakat, or Islamic alms or tithes, is one of the five mandatory obligations for Muslims. Islamic activists regard *zakat* a part of Islam's social justice for the poor, representing a form of income redistribution. It constitutes an income tax, which in Egypt is a voluntary donation at the rate of 2.5 percent. Contributors told me they paid their portion either directly to the mosque, if it was privately controlled, or else directly to known beneficiaries were the mosque operated instead by the state. Islamic investment companies also automatically withheld a 2.5 percent deduction on all monetary transactions for *zakat* donations, which had just been optional with government banks. Together, both individual and company donations generated ample funds that were used to finance numerous community development projects implemented through recipient mosques by local Islamic associations established by educated and pious professionals.

The quantity and quality of these small development projects far outweighed the meager efforts of government programs or even the lavishly funded attempts by state-authorized foreign agencies. In 1985 while directing a US-based community develop-ment program in the *Sa'id*, I had the opportunity to attend a regional conference of local development organizations that revealed the large proportion of Islamic efforts. Of 30 participating agencies, three were foreign-funded. The remainder consisted of privately financed local associations that operated on a much smaller scale and budget, but with a much greater success rate in establishing important services that were not available from government line ministries. These associations provided hospital beds for the poor, low-cost health clinics, affordable housing, after-school tutoring, complimentary text-books, clothing exchanges, veterinarian services, small-scale business assistance and low-cost credit, and guidance through the labyrinthine state bureaucracy for permits, licenses, and tax abatements. All of these constituted critically important services that the government in Cairo simply could not or would not provide.[41]

Nor was the foreign community any more successful, in spite of its ample resources. Most foreign development agencies (NGOs) were located in the *Sa'id*. Very few operated in the Delta, although a small number of programs were active in the poorer neighborhoods of Cairo. Yet placing the majority of these NGOs in the south had not simply been a serendipitous decision by government officials in Cairo. For these agencies seemingly offered impressive showcase examples of secular development in a region where the alternative was strongly identified with Islam. But, as I discovered, since secular foreign operations like the one I managed lacked the political insight and skills necessary to successfully implement their programs, the smaller but more astute Islamic organizations were much more effective. Moreover, sympathetic bureaucrats employed in provincial offices often favored local Islamic initiatives over those misconceived by overseas home offices.

The vast scope of these Islamic development activities, subsumed under the name of good deeds and pious acts, delivered a wide range of important social benefits otherwise considered the duty of the state but which had not been forthcoming. After the regional conference, I spoke with a number of agency directors who worked in the same city as I did. To them, Cairo had written off the south and neglected to provide essential social services. The gap was filled, not by a few inept foreign development agencies, but by the myriad of small community initiatives funded by labor remittances, *zakat* funds, and Islamic investment companies, and intended to provide a strong Islamic presence.

For example, by the early 1990s, government schools here had become so ineffective that many parents who had foregone family income in order to give their children an education were forced to sacrifice even more by enrolling them in after-school tutorial programs that could improve their chances for better scores on the Thanawiya 'Amma examination.[42] (There was a common rumor that government teachers purposely undertaught their charges in the morning and then retaught them in the afternoon as private tutors in order to augment their low salaries.) In order to provide better instruction unavailable from the Education Ministry, a number of Islamic associations built and operated five private, comprehensive schools. In a separate project, 15 devout Muslim teachers joined together under the auspices of the *Jama'iya al-Da'wa al-Islamiya*[43] to offer poor students private lessons at a nominal cost.

Since the 1970s, the cost of health and medical services had risen enormously. Geography fundamentally determined the availability of these high-priced necessities. Cairo had a disproportionately higher share of doctors, which then left even fewer available to service provincial cities, district towns, and the surrounding countryside. The last was especially avoided by Egyptian medical school graduates; only those under obligation to the government to repay their scholarships spent time in the villages before relocating to more prosperous urban clinics. Thus those who suffered the most from this maldistribution of medical specialists were also those who were least able to afford the cost of the relatively few professionals who remained. Consequently, a group of Muslim doctors, pharmacists, and clinicians established the *Jama'iya al-Muhamadiya al-Islamiya* and staffed an Islamic clinic. In 1994, they charged a £E3 fee for examinations, treatment, and prescriptions when other doctors were charging £E15 for examinations alone. They also admitted any and all patients, "regardless of what was on their wrist" – a reference to the Coptic custom of etching a cross on their lower arm – an indication that the clinic was open to both Christians and Muslims alike.

Other associations had similar, yet more specialized projects. *Jama'iya al-Tawhid wa al-Nur al-Khairiya* built an entire dormitory near the local university campus for rural students who did not have family in the city and therefore needed local accommodation. *Jama'iya al-Huda al-Khairiya* added a 24-bed wing to one of the city's private hospitals reserved exclusively for indigent patients. Every month, the *Jama'iya al-Sahwa al-Islamiya* distributed clothes, food, textbooks, and prescription medicines to neighborhood families. Arguably these endeavors just involved short-term charity, not long-term development, but such a debate is more academic than practical, for such projects provided beneficiaries with a range of services otherwise unavailable from large government or foreign offices. Many of the latter's development activities, despite their sophisticated planning, deteriorated in the long run due to mismanagement and improper funding, while those undertaken in the name of Islamic charity continued for as long as their endowment remained viable and their donors remained free.

The *Sa'id* was not alone in receiving Islamic philanthropy. In October, 1992, an earthquake caused unusual devastation throughout Egypt. I was in Cairo when it struck and damaged several poor urban neighborhoods. Old, neglected buildings were particularly susceptible, and the vibrations toppled a number of apartment complexes. When the general populace recovered from its shock, shelter, clothing, and food were foremost on people's minds. Yet the government was particularly slow in providing aid. Local Islamic organizations, on the other hand, rushed immediately to the stricken areas in order to deliver material assistance. Government officials defended their delay by pointing out that they needed time to investigate all the requests since many petitioners would present fraudulent claims to the government. The Islamic groups, however, had little need to investigate supplicants since they felt that few would lie before God.[44] Observers I talked to noted that both sides were probably correct. A year later, when a long-term instability brought about by the earthquake caused large mud slides beneath the Muqattam hills on the east side of the capital, government troops were ordered to assist the victims without delay, worried that another public relations blunder would once again help expand the influence of the Islamic opposition. The state then declared private aid and assistance illegal except through the Egyptian Red Crescent.[45] This effectively eliminated any Islamic philanthropy.

All these private-sector achievements, initiated by Islamic associations of devout and pious believers, clearly surpassed government and foreign undertakings in people's minds. Poor Egyptians received many essential services from these community projects, gratefully appreciated these efforts, and faithfully heeded the political message behind them. Pious acts of charity and community support seemed to make the difference in their lives between endurance and deprivation. This urban underclass gained tangible benefits from such programs, unlike the ineffective efforts of government offices or international agencies which mostly served the middle-class bureaucrats who staffed them. It was clear to me from visiting these projects and associations, and talking to their staff and members, that these professionals were Muslims seriously committed to easing the lives of those they served.

The religious benefactors who helped out the poor and needy under the banner of Islam benefited in turn from the allegiance they won from doing their good deeds and pious acts. The devotion and loyalty these workers were accustomed to bestowing on their patrons above them in the workplace flowed beyond the workshop, building site, or service activity, and even spilled over from the evening-school lessons and the medical check-ups to embrace the realm of radical activism within and outside the community. Whether these devout but déclassé professionals participated legally in community politics or else unlawfully in militant action, their supporters found it easy to transfer their paternalism to include these new patrons.

When Islamist technocrats entered political contests in numerous provincial-, city-, town-, and district-level election campaigns and partisan appointments, they received overwhelming support and loyalty from those they had once assisted. When pious but alienated professionals exhorted their followers to berate and attack the government for its fiscal corruption that had eliminated social services, working-class clients obliged and joined them to actively promote their agenda. Thus poor ex-villagers approved and followed those who had once helped them with difficult problems and who were now gaining their support in strengthening their religious message and in establishing what they saw as a virtuous and honest administration. So when the burning question turned to radically refashioning what many saw as a profoundly corrupt and dishonest government, the fundamental reply simply became "Islam."

After 1985, permanent labor repatriation, steady decreases in overseas remittances, and the government crackdown on Islamic investment companies generated major declines in funding for the vital services that compensated workers for their lack of sufficient income. As the government took over local private mosques and appointed new clerics,[46] it did more than just silence oppositional preachers. Before such takeovers, the local finance committees of private mosques, composed of educated, middle-class members, decided on how the *zakat* donations were to be distributed and chose which charitable activities were to receive funding. However, once the state controlled these mosques, I was told, it deposited most of their *zakat* donations into government banks and decided where the little that remained was to be distributed, frequently resulting in a precipitous decline in financing local social services.

Then, when the state reduced its budget, especially in social services, under pressure from IMF bailouts, many *Sa'idis* felt particularly upset and indignant. They felt even more powerless and frustrated when the political system prevented them from even voicing their concerns or further pressuring officials for better treatment.

A number of *Sa'idis* told me that a legal, religious-based political party could contain the angry and disaffected factions of young, provincial white-collar professionals and ex-rural workers. What they envisioned was an Islamic party that paralleled the Christian Democratic parties in Germany and Italy. Yet so long as the Egyptian government denied this movement a legitimate channel for influencing state policy, they argued, the more its collective alienation would turn to unlawful acts of violence.

Nationally, political participation remained limited, continuing a government policy that had begun shortly after the July, 1952 revolution. One of the first edicts issued by the new republican government was to abolish political parties, seeing them as both corrupt remnants of a decaying monarchy as well as likely avenues of counter-revolution. Egypt then experienced a number of one-party organizations to mobilize and lead the country on to greater development, culminating in the Arab Socialist Union (ASU).[47]

Immediately after the Corrective Revolution of May, 1971, al-Sadat reorganized the ASU in order to make it less threatening. But the triumph of the October 1973 war gave him a wider latitude which would have been previously unimaginable. In April 1974, he proposed major modifications in the ASU that essentially expelled recalcitrant factions – workers, peasants, students, academics, and their advocates – who opposed his new Open Door policy.[48] Since the state was abandoning the public sector and relying instead on private-sector investments to generate jobs, profits, and commodities, those segments harmed by this new policy who might protest and raise objections could prove embarrassing to the administration. This would also displease Cairo's benefactor, the United States, which had insisted not only on opening Egypt's trade door to the West but also on erecting an American-style, party-based democracy. By implementing a multiparty system, the administration won acclaim from Washington and still effectively silenced all but the most agreeable opposition.

Since they were too large to be censured outright, these troublesome factions instead were muzzled by affiliating them with new political parties entirely too weak to influence government policies and operations. Before the 1952 revolution, politics had been permeated by patron–client relations, but during the period of one-party organizations, this paternalism had ceased. It now reappeared, such that political success once again depended on displaying the right, servile deference to access powerful government officials. Those not in the new ruling party were denied such access and were therefore neutralized. So silenced, many members of the underclass who had previously spoken out through various ASU departments (*amanat*) were no longer able to bring attention to their critical conditions.

Then throughout the late 1980s and 1990s, the growing political gap between elite secular parties on the one hand, and both frustrated provincial professionals and the unorganized urban working classes on the other was filled in the *Sa'id* by local Islamic associations that then posed a serious challenge to the state.

In 1992 the government and its secular supporters mounted a major campaign against the Islamists who openly threatened its complacent and comfortable position underwritten by what activists saw as fraud and corruption. Already religious opponents dominated an impressive number of formal professional and university organizations. But discontent from the bottom of the social pyramid was beginning to incite the unorganized and to provoke even greater turmoil throughout the *Sa'id* but even in Cairo as well. The government responded defensively but ruthlessly, human rights organizations reported,[49] with arrests and detention, extra-judicial executions and torture, and official denunciations following one another in rapid succession. Compromise between the two sides seemed unthinkable.

Providing good deeds, charitable acts, and material welfare to those at the bottom of the social hierarchy seemed far removed from those engaged in senseless demagoguery or wanton terrorism. Indeed, the spiritual attitude and religious demeanor of the devout professionals I met appeared beyond reproach. Yet the accumulative effects of constant government arrest, torture, and humiliation in the *Sa'id*, I was told, pushed pious activists across the thin line that heretofore had separated them from those committed to mayhem. While many still remained hopeful that the political and election process would eventually establish a legitimate avenue for social change, a growing number moved beyond the limits of peaceful transformation as they began to realize that militancy offered the only practical way to fundamentally change the state and society.

Such a transition from pacifism to militancy sometimes seemed more a response to state persecution than due to any planned strategy for committing violence. The situation in Mallawi, a district town in the southern province of al-Minya, illustrates how good intentions changed into destruction.[50] In 1991, *al-Jama'a al-Islamiya* – and here it is difficult to distinguish between the generic term and the specific organizational offshoot of *al-Jihad*[51] – began as a nonpolitical charitable association. At first its relation with the

local town government was benign as its preoccupation with religious education and material welfare programs hardly constituted illegal crimes or acts of defiance. In May 1994, however, local security forces arrested two prominent members of the association, and while no mention of police misconduct was reported, the association's leader, Rajab 'Abd al-Hakim, an accountant by profession, was provoked enough to warn security officers to stop interfering with the group's activities. A month later, security forces "stormed Abdel Hakim's house and shot him." He died that evening in hospital. Three months later, association members attacked the local police headquarters, launching what became a small civil war.[52] Throughout 1994 and 1995, Mallawi remained under strict martial law and a harsh 12-hour curfew. What had once been harmless good deeds and charitable acts had been transformed into militancy and bloodshed.[53]

Throughout the *Sa'id*, men wearing full beards and white robes, and women dressed in the dark *naqab*, the complete Islamic covering, were routinely arrested, questioned, tortured perhaps, humiliated, jailed, or released. Homes of suspected militants were bombed and burned. Few *Sa'idi* militants came to trial – such a luxury was reserved mostly for their more prominent Cairene counterparts – but instead were either fatally shot in police crossfire when security forces came to arrest suspects or else were jailed indefinitely without appearing in court.[54] Many families became heartbroken and terrified by such government action. Neighborhoods became divided, sympathizing with those whose piety had earned them great admiration, frightened, however, that their sympathy might make them suspect as well. Anger swelled, and, in response, many acts of police misconduct were repaid by outraged relatives – not through organized retribution but by individual acts of revenge. That most religious violence erupted in the *Sa'id* may be more a testimony to this region's 'tribal' practice of seeking revenge for the dishonor of family members – al-th'ar – rather than as an exceptional concentration of state force.[55] Police misconduct also occurred in Cairo, Alexandria, and the Delta, but without this remnant of tribal tradition, such acts elsewhere went unavenged.

Thus Islamic radicals took up the cause of opposing what they saw as the ignorance, corruption, and injustice committed by the government in Cairo and by its representatives in the provinces. Pushed to the extreme, they crafted an ideology based on religion that justified what the state called terrorism, but what the militants called holy combat against abuse and persecution. Based on the writings of Sayyid Qutb, Muhammad 'Abd al-Salam Faraj, 'Umar 'Abd al-Rahman,[56] and others, a militant Islam arose that appealed to those persecuted for performing good deeds and charitable acts, and for enacting the compassion decreed by the basic tenets of their religious beliefs, but which the state was now violating in its zeal to silence opponents.

Of course, not all attacks against government forces were merely individual acts of retaliation for alleged injuries. Nor were they simply reactions provoked by the police harassment of otherwise blameless non-militant Islamic radicals. Informants reported that there may well have been clear cases of organized, intentional violence, perhaps even funded by foreign governments and sympathetic collaborators from outside Egypt.[57] Firearms and ammunition certainly flooded the Sa'id, yet this was not altogether new since old tribal vendettas, long antedating the rise of Islamic militancy, had once required such weapons for their execution.[58] Nevertheless, a significant portion of the violence that erupted in southern Egypt, it seemed to me, happened first in resisting arrest by those who otherwise desired just to lead a righteous life and practice their faith in a more devout and concrete way, and, second, in retaliation for the abuse and suffering that occurred when these pious Muslims were taken into police custody.

Immediately after the October, 1992 earthquake, when the prominent relief activities of the Islamic groups embarrassed the government and as religious violence began erupting in the Cairene suburb of Imbaba, the government chose to mount a full-scale military attack against the Islamists. State security had deemed Imbaba a "state within a state" for assuming many of the functions of government otherwise unavailable to local residents. Unable to cut down the movement in southern Egypt, it was more capable of eliminating it when it was so close to the seat of government power.

In an ironic sense, Imbaba and its neighborhoods, such as al-Munira al-Gharbiya, had experienced "reverse colonialism" as Sa'idis had migrated north to carve out impoverished replicas of their homeland.[59] Then, because the government was unable or unwilling to provide social and welfare services to these informal neighborhoods, Islamic development activities emanating from local mosques filled the gap, much as they had done back home. Centers such as health clinics, schools, and day-care were set up, and workshops for the unemployed and consumer stores for the underfed were established.[60] This assistance then served as a base for further mobilizing residents to a program of Islamic ethics and social justice that contrasted greatly with what was considered the decadent surroundings of unscrupulous wealth and secular power. The state claimed that Islamist leaders incited followers to attack cinemas, nightclubs, hotels, and other instances of moral corruption, like bawdy weddings or unveiled women. It also accused them of such crimes as petty theft, drug trafficking, and extortion.

In order to crush the Islamic movement in Imbaba, its leaders, members, and activities, the government ordered 15,000 troops to "invade" this Islamist semi-state on December 8, declaring war against al-Jama'a al-Islamiya which had, according to officials "seized control of the district" and the government intended to "take it back."[61]

The police broke into the houses of suspected militants, destroying the possessions inside. Dozens of Imbaba residents were arrested off the streets merely because their beards and Islamic dress looked suspicious. The wives, mothers, and sisters of wanted militants were arrested and detained for up to a month at a time. They complained of being tortured at the Imbaba police station and ordered to strip naked before giving forced confessions for crimes they had never committed. Children between eight and fifteen years old were beaten by security police aiming to coerce information from them about their wanted relatives.[62]

The "Battle of Imbaba" all but silenced militant Islamists, leaving the field (in Cairo at least) to apolitical moderates who aspired simply to establish (or reestablish) needed neighborhood services but who shunned the popular mobilization for radical programs. This siege may well have seen the last gasp of organized Islamic militancy, at least domestically. It was, thereafter, to rise to new heights (or sink to new depths), but outside Egypt's borders and far away from the immediate problems of state corruption and injustice. Shortly after the government withdrew from Imbaba, followers of Shaykh Umar Abd al-Rahman in New York City attempted to topple the World Trade Center (February 26, 1993). Two years later, on June 26, 1995, al-Jama'a attempted to assassinate President Mubarak in Addis Ababa, Ethiopia. And half a year after that, the Egyptian embassy in Islamabad, Pakistan, was truck-bombed.

Only on one more occasion did Islamic militancy rear its ugly head inside the country, when six men attacked and killed 58 tourists and 4 Egyptian guards at the Pharaonic sites in Luxor, and it was not clear if this was by order or from disorder. That is, was attacking foreigners a new strategic policy of devastating Egypt's tourist economy, or was it, as many claimed, a confusion between foreign-based, prison-based, or locally based leaders? Since such horror, however, concerted Islamist attacks have ceased.

This has not stopped the government from arresting its opponents, primarily from the more staid Muslim Brotherhood, nor has it discouraged prison-based leaders from both al-Jihad and al-Jama'a al-Islamiya from declaring a "unilateral and unconditional ceasefire."[63]

But the field of battle had shifted. And while the militants' goals and objectives as I uncovered them in the south had not changed, there were fewer now willing to achieve them. Perhaps this was due to arrest, perhaps to simple exhaustion, or perhaps it was merely a lull, the eye of a hurricane. Or conceivably there was the growing realization that such efforts were a waste, given the international political and economic forces of the times. A more thoughtful analysis might have produced a much more wide-ranging approach.

From among the hundreds of Sa'idis who were arrested in Imbaba and elsewhere that year under the pretext of suspicion or complicity,[64] a significant but unknown proportion crossed the line from nonviolence to militancy to enlist in the growing ranks of those who once had just performed good deeds and pious acts, but who were now provoked to engage in militancy and violence. Muslim radicals became Muslim militants, exchanging words for action in their campaign against a state that seemed to them unwilling to supply its citizens with their fundamental entitlements and basic social services, and against a state whose security forces committed what many viewed as ungodly acts against its own citizens.

Arrests and mistreatment intimidated and silenced many among those who participated in Islamic development associations. This reduced the provision of important welfare and charity services even more. In Imbaba and throughout the Sa'id, communities witnessed major declines in the local development projects that were closely connected to moderate Islamic associations. As successful programs and services closed for lack of funds and authorization, the government did nothing to compensate by providing its own. These

Islamic efforts had, in fact, first been initiated because of the absence of government action. Subsequently, the state did nothing to fill the vacuum left when it forced these associations and their members to suspend their activities. This in turn provoked even more anger and anxieties from those who had benefited from these charitable acts and good deeds. Many said that the termination of these religiously charged development projects had made life even more difficult and precarious for its working classes.

Yet state policies continued to generate poverty and anger at the bottom, and corruption and opportunism at the top that together eroded the state's ability to sustain solid economic growth and wore down the government's legitimacy in creating a national consensus. Increasingly, the state's security forces were called upon to buoy up the government's sagging authority. The Islamic opposition, unable to share power and peacefully alter the current configuration of economic policies and policy-makers, turned instead to more militant means to achieve its political goals.

Globalizing the Islamic Movement

On September 11, 2001, Islamism viciously and violently catapulted itself to the top of the American agenda. Nineteen Muslim members of a shadowy Islamist organization known only before in a few scattered attacks outside the United States now burst upon the American scene and burned their version of militant Islam deeply into the minds of somnambulant Americans. Osama bin Laden's al-Qa'eda network was a spinoff of the umbrella group, the World Islamic Front for Jihad Against Jews and Crusaders. The Front combined a number of disparate and desperate national organizations such as al-Jihad and al-Jama'a al-Islamiya from Egypt, the Armed Islamic Group from Algeria, the Ulama Association of Pakistan, and an assortment of other freelance militants and militant groups from Sudan, Mo-

rocco, Saudi Arabia, Yemen, and Somalia. First it established a base of operation in Afghanistan and then it raised a counter-attack against the paradoxically godless and godlike United States. As we know, they commandeered four aircraft and piloted two of them into the World Trade Center in New York City and a third one into the Pentagon in Washington, DC. The fourth apparently crashed prematurely in the Pennsylvania countryside.

September 11 was not the first attack by al-Qa'eda. The organization was also held responsible for the August 7, 1998, attack on US embassies in Kenya and Tanzania. Earlier, constituent groups also conducted daring attacks against what they considered as enemy targets. Al-Jama'a had been held responsible for the massacre of tourists in Luxor, in November, 1977; an aborted attack on Greek tourists in April, 1996; a suicide truck-bombing of the Egyptian embassy in Pakistan in November 1995; an attempted assassination of Egyptian President Mubarak in Addis Ababa, Ethiopia, in June, 1995; and at least eight minor attacks in Cairo and southern Egypt from 1993 to 1995. The Egyptian al-Jihad also mounted assaults, more against government officials than against the tourists targeted by al-Jama'a. It has also been held responsible for the first attempted attack against the World Trade Center in February, 1993.[65]

The roots of September 11 go back to 1979, when two important events took place just a month apart and, although thousands of miles from each other, they ultimately became strongly joined together and to the United States. In November, 1979 the Grand Mosque of Mecca was taken over by Saudi militants disgruntled over the moral corruption of the ruling regime despite its austere Wahhabi Islam.[66] In December, the Soviet Union sent troops to Afghanistan upon invitation of the ruling party, the People's Democratic Party. What connected these two events was one person: Osama bin Laden.

Shortly after the Soviet Union entered Afghanistan, bin Laden moved from his native

Saudi Arabia to Peshawar on Pakistan's north-west frontier. For the next ten years he set about bankrolling and then actively leading a *jihad* against the USSR. Using his family's resources amassed through lucrative construction contracts with the Saudi state, bin Laden financed the building of schools and shelters for Afghan refugees in Pakistan. His role soon shifted, however. In 1986 he and Abdalla Azzam, the Jordanian representative and recruiter for the Muslim Brotherhood in Pakistan, together defeated a Soviet military operation in the village of Jaji, an event that is now a veritable legend in the chronicles of the war. Bin Laden now began attracting a personal following of fighters, financed through family money, Muslim charitable donations, official Saudi finance, and US funds funneled through Pakistani intelligence agents. Huband reports[67] that after the Battle of Jaji, the number of Afghan Arabs jumped from 300 to around 7,000.

Bin Laden returned to Saudi Arabia a hero and a recruiter of more *mujahidin* fighters. His success on the lecture circuit was interrupted, however, by the 1990 Gulf War. Bin Laden's fervent and outspoken opposition to basing US troops in his country forced him to flee to Sudan in 1991. There he stayed as a businessman but also as a militant organizer until the Americans forced Sudan to evict him in 1996. He then moved back to Afghanistan.

The Soviets withdrew in 1989 and the government it supported fell three years later in 1992. Then, for the next five years, various Afghan factions fought a deadly civil war to capture control of the state in Kabul. First Gulbeddin Hekmatyar and then later Burhanuddin Rabbani presided over little more than poverty, chaos, and a weak factional army. They were more than outmatched by the well-financed, well-armed civilian army of Afghan refugees from Pakistan, the Taliban. In 1996, when bin Laden returned to Afghanistan, the Taliban took control of Kabul and declared Afghanistan an Islamic emirate, with just a small amount of fighting remaining in the northeast until they ruled

the entire country. The leader of the Taliban, Muhammad Umar Akund, and bin Laden soon became partners in furthering their Islamist political agenda. Although the principal focus of the program was defeating the Northern Alliance and subduing local tribes, a small contingent of zealous fighters were trained specifically to extend this *jihad* to global proportions well beyond Afghanistan's borders.

There seems to be quite some distance between Mallawi and Rajab 'Abd al-Hakim and the World Trade Center, the Pentagon, and Osama bin Laden. Yet the line also appears to be a fairly straightforward one. Still, given what we know about the very local nature of Islamic militancy in southern Egypt, how can we explain this sudden international prominence? A number of models have attempted to explain this complex shift. In the remainder of this chapter, I wish to explore these different accounts. There is probably not one single model that is absolutely correct; the combination of all these versions seems the best overall answer.

Perhaps the most attractive explanation is that bin Laden and al-Qa'eda represent the globalization of Islam.[68] Bin Laden himself appears as the Manichaean antithesis of today's George Soros, not so much because bin Laden challenged capitalism (for he did not), but because both men generated devastating world-scale consequences, though of opposite valorization, as the tentacles of their capitalist financial dealings reached out well beyond the personal and national borders which physically contained them. Similarly, but organizationally, bin Laden's network, al-Qa'eda, in turn becomes the contemporary equivalent of the Abraham Lincoln brigade that had operated in the 1930s in the Spanish Civil War. Like the Brigade, al-Qa'eda attracted volunteers from all over the Muslim world to converge on Afghanistan, which acted like a magnet to those thirsting for adventure, purpose, and employment. In its heyday of the 1980s, and particularly after 1986, when US funds channeled through Saudi Arabia and Pakistan were simply and plentifully sloshing around and finding deep pockets throughout Afghanistan, bin Laden and his *jihad* against the Soviet Union proved rather successful. "In the 1980s, the war in Afghanistan enjoyed fervent, almost giddy support across the Arab world, inspiring poetry, song and glowing accounts of courage and bravery in the name of Islam."[69]

Perhaps it was too successful, for it continued to attract adherents well after the Soviets admitted defeat in 1989 and went home. Thereafter, the Afghan Arabs grafted themselves on to the more indigenous Taliban who had been raised in the Afghan refugee camps in Pakistan, and together the two carved out a government and state limited only by a parcel of territory in the northwest still controlled by the Northern Alliance. As with many other groups trained to incite mayhem, the Afghan Arabs radicalized once they lost their raison d'être, much like US-trained Cubans after the Bay of Pigs. Many analysts employ the term "blowback" to describe the reversal as al-Qa'eda members shifted their gunsights from the Soviets to the Americans.

But perhaps this simplistic volte-face is far too mechanical and therefore suspect. After all, why would *jihad*ists just not declare victory and go home, much less decide to turn and bite the hand that fed (and financed) them? Another explanation, then, would be to see al-Qa'eda's mandate as a reflection of a home-grown anger and resentment that had become diverted from local concerns to refocus on suspected collaborators above and beyond the national boundaries. "Frustrated by repression at home, bleak economies and a helplessness bred by the close watch of security forces, they went to Afghanistan to take a place on the front line of a war for Islam."[70]

Thus as Islamic associations were crushed in Egypt, Algeria, Palestine, and Saudi Arabia, they and their members popped up in Afghanistan with renewed zeal and more intense anger. In a sense, then, this becomes a hydraulic model: pushed down (or repressed) "there," militancy then popped up and

emerged "here." Al-Qa'eda appears, then, as the outcome of Middle East governments being all too successful in stamping out domestic religious militancy. Many Islamists, of course, were arrested and jailed; some were killed, and others simply and unceremoniously dropped out and returned to "civilian" life. A fourth cluster, however – and perhaps the most zealous and vehement of them all – instead disappeared underground, slipped into hiding, and escaped the country. Stripped of all perspective and sense of community, they turned then to the only organization left open. Then, taking a page from 1970s dependency theory that had pinpointed the West and the United States specifically as the ultimate source of imperialism, it is not difficult to imagine militants condemning the only remaining superpower for supporting and even encouraging the shortcomings of their own comprador governments. As bin Laden noted later, why waste time with attacking autocratic Arab governments or even Israel, "the Zionist entity," when striking the United States at its core could be more effective?

These two models assume, then, a straight-line extrapolation from the horrors of Mallawi to the terrors of Kandahar. But it would be folly to assume that these account for all Islamists, particularly those who stayed home. Two other models can account for a more nuanced perspective of a globalizing Islamic movement. Anthony Shadid[71] employed a Durkheimian maturation model whereby militant organizations develop an increasingly more sophisticated program. The trajectory he envisioned went from militancy to welfare to participation in the formal political system. Shadid offered Lebanon's Hizbollah as an archetype; the Palestinian HAMAS and the Egyptian Muslim Brotherhood also come to mind. Thus al-Qa'eda and its constituents appear as stunted organizations retarded in their development by their incapacity to achieve local goals but also limited by the regional politics of Arab authoritarianism and Israeli intimidation from growing into "mature" democratic associations.

But the Muslim Brotherhood and its history in Egypt provides yet a fourth model. Here its moderate leaders and members gained dominance in the organization and marginalized the militants. The reasons for such marginalization may be the arrest and death of militants or else the state's support of moderates. In any event, internal machinations within various militant organizations take advantage of a growing polarization between radicals and moderates to oust the former and install the latter. Those who "lose," however, do not simply sulk and go away. Instead they leave to establish more militant offshoots that disagree as much with their former colleagues as they do with their declared enemies. The result is that even while the Muslim Brotherhood professed its desire to participate legally in Egyptian politics, its disaffected progeny stayed local or else expanded internationally to wreak havoc on both its parent and its adversaries.

A final model is a variation of the last. It suggests that such moderation is not just an evolutionary outcome but the result of government manipulation. This becomes an *agent provocateur* thesis whereby the state surreptitiously encourages false radicals and demagogues whose subsequent faulty planning and implementation outrage others and discredit the movement. At the same time, the government may well placate moderates in order to buttress the latter's claims to authority within their organization. The result is a weaker militant campaign but a stronger, moderate organization.

Thus we see a variety of different models that explain the transformation of Egypt's Islamist movement from a local campaign to a global crusade. First, there is a Globalization model of militants coming from all over the Islamic world attracted to a vital *jihad* in Afghanistan. Then there is a Hydraulic model, that argues that some Middle East governments actually succeeded beyond their wildest dreams in suppressing local militancy but only then to export it abroad where it could revive. There is

also an Immaturation model, based on modernization, that asserts that moderates drove the militants out of domestic Islamist associations who then became marginalized and went elsewhere, either within the country or outside to safer havens. Finally, there is the Manipulation model, that maintains that the state's hand played a substantial part in directing all these various outcomes.

But Osama bin Laden does not simply reflect a distorted version of the demands of Egypt's *al-Jihad* or *al-Jama'a al-Islamiya*. There is more than ending the corruption and injustice taking place in Cairo. In addition to ending support for Arab dictators, his other demands include ending the occupation of Islam's holy places – the US military presence in the Arabian peninsula and the Zionist–Israeli presence in Palestine. These, then, become a distillation, an even greater simplification, and hence a greater common denominator of militant movements from all over the Muslim world. At the same time, the anger that stokes such a global movement is still forged in the individual states that make up the region. Even as some moderate religious activists hope to integrate into the system, organizing, perhaps, the local equivalent of the Christian Democratic parties that participate in Germany and Italy, and become a part of the democratization movement,[72] others have turned their backs on such secular modernity and continue to espouse, instead, their radical version of Islamic politics. Conspiracy theorists, remnants of the corporatist Nasserist state who remain ever cognizant of the government's involvement in all political machinations, see behind this evolution, marginalization, exporting, and globalizing just Cairo's desire to crush its domestic opponents even if this means shifting the struggle to other, external venues. Egypt's government is all too ready to join the war against terrorism – a war it had been waging well before September 11 – and, in the process, even teach the United States a few lessons in this regard.

Conclusions

Since 1995 government repression in Egypt has prevailed and domestic militancy has gone into remission. But it would be foolish to count it out locally even as it erupts internationally. Government forces may have momentarily silenced the state's religious opponents, but it has not resolved the key economic, political, and ethical problems that gave rise to this crusade in the first place. For as long as there remains a shortage of good jobs and steady incomes, a narrow range of legitimate avenues for political dissent, and a desire for an honest and virtuous government, then Islamic activists will continue to mount a *jihad* of the heart, tongue, and hand to eliminate these gaps.

If those who undertake a militant *jihad* constitute a small tip of a huge iceberg, then it also seems important to consider that mass of people lying *below* this tip, those ordinary Muslim men and women who live quite ordinary lives and have quite ordinary jobs and who, like the militants, also oppose the state and its corruption and injustices, but who do not subscribe or resort to their violent methods and techniques. Although they condemn such tactics and pursue, instead, a *jihad* of words and good deeds, their grievances and goals strongly converge with those of a more militant persuasion.

What, then, has caused these moderates and non-violent radicals to move from below the tip of the iceberg, to cross the fine line that divides the pacifist radical from the militant, and to join forces with those intent on violently transforming society?

During the 1970s, the Islamic movement could be characterized as a middle-class crusade. It was not until after 1985, when a decline in oil prices generated a regional recession, that it began to mobilize rank-and-file members from Egypt's working classes. Both middle-class professionals and working-class indigents had originated in the countryside but had migrated to cities throughout the south and to Cairo. One important arena for their intermingling was the large number of small philanthropic social service associations that filled the void left by shrinking or nonexistent government assistance. These were financed and operated by devout university graduates and meant the difference between comfort and abject poverty for their beneficiaries.

But as the finances and operations of these Islamic organizations shrank with increasing government repression, these two segments linked up outside to force the state – legally or illegally – into a more equitable approach to national development and to install a more virtuous, God-fearing government. Together they fashioned an interpretation of Islam that struggled to overcome ignorance and unbelief and in their place establish the correct Islamic path defined by *shari'a* law and radical monotheism. Yet when these activists were attacked and arrested for simply practicing a more devout Islam, as evidenced in these acts of piety and charity, patrons and clients banded together in an Islamic crusade to permit the good and forbid the evil. The absence of legitimate channels for political participation and social protest funneled participants into applying their radical Islamic interpretation through violence.

In the last two decades, as the world has become phenomenologically smaller,[73] with advances in communication and transport technology, local Islamic conflicts against secular opponents have been able to expand without limits to envelope the entire global community. Local militants, pushed out by both government repression as well as by moderate colleagues, carried with them the anger and discontent fashioned at home and took advantage of the political chaos of Central Asia to emerge as a global movement.

Today, the battle lines seem even more starkly drawn, with the United States, Israel, and secular Middle East governments like Egypt on one side, and Islamic militants, ranging from the local urban neighborhoods of southern Egypt to al-Qa'eda at a global scale, on the other. But while the contestants are clearly identified, the outcome is far less marked. It may well become *the* major clash of the twenty-first century.

NOTES

1 Harris (1986:114–17).
2 Ibid.:165; Richards and Waterbury (1998:27).
3 Toth (1999:ch. 5).
4 Richards and Waterbury (1998:184).
5 CAPMAS (1990:7, 18; 1978a:54).
6 Farah (1986:21–2).
7 Waterbury (1983:402–4).
8 Ibid.:132–3.
9 François Burgat (1997) treats the Islamic movement as a newly emerging crusade (p. 1: "a new voice from the South") that absorbed activists disenchanted with the failures of the Arab socialism that had dominated this part of the world throughout the 1950s and 1960s. But the movement did not rise *de novo* in the 1970s, nor was it a reincarnation of a dispirited Left. The current movement only seems to have arisen from nothing – actually from its ashes – because it was crushed in Egypt from 1954 to the early 1970s by the secular nationalist government of Jamal 'Abd al-Nassir, a regime considered by many activists to be godless. Before that came the Muslim Brotherhood founded by Hasan al-Banna in 1928 and the *salafiya* movement under Muhammad Abduh in the 1880s. Thus the "current phase" appears only after a momentary hiatus. Bruce Lawrence (1998) discusses earlier types of movements: first a *revivalism* that occurs during the colonial period, then a *reformism* that coincides with the postcolonial nationalist period, ending with a *fundamentalism* in the strict sense, in the post-nationalist period. Richard Dekmejian (1995) goes even further in presenting a cyclical pattern for the Islamic movement, an alternation of decline and resurgence that commences shortly after the very founding of Islam itself in the seventh century. Birthdates are thus hard to pin down, demonstrating the dynamic and social nature of religion in general, and Islam in particular. Changes and counter-changes occur continuously.
10 Davis (1987).
11 See El-Hamamsy (1975:276–306) for details of these cultural categories.
12 John Esposito (1998:68) claims that the appropriate question in Islam is not what people believe (as in Christianity) but what they do (as in Judaism as well). That is, what counts is orthopraxy, not orthodoxy. While he is correct to say that Judaism is primarily a set of laws, and Christianity is a set of beliefs, Islam, as the last of the three Abrahamic religions, combines *both* belief *and* practice. Yet, as Ellis Goldberg concludes ("Smashing Idols and the State," p. 206), citing material from Hasan al-Banna and Sayyid Qutb, Islamic radicals and militants consider "good deeds" to be more important than "good words" in their efforts to reestablish *shari'a* law and the Right Path. That is, while correct belief *and* correct practice are both emphasized in Islam, the Islamic movement *per se* tends to emphasize orthopraxy over orthodoxy. This shift from "words" to "deeds" also paves the way, should it be necessary, for a shift in strategy from mere talk into militant action. On the other hand, *sufi* Islam, which is condemned by radicals and militants, reverses this emphasis, focusing instead on spiritualism and inner conviction.
13 Qutb (1978:ch. 5).
14 Qutb (2000:262).
15 Many activists employ this triptych, based on an Hadith, or authentic report, about the Prophet Muhammad, who said: "Whoever among you sees any evildoing, let him change it with his hand; if he cannot do that, let him change it with his tongue; and if he cannot do that, let him change it with his heart; and that is the minimum faith requires" (ibid., p. 87).

16 Gaffney1994:36–43.

17 This ambiguity is more than just following the standard anthropological tradition of keeping field-site names anonymous. It also avoids the identification of specific localities because of the real security risks to my informants whose residence and identity can be readily recognized from my work.

18 I know of three instances of such fieldwork in Egypt – Ibrahim (1980), Gaffney (1994), and Ansari (1986). Other analysts rely on these first-hand accounts, as well as secular commentators, government officials, and newspapers and journals, none of which appear particularly neutral or objective. Ibrahim and Ansari's material dates from the 1970s, when the government encouraged radical (but non-militant) Islamists on Egypt's college campuses to organize and mobilize, but before 1985, when middle-class radicals began to reach down and mobilize disaffected members of Egypt's working classes. Gaffney's information appears incidental to his principal intention of documenting various types of preachers and sermons.

Visits to southern Egypt involved constant government surveillance. Upon being escorted by state security officers and left at the residence or business of a small number of friends ("key informants"), I was able, however, to chat and interact with some latitude. Conversations ("interviews") with visiting activists were conducted at the sole discretion of these key informants – truly "gatekeepers" in the literal sense – who judged whether or not these discussions could take place at all, and to what extent. Background information about these partisans was gathered later. Formal research techniques were difficult, if not impossible, to follow. There was no universe of respondents, no sampling, and no formal interview schedules. Patterns did appear, however, which were consistent enough that an overall order eventually emerged.

19 When the Muslim Brotherhood began to expand its organization in the 1930s, after its founder, Hasan al-Banna, had moved from Ismailiya to Cairo, new branches and sub-branches were located primarily in the Delta. In the 1930s, the Delta was experiencing some of the same developmental forces – commercialization, urbanization, industrial and occupational specialization – now affecting the Sa'id. In listing new locations, Brynjar Lia mentions only one new branch in the Sa'id, in the relatively developed city of Asyut, the largest urban area south of Cairo. Otherwise, he records Delta provinces as the sites when new offices were opened outside of the major metropolitan areas. Lia (1998:121–2, nn.5, 8, 10).

20 CAPMAS (1978b:133); Toth (1999: 57–8, 105).

21 In the 1976 census, 30.5 percent of Sa'idis lived in cities as compared to 26.4 percent of those in the Delta. At the same time, 24 percent of Sa'idis engaged in agriculture and 2.4 percent in industry, as compared with 19.8 percent for the Delta in agriculture and 3.7 percent in industry. CAPMAS (1978b:85–96).

22 See Bakr (1994:101). Although Bakr focuses exclusively on Asyut Province, many of his conclusions, such as the importance of family relationships, can be generalized to other provinces within the Sa'id.

23 The proportion of the Coptic population in the Delta is 1.9 percent outside the large metropolitan areas across its borders. Approximately two-thirds of these are urban-based. In the Sa'id, the Coptic population is much higher – rising up to 14 percent when the percentage in the entire country was 6.2 percent in 1976. Of these, a little less than two-thirds live in the Sa'idi countryside, a pattern opposite that of the Delta. CAPMAS (1978b:73–84).

24 Yet it would be misleading to overemphasize the peculiarity of the Sa'id. Even though most Sa'idis hold Cairo and the north in disdain, they nevertheless are

strongly tied to it as part of a larger nation. Attempts such as Mamoun Fandy's to reduce the sociology of the Islamic movement to the contradiction of local tribal stratification among the Ashraf, the Arab tribes, and the *fellahin* (peasants) seem misplaced. For as I show here, it is more the politics and class character of rural-to-urban migration, the anti-*Sa'idi* development policies of Cairo, and most importantly, the moral outrage felt by *Sa'idis* toward state injustice and misconduct that can clarify the Islamic movement here. Tribal stratification may be at issue further south in the *Sa'id* where Fandy conducted his research, but I did not get the sense where I stayed further north that it had any impact on the perspective of the informants I met. Certainly the middle-class leadership was thwarted in their pursuit of upward mobility, but it was through the national class structure, not the local tribal system, that they wanted to rise (Fandy 1994:607–25).

25   Bakr (1994:194). Bakr lists unemployment as the single most important factor underlying organized political violence. As accurate as this might be, it is also the *injustice* of not having a job because government corruption reduced job-generating investment or else because social connections prevailed over achievement and expertise, that also infuriates frustrated job seekers.

26   *al-Wafd*, February 19, 1995.

27   Those who eschew class analysis in examining religious movements, like Martin Riesebrodt, criticize this approach by employing the same objections leveled at most second international Marxism: its excessive materialism, economism, and reductionism. Were Marxism to be frozen at the theoretical stage of the second international, then it would be well to throw it all out. But class is more than just economics; it includes politics and culture as well. More recent Marxists such as E. P. Thompson, Eric Olin Wright, and Anthony Giddens have injected culture,

social life, politics, and identity into the economism of earlier Marxist thinking and theorizing. Wright calls these updates a "Weberian Temptation" (1997:58). Riesebrodt (1993:27); Wright (1997:58).

28   Riesebrodt (1993:186) concludes that the rural-born urban-bound migrant constitutes one of the constant components of religious fundamentalist movements, if not worldwide, then at least in the two case studies he investigated, the United States and Iran. It certainly is the case in Egypt as well, to the extent that I would call Islamism the politics of rural-to-urban migration.

29   Goldberg (1992:211–13) argues that far from being in the grip of economic decline, middle-class migrants who became involved in the Islamic movement actually improved their lives by moving from the village to the city. The issue was not economic hardship – there wasn't any, he claims – but rather, it was political powerlessness. For one, Goldberg makes too great a distinction or separation between the political and the economic. Government corruption – a key complaint of my informants – is both: corrupt officials who embezzle state funds are then underfinancing the budgets of public services. For another, the notion of frustration here captures what appears as a contradictory movement: migrants desire, and expect, upward mobility, when they move. Instead, once in the city, they experience – and resent – downward mobility, often due to a stigmatization (as country bumpkins) over which they have no control. Also see Farah (1986:34) and Bakr (1994:172, 205).

30   Ibrahim (1980:430–2); Ansari (1986: chs. 9, 10).

31   The reasons behind working-class participation in such doctrinaire movements have been questioned. Riesebrodt (1993:158) argues that in the Iranian revolution, lower-class involvement was based less on abstract religious ideology and more on cliental ties to

charismatic, middle-class leaders. Asef Bayat (1997:ch. 3; 1998:136–69) further claims there were even two separate revolutions in Iran because class-segregated neighborhoods and the lack of "meaningful formal associations," such as mosques, seriously inhibited any cohesion between these two classes. However, urban Egypt lacks the occupational homogeneity found in Tehran neighborhoods. Moreover, mosques, service centers (e.g., schools and clinics), and coffee houses constitute important sites where both middle- and working-class men meet. Also see Toth (2000). Thus in Egypt, working-class participation was greater than in Iran, but like Iran, its involvement was based on cliental ties, not religious ideology. However, it was largely the effectiveness of this mobilization, more than any previous "populist" movement, that had government officials worried for fear that lower-class eruptions, like those in the January, 1977 riots, would (again) capsize their plans and policies.

32 Toth (1999:ch. 7).

33 Ibrahim (1996:100); Waterbury (1983:112–17).

34 Riesebrodt (1993:9) concludes that fundamentalism involves a struggle over the shift from personal, paternalistic ties to impersonal, bureaucratic relations that is involved in modernization. My earlier work on Egyptian rural workers confirms this. See Toth (1999). However, I have difficulty with Riesebrodt's use of the term "patriarchy" since this is a gender ideology. I prefer the term "paternalism" instead. The two are not always the same.

35 Toth (1999:ch. 7).

36 Ibrahim (1980: 452).

37 Gilsenan (1992:ch. 10).

38 al-Jihad ["(Religious) Struggle"] was the organization responsible for the assassination of President al-Sadat and holds sway primarily in Cairo. Al-Jama'a al-Islamiya ["(the) Islamic Association"] was its organizational offshoot that dominates the Sa'id, although earlier

organizations claim ancestry as well (see note 51 below). Both believe in a jihad of militant action to overcome the ignorance, or jahiliya, preached by Sayyid Qutb, although al-Jihad pinpoints just government officials as evildoers, while al-Jama'a al-Islamiya broadens its targets to include the larger Egyptian society as possible unbelievers. For an insightful examination of these and other militant organizations, see Bakr (1994). Bakr investigates fully developed Islamic associations, whereas here the emphasis instead is placed on a "preorganizational" process whereby radicals became transformed into militants who then may go on to join preexisting militant organizations like al-Jihad and al-Jama'a al-Islamiya.

39 Kuran (1993:308–10).

40 Sadowski (1991:231).

41 See also Bakr (1994:49), Sullivan (1994), Abu Zayd (1965), and Sullivan and Abed-Kotob (1999).

42 The Thanawiya 'Amma constitutes the large comprehensive examination at the end of high school that determines the discipline of beginning college students and hence their subsequent occupation.

43 This and other association names are pseudonyms.

44 Supplicants were also endorsed by two witnesses personally known to both benefactors and beneficiaries.

45 al-Sha'b, October 20, 1992.

46 Gaffney (1994:44, 91).

47 Gordon (1992).

48 Waterbury (1978:253–4).

49 EOHR (c.1994:1).

50 Middle East Times, 5–11 February 1995.

51 Gaffney (1994:329–30) notes that the Islamic Association, al-Jama'a al-Islamiya, in al-Minya was preceded by the al-Jam'iya al-Islamiya, also translated as the Islamic Association, but with a slightly different nuance in the Arabic. This is also the generic term for any Islamic association. The confusion is not just among foreign speakers; my informants also found it difficulty to

distinguish among these two different organizations and the generic term.

52 See Fisk (1995a:15, 1995b:14, 1995c:13).

53 Today, the HAMAS organization in Gaza and the West Bank of Palestine is in a similar contradictory position. It is engaged in so-called terrorist attacks against Israel while at the same time operating charitable programs for schools, clinics, welfare, and employment. HAMAS is an acronym for the Islamic Resistance Movement and is an offshoot of the Muslim Brotherhood. See Abu-Amr (1994). By US law, its funds have been frozen and donations to HAMAS are prohibited. Yet fungibility makes this financial situation difficult: it may well reduce violent attacks by cutting off funds budgeted for weapons and ammunition. But at the same time it also hurts those benefiting from its numerous non-violent programs. The situation in Palestine is much worse than in Egypt, for the Israeli government has much less interest in the welfare of Palestinians and the number of alternative agencies is much smaller.

54 Cf. Fisk (1995a, b, c).

55 Bakr (1994:38).

56 The last two are the ideologues behind al-Jihad and al-Jama'a al-Islamiya, respectively. Muhammad 'Abd al-Salam Faraj was executed as a result of the assassination of President al-Sadat in 1981. He argued that a jihad bi al-haraka (and only a militant jihad) was imperative for all Muslims who otherwise were unbelievers for rejecting it. 'Umar 'Abd al-Rahman is in prison in the United States for his part in the World Trade Center bombing in 1998. While teaching at Asyut University, he issued a number of fatwas, or religious pronouncements, justifying a militant jihad against Egyptian officials and civilians.

57 Bakr (1994:236–8).

58 Abu Zayd, al-Th'ar. Interestingly, Abu Zayd's ethnography about th'ar retaliation in the Sa'id alludes to local Copts

as armaments suppliers to rival Muslim tribal clans seeking mutual revenge. This points to the possibility that perhaps some of the sectarian violence in the Sa'id between Christians and Muslims was not altogether without cause, as militants targeted those who profited from equipping the violence. Bakr (1994:173–4) also points out the preponderance of Christians among Asyuti elites in more recent times.

59 Abdo (2000:26).

60 Weaver (2000:147).

61 Abdo (2000:20). It appears impossible to verify government reports of a single, overarching organization rather than a multitude of independent associations.

62 Ibid., 24. Abdo cites a March, 1993 report of the Egyptian Organization of Human Rights as the source of this information. Elsewhere, Weaver (2000:149) quotes an Islamist lawyer, Ali Ismail, whom she interviewed in November, 1994, that "[w]omen were tortured with electroshocks and beaten in the streets – dragged by their hair, after their hijabs were savagely torn off their heads." He goes on to tell her that there were no fewer than 5,000 people were arrested, of whom 4,500 were released over the next year. Of the remaining 500, only 100 have been brought to trial [Ibid.].

63 Abdo (2000:197).

64 EOHR (c.1994:2.)

65 This may well indicate the fluidity and confusion of these groups. Most US government officials attribute the first World Trade Center bombing attempt to al-Jihad but under the leadership of Shaykh 'Abd al-Rahman. However, Shaykh Umar 'Abd al-Rahman is the spiritual leader of al-Jama'a al-Islamiya.

66 Wahhabi Islam is similar to salafi Islam in that both condemn the worship of intermediaries between believers and God. But the overall doctrinal basis of each is different, as is the social milieu – one tribal and nomadic, the other urban and bureaucratic. Neither forms the basis of militant Islam until its adherents

feel attacked by non-Muslims. See Riesebrodt (1993).
67 Huband (1998:3).
68 *Ibid.*, p. 12.
69 Shadid (2001:80).
70 *Ibid.*, p. 82.
71 *Ibid.*, Ch. 8.
72 See Ibrahim (1996) and Harik (1994).
This is also Shadid's conclusion (2001).
73 What Anthony Giddens has called
time–space distanciation or what David
Harvey called time–space compression.
Giddens (1990) and Harvey (1989).

REFERENCES

Abdo, Geneive
  2000 No God but God: Egypt and the
  Triumph of Islam. Oxford: Oxford
  University Press.
Abu-Amr, Ziad
  1994 Islamic Fundamentalism in the
  West Bank and Gaza: Muslim Brother-
  hood and Islamic Jihad. Bloomington:
  Indiana University Press.
Abu Zayd, Ahmad
  1965 al-Th'ar: Dirasah Anthrupulujiyah
  bi-Ihda Qura al-Said. Cairo: Dar al-
  Maarif.
Ansari, Hamid
  1986 Egypt: The Stalled Society. Albany:
  State University of New York Press.
Bakr, Hasan
  1994 Political Violence in Egypt: Asyut as
  a Site of Tension. The Reasons and the
  Motives. 1997–93 (al-'Unf al-Siyasi fi
  Misr: Asyut: Bura al-Tawtir: al-Asbab
  wa al-Duwafiya'.) Cairo: Markaz al-
  Mahrusa li al-Bahuth wa al-Tadrib wa
  al-Nashr.
Bayat, Asef
  1988 Revolution Without Movement,
  Movement Without Revolution: Com-
  paring Islamic Activism in Iran and
  Egypt. Comparative Studies in Society
  and History 40(1).
——— 1997 Street Politics: Poor People's
  Movements in Iran. New York: Columbia
  University Press.

Burgat, François
  1997 The Islamic Movement in North
  Africa. Austin: University of Texas Press.
CAPMAS (Central Agency of Public Mobilization and Statistics)
  1978a The General Census of Residents
  and Residences. 1976. Population
  Census. Detailed Results. Cairo: Arab
  Republic of Egypt.
——— 1978b Population and Development:
  A Study of the Population Increase
  and Its Challenge to Development in
  Egypt. Cairo: Arab Republic of Egypt, Sep-
  tember.
——— 1990 Statistical Yearbook. Cairo:
  Arab Republic of Egypt, June.
Davis, Eric
  1987 The Concept of Revival and the
  Study of Islam and Politics. *In* The Is-
  lamic Impulse. Barbara Freyer Stowasser,
  ed. London: Croom Helm.
Dekmejian, R. Hrair
  1995 Islam in Revolution: Fundamental-
  ism in the Arab World. 2nd edition.
  Syracuse, NY: Syracuse University
  Press.
EOHR (Egyptian Organization for Human
  Rights)
  c.1994 Aliyat Intaj al-'Unf fi Misr:
  Asyut, Hala Numazhajiya (Tools of the
  Production of Violence in Egypt: the
  Asyut Case Study). Cairo: EOHR.
Esposito, John L.
  1998 Islam: The Straight Path. 3rd edi-
  tion. New York: Oxford University Press.
Fandy, Mamoun
  Egypt's Islamic Group: Regional Revenge.
  Middle East Journal 48(4).
Farah, Nadia Ramsis
  1986 Religious Strife in Egypt: Crisis and
  Ideological Conflict in the Seventies.
  New York: Gordon & Breach.
Fisk, Robert
  1995a Terror Stalks Egypt's Forgotten
  Towns. The Independent, February 8.
——— 1995b "Might of the Sword" Men-
  aces Christians. The Independent, February 9.
——— 1995c Cairo Puts Faith in Bullet
  and Bulldozer. The Independent, February
  10.

Gaffney, Patrick D.
1994 The Prophet's Pulpit: Islamic Preaching in Contemporary Egypt. Berkeley: University of California Press.

Giddens, Anthony
1990 The Consequences of Modernity. Cambridge: Polity Press.

Gilsenan, Michael
1992 Recognizing Islam: Religion and Society in the Modern Middle East. New York: I. B. Tauris.

Goldberg, Ellis
1992 Smashing Idols and the State: The Protestant Ethic and Egyptian Sunni Radicalism. *In* Comparing Muslim Societies: Knowledge and the State in a World Civilization. Juan R. I. Cole, ed. Ann Arbor: University of Michigan Press.

Gordon, Joel
1992 Nasser's Blessed Movement: Egypt's Free Officers and the July Revolution. New York: Oxford University Press.

El-Hamamsy, Laila Shukry
1975 The Assertion of Egyptian Identity. *In* Ethnic Identity: Cultural Continuities and Change. George DeVos and Lola Romanucci-Ross, eds. Palo Alto, CA: Mayfield Publishers.

Harik, Iliya
1994 Pluralism in the Arab World. Journal of Democracy 3(5):43–56.

Harris, Nigel
1986 The End of the Third World: Newly Industrializing Countries and the Decline of an Ideology. London: I. B. Tauris.

Harvey, David
1989 The Condition of Postmodernity. Oxford: Blackwell.

Huband, Mark
1998 Warriors of the Prophet: The Struggle for Islam. Boulder, CO: Westview Press.

Ibrahim, Saad Eddin
1980 Anatomy of Egypt's Militant Islamic Groups: Methodological Note and Preliminary Findings. International Journal of Middle East Studies 12(4): 245–66.
—— 1996 Cairo: A Sociological Profile. *In* Egypt, Islam, and Democracy: Twelve Critical Essays. Cairo: American University in Cairo Press.

Kuran, Timur
1993 The Economic Impact of Islamic Fundamentalism. *In* Fundamentalisms and the State: Remaking Politics, Economies, and Militance. Martin E. Marty and R. Scott Appleby, eds. Chicago: University of Chicago Press.

Lawrence, Bruce B.
1998 Shattering the Myth: Islam Beyond Violence. Princeton, NJ: Princeton University Press.

Lia, Brynjar
1998 The Society of the Muslim Brothers in Egypt: The Rise of an Islamic Mass Movement, 1928–1942. Reading, MA: Ithaca Press.

Qutb, Sayyid
1978 Milestones on the Road. Salimiah, Kuwait: International Islamic Federation of Student Organizations.
—— 2000 Social Justice in Islam. Trans. John B. Hardie, rev. trans. Hamid Algar. Oneonta, NY: Islamic Publications International.

Richards, Alan, and John Waterbury
1998 A Political Economy of the Middle East. 2nd edition. Boulder, CO: Westview Press.

Riesebrodt, Martin
1993 Pious Passion: The Emergence of Modern Fundamentalism in the United States and Iran. Trans. Don Reneau. Berkeley: University of California Press.

Sadowski, Yahya
1991 Political Vegetables: Businessman and Bureaucrat in the Development of Egyptian Agriculture. Washington, DC: Brookings Institution.

Shadid, Anthony
2001 Legacy of the Prophet: Despots, Democrats, and the New Politics of Islam. Boulder, CO: Westview Press.

Sullivan, Denis J.
1994 Private Voluntary Organizations in Egypt: Islamic Development, Private Initiative, and State Control. Gainesville: University Press of Florida.

Sullivan, Denis J., and Sana Abed-Kotob
  1999 Islam in Contemporary Egypt: Civil Society vs. the State. Boulder, CO: Lynne Rienner.
Toth, James
  1999 Rural Labor Movements in Egypt and Their Impact on the State, 1961–1992. Gainesville: University Press of Florida.
—— 2000 Rural-to-Urban Migration and Informal Sector Expansion: Impediments to Egyptian Development. First Mediterranean Social and Political Research Meeting, Robert Schuman Centre of the European University Institute, Florence, Italy, March 22–26.

Waterbury, John
  1978 Egypt: Burdens of the Past, Options for the Future. Bloomington: Indiana University Press, American Universities Field Staff.
—— 1983 The Egypt of Nasser and Sadat: The Political Economy of Two Regimes. Princeton, NJ: Princeton University Press.
Weaver, Mary Anne
  2000 A Portrait of Egypt: A Journey through the World of Militant Islam. New York: Farrar, Straus & Giroux.
Wright, Eric Olin
  1997 Rethinking, Once Again, the Concept of Class Structure. In Reworking Class. John R. Hall, ed. Ithaca, NY: Cornell University Press.

7

Nationalism and Millenarianism in West Papua: Institutional Power, Interpretive Practice, and the Pursuit of Christian Truth

Danilyn Rutherford

In the yard of the Three Kings Church in Timika, 20 meters from the church door, hundreds of Papuans had been gathering since November to voice their protest at Indonesian rule and their aspirations for self-determination. By December the gathering had become a densely populated micro-village of temporary dwellings and cooking fires. Tents decorated with painted depictions of the Morning Star flag bore banners identifying the tribal group or district of their occupants.

In front of a small parish building inside the yard an "administrative" area had been set up by Papuans to monitor visitors to the site. The area reflected the forms of external authority experienced by Papuans, first under the Dutch, and now under Indonesia. Here, tables covered with registration books were set in a line, a microphone was connected to a public address system, and name-cards on a table identified the secretary and chairman of the committee. The area was decorated with painted depictions of Christ, the Bible and other Christian images.

The impromptu iconography of the church-yard camp expressed the people's perspective of the struggle and the available means to resolve it. On the front wall of the church a huge, convincing portrait of a European-style Christ – arms wide, a friendly but worried face, a map of West Papua spread across the chest – was accompanied by the imperative in English: "Give us back our freedom." Adjacent, a depiction of traditional life portrayed an idyllic scene of sago-making watched over by a richly coloured bird of paradise. On one side of the church another large painting with the heading *Armi Papua Barat* (West Papua Army) showed a dark bird with spreading wings. Flanking the bird were three painted depictions of the Morning Star flag and an open Bible drawing attention to Efesus [Ephesians] 5, 8 ["For ye were sometimes darkness, but now are ye light in the Lord: walk as children of light"]. (van den Broek and Szalay 2001:83)

What is the relationship between people's experience of Christian institutions and the meanings they attribute to Christian texts?

Anthropologists have offered a straightforward answer to this question. Christian missions, schools, and churches promote particular interpretations of scripture and ritual in an effort to produce particular kinds of believers (see Aragon 2000, Asad 1993, Cannell 1999, Comaroff and Comaroff 1991, Rafael 1993 [1988], Schrauwers 2000; cf. Bowen 1993, Foucault [1975] 1979). Christian institutions achieve this "disciplinary" outcome because they are dense sites of power, "the effect of a network of motivated practices" ranging from brute force to spiritual and material sanctions and incentives, from ecclesiastical law to routinized habits of self-cultivation and control (Asad 1993:35).[1] Yet this straightforward answer does not offer us a way of accounting for the mixture of images and references deployed by the protestors in Timika. Timika is a mining town in the western half of New Guinea, an Indonesian province formerly known as Irian Jaya and now called Papua in an effort to appease its indigenous inhabitants, who would like to transform the territory into an independent West Papuan state. Although the town is home to just some of Papua's hundreds of ethnolinguistic groups, the "impromptu iconography" described above is far from limited to this community. Throughout the predominantly Christian province, pro-independence groups have resorted to texts, practices, and technologies associated with Christianity and the colonial and postcolonial state. To understand the conditions that have made it possible for Papuan separatists to read the Bible for signs of God's support for their struggle, we need to understand the history of Christian organizations in the province. But we also need to understand how such institutions can come to feature in people's lives and imaginations as something other than a disciplinary force. On the offshore island of Biak, the part of Papua that I know best, some prophets once accused foreign evangelists of tearing a page from the Bible – the one that accounted for the wealth and potency wielded by outsiders (see Kamma 1972:161). When it comes to the link between institutions and interpretations, our own approaches may be missing a page.

What is missing from these approaches can be stated plainly: people's treatment of the Christian message is surely related to the specific ways in which they have negotiated the traffic in people, practices, goods, and, often, violence, opened by organizations acting in the name of God. In this chapter, I explore this underexamined aspect of the link between institutional power and interpretive practice in the context of two episodes in western New Guinea's checkered history: a millennial movement known as Koreri that occurred on Biak between 1939 and 1943 and the campaign for West Papuan independence following the fall of Indonesian President Suharto's authoritarian New Order regime in 1998. In approaching these episodes, I take meaning not as the symbolic content of words, objects, or gestures, but as the lure that fuels efforts to order experience, efforts that can never fully succeed. The conventional threats to coherence described by Geertz (1973) certainly figure in my analysis: death, suffering, and injustice loom large in West Papua. But I intend to focus on dilemmas inherent to the institutions that disseminate Christian texts and rituals and attempt to control their meaning and use. I use the term "institutions" to refer to what Max Weber called "compulsory organizations" (1978:52) For Weber, these included the Church, which exercised "psychic coercion," and the state, which claimed a monopoly on the legitimate use of force. Like Weber, I view the actions undertaken by these organizations as fueled by a combination of abstract ideals and concrete motivations and constraints, including the collective interest of functionaries in a "secure existence" and the resources at their disposal for pursuing this end (1946:199). But unlike Weber, I don't sharply oppose the "ideological" and the "functional" purposes of an organization. "Ideas such as 'state,' 'church,' 'community,' 'party,' or 'enterprise'" only exist to the degree that they are evoked in social practice (ibid.). Purposes, including functional ones, are never simply given; these values and the subjects who pursue them are discursively produced. As such, institutions are subject to what Keane (1997) calls the "risks of representation": organizations depend for their authority – and their social reality – on instances of social interaction involving words, things, and forms of behavior that are always open to multiple uses, that can always be seen from multiple points of view. In the course of a Christian ritual, one such point of view might fix upon the officially sanctioned symbolism of an utterance, gesture, or object. Another perspective might foreground the ties between these phenomena and broader contexts and enabling conditions: the Sunday school or seminary where the participants learned these verses and movements, the money that paid for this bread and wine. A further perspective, which comes into focus in the cases I consider here, would highlight the links between the Christian institutions that introduced these texts and practices and other coercive organizations, including the colonial and postcolonial state. However official doctrine treats these ties – with some Protestant forms of Christianity doing their best to obscure the believer's dependence on established social forms – Christian genres of practice always *index*, that is, derive from and potentially point to, broader institutional orders (see Bauman 1983, Collins 1996, Mertz 1996, Shoaps 2002). Potentially a threat, but also a resource, for believers, this aspect of Christian ritual elicits interpretation, figuring in local struggles for authority derived from the divine.

These struggles are local because, as I hope to make clear in this chapter, historically particular understandings of the nature and powers of coercive organizations shape people's participation in Christian rituals and their interpretation of Christian texts.[2] One effect of such participation might be something akin to what Benedict Anderson (1991:55–8) describes as the consciousness born of the "bureaucratic pilgrimage."

Through their participation in a translocal institution, colonial officials develop a sense of "connectedness" and "interchangeability" with one another as they traverse the same administrative space. In the context of Christian institutions, which are almost always translocal and often transnational, a parallel instance might entail a situation in which participants, in imagining their global peers as equivalent "brothers and sisters in Christ," experience a sort of "practical transcendence" that calls to mind the divine transcendence of an otherworldly God. But other possibilities exist. Participating in a ritual can appear as a means of demonstrating one's privileged access to wealth and potency from beyond the reach of local worlds. The coexistence of these alternatives presents a dilemma to institutions whose pretensions to universality require them to extend personnel and resources across political boundaries. By virtue of an institution's role in the pursuit of status within a particular social context, Christian texts can appear as evidence of a limited good: a treasure possessed by outsiders, a stubbornly inscrutable truth, whose revelation unleashes extraordinary power.

Ever since European missionaries set foot in western New Guinea, the region's inhabitants have attempted to seize the potency of Christian institutions by laying claim to the truth behind official doctrine (see Giay 1986, 1995a, 1995b, Giay and Godschalk 1993, Kamma 1972, Rutherford 2000, 2003, Timmer 2000, 2001). In this chapter, my discussion of this dynamic begins with an analysis of Koreri, the movement on Biak, and its relationship to the islands' history of conversion and colonization. I then turn to my current research on the resurgence of Papuan nationalism in the province. In both cases, a particular orientation to officially sanctioned institutions may well have created a space for the pursuit of decidedly unsanctioned ends. In the conclusion, I explore the wider implications of these findings. But first, let us consider a case in which, for reasons related to the dynamics of a local society shaped by a particular experience of colonial expansion, the link between the power of Christian institutions and the secret meaning of Christian texts comes particularly vividly into view.

Koreri and the Power of the Foreign

In my previous writings, I have set the long tradition of Biak millenarianism, which dates back to the earliest days of colonial contact in New Guinea, in the context of the practices through which the people of these islands have pursued value, authority, and prestige (see Rutherford 2003). In arenas ranging from marriage to the performance of sung poetry, Biaks have reproduced an image of the so-called Land of the Foreigners as a source of excessive wealth, pleasurable surprises, and inscrutable texts. Under the New Order, this aspect of Biak social life had a corrosive effect on the identities imposed on the islanders by the regime. The islanders suppressed the referential meaning of official rhetoric by deploying it as evidence of a speaker's proximity to distant sources of wealth and power. This fetishization of the foreign, I have suggested, is the product of this region's history on the frontiers of powerful polities, beginning with the Moluccan sultanate of Tidore, where Biaks delivered tribute in return for trade goods and titles. This dynamic found its limits in the millennial movement, Koreri. Drawing on a myth that made a Biak ancestor, Manarmakeri, into the source of foreign potency, Koreri occurred at moments when Biaks were drawn to adopt the perspective of powerful outsiders on their society. Signaling a collapse in distances and differences, this recognition sparked expectations of Manarmakeri's imminent return. Whereas today's pastors present their sermons as glosses originating in an encounter with a sublimely alien original, Koreri prophets claimed to have discerned the Bible's secret significance: it was a rendering of Biak myth. Jesus Christ was really Manarmakeri, whose name means "The Itchy Old Man," an abject hero whose

potency resides in his scaly skin. This revelation heralded Manarmakeri's return and the opening of Koreri, a utopian state of endless plenty, which literally means "We Change Our Skin." Koreri prophets thus drew upon and superseded the strategies of leaders who used translation as a means not of overcoming, but rather of positing difference, that is, of creating the very "foreignness" that was the source of their prestige (see Rutherford 2000, 2003:ch.4).[3] But there is another way to look at Koreri, one that locates the movement in the context of the region's colonial institutions, which took a particular form.

The Netherlands Indies government laid claim to the western half of New Guinea in the early nineteenth century. The first missionaries to work in the region were two German cabinet makers, Carl W. Ottow and J. G. Geissler, who settled in Doreh Bay, on the Bird's Head Peninsula, in 1855.[4] They were the protégés of O. G. Heldring, the famous Dutch Pietist reformer, and Johannes Gossner, a defrocked German priest. Sharing a strong distrust of official institutions, Gossner and Heldring hit upon the idea of sending unpaid "Christian Workmen" to the colonies to spread the Gospel as they plied their trade. The local Papuans had little use for cabinets, but they did want trade goods, which the missionaries supplied in return for food and forest products, which they collected for a trader based in Tidore's sister polity, Ternate, seat of the residency that included western New Guinea. When the Utrecht Mission Society took over the field, its leaders pushed for the elimination of this practice. But the brothers in New Guinea found that they needed trade to attract the Papuans' attention. Very few Papuans converted to Christianity during the first 50 years of the mission; those who did were manumitted slaves. But coastal natives did take an interest in the mission post. Biak seafarers came to Sunday services, where they received tobacco and trade goods, along with snatches of sermons, which they repeated verbatim in their home communities or even sold for rice.

Needless to say, this tendency to turn Christian words into "booty" exasperated the missionaries. Even worse, would-be converts declared that Jesus belonged to the "Company," that is, the colonial state. That Papuans associated Jesus with the colonial government should come as little surprise, given the conditions in which the missionaries operated. Elsewhere I have described how the Dutch pursued a "policy of display" in western New Guinea during the nineteenth century (Rutherford 2003). Rather than investing in settlements in this vast and seemingly unprofitable land, officials traveled along the coasts erecting escutcheons and confirming the appointment of local chiefs. They also relied on the missionaries to create the impression of Dutch authority. Ottow and Geissler earned a small stipend from the government for rescuing shipwreck victims from competing colonial powers. Occasionally, the resident launched punitive expeditions, often to placate the missionaries, who kept the government informed of the Papuans' "evil" acts. The remarkable security enjoyed by the Protestants in this "unpacified" land attests in part to the value attributed to the commodities they traded, in part to their association with a violent colonial state.

By the end of the nineteenth century, the missionaries had become convinced that their efforts would never bear fruit until the government applied a firmer hand in New Guinea. Protestant pressure in the Netherlands contributed to the Dutch Parliament's decision to fund the expansion of the colonial bureaucracy into New Guinea. At the turn of the century, new victories for the mission accompanied the establishment of permanent government posts. North coastal communities suddenly took an interest in converting, and the demand for evangelists soon exceeded the supply. Having battled against prophets in the past, the missionaries worried that the "great awakening" might signal another round of Koreri. But as the Dutch lieutenant who "pacified" Biak in 1915 observed, Christianity's appeal lay in the

access the mission offered to evangelists fluent in Malay, the lingua franca and language of administration of the Indies, which later became Indonesian (see Feuilletau de Bruyn 1916:244; also Rutherford n.d.). Faced with a head tax, forced labor, and the prosecution of Papuan "criminals," Biaks no doubt felt the need for advocates who could speak on their behalf. As the same time, conversion gave Biaks access to Christian narratives, which they incorporated into Biak myth as a means of interpreting their changing experience of colonial power.

The Biak communities that requested evangelists got more than they bargained for. The first native teacher to visit Biak was a manumitted slave who had attended a native seminary in Java with a handful of other Papuan "foster children." But Papuan evangelists soon found themselves outnumbered by native Christians from Ambon and Sangir, whom the mission imported in large numbers to staff their government-subsidized schools. Natives from other parts of the Indies also monopolized the lower ranks of the colonial bureaucracy. The officials and teachers worked hard to suppress local practices, including "heathen" feasts and song and dance genres, which the missionaries associated with warfare, licentiousness, and other heathen "sins." By the 1920s, despite the missionaries' efforts to impose a division between the affairs of church and state, the two remained interchangeable in the local imagination. On Biak, people used the same word, *pandita* (Malay, "pastor"), to refer to colonial officials and mission teachers (see Hartweg 1926). Both were also known as *amberi*, a Biak term meaning "foreigner" drawn from the adjective *amber*, used in such expressions as "the Land of the Foreigners," *Sup Amber*.

At the same time, the intensified experience of colonial rule and mission guidance gave rise to new opportunities for the pursuit of status in Biak. One Papuan nationalist told me how his father, an evangelist trained in the 1930s, had managed to marry his mother, the daughter of a titled village chief.[5] Such a woman could only marry the son of a man with a similar Tidoran title, except if the suitor was a teacher, whose association with the mission and government gave him equivalent rank. The remarkably high literacy rates observed for Biak in the 1930s and 1940s indicate the attraction of these new ties (see de Bruyn 1948). Even coolies, stevedores, and mission carpenters enjoyed a certain cachet. Biak workers spent some of their wages buying the imported cloth and porcelain that circulated as bridewealth, along with silver bracelets made from colonial coins (see Rutherford 2001a). Commodities and money, often regarded as instruments for dissolving distinctions, became evidence of encounters in distant lands.

The outbreak of the millennial Koreri movement at the beginning of World War II must be set in this context, in which institutions that Biaks confronted appeared as source of both violence and value. I have argued elsewhere that the mission contributed to the movement by reviving *wor*, a forbidden song and dance genre, for use in church (see Rutherford 2003:ch.6). This surprising act of recognition occurred at a time when the colonial landscape was quickly changing. Although Koreri is sometimes called a "cargo cult," the movement had much in common with uprisings that occurred throughout the territory that later became Indonesia (see Lanternari 1963; Worsley 1968; also Kahin 1985). The Japanese occupation of the Netherlands Indies led to the destruction of the colonial administration. On Biak, as elsewhere, local people responded by attacking the elite natives through whom the Dutch had ruled.

The first stage of the movement, which began in 1939, was led by a former plantation coolie named Angganeta Menufandu.[6] Angganeta was critically ill when Manarmakeri appeared to her in a vision and explained his plans for her and "Papua," as he called her homeland. Angganeta miraculously recovered and soon was healing others, who gathered around her on a nearby island. She called for people to perform *wor*, the for-

merly banned genre, and drink palm wine, which was still forbidden. The faithful had to trade their imported clothing for loincloths and follow food taboos derived from the myth of Manarmakeri, who soon would return to his chosen land.

The encampment grew quickly, and soon thousands had gathered to drink and sing and dance to *wor* songs. While these practices reflected a certain "nativism," a closer look complicates the picture. For reasons I explore elsewhere, *wor*, which had attracted so much "foreign" attention, served as a privileged method for providing evidence of encounters with new and startling things.[7] Angganeta spent the nights crouched in what her followers called a "radio room," where she received transmissions that she turned into songs, which her followers repeated. Carried away by the music, some participants went into a trance and spoke English, Dutch, and Japanese, channeling the voices of outsiders and the dead. At a later stage, those who spoke in tongues earned the right to serve as the representatives of Angganeta and her successors: they were the *bin dame* (Biak/Malay, "women of peace") deputed to spread the movement and punish (perhaps "pacify") those who opposed it. Like Angganeta, their authority derived from their power to embody alterity. Their incomprehensible words made present absent worlds.

As the uprising progressed, its leaders increasingly laid claim to the authority of "foreign" institutions, as the *bin dame* example suggests. Angganeta, now known as the "Queen," held court in her hut, where Tidoran etiquette prevailed. After the Japanese arrested and executed Angganeta, some Biak warriors recently released from colonial jails wrote bylaws for the movement, supposedly inspired by rumors that the Japanese had promised to recognize existing nationalist organizations. Among other things, the bylaws designated an upside-down Dutch tricolor as the new Papuan flag. In addition to establishing an "army," one of the warriors founded a "city" where people from different

communities followed a strict schedule of
activities. Word spread that this warrior
owed his power to a tiny bible.[8] Another
leader built a replica of an airplane, around
which his followers drilled, danced, and
prayed.

Along with this recourse to objects, texts,
and practices associated with the colonial
church and state – and their Japanese and
Indonesian opponents – went a radical reversal of colonial hierarchies. When Koreri
came, the prophets proclaimed, all the
amberi would be Papuans, and all
the Papuans would be *amberi*. An Ambonese
teacher later described to the mission how a
huge band of believers had confronted him
(see Picanussa n.d.). After beating him up,
they forced the teacher to listen to a statement, which began with an announcement,
"Our movement is called the New Religion
and the New Government." The statement
went on:

*Our Manseren has returned from Holland,
so the Dutch people are now poor and the
Papuan people are going to become rich.
Queen Wilhelmina is now wearing a loin-
cloth and we Papuans are going to be wearing fine clothing. We also have a clothing
factory. The Dutch people now have to
work in the garden planting cassava, sweet
potato, taro and so forth, and we Papuans
are going to be eating the food Dutch people
usually eat.

*You *amberi* from Ambon, Java, Menado,
etc. who still remember and follow only
the Dutch Government, now we are going to
imprison all of you just like the Japanese have
imprisoned the Dutch. Now we want to chase
away all the Dutch people and other *amberi*
from our land because they have oppressed us
too much. Now we want to be free and stand
on our own.

*We want to become our own government
[Dutch, *Bestuur*], our own local head of
government [Dutch, *HPB*, acronym for
Hoofd Plaatselijk Bestuur] our own teachers
[Malay, *Goeroe*] and preachers [Malay, *Pen-
deta*].

*The Dutch people and you *amberies*, you
have deceived us Papuans. You have hidden
many secrets from us. (Picanussa n.d.)

In another report, also addressed to the mission, a Papuan elder recalled a similar ordeal
(see Mooiy n.d.). A crowd of Koreri believers
forced him to show them where the teacher
had hidden the school books and equipment,
which they destroyed. These items supposedly blocked Koreri, as did bridewealth,
which was also smashed. Then they took the
elder into the church and demanded that he
answer three questions. "1. Why don't you
believe in the Lord God? 2. Why did the
teacher hide the teaching equipment? 3. Are
you going to follow the *amberie* or are you
also a Papuan (servant of Koreri)?" They
stood beside him with a machete, ready to
strike if he refused to respond.[9]

On the face of it, this effort to clarify the
Bible's secret meaning seems at odds with
Angganeta's radio transmissions and her followers' outpourings of "foreign" words.
Where the crowd questioning the elder
focused on the significance of foreign discourse, the singers and dancers highlighted
its material qualities: its startling effects, its
strange sounds. Yet if we view interpretation
as itself a social act, then the paradox disap-
pears. Both sets of practices demonstrated
Angganeta and her successors' privileged
access to Manarmakeri and proved that the
Biak ancestor soon would return. In this way,
these prophets compelled their followers to
see themselves from a new perspective. The
missionaries who served in New Guinea envisioned their Papuan converts as submitting
to a similar force. For these Pietists, as for
Kierkegaard, Christianity's significance lay in
its implications for "existing individuals" and
their "eternal happiness," not in the abstract,
communicable logic of a doctrine.[10] Suddenly subjected to the gaze of an invisible,
inscrutable Other, the new Christians were
supposed to forgo worldly ties for spiritual
treasures stored up in an other-worldly realm
(see Derrida 1995, Kierkegaard [1843]
1985). The myth of Manarmakeri, I have

argued elsewhere, thematizes this transformation (see Rutherford 2003:ch.5). It describes startling moments of recognition and the "leap of faith" required to sacrifice old obligations on behalf of the new. But the Biak narrative results in a productive sort of failure. Manarmakeri leaves New Guinea after Biaks reject his offer of prosperity and eternal life, because these changes would have eliminated the conditions underlying Biaks' pursuit of prestige. Through Koreri, Biaks acknowledged a force that they had obscured by making the church and state into sites to raid. Refracted through a myth that deified the most degraded of characters, Biaks caught a glimpse of themselves as these institutions' official ideologies defined them: as ignorant and sinful, yet subject to salvation. But this acknowledgement could only occur at a millennial moment, spelling the end of the (colonial) world.

Koreri thus offered an account of biblical "truth" that laid bare an imperative embedded in the prewar mission and colonial government. The movement marked the limits of an approach to these institutions that made their "foreignness" into a source of value and prestige. Not surprisingly, Koreri left a lasting mark, not only within Biak society, but on the organizations established in its aftermath. With the Indonesian revolution raging in distant Java and Sumatra, postwar officials banned all "paraphernalia" associated with the movement and once again prohibited the performance of *wor* (see Galis 1946). These measures contributed to the success of Dutch efforts to retain western New Guinea as a separate colony after the Netherlands transferred sovereignty over the rest of the Indies to Indonesia in 1949. Indonesia disputed the Netherlands' claim that the "Melanesian" Papuans should eventually form a separate nation-state. A new understanding of Koreri soon emerged among Dutch officials, who cited the movement as evidence that the Papuans had an innate aversion to Indonesians – and not Dutch colonial rule.[11]

In August 1962, when the Netherlands submitted to US pressure and agreed to a settlement that entailed western New Guinea's transfer to the United Nations, then Indonesian control, this new reading of Koreri came to the fore. As part of the arrangement, Indonesia was to hold a consultation in which the Papuans would be given a chance to choose between independence and integration into the Republic. It quickly became clear that the Indonesian authorities were not going to risk the so-called "Act of Free Choice" yielding anything but one result (see Saltford 2000). Some of the Papuan nationalist leaders from Biak who emerged during this period of violence and repression presented Koreri as part of an age-old tradition of Papuan resistance (see, e.g., Sharp with Kaisiëpo 1994). But this vision of Koreri was not universally shared among Biak leaders, as I learned in a conversation with Seth Rumkorem, a Biak who long served as commander of an armed wing of the Free Papua Organization (Organisasi Papua Merdeka, or OPM).[12] Koreri was a "false religion" (Indonesian, *agama palsu*) that could only lead to death – as, indeed, it had, on a mass scale, when the Japanese military finally wiped out the movement. Rumkorem had spent much of his time in the forest fighting similar "false religions," movements led by people loosely affiliated with the guerrillas who suddenly became convinced that they themselves had become the embodiment of a divinely liberating force.[13] Rumkorem had little patience for such nonsense – nor for fellow exiles who have talked of reviving Koreri as part of the official culture of Papuan nationalism. Rumkorem's opposition to Koreri is not surprising, given his personal background; his father was one of the Biak teachers that the crowds attacked.

Clearly, when Papuan nationalists tap the power of the province's Christian institutions, they are doing so in a different fashion than their millennial predecessors and competitors. But rather than following Rumkorem in distinguishing "true" and "false" religions, we need to pay heed to the range of interpretive strategies that can coexist within a particular social field. The fact that both the Koreri prophets of 1939–42 and Seth Rumkorem have mobilized the term "religion" (Indonesian/Malay, *agama*), indicates that they all, in some fashion, have sought to tap this official category as a source of legitimacy (cf. Giay 1986, 1995a, 1995b, Giay and Godschalk 1993, Timmer 2001). Today's elite Papuan nationalists have faith that someday Jesus will free the Papuans. But, unlike the prophets, few have dared declaring how and when this will occur.

Something like the millennial "truth" of Koreri may well provide the horizon toward which contemporary nationalist performances gesture. In the second half of this chapter, I explore this possibility by examining the more recent history of Christian institutions in western New Guinea. I focus on the *Gereja Kristen Injili*, or GKI, heir to the Protestant mission whose authority Koreri leaders sought to supersede.

Papuan Nationalism and the Power of Prayer

In a 1973 study of the GKI, Ukur and Cooley (1977:27–9) point out that the Koreri uprising of 1939–42 is in part to be thanked for the speed with which the native Church gained autonomy during the 1950s. The Koreri movement traumatized the Protestant missionaries, who saw how quickly the local schools and congregations they had created could crumble. Before World War II, the missionaries failed to delegate any of their responsibility for performing Christian sacraments. When the Japanese military rounded up the European missionaries and sent them to distant camps, no one was on hand to baptize infants and serve communion or, even more importantly, to determine who would be allowed access to these rites. The Protestant mission's response to Koreri's call for a reversal of colonial hierarchies was to attenuate prior relations of inequality. As a result, growing numbers of Papuans did become *amber*, albeit without a radical transformation of the colonial conditions under which they lived.[14]

These changes entailed the expansion of opportunities for participation in Protestant institutions on all levels.[15] In 1918, the Utrecht Mission Society funded a school to train Papuan evangelists and teachers at the mission headquarters at Doreh Bay. In 1925, the mission moved the school to Miei, at the base of the Bird's Head, where it remained in operation until the 1950s under the guidance of Isak Semuel Kijne, a missionary from the Nederlandse Hervormde Kerk, which took over the New Guinea field after World War II. When Jan P. K. van Eechoud, the first Resident of Netherlands New Guinea after the war, began the task of cultivating a small corps of Papuan colonial officers, he recruited the school's best students (Derix 1987:133–56). Eventually, the school for teachers faced competition from the new educational opportunities offered by the colonial government and the Catholic Church.[16] But Protestant institutions still provided a privileged avenue to social advancement. The Protestant mission began ordaining Papuan ministers in 1952, beginning with a handful of experienced teachers and evangelists, then turning to graduates from a school of theology founded in 1954 (see Ukur and Cooley 1977:29–30). Although Ambonese and Sangirese church workers remained prevalent, Papuan pastors began to appear in greater numbers.[17] Among these early pastors was a Biak named William Rumainum, who became the first chairman of the GKI.[18]

At the same time, on a local level, the church created new possibilities for involvement. Before the war, mission evangelists and teachers exercised a great deal of control over the Papuan congregations. The congregations in turn were divided into resorts, each overseen by a European missionary, who answered to the chairman of the mission convention, the most senior Dutch pastor on hand. In 1956, when the GKI gained autonomy, this form of governance gave way to a Presbyterian system, in which a board of elders and male and female deacons governed the congregation (ibid.: 45–6, 53–72). Elders shouldered a range of responsibilities, from visiting the sick to leading Sunday services to enforcing policies laid down at higher levels of church organization. Local congregations elected their elders, who chose representatives to make up the parish governing body, which in turn sent representatives to the synod council, which met once every three years.[19]

Yet even if the mission satisfied, however partially, desires associated with Koreri, the missionaries who implemented these measures did so in the hope that the new order would undermine some of the presuppositions on which the movement rested. At the same time the church's Dutch advisors introduced new avenues to authority for Papuan villagers, they sought to deny that authority was primarily at stake. A booklet written by the mission anthropologist, F. C. Kamma, author of a seminal study on Koreri, reflects this contradiction. "Eldership is a form of service," as Kamma (n.d.:3) puts it at the beginning of the text, which contains frequent references to the Bible. "To serve means: to help, to provide everything that people need. Thus although eldership must also be called: a **position** or even often a **rank**, its meaning is **not** to command people, to seek or demand to be served, but rather just the contrary" (ibid.). Despite the fact that a congregation selected its own elders, these servants should always remember that their true source of authority lay elsewhere. "Elders are appointed by Jesus Christ through the intercession of the Congregation. Because of this, the choice is prayed for, so that Christ will use the Congregation to designate His servants. In this way, elders become the instruments of Christ. Christ governs the Evangelical Christian Church (GKI) by way of these office holders" (ibid.:6).

A similar publication for deacons makes much of the example provided by Christ, who served his disciples food – and even washed their feet – behavior that the booklet insists was utterly degrading at the time (see Teutscher 1961:1). In Biak, and perhaps else-

where, this effort to control the meaning of Christian "service" may well have had ironic effects. The very effort to limit the church officers' authority may well have provided a means of enhancing it, through proximity to Jesus, the ultimate "foreign" power. A similar possibility lies in the booklet's advice on conducting home visits, which are presented as occasions to comfort the suffering and reprimand sinners. The elder should bring along a list of suitable bible verses to read to the household, rather than speaking in his own words (see Kamma n.d.:52–5). As I have noted, such a displacement was key to the strategies of New Order-era Biak leaders, who sought to be recognized as purveyors of "foreign" words. Perhaps in response to this possibility, Kamma insists that the elder should neither present himself as a "spiritual policeman" (Malay, *polisi rohani*) nor as a "Christian magician" (Malay, *tukang hobatan kristen*), who in a heathen (Malay *kafir*) fashion presents himself as holding the monopoly on a community's religious resources; rather, every father should lead his family in prayer (ibid.:49–50). Again, this advice opens the way to its own subversion. The very move that would have the institution's authority penetrate ever more deeply allowed for the dispersal of spiritual skills.[20] The "democratization" of Protestant rituals also carried with it the danger that entrepreneurs could emerge outside the institutional boundaries of the church.[21]

A further set of productive contradictions comes into focus if one considers the ways in which Christian institutions responded to a changing political context during the period of post-war Dutch, then Indonesian, rule. During the same year that the GKI was founded, the Nederlandse Hervormde Kerk issued a Call to Reflection on the New Guinea question (see Generale Synode der Nederlandse Hervormde Kerk 1956; also Henderson 1973:84–5). The statement urged Dutch Protestants to carefully scrutinize the motivations behind the Dutch decision to retain western New Guinea, which, rather than serving a greater good – the

Papuans' right to self-determination – could be read as an effort to preserve Dutch national pride. But aside from the higher purposes that a negotiated settlement with Indonesia would serve, the Call appealed to more practical imperatives. The implications of the dispute for the Dutch Church's operations in Indonesia were potentially devastating. For Dutch missionaries working in New Guinea and their Papuan flock, the event revealed the risks that went along with the benefits of belonging to an organization that could channel resources from afar.[22]

In the aftermath of western New Guinea's transfer to Indonesia, the GKI's close relationship with the Indonesian Council of Churches (Indonesian, *Dewan Gereja Indonesia*), which was a legacy of the episode, helped the Church survive in tumultuous times (see Ukur and Cooley 1977:210, 295). Many Papuans in the colonial administration lost their jobs in the 1960s, when scores of Indonesia officials flocked to the new province of West Irian.[23] In contrast, the departure of Dutch missionaries vacated positions in the GKI hierarchy that were filled by the "Irianese," as the Papuans were now called. Similar pressures on the Catholic Church did not yield the same windfall for the indigenous faithful. European priests, many of whom became Indonesian citizens, were more willing to weather the change in administration than European pastors. Given the strict standards imposed for ordination, there were very few Papuan priests qualified to staff the dioceses, so the Europeans who did leave ceded their posts to Javanese and Eastern Indonesian colleagues (see Hadisumarta 2001). Under Indonesian rule, the relatively stronger European presence in the Catholic Church – and its relatively more formalized links to the outside world – provided Catholic leaders with more leeway to criticize the government. But both the GKI and the Catholic Church moved within a space of possibility that depended on their playing the role of mediator between the government and the population, rather than acting as the champion of either. Both insti-

tutions pursued this role not simply in the name of "peace," but because their institutional survival was at stake.

Official Indonesian state ideology played a key role in setting the rules of the game. In an effort to stem the growth of pro-Indonesian sentiment, Dutch propagandists had warned the Papuans that if Indonesia gained control of western New Guinea, the Indonesian government would force its inhabitants to convert to Islam, Indonesia's majority religion (see Ukur and Cooley 1977:285). In fact, a generalized "belief in God," rather than Islam per se, was and remains the first pillar of Indonesia's official state ideology, Pancasila, which was introduced by Indonesia's first president, Sukarno, and revised by Suharto, the general who replaced him in 1966 after an aborted "communist" coup and military-led massacres that cost close to a million Indonesians their lives (see Kipp 1996:107–8). Several months before the coup, an Indonesian brigadier-general explained to religious leaders from West Irian that "to pray for God's help and blessings for the good of mankind and the prosperity of the State is the essence of the Indonesian personality in everything they [sic] do."[24] Under Suharto's so-called "New Order" regime, "belief in God" was more than a description of the Indonesian national character – it was prescribed. All Indonesian citizens had to list an approved world religion on their identity cards, or risk being labeled communists. The central government's promotion of *agama*, that Indonesian term for institutionalized religion, served the regime's purposes (see Kipp 1996). Religious-based identities tempered the grip of those associated with ethnicity or residence suppressed allegiances based on class.

As a result, in Irian Jaya, as western New Guinea was once again renamed in 1973, Christianity provided a safe refuge for indigenous leaders and provided a passage into national networks through which New Order patronage freely flowed. Many members of the Papuan elite now participating in the movement have ties to Christian institutions: they include church officials, the rectors of schools of theology, graduates from Christian universities, and staff members from church-backed NGOs (see Rutherford 2001b:195–200; also Mote and Rutherford 2001). Since colonial times, Indonesian Christians have claimed more than their share of positions in the national elite by virtue of the opportunities for social mobility and alliance building offered by participation in church-based institutions.[25] Under the New Order, these pathways led in just one direction: to the center, where the regime used its control over export earnings, foreign investment, and military power to harness religiously based *aliran*, or "currents." Indonesians came to view the center as holding a monopoly on the sources of their life chances and status as legitimate social actors (see Pemberton 1994, Siegel 1997, 1998). But Irianese participation in the Catholic and Protestant "currents" seems not to have resulted in this level of subjugation. The churches in Irian Jaya operated in a different political environment from that found in other parts of Indonesia. Elsewhere, the lingering threat was "communism"; in Irian Jaya, the specter of Papuan separatism haunted the Indonesian nation-state.

The GKI came to occupy a particularly fraught position between the administrative and military apparatus and an often rebellious indigenous population. Intelligence officers attended church services during the 1960s to monitor the messages presented from the pulpit.[26] The authorities expelled some foreign pastors, including a German Lutheran, who reportedly gave a sermon in which he touched on the question of whether West Irian might in fact be God's chosen land. The government soon found uses for indigenous pastors, who risked being imprisoned, tortured, or worse, if they spoke out of turn. Early on during the Indonesian period, the Church distributed letters to local congregations, reminding the members of their duties "as Christians and citizens of the Indonesian Republic" (see Ukur and Cooley 1977:295). On the eve of the Act of

Free Choice, the GKI played an active role in promoting the Indonesian position. Many pastors served on the Consultative Councils that took part in the heavily manipulated event. One of the speakers at the GKI's Fifth Synod Convention called on the delegates to rise above any "personal disappointment" and place their trust in Jesus. After all, "Jesus already endured a choice that was free: to be crucified at Golgotha. Christ is the implementer of the *act of free choice*: for the salvation of people with faith" (ibid., emphasized words are in English).[27]

In a similar spirit, the GKI participated in military operations in which church officials distributed leaflets urging those who had joined the OPM to return to their communities and families (ibid.:289–90). But on occasion, the Church's authority was directed against the Indonesian military as well, as when one pastor saved some four hundred captured "rebels" from execution by begging for forgiveness, then kneeling to pray in front of the commanders and their troops (ibid.:290).[28] In addition to Protestant rituals, the GKI itself sometimes appeared to be up for grabs. This point was brought home to me when Seth Rumkorem, the OPM leader mentioned above, turned from "false religions" to speak of his own view of the place of faith in the struggle.[29] In the forest, he told me, the guerrillas always held Sunday services, divided according to denomination.[30] In the mid-1970s, Rumkorem went so far as to send a letter to the chairman of the GKI, urging him to send an official delegation to confer with the armed separatists. The pastors and the guerrillas would pray together, and if God indicated that the Papuan nationalist cause was just, then the GKI would agree to support the struggle openly; if not, the OPM would give up the fight.[31] New Order ideologies and imperatives clearly could not fully define Christian institutions in the eyes of the province's inhabitants; the churches' power still remained, in some sense, at large.

Perhaps for this reason, the post-Suharto period in Papua has yet to see the religious

violence that has plagued other parts of Indonesia. Elsewhere, the sudden collapse of
the institutional networks that connected
local communities and the national center
has given rise to intense anxieties about identity. A key theme in nationalist literature is
the fear that one could be a traitor to the
nation without knowing it (see Siegel 1997).
Under the New Order, one was either recognized as a proper Indonesian, or one stood
with the forces of disorder and death. These
anxieties arguably account for the ferocity of
conflicts in places like Ambon and Poso,
where, under conditions of democratization,
being Muslim or Christian entails membership in potentially threatened political "currents" (see Sidel 2003, van Klinken 2001).
But in Papua, the possibility of seeing something unexpected in oneself is not unwel-
come: Papuanness is what has suddenly
come (back) to light.

This moment of recognition has resulted
not in the suppression or replacement of
existing institutions. Instead of founding a
new religion, the current movement's leaders
have recontextualized the old, turning the
churches and practices associated with them
into a source of legitimacy for a new national
order. FORERI, the Forum for the Reconciliation of the People of Irian Jaya, was
founded at the instigation of the churches to
open a dialogue between provincial leaders
and the central government following a series
of flag raisings that ended with the death of
demonstrators in July, 1998. In February,
1999 a Team of 100 representatives met
with then President Habibie, whom they
startled by announcing that the province's
population wanted to secede. Reportedly,
the delegates' main activity in Jakarta was
prayer, including at a service led by a famous
Indonesian evangelist (Mote and Rutherford
2001:126). Upon their return to the province,
the delegates "socialized" – that is, broad-
casted and explained – their message by
urging their constituents to pray for the non-
violent movement's success. Theys Eluay, a
charismatic Sentani chief who participated
in the Act of Free Choice, assumed the role

of "Great Leader" at a birthday celebration
in November, 1999, which no doubt included
prayers to his good health. The period of
relative openness that followed culminated
in June, 2000 in the Second Papuan National
Congress in Jayapura, which was attended by
thousands of participants from throughout
the province and beyond (see King 2002,
van den Broek and Szalay 2001:89–90).[32]
Prayer was in abundance at this event, with
representatives of each of the provinces' religions and denominations opening each day's
session by leading a brief devotion. The secretary of the Presidium, the executive branch
confirmed during the Papuan congress, is a
Papuan Muslim, whom, I have been told,
prays for West Papua's liberation, along
with everyone else.[33]

I have heard rumors of strange occurrences
associated with the contemporary Papuan
nationalist movement. A group of Papuans
near Wasior, where an attack on a military-
controlled logging concern led to harsh re-
prisals and many civilian deaths, supposedly
found the "original" Bible in a cave.[34] But the
movement's institutionally sanctioned invo-
cations of Christianity are worth scrutiny as
well. Those who organized the Congress
seemingly followed the lead of Indonesian
ideology in deploying a generalized notion
of religion as one of the "pillars" established
to represent the new nation's bases of support
(see King 2002:101) But at the same time,
like the Koreri prophets, they gave new
meaning to Christian practices and texts. As
one consultant told me, "All the people pray
for independence, the Presidium, everyone.
They also hope and depend on God. They
always pray for this. They have the hope,
the faith, that someday it will arrive. Faith
that what they are struggling for is right, and
because it is right, God is on their side."[35]
Speaking in English and Indonesian, he concluded by calling this faith a "force within
the heart of every Papuan" that "military
weapons" would never "kill." Papuan nationalist prayer evokes the checkered history
of Christian institutions in the province. But
in doing so, like Koreri's millennial rituals, it

gestures towards the moment when God's true intentions will be revealed.

Conclusion: The Politics of Transcendence

And so we return to the churchyard in Timika. I am not an expert on the Amungme, the highland tribe most affected by the enormous gold and copper mine operated by US-owned Freeport Indonesia not far from this town. But other observers have suggested factors one might consider in order to make sense of this scene. Chris Ballard (2002) has described the "signature of terror" inscribed on the Amungme landscape, which has been the site of torture, killings, and disappearances by the Indonesian military, which provides security for the mine. Village-based troops have painted murals featuring divisional names and insignia over nature scenes and portraits of "traditional" warriors, as well as more grisly images, such as a bleeding skull wearing a special forces beret. The murals in the churchyard, including the one labeled "West Papua Army," arguably offer what Ballard calls a "counter-iconography" to these military images. Obliquely recalling the Indonesian state's deathly violence, the churchyard paintings conjure transcendent forces: those embodied in the Gospel and the international community, which many hope will intervene to set West Papua free.

One could place this vision in the context of the millennial traditions that anthropologists have documented among the Amungme (Widjojo 2002). Amungme narratives describe the quest for *Hai*, the land of peace and plenty, which involves an arduous journey and a series of trials and temptations endured with the help of a "foreign" dwarf. But one would need to pay heed to the relationship between these narratives and a particular history of engagement with church and state. Akiguma, the lowland Amungme community that has produced some of the province's most respected leaders, was created in 1959 at the initiative of Dutch

missionaries and officials, who, following decades of sporadic contact, relocated highland Papuans to bring them within reach of schools, development projects, and the law (see Widjojo 2002). The most famous of these leaders is undoubtedly Tom Beanal, the Catholic lay priest turned environmental advocate, customary chief, and, most recently, Freeport commissioner, who is the vice-chair of the Papuan Presidium. Although not as well educated as Tom, Yosepha Alomang, the Amungme activist who organized the churchyard protest, has traveled the same organizational paths. Yosepha came to prominence as the leader of a women's prayer group-cum-cooperative, founded with the support and encouragement of a series of Catholic priests (see Giay and Kambai 2003).[36] She participated with Tom in the compilation of a highly publicized human rights report documenting military abuses around Timika (including Yosepha's own imprisonment and torture), which was released in 1995 under the name of the province's Catholic bishop (see Ballard 1997). She has received international acclaim for her activism, including the 2001 Goldman Environmental prize.[37] At the same time as the protestors' "counter-iconography" recalled military violence and millennial dreams, it also arguably pointed to the "conveyor belt" to social standing and influence provided by the Catholic Church (see Sidel 2003). When Tom discussed the demonstration with me, he criticized Yosepha's "cargo cult-like beliefs."[38] But these leaders are fighting over shared terrain. In Timika, as elsewhere in Papua, a particular orientation to Christian institutions has made them a resource in struggles for status and prestige.

In this chapter, I have dwelt upon the conditions that have enabled Papuan leaders to turn Christian texts and rituals toward their own ends. These conditions include the materiality of institutions – their dependence on concrete acts and objects – and their embeddedness in wider social and political fields. In paying heed to these aspects of institutions in a context that has brought them to the fore,

I have sought to illuminate how institutional power can be appropriated. But my materials at the same time shed light on some of the ways in which institutional power is produced. The traffic in authority between official institutions and unofficial practices runs in both directions, as Steve Caton (n.d.) suggests.[39] By turning Christian prayer into a separatist weapon, today's Papuan nationalists have reinforced the churches' authority, even as they have run foul of these organizations' officially neutral stance. In the same fashion, Indonesian leaders have created a resource for Papuan separatists through their own deployment of Christian practices and texts. Even the practices of Koreri prophets, who radically rejected the mission's legitimacy, had a constitutive effect on the province's religious institutions. As I have suggested, coercive organizations owe their authority – and their very existence – to such concrete practices and evocations. Institution, after all, is a word with two meanings: an instituted order and the instituting processes through which such an order, however provisionally, comes into force (see Weber 2001).

The interpretive practices described in this chapter have played a critical role in shaping Papua's religious institutions as sites of contestation. Human rights workers who have visited OPM groups still at large in the province report that their commanders now spend much more time preaching than planning attacks.[40] Against these guerrillas-turned-pastors, the Indonesian authorities are currently deploying their own version of Christian truth. A crackdown against separatists is underway in Indonesia, where a massive military campaign is being waged in another restive province, Aceh. On Biak, Papuan separatists have been given three months to turn in their weapons and insignia, or else face the full force of the law.[41] The Indonesian police are "socializing" the call for surrender by way of the island's Protestant congregations. The letter inaugurating the operation ends with three bible verses: Matthew 5:9, Hebrews 12:14, and Psalms 34:15.[42]

With the US-led "war on terror" reshaping global realities, the future looks grim for the current generation of Papuan nationalists. This is not to say that, when it comes to the true meaning of the Bible, the Indonesian authorities are sure to have the final word. I hope I have made one thing clear. Institutional power both shapes and is subject to interpretive practices. This is why, some fifty years after Koreri, the forces capable of making West Papua a reality still go by the name of the Lord.

NOTES

1   Asad shows how the medieval church set the boundaries of proper worship through "authorizing discourses" that at the same time represented the clergy's measures as "instruments of God" (1993: 35). Compare Rappaport (1999) and Leach (1983).

2   Much as linguistic ideologies present a partial image of the "multi-functional nature of linguistic communication," ideologies of institutionality present a partial view of the social, technological, and material preconditions and effects of actions undertaken in the name of church and state. See Kroskrity (2000), Woolard and Schieffelin (1994); also Silverstein (1976).

3   This orientation to translation would be at odds with that classically associated with the Protestant vision of the Word as a bearer of a universally transmissible meaning. See Rutherford (n.d., 2003: 250 n.16).

4   The following account draws on Rutherford (2003:ch.6 and 2005).

5   Interview, Seth Rumkorem, Wageningen, October 14, 2002.

6   The following account is drawn from Kamma (1972) and Rutherford (2003: ch.6).

7   See Rutherford (1996, 2003:3). *Wor* composers invent songs instantly and automatically after they experience

something startling or striking. Their lyrics take the form of almost identical couplets. The second couplet fills in words that are omitted in the first: place-names, personal names, and nouns that specify the meaning and origin of the song.

8   The man's relatives reported that he had received in a colonial prison from Indonesia's first president, Sukarno, who was then a famous nationalist.

9   The Papuan teacher answered, "Only the Lord God made the heavens and earth." The crowd beat the man until he thought he was dead. When he awoke and saw that he was still alive, he answered "with my lips (Malay, dengan bibir mulut) that I was willing to follow their religion." As soon as he said this, they let him go. See Mooiy (n.d.).

10 See Rutherford (2005). Kierkegaard insists upon the paradox embedded in Christianity's proposition that "the individual's eternal happiness is decided in time through a relation to something historical that furthermore is historical in such a way that its composition includes that which according to its nature cannot become historical and consequently must become that by virtue of the absurd" ([1846] 1992:385). By contrast, the Biak response to Christianity outlined here and in Rutherford (2003: ch.5) does not presume the sheer division between the temporal and the eternal on which this paradox turns. Koreri and the narratives associated with it in large part account for how Biak's God has remained a divinity whose power is "of this world."

11 De Bruyn (1948:22) refers to Koreri as an expression of "self-conscious Papuan nationalism." See also van Baal (1989, vol. 2:167).

12 Interview, Wageningen, October 14, 2002.

13 Rumkorem is a member of the Calvinist Gereformeerde Kerk in the Netherlands, where he lives in exile. He recounted his troubles with a group of Catholic villagers who staged a crucifixion, promising that the victim would rise in three days, at which time Papua would be free. He told me of other villagers who tried to recruit the guerrillas to submit to a scheme in which they would lay down their arms, pray, and sound a trumpet outside the provincial capital, Jayapura, which, like Jericho, would fall. Rumkorem was sometimes inclined to trace these disturbances, if not to Satan, then to the Indonesian special forces, who sought to discredit the OPM internationally by portraying it as a cult.

14 Biaks first used the term, amber, to refer to themselves in the early 1960s, I was told; at first it was a joke. Zachi Sawor remembered the names of the two Biak students who started the habit, jokingly calling out, "Hey amberie!" (interview, Wageningen, October 11, 2002). But this practice, of calling elite members of one's group by the name used for non-Papuan Indonesians and other foreigners, may be prevalent elsewhere in the province. See, e.g., Giay (1995a).

15 See Kamma (1977), Ukur and Cooley (1977).

16 The Catholic Church established a mission in the south at Merauke in 1905, then expanded into the mostly Protestant north in the late 1930s, when territorial restrictions on evangelization were lifted. See Hadisumarta (2001), Mewengkang (2001). Members of several different religious orders proselytized in New Guinea, including the Jesuits, the Augustinians, and the Franciscans. The province is now divided into four dioceses, with bishops based in Jayapura, Sorong, Merauke, and Agats.

17 Scores of Christians from Ambon, in particular, flooded into Netherlands New Guinea after the Indonesian Republic crushed a separatist rebellion in the southern Moluccas.

18 Rumainum was the descendant of a Papuan evangelist of Petrus Kafiar's generation, also trained in Depok.

19 Henderson (1973:90) notes that the Protestant church was the first institution in the colony to entrust the average Papuan "with the promotion of his [sic] own interests via a democratic system."

20 The long-term effects of these policies were evident on Biak in the early 1990s, when lay people regularly mounted the pulpit to deliver sermons, and everyone, myself included, was expected to be able to lead a prayer. See Rutherford (2003:125–6).

21 There is evidence for the lasting effects of these policies. The early 1990s saw the emergence of vaguely millennial "prayer groups" on Biak, which attracted the suspicion of church officials and the military (ibid.:129). My initial research suggests that lay participation is equally important in the functioning of Catholic institutions in the province, despite the very different model of mediation and authority Roman Catholicism is generally understood to promote. See Hadisumarta (2001).

22 Although Catholic leaders in Java supposedly engaged in a similar lobbying effort, their initiative was much less open. Interview with Nicolaas Jouwe, Leiden, October 17, 2002.

23 West Irian was a relatively attractive posting for Indonesian officials, given the economic crisis then underway in the rest of the Republic.

24 Sutjipto (1965:10). Sutjipto gave this address during an "Orientation Week on the Aims and Means of the Indonesian Revolution."

25 Some analysts have gone so far as to argue that the rise of reformist Islam in the 1990s represented an attempt on the part of elite Muslims to compete with elite Christians on the same terrain. See Sidel (2003); also Schrauwers (2000:14). An example is the founding of ICMI (Ikatan Cendiakawan Muslim Indonesia, Indonesian Muslim Intellectuals Network) in the early 1990s. This initiative was originally supported by Suharto, who used the group to offset rival factions within political and military circles. ICMI's chair was B. J. Habibie, Suharto's vice-president and longtime protégé, who assumed office after his mentor resigned.

26 Some Papuans left the GKI as a result of the incident, joining the growing ranks of Papuan evangelicals or converting to Catholicism (interview with Nicolas Jouwe, Leiden, October 17, 2002).

27 Tjakraatmadja also warned the delegates not to let anyone "turn the Act of Free Choice into a determination of the future made on the basis of personal disappointment uninformed by just consideration, revenge, tribal or ethnic hatred."

28 For GKI members, this story would recall the tale of Ottow and Geissler's arrival in New Guinea, which has the Germans dropping to their knees to thank the Lord and ask for his help. See Kamma (1976).

29 Interview, Wageningen, October 14, 2002.

30 Whether they were Catholic, Protestant, Seventh Day Adventists, or Pentecostals, all the freedom fighters worshiped God in their own (institutionally) sanctioned ways.

31 If God was not behind them, why should they risk their lives? Seth pointed out. This proposal calls to mind one of the demands made by today's Papuan leaders. In official statements, they have called on members of the Indonesian central government to sit down with them to consult, not God, but the historical record, with the understanding that if history shows that the Papuans are really Indonesians, the separatists will give up their struggle. See Mote and Rutherford (2001:128).

32 The event's emotional climax was the raising of the Morning Star flag and the singing of the national anthem, "Hai Papua Tanahku." Introduced in 1961 by a colonial advisory body, the New Guinea Council, set up in a last-ditch effort to accelerate the territory's progress towards self-rule, the flag features a design supposedly inspired by the

Christian triad of virtues, faith, hope, and love, with the single star representing hope.

32 For its part, the national anthem, a song composed by Kijne during the 1930s, begins with a pledge of loyalty and ends with a prayer (Nicolaas Jouwe, Interview, Leiden, October 17, 2002).

33 Interview, Washington, DC, October 3, 2002.

34 Interview with Seth Rumkorem, Wageningen, October 14, 2002.

35 Interview, Washington, DC, October 3, 2002. A non-Papuan pastor who advocates on behalf of the Papuan cause described trying to convince the Papuans that it would take more than prayer to win their liberation. God had already granted them their rights; now they had to struggle to realize them. (Interview, Jakarta, June 6, 2003.)

36 In this capacity, she spoke out boldly against Freeport's policy of importing food, rather than supporting local producers, the company's failure adequately to compensate local landowners, and the damage the company has done to the local environment.

37 See "Papuan Housewife Tells Sufferings of Her People," Kyodo News, June 14, 2000. See also Press Release, April 23, 2001, Goldman Environmental Prize, www.goldmanprize.org.

38 Interview, New York, December 11, 2002. "She wants, she's trying to bring the people to M [DR: merdeka or freedom], but she herself cannot do it, so she has to mix it up with matters that are, what, beyond her capabilities. Supernatural. Then only can she succeed."

39 Caton (n.d.) argues that institutions and the traditions they promulgate depend for their authority on what Volosinov called "behavioral ideology": their tacit invocation in practices that are always "dialogic" to the degree that they consist of a range of contending "voicings," that is, socially locatable points of view.

40 Papua's premier human rights organization, ELSHAM, has led a campaign to transform Papua into a zone of peace.

As part of this campaign, human rights workers have visited some of the OPM commanders still at large in the province's dense forests. To their surprise, these commanders responded enthusiastically to the human rights workers' call to lay down their weapons. Many no longer behave as military commanders, but rather as the leaders of religious communities whose main function is to pray for Papua's salvation. (Personal communication, John Rumbiak.)

41 In fact, Koru Konsup, the aging OPM fighter who recently resurfaced to found a pro-independence community in West Biak, has no weapons. The community's main activities are marching and prayer.

42 See "Semua Warga Biak yang Terlibat Separatis OPM Diancam Menyerah Sebelum Batas waktu yang Ditetapkan Berakhir," Elsham News Report, 28 Juli 2003. The verses are, "Blessed are the peacemakers, for they shall be called sons of God," "Strive for peace with all men, and for the holiness without which no one will see the Lord," and "The eyes of the Lord are toward the righteous, and his ears toward their cry."

REFERENCES

Anderson, Benedict
    1991 Imagined Communities: Reflections on the Origin and Spread of Nationalism. London and New York: Verso.

Aragon, Lorraine V.
    2000 Fields of the Lord: Animism, Christian Minorities, and State Development in Indonesia. Honolulu: University of Hawai'i Press.

Asad, Talal
    1993 Genealogies of Religion: Discipline and Reasons of Power in Christianity and Islam. Baltimore, MD: Johns Hopkins University Press.

Ballard, Chris
    1997 Irian Jaya. The Contemporary Pacific 9(2):468–474.

Ballard, Chris
2002   The Signature of Terror: Violence, Memory, and Landscape at Freeport. *In* Inscribed Landscapes: Marking and Making Place. Bruno David and Meredith Wilson, eds. Pp. 13–26. Honolulu: University of Hawai'i Press.

Bauman, Richard
1983   Let Your Words Be Few: Symbolism of Speaking and Silence among Seventeenth Century Quakers. Cambridge: Cambridge University Press.

Bowen, John R.
1993   Muslims through Discourse. Princeton: Princeton University Press.

Cannell, Fenella
1999   Power and Intimacy in the Christian Philippines. Cambridge: Cambridge University Press.

Caton, Steven C.
n.d.   What is an "Authorizing Discourse"? Unpublished manuscript.

Collins, James
1996   Socialization to Text: Structure and Contradiction in Schooled Literacy. *In* Natural Histories of Discourse. Michael Silverstein and Greg Urban, eds. Pp. 203–228. Chicago: University of Chicago Press.

Comaroff, John L., and Jean Comaroff
1991   Of Revelation and Revolution. Volume 1: Christianity and Consciousness in South Africa. Chicago: University of Chicago Press.

de Bruyn, Jan Victor
1948   Jaarverslagen 1947 en 1948 van Onderafdeling Biak. Nummer Toegang 10-25, Stuk 188. Nienhuis Collectie van de Department van Bevolkingszaken Hollandia Rapportenarchief. The Hague: Algemeene Rijksarchief.

Derix, Jan
1987   Bapa Papoea; Jan P. K. van Eechoud, Een Biografie. Venlo: Van Spijk.

Derrida, Jacques
1995   The Gift of Death. David Wills, trans. Chicago and London: University of Chicago Press.

Feuilletau de Bruyn, W. K. H.
1916   Militaire Memorie der Schouten-eilanden, 31 August, Nummer Toegang 10-25, Stuk 183. Nienhuis Collectie van de Department van Bevolkszaken Hollandia Rapportenarchief. The Hague: Algemeene Rijksarchief.

Foucault, Michel
[1975] 1979   Discipline and Punish: The Birth of the Prison. Alan Sheridan, trans. London: Penguin.

Galis, K.W.
1946   Dagboek over April 1946. Nummer Toegang 10-25, Stuk 179. Nienhuis Collectie van de Department van Bevolkingszaken Hollandia Rapportenarchief. The Hague: Algemeene Rijksarchief.

Geertz, Clifford
1973   Religion as a Cultural System. *In* The Interpretation of Cultures. Pp. 87–125. New York: Basic Books.

Generale Synode der Nederlandse Hervormde Kerk
1956   Oproep van de Generale Synode der Nederlandse Hervormde Kerk tot bezinning op de verantwoordelijkheid van het Nederlandse volk inzake de vraagstukken rondom Nieuw-Guinea. No. 825.35/3690. June 27. The Hague.

Giay, Benny
1986   Kargoisme di Irian Jaya. Sentani, Irian Jaya, Indonesia: Region Press.
—— 1995a   Zakheus Pakage and His Communities: Indigenous Religious Discourse, Socio-political Resistance, and Ethnohistory of the Me of Irian Jaya. Amersterdam: VU University Press.
——1995b   The Conversion of Weakebo: A Big Man of the Me. Journal of Pacific History 34(2):181–190.

Giay, Benny and Jan A. Godschalk
1993   Cargoism in Irian Jaya Today. Oceania 63:330–344.

Giay, Benny and Yafet Kambai
2003   Yosepha Alomang: Pergulatan Seorang Perempuan Papua Melawan Penindasan. Jayapura: Elsham Papua.

Hadisumarta, Mgr. F. X., and O. Carm.
2001   Keuskupan Manokwari-Sorong Gerak dan Perkembangannya. *In* Bercermin pada Wajah-Wajah Keuskupan Gereja Katolik Indonesia. Dr. F. Hasto Rosariyanto, SJP. Pp. 49–75. Yogyakarta, Indonesia: Kanisius.

Hartweg, F. W.
  1926 Letter to the Board of September 23. UZV K31, D12. Oegstgeest, the Netherlands: Archives of the Hendrik Kraemer Institute.
Henderson, William
  1973 West New Guinea: The Dispute and Its Settlement. South Orange, NJ: Seton Hall University Press.
Kahin, Audrey R., ed.
  1985 Regional Dynamics of the Indonesian Revolution: Unity from Diversity. Honolulu: University of Hawai'i Press.
Kamma, F. C.
  n.d. Hollandia: Panitia Pembangunan Djemaat. Pembangunan Djemaat: Tentang Kepenatuaan
  —— 1972 Koreri: Messianic Movements in the Biak-Numfor Culture Area. The Hague: Martinus Nijhoff.
  —— 1976 Dit Wonderlijk Werk. Vol. 1. Oegstgeest: Raad voor de Zending der Nederlandse Hervormde Kerk.
  —— 1977 Dit Wonderlijk Werk. Vol. 2. Oegstgeest: Raad voor de Zending der Nederlandse Hervormde Kerk.
Keane, Webb
  1997 Signs of Recognition: Powers and Hazards of Representation in an Indonesian Society. Berkeley: University of California Press.
Kierkegaard, Søren
  [1843] 1985 Fear and Trembling. Alastair Hannay, trans. London: Penguin.
  —— [1846] 1992 Concluding Unscientific Postscript to Philosophical Fragments. Howard V. Honig and Edna H. Honig, trans. Princeton, NJ: Princeton University Press.
King, Peter
  2002 Morning Star Rising? Indonesia Raya and the New Papuan Nationalism. Indonesia 73:89–127.
Kipp, Rita Smith
  1996 Dissociated Identities: Ethnicity, Religion, and Class in an Indonesian Society. Ann Arbor: University of Michigan Press.
Kroskrity, Paul V.
  2000 Regimenting Languages: Language Ideological Perspectives. In Regimes of Language: Ideologies, Polities, Identities. Paul V. Kroskrity, ed. Pp. 1–34. Santa Fe, NM: School of American Research Press.
Lanternari, Vittorio
  1963 The Religions of the Oppressed: A Study of Modern Messianic Cults. London: McGibbon & Kee.
Leach, Edmund
  1983 Melchisedech and the Emperor: Icons of Subversion and Orthodoxy. In Structuralist Interpretation of Biblical Myth. E. Leach and D.A. Aycock, eds. Pp. 67–88. Cambridge: Cambridge University Press.
Mertz, Elizabeth
  1996 Recontextualization as Socialization: Text and Pragmatics in the Law School Classroom. In Natural Histories of Discourse. Michael Silverstein and Greg Urban, eds. Pp. 229–252. Chicago: University of Chicago Press.
Mewengkang, Jus F., MSC
  2001 Arah Dasar Keuskupan Agung Merauke. In Bercermin pada Wajah-Wajah Keuskupan Gereja Katolik Indonesia. Dr. F. Hasto Rosariyanto, SJ. Pp. 34–48. Yogyakarta, Indonesia: Kanisius.
Mooiy, D.
  n.d. Perhambatan Koreri. Files of F. C. Kamma, Hendrik Kraemer Institute, Oegstgeest, the Netherlands, unpublished manuscript.
Mote, Octovianus and Danilyn Rutherford
  2001 From Irian Jaya to Papua: The Limits of Primordialism in Indonesia's Troubled East. Indonesia 72:115–140.
Pemberton, John
  1994 On the Subject of Java. Ithaca, NY: Cornell University Press.
Picanussa, J.
  n.d. Soetoe Ibarat dari Hikajat Manseren Manarmaker (Manseren Konori). Files of F. C. Kamma, Hendrik Kraemer Institute, Oegstgeest, the Netherlands, unpublished manuscript.
Rafael, Vicente L.
  1993 [1988] Contracting Colonialism: Translation and Christian Conversion in Tagalog Society under Early Spanish Rule. Durham, NC and London: Duke University Press.

Rappaport, Roy A.
1999   Ritual and Religion in the Making of Humanity. Cambridge: Cambridge University Press.

Rutherford, Danilyn
1996   Of Birds and Gifts: Revising Tradition on an Indonesian Frontier. Cultural Anthropology 11(4):577–616.

—— 2000   The White Edge of the Margin: Textuality and Authority in Biak, Irian Jaya, Indonesia. American Ethnologist 27(2):312–339.

—— 2001a   Intimacy and Alienation: Money and the Foreign in Biak. Public Culture 13(2):299–324.

—— 2001b   Waiting for the End in Biak: Violence, Order, and a Flag Raising. In Violence and the State in Indonesia. Benedict R. O'G. Anderson, ed. Pp. 189–212. Ithaca, NY: Cornell Southeast Asia Program Publications.

—— 2003   Raiding the Land of the Foreigners: The Limits of the Nation on an Indonesian Frontier. Princeton, NJ: Princeton University Press.

—— 2005   The Bible Meets the Idol: Writing and Conversion in Biak. In The Anthropology of Christianity. Fenella Cannell, ed. Durham, NC: Duke University Press.

—— n.d.   Frontiers of the Lingua Franca Department of Anthropology, University of Chicago, unpublished manuscript.

Saltford, John
2000   United Nations Involvement with the Act of Self-Determination in West Irian (Indonesian West New Guinea) 1968–1969. Indonesia 69:71–92.

Schrauwers, Albert
2000   Colonial "Reformation" in the Highlands of Central Sulawesi, Indonesia, 1892–1995. Toronto: University of Toronto Press.

Sharp, Nonie, with Markus Wonggor Kaisiëpo
1994   The Morning Star in Papua Barat. North Carlton, Australia: Arena.

Shoaps, Robin A.
2002   "Pray Earnestly": the Textual Construction of Personal Involvement in Pentecostal Prayer and Song. Linguistic Anthropology 12(1):34–71.

Sidel, John T.
2003   Other Schools, Other Pilgrimages, Other Dreams: The Making and Unmaking of Jihad in Southeast Asia. In Southeast Asia over Three Generations: Essays Presented to Benedict R. O'G. Anderson. James T. Siegel and Audrey R. Kahin, eds. Pp. 347–382. Ithaca, NY: Cornell Southeast Asia Program Press.

Siegel, James T.
1997   Fetish, Recognition, Revolution. Princeton, NJ: Princeton University Press.

—— 1998   A New Criminal Type in Jakarta: Counter-revolution Today. Durham, NC: Duke University Press.

Silverstein, Michael
1976   Shifters, Linguistic Categories, and Cultural Description. In: Meaning in Anthropology. K. H. Basso and H. A. Selby, eds. Pp. 11–55. Albuquerque: University of New Mexico Press.

Sutjipto S. H., Brigadir Djendral TNI
1965   Irian Barat: Agama dan Revolusi Indonesia. Address given by the Sekretaris Koordinator Urusan Irian Barat/Sekretaris Umum Musjawarah Pembantu Pemimpin Revolusi/Ketua Gabungan V Komando Operasi Tertinggi at "Pekan Pengenalan Tudjuan dan Upaja Revolusi Indonesia" bagi Rochaniawan dan Rochaniawati Daerah Propinsi Irian Barat, sponsored by the Sekretariat Koordinator Urusan Irian Barat in Jakarta, June 2–10. Jakarta: Projek Penerbitan Sekretariat Koordinator Urusan Irian Barat.

Teutscher, H. J.
1961   Pembangunan Djemaat: Katechismus Ketjil tentang Kesjamasan. Unpublished manuscript.

Timmer, Jaap
2000   Living with Intricate Futures: Order and Confusion in Imyan Worlds, Irian Jaya, Indonesia. Doctoral thesis, Centre for Pacific and Asian Studies, University of Nijmegen, the Netherlands.

—— 2001   Government, Church, and Millenarian Critique in The Imyan Tradition of the Religious Papua. Antropologi Indonesia 65:40–59.

Ukur, F. and F. L. Cooley
1977 Benih Yang Tumbuh VIII: Suatu Survey Mengenai Gereja Kristen Irian Jaya. Jakarta: Lembaga Penelitian dan Studi Dewan Gerja-gereja di Indonesia/ Ende, Flores, Indonesia: Percetakan Arnoldus.

van Baal, Jan
1989 Ontglipt Verleden. 2 vols. Franeker: van Wijnen.

van den Broek, Theo, and Alexandra Szalay
2001 Raising the Morning Star. Journal of Pacific History 36:77–91.

van Klinken, Gerry
2001 The Maluku Wars: Bringing Society Back In. Indonesia 71:1–26.

Weber, Max
1946 From Max Weber: Essays in Sociology. H. H. Gerth and C. Wright Mills, eds. New York: Oxford University Press.
—— 1978 Economy and Society. Guenther Roth and Claus Wittich, eds. Berkeley: University of California Press.

Weber, Samuel
2001 Institution and Interpretation. Stanford, CA: Stanford University Press.

Widjojo, Muridan Satrio
2002 Strategi Amungme untuk Memperoleh Pengakuan di Mimika, Papua. Master's Thesis, Department of Anthropology, University of Indonesia.

Woolard, Kathryn A., and Bambi B. Schieffelin
1994 Language Ideology. Annual Review of Anthropology 23:55–82.

Worsley, Peter
1968 The Trumpet Shall Sound. New York: Schocken Books.

8

The Sarvodaya Movement's Vision of Peace and a Dharmic Civil Society

George D. Bond

Introduction

The Sarvodaya Shramadana movement began as a grassroots development movement in the 1950s in post-independence Sri Lanka and has grown to be one of the largest NGOs in Asia. In recent years, as a violent ethnic conflict has simmered and erupted in Sri Lanka, Sarvodaya has become one of the major voices for peace in the country. Since 1983, the movement has organized major peace marches and meditations. It has lobbied for peace as part of its larger campaign to bring about a Dharmic civil society that will liberate the people at grassroots level. Both Sarvodaya's vision of peace and its ideal of civil society have been shaped by Gandhian and Buddhist sources. Sarvodaya has sought to empower people to rebuild the kind of civil society that it believes colonialism destroyed. By reconstructing the horizontal axis of village power, Sarvodaya hopes that the people can realize the kind of "holistic social health" that will produce peace.[1]

A Brief History of Sarvodaya's Peace Activities

- Following the 1983 riots that marked the escalation of the current ethnic conflict, Sarvodaya established camps for the Tamil refugees and was one of the main organizers of a major peace conference that adopted a "People's Declaration for National Peace and Harmony."

- After this conference, Sarvodaya sought to implement the spirit of the conference by undertaking a peace march or "peace walk" in Sri Lanka, from Kataragama in the south to Jaffna in the north. This march, however, was halted because of a request from President J. R. Jayawardene, who said that he feared for the safety of the marchers.

- Since that first march, Sarvodaya has organized numerous other peace marches, including what it described as a People's Peace Offensive in 1987.

- Sarvodaya has also operated a program of relief in the areas of unrest.

- Sarvodaya established a Peace Center, Vishva Niketan, in 1987, to serve as a place of meditation and peace.
- Sarvodaya has continued to hold peace marches and peace meditations. In 1999, it assembled 170,000 people to contemplate peace in Vihara Maha Devi Park in central Colombo.
- On March 15, 2002, Sarvodaya organized an even larger gathering when some 500,000 people assembled in Anuradhapura to meditate for peace.

The Three Sources of Sarvodaya's Peace Campaign

Sarvodaya's campaign for peace and non-violence reflects the three influences that have shaped the movement: Gandhian ideals, Buddhist teachings, and a belief in an ecumenical spirituality.

Gandhian ideals

From the Gandhian side, Sarvodaya's vision of peace draws on Gandhi's commitment to non-violence (*ahimsa*) and self-realization (*swaraj*). Gandhi understood clearly that these values could not exist without changing the violent and oppressive structures of society. His "Constructive Program" sought to address these structures and reestablish traditional values. As Kantowsky has noted, Gandhi believed that "Only when an equal share has been given 'unto this last,' is a non-violent social order (*Ahimsa*) possible; only in such a society can Truth (*Satya*) and Self-Realization (*Swaraj*) grow."[2]

Buddhist teachings

From the Buddhist side, Sarvodaya's vision of peace finds a rich resource in the classical Theravada teachings and also in the ideology of Sinhala Buddhism. Sarvodaya discusses Buddhist teachings such as the opening verse of the *Dhammapada*, which says:

"Mind is the foremost of all realities. Mind is the chief and all are mind-wrought. Whoever speaks or acts with an impure mind, suffering follows him as the wheel of the cart follows the foot of the ox." Conversely, the *Dhammapada* also says that if one has a pure mind, contentment and peace (*sukha*) will surely follow. Sarvodaya regards this teaching as an answer to the question of "What is the source of individual and social suffering or happiness?" or "What is the source of violence or peace?"

Ecumenical spirituality

A third factor in Sarvodaya's peace discourse stems from A. T. Ariyaratne's basic belief that there is an underlying spiritual unity to all religions and that the achievement of peace depends on being able to actualize this unity. He speaks about "universally just spiritual laws" that transcend the historic religions and he describes all religions as "intrinsically messages of peace and brotherhood."[3] This view could be described as a Victorian spirituality, because it resonates with elements of nineteenth-century movements such as the Theosophical Society.[4] But the approach also reflects the influence of the new-age spirituality of the postmodern period. This kind of ecumenical spirituality in the Sarvodaya movement represents another link to the Gandhian heritage, for both Gandhi and Vinoba Bhave also regarded all religions as equal paths to God and liberation.[5]

Sarvodaya's peace movement seeks to awaken the people's spiritual consciousness and restore what it regards as Buddhist and ecumenical spiritual values in order to counter the dominant materialist values that have led to the violent structures and the oppression of the people. Sarvodaya holds that lasting peace and justice depend on this kind of people's revolution in society, economy, and politics and it draws on its three sources – Gandhian, Buddhist, and spiritual – to envision this revolution.

Sarvodaya's Vision of a Village Social and Economic Revolution

For Ariyaratne, as for Gandhi, the village represents the heart of the nation and the source of its spiritual and moral vision. Ariyaratne's book, *The Power Pyramid and the Dharmic Cycle*, reflects Gandhi's essay, "The Pyramid and the Oceanic Circle," in which Gandhi argued that society should not be like a pyramid with the many at the base supporting the few at the top, but it should be an "oceanic circle" of individuals and villages.[6] Ariyaratne interprets Gandhi's model for social change and focuses on the village to emphasize the need for decentralization and a bottom-up approach. He sees the village to be the area of Sri Lankan society most adversely affected by the government's policies. He argues that "full human development and happiness cannot be achieved by centralization...[because] centralisation as a system is inconsistent with a non-violent structure of society."[7]

To a certain extent, Sarvodaya adopts an idealized view of the ancient Sri Lankan village as its model for the future. This approach is problematic, as Obeysekere and Gombrich have pointed out.[8] But Sarvodaya idealizes traditional village life as a means of authorizing Buddhist and spiritual values as alternatives to the materialistic values that it sees to be the source of the systemic problems in the country.

In its recent plans and programs to empower a new, village-centered social order and a civil society, Sarvodaya has emphasized two key terms: *Gram Swaraj*, village self-rule, and *Deshodaya*, the awakening of the nation. Both of these terms reflect Sarvodaya's Gandhian heritage, and both have to do with transferring power to the people at the village level. In Sarvodaya's usage, the terms are closely related, with *Gram Swaraj* signifying the liberation of the village through the creation of economic and social programs at the grassroots level and *Deshodaya* signifying the national and

political outcome of this village liberation process.

In effect, what Sarvodaya proposes with these terms is to empower the people at the grassroots to construct a civil society that will bring a new social order embodying Gandhian and Buddhist ideals. Sarvodaya's conception of a civil society agrees to some extent with the definition suggested by Walzer: "The words 'civil society' name the space of uncoerced human association and also the set of relational networks – formed for the sake of family, faith interest and ideology – that fill this space."[9]

Sarvodaya's idea here also resembles the conception of civil society proposed by Gordon White, that "civil society represents an intermediate associational realm between the family and the state populated by organisations which are separate from the state, enjoy autonomy in relation to the state and are formed voluntarily by members of society to protect or extend their interests and values."[10] Neither of these definitions, however, fully captures the distinctive conception of civil society that Sarvodaya has developed. Sarvodaya seeks to empower not just any civil society that will stand over against the state and the market, but it seeks to create a citizenry that will embody Gandhian and Buddhist "interests and values" in generating alternatives to the state and the market. Sarvodaya needs a Dharmic citizenry that will generate a cultural-spiritual revolution to generate a Dharmic civil society.

Sarvodaya wants to empower the people how to build – or, rather, in Sarvodaya's view, rebuild – a Dharmic civil society by reconstructing the horizontal axis of village or people's power. By liberating the village, *Gram swaraj*, the people can free themselves from the hierarchical forces of the state and the market and take charge of their own governance by creating an alternative economic and political system, *deshodaya*. This vision of liberation has been part of Sarvodaya's ideology for many years, although it has taken on a new urgency in the present context. Sarvodaya has contrasted the existing social order with an ideal Sarvodaya social order in a chart published in its literature and displayed in its community centers since 1960.[11] According to this chart, the present social order is characterized by "import–export economy...foreign debts, and subjugation to neo-colonialism." In such a society, Sarvodaya notes, "the law of enforcement and state power increase, the laws of Dharma and power of the people diminish. The Rulers are all powerful and the people powerless." By contrast, Sarvodaya's vision of the ideal social order calls for a society based on spiritual values, simplicity, self-sufficiency, decentralization, and people's power.

Sarvodaya's program today continues to focus on a simple and sustainable Buddhist lifestyle. Sarvodaya seeks to prepare the villages that are participating in the movement to be both self-reliant and capable of participating in a "Dharmic circle" of villages that will buffer the pressures and uncertainties of the national and global economies. Ariyaratne anticipates that Sarvodaya's economic programs will "organize the production, distribution and consumption in the Sarvodaya villages and village clusters...so that they [can] effectively confront the onslaughts of the violent and capitalist commercial economy invading them from without and build an economic cover through that to protect the common man."[12]

In this way, Sarvodaya calls for a revolution to build what it describes as "a society whose value system is based on Truth, Non-violence, and Self-denial...a no-poverty, no affluence society."[13] This aim represents both an interpretation of the Gandhian ideal and an application of the Buddhist Middle Way to social and economic life. This is Sarvodaya's vision of a Dharmic civil society.

To accompany and facilitate the economic revolution in the village, Sarvodaya has also called for the political empowerment of the grassroots. Ariyaratne foresees the villages uniting and liberating themselves from the power of both the government and the global economy. In his book, *The Power Pyramid and the Dharmic Cycle*, Ariyaratne expresses the hope that the Sri Lankan Sarvodaya movement can facilitate a network of 25,000 independent village republics to harness the power of the people.[14]

Sarvodaya has articulated and is attempting to implement an ambitious plan that goes well beyond village development and requires a reshaping of the economic and political realities of the country. Sarvodaya's conception of reform, which follows Gandhi's ideas for a village political system, seems open to the same criticisms that Gandhi's conception received. Nehru and the Congress Party leaders who sought to industrialize India viewed Gandhi's idea of a network of village republics as "utopian" and unrealistic in the modern context. Some critics have regarded Sarvodaya's proposal for a polity based on a circle of self-sufficient villages as similarly utopian and improbable in the twenty-first century. Kantowsky noted that "Gandhi's solution to the conflict between man and the institutions that he creates as a social being was the abolition of the state."[15] Ariyaratne does not exactly call for the abolition of the state, but in the *The Power Pyramid and the Dharmic Cycle*, and in other writings he has made millennialist predictions that the current political and economic systems will collapse from their own weight, leaving only the villages standing.[16] Some critics have referred to Ariyaratne as the last living Gandhian.[17]

Conclusion

Although Sarvodaya's vision of reform and peace may seem idealistic, it can also be regarded as appropriate for the situation in Sri Lanka in a couple of ways. First, Sarvodaya should be commended for standing up for peace. In a South Asian region that has been wracked by conflict and violence in recent years, Sarvodaya has been one of the few groups actively calling for peace and seeking to build a consensus for peace.

Second, although Sarvodaya's ideas for a non-violent revolution may appear to some as naïve and utopian, they are naïve and utopian in a prophetic sense. They point to other and more hopeful alternatives to the violent paradigm of global materialism and consumerism that threatens to undermine cultural values and bring about the destruction of both society and the environment. Sarvodaya invokes Buddhist and spiritual values not in order to return to the past or to build up a Sinhala Buddhist identity but to orient society toward these ideals of spirituality, equality, simplicity, and conservation. These are ideals that in the context of the twenty-first century could apply far beyond the shores of Sri Lanka. Sarvodaya seeks to realize these ideals today in order to build an infrastructure for peace. Affirming Schumacher's ideal of "Small is Beautiful," Sarvodaya seeks to transform the values that inform both Sri Lankan society and the larger global society.

NOTES

1 Portions of this chapter are related to Bond (2003). Please refer to this for a more detailed discussion of the history of the Sarvodaya Movement.
2 Kantowsky (1980).
3 Ariyaratne (1987:14).
4 The Theosophical Society, for example, believed in an eclectic spirituality involving great spiritual teachers or Mahatmas.
5 Wismeijer (1981:41).
6 Gandhi (1997:188). The original essay was written in 1946.
7 Ariyaratne (1995:12). As a movement, Sarvodaya seeks liberation and awakening, which can be defined by qualitative states such as happiness, peace, and non-violence, states best developed and nurtured in a decentralized system focusing on the family and the village.

8 Gombrich and Obeyesekere (1988: 243f.).
9 Walker (1995:7).
10 White (1998:379).
11 This chart appears in many places in Sarvodaya literature. This version is from Ariyaratne (1990b:7). See Goulet (1981:11) for his summary of this chart.
12 Ariyaratne (1988b:11).
13 "An Endowment Fund for the Sarvodaya Shramadana Movement"(unpublished document, November, 1996), p. 2.
14 (1988a:99). Ariyaratne recognizes that the urban areas are also important and he later spells out how they can be divided into groups of 250 families that function like village communities within the urban areas. (See "An Endowment Fund for SSM," Sarvodaya publication, November, 1996, p. 2.)
15 Kantowsky (1980:75).
16 (1988a:17).
17 Newspaper editorial, *The Island*, Colombo, September 1, 1999.

REFERENCES

Ariyaratne, A. T.
1987 Peace Making in Sri Lanka in the Buddhist Context. Ratmalana, Sri Lanka: Sarvodaya Vishva Lekha Press, published speech/article.
——1988a The Power Pyramid and the Dharmic Cycle. Ratmalana, Sri Lanka: Sarvodaya Vishva Lekha Press.
——1988b Sarvodaya and the Economy. Ratmalana, Sri Lanka: Sarvodaya Vishva Lekha Press, published speech/article.
——1989 Politics, Politicians and Sustenance of a Contented Civil Society. Ratmalana, Sri Lanka: Sarvodaya Vishva Lekha Press, published speech/article.
——1990a Living with Religion in the Midst of Violence. Bulletin of Peace Proposals 21(3): 275–290.
——1990b The Vision of a New Society. Moratuwa, Sri Lanka: Sarvodaya Press.

—— 1995 Buddhist Thought in Sarvodaya Practice. Ratmalana, Sri Lanka: Sarvodaya Vishva Lekha Press.

—— 1996 The Greatest Tribute to Mahatma Gandhi is Building a Sarvodaya Society in the 21st Century. Ratmalana, Sri Lanka: Sarvodaya Vishva Lekha Press, published speech/article.

Bond, George D.
1988 The Buddhist Revival in Sri Lanka. Columbia: University of South Carolina Press.

—— 2003 Buddhism At Work: Community Development, Social Empowerment and the Sarvodaya Movement. Bloomfield, CT: Kumarian Press.

Gandhi, M. K.
1997 Hind Swaraj and Other Writings. A. Parel, ed. New Delhi: Cambridge University Press.

Gombrich, Richard, and Gananath Obeyesekere
1988 Buddhism Transformed: Religious Change in Sri Lanka. Princeton, NJ: Princeton University Press.

Goulet, Denis
1981 Survival with Integrity: Sarvodaya at the Crossroads. Colombo, Sri Lanka: Marga Institute.

Kantowsky, Detlef
1980 Sarvodaya the Other Development. New Delhi: Vikas Publishing House.

Sarvodaya
1994 Sarvodaya Strategic Plan for 1995–98. Ratmalana, Sri Lanka: Sarvodaya Vishva Lekha Press.

Sivaraksa, Sulak
1992 Sivaraksa, Seeds of Peace. Berkeley, CA: Parallax Press.

Walker, M.
1995 Toward a Global Civil Society. Oxford: Berghahn Books.

White, Gordon
1998 Civil Society and Governance. Proceedings of a workshop by the Institute of Development Studies, University of Sussex, June.

Wickremeratne, Ananda
1995 Buddhism and Ethnicity in Sri Lanka: A Historical Analysis. Kandy, Sri Lanka: International Centre for Ethnic Studies and Vikas Publishing House.

Wismeijer, Hans
1981 Diversity in Harmony: A Study of the Leaders of the Sarvodaya Shramadana Movement in Sri Lanka. Privately published dissertation, University of Utrecht, the Netherlands.

Part III

Deterritorialization and the Politics of Place

9

Defying Deterritorialization: Autonomy Movements against Globalization

June Nash

The emphasis in globalization discourse on the flow of goods, capital, and services leaves little room for the observation of resistance and protest in places that are marginalized by those processes. Yet these are the areas that are becoming the center of dissent in day-to-day protests against the dislocations and environmental contamination caused by global enterprises. At the same time that populations are forced to migrate in search of work, global enterprises are going underground, buried in the underworld of dotcoms and obliterating their tracks with multiple conglomerate identities.

The elusive practices of what has become known as flexible capitalism add to the problems of ethnological research. If we look straight ahead with the tunnel vision of disciplines that concentrate on core institutions in the centers of global power we miss the manifold processes known as globalization that occur on the margins. These core institutions are so intertwined with regional, national, and local clusters that it is difficult if not impossible to perceive the macro-formations. Instead we might go to any one of the multiple sites where the impact of globaliza-

tion is felt directly by people whose survival is at stake.

Anthropologists are by inclination and profession predisposed to study the peripheral phenomena of everyday life everywhere in the world, and especially in marginal areas. Our hidden bias for Third World perspectives is becoming more explicit as the failure of modernity projects becomes explicit. With the widening gap between rich and poor – countries, regions, and people – during the recovery from the debt crisis of the 1980s, anthropologists developed stinging critiques of development projects pursued in the 1990s (Arce and Long 2000, Escobar 1995). Many of these formerly marginalized areas have become frontiers of the latest capitalist advances, where we find indigenous people engaged in a fight for their territories and their way of life.

I will focus on the people that Darcey Ribeiro (1971) calls "testimonial people," or "the modern representatives of old original civilizations" whose cultivated historical memories and everyday lived practice enable them to attest to ways of life that are alternatives to capitalism. The resurgence of ethnicity witnessed by anthropologists throughout the Western hemisphere – particularly since the organization of the quincentennial celebration of 500 years of resistance in 1992 – places the testimonial people in the vanguard of resistance and protest to many of the globalization processes that concern anthropologists. Many continue to practice collective lifeways and to relate to cosmic powers in ways envisioned by their ancestors. These normative practices are not the result of passivity, but rather the product of practiced resistance by those who have experienced the trauma of conquest and colonization. This ritual reinforcement and daily enactment of their sacred tie with the land cultivates an environmental ethic of conservation and sustainability among testimonial peoples. In recognition of the unique contribution they can make because of this, participants at the Conference on Environment and Development at Rio de Janeiro in 1992 adopted a comprehensive program for sustainable development with indigenous stewardship.

Paradoxically, the resurgence of ethnic identity in the struggle to retain ancestral lands and the recognition of their claims by United Nations covenants coincides with the anthropological critique of essentialism and the deconstruction of "peoples and places." Now that anthropologists are alerted to global trends resulting from flexible deployment of capital, labor, and markets, they have begun to address issues of (1) the "deterritorialization" of peoples, communities, and industries forced to migrate either because of land seizure, pollution, or the search for wage work (Appadurai 1991a, Gupta and Ferguson 1997); (2) the "deculturation" or homogenization of cultures with the loss of the symbolic and material reference points to cultural identity (Garcia Canclini 1990); and (3) the fragmentation of social relations promoted by the commodification of social exchange (Nash 1993, n.d.) or by divisive state policies (Nash n.d.). Focus on the "transitory, deterritorialized, unfixed, processual character of much of what we study" (Malkii

1997a) has cultivated a critique of the "peoples and places" approach to anthropological representation. Except for textbook summaries, that approach had long been superseded by fieldwork on rural to urban and global migrations, the intrusion of communication media and transportation that bring with them new conceptions of the world, and technology that transforms the speed and social organization of production. Nonetheless, the critique brought together in the anthology edited by Gupta and Ferguson (1997) promoted the problematizing of the relation of people to place.

Yet in the postmodern vein of inquiry, the terms of discourse – deterritorialization, creolization, hybridization, or fragmentation – often become reified as processes and cut off from the political and economic context in which the contradictions between capital and human communities are affected. Appadurai (1991b) opened this discourse with the statement "It is this fertile ground of deterritorialization in which money, commodities and persons unendingly chase each other around the world that the group imaginations of the modern world find their fractured and fragmented counterpart." As Appadurai warns (1991a:191): "The *ethno* in ethnography takes on a slippery, nonlocalized quality to which the descriptive practices of anthropology will have to respond." Unfortunately this has instead fostered a slide into the nearest convenient ethnoscape, often forgetting the capitalist framework that propels mobility. In so doing some ethnographers have come to treat deterritorialization as a force in itself.

Given this mode of inquiry, the resistance and protest of people confronting globalization processes may be ignored in the rush to affirm what become the imperatives of the new discourse on globalization. Attempts to bring the conflict into focus are cast as naïve or, even worse, essentializing. Responding to macro-analyses of globalization that stress the mobility of people and the homogenization of culture, some anthropologists deny the premises of testimonial peoples to validate the continued occupation of their ancestral lands as "essentialist" and the anthropologists who quote them as romantics.

Defying charges of essentialism, indigenous organizations often continue to assert that the selection of defining traits to identify a people is the simplest and most practicable means of identifying a group's claims to cultural property. Others are learning constructivist approaches that relate to universal juridical premises or historical events of indigenous resistance as a definer of identity (Dover and Rappaport 1996, Field 1999, Jackson 1996, Warren 1992). Australian aborigines appeal to the sanctity of sacred sites to ward off dam builders and maintain their aboriginal identity in a post-colonial conflict between whites and blacks (Bell 2001, Morphy 1995); in the Amazonian region threatened by large-scale gold mining, Tukanoan Indians enhance the cosmological ideals of spiritual territory and locality in the mobilization of political responses (Arhem 1998), while the Kayapo regroup traditional ceremonial hunting associations to overcome divisions and negotiate with the gold-mining companies (Turner 1996); Wachti of the Congo transport trees rooted in the clay pots that symbolize maternal wombs when they are forced to migrate (Lovell 1998). Until we resolve the tensions in each camp, the destructive tendency implicit in the argument against essentialism can, as Kay Warren (1992) points out, disorient attempts to operationalize the cultural guidelines for indigenous political organizing. In the interim, both approaches are valid in affirming the universal right of all people to their cultural practices.

Despite the many signs of alienation from community or place in societies around the globe, it is also apparent that identification with locality becomes increasingly important with globalization. People who are uprooted, forced to migrate in search of employment, or exiled for political reasons go to extraordinary lengths to retain their ties to home. The contribution by migrants to the United States of billions of dollars in remittances to families and communities provoked President Fox of Mexico to call them national heroes. Migrations now tend to be transnational, with immigrants oscillating back and forth from their home country to *their* work sites (Kearney 1995, Schiller et al. 1992), often re-creating in each site cultural spaces that share common elements. As ethnographers rise to the challenge of defining new ethnographic sites among displaced and dislocated populations, they are discovering ethnographic sites in homeless shelters and refugee camps. Although these sites appear to be diametrically opposite to conventional field sites in communities, ethnographers are discovering that, like communities, they share persistent patterns in gender, ethnic, and class correlates that contradict the assumed trends in globalization (Malkii 1997b, Passaro 1997).

These global issues of deterritorialization, hybridization, and fragmentation occur in the context of flexible global capitalization. Analyzed within that global context they promote a more dynamic view of the dialectical relationship between human consciousness and place that responds to the innovative pathways that indigenous people are creating to anchor their communities to localities. Here I shall consider the importance of retaining our peripheral perspective on local and regionally situated ethnographic studies because – not in spite – of the global flows that threaten to erase boundaries. I shall draw upon my own experiences over forty years with Mayas in the borderlands between Mexico and Guatemala to demonstrate how they are reasserting control over the spaces they occupy in spite of capitalist penetration and military invasion. Parallel developments among Mayas in this porous borderland demonstrate the importance of retaining the framework of capitalist processes conditioning the cultural responses.

Mayas across the Border

Mayas are among the indigenous peoples of the western hemisphere, defined by the United Nations Inter-Commission Task

Force on Indigenous People as "those which, having a historical continuity with pre-invasion and pre-colonial societies that have developed on their territories, consider themselves distinct from other sectors of the societies now prevailing in those territories or parts of them" (IUCN 1997:27). In their 500 years of contact and colonization, Mayas have resisted assimilation to the dominant European and *mestizo* (mixed-blood) society by holding on to the small plots of land they cultivate and rejecting the intrusion of developers who would change their way of life. When forced to move, they have cultivated ways of reestablishing community and cosmic orientations.

My first acquaintance with Mayas comes from highland Mayan communities of Chiapas, Mexico where I lived for over two years in the late 1950s and 1960s and to which I have returned periodically. These small plot cultivators and artisans were able to operate with some autonomy within their communities when I first arrived, in part because the Land Reform Article 27 of the 1917 Constitution restored lands that had been expropriated during the 1871–1910 liberal regime of Porfirio Diaz. With rising populations and a shrinking land base, indigenous people are now losing control over the semi-subsistence economy that ensured their survival. Some are colonizing the Lacandón rainforest, where, since 1970, 200,000 settlers speaking five distinct Mayan dialects have resettled from the coastal plantations and highland villages. There the settlers are in competition to secure land titles with cattle ranchers, oil explorers, and hydroelectric engineers who have flooded hundreds of thousands of hectares by damming the rivers. Rising populations and a diminishing land base, combined with the neoliberal trade and domestic policies adopted during Salinas's presidency and pursued by his successor Zedillo, threaten the household organization of production geared to semi-subsistence strategies of survival.

Mayas on both sides of the border are confronting the threat of dislocation with the termination of land reform claims and markets for their cash crops promoted by neoliberal trade and economic policies in a resurgence of ethnic identification that challenges assumptions about the inevitability of cultural homogenization and the loss of local control (Nash 1995, Warren 1998). They have done this in distinct ways that conform to different levels of indigenous autonomy in each country. In Mexico, the PRI government co-opted native officials with funds diverted from public projects to further their control of highland villages. Following the first Chiapas National Indigenous Congress in 1974, *campesinos* formed independent agrarian organizations that broke away from official PRI confederations. These organizations provided the impetus for the celebration of 500 Years of Resistance on October l2, 1992, as indigenous *campesinos* of Chiapas assumed an increasingly independent role, moving from a position of the right to land for those who work it to the right for indigenous people to govern themselves in the regional territories in which they constitute a majority.

Like the Mayas of Chiapas, Guatemalan Indians bore the brunt of neoliberal trade policies of the 1970s and 1980s that opened their borders to investment in commercial crop cultivation, cattle raising, and tourism. Few Indians benefited from capitalist penetration. Their attempts to develop cooperatives and to unionize wage workers were met by armed repression. In Guatemala, where the Mayas constitute a majority of the population, they have little entry into political office, and until recently they rarely succeeded in gaining an education beyond primary grades. Small plot cultivators of the western highlands of Guatemala migrated to the Ixcán rainforest contiguous with the Lacandón rainforest, where they were promised title to the land. Practicing a communal form of life, they organized cooperatives linked in a loose network called Communities of Populations in Resistance (CPRs) (Sinclair 1995:75). Even in these newly constituted communities, indigenous people of Guatemala could not escape the internal class conflicts endemic in a nation structured in racist as well as classist terms.[1] Following the militarization of the area in 1975, the Guatemalan Mayas were caught in a near-genocidal conflict.

The colonizers of both the Lacandón and of the Ixcán rainforests took a stand against deterritorialization when the promises to the lands they colonized were revoked. This happened first in Guatemala in 1975 when oil was discovered and the oil companies – Getty Oil, Texaco, Amoco, and Shenadoah Oil – extended their drilling into settled areas of Ixcán. The army and paramilitary forces backed up the companies against the settlers when the tried to defend their lands (Sinclair 1995:85 ff.). Some joined the Committee of Campesino Unity (CUC), a broadly based community-action organization of indigenes and *mestizos*; others joined the Guerrilla Army of the Poor (EGP), especially after the massacre in Rio Negro in 1982 when over half the villagers were killed after they opposed the damming of a river for an international hydroelectric company (Alecio 1985:26).

In Mexico President Salinas ended the promise of land titles for the colonizers of the Lacandón in 1992 with the Reform of the Land reform Article 27 of the Constitution. The North American Free Trade Agreement (NAFTA) exacerbated the problems of small plot cultivators, some of whom were having difficulty in marketing the cash crop of coffee that the government had promoted in order to meet the growing needs for chemical fertilizers and pesticides. These events precipitated the January 1, 1994 uprising of the Zapatista Army of National Liberation (EZLN) in the Lacandón jungle where the government rarely funded medical or educational facilities in villages and where they never sent ballot boxes. There the PRI officials of the major towns in which the new settlements were subsumed relied on paramilitaries hired by ranchers and often armed by federal forces to thwart *campesino* protests against arbitrary governance and raids on their land. The Zapatista uprising offered

an opportunity to militarize the area, with federal troops building up from the 37,000 that controlled the Lacandón colonizers during Salinas's presidency to an estimated 70,000 under Zedillo.

The contest for control of the Lacandón area was intensified after French oil explorers discovered what *El Financiero* (February 28, 1995) called "an ocean of oil" under cover of the forest, the same ocean that flowed beyond the border into Guatemala. Clearly this was a known factor by Zedillo when he ordered the invasion of the Lacandón rainforest on February 9, 1995 in an operation that was called the apprehension of subcommander Marcos and other "terrorists." Many civil society activists considered that the invasion was prompted by the oil discoveries, since the EZLN had not violated the conditions of the ceasefire agreement signed twelve days after the uprising.

An ongoing dialogue between the Zapatistas and the government begun in March 1994 was interrupted by the assassination of Donaldo Colosio during his election campaign for the presidency. When the dialogue was resumed in April 1995, thousands of Indians from throughout the highland towns and Lacandón settlements congregated in San Andrés Larrainzar in April, 1995 to offer support and protection for the Zapatistas. Although the meetings then and subsequently in September were aborted by the intransigence of government representatives in the Commission for Agreement and Peace (COCOPA), the dialogue seemed to reach a successful conclusion when a reconstituted COCOPA signed the San Andrés Accord in February, 1996.

As support for the Zapatistas spread in the highland indigenous towns where people urged the government to implement the Accord, paramilitary bands trained and equipped by federal troops attacked the Catholic catechist groups in the diocese of Bishop Samuel Ruiz. On December 22, 1997 one of these bands, called the Red Masks, attacked kin and neighbors of their town who had exiled themselves in a

Christian Base Community called Acteal, a hamlet in the mountainous periphery of the town. The band killed 45 of the people joined in prayer in a rude wooden chapel. News of the massacre spread throughout the world, having a negative impact on Mexican stock-market ratings and tourism, which had declined with the longstanding conflict in the region. The survivors are now trying to avert further bloodshed as they seek political and spiritual reconciliation. With donations from throughout the world, they have built a cement mausoleum for the victims, whose names are inscribed on the walls, along with photographs. Leaders of the community conduct tours of their small community for foreign guests, who arrive daily,[2] reciting the horrifying events of the massacre in daily memorial services. Acteal now epitomizes a new place for resistance, now directed against the *caciques* – indigenous leaders co-opted by the PRI.

Mayas are among those world populations who are intensely aware of the threat posed by globalization because their small plot cultivation practices are at odds with government plans in both Mexico and Guatemalan for the development of energy resources. For indigenous people, security is located in the land that provides them with the potential for regeneration of life, not the ephemeral profits from capitalizing on their land or hydraulic resources. They are utilizing solar energy to power their computers and other technology provided by NGOs.

Combining preconquest powers with saints and spirits from the Christian religion, Mayas of both countries still maintain a cosmogony that holds humans responsible for the balance in the universe. This has profound consequences for their preference for collective projects in development and for their daily behavior. During the 1990s, as Guatemalan Mayas entered into peace negotiations with their government, they focused increasingly on issues of indigenous land claims, evoking Ruwach'ulew (The Earth/ the World), or Quate' Ruwach'ulew (Our Mother the Earth) in what Kay Warren calls

"an indigenous ecological discourse in overlapping ways to interconnect Maya cosmology, agricultural rituals, strategies for socioeconomic change, land issues, and rights struggles" (Warren 1998:65) Chiapas Mayas have always invoked preconquest cosmic powers as they try to achieve a balance with nature. Zapatistas often contrast this reverence for nature in opposition to neoliberal policies of death, as during the Intercontinental Convention for Life and Against Neoliberalism in late July and early August 1996. When many fires blew out of control during the planting season in March, 1998, Tzeltal-speaking Zapatista supporters in the highlands attributed the loss of forest lands in the Lacandón to an upset in the balance between the sun and the moon caused by the rape and pillage carried out by the army and paramilitary troops in full view of the Tatik Sol.

With the advent of the millennium and the newly elected President Vicente Fox promising to resolve the conflict, Zapatistas and their supporters planned a campaign to bring their demands to the federal capital. In January, 2001 Zapatistas congregated in San Cristóbal in the square in front of the cathedral, where they had protested on so many occasions the presence of the army in the Lacandón rainforest in the years after the uprising. The square had become the contested arena for civil society to articulate their sentiments where peace marchers and the national consultations with civil society congregated to speak. There had been clashes between the ranchers calling for the hanging of Bishop Samuel Ruiz and the Zapatista supporters calling for resumption of the dialogue and peace with dignity after the army invasion of the jungle in 1995. It was an appropriate place for Zapatistas and their supporters to congregate as they announced their departure to Mexico City. They arrived in late afternoon as the winter sun set the ochre tones of the cathedral ablaze. They were still masked but bearing banners with their messages clearly articulated: President Fox should carry out his promises to withdraw troops from the rainforest, to implement the San Andrés Agreement, and to release Zapatistas incarcerated without charges brought against them.

After many stops visiting with indigenous groups en route, the Zapatista convoy, with foreign supporters, arrived in Mexico City in March. There they were hosted by the Institute of Anthropology and History in the Universidad Nacional Autónoma de Mexico where Subcomandante Insurgente Marcos addressed the community of scholars and activists in his inspired poetic vein, affirming, "Perhaps the only thing it [the Zapatista uprising] did was to organize what each one had decided, to listen and to make themselves echo and voice of what we are." The leaders of the EZLN high command spoke in the public squares of the city that were filled with tens of thousands of their supporters. Commander Esther reaffirmed the Mexican civil society claim, "There will never be a Mexico without Indians," asserting, "There will never again be a Mexico without women!" Commander David inveighed against the continued military posts in indigenous zones, calling upon President Fox to fulfill his commitments to meeting the conditions for resuming the dialogue interrupted in 1996.

On March 11, for the first time in the history of the republic, indigenes spoke in the federal congress. Many of the congressmen of President Fox's own Party of National Action (PAN) boycotted the meeting and the autonomy bill they approved was gutted, leaving indigenous peoples even more subject to state control than before. President Fox admitted that they were justified in their position, although he had at first acclaimed the bill as an historic victory.

Commander Tacho's message to the Congress acclaiming the roots of the resistance and survival in the past 500 years will probably become a reference point in Mexico's history:

> We fled far to defend ourselves from the great oppressor in order not to be exterminated unjustly. With their intelligence and

knowledge our first grandparents thought that they would find refuge in the farthest mountains where they could promote their resistance where they could survive with their own forms of government politically, socially, economically, and culturally, so that our roots would not be ended, so that our motherland would never die, nor our mother moon, nor our father sun. And so our roots could never be torn out and die, these deep roots that survive in the deepest heart of these lands that take on the color that we are, the color of earth. (EZLN 2001, my translation)

If we were to subject the poetic expression of a people who are caught in a revolutionary process to the sterile deconstruction of postmodern discourse, we are in danger of cutting ourselves off from the transformative course of social change undertaken by testimonial people.

Conclusions

Anthropological critiques of the link between peoples and places have questioned the homologous relation between culture and habitat as a result of global processes accelerating the mobility of people, production sites, and products. It is important for anthropologists to bring this awareness of macro-trends into our perceptions of local resistance movements that reject the normativity of deterritorialization and disintegration of cultural cohesiveness. As we problematize issues of the association of place and culture, the tendency to deny any consistent relationship between people and places as invalid eclipses the efforts of some indigenes and their allies to reassert the validity of their claims to cultural integrity and territory.

I have chosen a peripheral vision of testimonial peoples who reiterate the ongoing struggle to remain in place or to make the new spaces to which they migrate their own. The struggle in which Mayas are engaged on both sides of a national border reminds us of what locality means as a lived – and contested – experience in a globalizing world. This experience intensifies Mayan peoples' sense of being a part of a particular place. Indigenous people on both sides of the Mexico–Guatemala border illustrate distinct aspects of cultural identification with space, yet they share similar commitments. They show both the resistance of many indigenous peoples to the deterritorialization implied by globalization processes, and the resilience to resettlement in new environments where they re-create the communities they were forced to abandon. Paradoxically, the very processes of globalization that threaten the world they live in also generate the human rights movement of NGOs that help them to further their goals.

At a point in time when distinctive ethnic groups are challenging the monocultural construction of nations, the anthropological link of culture areas and people has come under fire. Intellectual elites who dominate the global discourse tend to normalize the dislocations that disrupt families and communities. In order to reconstitute our understanding of people and locality we can learn from the initiatives of indigenous peoples how they intend to achieve a balanced relation with nature and at the same time live in a pluricultural world that respects alternative ways of seeking survival and living. Their dialectical understanding of the mutual penetration of human activity with landscapes and how this generates a participatory ontological stance provides not only a powerful theoretical understanding of consciousness, but a key approach to substantiating claims in western courts. The Mayas ability to survive in place after 470 years of colonization and subordination is presumptive evidence for the validity of their stewardship of the land.

NOTES

1   Susanne Jonas (1991) develops a structural analysis of ethnic and class antagonism, showing the persistent tendencies toward violence to ensure the rule of a narrow elite in Guatemala.
2   Among the international visitors was Congressman Luis Gutierrez, who saw the importance of this event for his Mexican American constituency in Chicago, Illinois in 1998.

REFERENCES

Alecio, Rolando
    1995   Uncovering the Truth: Political Violence and Indigenous Organizations. In The New Politics of Survival. Minor Sinclair, ed. Pp. 25–46. New York: Monthly Review Press.
Appadurai, Arjun
    1991a   Disjuncture and Discontinuity in the Global Cultural Economy. Public Culture 2(2):1–24.
    1991b   Global Ethnoscapes: Notes and Queries for a Transnational Anthropology. In Recapturing Anthropology: Working in the Present. R. G. Fox, ed. Pp. 191–210. Santa Fe, NM: School of American Research Press.
Arce, A. and N. Long
    2000.   Negotiating Agricultural Development: Entanglements of Bureaucratic and Rural Producers in Western Mexico. Wageningen Studies of Sociology.
Arhem, Kaj
    1998   Powers of Place: Landscape, Territory and Local Belonging in Northwest Amazonia. In Locality and Belonging. N. Lovell, ed. Pp. 78–103. Oxford: Berg.
Bell, Diane
    2001   Talk given at the Conference on Indigenous Women and Religion, Scripps College, Claremont, CA, May 24–27.
Dover, Robert V. H., and Rappaport, Joanne
    1996   Introduction. In Ethnicity Reconfigured: Indigenous Legislators and the Colombian Constitution of 1991. Special issue. Journal of Latin American Anthropology 1(2):2–17.
Ejército Zapatista de Liberación Nacional (EZLN)
    2001   Ya Basta!, http://www.ezln.org/, March 17.

Escobar, Arturo
1995 Encountering Development: The Making and Unmaking of the Third World. Princeton, NJ: Princeton University Press.
Field, Les W.
1999 Complicities and Collaborations: Anthropologists and the "Unacknowledged Tribes of California," Current Anthropology 40(2):193–209.
Garcia Canclini, Néstor
Hibridas: Estrategías para entrar y salir de modernidad. México, DF: Grijalbo.
Gupta, Akhil, and James Ferguson
1997 Culture, Power, and Place. Ethnography at the End of an Era. In Culture, Power Place: Explorations in Critical Anthropology. A. Gupta and J. Ferguson, eds. Pp. 1–29. Durham, NC: Duke University Press.
IUCN (Inter-commission Task Force on Indigenous Peoples)
1997 Peoples and Sustainability: Cases and Actions. Utrecht: International Books.
Jackson, Jean
1996 The Impact of Recent National Legislation in the Vaupés Region of Colombia. Journal of Latin American Anthropology 1(2):120–51.
Jonas, Susanne
1991 The Battle for Guatemala: Rebels, Death Squads, and U.S. Power. Boulder, CO: Westview Press.
Kearney, Michael
1995 The Local and the Global: The Anthropology of Globalization and Transnationalism. Annual Review of Anthropology 324: 547–65.
Lovell, Nadia
1998 Wild Gods, Containing Wombs and Moving Pots: Emplacement and Transience in Watchi Belonging. In Locality and Belonging. N. Lovell, ed. Pp. 53–77. London and New York: Routledge.
Malkii, Liisa
1997a News and Culture: Transitory Phenomena and the Fieldwork Tradition. In Culture, Power, and Place: Explorations in Critical Anthropology. Akhil Gupta and James Ferguson, eds. Pp. 86–101. Durham, NC: Duke University Press.

1997b Ethnography at the End of an Era. In Culture, Power Place: Explorations in Critical Anthropology. A. Gupta and J. Ferguson, eds. Pp. 1–29. Durham, NC: Duke University Press.
McIntosh, Ian S., and David Maybury-Lewis
2001 Cultural Survival or "Cultural Survival?" Cultural Survival 25:4–5.
Morphy, Howard
1995 [1993] Colonialism, History and the Construction of Place: The Politics of Landscape in Northern Australia. In Landscape: Politics and Perspectives. Barbara Bender, ed. Pp. 205–44. Oxford: Berg.
Nash, June, ed.
1993 Crafts in the World Market: The Impact of Global Exchange on Middle American Artisans. Albany: State University of New York Press.
1995 The Reassertion of Indigenous Identity: Mayan Responses to State Intervention in Chiapas, Mexico. Latin American Research Review 30(3):7–42. Reprinted in Mexico, Central and South America: The Scholarly Literature of the 1990s. Jorge Dominguez, ed. New York: Garland Press.
2004 Beyond Resistance and Protest: The Mayan Quest for Autonomy. In Proceedings of a School of American Research Conference on Mayas Across the Border. John Watanabe and Edward Fischer, eds. Santa Fe, NM: School of the Americas.
Passaro, Joanne
1997 "You Can't Take the Subway to the Field!" Village Epistemologies in the Global Village. In Anthropological Locations: Boundaries and Grounds of a Field. Akhil Gupta and James Ferguson, eds. Pp. 147–62. Berkeley: University of California Press.
Ribeiro, Darcy
1971 Americas and Civilization. New York: Dutton.
Schiller, Nina Glick, Linda Basch, and Christine Blanc-Szanton
1992 Toward a Transnational Perspective on Migration: Race, Class, Ethnicity, and Nationalism Reconsidered.

Annals of the New York Academy of Sciences 645. New York: New York Academy of Sciences.

Sinclair, Minor
1995 Faith, Community and Resistance in the Guatemalan Highlands. *In* The New Politics of Survival: Grassroots Movements in Central America. Minor Sinclair, ed. Pp. 75–108. New York: Monthly Review Press.

Turner, Terry
1996 An Indigenous People's Struggle for Socially Equitable and Ecologically Sustainable Production. Journal of Latin American Anthropology 1(1): 98–121.

Warren, Kay B.
1992 Transforming Memories and Histories: Meanings of Ethnic Resurgence for Maya Indians *In* Americans: New Interpretive Essays. A. Stepan, ed. Pp. 189–219. Oxford and New York: Oxford University Press.
1998 Indigenous Movements and their Critics. Princeton, NJ: Princeton University Press.

10

The Resilience of Nationalism in a Global Era: Megaprojects in Mexico's South

Molly Doane

Introduction

Since his election in July 2000, Mexican President Vicente Fox has been promoting the Plan Puebla-Panama (PPP), a plan to strengthen the regional infrastructure and economy of southern Mexico and to improve communication among the Central American nations. The PPP seeks to modernize existing petrochemical industries in the region, expand industrial forestry and agricultural production, bring in new *maquila*-style firms,[1] and substantially increase the number of major arterial highways in southern Mexico. By linking Mexico's poorer states and its resources, including Puebla, Tabasco, Oaxaca, Yucatan, and Chiapas, to its international neighbors to the south, the PPP would, in theory, improve the economic situation of southern states at the same time as it laid the groundwork for a Central American alliance formidable enough to improve the region's bargaining position in future trade negotiations. At the same time, improved transportation across the Isthmus of Tehuantepec would create a new transportation corridor between the Pacific and Atlantic Oceans, making Southern Mexico a central node in international trade routes linking North America to Europe and Asia. In sum, the PPP seeks to usher in a new era of Mexican development in which national fortunes are tied to the strengthening of the Central American region as a whole, where Mexico, not the United States, will take a leading role in directing the course of development.

President Fox's reluctance to embrace the proposed Free Trade Area of the Americas (FTAA) and his campaign promise to open the US/Mexican border on the surface constitute a break from the accommodationist policies of his predecessors (Henwood 2000). But if Fox's policies challenge US political-economic imperialism, they do not constitute a paradigm shift in the dominant neoliberal model of economic development. Rather, they are an attempt to engineer a spatial relocation of global economic flows to shore up the rhetorical and political power of the nation-state. This strategy reinvigorates nationalism using a globalization paradigm that, according to theoretical conceptualizations, is generally destructive to the nationalist hegemony of the state.

Of course, not everyone embraces this globalism nor believes in the national benefits of the PPP. At the international level, the PPP has become a rallying point for anti-globalization protests around the FTAA. At the national level, the plan is regarded by many indigenous, professional, and *campesino* activists as a form of neoliberal imperialism and a violation of recent autonomy legislation passed by the Mexican Congress that was intended by its proponents to strengthen local, indigenous priorities for development (Machuca n.d., Podur 2001). In fact, the PPP is an expanded and updated version of an earlier "Megaproject," against which opposition is already strong and organized in the affected states of Veracruz, Oaxaca, and Tabasco. The Megaproject was presented to the public in early 1997, and aspects of it had already been implemented by the time of Fox's election.

This chapter draws from ethnographic fieldwork on the "Megaproject" conducted in Oaxaca between 1996 and 1998. It explains the contested nature of neoliberal development in Mexico, and how government officials promote neoliberal governance as the only reasonable solution to poverty in Mexico's underdeveloped southern region. Opponents of neoliberal development and proponents of the Megaproject alike invoke the national historical legacy to legitimize their respective positions. Whereas anti-development activists draw from the 1910–17 Revolution to define their nationalism, interpreting the Revolution as a rejection of free-market capitalism, government representatives locate their nationalism in the liberal period, emphasizing the Enlightenment ideals of free markets, democracy, and universalism that were the hallmark of the period. If activists against development use nationalism as a hedge against global capitalism, government spokespeople use nationalism as rhetorical cover, suggesting that their transnational development projects are nationalist ones designed to boost local economies.

Background: Social Movements in Mexico

Contemporary social movements in Mexico inhabit a moment where the contradictions between struggles over democratization and economic development are particularly acute. In the past few decades, both the theory and practice of social movements have undergone a notable and much discussed transformation, turning away from an earlier engagement with socialist politics and the discourse of class in favor of a politics of democratization couched in terms of civil society (Alvarez et al. 1998, Doane 2001, Nash 2001). The beginnings of this transformation are generally traced to 1968, when violent state repression of student protests in Mexico coalesced with international events, such as the protests against the Vietnam War, the invasion of Czechoslovakia by the Soviet Union, and the refusal of the International Communist Party and intellectuals linked to it to support the massive student uprisings of the Paris Summer. The global paradigm shift of 1968 was characterized by, on the one hand, a distrust of authoritarianism in any form, whether socialist or capitalist, and on the other, an intellectual retreat from structural Marxism among student intellectuals (Edelman 2001, Escobar and Álvarez 1992, Harvey 1990, Warman 1988). Foucault's *oeuvre*, which provided a new harbor for disaffected Marxists, was forged within this intellectual and political milieu (Miller 1993).

Evalina Dagnino (1998) summarizes the changes that have occurred in Latin American social movements in terms of the rise of post-1968 non-party, democratizing, grass-roots activism. The influence of structural Marxist theory, rooted in party politics, has given way to Gramscian concepts of hegemony rooted in a politics of democratization and, to a lesser extent, Foucauldian emphases on decentered power and the politics of everyday life (Álvarez et al. 1998, Escobar and Álvarez 1992, Joseph and Nugent 1994). This politics of democratization is voiced through "civil society," which in simplified Gramscian terms refers to a realm that lies outside of the formal mechanisms of the state, and as such can generate counter-hegemonic claims that transform the state and its ideology partly through instituting and practicing democracy at the local level. This "war of position" seeks not to topple the state but rather to democratize it incrementally and "from below" (Álvarez et al.1998). The turn toward a politics of democracy suggests a rejection of authoritarian, universalistic models of social change, and is often referred to as cultural politics because of its emphasis on cultural pluralism, as, for example, promoting models of political participation based on indigenous customary law, local economic development based on women's participation, or traditional methods of production (Nash 2001, Nigh and Rodriguez 1995, Rubin 1997, Stephen 2002).

This turn toward a cultural politics does not necessarily imply a rejection of "material" concerns nor distancing from the politics of work and production, as New Social Movements Theory sometimes seems to suggest (Laclau and Mouffe 1985). As June Nash (1994a, 1994b, 2001) and others have shown, struggles for democracy revolve around issues of survival, subsistence, and local development, and traditional struggles around work or the site of production are also interpreted through particular cultural experiences (see for example, Bray 1995, Hernández Castillo and Nigh 1998, Moguel et al. 1992, Nigh 1992). Moreover, many civil society activists regard their movements as a challenge to the authority of the state. However, it is certainly true that the socialist vanguard has been superseded by a civil society model of organizing that is at once more inclusive – bringing together women's organizations with *campesino* unions and environmentalists – yet politically more elusive, in the sense that it avoids strong party ties, makes cross-class alliances, and looks for local solutions to "structural" problems.

The social movement against the Megaproject is in many ways typical of the new cultural politics of democracy in Latin America. Insofar as it does not challenge "structure," it seeks to effect a transformation of the national/global economy by creating alternative spaces "from below." This politics, by adopting a scalar hierarchy, produces a new set of strategic challenges and reveals the particular contradictions of social struggle in the neoliberal era. Specifically, these politics attempt to alter particular "local" political or economic relations with respect to the national and international scenes without revolutionizing the national and international structures in which they are nested, posing the question of whether popular movements can create new spaces of autonomy as fast as the state can fill them in again.

The Megaproject case also demonstrates some of the emerging potentials and limitations of transnationalism within social movements. Activists involved in the Megaproject were tied to larger networks of nongovernmental organizations (NGOs) and indigenous unions with transnational links to activists working on similar issues in Europe, the United States, and Latin America. Thus, it is possible to do an internet search that yields synopses of the environmental and development issues at stake posted by a variety of internationally linked social justice groups. However, their knowledge of the specific political dynamics of particular cases is limited by the number of movements to which they have ties and sporadic communication with local actors. This is consistent with the findings of Khagram et al. (2003) who argue that, although social movements often utilize transnational networks, there are few examples of truly transnational movements.

Neoliberalism and Social Protest

Although struggles against neoliberalism are on the rise, the global integration of the Mexican economy is not new. In the Liberal era, Mexico allowed direct foreign investment as an avenue toward modernization (Coatsworth 1981, Esparza 1988). After the Mexican Revolution of 1910–17, foreign investment continued, but was controlled by protectionist policies of the state that favored domestic industry (Hellman 1994). These programs for domestic industrialization and infrastructural development greatly expanded during the oil-boom years of the 1970s, when private banks loaned Mexico millions of dollars against future oil revenues to fund rapid modernization programs. In 1982, oil prices crashed and Mexico's financial bubble burst, making it impossible to meet loan payments. The national debt was subsequently refinanced through the International Monetary Fund (IMF), ushering in a period of structural readjustment. IMF austerity programs led to the retraction of protections long afforded to the agrarian sector, national industries, and organized labor (Barkin et al. 1990, Fox 1993). Real wages fell, unemployment rose, and inflation skyrocketed, leading to a decline in living standards for the middle classes and a condition of "subsistence insecurity" for the agrarian sector (Nash 1994a, 1994b, 1995). In order to meet this crisis, Mexico opted for trade liberalization. In preparation for the North American Free Trade Agreement (NAFTA), modifications were made to Article 27 of the Mexican Constitution in favor of private property, effectively ending provisions for agrarian redistribution that were the cornerstone of the Revolutionary social contract (Collier and Quaratiello 1994, Dewalt et al. 1994, Hellman 1994). Although the Zapatista rebellion had long been brewing, rebels chose NAFTA's ratification date, January 1, 1994, to mark their opposition to the neoliberal direction of the State. Manuel Castells (1997) has called the uprising the "first informational guerrilla movement" insofar as its power lay not in armaments but in its ability to use the media to create global recognition and allegiance to the Zapatista cause. But Zapatista priorities, like their name, from revolutionary hero, Emiliano Zapata, are grounded in the nation (Collier and Stephen 1997).

The Zapatistas' ongoing rebellion became an issue in Fox's campaign, whose populism came out in his statements of sympathy toward them. He criticized President Zedillo for failing to negotiate with the rebels and expressed a commitment to resolving Zapatista demands, promising to dismantle military checkpoints and demilitarize Zapatista communities (Espinoza 2000). Two years later, the Zapatista uprising remains unresolved and negotiations with the Fox Administration have been unsatisfactory to the rebels, whose demand for an indigenous autonomy law has been met with a "compromise" version that has the potential to seriously weaken communal indigenous rights that were already in place (Podur 2001). In fact, it would be hard to mesh the kind of growth model promoted by Fox with either the social programs or the development autonomy demanded by the Zapatistas. It is worth remembering an infamous Chase Bank memo from 1995, which noted that for Zedillo to placate Zapatista demands would require expensive social programs, a direction not promising for free-marketeer investors. The memo goes on to say, "while Chiapas, in our opinion, does not pose a fundamental threat to Mexican political stability, it is perceived to be so by many in the investment community. The government will need to eliminate the Zapatistas to demonstrate their effective control of the national territory and of security policy" (Silverstein and Cockburn 1995). The memo is a stark reminder of the uncompromising nature of the neoliberal growth model and calls into question the integrity of current provisions made for "local" development included in Fox's recent economic expansion plans for Mexico's southern states.

The Megaproject in Oaxaca and the Meaning of "Mexican"

The Megaproject case provides a particularly good example of the dynamic positioning of activists and representatives of the state in relationship to each other. Activists framed their protest against the international aspects of the project within a discourse of anti-imperialism, and their protest against the state within a discourse of revolutionary nationalism that exposed the contradictions of the neoliberal policies of the state. At the same time, proponents of neoliberal development used nationalist rhetoric to promote their projects, often co-opting the Left's language of local development to promote their globalizing projects.

Officially known as the Program for the Integrated Development of the Isthmus of Tehuantepec, the Megaproject was initially planned in relative secrecy in the mid-1990s. Even as local and national newspapers began to leak stories about its existence, officials in local state development agencies trenchantly denied any knowledge of it. But early in 1997, a report commissioned by the Development and Planning Commission was leaked to key NGOs in the region, and government spokespeople issued statements about the benefits of the proposed project to the press, which for the most part printed the press releases sent to them by state development agencies. According to these reports, the project was intended to expand industry, modernize oil production and processing plants, develop agribusiness and industrial forestry, and improve transportation to facilitate the development of the Isthmus, until now an economically stagnant region. Although newspaper reports noted that one goal of the internationally financed project was the rapid movement of goods from the Isthmus of Tehuantepec (primarily Veracruz and Oaxaca) to the world market, these patently global aspects of the project, certain to raise fears about the integrity of national sovereignty and competitiveness, were downplayed, and the project was marketed as a local/regional endeavor. It promised to modernize and democratize an area of southern Mexico so indigenous, rural, and poor that urban Mexicans jokingly insist it belongs to Guatemala – and by modernizing it to make this region more Mexican. An editorial comment entitled

"Maquiladoras in the Future of Oaxaca" illustrates this logic. Mentioning that fifty national and international companies were interested in investing in the Isthmus region, the author opines: "Maquiladoras would reactivate the economy at all levels, would allow for the entrance of foreign capital and translate into a source of jobs and a higher level of life for the family. Maquilas would prevent Oaxaca's youth from having to migrate to the United States" (Aranda Villamayor 1997). More than any other state in Mexico, Oaxaca has witnessed profound transformations at the village level as a result of migration of men to cities in the north, and to the United States. Its deserted towns repatriate themselves in places as far away as Los Angeles and Chicago. Michael Kearney (1998) writes about the effect of migration on Mixtec populations from Oaxaca. He describes how the experience of migration has made Mexican national identity secondary to their ethnic identities, which get reinforced in the context of diasporic community formation in California. If foreign investment in the form of *maquilas* would prevent this migration, as the editorial above suggests, then the Megaproject would tend to reterritorialize citizenship within Mexico's south. In fact, this is not the most likely outcome. It is well documented that *maquilas* prefer to hire women – female labor commands lower wages, is less likely to be organized, and is regarded as more docile and compliant (Cravey 1998, Iglesias Prieto 1997). As Nash and Fernández-Kelly have shown (1983), this consistently gendered dimension of male migration and female *maquila* labor is a direct result of the new international organization of labor in the context of neoliberal development, as well as a major factor in the depopulation of rural villages. These facts are turned on their ear in official representation of the project and the causes of migration are presented as its solution. The Megaproject is presented in nationalistic terms in spite of its globalizing implications, and has the effect of recasting the Mexican national program as an essentially neoliberal one.

Yet the construction of the "neoliberal Mexican" is a highly contested process. At stake is the meaning of Mexico's national heritage and the true goals of the Mexican Revolution, which has been interpreted, at one extreme, as a victory for Mexico's modernizing bourgeoisie and, at another, as a true agrarian revolution. Many scholars have observed that the agrarian reforms ushered in by the Revolution did not in fact prevent the development and expansion of capital-intensive agriculture in Mexico (Gledhill 1995, Grindle 1986, Thiesenhusen 1995), and others have emphasized the relative continuity of Mexico's development trajectory by referring to the present neoliberal period as Mexico's "third wave" of development after liberalism and agrarian socialism (Phillips 1998). Despite the critique of the shortcomings of the Mexican Revolution among left activists, a common strategy has been to fall back on what Carr and Ellner (1993) refer to as "revolutionary nationalism": locating authentic Mexican values in the ideals of the Mexican Revolution and the promise of agrarian socialism. As Carr and Ellner point out, this puts the left in the untenable position of eliding the limitations of the revolutionary state, which did not break with the modernizing political economic agenda of the preceding liberal period.

In fact, nationalism is an important ideological and rhetorical tool in the fight against neoliberalism (see Collier and Stephen 1997, Stephen 1997, 2002) and a rallying force for both the Right and the Left in Mexico. Opposition to the Megaproject fought neoliberalism rhetorically by invoking the liberal period of Mexican history; thereby exposing the contradictions between free-market economics and democratic politics. This opposition came from organized social groups in the Isthmus region, including *campesino* and indigenous unions, and a variety of national environmental and human rights NGOs, some of which have international links. These activists regarded the proposed project as an imperialist intervention, a force of underdevelopment, and framed foreign investment in the area as a threat to local sovereignty. Invoking the Liberal period (1854–1911) of Mexican history, when financial speculators from the United States and other foreign nations set their sights on southeastern Mexico as a global transportation link, the activists argued that the project would benefit investors at the expense of the environment, local self-determination, and community development. Because the Megaproject was recognized as transnational in scope, opposition was consistently framed within a rubric of revolutionary nationalism. That is, neoliberal projects were regarded as a return to a less progressive social era predating the social and agrarian protections put into place by the Mexican revolution.

But government officials and other proponents of the neoliberal view also invoke the liberal period of Mexican history to legitimize their projects. In contrast to activists, who use the dictator Porfirio Díaz as a symbol of liberal decadence, they appeal to the legacy of the Mexican President Benito Juárez, who established a modern republic, instituted universal education, curtailed the power of the Church, and ousted Emperor Maximilian, ushering in a period of modernization and growth. By invoking the heroic figure of Benito Juárez, it is possible to cast the present period as one of progress and growth, and elide the nominal agrarian socialism that intervened between the two liberal eras.

Interpreting the Megaproject: Two Uses of History

Liberal-era nation-building projects, coming at the time of independence from Spain, provide some of the foundational nationalist stories for both proponents and opponents of neoliberal development. Brian Hamnett (1999) shows that Mexican nationalism was formed in the context of a massive political-economic reversal between the United States and Mexico that plummeted Mexico from its status as a world power at the time of independence from Spain in 1821 to a position of geopolitical subordination to the United States. Mexico's fall from empire had to do with the burden of an external debt inherited from Spain and the incomplete consolidation of the northern frontier, leading to the loss of two-thirds of its territory to the United States after the Mexican–American War (1846–8). This dramatic reversal of fortunes is poignantly illustrated by the fact that in 1821, when Mexico stood on the brink of empire, the American dollar was calibrated against the peso (Hamnett 1999).

Before this reversal, a canal or railroad across the Isthmus of Tehuantepec in Mexico was a significant part of the strategy for domestic territorial and economic expansion. Mexico had already commissioned a geographical survey to assess the advantages of a water canal or railroad through the Isthmus of Tehuantepec (Moro and de Garay 1844, Toledo 1995). By the time the Mexican–American War intervened in national development plans, transit rights across the Isthmus of Tehuantepec had become an international issue (Reina and Piñón Jiménez 1994, Toledo 1995). Geographical inquiries into a possible canal were initiated by the governments of Spain and the United States. In 1848, the Treaty of Guadalupe–Hidalgo ceded California and the southwestern states to the United States. In order to avoid further territorial loss to the United States and damage to the nationalist reputation of the Liberal regime, President Juárez granted the country transit rights in its Pacific ports and across the Isthmus of Tehuantepec in the McLane–Ocampo treaty of 1859. However, the treaty was never ratified by the US Congress because of the outbreak of the Civil War. Soon after, the French invaded Mexico, installing Maximilian, Archduke of Austria, as Emperor and briefly ousting President Benito Juárez. Although the legacy of Benito Juárez is highly contested, the struggles of the emergent Mexican nation against foreign imperialism during his administration are

powerful nationalist stories for all Mexicans (Hamnett 1999).

After the defeat of Maximilian, Juárez and later Porfirio Díaz embarked upon a modernizing project, through which Mexico inserted itself into the world market. Liberal theorists thought that building infrastructure such as transportation and industrial expansion in the agriculture sector would stimulate stagnant economies. Under the Porfiriato the southeastern states of Oaxaca and Chiapas were especially targeted for development (Coatsworth 1981). Although Juárez was interested in attracting foreign capital, it was Porfirio Díaz who was responsible for dramatically increasing foreign investment, from 200 million pesos in 1857 to over one billion in 1911 (Chassen 1990). During the Porfirian era, railroad construction was a national priority. Liberal policy-makers explicitly connected railroad construction in southeastern Mexico to their project to stimulate the economies of Oaxaca and Chiapas. The railroad system increased from 1,074 kilometers of track in 1880 to 19,280 kilometers in 1910 (Chassen 1990).

John Coatsworth has argued that railroad construction failed to stimulate economic growth. Instead, it served as a conduit for the export of raw materials to the United States, stimulating US mineral companies and other industries profiting from cheap natural resources. Moreover, rail lines constructed in remote areas of the southeast, rather than having a modernizing effect on production and social relations, actually served to revivify a disintegrating hacienda system, which remade itself in the form of modern agribusinesses. Combined with a dependency on the flow of foreign capital, the Porfirian development agenda contributed to a regressive redistribution of wealth and investment in Mexico (Coatsworth 1974).

The contradictions within the Liberal period provide a see-saw of interpretations for proponents and opponents of neoliberal development and provide a powerful nationalist script through which globalization and neoliberal development in Mexico are debated. On the one hand, for most Mexicans Benito Juárez is a nationalist hero. He set out to modernize the nation by disempowering the Catholic Church and breaking up latifundios. He sought to balance the threat of foreign intervention with the need for foreign capital, and he wrested control of the country away from Maximilian. Thus, modernization serves as a legitimate discourse tied to nationalist dreams for proponents of the project. Mainstream or government forces use liberalism to evoke the democracy of the market and to discredit the agrarian socialism and socialists that have come between the nation and its freedom. On the other hand, Porfirio Díaz tipped the balance of national policy toward foreign investment and reinforced the power of large landholders. His thirty-year dictatorship undermined the Republican values promoted by Juárez.

Activists use this script to link nationalism to anti-imperialism, locating threats to Mexican sovereignty in foreign capital invasion, as well as complicity of national elites (read neoliberals) in selling off their country to foreigners. Because Porfirio Díaz allowed the sale of land to foreigners, his version of liberalism is a threat to sovereignty. Moreover, because the Porfiriato was a dictatorship, associating liberalism with the Porfiriato suggests that neoliberalism is not to be logically associated with democracy: it raises questions about the neoliberal tendency to assume that electoral democracy flows naturally from free markets, and suggests that neoliberalism is a step backward for democracy in Mexico. The alternative reading compares current development projects to the development scams and land grabs of the Porfirian period that were one catalyst for the Mexican Revolution and its call for land redistribution and a protectionist state, by implication warning that contemporary abuses might bring about another revolution.

This full circle – from liberal to neoliberal development and from the revolution of Zapata to the revolution of the Zapatistas (Stephen 2002) – was symbolized most powerfully for activists by the transportation aspect of the Megaproject. As mentioned previously, during the Porfirato railroad construction was a major priority and new rails in southeast Mexico were a conduit for the export of raw materials to the United States. Since the Megaproject proposes a railroad or highway to modernize transportation across the Isthmus of Tehuantepec, its opponents represent this neoliberal project as a resurrection of liberalism that undermines the true (revolutionary) nation. In a conference hosted by activists and intellectuals called the "Transisthmenic Megaproject: the Other Side of the Mirror," the absurd and surreal world of *Alice in Wonderland* was invoked to connect the two historical periods.

A perusal of Liberal-period development plans for the Isthmus of Tehuantepec does in fact impart a sense of the surreal. Alejandro Toledo has summarized the extensive geographical reports on the Isthmus era from the nineteenth century and has documented the sundry uses imagined for the Isthmus. It was considered as a potential transportation corridor between the Pacific and Atlantic Oceans, and to the southern states of the United States. Because the United States had recently annexed California, sea routes between the east and the west coasts were being considered as a way to encourage the speedy settlement of this new territory. The violation of sovereignty implied in these explorations was apparently not lost on the Mexican press, which reprinted a selection from American Admiral Robert Schufeldt's 1872 Report to Congress: "a canal across the Isthmus of Tehuantepec is a prolongation of the Mississippi river toward the Pacific Ocean. It converts the Gulf of Mexico into an American lake. In time of war it closes the Gulf to all enemies" (Schufeldt 1872: 20).

The report goes on to explain that the Tehuantepec canal "brings New Orleans 1,400 nautical miles nearer to San Francisco than a canal via Darien [Panama]" and very explicitly invokes Manifest Destiny:

It may be that the future of our country lies hidden in this problem – whether . . . our principles of government, and our commerce under the flag . . . are to go hand in hand to further development, until are reached and taught the remotest corners of the East and the rudest barbarians of the Pacific Isles, or whether, resisting the struggles and checking the aspirations of the American heart for space and freedom, we are to live in disregard of natural law, and leave to another nation a glorious mission unfulfilled. (Schufeldt 1872: 20)

It was Panama that was eventually selected for the canal site, financed by the United States in return for a hundred-year concession and reversion to Panamanian control in 1999. The fact that the Panama Canal can no longer keep pace with the volume of shipping traffic in the region has revivified the intracontinental competition among Mexico, Nicaragua, and Columbia to host the next and best Isthmenic "dry" canal (a highway or railroad), witnessed by the numerous reports on potential canal sites that came out in the 1980s and 1990s. In the Isthmus of Tehuantepec, a railroad was eventually completed in 1907. Although not the interoceanic passageway originally envisioned, it was financed by a British company, Pearson & Son. Pearson was a close friend of President Díaz. Badly constructed by the standards of its day, the railroad was almost immediately nationalized, and Mexico acquired the huge debt incurred by its construction, leading to speculation that the whole project had been a sinecure for Pearson and his investors (Toledo 1995). In the Isthmus of Tehuantepec today, plans for a highway or a high-speed railroad are an echo of the plans laid for development during the liberal period. This history raises concerns that current projects are similarly designed to benefit wealthy investors, and that the Isthmus might become the next Panama, a militarized zone serving US interests, stripped of its territorial sovereignty. But transportation is merely one aspect of the Megaproject; and among activists, the project is considered much more than a foreign intervention. Its international investors represent the new "transnational enemy."

Transnationalism and the Repatriation of Struggle

"Carlos Slim [The richest man in Latin America] is Mexican, but he is more transnational than many foreign capitalists, that's why today, with these projects, its no longer a struggle against one foreign power, we are not in the age of imperialism, when Maximilian governed, its is a struggle against transnational capital" (Miguel Ángel García, quoted in El Imparcial, August 26, 1997: 3).

Miguel Ángel, the director of an environmental NGO active in the Chimalapas forest of Oaxaca, an area affected by the Megaproject and now by the PPP, went on to explain that although global capitalists may have been born Mexican, they have lost their culture and their identity. As a result, they will think nothing of selling their own lands, nation, and peoples. At a community meeting, Luis Miguel, also of Maderas del Pueblo, remarked: "If we don't stop the Megaproject, we will have to ask Molly here to teach us English – let's hope so, anyway; it's easier than Japanese." These remarks suggest that what is really insidious about imperialism is its deterritorialized or denationalized nature. Global actors are removed from a meaningful connection to their nation. By representing transnational capitalism as antithetical to nationalism, activists transform local cultures and the community "beneath the state" into the real locus of nationalism.[2] National elites, by engaging global economics, become honorary foreigners. This is important in two respects: (1) transnationalism is still largely represented as the struggles of a nation against its foreign enemies; and (2) nationalism, a statist ideology useful for creating relatively homogeneous identities, is recast as pluralistic, local, and culture-bearing. Nationalism is thus rescaled to inhabit a space beneath the reach of the transnational state itself.

In contrast, the governmental proponents of neoliberalism represent development as a hedge against internal fragmentation that would shatter the nation from within. In 1997 representatives of the state government of Oaxaca went on tour to promote the Megaproject, making stops at some of the major municipalities on the Isthmus. They arrived in the dusty, hot windblown towns toting a bewildering array of computers and, armed with *PowerPoint*, they generated a slick slide-show worthy of Madison Avenue. In Matías Romero, their audience was a mixed crowd of local professionals, workers, *campesinos*, activists, and municipal authorities. The speakers emphasized that the proposed transportation project was *not* intended to compete with the Panama Canal – but rather to make the Isthmus itself a competitive region. The transportation project would complement an ambitious industrialization plan designed to provide new jobs and economic security. The goods produced and processed in *maquilas*, forest plantations, and petrochemical plants would be brought to market via the new high-speed railroad. Far from transforming the Isthmus into another Panama, the Megaproject would boost local prosperity by linking the Isthmus to world markets. Rather than compromise national sovereignty, it would bring the region up to par with the rest of Mexico – thus making it more a part of the nation. The presentation was designed to meet dissent that was known to be brewing.

In fact, a great deal of opposition has arisen to the very idea of "Megaprojects." Between 1940 and 1970, Mexico underwent dramatic industrial development, transforming itself from a rural to an urban nation. During this period, the tropics of southeastern Mexico, as elsewhere in Latin America, were systematically deforested in colonization projects that opened new lands for *campesino* settlement and monocrop production, and timber, mineral, and water resources were tapped to provide for the growing needs of the nation (Bray 1991, Collier et al. 1994, Downing et al. 1992). In Oaxaca, huge, inefficient and technically flawed dam projects resulted in much loss of property and the relocation of 35,000 people to Uxpanapa, a forest that is now deforested, dry, and infertile (Bárabas and Bartolomé 1973). Mexican ecologist Alejandro Toledo has called the development of the Isthmus "one of the greatest social and ecological tragedies in the history of the modernization of Mexican society" (Toledo 1995:139).

Even community members hostile to the activists in the area were suspicious of the Megaproject and its goals. The railroad that now winds through the Isthmus was built behind the standards even of its day in 1907, contributing to the curtailment of Matías Romero's glory days as a thriving railroad hub in the first half of the twentieth century. Regarding the proposed plan to build a high-speed train in place of the present obsolete system, the former Mayor of Matías Romero offered the following observation:

> They are always saying that the railway is going to be fixed.... [When the Engineer Olguin visited recently proposing to renovate the railroad] I asked him through which route the railway would pass. He said in the same place it is now. We are going to use the [existing] infrastructure. Which is to say that this Engineer hasn't ridden a train.... If the engineer who came as the governor's representative would ride the train, he wouldn't need to ask the railway workers about anything, he would notice. But if he were to have asked the railway workers about the tracks, the workers would have told him that the tracks have many curves and a few very steep hills and this impedes the rapid transit of the train. (Smith [pseudonym] 1997; recording of presentation by the state government, public meeting, January 30)

Organized resistance to the Megaproject became publicly manifest in 1997, when the environmental NGO, Maderas del Pueblo, and human rights NGO UCIZONI co-hosted a conference about the Megaproject. Attended by about a thousand people from NGOs, local communities, and universities, "The Isthmus is Ours" was very effective in putting the Megaproject on the public agenda. Thus, whereas there had been little news coverage of the proposed project in the preceding months, the Megaproject was almost daily in the news for the weeks just before and after the conference. Here it was stressed that government estimates of the benefits of the project were overblown and environmental damages underestimated. Instead of pork-barrel development fiascos, it was argued, capital should be put toward local projects to reinforce and strengthen local cultures and land-use patterns. Thus, like the Zapatistas in Chiapas, the social movement against the Megaproject in the Isthmus has linked ethnic identity and local development with sovereignty and political autonomy. In the context of the conference, national sovereignty was again rescaled – transformed from a problem of autonomy of one nation against others into the autonomy of local cultures from a neoliberal state.

The significance of social protest over the Megaproject for its longer-term goals and projects was not lost on observers and commentators. Responding to the common accusation that neoliberalism and structural adjustment policies pursued in the 1980s and 1990s had deepened poverty in Mexico, the President of the Association of Mexican Bankers offered this observation:

The poverty that forty million Mexicans suffer is the result of [both] the populist social policies and the great increases in population of the seventies. Some people with bad intentions or who are ignorant of the real issues attribute the origin of the current political economic crisis to the free market policies Mexico has been employing in the last few years, and they call this neo-liberalism. But neoliberalism in Mexico is a myth. When traditional communist and so-cialist doctrines came crashing down, the followers of these doctrines were left without banners; they didn't know what to say or who to attack. (Del Valle, quoted in *La Jornada*, October 17, 1997:18)

Of course, neoliberalism in Mexico is not a myth, but a pervasive reality that affects Mexican society at every institutional level. Just as constitutional reforms in 1992 denationalized lands in order to make property available on the free market, changes to legislation and agencies in the past decade have responded to a drive for decentralization.

Decentralizing the Environment for the Megaproject

New federal environmental legislation passed in 1995 reflects the general decentralizing trend in Mexican policy. The new laws set out new specifications for the ratification of land-use plans in ecologically sensitive areas that come under federal jurisdiction. During a course offered at the Autonomous University of Mexico (UNAM) in 1997 concerning how to use and interpret aspects of the new legislation, lecturers stressed the grassroots nature of the new law, claiming it would put more power into local hands concerning decisions about development. However, several government officials working in the federal environmental agency (SEMERNAP) cautioned that community land-use plans could be overridden by the eminent domain privileges of agencies like the Ministry of Transportation. Moreover, SEMERNAP had been unable to process and implement the backlog of community land-use plans that had been pouring in, many of which overlapped or conflicted with development plans proposed by the state-level environmental and development agencies that proliferated as decentralized planning proceeded apace. Nevertheless, the creation of laws that strengthened community-level decision making were lauded by environmentalists working at the community level, who began to investigate how the law might be used to impede large-scale development interventions like the Megaproject.

At the same time, in response to the requirements of the new environmental laws, a new government agency in Oaxaca, the State Institute of Ecology, was charged with carrying out the regional-level territorial land-use plan for Chimalapas. Although the agency was established in response to pressure on the federal government from local environmental activists, its staff was handpicked by the conservative state governor. That the agency was directed by an urban planner and staffed by architects was symptomatic not only of the recent change in vogue from urban development to ecology, but also of the cynicism of the governor toward environmental protection as a whole. Upon inquiries about the ecological advisability of the Megaproject, a representative of this agency responded "the project comes from the federal government. They wouldn't suggest doing it in the first place if it were going to be harmful to the environment." Although the agency had no technical staff – which would include geographers, agronomists, foresters, anthropologists, etc. – it completed a land-use plan for the entire Isthmus region. This plan, under Federal law, now had to be approved by the affected municipalities of Chimalapas.

Meanwhile, the ecological NGO, Maderas del Pueblo, with support from the WWF (World Wide Fund for Nature) and USAID (the US Agency for International Development), completed several ecological land-use plans for communities in Chimalapas. These plans, if accepted by the communities, would encourage small-scale production and ecological forestry, and would make forestry plantations, such as those proposed by the Megaproject, illegal. In 1997, Maderas del Pueblo was doing political work in Chimalapas to get these ecological measures implemented in local law.

In this same year, in town elections in San Miguel Chimalapa, a pro-PRD (center-left party) government, sympathetic to the

NGO, was replaced by a pro-PRI one, sympathetic to government projects. According to a number of community members and activists, community members were given 200 pesos each (US$25) and a machete per household to vote for the PRI-supported (centrist majority party) candidates. The consensus seems to be that the state and federal governments rigged the elections in order to install puppets, and that these puppets would be manipulated into ratifying a land-use plan that would give the green light to the Megaproject. This turn of events coincided with a series of events I have discussed elsewhere (Doane 2001) that eventually led to a rupture between international funders and ecologists in Chimalapas in favor of an alliance between the state and federal environmental protection agencies and international funders. That is, monies intended to fund nongovernmental initiatives began to be channeled directly to the state. Activists complain that the government has co-opted the terminology and practices of the opposition, representing themselves as activists for the people. More seriously, this turn of events shows that not only discourse but local democratic process can be co-opted to strengthen authority at the level of the local state, thus generating the appearance of consent at the local level for neoliberal globalization.

Conclusion

Now that the Megaproject has been subsumed under Vicente Fox's Plan Puebla-Panama, the original development plan for the Isthmus is unequivocally linked to a global regionalization plan, subsuming the Isthmus into a Central American region modernized enough to take its place as a viable economic partner with the United States. The PPP is significant on several fronts. First, improved transportation and infrastructure will certainly encourage the growth of transnational firms at the expense of less competitive national and local ones, making way for the monopolization of local economies by fewer and larger enterprises. Second, although the PPP indicates an embrace of neoliberalism only hinted at under the Megaproject, it is a still a *national* neoliberal project. The 2002 Mexican federal budget, in an era of drastically curtailed social subsidies, earmarks almost US$1 billion for the PPP. This is hardly matched by the US$4 million collected from assorted banks and international investors by the Inter-American Development Bank.[3] Of course, there is a great deal of opposition to the PPP to be reckoned with. In Oaxaca, activists who link neoliberal projects to the Porfiriato are by extension suggesting that projects like the PPP will lead to a new kind of revolution. International awareness of and opposition to the PPP has grown in the context of antiglobalization protests, and the Mexican government has removed its *PowerPoint* presentation showcasing the PPP from its webpage and moved information relating to the project to the Department of Foreign Relations. This relates to the third major implication of the PPP. As international and national protests build against it, Fox may find that the PPP will not serve as a centerpiece for national regionalization, and that remaking globalization in a Mexican image faces challenges from not only the lobbyists for the FTAA "above" but also the supposed beneficiaries "below."

In this chapter I have argued that nationalist discourse plays an important role in generating consent for neoliberal projects; and the state, its agencies, and political parties institute the necessary reorganizations at the local level to put those projects into practice. In order to make way for global free markets, the nation is rescaled into decentralized units. This rescaling is generally regarded as a move toward democratization and away from the centralized, authoritarian state model. Local agencies charged with decision making at the local and regional levels should be more efficient and more responsive to local demands. In fact, proliferating state agencies imposed a bureaucratic disorder at the level of the local state that made rational planning difficult and accountability impossible. The rescaling of the state, answering the call of democracy and free market, has the paradoxical effect of empowering interests at the supranational level – in this case, making it difficult for local activists to defeat the Megaproject or the PPP in spite of the unpopularity of these projects.

At the same time, activists on the left rescale nationalism to fit their own pluralistic vision of the decentralized state. Nationalism refers not to a homogenizing ideological construct, but rather signifies cultural authenticity and sensitivity to the local. This nationalist discourse is used to mobilize opposition to transnational interests within the state. One of the challenges for *campesino* movements in Mexico struggling to escape the morass of neoliberalism is to distinguish, rhetorically and legally, their spaces of autonomy from the hidden, decentered fiefdoms of rule that are augmented, not broken down, by the restructuring state.

Moreover, local movements will need to manipulate their rescaled nationalism in such a way that it continues to strengthen pluralism and autonomy without rejecting alliances with other social movements – both national and international – that engage the same fight against Megaprojects and other top-down initiatives.

NOTES

The author would like to thank the Wenner-Gren Foundation, the National Science Foundation, and the Institute for the Study of World Politics for kindly and generously supporting the dissertation research on which this chapter is based.

1   *Maquilas* are factories set up by foreign investors on Mexican soil. Factory infrastructure is minimal to allow for mobility; workers are unskilled and often female. Manufacturing materials are imported, and finished goods are exported (Nash and Fernández-Kelly 1983, Iglesias Prieto 1997).

2 Leslie Gill (2000) observes that protests against neoliberalism in Bolivia often take the form of a protest against US imperialism, thus eliding the essential role of national elites in promoting and implementing free-market policies.

3 These figures were compiled by the Maquila Solidarity Network, March 2002 (http:/mexico.indymedia.org:8081).

REFERENCES

Álvarez, Sonia E., Evelina Dagnino, and Arturo Escobar
  1998 Cultures of Politics, Politics of Cultures: Re-visioning Latin American Social Movements. Boulder, CO: Westview Press.
Aranda Villamayor, Carlos
  1997 Las Maquiladoras en el Futuro de Oaxaca. Notícias, Oaxaca, October 1.
Bárabas, Alicia, and Miguel Alberto Bartolomé
  1973 Hydraulic Development and Ethnocide: The Mazatec and Chinantec People of Oaxaca, Mexico. Copenhagen: International Work Group for Indigenous Affairs.
Barkin, David, Rosemary L. Batt, and Billie R. DeWalt
  1990 Food Crops vs. Feed Crops: Global Substitution of Grains in Production. Boulder, CO: Lynne Rienner.
Bray, David Barton
  1991 The Struggle for the Forest: Conservation and Development in the Sierra Juárez. Grassroots Development 15(3):13–25.
——1995 Peasant Organizations and the "Permanent Reconstruction of Nature": Grassroots Sustainable Development in Rural Mexico. Journal of Environment & Development 4(2):185–204.
Carr, Barry, and Steve Ellner, eds.
  1993 The Latin American Left: From the Fall of Allende to Perestroika. Latin American Perspectives Series 11. Boulder, CO: Westview Press.
Castells, Manuel
  1997 The Power of Identity. Malden, MA: Blackwell.
Chassen, Francie R.
  1990 Regiones y Ferrocarriles en la Oaxaca Porfirista. Oaxaca: Carteles.
Coatsworth, John H.
  1974 Railroads, Landholding, and Agrarian Protest in the Early Porfiriato. Hispanic American Historical Review 3 (August):48–71.
——1981 Growth Against Development: The Economic Impact of Railroads in Porfirian Mexico. DeKalb: Northern Illinois University Press.
Collier, George A., with Elizabeth Lowery Quaratiello
  1994 Basta! Land and the Zapatista Rebellion in Chiapas. Oakland, CA: Institute for Food and Development Policy.
Collier, George A.; Daniel C. Mountjoy, and Ronald B. Nigh
  1994 Peasant Agriculture and Global Change. Bioscience 44(6):398–407.
Collier, George, and Lynn Stephen, eds.
  1997 Ethnicity, Identity and Citizenship in the Wake of the Zapatista Rebellion. Theme issue. Journal of Latin American Anthropology 3(1).
Cravey, A. J.
  1998 Women and Work in Mexico's maquiladoras. Lanham, MD: Rowman & Littlefield.
Dagnino, Evelina
  1998 Culture, Citizenship, and Democracy: Changing Discourses and Practices of the Latin American Left. In Cultures of Politics, Politics of Cultures: Revisioning Latin American Social Movements. Sonia E. Alvarez and Arturo Escobar, eds. Pp. 33–63. Boulder, CO: Westview Press.
DeWalt, Billie R., Martha W. Rees, and Arthur D. Murphy
  1994 The End of Agrarian Reform in Mexico: Past Lessons, Future Prospects. San Diego, CA: Center for US–Mexican Studies UCSD.

Doane, Molly
2001 A Distant Jaguar: The Civil Society Project in Chimalapas. Critique of Anthropology 21(4):361–382.

Downing, Theodore E. et al., eds.
1992 Development or Destruction: The Conversion of Tropical Forest to Pasture in Latin America. Boulder, CO: Westview Press.

Edelman, Marc
2001 Social Movements: Changing Paradigms and Forms of Politics. Annual Review of Anthropology 30:285–317.

Escobar, Arturo, and Sonia E. Álvarez
1992 The Making of Social Movements in Latin America: Identity, Strategy, and Democracy. Boulder, CO: Westview Press.

Esparza, Manuel
1988 Los Proyectos de Los Liberales en Oaxaca. In Historia de la Cuestión Agrária Mexicana. Leticia Reina, ed. Pp. 269–330, Vol. 1. México, DF: Juan Pablos Editor.

Espinoza, Martin
2000 Could Zapatistas Lose Out to Fox in War of Ideas?" December 5. http://www.pacificnews.org/jinn/stories/6.24/001205_could.html

Fox, Jonathan
1993 The Politics of Food in Mexico: State Power and Social Mobilization. Ithaca, NY: Cornell University Press.

Gill, Lesley
2000 Teetering on the Rim: Global Restructuring, Daily Life, and the Armed Retreat of the Bolivian State. New York: Columbia University Press.

Gledhill, John
1995 Neoliberalism, Transnationalization and Rural Poverty: A Case Study of Michoacán, Mexico. Boulder, CO: Westview Press.

Grindle, Merilee Serrill
1986 State and Countryside: Development Policy and Agrarian Politics in Latin America. Baltimore, MD: Johns Hopkins University Press.

Hamnett, Brian
1999 A Concise History of Mexico. New York: Cambridge University Press.

Harvey, Neil
1990 The New Agrarian Movement in Mexico, 1979–1990. London: Institute of Latin American Studies.

Hellman, Judith Adler
1994 Mexican Lives. New York: New Press.

Henwood, Doug
2000 Profiteering in the Hemisphere. NACLA Report on the Americas 34(3):49–55.

Hernández Castillo, Aida, and Ronald Nigh
1998 Global Processes and Local Identity among Mayan Coffee Growers in Chiapas, Mexico. American Anthropologist 100(1):136–147.

Iglesias Prieto, Norma
1997 Beautiful Flowers of the Maquiladora: Life Histories of Women Workers in Tijuana. M. S. w. G. Winkler, trans. Austin: University of Texas Press.

Joseph, Gilbert and Daniel Nugent
1994 Everyday Forms of State Formation: Revolution and the Negotiation of Rule in Modern Mexico. Durham, NC: Duke University Press.

Kearney, Michael
1998 Transnationalism in Mexico and California at the End of Empire. In Border Identities: Nation and State at International Frontiers. Tom Wilson and Hastings Donnan, eds. Pp. 117–141. Cambridge: Cambridge University Press.

Khagram, Sanjeev, Riker, James, and Kathryn Sikkink
2003 From Santiago to Seattle: Transnational Advocacy Groups Restructuring World Politics. In Restructuring World Politics: Transnational Social Movements, Networks, and Norms. Sanjeev Khagram, James V. Riker, and Kathryn Sikkink, eds. Pp. 3–23. Minneapolis: University of Minnesota Press.

Laclau, Ernesto, and Chantal Mouffe
1985 Hegemony and Socialist Strategy. London: Verso.

Machuca, Jesús Antonio
n.d. El Plan Puebla-Panamá y el Patrimonio Cultural en el Sur de México.

http://www.ciepac.org/otras%20temas/memorias/cultur.htm

Miller, John
1993 The Passion of Michel Foucault. New York: Simon & Schuster.

Moguel, Julio et al., eds.
1992 Autonomía y Nuevos Sujetos Sociales en el Desarrollo Rural. Mexico: Siglo XXI.

Moro, Cayetano, and José de Garay
1844 Survey of the Isthmus of Tehuantepec, executed in the years 1842 and 1843, with the intent of establishing a communication between the Atlantic and Pacific Oceans, and under the superintendence of a scientific commission, appointed by the projector Don José de Garay. London: Ackermann.

Nash, June
—— 1994a The Challenge of Trade Liberalization to Cultural Survival on the Southern Frontier of Mexico. Indiana Journal of Global and Legal Studies 1(2):367–395.
—— 1994b Global Integration and Subsistence Insecurity. American Anthropologist 96(2):1–31.
—— 1995 The Power of the Powerless: Update from Chiapas. Cultural Survival 19(1):14–18.
—— 2001 Mayan Visions: The Quest for Autonomy in the Age of Globalization. New York: Routledge.

Nash, June C., and María Patricia and Fernández-Kelly
1983 Women, Men, and the International Division of Labor. Albany: State University of New York Press.

Nigh, Ronald
1992 La Agricultura Orgánica y el Nuevo Movimiento Campesino en México. Antropológicas 3:39–49.

Nigh, Ronald, and N. J. Rodríguez
1995 Territorios violados: indios, medio ambiente y desarrollo en América Latina. México, D.F., Dirección General de Publicaciones del Consejo Nacional para la Cultura y las Artes: Instituto Nacional Indigenista.

Phillips, Lynne
1998 The Third Wave of Modernization in Mexico: A Cultural Perspective on Neo-Liberalism. Wilmington, DE: Scholarly Resources.

Podur, Joshua
2001 Mexico's "Modern Right." ZNet Daily Commentaries, June 11, www.Zmag.org/chiapas/index.htm

Reina, Leticia, and Gonzalo Piñón Jiménez
1994 Economía contra Sociedad: el Istmo de Tehuántepec, 1907–1986. México, DF: Nueva Imágen.

Rubin, Jeffrey W.
1997 Decentering the Regime: Ethnicity, Radicalism, and Democracy in Juchitán, Mexico. Durham, NC: Duke University Press.

Schufeldt, Robert
1872 Reports of the Tehauntepec Canal Survey. Forty-Second Congress, second session. SS 1480, s.exdoc.6.

Silverstein, Ken, and Alexander Cockburn
1995 Major U.S. Bank Urges Zapatista Wipe-Out: "A litmus test for Mexico's stability." Counterpunch 2(3), February 1.

Stephen, Lynn
1997 Redefined Nationalism in Building a Movement for Indigenous Autonomy in Southern Mexico. Journal of Latin American Anthropology 3(1):72–101.
2002 !Zapata Lives! Histories and Cultural Politics in Southern Mexico. Berkeley: University of California Press.

Thiesenhusen, William C.
1995 Broken Promises: Agrarian Reform and the Latin American Campesino. Boulder, CO: Westview Press.

Toledo, Alejandro
1995 Geopolítica y Desarrollo en el Istmo de Tehuantepec. [Mexico]: Centro de Ecología y Desarrollo.

Warman, Arturo
1988 Los Estudios Campesinos: Véinte Años Después. Comercio Exterior 38(7):653–658.

11

The Politics of Place: Legislation, Civil Society and the "Restoration" of the Florida Everglades

Max Kirsch

Introduction

The Everglades has long been the site of culture wars over the future of environmental standards in the United States and in Florida. Environmental and development issues are continuing to generate increasing conflict in Everglades communities, which are already under stress from rapid social change. The current restructuring of the agricultural industry and new environmental legislation have highlighted the differences in approaches to the maintenance of place that exist within Everglades communities and the proposals for development that are being presented by industries and governmental agencies. These differences are challenging communities to respond to changes initiated from outside their boundaries.

There has been a substantial effort on the part of community-based organizations to engage citizens in the decision-making process of legislative policies. These organizations and voluntary associations are reacting to the current threats to environmental justice, community, equity, and participation in the formulation of environmental planning. At the same time, the managerial strategies of "verticality" and "encompassment" (Ferguson and Gupta 2002) pose obstacles to the elements of community and civil society attempting to garner significant participation in the planning process.

This chapter will explore the position and interaction of Everglades communities and their wider elements of civil society as they struggle to maintain a sense of place in the contested arena of Everglades restoration, for which the federal and Florida state governments have pledged to spend an estimated US$8 to $10 billion over the next ten to thirty years. It argues against a perspective of neo-globalism that presents abstractions rather than grounded analyses of "communities of practice" (Gupta and Ferguson 1997, Nash 2001a:219), proposing instead that more localized descriptions and histories are needed to interpret the relationship between global forces and local developments.

Globalism and the Florida Everglades

The restoration of the Everglades is necessarily framed by global, national, and local forces. Tardanico and Rosenberg (2000) point out that processes of globalization, particularly in the name of the North American Free Trade Agreement (NAFTA), incorporate both underdeveloped economies such as those of southern Mexico and the rich economies of the north, including the southern United States. This marginalization of indigenous and local groups feed into the global and continental shifts that are "segmenting societies and linking up valuable functions, individuals, social groups, and territories, while excluding others" (Tardanico and Rosenberg 2000:4, Castells et. al. 1995–6: 33). As they also point out, the US South does not fare well in comparison to the northeast corridor. Differences in the "New South" are acute: telecommunications in North Carolina's Research Triangle do not compare with the poor agricultural areas of the "Old South," which harbor far more migrant and poorly paid labor than NAFTA's documents would suggest (Tardanico and Rosenberg 2000:4–5).

Everglades communities contain their own history and responses to the processes of globalization and practices of capitalist management. The time–space compression that Harvey (1990, 1998) refers to as the condition of late capitalism is not clearly apparent in the vegetable and sugar fields of the Everglades, nor can it explain the labor practices or the mechanization of cultivation that have been introduced during the past decade. Also, the recent and popular postmodern discussions of the inevitability of "capital fluidity" tend to produce a neo-globalism that naturalizes the break between people and place, failing to indicate the resistance to such exogenous forces by local communities (cf. Nash 2001a, 2001b). Appadurai (1991), for example, views "deterritorialization" as a dominant mode of our present condition, where "money, commodities and persons unendingly chase each other around the world that the group imagination of the modern world find their fractured and fragmented counterpart." Likewise, Inda and Rosaldo tell us that

> as a result of all this back and forth movement, from the West to the rest and vice-versa, the familiar lines between "here" and "there," center and periphery and vice versa, West and non-West have to some extent become blurred. That is to say, insofar as the Third World is the First and the First World is the Third, it has become difficult to specify with any certitude where one entity begins and the other one ends.... Where, for example, does one draw the boundaries of Mexico when so many of "its people" live in the U.S.? Or where does one draw the boundaries of the U.S. when "its capital" has such a strong presence in Mexico? (Inda and Rosaldo 2002:22)

Both Nash (2001a, 2001b) and Mintz (1998) warn that this fascination with deterritorialization and deculturalization focus analyses on the abstraction of capital and its control over global accumulation, leading to the conceptual loss of agency in communities and regions disaffected by organizational changes in production. These debates are reminiscent of the differences presented in the debates over Wallerstein's The Modern World System (1974), which posited the structural binaries of "core" and "periphery" as primary units of analysis, often forgetting the "periphery" had much to do with how the "core" countries organized their intrusions into uncolonized, and later colonized, regions of the world. The argument has evolved so that the "core" is now described as "ethnoscapes," "technoscapes," and "financescapes" (Appadurai, 1986, 1990), and the periphery as the world at large.

The creation of a binary between space as fluid and place as decentered has taken the role of the social scientist outside the community and into the world of power as an abstraction. The people who inhabit these spaces are easily identified as spokes in the global wheel, reacting solely to the forces of capital surrounding them rather than to their own histories, religions, families, and beliefs. What is forgotten is the increasing fragmentation of regions and communities and, often, the violence that accompanies the attempt to recapture identity through the political maze of global politics. As the personnel involved in these new descriptions of capital flows constitute a kind of global network entrenched in a narrow cosmopolitanism, we run the risk of creating a novel class-based centrism that focuses on the managers of capital rather than the communities of place. In addition, the Balkanization of many parts of the world attests to the danger of viewing the world in Inda and Rosaldo's terms. There is resistance to attempts at deterritorialization, proving it to be much more a category of political strategy than a holistic analytic process. The Zapatista uprising is one of many instances Nash (2001a, 2001b) cites to show the importance of territorial resistance to globalization that denies the continuing priority of peoples' association with place. Those who naturalize the forced relocation of people undermine the basis of such struggles.

"We are never anywhere, anywhen, but in place," Englund reminds us, where "the subject is inextricably *situated* in a historically and existentially specific condition, defined, for brevity, as a 'place'" (Englund 2002:267). These places are the communities of practice that take into account all of the places in which people that are the subjects of study engage in and interact in the process of social reproduction. Analyses of these communities now often include "civil society," a concept reintroduced both in academic circles and popular culture during the 1980s to illuminate the phenomenon of independent organizations and affiliations that challenge the mechanisms of corporations and the state in controlling public debate and action. But beyond the common usage of the concept, the term can be useful for analyses of infor-

mal practices that include interpersonal relations (Hann and Dunn 1996:3), and the development of grassroots movements that are designed to be separate from either local or external governing forces.

In the language of neo-globalism that stresses deterritorialization and the free movement of capital and peoples, it is easy to view community-based organizations and the people who constitute them as inconsequential remnants, if not cultural survivals of the past, unable to confront the onslaught of the many levels of multinational or provide comfort and resistance to community oppression or destruction. But communities are vibrant and changing sources of place, as Mintz (1998) cautions, and the Everglades has a long history of organizations that provide services and support to both visiting and stable local populations.

The migrants, farmers, and other residents of the Everglades, of course, have been and continue to be deeply affected by changes in global strategies for capitalist accumulation. But as we shall see, these changes are substantially modified by national, local, and community forces that call into question the neo-global analyses of communities, capital, and production.

The Restoration of the Everglades

The restoration of the everglades has been repeatedly hailed as the most significant environmental reconstruction project in the history of the United States. Reference to the restoration by federal and state authorities is entwined with environmental-speak – homage to the growing concerns at home and abroad about the fate of the Earth's biosphere and the effects of industrial development and residential growth on what is left of the Earth's habitat. Seemingly brought about by international concern that one of the Earth's rare treasures is being rapidly destroyed, the real winners in the restoration process may well be the same development interests that are often accused of devastating these wetlands. These developers are responding to the opportunities presented by the urban sprawl and growth of suburban enclaves that has doubled Florida's growth several times since the 1960s and that has created an infrastructure crisis – jammed highways, substandard schools, and overcrowded prisons being among the most discussed. The other, overarching problem is water.

The Everglades Agricultural Area (EAA) is a drained swamp bordering Lake Okeechobee, established by government decree in the mid-nineteenth century when twenty million wetland acres were handed over to Florida lawmakers, and "reclamation" became a statewide rallying cry (cf. Roberts 1999). Reclamation meant turning the land from swamp into cultivable farmland that could support rice, cotton, citrus, and sugar cane. The land was restructured by the construction of canals that drained the swampy water into the Atlantic Ocean, thus exposing a mucky soil inhabited by saw grass. By the 1920s development of the area was in full swing, with the population growing tenfold between 1900 and 1930 (Roberts 1999). In 1947, Congress allocated an additional $200 million to the Army Corps of Engineers to build levees and dams in the southern Everglades, thus providing Miami's growing population with flood-free drinking water. Once labeled "unfit for man or vermin," the area between Interstate 75 and the Fort Meyers airport now boasts the highest concentration of golf holes per capita on earth (Grunwald 2002c). By the end of the drainage project in the 1960s, over 18,000 square miles had been drained, utilizing 1,000 miles of canals, 720 miles of levees, and over 200 water-control structures (Scully 2001). The result was the effective elimination of the Everglades. While wetlands are still part of the landscape of South Florida's ecology, the biodiversity of the area has been restructured, and its heterogeneity substantially reduced.

Despite the many obstacles that confronted the early farmers on what turned out to be a low-nutrient soil, sugar production in the area began to increase, particularly with the development of new strains of sugar crops that were more adaptive to the local environmental constraints. Sugar is a dry-land crop, and the muck created by the draining was not suitable for cane growth. The problem was solved with the breeding of new strains of cane, and the enormous applications of phosphorus and nitrogen. As a result, the area began to commercially thrive. But the US sugar crop remained small, with the US Sugar Corporation, owned by the Mott family, the primary benefactor of the reclamation efforts.

The story changed in 1959 with the Cuban Revolution. Cuban sugar was banned from sale in the United States, and with substantial federal incentives for sugar production, more outsiders were attracted to the area. The Army Corps of Engineers drained more swamp for cultivation, and by the mid-1960s Florida's sugar production had increased tenfold. With the help of Washington, the sugar industry became the major player in Florida politics (Roberts 1999:58).

Along with the expansion of sugar production came former Cuban sugar producers, the most influential among them Alfonso Fanjul, who bought 4,000 acres of drained farmland. By 1990, the company had bought Domino Sugar and 90,000 new acres in Florida, along with 110,000 acres in the Dominican Republic, forming the Florida Crystals Corporation. Florida Crystals is now the largest sugar producer in the United States.

The Fanjuls became a major force in national and Florida politics. The movie *Striptease* was based on the Fanjul family, and their influence over national environmental policy has become legendary. The Clinton Administration's adopted plan for the restoration of the Everglades bears an uncanny resemblance to a plan championed by the sugar industry, and in particular, the Fanjul's Florida Crystals. The plan calls for restoration to begin south of the sugar farms and requires that Florida taxpayers pay half the $700 million cost for filtration marshes.

In a highly politicized move also initiated by Florida Crystals, the sugar industry was exempted from the NAFTA deregulation of industry until at least 2008, while its production continues to be subsidized. The arrangement defies free-trade logic, while irking refiners and consumers (Barboza 2002).

The history of sugar, vegetable production, and Everglades environmental policy is global, national, and local in scope, but none has had a more powerful presence than the federal government and the halls of Washington. Congress passed the Everglades Restoration Plan in 2000, and to date over US$1 billion in funding has been granted. The Plan is under the direction of the same federal agency charged with initially draining the swamps in the 1940s, the Army Corps of Engineers. The current plan sounds eerily familiar to the first plan, and this is no accident. The Army Corps of Engineers is again involved in a re-plumbing project, a plan that is designed more to provide water to Florida's growing population than to "restore" what was the Florida Everglades. The region's population is expected to double again by 2050. Nationally, the Army Corps approves proposals for the draining and filling of streams, marshes, and other wetlands, and regularly approves over ninety-nine percent of such requests, destroying more wetlands than any developer (Grunwald 2002d). As Grunwald reports, "This mind-set was on display after September 11, when the Chief Corps regulator sent on e-mail to staff nationwide: 'the harder we work to expedite the insurance of permits, the more we serve the nation by moving the economy forward'" (ibid.). Indeed, while the Army Corps initially questioned a mining plan that is now destroying more wetlands than was permitted nationwide in 2001, as Grunwald tells us, "the Corps is not blocking the plan, or even fighting the plan. The Corps is promoting the plan as a key element of its 7.8 billion Everglades restoration project" (Grunwald 2002e). The fate of the Everglades is now in the hands of a new administration in Washington closely tied to development interests

in the state of Florida. In a recent editorial, the *New York Times* publicly worried about the fate of the restoration project, when Gale Norton, Bush's Interior Secretary, removed Michael Davis, the Clinton Administration's point man on the Everglades (*New York Times* 2001).

Communities and Civil Society

The principal destination into the Everglades is Belle Glade, a city of 14,000 people and 2,862,000 acres of subtropical Everglades. Founded in 1928, the area was first inhabited by the Calusa Indians, and later by the Seminole Indians, who gave Lake Okeechobee (Land of Big Water) its name. Today it houses farmers (those who stay in the area year round) and migrants (those who travel for agricultural work) and the auxiliary services needed to maintain their presence. Noticeable as one enters Belle Glade are the ramshackle houses and the number of churches of every denomination. Social agencies that service the area are prominent in number and in diversity. Belle Glade is a town that has long experienced the need for supportive community organizations and social service agencies, both public and privately funded.

The stark transition between the growing developments of the east and the agricultural fields and towns of the Everglades symbolizes the contradictions inherent in Florida's development and the current strategies to address differing interest groups and communities. The politics that are played out in the media and the halls of government often obscure the current state of community participation in decision making, and the attempts by community-based organizations to maintain a sense of place and history in these processes.

Like Sassen's (1998) discussion of the telecommunications industry in New York City, *place* in the Everglades is determined by the necessity of geographic locale and by the product it supports. But beyond the importance of locale and product, there were strong fluid communities long before the advent of agricultural conglomerates. The presence of African-American and American Indian populations, along with the newer Mayan-speaking Guatemalans, Caribbean immigrants and white enclaves speak to the structures of community maintenance that exist beyond the realm of the production line. Kinship and family and the organizations that support them are the buffer between the local population and the changing hands of corporate multinationals and legislation that now dominate the headlines.

The sheer number of community-based organizations in the EAA speaks to the involvement of the community in global, national, and local affairs. The Glades Interagency Directory lists 92 service-provider agencies, or one agency for every 152 residents, one of the highest per-capita ratios in the country. These agencies are overwhelmingly grassroots-based, ranging from the Belle Glade Housing Authority to Centro Campesino and Florida Rural Legal Services. Most are funded by grants and donations, as well as widely fluctuating federal and state funding. Most of the agencies are housed in small, run-down offices that service walk-ins looking for help. As I arrived to interview one agency head, she asked me to wait while she e-mailed a friend of hers who she thought might be able to help a recent walk-in who was hysterical but could not tell her why. As in this case, much of the help provided is accomplished through personal and professional networks that exist within the community. Participation by community members is informal and by word of mouth. This is the civil society of interpersonal relations, one that is maintained by strong community ties. Some of the more active organizations attend inter-agency and state and federal outreach meetings. By and large, they frustrate them. All of the organizations, from housing to AIDS, are affected by the restoration process and the politics that is integral to its development and implementation. Funding is being diverted while the community is faced with a deluge of information and attention needing to be negotiated. The fate of

skill-specific workers and the migration patterns of workers affect families and their support systems – the community as a whole.

These community and advocacy organizations act as a new kind of social movement based on informal and loosely knit organizations that are maintained over time. More than the new social movements (NSMs) illustrated by Eder (1985) and analyzed by Edelman (2001), they reach beyond the activities of political pressure groups to act as advocacy organizations and community defenders against a constant barrage of federal and state actions that would weaken community maintenance, from lower standards for drinking water to the reduction of funds for AIDS treatment and services.

At the same time, these organizations operate within an arena that works to incorporate their resistance and demands through the verticality and encompassment that Ferguson and Gupta describe (2002). They define verticality as "the central and pervasive idea of an institution as somehow 'above' civil society, community and family...[and] *encompassment* [as where the] state (conceptually fused with the nation) is located within an ever widening series of circles that begins with family and local community and ends with the system of nation states" (2002: 982).

Aspects of verticality and encompassment are accomplished through the federal and state laws that mandate community-outreach programs. This is particularly true of the agencies that are directing the Everglades restoration project, which must show that they have implemented standards for participation by community members. How this mandate is interpreted by the agencies and by community organizations differs by stakeholder, although it is fair to conclude that the integration of community concerns has not been a priority for planning purposes, and at times, has been actively subverted.

The Public Outreach Program Management Plan for the CERP, produced in August 2001 by the Army Corps of Engineers and the South Florida Water Management

District, defines the components of public outreach as "information and involvement." Included in the reasoning for these components are media attention and legal mandates. The Plan cites expanding outreach through colleges and other educational institutions and the South Florida Water Management District entered into an agreement with Florida Memorial College in late 2000. Florida Memorial is a small Baptist college in Miami that has scant resources for environmental studies and even fewer for advocacy and coalition building. The agreement serves to provide as low a profile as possible, excluding formal relationships with community organizations and others who may have differing viewpoints from those of the federal and state agencies. As such, there is often an appearance of compliance with regulations regarding community input without actually soliciting differing points of view.

The organizational chart for the South Florida Ecosystem Restoration depicts the attempts at diffusion made by federal agencies. The chart, produced by the Environmental Protection Agency (EPA), consists of a series of arrows pointing in various directions and ending up in a circle. Meant to represent the working consensus of stakeholders, it includes a "task force," a "working group," and various "teams." The chart was distributed at an "outreach" meeting called by the Army Corps of Engineers, held at 9:00 AM on a Tuesday morning in Fort Lauderdale, far from any community stakeholders and ensuring that only civil service members of the federal agencies could attend. It consisted of speeches by various officials of the Army Corps about general planning, funding, and timetables, but did not actively seek comments from members of the audience. It was what one community-based activist called "manufactured participation."

Community organizations are not united on what is needed and how to accomplish participatory goals, making it easier for individual demands to be subverted by restoration planning agencies, who cite the need for consensus and understanding. Like the differences in the sectors of mainstream environmental organizations, some strongly believe that they should work with those that hold power, while others are more comfortable expressing their points of view by building grassroots efforts. Many of the differences are based on the insecurity about economic sustainability and employment in the area, including the future fate of those that have been displaced by mechanization or will be displaced by the restoration process. The primary community development corporation, for example, is focused on the development of tourism, the magic bullet for many communities around the world that are undergoing transformations in the productive sphere (Kirsch 1998). As one organization's manager told me, "People need to be aware of how quaint the community is." But even she becomes frustrated at the process in place. "We're sick and tired of being assessed," she complained, "people are getting frustrated with systems."

It is noteworthy that most of the leaders of community-based organizations are African-American women. There is agreement among community-based organizations that the area is underserved and by some descriptions, oppressed. "It's like a Third World country," one agency director remarked, commenting on the relationships of power that exist among the various federal, state, and local agencies. In addition, many do not trust the motives of the larger environmental organizations, who they view as naïve and uninformed. One officer of an activist organization quipped,

It's the "stupidity position" of the traditional environmental groups, who thought that they were going to be getting something, and didn't. In their arrogance, being predominately white, they thought they would be treated differently, told the truth. They presume that we aren't them, so we can't collaborate. They didn't take into consideration that this it the United States of America, it's a process. They thought they were having conversations in good faith, and they became part of the problem and the victim of action to which I am unsympathetic towards.

This director believes in coalition building, but not with the agencies of power. She believes that the restoration managers are focusing on wildlife, "because birds and fish can't talk." The funding agencies, she maintains, don't care about people. "They're just doin' their job...the fight for community is continually undermined because they are those experts who think they know how and can do it better." Despite the negative tone of her remarks, this director is optimistic about the possibilities for building sustainable opposition and gaining input into the process. Part of the optimism comes from what many community leaders recognize as the bad science inherent in the restoration plan, which will have to be addressed and will leave new openings for counterpoint perspectives. Their view is backed by the National Academies' National Research Council, whose report released on December 18, 2002, concluded that more money for scientific reviews of the restoration process is necessary, along with significant management improvements in conducting scientific reviews (Lipman 2002). "The process has to play itself out," the director pointed out, "over and over and over again." The challenge, as she sees it, is

> having everyone know that we're here and that we're here to stay. The tendency in oppressed communities is that once our light bulb goes off to not acknowledge what's occurred and discount the history – we therefore repeat history, mistakes are continually repeated. The challenge here is to go forward because of the road and the vastness of the project.

Encompassment

Sugar companies were a major contributor to the Clinton, George W. Bush, and Jeb Bush

election campaigns. Bruce Babbitt, the Clinton administration's environmental chief, managed to win over the support of the World Wide Fund for Nature, the National Wildlife Federation, the Nature Conservancy, and the Wilderness Society, despite the harm many environmental critics and local communities claimed the Clinton policies would cause. This was the same Bruce Babbitt who devised a market-oriented environmentalism that negotiated with and then included environmental groups, ultimately convincing the Sierra Club to work with him to pass legislation that halved the old growth that remained in the Pacific Northwest.[1] The Sierra Club had initially taken a stand against but did not actively oppose NAFTA, which by general agreement of environmental scientists and activists weakened existing environmental policies. All of these environmental organizations receive large corporate contributions, and positions that threaten corporate funding also threaten organizational viability.

Contradictions in stated policy and local reasoning have become acute. While Vice-President Gore was campaigning on a platform that stressed the importance of the environment – a primary component of the Democratic Party's Platform – he refused to denounce plans for an airport at the edge of the Everglades because it was being proposed by powerful Cuban–American business organizations (Grunwald 2002a). Many believe that this refusal to defend environmental standards cost him the election, and environmental organizations split over the decision by many to campaign for Ralph Nader, who received more than 96,000 votes in Florida.

Further complicating the situation is the lack of knowledge about how true restoration would work. The Corps of Engineers has proposed numerous projects that have been criticized both by environmental organizations and by other federal agencies, such as the Fish and Wildlife Service, although the current director never forwarded staff critiques to Congress. Richard Harvey, the EPA's South Florida manager, has argued that the plan focuses on water quantity rather than water quality. He stated in an internal e-mail that "Getting the water quality right is critical to the restoration of the ecosystem and yet the two lead agencies – the Corps and the [South Florida] Water Management District – don't seem to have a clue about how to do it – and therefore choose to virtually ignore/hope it will go away – unless they are sued" (quoted in Grunwald 2002d).

Gore championed the Everglades Restoration plan to Congress, with the assistance of US Senator Bob Graham (D-FL) and Representative Clay Shaw (R-FL). The plan and the politics surrounding it were shepherded through the initial stages by Bruce Babbitt. Among Babbitt's greatest concerns was the pivotal role of Florida in both the 1996 and 2000 elections, moving him to lobby hard with stakeholders in the restoration process, including legislators, industry, and developers. As the plan stands, its wording is reverent to the need for water redirection to the developing coast. In its first section justifying the plan, the House version of the bill declares: "the plan is approved as a framework for modifications and operational changes to the Central and Southern Florida Project that are needed to restore, preserve, and protect the South Florida ecosystem *while providing for other water-related need of the region, including water supply and flood protection*" (United States Congress 2000; my emphasis).

The relationship between the federal agencies, the Florida state legislature, environmental groups, and community-based organizations is multifaceted. While Congress and federal agencies define the playing field, some environmental groups fear that if they do not engage these sources of power, they will lose all voice. Organizations such as the Audubon Society believe that they have a say in the making of environmental policy, as long as they stay on the good side of federal environmental chiefs. Others, such as Friends of the Everglades, a large coalition of environmental activists, decry the collaboration of environmental organizations with federal and state governments, claiming that

working within the system will only hurt the cause of true restoration.

The growing divide among environmental groups and community organizations attests to the complexity of local integration into national policies. "There is a growing rift within the Everglades Coalition, the network of conservation groups that helped push restoration into law," Grunwald reports. "Some environmentalists want to work with the system to persuade the Army Corps of Engineers and the South Florida Water Management District to improve the plan. Others say the only hope for real ecological benefits will be tough legal requirements of restoration progress, or barring that, public opposition and litigation. As Grunwald continues,

> The most enthusiastic environmentalist advocates for the plan work for the National Audubon Society and its Florida chapter, Richard Pettegrew, the chairman of the commission that proposed the plan's blueprint, is on Audubon's Board; former Audubon staffer Naciann Regalado is head of the Everglades outreach for the Corps.
>
> But several environmental groups, including Friends of the Everglades and the Biodiversity Legal Foundation, opposed the plan in 2000, and now fed-up officials at such groups as Environmental Defense and the National Resources Defense Council also criticize it. (Grunwald 2002b)

The influence of the sugar companies in the halls of Congress and the federal agencies in Washington is now legendary. Not only did the final plan unveiled by Babbitt and Gore closely resemble the suggestions made by the sugar industry, but the $2 million that the US Sugar Corporation and the Fanjul-owned Florida Crystals have pumped into federal election campaigns helped them to negotiate the placement of the restoration so it would not interfere with sugar cane production.

The Comprehensive Everglades Restoration Plan (CERP) integrates levels of policy and decision making that tie community interests to the concerns of industry and developers. The mining, agricultural, and development companies that are fighting for environmental control are global and national; the labor that supplies agricultural and development companies is local in scope. Jobs and tax revenues in a state that boasts no income tax are pitted against the more abstract notion of what the environment represents. While communities measure survival in terms of both their ability to function and maintain sustainable infrastructures, corporations and government agencies take the cost-accounting approach, testing possible costs of cleanup and lawsuits against the profitability of their businesses and their ability to show growth in the next accounting quarter.

Still, they face obstacles. Sued by environmental and labor organizations for both their mistreatment of migrants and the pollution caused by phosphorus, the Fanjuls, along with US Sugar, have sustained a political and media campaign to absolve themselves of any responsibility for the environmental problems that have occurred since the draining of the wetlands. Using the discourse of science, the sugar industry has claimed that phosphorus levels are not dangerous. Robert M. Baker Jr., a prominent sugar industry spokesman, has gone so far as to claim that

> Farming will have been taxed and regulated out of business in order to achieve water quality that is twice as pure as rain, while government policy encouraged suburban sprawl whose runoff has at least four times as much phosphorus as sugar cane's. And the discharge from the best sewage plants has six times as much... The Everglades need a solution, not a scapegoat. (Sugar y Azúcar 1992).[2]

But community and environmental organizations disagree. Phosphorus levels have been blamed for a multitude of diseases and disorders, including not only the generally recognized skin rashes and asthma, but arthritis and cancer as well. The Everglades vegetation sensitive to phosphorus contamination,

such as saw grass, has quickly died out in favor of more phosphorus-adaptive plants, such as cattails. The draining of the saw grass exposed the soil to the air, allowing fertilizers from the farms and natural nutrients to oxidize and stay in place rather than blow away or float off in rainstorms. Over time, Roberts (1999:60) reports, up to six feet of phosphorus-tainted topsoil has settled in the Everglades.

Meanwhile, as if to flaunt the relations of power in the discourse of environmental policy, limestone mining that will destroy 4,500 acres of wetlands was approved by the Army Corps of Engineers in August of 2002. The limestone will be used for housing developments and roads. As the attorney for the Natural Resources Council put it, "We're committing an act of environmental cannibalism of really historic proportions" (Flesher 2002:1A). Like the standard rebuttal to issues of development, the answer lies in jobs. The mining companies claim that the mines employ 7,000 people, and another 7,000 jobs in trucking, construction, and allied work. The immediate explanation is that they must expand their quarries or go out of business, at great cost to Florida's economy. The mining companies, which are based from West Virginia to as far away as Athens, Greece, argue that "if you want Florida to continue to grow, if you want tourists, if you want jobs, you've got to have new schools, churches, shopping centers" (Flesher 2002:14A).

The mining industry has also been a major contributor to Florida's political campaigns, among them Senator Bob Graham, and Representative Clay Shaw, both of whom played a major role in the development of the restoration plan. The Florida newspaper, the *Sun-Sentinel*, reports that the state legislature stripped local communities of the right to set environmental standards for blasting, and Congress in 2000 declared the mining pits "reservoirs" for Everglades restoration. "It's horrendous," said the chair of the Florida Sierra Club. "If you have the right lobbyists and the right politicians, you can get anything you want. You can turn mining the Everglades into Everglades Restoration" (Flesher 2002, 14A).

Conclusion

A current story in the Florida media describes a "cultural divide" that exists in south Florida. The divide is represented by a tragedy that involved a young Mayan illegal immigrant. If she had been about to give birth in her own country of Guatemala she would have been surrounded by family and generations of experience in child-bearing. Alone in the United States and unable to speak English, she had no one with her when her labor started and did not know how to call for help. The baby died, and she is being charged with murder. The police provided her with a Spanish interpreter, a language that she does not speak. The incident symbolizes the contradictions that characterize South Florida and is very much the story of the Everglades. While the area is growing exponentially, and new urbanism and shopping centers proliferate, so does the migrant labor that supports their growth, and the drive for profit that militates against true restoration. Migrant labor arrives with dream of finding a safer and better life. They come to find that until they are integrated into their own cultural communities, there is no social support or safety net. Mayans, many of whom emigrated from Huehuetenango, the poorest province in Guatemala during the period of the country's civil war, maintain their ties with each other through fierce obstacles. While the men often learn Spanish in the fields to which they must migrate, the women are confined to the domestic household and community, where they speak their own language. There is severe discrimination. Yet, in this area, as in areas around the globe, indigenous groups, even outside their home countries, are starting to agitate for their rights and their dignity. While illegal status often makes individuals hesitant to organize, community-based organizations and other elements of civil society are forming to represent their rights and to defend their status.

The new language of neo-globalism transfer and deterrorialization rarely conveys the complexity of local communities and their maintenance. A level of analysis that relies on the global transfer of capital and power is consistently depressing, as it most often results in an analysis that overplays the power of capital to overwhelm community maintenance and localized needs. Particularly in the Everglades, where community, crops, and labor are all integrated on multiple levels of local, national, and supra-national organization, it is easy to forget that local populations still participate and influence the policies that are developed around them. Attempts at verticality, while prominent, are not always successful. Even when there is a significant attempt to exclude localized voices, communities invariably still manage to demand input into the process.

The restoration of the Everglades has opened up long-standing discontinuities between the communities and their inhabitants that exist in the area, and the industrial corporations and developers that have interests in expanding their control over the region's resources. The active participation by local and national government agencies and their differences with the civil society that opposes them has exacerbated these differences. While the effect of localized organizing on the planning and implementation process and the contention over voice remains to be seen, the result will be no less than the fate of the Everglades, and South Florida.

NOTES

1 For a full discussion of Babbitt's environmental strategy, see Cockburn (1995).

2 It is an interesting paradox that while the philanthropic foundation created by the Mott family supports environmental issues, including a US$900,000 grant to

save wetlands in Latin America, they have not contributed to any environmental efforts in the Everglades.

REFERENCES

Appadurai, A.
1986 Introduction: Communities and the Politics of Value. *In* The Social Life of Things: Commodities in Cultural Perspective. Arjun Appadurai, ed. Pp. 3–63. Cambridge: Cambridge University Press.
—— 1990 Disjuncture and Difference in the Global Cultural Economy. Public Culture 2: 1–24.
—— 1991 Global Ethnoscapes: Notes and Queries for a Transnational Anthropology. *In* Recapturing Anthropology: *Working in the Present*. R. G. Fox, ed. Pp. 191–210. Santa Fe, NM: School of American Research Press.
Barboza, J.
2002. Everglades Plan Defies Free Trade Logic. New York Times, May 6, p. 1.
Castells, M. S. Yazawa, and E. Kiselyova
1995–6 "Insurgents Against the New World Order": A Comparative Analysis of the Zapatistas in Mexico, the American Militia and Japan's Aum Shino. Berkeley Journal of Sociology 40:26–47.
Cockburn, A.
1995 "Win-Win" with Bruce Babbitt: The Clinton Administration Meets the Environment. New Left Review 201: 43–55.
Edelman, M.
2001 Social Movements: Changing Paradigms and Forms of Politics. Annual Review of Anthropology 30:285–317.
Eder, K.
1985 The New Social Movements: Moral Crusades, Political Pressure Groups or Social Movements. Social Research 52(4):28–42.
Englund, H.
2002 Ethnography After Globalism: Migration and Emplacement in Malawi.

American Ethnologist 29(2): 2261–2286.
Ferguson, F., and J. Gupta
2002 Spatializing States: Toward an Ethnography of Neo-liberal Governmentality. American Ethnologist 29(4): 981–1002.
Flescher, I.
2002 Mining the Everglades. Florida Sun-Sentinel, August 23, p. 1A.
Grunwald, M.
2000. "Pentagon Rebukes Army Corps" Washington Post, December 7, p. AO1.
—— 2002a A Rescue Plan, Bold and Uncertain. Washington Post, June 23, p. A16.
—— 2002b Among Environmentalists, The Great Divide. Washington Post, June 25, p. A13.
—— 2002c An Environmental Reversal of Fortune. Washington Post, June 25, p. AO1.
—— 2002d Water Quality is Long-Standing Issue for Tribe. Washington Post, June 24, p. A11.
—— 2002e "Between Rock and a Hard Place," Washington Post, June 24, p. AO1.
Gupta, A., and Ferguson, J.
1997. Culture, Power and Place: Ethnography at the End of an Era. *In* Culture, Power, Place: Explorations in Critical Anthropology. A. Gupta and J. Ferguson, eds. Pp. 179–208. Durham, NC: Duke University Press.
Hann C. and E. Dunn, eds.
1996. Civil Society. London: Routledge.
Harvey, D.
1990. The Condition of Postmodernity. Malden, MA: Blackwell.
—— 1998. What's Green and Makes the Environment Go Round. *In* The Cultures of Globalization. Frederic Jameson and Masao Miyoshi, eds. Pp. 327–355. Durham, NC: Duke University Press.
Inda, J. X., and R. Rosaldo, eds.
2002. Introduction. *In* The Anthropology of Globalization: A Reader. Pp. 1–36. Malden, MA: Blackwell.
Kirsch, M.
1998 In the Wake of the Giant: Multinational Restructuring and Uneven

Development in a New England Community. Albany: State University of New York Press.

Lipman. L.
2002 Report: Everglades Science Needs more Money. Palm Beach Post, December 19, p. 10.

Mintz, S.
1998. The Localization of Anthropological Practice: From Area Studies to Transnationalism. Critique of Anthropology 18(2):117–133.

Nash, J.
2001a Mayan Visions: The Quest for Autonomy in an Age of Globalization. New York: Routledge.
——2001b Globalization and the Cultivation of Peripheral Vision. Anthropology Today 17(4):15–22.

New York Times
2001 Editorial. November 23, p. A32.

Roberts, P.
1999 The Sweet Hereafter. Harper's 299(1794):54–68.

Sassen, S.
1998 Globalization and its Discontents. New York: The Free Press.

Scully, J.
2001 Restoring the Fragile Everglades, Evermore. Chronicle Review, January 12, pp. B13–14.

Sugar y Azúcar
1992 Has Sugar Harmed the Everglades?" March, p. 1.

Tardanico R., and M. B. Rosenberg, eds.
2000 Poverty or Development: Global Restructuring and Regional Transformations in the U.S. South and the Mexican South. New York: Routledge.

United States Congress
2000 106th Congress, 2nd Session, H.R. 5121 (House Plan), September 7.

Wallerstein, I.
1974 The Modern World System: Capitalist Agriculture and the Originals of the European World Economy in the Sixteenth Century. New York: Academic Press.

12

"Land, Water, and Truth": San Identity and Global Indigenism

Renée Sylvain

Introduction

In 1999 approximately sixty-five thousand hectares of traditional territory in and around the Kalahari Gemsbok National Park were returned to the ≠Khomani San by the South African government. This land claim victory was significant, both because it signaled the presence of a hospitable political climate for restitution claims and because it illustrated the ability of the San to assert their rights, as indigenous people, vis-à-vis the state. One elderly ≠Khomani woman explained the struggle of indigenous people in southern Africa as follows: "we need land, water, and truth". In this chapter I discuss the connection, suggested by her list of needs, between rights to resources and current debates about the "truth" of indigenous identities.

International discourse on indigeneity, reshaped for a southern African context, sets the terms under which San struggles for land and resources are recognized as struggles of indigenous peoples. As the criteria for recognition increasingly focus on "cultural" features of indigeneity, to the exclusion of socioeconomic and political features, the majority of contemporary San find themselves compelled to choose between being excluded from the debate and asserting themselves in essentialist and primordialist vocabulary. I illustrate the dilemma with examples drawn from San groups in Namibia and South Africa.

The San of Southern Africa

There are approximately ninety thousand San in southern Africa; the largest number live in Botswana and Namibia, and a few smaller groups live in South Africa, Angola and Zimbabwe. Only a handful of San continue to live on (dramatically diminished portions of) their traditional territories. Traditional hunting and gathering is, in most places, no longer a viable subsistence strategy, and most San live in conditions of marginalization and poverty on the periphery of the global capitalist and state systems. The majority of San are farm workers and domestic servants on Afrikaner-owned cattle ranches or are casual laborers on the cattle posts of Bantu-speaking pastoralists. Others struggle to subsist as part-time foragers, relying on government relief in village settlements.

The San are widely recognized as the most impoverished, disempowered and stigmatized ethnic group in southern Africa. To address systemic and widespread discrimination and marginalization, they began to mobilize in 1996 under the auspices of a regional pan-San organization – the Working Group of Indigenous Minorities in Southern Africa (WIMSA) – which networks with regional human rights and development NGOs and facilitates San participation in international indigenous peoples' rights forums. This regional and international networking is enabling the San to articulate their collective goals: to secure land rights and control over natural resources, to gain government recognition of their community leaders, to protect their interests in their relationships with agents of capital, and to empower themselves through self-directed development projects. The San are only now beginning to struggle for rights and to renegotiate their relationships with the state as *indigenous peoples*. So we should ask: What does indigenism mean in an African context?

Global Indigenism and African Indigenism

The status of the San as indigenous peoples is not seriously in question. My concern here is with the expectations their classification as "indigenous" places on them and, in particular, with the preconceptions about San culture that are imposed along with the recognition of their indigeneity. For, despite the laudably flexible criteria for indigenous status employed in international forums, at the local level – in the context of post-apartheid southern Africa – the criteria for indigenous status tend to become ontologically saturated with essentialist and primordialist conceptions of culture.

Currently, the only definition of indigenous peoples that is legally binding (for its signatories) is the one provided by the International Labour Organization Convention (ILO) 169 (1989) (Saugestad 2001:44). According to Article 1 of the convention, indigenous peoples are

> peoples in independent countries who are regarded as indigenous on account of their descent from the population which inhabited the country, or geographical region to which the country belongs, at the time of colonization or conquest or the establishment of present state boundaries and who, irrespective of their legal status, retain some or all of their own social, economic, cultural and political institutions. (ILO 1989: pt .1)

Article 2 makes self-identification a fundamental criterion for the recognition of indigeneity. The most significant site for the formation and articulation of global indigenism is the UN Working Group on Indigenous Populations (Muehlebach 2001), which, while resisting overly precise and inflexible definitions, draws from the ILO convention and from the working definition provided by UN special rapporteur José Martínez Cobo:

> Indigenous communities, peoples and nations are those which, having a historical continuity with pre-invasion and pre-colonial societies that developed on their territories, consider themselves distinct from other societies now prevailing in those territories, or parts of them. They form at present non-dominant sectors of society and are determined to preserve, develop and transmit to future generations their ancestral territories and their ethnic identity, as the basis for continued existence as peoples in accordance with their own cultural patterns, social institutions and legal systems. (Cobo 1986:1)

These definitions provide four broad criteria for identifying indigenous peoples: (1) genealogical heritage (i.e., historical continuity with prior occupants of a region); (2) political economic or "structural" marginalization (i.e., non-dominance); (3) cultural attributes (i.e., being "culturally distinct"); and (4) self-identification. At the international level of discourse, there are neither substantive claims made about the ontological significance of prior occupancy or genealogical heritage nor are there any substantive claims about the content of indigenous peoples' distinct cultures or their modes of self-identification (see Anaya 2000, Barsh 1996, Grey and Dahl 1998:352). The definition is multidimensional enough to be serviceable to a fairly wide range of rights issues. Different criteria can be highlighted depending on the priorities and agendas of advocacy organizations and the criteria themselves are malleable enough for advocacy organizations to elaborate on their ontological significance in different ways for different contexts.[1] But, because land rights are a priority in indigenous peoples' struggles, we find essentializing tendencies in which the criteria for indigenous status emphasize a unique relationship to the land.[2]

The highly flexible and generic criteria provided by international forums gain more substantive content when they are applied to local situations. Many have noted that applying the term *indigenous* to an African context is problematic since the colonial encounter tended to make all Africans "indigenous" relative to the colonizing powers (see Maybury-Lewis 1997:7–8, Veber and Wæhle 1993:9–15). However, in the postcolonial context, finer distinctions are being drawn in order to describe and address current power asymmetries among various ethnic communities. In order to sharpen the contrast between "indigenous" Africans and other Africans, indigenous peoples' forums stress cultural distinctness and link it directly to prior occupancy. As a result, two connected trends have emerged in the discourse that adapts global indigenism to African indigenism.

First, the concern to distinguish indigenous Africans from other Africans has resulted in an overdrawn distinction between the "cultural" features of indigeneity and the political-economic features that indigenous peoples share with marginalized minorities – namely, non-dominance. Second, political economy gets pushed further into the background as essentializing ontological connections among prior occupancy (and genealogical heritage), cultural distinctness, and self-identification are foregrounded to become the core features of African indigenous identity. Encouraging this second trend are pressures brought to bear by local conceptions of "culture" and racial identity that continue to shape the political landscape of postapartheid southern Africa.

One finds varying degrees of essentialism in the Africanist-indigenist literature. I will highlight one dimension of this trend. At a joint conference of the International Work Group for Indigenous Affairs and the Centre for Development Research a definition was accepted which added only slightly more ontological weight to the criterion of prior occupancy. Here, indigenous peoples in Africa "implies *peoples with strong ties to their lands*, who have been in their region since before colonization, [who] were now dominated by other peoples from whom their cultures were markedly different and who identify as 'indigenous'" (Veber and Wæhle 1993:10, emphasis added). A more extreme essentializing emphasis on genealogical heritage is found in the criteria provided by the Indigenous Peoples of Africa Co-ordinating Conference (IPACC), which includes, inter alia, "a claim to specific ancestral land *linked to their cultural identity* and economic survival; a distinct and identifiable genealogical bloodline; modes of production such as hunting-gathering-foraging and pastoralism; and a close link between the natural world ... and their cultures, intellectual resources and identities"(IPACC n.d.; emphasis added).[3] For IPACC, what makes indigenous Africans distinct are "ancient economies and cultural systems" (IPACC n.d.), and what began in international discourse as "prior occupancy" is now an overt, primordializing link between cultural identity and ancestral lands.

The implications of this move may be illustrated by Saugestad's (2001) recent work on San indigeneity in Botswana. On the one hand, she provides a broad definition of indigeneity that emphasizes political economic features, but on the more particular question of what makes indigenous peoples *culturally* distinct, she claims: "Many of the cultural practices of indigenous populations are reflections of ways they use or once used the natural resources around them. If their cultural rights are to be respected, this may imply that their rights to land and other natural resources have to be respected *so that they can continue their way of life*" (Saugestad 2001:43; emphasis added). I have neither quarrel with her claim that respecting cultural rights must include protecting rights to natural resources and land or with her characterization of indigenous culture as reflecting past subsistence patterns. But two implications of her statement are important for my purposes here. First, pegging culture to natural resource use may suggest that indigenous peoples' cultural rights are limited to the preservation of their (traditional) culture ("continuing their way of life"). Second, limiting a definition of indigenous culture to a particular relationship to the land precludes any role for political economy in the historical formation of cultural identities or cultural practices. The essentializing tendencies to which I refer are ultimately a result of an overdrawn distinction between political economy and "culture." Insofar as indigenous culture is rooted in the land, separable from other important political and socioeconomic relationships, indigenous culture becomes defined in essentialized and static terms. The more essentialized the "cultural" features become, the more they are seen as contrary to the historically transitory features of political economy.

This trend is reflected in the description, provided by the South African San Institute (SASI), of the situation of the South African ≠Khomani San. SASI recognizes that "A significant proportion of southern Kalahari [≠Khomani] San are no longer dependent on the land or traditional ways of making a living, and are, therefore, forced to eke out an existence within the market economy" (1999:6). Yet, according to SASI, the primary distinction between marginalized minorities and indigenous people is the latter's "relationship to the land" (SASI 1999:6). So the San's status as laborers or unemployed squatters results in the "*loss* of culture" (SASI 1999:6). The problem with pegging cultural identity to a unique relationship to the land – and associating political economic context with culture *loss* – is that we are compelled to conclude that the ≠Khomani San (along with a great many other San) have already been "deculturated," and so no longer possess a culture that could count as "indigenous."

As we shall see, the ontologically saturated criteria for African indigeneity are more obviously applicable to some San groups than to others. This is because the socioeconomic conditions the San cope with and struggle to change are not uniform – the rights issues that occupy their attention differ according to context, and the ways they self-identify differ with their histories and current socioeconomic circumstances.

Land and Labor: Identifiable Indigenism and Invisible Identities

Very broadly, the San in southern Africa travelled along two different historical trajectories of colonial rule and identity formation. For some groups, colonial rule and apartheid took the form of geographical, political, and economic segregation, through containment in reserves and ethnic homelands (or in game parks). For other San people, the consequences of colonization and apartheid were complete land dispossession and incorporation into an ethnically hierarchical class system. The current struggles of the first group – the "segregated" San – focus on land rights, control over natural resources, and local self-government and are easily recognizable as the struggles of indigenous peoples.

The struggles of the second group – the "incorporated" San – are more complicated.

Land and Local Identities: the Nyae Nyae Ju/'hoansi

The Ju/'hoansi of the Nyae Nyae area of Namibia, and the Dobe region of Botswana, have long been established as the paradigms of "authentic" Bushmen (Gordon 1992). Both in the vast anthropological literature on southern Africa and in popular media representations, they provide us to this day with the best picture of "pristine" hunter-gatherers living in splendid isolation from the forces of the global economy.[4] Although this image has been exaggerated in the popular media, it is not entirely without foundation.

The Ju/'hoansi of Nyae Nyae were, until the 1920s, strictly hunter-gatherers. Until 1959, when they were brought under the jurisdiction of a Native Commissioner, they had lived largely beyond the scope of state authority and enjoyed a relatively high level of political autonomy (Marshall 1976, Marshall and Ritchie 1984:2–3).[5] After the establishment of an administrative post at Tsum!kwe, they were encouraged to adopt a sedentary lifestyle, raising livestock and cultivating crops. By the mid-1970s, after the creation of the Bushmanland homeland, the Ju/'hoansi lost 70 percent of their foraging territories. By the early 1980s, they were facing widespread poverty, starvation, and alcoholism and so were vulnerable to recruitment efforts by the South African Defence Force, which offered them large salaries to fight in covert operations units against the South West Africa Peoples Organization (SWAPO) (see Biesele and Weinberg 1990, Gordon 1984, Lee 1988b, Lee and Hurlich 1979, Marshall and Ritchie 1984). In the early 1980s, overpopulation, poverty and conflict compelled a few groups of Ju/'hoansi to leave Tsum!kwe and return to the bush, where they engaged in a mixed subsistence strategy of foraging and livestock raising (Bixler et al. 1993:26). The Nyae Nyae Development Foundation assisted the Ju/'hoansi

with securing development inputs and establishing their own organization, the Nyae Nyae Farmers Cooperative (NNFC). The NNFC reestablished the Ju/'hoansi's traditional land tenure (n!ore) system, oversaw land management strategies, and negotiated with agents of the state to protect the Ju/'hoan communities' interests regarding natural resource management and development projects (Bixler et al. 1993: 25–9).

The situation of the Nyae Nyae Ju/'hoansi improved after Namibian independence in 1990. A major victory came in 1991, when the SWAPO government tacitly recognized the Ju/'hoansi's traditional n!ore system (Biesele 1992, Brown 1991). The next task for the Ju/'hoansi was to secure legal control over the area, to protect themselves from the encroachments of Bantu-speaking pastoralists and tourism companies (Hitchcock 1993:121). This was achieved in 1998, when the Ju/'hoansi were granted rights under the Communal Areas Conservancy Program to 9,000 square kilometers of land and a role in managing the natural resources within their territory (now called the Nyae Nyae Conservancy) (Brörmann 1999:41).

The Ju/'hoansi also reached an agreement with La Rochelle Hunting and Guest Farm worth N$170,000 (US$34,402). According to the terms of the agreement, La Rochelle is entitled to hunt a quota of wild game (which it will restock), and will provide employment opportunities to the Ju/'hoansi. The income from this agreement will be divided among the Ju/'hoan communities inside the conservancy and will be invested in development projects (WIMSA 2000:36–37).

The Nyae Nyae Ju/'hoansi present us with a familiar case of indigenous peoples' issues; their struggles are over land rights and control of natural resources. Furthermore, because they enjoyed de facto land rights under apartheid, their identity as "Bushmen" is not in question. The situation of a group of "incorporated" San – the San of the Omaheke Region of Namibia – is more complex.

Exploitation and Exclusion: the Omaheke San

Unlike the Nyae Nyae Ju/'hoansi, the San in the ethnically and linguistically heterogeneous Omaheke Region were completely dispossessed of their land and incorporated into a rural class system as a result of first German (1884–1915), and then South African colonization (1915–1990).[6] The European population of the Omaheke includes Afrikaner and German settlers; among the African population are Bantu-speaking Hereros, Tswanas, and Ovambos, as well as Khoi-speaking Namas-Damaras, "Coloureds" (or "Basters"), and the San.[7] The Omaheke San are themselves divided into three main language groups: the Ju/'hoansi, the Nharo, and the !Xûn.

Beginning as early as 1914, large tracts of the Omaheke were set aside as reserve land for Hereros and Tswanas. The reserves became apartheid homelands in the 1970s, and after Namibian independence, they became known as the "communal areas," and now comprise about 35 percent of the total land area in the Omaheke. The remaining 65 percent of the Omaheke is a "commercial farming block," dominated by Afrikaner and German cattle ranchers, who occupy 900 farms averaging about seven thousand hectares. No land in the Omaheke was set aside for the San.

Two features of the Omaheke socioeconomic context structure the lives of the farm San: First, their landlessness makes them vulnerable to extreme class exploitation and poverty; second, the ethnic heterogeneity of the Omaheke, combined with the racial attitudes of the white farmers and of Bantu-speaking stock owners, has resulted in an ethnic labor hierarchy in which the San are relegated to the lowest rank.

Approximately four thousand (of 6,500) San in the Omaheke live and work on white-owned farms, where they comprise about 25 percent of the labor force (Suzman 1995:5). Today, the San in the region are third- and fourth-generation farm laborers and domestic servants; some of them continue to work on the same farms on which their parents and grandparents were born, while others have spent their working lives on as many as ten different farms.

Remuneration for farm work consists of a balance between monthly wages and weekly rations. The wages and rations given are usually inadequate to support an entire household, and so the San are compelled to purchase food from the farmer on credit, leaving many San families tied to the farms through a system of debt-bondage.[8] On the white farms, San workers are paid less than non-San workers for two reasons: On farms with both San and non-San workers, the non-San typically occupy positions of authority over the San (e.g., as foremen), and farmers who are willing to pay higher wages for labor typically prefer to hire non-San workers. Farmers justify this wage discrimination by referring to the "traditional" culture and "ethnic character" of the "Bushmen." For example, farmers claim that the San are incorrigibly nomadic and are therefore unreliable workers – they often disappear without notice. While the farmers explain the "unreliability" of their San workers in cultural terms, the San themselves offer job-related explanations: Poor wages or rations, or excessive beatings at the hands of the farmer, lead them to seek work elsewhere. Farmers also see the Bushmen as "primitive" and "childlike" – they lack a proper grasp of the value of money and lack the foresight to save money. Low wages and accumulated debt-for-food purchases usually suffice to explain their inability to save. Although working on white-owned farms often means debt and dependency, most San recognize that working for whites is, so far, their best option.

Approximately one-third of the Omaheke San work on Herero or Tswana cattle posts in the "communal areas." Here San men tend livestock, chop wood, collect water, and perform other menial tasks. San women cook, do laundry, and do housecleaning. On the

Bantu cattle posts the San are typically not paid for their work but receive only small ration packages, and sometimes only alcohol, for their labor. San children, usually girls, are recruited by Hereros and "adopted" as servile household members.

Because jobs on white farms are scarce, and working for Hereros or Tswanas often means no pay, little food, and eventual alcoholism, many San are "on the road" in a perpetual search for employment, which means moving from farm to farm, usually where one has kin, asking farmers for work, and settling down briefly to visit friends and family who can provide food and shelter. On the farms, this often means that unemployed visitors are "squatting," because farmers discourage extended visits from their workers' kin. The most easily accessible sites to visit and receive short-term support are resettlement camps, or squatters' villages along the edges of urban centers.

Shortly after independence the SWAPO government established two resettlement camps in the Omaheke for indigent people. The majority of the resettlement camp residents are San, who are mostly too old or too sick to work on the farms. The camps provide San with access to sporadic supplies of drought relief food, water, housing, small plots of land for kitchen gardens, and grazing land, for the few who have livestock. The main sources of personal income are old-age pensions. A few San men tend livestock for absentee Herero, Tswana, or Nama-Damara stockowners in return for milk and a small wage. However, the wages are often not paid, or are paid infrequently, and the San must get by without money. San women are able to get extra food by tending the gardens and doing the laundry of non-San camp residents.

After several generations as a landless underclass of farm laborers, domestic servants, and squatters, the Omaheke San have managed the feat of becoming nearly invisible. The general consensus among non-San in Namibia is that there are no "real" or "authentic" Bushmen in the Omaheke anymore; since they no longer hunt and gather,

they have lost their cultural identity. The farmers see their San workers as "detribalized," and so no longer "authentic" Bushmen. However, the attitude of the farmers is discordant, since they also opportunistically see the San as *Bushmen* rather than as workers to whom they would have obligations to provide adequate remuneration.

The Omaheke San do not consider themselves "detribalized." A large part of what it means to them to be "San" in the Omaheke today comes from *their culturally unique ways* of resisting and coping with their experiences of class exploitation. San healers claim to be able to transform themselves into predatory animals, which they say enables them to steal livestock without getting caught.[9] They are particularly active in marginal areas off the farms where they conduct trance dances for those suffering from poverty-related diseases and from general psychological distress. The trance dances themselves reflect the local realities of the capitalist system. Most healers charge between N$10 and N$50, and ritualistically incorporate currency into the trance dance as a ceremonial object.

Their cultural life also has more mundane manifestations in daily patterns of social interaction and survival. Their traditional sharing ethos continues to be powerfully present, so that there are few unemployed San who do not have a place to sleep, nor kinfolk who will provide food. The San mobilize their traditional kinship systems to provide a social safety net to cope with poverty, unemployment and homelessness.

For example, the Ju/'hoansi in the northern Omaheke follow a pattern of joking with people in their own and alternate generations and avoiding (showing respect) toward people in adjacent generations.[10] This joking/avoidance pattern is sustained by a unique naming system. Thus, a firstborn daughter is named after her father's mother, a second-born daughter after her mother's mother. Similarly, a firstborn son is named after his father's father, and a second-born son after his mother's father.[11] These "namesakes" refer to each other as *!kun!a* (old name) and *!kuma* (young name), and enjoy a special, affectionate, joking relationship. The naming system in the Omaheke, although largely conforming to the system followed by the segregated Ju/'hoansi in Nyae Nyae (see Marshall 1976, and Lee 1986, 1993), operates with a unique twist. In the past, farmers gave Ju/'hoan servants European names and, over the years, the Ju/'hoansi have appropriated these names and assimilated them into their naming system. Thus in the Omaheke, specific Afrikaans names are linked with specific Ju/'hoan names: If a woman is called N!ukxa-Sara, her granddaughter will also be called N!ukxa-Sara.

Non-kin who happen to share the same name often treat each other as close kin and enjoy a supportive, joking relationship with each other. When nonrelated Ju/'hoansi with the same name meet, the younger !kuma assumes the kin relations of her !kun!a. Thus, the !kuma addresses her !kun!a's husband as "my husband," her !kun!a's brother as "my brother," etc. (see Lee 1986:76–8).[12] Similarly, when a Ju/'hoan meets someone with her sister's name she may joke with her and address her as "sister," and anyone with her father's name she may address respectfully as "father." This extended use of kin names is not, however, purely fictive. For Ju/'hoansi who live far from genealogical kin and in conditions of extreme poverty and marginalization, name-relations facilitate "making family" and sustain expectations of familial assistance. For example, two Ju/'hoan women living in a resettlement camp described themselves to me as "sisters." They shared household tasks, food, clothes and what money they could scrape together, and the people who lived in their two houses "shared a fire" (i.e., formed a household). It turned out that they did not have a common parent, but both of their mothers were named "//Uce", and that sufficed to make them "sisters." On the basis of this name-relationship, they formed a bond of mutual support and assistance to cope with the hardships of camp life.

The San scattered throughout the commercial and communal farms, squatters' villages and resettlement camps maintain an extensive, kin-based network of mutual assistance and support, which supplies the infrastructure for a landless "community." They are also highly mobile as San households redistribute people as well as resources to cope with poverty: Children are fostered out to kin who can support them, and San women and children station themselves with kinfolk on farms or in resettlement camps while their menfolk go "on the road" to search for work. Usually San men seek work on farms on which they have kin who will speak to the farmers on their behalf. San mobility – their almost constant effort to find adequate employment – has contributed, not only to a "subterranean" community infrastructure, but also to a unique adaptation of their traditional *n!ore* system. Ju/'hoansi who spent most of their lives on one farm insisted that their *n!ores* are the farms on which they were born, while other Ju/'hoansi described their *n!ores* as including the areas they traveled as they moved from farm to farm looking for work.

The Omaheke San thus express a class-shaped conception of their territorial identity. However, while indigenous discourse has politicized "culture" to great strategic advantage, "class" has become depoliticized and, in order to be recognized as indigenous people, the San are compelled to present themselves as largely uncorrupted by historical and political economic context. As I have already suggested, one important component of this essentializing move has been to insist on a special relationship to the land. Thus, we find that struggles over land rights are often couched in terms of retaining or regaining a "traditional" (primordial) cultural identity. But, in the Omaheke, San calls for land reflect their self-consciousness as an underclass. !Xabon, a middle-aged San woman living on a resettlement camp near the Botswana border, described her situation this way:

There is no change since independence.... We are in a place here [off the farms], but

there is no way we can survive – no way to
make a garden and survive from it. It's only
the black people [Nama-Damaras] who can
do anything in this place to survive – not us.
They don't want us to survive. We must stay
under them [in servitude]....Where will we
have a place to stay? There are more black
people now and fewer white people, and the
San will always be under the black people –
low and under them. And when will we have
a place to stay? [personal communication,
June 2001]

The San's class status is also reflected in their
struggles for political representation, as another San woman, N/isa, pointed out: "the
San people of this place must have a leader
who will work with them and help them
come out from under the black people."
The class exploitation and oppression
!Xabon and N/isa describe is common in
the small "resettlement" pockets off the
farms, where resettled Nama-Damaras, Hereros, and Tswanas often take advantage of
the lack of clear administrative structures to
claim leadership positions and assume control over the distribution of land, water, and
other resources. The San are denied independent access to resources and are forced
to herd cattle, tend gardens, and clean
house for non-San in return for water, food,
and occasionally a small wage.

As these examples only begin to illustrate,
the Omaheke San have a rich and distinctive
cultural life. Their culture has been shaped
by several generations as a landless underclass and so looks very different from the
more recognizably "indigenous" Ju/'hoansi
of Nyae Nyae. The recognition of the distinct
cultural identity and indigenous character of
the incorporated farm San is complicated by
two things: Not only do these San, because of
their landless underclass status, not conform
to the image of indigeneity drawn by indigenist discourse but they also fail to conform
neatly to the dominant definition of *Bushmen*, as it is articulated by farmers, by non-
San Africans, and by the Western media, all
of which define *Bushman* identity in terms of

the paradigm established by the segregated
Nyae Nyae Ju/'hoansi. Underlying both the
international image of indigeneity and the
image of "Bushmanness" is a shared conception of what constitutes an *authentic* cultural
identity for indigenous peoples. This shared
conception can be examined in terms of the
meaning San land rights have acquired – specifically, the idea that land rights are a means
of national or cultural regeneration, rather
than a means for achieving social and economic justice.

Cultural Survival and Class Struggle

There are two general trends in international
discourse on indigenous rights. One trend
emphasizes self-determination, which is
broadly construed to mean indigenous control over local political processes, control
over natural resources, and control over the
definition and representation of their own
identity; here land rights provide the basis
for local autonomy and for self-directed
development. The second trend emphasizes
"cultural survival."[13] In the South African
and Namibian contexts, where "culture"
has been, and continues to be, conceived in
essentialized and static terms, "culture survival" assumes primordialist implications.
Adam Kuper cautions that when culture is
reified and naturalized, as it is in South
Africa, commendable multiculturalist aspirations can too easily be read as an apology
for apartheid (1999:xi). In the postapartheid
context, land is seen as providing the basis
for a cultural or national identity, which is
often defined in static terms as a "traditional" identity.

According to the "cultural survival" paradigm, a core feature of indigenous identity is
a unique (often spiritual) relationship with
the land. For example, Richard Lee sees
cultural survival as a struggle to retain a
traditional culture based on hunting and
gathering; what makes the San distinct is
a "way of life" that is "communally based,

that speaks of spirituality, non-capitalist values...harmony with nature" and most importantly, "their sense of place" (2000:8; see also Lee1988a:263).

However, there is evidence that the San did not self-identify in quite the way Lee describes until fairly recently. In 1984, prior to Namibian independence, researchers reported that the Ju/'hoansi of Nyae Nyae (in the Bushmanland homeland) "never defined themselves as hunters and gatherers.... Sometimes they called themselves the owners of N/um – a spiritual healing power... [or] the owners of argument, or the people who talk too much" (Marshall and Ritchie 1984:2). By 1997 – after independence created opportunities for land claims – an important change occurred in the way that the Nyae Nyae Ju/'hoansi began talking about their cultural identity. Anthropologists now reported that "at the most basic level of existence sits the land – their home, what the Ju/'hoansi call their n!ore"; according to their informant, ≠Oma Djo, "Our n!ore is who we are" (Katz et al. 1997:65).

Because the segregated San must defend their land claims, their relationship to the land understandably moves to the forefront of their own sense of cultural identity. But the cultural survival agenda, now being successfully co-opted by the Nyae Nyae Ju/'hoansi, obscures the collective goals of economic justice that many San, especially those who work on farms, are seeking to achieve. The Omaheke San are also seeking land rights, but they are not trying to restore a hunting and gathering lifestyle or regain an evolutionary heritage; rather, they are struggling for access to development resources (land, livestock, boreholes), for better working conditions and for political representation. In short, they are struggling for economic and social justice. Reducing land claims to the preservation of cultural objects, and promoting primordialized forms of ethnonationalism makes the struggles of the Omaheke San less visible as the struggles of indigenous peoples and makes their identity less recognizably indigenous.

The emphasis on "cultural survival" – with its metaphysical connection between indigenous identity and a unique relationship with the land – also perpetuates the local ideological conditions that keep the incorporated, landless farm San invisible. The only way to make themselves visible, and earn a living off the farms, is to conform to popular stereotypes, which in turn reproduces the very class inequalities that these stereotypes help to sustain.

Cultural Identity as Commodity: the !Xûn

In August 1998, members of the !Xûn community – a group of unemployed farm workers in the southern Omaheke Region – entered into a joint tourism venture with Intu Afrika Lodge (located outside of the Omaheke Region). This group of San, with the assistance of WIMSA, drew up a contract to ensure appropriate housing and remuneration for the San and to secure a share in the returns from the venture (Brörmann 1999:40).

Intu Afrika's brochure starts off with familiar romantic stereotypes of "Stone Age" hunter-gatherers. They do acknowledge the rather brutal colonial history of the San, and their present problems of landlessness and exploitation as cheap laborers, but their answer to these contemporary problems has been to install them in a game reserve, where the San can "regain dignity and pride" and be given the "scope to practice cultural activities that utilize traditional Bushmen skills."

Ethnotourism does present an important economic opportunity for the Omaheke farm San, but there are grounds for reservations. First, the only identity given "scope" for expression here is the one that is marketable – that is, the traditional foraging identity as it is defined largely by stereotypes feeding the demand for this kind of ethnotourism.

This problem is not merely an academic one. In 1999, the !Xûn San lodged a legal complaint against a South African photographer and the manager of Intu Afrika

Lodge over a brochure featuring a photograph of the !Xûn community's highly respected, and recently deceased, leader. The primary complaint was that their leader's image was used without authorization, but a corollary issue was the misrepresentation of the San as "primitive" and still living a traditional foraging life in the bush. Ironically, the point of !Xûn San's complaint was completely lost on the South African *Sunday Times*, 31 October 1999, which reported the case in the following way:

> A tiny band of San Bushmen, who still hunt wild animals with poison arrows in the Kalahari Desert, could become the centre of a landmark intellectual property rights court case.... Angry members of the !Xoo [*sic*] community are crying foul over "insulting" photographs – depicting them as primitive hunters – distributed and sold without their permission [Jordan 1999].

My second reservation brings me back to the issue of class exploitation. The transformation of the San from farm workers to culture workers, and commoditization of San culture, need not (and has not) removed the potential for exploitative class relationships. In fact, WIMSA, on behalf of the !Xûn, has filed a legal claim against Intu Afrika because the lodge owner has withheld wages, levied unilateral deductions from their pay, and prohibited contact between the San role-players and other members of their community (WIMSA 2000:31). Labor conditions at this lodge simply duplicated those on many commercial farms in the Omaheke. As one former role-player told me:

> The owner of Intu Afrika showed me that I am a Bushman and that I have no say in anything....Even if the tourists gave us money as a gift, the money didn't come to us. The white people just took it for themselves... The tourists gave us blankets and clothes, which the owner took and sold to the Ovambo workers. (personal communication, June 2001)

The public face of Bushman identity (as "people who still hunt wild animals with poison arrows,") and the public face of corporate development ventures (as empowering the San to "regain dignity and pride,") are clearly at odds with the personal realities of Bushmen who "have no say in anything." Even the valorization of San "traditional" culture was, once again, the means for further class exploitation.

Apartheid and Assimilation: the ≠Khomani

The case of the ≠Khomani San, with which I began this chapter, provides a clear example of the rhetoric of the "cultural survival" agenda. After white and "Coloured" settlers moved into their foraging territories in the mid-19th century, the ≠Khomani were pushed deeper into the Kalahari or were forced into servile relationships with white farmers and Coloured stockowners. Those who chose not to work for Coloured or white farmers became clients of white academics and state officials and were allowed to live in the Kalahari Gemsbok National Park (KGNP), where they worked as game wardens and herders in return for limited hunting rights, clothes, and a small wage (White 1995:32). Between 1937 and 1973, the ≠Khomani lost their traditional territories in the KGNP when they were relocated to the Mier reserve and reclassified under Apartheid law as "Coloured." During the 1970s and 1980s, most ≠Khomani worked for Coloured stockowners, while the rest roamed among the white farms seeking jobs (White 1995:33).

In August of 1995, a restitution land claim was launched on behalf of the descendants of the ≠Khomani living near the KGNP. In March of 1999, an agreement was signed giving the San 25,000 hectares of land inside the KGNP and 40,000 hectares of farmland outside the park, where they will be able to keep game and engage in subsistence farming. It is also expected that they will set up a tourism camp as a community income-generating project (SASI 1999:6). In a speech delivered in celebration of the ≠Khomani San victory, the South African Minister of Agriculture and Land Affairs (Hon. Derek Hanekom) stated, "We are here today celebrating more than just the settlement of a land claim: we are here celebrating the rebirth of the ≠Khomani nation" (Brörmann 1999:43).

The ≠Khomani case received a lot of press both in Africa and in the West, and this media coverage provides important insights into what their newly recovered national identity is supposed to look like. For example, an article in a Ugandan newspaper, the *Monitor*, for Tuesday 25 March 1999, describes the San as "a nomadic tribe of stone age hunters and gatherers" (*Monitor* 1999), and the South African *Daily Dispatch*, for Tuesday March 16 1999, describes them as "the remnants of a Stone Age culture" (*Daily Dispatch* 1999). An article in the Canadian *Globe & Mail*, Saturday March 20 1999, begins by describing the San as "the last remnants of an ancient African people ..." (Barnett 1999:A17) – a description to be read in the context of a large photograph of barefoot "Bushmen" clad in loincloths walking through the Kalahari. Interestingly, the article goes on to acknowledge "the San are no longer spear-carrying barefoot hunter-gatherers clad in loincloths. Only a few scattered groups now live a traditional lifestyle, but Mr. Chennells [the Khomani San's lawyer] said that a return to their land will give them back their identity"(Barnett 1999: A17). The clear implication is that the identity that will be returned to them with the land is their "traditional lifestyle," as "spear-carrying barefoot hunter-gathers clad in loincloths." In this case successful land claims – when they are interpreted conservatively in terms of "cultural survival" – do nothing to undermine the very stereotypes that continue to be used to exploit and oppress the San. Claiming that a group *lacks* a cultural identity until it becomes landed creates unnecessary confusion as to whom land rights were given in the first place. Confusing the goal of

indigenous activism with the criterion for recognizing indigenous identity may have the unfortunate consequence of encouraging a discourse on indigeneity that excludes landless farm San.

Unlike the Omaheke San, the incorporation of the ≠Khomani San into broader South African society meant pressure to assimilate into the "Coloured" community. As a result, ≠Khomani identity must be more deliberately reinvented. To do this, the ≠Khomani rely heavily on primordialist elements of indigenist discourse, which mesh well with local, popular conceptions of cultural identity. To distinguish themselves from the Coloured community, the ≠Khomani assert an identity as "primordial Bushmen," buttressed by popular notions that "Bushmen" are genetically and culturally "pure," while "Coloureds" are racially mixed, and therefore "deculturated."

Hylton White notes that while "their primordial connections with the [precolonial] ≠Khomani Bushmen are tenuous at best" (1995:25) their self-representations "as pristine hunter-gatherers – and their assertion that they are thus distinct from Basters ["Coloureds"] – marks a strategic attempt on their part to position themselves as authenticated subjects of the global Bushman image"(1995:35).

While this kind of "strategic essentialism" is effective for securing rights in the short term, it also reveals the asymmetrical power relationship between the San and agents of the national and international political economic system. The San are being compelled to conform to identity expectations placed on them by states and the international donor community, all of whom expect to find a bounded cultural entity to which rights can be attached, and a culturally discrete "target community" for development funding (Robbins 2001:849). The ≠Khomani San, and the activists and lawyers working on their behalf, recognize that the legitimacy of their claims for land and resources requires concealing the truth about who they have become after a history of colonization and apartheid.

Conclusion

In southern Africa, the category of "indigenous" is superimposed on a political and cultural landscape that continues to be shaped by the legacy of apartheid. Unlike the peoples whose activism established the paradigm of indigeneity – Native North Americans, South American indigenous peoples, and Australian Aborigines – most San are not struggling against a legacy of integrationist and assimilationist state policies; rather, they are fighting against a converse legacy of racial segregation and class exploitation, based on deeply essentialist conceptions of what constitutes cultural or ethnic difference. Those San who did face assimilationist policies are compelled to draw from apartheid definitions of culture in order to assert their rights, with the consequence that they continue to be seen as radically "Other" – as people struggling to regain their "primitive" identity and lifestyle (see Kymlicka 1999).

The essentializing and primordializing tendencies evident in the public discourse on indigenous identities is in part owed to the reductionist and reifying requirements of legal discourse (Coombe 1999, Sieder and Witchell 2001). However, in southern Africa, these tendencies are reinforced by local conceptions of "authentic" Bushman identity that limit the recognition of San identity to a "traditional" one, uncontaminated by political economic and historical contexts. Thus, the most significant ideological connection the San have with the international indigenous peoples' movement is a shared ontological premise that what distinguishes indigenous peoples from the masses of the world's impoverished "marginalized minorities" is a unique (spiritual) relationship to the land. The distinction between indigenous peoples and marginalized minorities is important here because it effectively separates indigenous peoples' issues from class issues, and so the scope of indigenous peoples' issues risks becoming narrowly focused on the cultural politics of micronationalism.

The legacy of colonization and apartheid has two important consequences for how the elderly ≠Khomani woman's call for "land, water, and truth" is received. First, San struggles for social and economic justice – the struggle for land and water – are consistently portrayed as struggles to preserve an archaic lifestyle, a mere cultural anachronism. Secondly, the truth – the complex, class-shaped cultures of most contemporary San – is kept hidden. She cannot have all three – land, water, *and truth* – unless we rethink current definitions of "indigenous culture."

A great deal of ambivalence has been expressed about the ways in which indigenous activism has politicized culture: Some see the promotion of essentialized conceptions of culture as strategically useful and as components of a potentially subversive counter-hegemonic discourse (see, for example, Coombe 1999, Lattas 1993, Lee 2000, Turner 1993); others see essentialist strategies as potentially trapping indigenous actors in stereotypical definitions of their cultural identity, or at least limiting the potential for building alliances along class lines (see, for example, Gledhill 1997, Ortiz 1984, Robbins 2001, Sieder and Witchell 2001). However, mobilizing "culture" as a platform for rights activism need not lead to the promotion of stereotypical, primordial identities, nor to the exclusion of class interests – so long as indigeneity is rethought with a greater sensitivity to the mutual accommodation between culture and class that we find in the lived practices and beliefs of contemporary San.

NOTES

1   The International Work Group for Indigenous Affairs (IWGIA) adopts a definition of indigenous peoples drawn from Cobo and the ILO, but they emphasize non-dominance and add slightly more ontological substance to prior occupation: "Indigenous peoples are the disadvantaged descendants

of those peoples that inhabited a territory prior to the formation of a state. The term indigenous may be defined as a characteristic relating the identity of a particular people to a particular area and distinguishing them culturally from other people or peoples" (IWGIA n.d.).

2 Cobo (1986) notes: "It is essential to know and understand the deeply spiritual special relationship between indigenous peoples and their land as basic to their existence as such and to all their beliefs, customs, traditions and culture" (para. 196). Article 13 of the ILO Convention 169 refers to the "special importance for the cultures and spiritual values of the peoples concerned of their relationship to the lands or territories, or both as applicable, which they occupy or otherwise use, and in particular the collective aspects of this relationship." Article 25 of the UN Draft Declaration states that "Indigenous peoples have the right to maintain and strengthen their distinctive spiritual and material relationship with the lands, territories, waters and coastal seas and other resources which they have traditionally owned or otherwise occupied or used, and to uphold their responsibilities to future generations in this regard" (United Nations 1995).

3 IPACC places "a situation of non-dominance in their national economies and political systems" as the last item on their list.

4 The renown of this group of San is owed largely to the ethnographies, first of the Marshall family (see Marshall 1976, Marshall Thomas 1959) and later, to the work of the Harvard Kalahari Research Project (see, for example, Biesele 1993; Draper 1976, 1975; Katz 1984; Lee and DeVore 1976; Lee 1993, 1979; Shostak 1981). For the lay population the primary sources of information about the Ju/'hoansi are such images as the block-buster movie, *The Gods Must Be Crazy* (see Gordon 1992), and fictionalized representations, such as Laurens van der Post's *The Lost World of the Kalahari* (1958).

5 My claim that the Nyae Nyae Ju/'hoansi lived a relatively autonomous lifestyle could be seen as contentious in light of what became known as "the Great Kalahari Debate." One side of this debate, the "traditionalists" argue that the San were, until very recently, an autonomous ethnic group, living a foraging lifestyle with roots in the paleolithic (see, for example, Lee and Guenther 1991, Solway and Lee 1990). On the other side, the "revisionists" argue that the San are now, and have for a millennium been, a dependent underclass, and their ethnic status was imposed through the process of rural class formation (see Wilmsen 1989). I am inclined to accept the tacit conclusion that most Kalahari scholars have drawn: the revisionist argument is applicable to some groups of San, while the traditionalist argument is applicable to others.

6 Much of the following is drawn from my dissertation (Sylvain 1999); on the mutual constitution of class and culture among the Omaheke San see also Sylvain (2001).

7 The Herero-speakers represent 43 percent of the Omaheke population; the Nama-Damaras 24 percent; the San 12 percent; the Tswana seven percent; the Afrikaans-speakers 8 percent; Ovambo 3 percent; and others 3 percent (Suzman 1995:4).

8 On farms I surveyed (in 1996–7) the average wage for San male workers was N$82 per month. This compares to an average monthly cash wage of N$166.12 for non-San farm workers (Devereux et al. 1996:x, 23). The average wage for San domestic servants was N$45 per month, while wages for non-San domestic servants averaged N$221.90 per month (Fuller and Hubbard 1996:114–15).

9 Stock theft was historically, and remains today, not only a way for the San to cope with poverty and hunger, but also to exact retribution from farmers who are known to mistreat their workers (see also Gordon 1992, Suzman 2000).

10 This pattern holds except where one's name alters the arrangement (see Lee 1993).
11 Additional children are named after their parents' siblings (see Lee 1993:71).
12 One significant difference in the Omaheke version of the name-relation terms was the discontinuation of the female equivalent of *!kun!a* and *!kuma* – *tun* (old name) and *tuma* (young name) for grandmothers, granddaughters, and other female name-sharers. Older women I spoke to knew the terms *tun* and *tuma* and sometimes still used them, while many younger women I spoke to had not even heard of the terms.
13 The term "cultural survival" has been used by a number of indigenous advocacy organizations – most obviously by Cultural Survival. As a recent issue of *Cultural Survival Quarterly* (Lee et al. 2002) shows, the term does not necessarily imply the preservation of fossilized cultures (see Wright 1988:384, also Anaya 2000).

REFERENCES

Anaya, S. James
  2000 Indigenous Peoples in International Law. Oxford: Oxford University Press.
Barnett, Denis
  1999 South Africa. Bushman Tribe Agree on Land Claim. Globe and Mail, March 20:A17.
Barsh, Russell Lawrence
  1996 Indigenous Peoples and the UN Commission on Human Rights: A Case of the Immoveable Object and the Irresistible Force. Human Rights Quarterly 18(4):782–813.
Biesele, Megan
  1992 Changing Human Rights for the San in Namibia. Namibia Brief 16:33–38.
——— 1993 Women Like Meat: the Folklore and Foraging Ideology of the Kalahari Ju/'hoan. Johannesburg: Witwatersrand University Press.

Biesele, Megan, and Paul Weinberg
  1990 Shaken Roots: The Bushmen of Namibia. Marshalltown, South Africa: Environmental Development Agency.
Bixler, Dori, Megan Biesele, and Robert K. Hitchcock
  1993 Land Rights, Local Institutions and Grassroots Development among the Ju/'hoansi of Northeastern Namibia. IWGIA Newsletter 2(April/May/June): 23–29.
Brörmann, Magdalena
  1999 Working Group of Indigenous Minorities in Southern Africa, Report on Activities, April 1998 to March 1999. Windhoek: WIMSA.
Brown, Susan
  1991 Land in Namibia: Rhetoric, Reform or Revolution? Southern Africa Report 7(2):7–10.
Cobo, José Martínez
  1986 The Study of the Problem of Discrimination against Indigenous Populations. United Nations Document E/CN.4/Sub.2/1986/7/Add.4.
Coombe, Rosemary
  1999 Culture: Anthropology's Old Vice or International Law's New Virtue? 1999 Proceedings of the American Society for International Law. Electronic document, http://culturalpolicy.edu/workshop/coombe.html, accessed September 2001.
Daily Dispatch
  1999 Khomani Bushmen Come Home. Daily Dispatch, Tuesday, March 26. Electronic document, http://www.dispatch.co.za/1999/03/16/features/Khomani.htm, accessed February 2, 2001.
Devereux, S., V. Katjiuanjo, and G. van Rooy
  1996 The Living and Working Conditions of Farmworkers in Namibia. Windhoek: Legal Assistance Centre, Farmworkers Project and Social Sciences Division, Multi-Disciplinary Research, Centre, University of Namibia.
Draper, Patricia
  1975 !Kung Women: Contrasts in Sexual Egalitarianism in Foraging and Sedentary Contexts. *In* Toward an Anthropology of

Women. R. Reiter, ed. Pp. 77–109. New York: Monthly Review Press.

—— 1976 Social and Economic Constraints on Child Life among the !Kung. *In* Kalahari Hunter Gatherers: Studies of the !Kung San and their Neighbors. Richard B. Lee and Irven DeVore, eds. Pp. 199–217. Cambridge MA and London: Harvard University Press.

Fuller, B., and D. Hubbard
1996 The Living and Working Conditions of Domestic Workers in Namibia. Windhoek: Legal Assistance Centre.

Gledhill, John
1997 Liberalism, Socio-Economic Rights and the Politics of Identity: From Moral Economy to Indigenous Rights. *In* Human Rights, Culture, and Context: Anthropological Perspectives. Richard Wilson ed. Pp. 70–110. London and Sterling, VA: Pluto Press.

Gordon, Robert
1984 What Future for the Ju/Wasi of Nyae Nyae? The San in Transition. Cambridge, MA: Cultural Survival.

—— 1992 The Bushman Myth: the Making of a Namibian Underclass. Boulder: Westview Press.

Gray, Andrew, and Jens Dahl
1998 UN Declaration Enters a Third Year at the UN Commission on Human Rights. *In* the Indigenous World, 1997–1998. Pp. 347–363. Copenhagen: International Work Group for Indigenous Affairs.

Hitchcock, Robert
1993 Indigenous Peoples, the State and Resource Rights in Southern Africa. *In* "... Never Drink from the Same Cup": Proceedings of the Conference on Indigenous Peoples in Africa. Tune, Denmark, 1993. Hannes Veber, Jens Dahl, Fiona Wilson and Espen Waehle, eds. Pp. 119–132. IWGIA Document 74. Copenhagen: IWGIA and the Centre for Development Research.

Indigenous Peoples of Africa Co-ordinating Committee (IPACC)
n.d. Who are indigenous Africans? Electronic document, http://www.ipacc.org.za/who.html, accessed December 4, 2001.

International Labour Organization (ILO)
1989 Convention No. 169. Convention Concerning Indigenous and Tribal Peoples in Independent Countries. Geneva.

International Work Group on Indigenous Affairs (IWGIA)
n.d. Indigenous Issues: Indigenous Peoples – who are they? Electronic document, http://www.iwgia.org/pop_up.phtml?id = 3, accessed December 4, 2001.

Jordan, Bobby
1999 San people in legal action over 'insulting' ad. Sunday Times. October 31. Electronic document, http://www.suntimes.ca.za/1999/10/31/news/news05.htm, accessed January 15, 2001.

Katz, Richard
1984 Boiling Energy: Community Healing Among the Kalahari Kung. Cambridge, MA: Harvard University Press.

Katz, Richard, Megan Biesele and Verna St. Denis
1997 Healing Makes Our Hearts Happy: Spirituality and Cultural Transformation among the Kalahari Ju/'hoansi. Rochester, VT: Inner Traditions.

Kuper, Adam
1999 Culture: an Anthropologist's Account. Cambridge, MA and London: Harvard University Press.

Kymlicka, Will
1999 Theorizing Indigenous Rights. University of Toronto Law Journal 49:281–293.

Lattas, Andrew
1993 Essentialism, Memory and Resistance; Aboriginality and the Politics of Authenticity. Oceania 63(3):240–268.

Lee, Richard
1979 The !Kung San: Men, Women and Work in a Foraging Society. Cambridge: Cambridge University Press.

—— 1986 !Kung Kin Terms, the Name Relationship and the Process of Discovery. *In* The Past and Future of !Kung Ethnography: Critical Essays in Honour of Lorna Marshall. Megan Biesele, ed., with Richard Lee and Robert Gordon. Pp. 77–102. Hamburg: Helmut Buske Verlag.

—— 1988a Reflections on Primitive Communism. *In* Hunters and Gatherers, vol. I: History, Evolution and Social Change. T. Ingold, D. Ritchie, and J. Woodburn, eds. Pp. 252–268. Oxford: Berg.

—— 1988b The Gods Must Be Crazy But the State Has a Plan: Government Policies toward the San in Namibia. *In* Namibia: 1884–1984, Readings on Namibia's History and Society. Brian Wood ed. Pp. 540–543. Namibia Support Committee in co-operation with the United Nations Institute for Namibia.

—— 1993 The Dobe Ju/'hoansi. 2nd edition. Fort Worth, TX: Harcourt Brace.

—— 2000 Indigenism and its Discontents: Anthropology and the Small Peoples at the Millennium. Paper presented as the 2000 Keynote Address at the Annual Meeting of the American Ethnological Society, Tampa, March 25.

Lee, Richard, and Irven DeVore
  1976 Kalahari Hunter-Gatherers: Studies of the !Kung and Their Neighbors. Cambridge, MA and London: Harvard University Press.

Lee, Richard B., and Mathias Guenther
  1991 Oxens or Onions? The Search for Trade (and Truth) in the Kalahari. Current Anthropology 32(5):592–601.

Lee, Richard B., Robert Hitchcock, and Megan Biesele, guest eds.
  2002 The Kalahari San: Self Determination in the Desert, special issue, Cultural Survival Quarterly 26(1).

Lee, Richard, and Susan Hurlich
  1979 Colonialism, Apartheid and Liberation: a Namibian example. *In* Challenging Anthropology. D. N. Turner and G. A. Smith, eds. Pp. 353–371. Toronto: McGraw-Hill; Cambridge, MA: Harvard University Press.

Marshall, John, and Claire Ritchie
  1984 Where are the Ju/wasi of Nyae Nyae? Changes in a Bushman Society: 1958–1981. Cape Town: Centre for African Studies, University of Cape Town.

Marshall, Lorna
  1976 The !Kung of Nyae Nyae. Cambridge, MA: Harvard University Press.

Marshall Thomas, Elizabeth
  1959 The Harmless People. New York: Vintage Books.

Maybury-Lewis, David
—— 1997 Indigenous People, Ethnic Groups and the State. Boston: Allyn & Bacon.

Monitor
  1999 San Bushmen Get New Lease for Survival. Tuesday, March 25. Electronic document, http://www.africanews.com/monitor/freeissues/25mar99/interhtm#anchor7, accessed January 20, 2001.

Muehlebach, Andrea
  2001 "Making Place" at the United Nations: Indigenous Cultural Politics at the U.N. Working Group on Indigenous Populations. Cultural Anthropology 16 (3):415–448.

Ortiz, Roxanne Dunbar
  1984 The Fourth World and Indigenism: Politics of Isolation and Alternatives. Journal of Ethnic Studies 12(1):79–105.

Robbins, Steven
  2001a NGOs, "Bushmen" and Double Vision: the ≠Khomani San Land Claim and the Cultural Politics of "Community" and "Development" in the Kalahari. Journal of Southern African Studies 27(4):834–853.

Saugestad, Sidsel
  2001 The Inconvenient Indigenous: Remote Area Development in Botswana, Donor Assistance, and the First Peoples of the Kalahari. Uppsala: Nordic Africa Institute.

Shostak, Margorie
  1981 Nisa: The Life and Words of a !Kung Woman. Cambridge MA: Harvard University Press.

Sieder, Rachel, and Jessica Witchell
  2001 Advancing Indigenous Claims through the Law: Reflections on the Guatemalan Peace Process. *In* Culture and Rights: Anthropological Perspectives. Jane K. Cowan, Marie-Bénédicte Dembour, and Richard A. Wilson, eds. Pp. 201–225. Cambridge: Cambridge University Press.

Solway, Jacqueline S., and Richard B. Lee
  1990 Foragers: Genuine or Spurious? Situating the Kalahari San in History. Current Anthropology 31(2):109–122.

South African San Institute (SASI)
1999 Annual Report, April 1998–March 1999. Cape Town: South African San Institute.
Suzman, James
1995 Poverty, Land and Power in the Omaheke Region. Windhoek: Oxfam.
——— 2000 Things from the Bush: a Contemporary History of the Omaheke Bushmen. Switzerland: P. Schlettwein.
Sylvain, Renée
1999 "We Work to Have Life": Ju/'hoan Women, Work and Survival in the Omaheke Region, Namibia. Ph.D. dissertation, Department of Anthropology, University of Toronto.
——— 2001 Bushmen, Boers and Baasskap: Patriarchy and Paternalism on Afrikaner Farms in the Omaheke Region, Namibia. Journal of Southern African Studies 27(4):717–737.
Turner, Terence
1993 Anthropology and Multiculturalism: What is Anthropology That Multiculturalists Should Be Mindful of It? Cultural Anthropology 8(4):411–429.
United Nations
1995 Declaration on the Rights of Indigenous Peoples. United Nations Documents E/CN.4/1995/2, E/CN.4/Sub.2/1994/56.

van der Post, Laurens
1958 The Lost World of the Kalahari. Harmondsworth: Penguin.
Veber, Hannes, and Espen Waehle
1993 An Introduction. In "...Never Drink from the Same Cup": Proceedings of the conference on Indigenous Peoples in Africa. Tune, Denmark, 1993. Hannes Veber, Jens Dahl, Fiona Wilson and Espen Waehle, eds. Pp. 9–19. IWGIA Document 74. Copenhagen: IWGIA and the Centre for Development Research.
White, Hylton
1995 In the Tradition of the Forefathers: Bushman Traditionality at Kagga Kamma. Cape Town: University of Cape Town Press.
Wilmsen, Edwin N.
1989 Land Filled with Flies: a Political Economy of the Kalahari. Chicago and London: University of Chicago Press.
Working Group of Indigenous Minorities in Southern Africa (WIMSA)
2000 Working Group of Indigenous Minorities in Southern Africa, Report on Activities, April 1999 to March 2000. Windhoek: WIMSA.
Wright, Robin
1988 Anthropological Presuppositions of Indigenous Advocacy. Annual Review of Anthropology 17:365–390.

Part IV

Privatization, Individualization, and Global Cosmopolitanism

13

Changing the Rules of Trade with Global Partnerships: The Fair Trade Movement

Kimberly M. Grimes

We are women working to build our lives.
Together we have overcome many problems.
We will send our children to school with our earnings.
We purchase our food and clothing,
we plant our gardens and cultivate our crops,
we repair our houses and we plant trees.
By working together, we become united in one mind.

    (working song of the 75 women of the Keya Palm project in Agailjhara, Bangladesh[1])

In the face of rapid globalization and increasing international trade, questions and concerns about the damages of market liberalization and the free-trade agenda are being voiced by people throughout the world. From Seattle, to Washington, DC, to San Salvador, to São Paulo, to Paris, to Salzburg, to Cape Town, to Istanbul, to Azad Maidan, to Prague, to Calcutta, and many other cities, people are taking to the streets in protest at the WTO (World Trade Organization), the World Bank/International Monetary Fund (IMF), and the policies and practices of transnational corporations which have rapidly amplified global insecurity and the disparity between First and Third World nations, and continue to wreak havoc on the lives of the poor.

In the search for viable alternatives to the monolithic draconian policies, a decentralized, grassroots citizen movement born some fifty years ago is burgeoning. The fair trade movement offers producers, consumers, and business people the opportunity to expand economically just and environmentally sustainable international production and trade. The movement is strikingly heterogeneous in composition with a wide variety of small-scale craft, clothing, and agricultural producers throughout the world trading with US, Canadian, European, Japanese, Australian, and New Zealand fair trade marketers of diverse origins. Together they are challenging the structural conditions of inequality by increasing producers' incomes, empowering their decision making and autonomy, providing opportunities for education and health care, and improving local living conditions.

As a social movement, fair trade is exemplary of participatory democracy.[2] Women and men collectively negotiate their patterns of work, mixing the production of goods for sale or cash crops while maintaining and creating individual and community activities and strategies that help to resist their exploitation and homogenization in the global marketplace. Women producers have been especially empowered through earning hard currency, and connecting with other women who may be of a different religion or class, yet share many of the same problems arising from oppression and little or no say in local and national affairs. Fair trade creates a bridge between the peoples of the developing nations and those of the developed ones. For consumers in First World countries, fair trade gives people the opportunity to not only purchase products that support their values of a more socially just and equitable world trade order, but to also learn about the producers' lives, their struggles, and our mutual interdependence.

The Essence of Fair Trade

The roots of the fair trade movement date back to the late 1940s with the founding of Mennonite- and Brethren-affiliated fair trade businesses in the United States. To honor their beliefs and obligations as Christians by assisting those in need, the church organizations began marketing products from impoverished artisan groups in developing nations through their congregations. They established the first network of fair trade stores, organized local fundraisers, and later produced a retail mail-order catalog. As well as selling products, they developed ways of telling consumers the artisans' life stories. In Europe fair trade began with Oxfam, the grassroots community-based development organization. Founded in 1942 as the Oxford Committee for Famine Relief, in the 1950s Oxfam UK sold products made by Chinese refugees which ultimately led to the creation of the first Alternative Trade Organization (ATO) in Europe in 1964. The second arose in the Netherlands in 1967. Over the next 30 years, fair trade expanded in

the United States, Canada, and throughout Western Europe with the birth of several large importing organizations and numerous small retail shops.

In the Pacific rim, fair trade began in Australia and New Zealand soon after Europe, with the first outlets opening in the early 1970s. Oxfam Australia is the largest group in the country with its online shop and 17 retail stores. Tradewinds, the other large fair trade organization, distributes fair trade coffee and tea to numerous health and fair trade stores. The number of retail shops in New Zealand has grown to a current total of 30. The fair trade movement started later in Japan, with the founding of the Dai-San Sekai shop in 1986 as a department within the larger nongovernmental organization (NGO), Press Alternative. In that same year, a citizens' group established the "Japan Committee for Negroes Campaign" and started importing fair trade muscovado sugar in 1987. Currently there are five large fair trade importing organizations and an additional three NGOs that employ fair trade as a fundraising tool. Hundreds of smaller citizens' groups sell handicrafts under the banner of fair trade.

In response to the growing number of fair trade producers and marketers, by the late 1980s and early 1990s the loose association of fair trade groups became formally organized, with the creation of umbrella organizations to link fair traders. The first, established in 1989, is the International Federation of Alternative Trade (IFAT), which links producer associations in Latin America, Africa, and Asia with the marketing nations mentioned above. Today it has over 160 members from more than fifty countries who meet annually at a conference held in a different country each year.[3] Within continents, other umbrella organizations have been created, such as the Fair Trade Federation (FTF) in North America, and the European Fair Trade Association (EFTA), the Network of European World Shops (NEWS!), and the International Fair Trade Labeling Organization (FLO) in Europe.

Australasian operated as an umbrella organization for Australia and New Zealand, but folded after a few years primarily due to the small size and number of fair trade shops which lacked sufficient funds and staff to attend meetings. Currently a new initiative is in the works, the Fair Trade Alliance of Australia (FTA), which, with the support of other social responsibility groups and individuals, hopes to unify and expand the fair trade movement in Australia. It is working on creating a branch of the FTA to be the FLO member initiative for labeling products in Australia similar to Transfair USA and Max Hvelaar in the Netherlands, who certify and label fair trade coffee. Japan has no mother organization, although three of the largest fair trade groups are members of IFAT. In the United States and Europe many of the larger fair trade organizations are members of several umbrella groups; this overlap strengthens the movement as a whole with information and assistance constantly shared.

While each organization has its own specific mission statement and criteria, the following basic principles underlie all fair trade partnerships. The marketers agree to pay fair wages to the artisans and farmers (based on the producers' basic needs, costs of production, and margins for investment); provide advance payments for working capital; purchase goods directly from the producers, eliminating the chain of middlemen and speculators; and provide technical and financial assistance when necessary. The producers agree to work in an economically, socially, and environmentally sustainable manner; ensure healthy and safe working conditions; support democratic participation of all members, and contribute to the development of the community by increasing jobs and by building schools, health-care centers, and other infrastructure projects that a particular community deems a priority.

In general, people involved in fair trade believe that optimizing profits to the detriment of workers and the environment is not only unethical but a shortsighted, inane strategy. They maintain that businesses must champion human rights, highlight labor issues, ensure the wise use of natural resources, promote economic justice and, where pertinent, work to preserve culturally embedded craft traditions. Fair traders recognize the new world order in which the powers of government have shrunk as the unelected officials of the WTO, transnationals and financial speculators, have, for the most part, unfettered control of international production, trade, and financial flows. Thus fair traders believe it is up to citizens to create new enterprises which are based on sustainable global partnerships to meet the needs of society. Anita Roddick, founder of the Body Shop, states: "Many governments' economic agendas seem to take no account of caring for the weak and frail and the marginalized. If governments are not interested, then I believe that business – rich, powerful and creative – has to take responsibility. If not us, who?" (Roddick 2000:90).

The Variety of Fair Trade Businesses

One of the strengths of the fair trade movement is its heterogeneous make-up. The number of workers in a fair trade business in North America and Europe range from two to hundreds. While some companies use only full-time employees, others depend on a mix of full-time, part-time, and volunteer labor. Annual gross sales of these businesses range between tens of thousands to millions of dollars. Some groups focus on a particular commodity, such as coffee, tea, chocolate, bananas, sugar, or cotton, whereas others work directly with diverse craft, textile, clothing, and art producers. The political vision of fair trade organizations varies as well, from leftist, activist positions to more moderate ones. For example, at Global Exchange in San Francisco, fair trade is one section of its broader human rights mission, which includes a corporate accountability program (targeting transnationals with repressive labor practices); the organizing of boycotts, protests, and acts of civil disobedience; and the production of educational programs, such as lecture tours, "reality" travel tours, and printed materials.[4] At the other end of the spectrum, faith-based fair traders do not organize protests but rather focus on their beliefs of solidarity to change the world with artisan and farmer partnerships and consumer awareness programs. Fair traders as a group tend to be unhappy with the dominant national political parties and are searching for a progressive politics that seriously addresses growing global social and environmental problems.

The movement is the largest in Europe with 12 large fair trade importing organizations and a network of over 2,700 shops in 15 national associations in 13 European countries. Fair trade commodities are stocked in some 13,000 commercial shops and 30 supermarket chains. A conservative estimate of the annual aggregate net retail value of fair trade products sold in 2001 exceeded $260 million, through over 64,800 points of sale (Bowen 2001:22–3). The organizations receive some financial support from the European Union and voice their views and concerns through campaigns and petitions when the Union is negotiating trade agreements. Fair trade is expanding so that currently every major town in England and in the Netherlands has at least one supplier of fair trade products, with cities having several.

In the United States and Canada, the Fair Trade Federation's *2002 Report on the Fair Trade Industry* in North America reveals a large increase in fair trade sales over the last few years, primarily due to a national fair trade coffee campaign in the United States. Global Exchange, Oxfam USA, university student groups, and other organizations began the campaign by threatening Starbucks, the largest gourmet coffee importer in the United States, with protests in front of their cafés if they did not start buying a percentage of fairly traded coffee; the campaign has grown and continues to pressure other coffee buyers and distributors. In 2001

gross sales topped $100 million, with coffee accounting for $57 million and the rest for all other fair trade products combined. Outlets retailing fair trade products jumped 271 percent from a total of 2,575 retail outlets in 2000 to 7,000 in 2001, a marked increase, again primarily due to the growth of coffee outlets. In examining all fair trade products except coffee, the two largest organizations, Ten Thousand Villages and SERRV International, account for about half of fair trade sales in North America. The number and volume of sales of smaller fair trade businesses are expanding rapidly, however, most notably with the appearance of more e-businesses (see Grimes 2000:17–19).

Producer groups differ from one region to another, depending on the number of years in business, the type of good(s) produced and their organizational structure. From the largest association, Frente Solidario de Pequeños Cafetaleros de América Latina, comprising 200,000 coffee farmers, to small family-based craft workshops of a couple dozen members, fair trade producer groups include co-ops, associations, family groups, workshops for the handicapped, state organizations, and private businesses. What the groups have in common is meager incomes, lack of direct access to markets, no social benefits, and difficult working conditions – conditions their fair trade partners help them to surmount (Bowen 2001:28–9).

Work and market relations for those producing commodities differ from those producing crafts, textiles, clothing, and art. Fair trade marketers establish minimum fair prices for commodities – regardless of how low the world commercial market price falls.[5] They provide advance payments so small farmers can avoid borrowing money before the harvest and paying exorbitant interest payments to moneylenders. Apart from these basic principles, particular farmer–marketer relations differ within commodity-producing groups. For example, the 35,000 cocoa farmers of the Kuapa Kokoo cooperative in Ghana not only receive fair payments for their beans but they are also stockholders in the British Day Chocolate Company, which turns the beans into Divine chocolate bars. The farmers vote for regional representatives who attend the company's Annual General Meeting to decide policy for the company. As shareholders their income is greater, since most of the profits are made from the finished product. The Dominican cocoa producers, CONACADO (Confederación Nacional de Cacaocultores Dominicanos/National Dominican Federation of Cocoa Producers), working with Canadian marketers, receive the guaranteed minimum fair price and, in addition, a bonus to be used for community projects (SERRV 2002). Each group of farmers determines their own terms for sale and support.

For crafts, textiles, and clothing, fair traders work with individual groups to help work out the production cost and fair price of each particular item. Often when a group begins working with fair traders, one of the difficulties is to get producers to increase their prices, since they are accustomed to receiving so little for their products from mainstream commercial buyers. Some producers trade with other fair trade producers to get materials, such as the women's cooperative, UPAVIM (Unidos Para Vivir Mejor/ United to Live Better) in Guatemala City, which buys bulk cloth at fair prices from rural Maya women to make into household items (Rosenbaum 2000). Many groups work with NGOs and fair traders, such as several Nepali artisan cooperatives (MacHenry 2000). In other cases, producers sell as much as they can to fair traders and then the rest to regular commercial buyers, since fair trade marketers often cannot absorb all of the goods they make.

"Partnering" with Consumers

The fair trade movement goes beyond producers and marketers, since ultimately it is consumers armed with their dollars, euros, or yens which make the movement grow. The emergence of "ethical" shopping has corres-

ponded to the growing rise in socially responsible businesses and their increase in gross sales. As the Dutch philosopher Michiel Korthals reports:

> Consumers are not only becoming more concerned about the safety of products for humans, animals, and the environment, but also attach moral significance to the way each product is being produced and the norms and values involved. And what is even more striking, they also think it important to express these 'ethical' and political preferences in the market itself and not solely on the political forum. (Korthals 2001:203)

Ray and Anderson's (2000) study reveals that over 50 million adults in the United States and some 80 to 90 million adults in Western Europe are questioning the dominant social order with profound concerns for the environment; for peace, jobs, and social justice; for women's rights; for spirituality and personal growth; and for stopping corporate globalization. Named "cultural creatives," Ray and Anderson found that these adults are in a transition, working to bring their values and beliefs into alignment with the way they live. And part of this transition includes changes in people's purchasing habits, switching to fairly traded goods, organic foods, items made from recycled materials, alternative health products, and spiritual goods. The strength of this new cultural movement is found in its diversity of concerns and strategies for changing the predominant social order. It has grown out of many earlier struggles of the twentieth century, yet no one orthodoxy or worldview is restraining it.

The media in the mid-1990s began paying more attention to the worldwide problems of sweatshops, unfair labor practices, and enslaved children who weave rugs or pick cocoa beans. Kathie Lee Gifford's tearful admission in spring 1996 of her ignorance of the sweatshop conditions in the factories which produce her brand-name clothes set off a chain reaction in the media. Campaigns against Nike, Disney, Wal-Mart, and others for using sweatshop labor became news and other prominent media stars, such as Oprah Winfrey, increased consumer awareness of the problems. As a result many consumers are now considering the social conditions in which a product is made. Surveys conducted in Europe and North America reveal that over seventy percent of consumers want the products they purchase to be made in a safe and fair working environment (Barlow and Clark 2001; Klein 2000; Ross 1997). Labor supporters are urging unions to organize at the international level and to demand core labor standards in hemispheric and global trade agreements (Frundt 2002:37–42). A survey conducted by Christian Aid and Cafédirect in the United Kingdom showed that consumers are willing to pay more for products if the money goes to the producers; they believe that "trading fairly with the developing world is a better way to help poorer countries than giving aid" (Miller 1993:16). One of the issues that the "cultural creatives" agree upon is a willingness to pay more taxes or more for consumer goods if the money supports ecological and social sustainability. In fact, most already do (Ray and Anderson 2000).

For the fair trade movement consumer support has meant rapid growth, even as the annual growth of world trade declines. Rugmark, an international organization that labels fair trade carpets, reports that "ethical" purchases' growth equaled six times that of the market as a whole in 2001 (Rugmark 2002:1).[6] Many consumers are demanding change and are carefully using their purchasing power to support the various directions of this change. This "global backlash" to the dominant economic order is no longer a "fringe" movement but rather a "harbinger of things to come" (Broad 2002:9).

Creating Equity and Social Services with Fair Trade

As the gap continues to widen between the wealthy and the poor, Third World populations are hardest hit, because the poorer the country, the smaller the share of national income distributed to the poorest groups in that country.[7] Moreover, since the 1970s, the percentage of national income distributed to the poorest populations in all countries has been decreasing (Brown 1993). According to the United Nations, women constitute more than seventy percent of the world's poorest citizens. They are even more disenfranchised since patriarchal structures and practices within nations and local communities further magnify their invisibility and exclusion.

Excluded from discussions on issues and decisions that directly impact their lives, more and more producers, especially women, are turning to fair trade to strengthen their positions at home and in the world market. Fair trade helps people to embark on their own path of independent development rather than remain dependent on the exploitative relationships with transnationals and middlemen, or the charity of aid-relief organizations. For example, SERRV International is launching "an innovative model for empowering producer–partner organizations as they seek to overcome obstacles and capitalize on opportunities in the global economy" (Backe 2002:1). The three-part integrated approach includes: expanding the US market for products; expanding capacity-building services by working with individual groups to develop long-term growth plans and a multifaceted package of business development services which will allow groups to achieve complete economic self-sufficiency; and reaching out to the most marginalized groups with the provision of technical and financial support for several years until they can develop their capacity to produce and market products at the international level (Backe 2002). As shown in this example, as fair trade marketing organizations grow and obtain more resources, they continually seek new ways to attack global poverty and create possibilities for their partners to attain self-sufficiency.

One of the most important benefits to producer groups from fair trade is direct access to markets with which they otherwise would never have had contact. Once involved in fair trade, they often meet with other commercial buyers in developed nations while visiting these countries, and at times create direct south-to-south trade by meeting other producers at annual conferences and trade shows. Fair traders encourage the making of many contacts to avoid overdependence on one or a few marketers. Fair pay includes working capital for investment in their organizations to develop new products, meet changing market demands, and survive crises. Prepayment means they can avoid the downward spiral of indebtedness. Along with financial assistance, marketers often provide technical assistance including designers, consultants, research, and training workshops.

Most importantly, fair trade gives producers the confidence to trade in the global marketplace. Many groups at first are literally frightened and lack the knowledge to even approach national trading associations and government officials, whose prejudices make them feel inferior. The producers cannot imagine being able to understand the national export and foreign import requirements needed to participate in the international market. With their fair trade partners, however, the groups overcome these feelings and gain the necessary skills to trade globally.

When producer groups enter the fair trade movement, monies earned are first spent on basic needs: food – since many families are malnourished – clothing, and shelter. Once basic needs are met, most often their next priority is education for their children, who previously had to go out to work at a young age to help support the family. As the amount of time in the fair trade partnerships increases, so too do the earnings that can be used for community-based projects. Each community decides which needs are most pressing and often works on several infrastructure projects concurrently, as demonstrated by the following examples.

The women of UPAVIM who live and work in a squatter settlement in Guatemala City have constructed a three-story building to house their craft-making center, a children's center (day care and Montessori preschool), a dental clinic, and a scholarship/tutorial program (Rosenbaum 2000:94–5). They are currently raising funds from the production of angel pins to purchase a tortilla-making business and are buying land to grow herbs and crops in order to lower the costs of food consumption. The use of these facilities and programs are shared with all those in the squatter settlement, not just the members of the craft cooperative.

Maya Traditions, based in San Francisco and Panajachel, Guatemala, partners with three rural Maya weaving groups. Since their partnership began, the groups and Maya Traditions together have initiated a scholarship program and an integrated health program. The women have participated in various workshops on livestock fattening, analysis of human rights issues, development of business skills, and the contemplation of Maya cosmo-vision. One group paid off a loan for land used in common to grow corn and other vegetables (Lynd 2000).

UNICEF and fair trader Ganesh Himal located in Spokane, Washington, partners with Bhaktapur Craft Printers (BCP) in Nepal to market handmade paper products. With the Chinese takeover of Tibet, the papermaking industry was threatened with extinction owing to the loss of the Tibetan market. With a new market, women now gather tree bark to make paper journals, stationery, and other paper goods, and at the same time, preserve the trees in the fragile forests of western Nepal. They use the profits from paper-product sales to fund potable water, sanitation, education, irrigation, forestry, and environmental programs. Over ten million Nepalese rupees were generated between 1987 to 1993 to support the programs (Ganesh Himal 1995).

Fair traders' partnerships extend to marginalized groups within developed nations as well. The Enterprising Kitchen, based in Chicago, is a nonprofit organization that provides employment and life skills training to impoverished, and often abused, women who are working toward self-sufficiency and independence. With fair trade partners marketing and providing some development funds, the Kitchen has grown in six years from employing four women with some Tupperware molds and one hand mixer to 100 employees that produce thousands of natural bath products annually.[8] The women obtain more than income; they gain self-esteem and the knowledge that they are valuable people. Fair traders in the United States also partner with other impoverished women's groups who make bean and bread mixes or beeswax candles, and Native American communities, selling their teas, honeys, wild rice, and other foods in order to create economic opportunities that can support families on the reservations.

The projects are as numerous as the everyday life problems the groups confront. Fair trade does not promote the "one-size-fits-all" solution to problems in the way that the IMF, WTO, and other free-trade policy-makers do. Fair trade is attentive to communities' differing cultures, environmental situations, and histories, and to the producers' differing religions, ethnicities, and gender ideologies and roles. Appropriate solutions to social, economic, and ecological problems are determined at the local level and assisted at the global level. It is this consciousness that enables fair trade partnerships to dramatically improve people's living conditions and to build a global solidarity that is based on dignity and respect.

The Challenges Faced by the Fair Trade Movement

The challenges the movement faces are numerous. While fair trade sales are substantial and on the rise, they still comprise a small percentage of the whopping trillions of dollars in total goods exchanged globally.[9]

An examination of the major commodities entering world trade during the 1980s shows that just 15 transnationals market 70 to 90 percent of the world's production, and for each particular commodity only three to six corporations dominate the entire market (Brown 1993:50–1). In the 1990s the trend for further concentration of wealth and power in the commodity market continued with mergers and hostile takeovers. The result, for example, in the two markets of coffee and chocolate, are four transnationals controlling each; Nestlé, Mars, Hershey, and Cadbury dominate the cocoa bean–chocolate market and Kraft, Nestlé, Procter & Gamble, and Sara Lee, the coffee market (Gresser and Tickell 2002:25; SERRV 2002:2). International trade agreements, the expansion of free-trade zones, and the hegemony of global financial and trade institutions continue the trend that began several decades ago to increase richer nations', their transnationals' and their elites' share of global profitability at the expense of impoverished peoples whose countries are drowning under the burden of debt (George 1988).

In a time when neoliberalism is destroying social, ethnic, and political consciousness in the guise of "freedom," fair trade plays an important role in preserving and promoting cultural traditions and the diversity of identities in the world of increasing homogenization. Moreover, it provides a sustainable, proven, global alternative economic model which demonstrates how production and trade can work at the grassroots and international levels and how it can benefit all people, not just the elites of the world. However, in order to have a greater impact to change the dominant economic order, fair trade must overcome many hurdles. First is the need to increase fair trade outlets and sales so that many producer groups who currently want to join the movement can have direct access. It is difficult for marketers to absorb all of the production capabilities of groups with whom they are currently working, let alone take on the many who have yet to find a partner.[10] Thus the push among supporters of fair trade and fair traders themselves to influence conventional companies, such as Starbucks, to commit to buying fairly traded goods.

The public must be educated to understand what fair trade is exactly and how it differs from free trade. Fair trade standards must be clear to industry and consumers. If not, confusion could cause damaging controversy to the movement. As fair trade increases, companies threatened by it could release misinformation in response. To address this issue of public education, a new organization, the Fair Trade Resource Network (FTRN), was born in 1999 in the United States. Its educational mission is to raise consumer awareness about fair trade by gathering and compiling all the research and data on fair trade; providing fair trade information to schools, universities, the media, and the general public through campaigns, printed materials, and other resources; and hosting an online bookstore. Based in Washington, DC, the nonprofit institution is currently corresponding and working with the movement in Europe and plans in the future to work with Japanese and Australian fair traders in order to educate people worldwide.[11]

The fair trade movement needs to continue to build coalitions with other labor and environmental groups who share many of the same concerns to reach and educate a larger segment of the general population. The movement also must continue developing fair trade labels for commodities to help consumers distinguish fairly traded products. European fair traders were the first to develop three fair trade seals for food products and have created a specific fair trade labeling institution, the FLO, to address the development of certifications and labels for both food and nonfood products. Transfair, the first fair trade certification organization in North America, has developed a seal for fair trade coffee and hopes to expand to other food products over the next few years. An immense fight over the issue of labeling is imminent as the WTO insists that labels give "unfair advantage" to particular groups.

Fair traders will have to mount a large campaign with many other groups who have a vested interest, such as the organic foods movement, if they are to challenge the WTO's interpretation.

Many fair trade producer groups lack sufficient market information, business expertise, and technical skills. Consumer demand can and does change quickly, especially in the clothing industry; producers need to be able to respond as quickly. Some groups that have been involved in fair trade for over a decade have reached the point where they are able to obtain the information they require through their own skills, yet many others do not have this capability. Strategic plans, like the one by SERRV International discussed previously, are addressing these problems, and other marketers are also continuing to increase technical and business assistance. The survival of producer groups depends on this information.

In the marketing countries, fair trade businesses face the hardships of small businesses (which cause half such businesses in the United States to fold in their first three years). Some fair trade retailers who were undercapitalized have had to close. Most people enter fair trade due to their commitments to social justice and their environmental concerns, and they often lack business skills and underestimate the costs of running a retail shop. In the United States, for example, most people do not realize that small businesses have the heaviest tax burden, making up for tax revenues that transnationals avoid by moving their money to offshore accounts and other countries. In Europe, there is more support for retailers with the Network of European World Shops (NEWS!) organization, which addresses the needs of retailers specifically with all sorts of business information. The US, Canadian, Japanese, and Australian retailers lack this type of parent organization, although in North America the FTF is working to give current and prospective retailers more professional support, such as the development of a video and booklet designed to teach people how to start and run a successful fair trade retail store. Overall, networking and parent organizations must increase throughout marketing nations if fair traders are not only to augment sales and the number of outlets, but to also have sustainable businesses that can provide a living for the employers and employees.

Fair Trade in the Twenty-First Century

> Poverty is not only about a shortage of money. It is about rights and relationships; about how people are treated and how they regard themselves; about powerlessness, exclusion and loss of dignity. Yet the lack of adequate income is at its heart.
>
> Mahatma Gandhi[12]

The bipolarity of the struggle between fair trade proponents and those pushing the free-trade agenda marks a critical moment in human history. In the late twentieth century we witnessed a dramatic change in Western consumption patterns in which shopping became more than the means to acquire basic necessities. Shopping now ranks as the number two leisure activity as people search for their wants, desires, and images in the maze of tastes and styles offered by modern consumer culture (Lury 1996).[13] People's responses in these Euroamerican societies to the flood of products range from one of never-ending desire for more "stuff" to an outright rejection of vulgar consumerism. Fair traders realize that corporations' promotion of material goods as the road to happiness is untrue and unhealthy for people and the planet. Yet they, too, promote the purchasing of goods.

The issue for the movement is one of equity and sustainability. As a fair trade storeowner told me, "We all drink coffee or tea and are gonna buy it somewhere, so why not here, where farmers can be paid enough

so they can have a cup, too?" Another shop-owner explained, "If we keep cutting down the rainforest to grow coffee on monocrop plantations, we won't be able to grow anything soon. It should be grown in the rainforest as nature intended it to – heck, there it even produces better-tasting coffee – what more could you want?"[14] The outcry against neoliberal, "trickle-down" economic policies is growing worldwide and more people are looking for a viable alternative. The fair trade movement positions itself as the alternative, one that recognizes the interconnectedness of all peoples in the world and one that wants to create income for the majority rather than concentrating wealth in the hands of a few. It is not anti-globalization, as the media has often incorrectly represented the advocates of fair trade. On the contrary, fair trade partnerships are international partnerships.

For many, the most important question is that of time. Destruction of natural and human resources is proceeding at an unprecedented rate. Advocates of fair trade worry that they are running at too slow a pace and are getting left behind. They are very concerned about their ability to make their alternative model of international production and trade grow fast enough to compensate for, and eventually hope to end, the damage that the free-trade system is causing. Just how much influence the movement will be able to assert in the politics of production and consumption remains unanswered. Yet if the vision, persuasiveness, and determination of the variety of peoples and groups which comprise the fair trade movement are any indication, profound change could be right around the corner.

NOTES

1   From the brochure for Ten Thousand Villages, the largest fair trade organization in the United States, www.tenthousandvillages.org, 704 Main Street, Akron, PA 17501, USA.

2 I follow the use of the term as Stephen understands it, in that it "denotes widespread citizen participation. It is not confined to electoral democracies in which the primary exercise of citizenship is voting" (1997:277).

3 For more information on IFAT's mission and program, see www.ifat.org

4 For more information on Global Exchange's mission and program, see www.globalexchange.org

5 For example, since the 1990s the set price for coffee has been $1.26 per pound; $1.41 for organic. The major multinationals that control the coffee market have dropped the price to its lowest in 30 years (US14c. per kilo for green beans in 2001). It now costs coffee farmers more to pick the beans than they receive. The coffee crisis has resulted in a dramatic increase in malnutrition, the forcing of children out of school, worsening healthcare, and other miseries (Gresser and Tickell 2002). The same is true for the four giant chocolate companies (Nestlé, Mars, Hershey and Cadbury) who control the cocoa bean market. Only in the case of chocolate, children are being enslaved to pick the beans in Ghana and other countries.

6 Rugmark is an international certification program which labels rugs made by fairly paid adults and without illegal child labor; they also have other programs to support rugmaking communities. For more information on Rugmark's mission and program, see www.rugmark.org

7 In many Third World countries such as Brazil, India, Mexico, Malaysia, and Peru, the poorest 40 percent of households received less than 10 percent of the total income, whereas in First World countries the poorest 40 percent got at least 20 percent (Brown 1993:117).

8 www.theenterprisingkitchen.org, The Enterprising Kitchen, 4545 North Broadway, Chicago, IL 60640.

9 Oil accounts for much of this, since it is the number one commodity traded. Coffee is number two, which is why fair trade devotes so much of its time and resources to it. Still less than a million coffee farmers sell to fair traders out of the 25 million producers globally.

10 Page-Reeves (1998) discusses this problem in her research on Bolivian handknit sweater makers who sell about thirty percent of their production to fair traders and then end up selling the rest to commercial buyers who pay miserable wages to the knitters.

11 For more information on FTRN's mission and program, see www.fairtraderesource.org, Fair Trade Resource Network, PO Box 33772, Washington, DC 20033, USA.

12 Quoted on the home page of a New Zealand fair trade organization, Trade Aid Importers, www.tradeaid.co.nz

13 Watching television is the number one leisure activity (Lury 1996). Obviously there is a connection between the two since television's primary purpose is to sell advertisers' products.

14 From interviews I conducted with members of the Fair Trade Federation.

REFERENCES

Backe, Brian
  2002 Taking an Integrated Approach to Expanding Opportunities for Grassroots Enterprises in the Developing World: Alternative Trade and Capacity-Building. Long-Range Strategy Paper, Resource Development Section, SERRV International. October. www.serrv.org

Barlow, Maude, and Tony Clark
  2001 Global Showdown. Toronto: Stoddart.

Bowen, Brid
  2001 Let's Go Fair! In Fair Trade Yearbook: Challenges of Fair Trade 2001–2003. European Fair Trade Association, ed. Ghent, Belgium: Druk in de weer, pp. 21–41 (available via www.fairtraderesource.org).

Broad, Robin
  2002 Global Backlash: Citizen Initiatives for a Just World Economy. New York: Rowman & Littlefield.
Brown, Michael
  1993 Fair Trade: Reform and Realities in the International Trading System. London: Zed.
Frundt, Henry
  2002 Central American Unions in the Era of Globalization. Latin American Research Review 37(3):7–53.
Ganesh, Himal
  1995 Bhaktapur Craft Printers: Handmade Paper Products from Nepal. Ganesh Himal Newsletter, July, p.1.
George, Susan
  1988 A Fate Worse than Debt. New York: Grove Weidenfeld.
Gresser, Charis, and Sophia Tickell
  2002 Mugged: Poverty in your Coffee Cup. Boston: Oxfam International.
Grimes, Kimberly
  2000 Democratizing International Production and Trade: North American Alternative Trade Organizations. In Artisans and Cooperatives: Developing Alternative Trade for the Global Economy. Kimberly Grimes and Lynne Milgram, eds. Pp. 11–24. Tucson: University of Arizona Press.
Klein, Naomi
  2000 No Space, No Choice, No Jobs, No Logo. New York: Picador.
Korthals, Michiel
  2001 Taking Consumers Seriously: Two Concepts of Consumer Sovereignty. Journal of Agricultural and Environmental Ethics 14:201–215.
Lury, Celia
  1996 Consumer Culture. New Brunswick, NJ: Rutgers University Press.
Lynd, Martha
  2000 The International Craft Market: A Double-Edged Sword for Guatemalan Maya Women. In Artisans and Cooperatives: Developing Alternative Trade for the Global Economy. Kimberly Grimes and Lynne Milgram, eds. Pp. 65–84. Tucson: University of Arizona Press.

MacHenry, Rachel
  2000 Building on Local Strengths: Nepalese Fair Trade Textiles. In Artisans and Cooperatives: Developing Alternative Trade for the Global Economy. Kimberly Grimes and Lynne Milgram, eds. Pp. 25–44. Tucson: University of Arizona Press.
Miller, Nicholas
  1993 Conscious shoppers vote for fairer trade: British consumers offer to pay more for products to encourage better conditions for exploited workers in developing world. Weekly Journal 82:16.
Page-Reeves, Janet
  1998 Alpaca Sweater Design and Marketing: Problems and Prospects for Cooperative Knitting Organizations in Bolivia. Human Organization 57(1): 83–93.
Ray, Paul, and Sherry Anderson
  2000 The Cultural Creatives: How 50 Million People are Changing the World. New York: Harmony Books.
Roddick, Anita
  2000 Business as Unusual. London: Thorsons.
Rosenbaum, Brenda
  2000 Of Women, Hope, and Angels: Fair Trade and Artisan Production in a Squatter Settlement in Guatemala City. In Artisans and Cooperatives: Developing Alternative Trade for the Global Economy. Kimberly Grimes and Lynne Milgram, eds. Pp. 85–106. Tucson: University of Arizona Press.
Ross, Andrew, ed.
  1997 No Sweat: Fashion, Free Trade and the Rights of Garment Workers. New York: Verso.
Rugmark
  2002 It's a Fact: Consumers are Concerned about Ethics. Rugmark News, January, p.1.
SERRV International
  2002 Dominican Cocoa Farmers Unite. Partnerships Newsletter, October, p.3.
Stephen, Lynn
  1997 Women and Social Movements in Latin America: Power from Below. Austin: University of Texas Press.

14

"The Water is Ours, Carajo!" Deep Citizenship in Bolivia's Water War

Robert Albro

"The Wars of the [21st] century will be about water."
  – Ismail Serageldin, World Bank vice-president

In September, 1998, the International Monetary Fund (IMF) approved a $138-million loan for Bolivia, to encourage the country's economic growth. In order to comply with the IMF's conditions for the loan, Bolivia's government agreed to sell off its remaining public enterprises, including both the national oil refineries and the municipal water system of the department of Cochabamba, SEMAPA. This policy was fully consistent with the precedent established by the Bolivian government in 1985 through the ruling *Movimiento Nacionalista Revolucionario* (MNR) party's New Economic Plan, a policy that has embraced the neoliberal orthodoxy of selling off Bolivia's public sector to private corporations (see Bailey and Knutsen 1987, Gamarra 1994, Healy and Paulson 2000).[1] In June, 1999, the World Bank followed up with a report called the *Bolivia Public Expenditure Review*, recommending that "no

subsidies should be given to ameliorate the increase in water tariffs in Cochabamba,"[2] a recommendation paving the way for SEMAPA's eventual privatization.

But to the surprise of those cutting the deal, the circumstances of the privatization of SEMAPA provoked a civic revolt in the region of Cochabamba, Bolivia. In this chapter, I explore how to understand this civic revolt, called the Water War, as a grassroots response to 17 years of neoliberal, democratic, and multicultural reforms in Bolivia. The Water War also illustrates the agency of a "plural popular" subject in Bolivia, neither "elite" nor "Indian." I argue for a view of popular movements in terms of a pluralistic appreciation of diverse constituent networks, taken together, as a political subject position. This chapter offers an account of popular mobilization in Bolivia that includes not just the regional scene of revolt, but also the transnational dimensions of popular agency. It examines the negotiation of conjunctural relations between regional and global activist networks as a part of this response, in particular the key contexts of translatability and mutual recognition of the cultural codes

informing collaborating networks. I discuss
the Water War as a shared challenge of democratic renewal – which I label utopic recovery
– not simply for Bolivia's hard-pressed popular sectors, but also for international anti-
globalization activism. While I note the
distortion effects that occur when moving
between these arenas, both converge in
the shared goal of an expanded idiom of
citizenship.

Taking Back the War

After closed-door negotiations – described by
observers as "a totally irregular and obscure
process" (Vargas and Kruse 2000:9) – in September, 1999 the Bolivian government signed
a contract to hand over SEMAPA to the company Aguas de Tunari, a multinational con-
sortium that is a subsidiary of the San
Francisco-based construction giant, Bechtel.
It was later revealed that Aguas de Tunari
was the only company that offered a bid,
for which it was awarded a 40-year concession to provide water and sanitation services
to the residents of Cochabamba, as well as to
generate electricity and irrigation water for
the region's agricultural sector. The sale of
SEMAPA to foreign investors continued a
14-year process of the shrinking of the state,
which one analyst charitably has called the
"friendly liquidation" of Bolivia's public
commons (see Van Cott 2000). The attempted privatization of SEMAPA also
carried with it an assumption about Bolivia's
"water": as a question of the technical development and commodification of a formerly
public national resource, in terms of its potential economic value, to be regulated, and
to be sold to prospective individual consumers (see Flórez and Solón 2001, Marvin
and Laurie 1999, Nickson and Vargas 2002).

Concurrent with the sale of SEMAPA, the
Bolivian parliament hurriedly passed a new
Water Law (law 2029). This law, effectively
legalizing the new contract with Aguas de
Tunari, appeared to give a potential monop-
oly to Aguas de Tunari over all water

resources, including those used by "peasant"
(*campesino*) farmers for irrigation, as well as
those community-based water resources paid
for, built, and maintained by rural and periurban communities previously independent
of state regulation. The new *Federación
Departamental Cochabambina de Regantes*
(FEDECOR) was immediately concerned
that this Water Law appeared to spell a loss
of ancestral "uses and customs" (*usos y costumbres*) for rural water users, enabling the
sale of water resources that had never really
been a part of SEMAPA in the first place. The
same went for the many independent communal water systems of peripheral urban
communities, built by the residents and not
yet connected to SEMAPA, now threatened
with being summarily appropriated by the
new concession (Vargas and Kruse 2000:10).

Founded in 1996, FEDECOR functions as
an independent organization of "peasant irrigators," operating parallel to the traditional
agrarian union hierarchy, which in FEDE-
COR's view has long been hopelessly infil-
trated by political party interests. This new
federation of farmers has "gained strength
from the rich associative tradition that sus-
tains Andean organization in the countryside." Basic to this tradition is the
conviction that "water" is first a sacred and
inalienable social and public resource, vital
to "life," and managed through reciprocal –
usually ritualized – obligations between local
communities and the cultural and cosmological sources of such vitality (see Chanez
Mendia n.d., Crespo 1999). As a slogan of
the water warriors bluntly put it, "Water is
Not for Sale!" (Coordinadora 2000b), because no one could claim exclusive ownership over water, the basis for life, which is
considered a sacred and collective resource.[3]

On January 11–13, 2000, and after holding a public "assembly," the newly created
Coordinadora (Coalition for the Defense of
Water and Life) engineered a blockade of the
city to protest the inflationary rate hikes
which had doubled, even tripled the ordinary
citizen's water bills. Led by labor union
leader Oscar Olivera, FEDECOR leader

Omar Fernandez, and others, the Coordinadora quickly became the organizational lightning rod for the Water War. Organized on November 12, 1999, the Coordinadora came to exist in direct response to the "generalized popular discontent" caused by the extreme rate hikes and new Water Law and the pervasive interclass "perception of social injustice" about the lack of public consultation with the government's sale of SEMAPA (Vargas and Kruse 2000:11). It took advantage of the "dense organizational structure" of FEDECOR (led by Omar Fernandez), the departmental worker's federation (led by Oscar Olivera), and rural and urban teachers, as well as university students. In its later actions, the regional federation of coca-leaf growers (led by Evo Morales) and the regional transporter's union were critical in adding their rank-and-file to the struggle (see Gutiérrez Aguilar, 2001:195).

But in the heat of the struggle and mobilization, the Coordinadora brought together rural farmers, industrial proletariats, disillusioned recent in-migrants, largely invisible members of a growing informal economy, environmentalists, retirees, left-leaning economists and technocrats, as well as sympathetic foreigners, in provincial towns, peripheral shantytowns, and the urban streets, in an ultimately successful and spectacular street-level demonstration of popular consensus. Explanations of the singular success of this coalition have emphasized its "capacity for bringing together popular discontent" (Gutiérrez Aguilar 2001:196) in an effective representation of a wide range of ideological positions. Vargas and Kruse (2000:11) note the Coordinadora has proven exceptional "in its capacity to absorb and give roles, space, and a way to act to all the sectors that added themselves to the fight." As the political instrument of multiple popular sectors, the Coordinadora is at once rural and urban, multiclass and multiethnic, straddling what have historically been often fractious divides.

The interventions of its chief spokesperson – Oscar Olivera – routinely call for the restoration of the collective "rights" of Bolivian citizenship. This was most forcefully stated in a communiqué by the group titled "We Bolivians have never had the souls of slaves" (January 15, 2000). The Coordinadora assumes the inclusion of the resistors to water privatization in the Bolivian body politic, but protests the lack of popular influence over this body. As with FEDECOR, the Coordinadora rejects the national political establishment as a responsible mediator of the interests of Bolivian society at large. In a rally I attended organized by the Coordinadora in July, 2001, condemnation of the national government and political party interests was ubiquitous, in placards, in the private comments of protestors, and in the speeches offered by Olivera, Morales, and others. For example, one ex-miner who marched expounded a popular theory that "the government is concealing" from fired miners and from the general population that the mining industry is still potentially rich and economically viable. Also, among others, there were placards reading: "Viva la unidad del pueblo contra los sirvientes del neoliberalismo!" ("Long live the unity of the people against the servants of neoliberalism!"), "Contra el gobierno vende-patrias!" ("Against our sell-out government!"), and "Muere este gobierno asesino y corrupto!" ("Die, corrupt assassin government!")

Finally, successive speakers voiced their convictions that the current government is a "slave" government, "poisoning" the country, filled with "shameless" and "worthless" people. A communication from the Coordinadora during the Water War insisted, "We need respectful leaders of the people who listen, and who carry out their wishes, and who do not sell themselves and who do not have fear" (Coordinadora 2000b).

The restoration of rights is not envisioned for any one community or social sector, but interpreted inclusively in pluralistic terms as a "patrimony" of the Bolivian people. The Coordinadora has acted to create an alternate significance to citizenship in Bolivia around explicitly collective cultural heritage or property rights, in order to arrest the "robbing of the country, the sacking of its patrimony" (Calderón 2002:140). In this sense, both the Water War and Bolivia's recent indigenous movements reject a potentially formal participation within the strictures of the nation-state. However, while indigenous movements have insisted upon an indigenous "nation" as distinct from the Bolivian "nation" (see Bigenho 1996), the Water War firmly claims popular "citizenship" as Bolivians, criticizing, as their spokesperson Olivera has put it, "the way this so-called democracy is run" (quoted in Neary 2001). The coalition labels this problem the "simulation of democracy, which only renders us obedient and impotent, and turns us into obliged voters and taxpayers for the benefit of the rich" (Coordinadora 1999).

As Olivera has reflected elsewhere, "Behind the Water War lies the call for a true democracy in which one can participate, think, and decide" (quoted in Calderón 2002:142), an idea expressed in the routine practice of communal assembly and decision-making (*consulta popular*), a case of what Rivera (1990:109) has called "direct democracy" – circumventing the logic of parliamentary representation and the equation between "individuals" and "citizens." As a leader, Olivera has rejected the proffered mantle of the "voice of the pueblo." He insists, instead, "It is important that I at least listen to what they are saying, and let them unburden themselves of their anxieties," even if there is no clear solution. Such an injunction, in Olivera's words, "not to speak, but instead to listen," is an inversion of the traditional vertical hierarchy of patronage and clientage of the national political elite.[4]

Exasperated with government inactivity and ineffectual negotiations, on February 4–5, 2000, the Coordinadora organized a peaceful "taking of the city," with a march to Cochabamba's central plaza. The march was met with violence and tear gas by riot police, which produced an estimated 175 injuries, included two people who were blinded (see *Asamblea Permanente de Derechos Humanos de Cochabamba*, February

2000). Riot police also refused to let protesters enter the symbolic space of the plaza. The Coordinadora held another referendum on March 22, where more than 90 percent of the estimated 50,000 voters – an overwhelming majority – registered their disapproval at the sale of SEMAPA (Vargas and Kruse 2000:12). By early April the region's water protest galvanized protests and clashes with the police and army in other regions of the country around a plethora of festering issues.

On April 4 the Coordinadora declared a "final battle," with the new goals of reforming the new Water Law, and of kicking Aguas de Tunari entirely out of Bolivia. The new protest included the symbolic occupation of the new headquarters of Aguas de Tunari, marches and rallies of thousands of people in the central plaza, and both rural and urban blockades. On April 6 Olivera and other leaders of the Coordinadora were arrested by police while attending a meeting to "negotiate" with city and government officials, precipitating a ferocious response from the assembled protestors, who renewed their protests and were engaged in a pitched battle with the police and army over the next several chaotic days. On April 8 Bolivia's president, Hugo Banzer, declared martial law. That day a 17-year-old boy was shot dead by a plain-clothed army sharpshooter. Protests, blockades, and violent confrontations continued throughout April 9–10, as police assaulted the "water warriors" with live ammunition.

Once the dust cleared, six people had died nationwide, with hundreds more injured and dozens forcibly detained by the police authorities (see *Asamblea Permanente de Derechos Humanos de Cochabamba*, April 2000). But this latest wave of protests, spearheaded by the Coordinadora, produced an unexpected victory. After four days in hiding, the Coordinadora leaders signed an agreement with the Bolivian government that guaranteed the withdrawal of Aguas de Tunari and annulled the previous contract, granting total control of SEMAPA to a regional directorate. Perhaps unique in the recent annals of struggle against neoliberal regimes in Latin America, a popular coalition in Bolivia had successfully kicked a transnational corporation out of the country, in the process reclaiming a say in deciding what should happen to the country's own "national patrimony."[5] Furthermore, the international arena of so-called anti-globalization activism took immediate notice. If the shattered windows and gutted interiors of a Starbucks symbolized 1999's "Battle in Seattle," Bolivia's Water War in the following year quickly became the next symbol. As a civil revolt against the privatization and mercantilization of citizenship life, the Water War became the "poster child for what happens when a poor country is left to the whims of global economic planners" (Shultz 2000), and a "global wakeup call against economic oppression in the world" (Sterling 2000).

The Coordinadora: Popular Recognition and Utopic Recovery

Why did the Water War ignite in the region of Cochabamba? An influential consensus about Cochabamba's *vallunos* (valley-dwellers) treats them as a "class" of long de-indianized penny capitalists who over time have successfully manipulated vertical ties as clients of urban elites and state politicians, to solidify their own access to land, material, and capital (Dandler 1983, Larson 1998). As a regional case study, Cochabamba has thus reflected the "peasant community study" trend within Latin Americanist anthropology, where "class differences and differentiation remain the basic theoretical issue" (Kearney 1996:173). This has been nurtured in commitments of the Bolivian nation-state and of social scientists to apprehend the region through the twin lenses of class identity and of racial and cultural *mestizaje* (mixture) (Albó 1995, Rivera 1984). For these reasons, research on the "Andean community" has been carried out elsewhere, with Cochabamba written off as a crossroads defined by its "lack of an identity" (Albó 1987:46).

As a teleological discourse of nation-building, the new MNR government of 1952 equated a process of social and cultural mestizaje – the assimilation of Andean "others" through the erasure of disruptive internal differences – with the successful construction of a "national-popular" citizenry (see Laclau 1977, Zavaleta 1986). Martínez-Echazabal (1998:21) recently put it this way: "Mestizaje underscores the affirmation of cultural identity as constituted by 'national character,'" a cultural identity considered necessary for the creation of a "middle class." And as Mallon (1996:170) and others have also observed, being a "mestizo/a is, by definition, betwixt and between, neither Indian nor Spanish." Of course this very attempt to deny colonial forms of racial/ethnic hierarchy and oppression holds out the promise of "inevitable cultural homogenization" (Lienhard 1997:190), potentially all but eliminating the politicization of culture as a way to contend with the state.

But despite the region's long association with mestizaje, historians like Brooke Larson are now calling attention to the importance of the cultural identities of its rural-urban popular sectors. She draws attention to the "multiple, overlapping sites of work, ceremony, and struggle" (1998:349) of the lower valley towns and nearby city. Altogether, these overlapping sites promote a fundamental identification between the new *cholos* (upwardly mobile former Indians) of the city and the citified "peasants" of the nearby provinces that facilitated the emergent popular "problem-solving networks" (see Auyero 2000) instrumental in the Water War. In the terms of Javier Sanjinés (2001:292), in Cochabamba, too, we should recognize "the development of a vibrant cholo/Indian urban culture" which carries with it the potential for "an alternative public sphere."

As a coalitional instrument, the Coordinadora has been approvingly credited with the lack of a clear identity: "No one knew in reality who or what the said 'Coordinator' was, it being in reality the name for the union of all" (Gutiérrez et al. 2000:137). Oscar Olivera's sister, Marcela, defined the Coordinadora for me as "a mixture of lots of things." She continued, "The Coordinadora is legitimate because it has had the support of *the people*. But it can also disappear when the people are gone" (my emphasis). In contrast to both government and established political parties, the coalition has been called an alternative "public space," or an instrument of "popular mobilization," identified as a spontaneous expression of "popular sentiment," of "popular unity," of the "common good," and "popular resistance" (Coordinadora 2000c). One analysis of the Coordinadora describes it as "the people's tool for creating its own unity" (Gutiérrez Aguilar 2001:201), while another extols it as a "democracy of the plebe" (Gutiérrez et al. 2000:173). The many equations between the Coordinadora and the will of "the people" make clear that for those involved its "popular" character is what marks it as a worthwhile alternative. This, in turn, departs from a decades-long identity politics in Latin America, carried out "from a particular location within society, in direct defiance of universal categories" (Hale 1997:568), typically in the terms of a particular race, ethnicity, gender, or cultural identity.

Too often the "popular" qualities of such movements are treated as byproducts of the political process, the outcome of a populist "leadership style" (see Bailey 1988; Conniff 1999; de la Torre 2000). In just this way, critics from within and without have dismissed neopopulism in Bolivia as imposed from on high and as expressing the programs of national leaders. It has been dismissed as mere "political demagoguery" (Lagos 1997), and as substituting substantive ideological content for "tactical flexibility" (Mayorga 1991). Recent sympathetic scholarly discussion about the Water War has similarly identified the Coordinadora as an instrument of "the plebe" or "the multitude" (Gutiérrez et al. 2000:158), a view likely to feed uncritical accounts that dismiss popular movements as diffuse action by "the people"

as an anonymous and "amorphous mass" (Weyland 2000).

Critics of the Coordinadora strike this note, pigeonholing it as an anachronistic instrument of class warfare of the defunct national Left, just one more "sectarian" and "opportunistic" attempt by a group of demagogues with self-interested political aspirations to bend the public's ear and to establish "spaces of power" for themselves (see Crespo 2000; García Mérida 2002). For critics, the Coordinadora shows a "lack of a serious and coherent discourse" as it opportunistically uses "demagogic slogans" (Salinas 2002). Nor is it an effective instrument of struggle, but a handful of intransigent and "proud vanguardists" (*Los Tiempos* 2001a), or a "multitude of individual demagogues incapable of providing practical solutions" (*Los Tiempos* 2001b). As a gathering of "strong men of the pseudo-Left" (de Ugarte 2001), who peddle their sterile "radical Marxism" (Varnaux Garay 2001), the Coordinadora has evident skill only in irresponsibly stoking "the fury of the masses" (Gonzáles Quintanilla 2001). Descriptions of the Coordinadora like these – both positive and negative – reveal a superficial tendency to caricature "the people," "the masses," or "the multitude," while never identifying the sources of the coalition's collective vitality.

When confronted with events like the Water War – where diverse popular sectors and their respective cultural tactics combine as a plural political subject – the analysis of current social movements is hindered by a lack of imagination in relating the "plural" to the "popular." Prevailing views often assume ideas that share a great deal with the sort of political character assassination just noted. As with a recent constitutional reform that labels Bolivia a "multiethnic and pluricultural" state (D'Emilio 1997), a pluralistic stance typically assumes the recognition of multiple collective entities participating together in a larger body politic (McLennan 1995:33). Meanwhile, notions like the "popular" (particularly when labeled "populism") usually withhold any real agency from collective popular actors. Stuart Hall's (1981) influential account – comparable to similar Latin American definitions of the "national popular" – defines the popular as taking shape only in negative relief, against some "power bloc." Popular identity can thus only be a marriage of convenience, or temporary coalition of heterogeneous social "classes" that briefly joins for one specific purpose, after which it fragments.

But I argue that we need to look for the "plural" in the popular as a potentially transformative and liberatory agency, and as foundational to the Water War as a regional citizen's revolt. Instead of equating the "popular" with any particular identity politics, a cultural content, or specific community, we should look for cultural zones of translatability across or between "communities," "classes," or social "sectors," as points of potential articulation and co-alignment. Pluralism, in this sense, refers less to the democratic co-participation of difference collective entities as to what Taylor (1994) calls a "politics of recognition," that is, the cultural tactics of plural political subjects enabling collective action. As Laclau and Mouffe (1985:138) have argued with their notion of a "radical and plural democracy," popular identity is best conceived as "the meeting point for a multiplicity of articulatory practices."

A first point of mutual recognition was the shared material and symbolic urgency of water, itself, as part of the public commons. In this progressively water-poor region, conflicts over water have flared over the last quarter-century, fueled by increased scarcity, the failure of local government to deliver on its many promised solutions, and the haphazard drilling of new water wells (see Kruse 2002:13–33), most recently in what Crespo (1999) calls the "War of the Wells" in nearby Vinto and Sipe-Sipe in 1995. For the Water War, this included the rural peasant irrigators, who understood the Aguas de Tunari concession as a usurpation of their customary ancestral rights. It also included peripheral

urban communities, who feared a loss of ownership over independent communal water systems that they, themselves, had built. It further included lower- and middle-class urban consumers, who received inflationary water bills without warning. Finally, "water" fitted smoothly into the discourse of Bolivian oppositional politics – among the coca growers and others – alongside such hot potatoes as land reform, coca leaf, and political and cultural patrimony rights.

A second point of recognition for the diverse social sectors participating in the Water War was a shared orientation of disenchantment and resentment toward the "culpable state" (Yashar 1998:36), based upon the conviction that the state had withdrawn its historical patronage along with many of the public rights of its own citizens. For the case of organized labor, the austerity measures since 1985 have severely crippled the national workers' movement, hastening a "collapse of the class-based model of the traditional left" (Albó 1996:16). The reduction of Bolivia's workforce in the emergent "flexible" global economy has, in the words of Oscar Olivera, meant a "systematic loss of our rights" (quoted in Calderón 2002:139). Another recognition point was a shared commitment to collective political action and protest, whether by members of peripheral barrios filled out by families of ex-miners trying to make ends meet in the precarious informal and economy engaging in community vigilantism against petty crime (see *Los Tiempos* 2001c), or by the militant coca growers' movement, which has made routine use of forms of communal protest and dissent over the years in repeated standoffs with a hostile government (see Healy 1989, 1991). These points of recognition refer less to a shared cultural identity or values and more to shared predicaments and tactics of mutual engagement across distinct networks.

A fourth recognition point was the strategic use of Andean identity frames. For underdeveloped peripheral urban barrios, a highland Andean cultural identity has become an effective instrumental idiom of distinction in directing claims for community resources (see Goldstein 1998). For coca growers, the traditional chewing of the "sacred leaf," together with the *whipala* (the flag of indigenous "nations"), has anchored the call for national cultural sovereignty (see Stephenson 2003). For an emergent population of "cholo professionals" and the regional "cholo bourgeoisie" (see Toranzo 1991), the historically pejorative term "cholo" has undergone a shift in signification, referring to pride in one's "humble" ancestry, and is now performed almost weekly in the myriad folklore festivals sponsored by regional municipalities and showcasing the region's "typical food," music, dancing, or agricultural products (see Carpio San Miguel 2001). Such a strategy of valorizing regional cultural producers makes the urban popular sectors heirs to a primordial Andean tradition and its "carnal interpretation of society" (Sanjinés 2001:304). A humble ancestry, cultural sovereignty, and community resources all represent what must be "recovered" after the successive shocks of neoliberal and democratic reforms (see Albó 1996:17).

Local businesses or nongovernmental organizations (NGOs) are often responsible for the planning and financing of these folklore festivals. Partially filling the void left by retreating government, NGOs have now started to practice what Kevin Healy calls "people-centered development" (2001:95), which strives for the revitalization of Bolivia's own economic and "cultural patrimony," rather than the imposition of a technical regime of modernization. In turn, local networks of intermediary popular leadership cadres are increasingly hooked into an expanding regional NGO network. A fifth recognition point, then, was the NGO network, bringing together labor leaders, foreign activists and researchers, and periurban shantytown dwellers, as well as new "cholo" professionals, in different forums, meetings, colloquia, or projects. The regional NGO network played a crucial role in the formation of working relationships between local leaders and activists both before the

Water War, and as I subsequently explore, after the regional events of April, 2000. These NGOs enjoy links to a vast global arena of cyberactivism and its hypertext-linked information networking (Lins Ribeiro 1998), available to local popular movements. These links would enable Oscar Olivera to bypass a Bolivian nation-state that increasingly lacks a monopoly over information power, giving him timely access to issue-specific nodes of the "transnational social movement network" (Brysk 1996).

For the Water War, popular identity is plural, in the sense that it is collectively constituted through these five (and other) channels of mutual recognition, all shared by the distinct networks of participating social sectors. Melucci (1996:4) refers to contemporary social movements as "solidarity networks entrusted with potent cultural meanings." The "plural popular," then, is less an identity so much as it pragmatically *brackets a process of identification*, catalyzing mutually overlapping networks to action. In April of 2000 in Cochabamba, this process was driven by the shared experiences of people suffering disenfranchisement under the state's ongoing neoliberal policies and articulated around a shared concern for a the shrinking public commons, in this case, water. If this is the regional picture, I now go on to explore how the construction of political subject positions in popular movements like Bolivia's Water War problematically incorporates in this bracketing process the discourses and practices of an emerging international activism.

Oscar Olivera, International Water Activist

Doubling back to the thick of things in the middle of April, 2000, after the unexpected victory in Cochabamba of April 10, Oscar Olivera surprisingly arrived in Washington, DC on April 14, to be in solidarity with "anti-globalization" activists gathered there to protest the A-16 meeting. While thousands of protestors attempted to blockade the IMF and World Bank meetings in downtown Washington, and amid calls for the cancellation of hundreds of billions of dollars in debt owed by the world's poorest nations, the Water War was repeatedly cited at the rally as an example of victory over growing corporate greed in the global marketplace (Weiss 2000b). In the words of a close collaborator, Olivera's case was "right story, right time!," and his "star soared within international circles of diverse anti-globalization activists," as Olivera now began actively to participate in what Brysk (1996:45) has labeled the new "transnational social movement network."

On the eve of "the ultimate battle," Jim Shultz and Tom Kruse – two "activists beyond borders" living in Cochabamba (Keck and Sikkink 1998) – conferred and agreed "to get the word out" about the Water War. Both proved instrumental in facilitating Olivera's access to a sympathetic international community. With an e-mail list of over two thousand names and years of experience as a consumer lobbyist, Shultz became, in his words, the "designated get-the-word-out guy." Through the Democracy Center and as a writer for the Pacific News Service, Shultz had been chronicling the unfolding events of the Water War since early February. For Shultz, the plot line was clear: "the battle between arrogance and democracy." His barrage of alerts, dispatches, and bulletins quickly made its way around the Web. Shultz's piecemeal account – "Bolivia's War over Water" – placed the events of Cochabamba between February and April of 2000 under an international web-linked spotlight. Many of Shultz's articles were later reprinted in newspapers and magazines in Canada and in the United States, though ignored by wire services like the AP (http://www.democracyctr.org/water-war/index.htm).

In 1992 while living in San Francisco, Shultz founded the Democracy Center, a nonprofit organization dedicated to working with "community leaders" and NGOs in the United States and abroad on questions of social and economic justice. In 1998 he moved his base of operations to Bolivia, where he now lives. An important project for the Democracy Center has been the publication of *The Democracy Owner's Manual* in 2001, a how-to guide for political lobbyists. The *Owner's Manual* was the fruit of Shultz's many years spent as a consumer lobbyist in California. Although from the United States, Shultz shares with Olivera and the Coordinadora a commitment "to resignify the very meanings of received notions of citizenship" (Alvarez et al. 1998:2). Shultz describes his own approach to me as one of "active citizenship," rooted in strategies of consumer advocacy.

But concepts like "active citizenship" have their own genealogies within an established US tradition of movements of "democratic renewal." If Ralph Nader's Public Citizen is the best-known current heir to a US "new populism," strategies of active citizenship can be traced to Saul Alinsky, Hull House, and others dedicated to reinventing American democracy from the bottom up using the tactical toolkit of grassroots citizenship in the 1940s and 1950s. While active citizenship assumes the erosion of traditional mediating institutions like political parties, it starts from the "individual citizen" as a point of departure. For collective rights movements like the Water War, this genealogy poses a potential risk of distortion. "Community organizing" is threatened with becoming little more than citizens as "clients and customer" (Boyte 2001:6), encouraging consumers to act only with their pocketbook. "Citizenship" as a radical individualism of the consumer at once fits with the expectations of privatizing companies like Aguas de Tunari, even as it is potentially at odds with the collective popular sovereignty exhibited in the citizen's revolt of the Water War. "Citizenship," then, can be a problematic point of recognition between local movements with specific agendas and international activist currents.

Shultz realized the Water War had a "clear US angle." Crucial to the developing plot was

Shultz's success in "documenting the Bechtel connection," the "hidden-hand" owners of the subsidiary Aguas de Tunari. He realized that Bechtel was the "perfect target for a protest movement." Armed with the new Bechtel information, Shultz sent out an "alert" saying: "Bechtel! Hammer them." Newly armed with the personal e-mail address of Bechtel's chairman, "people hammered away." Among the weirder results was a group of "water activists" from New Zealand who responded by obtaining a fire truck and hosing down the Bolivian consulate in Auckland! Eventually Shultz's corpus of frontline reportage earned him the 2001 "Project Censored Award," which is given annually to the most compelling yearly story ignored by the news establishment. This is one indicator of the strong reaction to the Water War on the internet (see http://www.projectcensored.org/stories/2001/1.html),[6] acting as what Lins Ribeiro (1998:329) calls a "global virtual archipelago," circulating information using a "networking pragmatism" (1998:355) of internet-aided, hypertext-linked, ad-hoc coalition building.

Olivera landed in Washington, DC in the company of Tom Kruse. In Washington, Olivera was the recipient of a "quality of global solidarity possibly unique in all of history" (Korten 2000). Olivera and Kruse had first met in the late 1990s, when they served together on a panel on the spiraling fortunes of the labor sector at the *Centro de Documentación e Informacion, Bolivia* (CEDIB), an NGO and provider of news and hard-to-get documentation based in Cochabamba. A thirty-year-old center, CEDIB "seeks to support the different processes of construction of a citizenry, democracy, and popular participation with programs of information" (http://www.cedib.org/cedib/index.html). Kruse recalls that each told the same story about both US and Bolivian labor on their panel: "The rich getting richer, the poor getting poorer, the world getting uglier, and labor density getting lighter!" Based on their shared commitment to combating the downturn in

the fortunes of international organized labor, Olivera and Kruse began to collaborate on post-neoliberal alternatives.

Married to a Bolivian anthropologist, Kruse has lived in Bolivia since 1993. Over the years, he has worked extensively as a consultant and investigator for different research-based NGOs in Bolivia. He is currently working with the *Centro de Estudios para el Desarrollo Laboral y Agrario* (CEDLA), a labor and economics research center in La Paz. Founded in 1985, CEDLA has sought to assist in the construction of a grassroots response to the crisis within organized urban and rural labor created by the MNR's neoliberal reforms, also a focus of Kruse's own ongoing research (see http://www.cedla.org). One priority of CEDLA is to define an "agenda for public debate" and to make such an agenda available to organizations within the labor and agricultural movements, as well as within the informal urban sector, so that they might better "defend their own interests," primarily against ongoing state-driven policies.

Tom Kruse, then, was well connected within the local world of "policy-," "information-," and "social science-" type NGOs, enjoying contacts with the left-leaning self-identifying cholo professionals often employed there. Dedicated to supporting "popular participation" – though not necessarily in terms of the government's own model for such a thing – these "policy"-type NGOs are a networked forum of ongoing colloquia, seminars, congresses, festivals, and the like, bringing grassroots leaders like Olivera and activists like Kruse together. Both Kruse and Olivera have sought a way out of the "old vanguardist discourse" characteristic of the crisis of Bolivia's much diminished labor movement, by linking it to other parallel currents in civil society increasingly outside of the official governmental orbit also critically hit by neoliberal policies like privatization.

As things started to heat up over water, Kruse became an informal facilitator. He was the "international liaison" for the Coordinadora. If Shultz got the word out, Kruse "made the phone calls." He was able to help facilitate Olivera's departure from the country and then to help line up "a network of people to receive Olivera in DC." This included Larry Weiss, for example, the executive director of the Minnesota Fair Trade Coalition and coordinator of (as well as writer for) the "Labor, Globalization, and Human Rights Project" for the Resource Center of the Americas. Weiss, in his own words, soon became "part of an impromptu advance team scrambling to line up meetings and speaking venues for Olivera" (http//: www.americas.org/News/Features/200005_ Protest_DC/Index.asp). These included timely meetings with Ravi Khanna of 1WorldCommunication (see below), representatives of the group Hemispheric Social Alliance, and AFL–CIO officials, who, in turn, put Olivera in touch with water activists from other countries. Bolivia has subsequently become a key example in Public Citizen's current campaign against corporate greed in privatizing the world's fresh water supply (see Public Citizen 2002).

As part of his new activist's traveling roadshow, Olivera was in North America again between October 16 and November 1, 2000, making stops in 13 different cities in Canada and the United States. This barnstorming trip began in Washington, DC, where Olivera received the Letelier–Moffit prize from the Institute for Policy Studies (IPS).[7] As the director of the IPS stated, "The Coordinator, with Olivera at its head, is an inspiring symbol of the growing international resistance to the devastating impacts of World Bank and IMF-promoted policies throughout the world" (Institute for Policy Studies 2000:4). The Letelier–Moffit prize is one of two international awards Oscar Olivera has received since the events of the Water War. The other is the Goldman Environmental Prize (see http://www.goldmanprize.org), which is awarded yearly to outstanding "grassroots heroes" in the fight for the world's environment. Other ostensible reasons for the trip included follow-up meetings with representatives of the AFL–CIO in Washington,[8] and opportunities to offer his testimony to "unions, religious groups, community reps, and university students" in the United States and Canada about the Water War, as a successful example of the new "resistance to globalization from below" (Coordinadora 2000d). The trip, funded by the Center for Economic Justice and 1World Communication, built directly on contacts Olivera had made in his previous visit to Washington to join protestors of the A-16 meeting.

This tour included the "American premiere" of a 33-minute documentary on the conflict, "The Water is Ours, Damn It!" The film was produced by 1World Communication.[9] The brainchild of Ravi Khanna, an activist of south Asian Indian origin with a desire to unify the "Global South," 1World is a web-based alternative "weekly news digest." According to Khanna, 1World seeks to "bridge the digital divide," taking inspiration from mid-1990s web activism in support of the Zapatistas in Chiapas.[10] The film, itself, is a series of simultaneously translated interviews with local "water warriors" of different social backgrounds, interspersed with graphic images of the convulsive days of conflict taken from available local news footage. Oscar Olivera appears as the conflict's main interlocutor and the film's indisputable star.

There was also the third international meeting of the People's Global Action (PGA), held in Cochabamba in September, 2001, because of the Water War. Founded in 1998 as a "worldwide coordination network of resistance to the global market" (http//:www.nadir.org/nadir/initiativ/agp/en/), the PGA functions as a "global tool for communication and coordination for all those who fight the destruction of the planet by capitalism and build local alternatives to globalization." It has since met in Bangalore, Seattle, Washington, Prague, Quebec, Genoa, and Qatar, as part of the protests held in these cities.[11] Both Evo Morales and Oscar Olivera addressed the PGA crowd. Statements issued by the Coordinadora during the Water War were included in the meeting's minutes and on the website. New PGA goals foregrounded in Cochabamba built on the Water War, including a campaign for the "defense and recognition of self-determination and land sovereignty of all people" and the call to resist corporate domination with "civil disobedience."

As recently as April 23, 2002, Olivera was again in the United States, this time in San Francisco, to belatedly receive his Goldman Environmental Prize. His visit – and the Water War more generally – received significant recognition in both the *San Francisco Chronicle* and *San Francisco Bay Guardian* (Dolinsky 2001, Juhasz 2002, Langman 2002, Zoll 2000). On July 1, the San Francisco Board of Supervisors passed a resolution in support of Bechtel dropping litigation procedures against Bolivia for potential profit losses stemming from Aguas de Tunari's exit. While there, Olivera led a protest march to Bechtel's international headquarters, organized by Nader's NGO Public Citizen (see http//:www.citizen.org). The protest combined solidarity with Cochabamba and a demonstration "against a possible privatization of San Francisco's water and takeover by Bechtel" (Dolinksy 2001). Fliers for the protest at Bechtel headquarters read, "Join Oscar Olivera/winner of the Goldman Environmental Prize/and Hero of the Cochabamba struggle." The protestors marched to Bechtel's headquarters dressed in blue, as a "human river," carrying such signs reading: "Water is Not a Private Commodity. Bechtel: Stop Extorting Bolivian People!"

If Olivera's case is representative, his engagement as an anti-privatization water activist in the international human rights arena deeply involved him in an "issue-specific node" (Brysk 2000:86–97, Keck and Sikkink 1998) of a vaster archipelago of international anti-globalization activism. However, if what I called his "plural popular" networking in Cochabamba's regional arena was a crucial politics of recognition for the collective mobilization of the region's diverse popular

sectors, Olivera's role looks very different on the global activist stage. On the one hand, I have pointed out potential points of mutual recognition between Olivera's Coordinadora and other "transnational social movement networks" – as with a shared commitment to citizenship rights. On the other hand, local activists engaging in the arena of global activism are subject to specific forms of representation and recognition that prevail in that context. These include easily downloadable hypertext-linked photos and out-of-context quotes from Coordinadora communiqués, notoriety from winning prestigious awards as a "symbol" of "resistance to globalization from below," star protagonism in documentary films and TV specials, and a new international role as "spokesperson" for both local and international movements. But this sort of participation raises questions about the nature of the representation of popular movements. Despite protests to the contrary, while overseas Olivera is the exclusive "voice of the pueblo," a role potentially at odds with his organic involvement in the Water War itself. At the same time, the insertion of local issues and protagonists into the spectacles of global activism inevitably produces a distortion effect.

Oscar Olivera and Pan-Indigenism

I want to point out the ways that a particular indigenous-environmentalist equation has been applied to Olivera's international activism, perhaps at the expense of the regional civic revolt. Olivera's most instrumental contact in Washington was Maude Barlow, a citizens' rights activist who Weiss describes as "Canada's Ralph Nader," and who elsewhere has been called Canada's "best-known voice of dissent."[12] Barlow has chosen, as one career profile put it, "the global citizen activist route" (Inter Press Service 2000), and her political activism is frequently coordinated with Nader's own organization, Public Citizen. Meeting Barlow was a linchpin for

Olivera's entrance into the worldwide "anti-globalization" effort. As chairwoman of the Council of Canadians, a "citizen's watchdog organization," Barlow has dedicated herself to "promoting economic justice, renewing democracy, asserting Canadian sovereignty, advancing alternatives to corporate-style free trade, and preserving our environment" (http//:www.canadians.org). The Council of Canadians had earlier actively campaigned against the adoption of the North American Free Trade Agreement (NAFTA), and has recently launched a campaign to prevent the bulk export of Canada's fresh water. Barlow had also been present at the anti-WTO rally in Seattle in 1999. Through such networks of contacts, then, Cochabamba's Water War was more than rhetorically linked with events in Seattle, and subsequent protests in Prague, Milan, or Quebec.[13]

As Olivera's plane touched down in Washington – his first time ever outside of Bolivia – Barlow was leading a teach-in on behalf of the "International Forum on Globalization" for approximately 2,000 people at the Foundry United Methodist Church. Some of the premier names of the "global justice movement" spoke out at this meeting against the "robber-baron version of globalization" practiced by the WTO and World Bank, including Ralph Nader and India's Vandana Shiva. Barlow had planned to talk about the recent "victory in Bolivia" even before she learned that Olivera would be there in person. When he entered the church straight from the airport, Barlow announced to the audience, "Our hero from Bolivia has arrived!" She welcomed Olivera as a "45-year-old mechanic from Bolivia." In a subsequent written report, Barlow would refer to Olivera as "the humble shoemaker who led the fight" (Barlow 2000).

Entering the church, Olivera was met with a three-minute standing ovation. According to Shultz, he then delivered "the ten-minute speech of his life": "My name is Oscar Olivera. I'm a worker in a shoe factory in Cochabamba, Bolivia. Bolivia is one of the poorest countries in Latin America. We have

had a heroic victory against a transnational corporation." In this speech, Olivera contrasted Bolivia's "David" to the "Goliath" of the global economy, with himself a genuine representative of a victimized "testimonial people" (Ribeiro 1971).[14] Olivera's self-consciously testimonial style, like Rigoberta Menchú's (1984) famous account, is a "popular" reportage likened to oral history. Representing a "community of witness" (Gugelberger and Kearney 1991:9), the subjects of these testimonies are frequently contrasted with the "bourgeois individual." As one tactic of drawing public attention to a threatened collective identity in the international human rights arena, the testimonial is a strategic politics of recognition turning on the authority of a lived experience. As it was bluntly put to me by one of Olivera's handlers, "Here's this little brown guy who says things like 'compañero.' Liberals eat that shit up!" This approach also confers a monopoly to Olivera as an exclusive narrator of the negative effects of corporate immorality in the "Global South," a departure from his own "plural popular" injunction to "listen."

Olivera flatly asserted: "Now Bolivia is no longer an owner [dueño] of anything!" He then proceeded to tick off all of the formerly public assets that are "now owned by foreigners." He pointedly emphasized: "Now all that we own is the air and the water. We have become more individualists than before, people who no longer think about their neighbor. But in our hearts and souls we preserve the solidarity, the dignity, and the desire to lose our fear." His account was vividly dramatic: Bolivia's "traditional" communitarian values are under attack by the corrosively individualizing hand of the market, while "we Bolivians" have been stripped to our very essence: hearts and souls "owning" only the air and water. An earlier statement from the Coordinadora insisted, "We occupy the streets and the roads because we are the true owners" (February 6, 2000). It is clear Olivera emphasizes an idea of citizenship hinging on the issue of collective "ownership," which is quite different from the potentially radical individualism of citizenship as consumer advocacy. Olivera's international speeches also express a "popular ecology" (Crespo 1999) that echoes the environmentalism implicit in the anti-WTO crowd, an identity with a similar moral authority to that of the "noble eco-savage" (see Conklin and Graham 1995).

Olivera has described the perceived collusion between Bolivian elites and global capital as a case of "the old prejudice the powerful feel against the polleras and the abarcas" (quoted in Calderón 2002:143). In a later interview with the *Multinational Monitor*, Oscar emphasized the unilateral nature of the government's new law 2029 – the "Water Law" – as a direct affront to collective indigenous cultural rights. He criticized a disregard for the long established precedents of ancestral "usage and custom" (*usos y costumbres*) by rural communities, clarifying for an international audience, "The people [*la gente*] look at water as something very sacred. Water is a right, not something to be sold. It is also tied to traditional beliefs for rural people, since the time of the Incas." Olivera equated the Inca past with the Indigenous present, while asserting the primacy of ancient and communal cultural practices over and above transient state power. "Customary law" (as *usos y costumbres*), together with collective "ownership," become an essentialized basis for cultural rights to water as a primordial sentiment (Geertz 1963). "The people" take on an inclusive and global populist usage, as one half of a dichotomy – widespread in the international environmental movement – between all native peoples viewed as original "owners" and unscrupulous corporate raiders.

As a middle-class labor leader, Olivera cannot credibly claim a status as an indigenous leader. Yet in his different interventions destined for international crowds, Olivera is at pains to link the Water War, and his role in it, to a Bolivian "indigenous movement."[15] In the documentary film produced by 1World,

he makes a point to emphasize his regular and respectful participation in Aymara and Quechua Indian customs, as a key part of the struggle:

> On Friday the 8th, the government announced that Aguas de Tunari was going. And this signified a great joy for the people. We celebrated, and I was invited to an Aymara ritual, called a *q'oa*, carried out every first Friday of the month. A rite carried out to the *Pachamama* [an Andean space–time and fertility figure]. And that Friday coincided with Aguas de Tunari's exit from Cochabamba. So I went to the q'oa and very late we hear that, evidently, it had been decided that Aguas de Tunari was to stay, that a state of siege had been declared, and we saw on the TV how government agents had gone to my parents' house, where in fact I had planned to sleep that very night. But because of the q'oa, I hadn't gotten there yet. (quoted in Franklin 2000)

In his comment, Olivera is careful to point out the cultural relevance of the ritual. Olivera's sister Marcela reported to me that, although such rituals have never been a part of their own family's life, afterward her brother promised "never to miss any such ritual since it was because of this that he was saved!" Olivera's protagonism followed the activities and routes of the "global panindigenous movement" (Brysk 2000:97–104). Olivera's initial participation in the protest events in Washington during April, 2000 led to a series of smaller-scale get-togethers over the next several years and on several continents between leaders of the Coordinadora and groups eliding the questions of "global citizenship" with "environmentalism" and "indigenous rights."

This included an "International Solidarity Trip" by Barlow and others to Cochabamba, on December 6–11, 2000, organized by the Council of Canadians. Olivera served as local host to the delegation, which came to join in a seminar organized by the Coordinadora called "Water: Globalization, Privatization, and the Search for Alternatives." In Barlow's account, they listened to "music from an in-digenous anti-globalization youth group." They also made visits to some peripheral urban zones and rural communities in Cochabamba, each filled with "speeches and testimonies, most given through tears," and "followed by sharing chicha." A delegation member, Chief Gary John (a spokesman and member of the Lillooet Chiefs Council from British Columbia), performed for the cocha-bambinos who met with them, most of whom live in the city:

> Everywhere we went, Chief Gary John brought out his drum, with its drawing of a grizzly – his totem – and sang his heart out for the people; everywhere, they fell in love with him. But at this one visit, high on a dusty hill overlooking this vast Andean valley, sur-rounded by inquisitive children and older women sitting in their best colors on the ground, Gary particularly shone. One man had wept as he told us that the browner your skin, the less likely you were to receive water under the old system . . . . Gary took his drum and sang a warrior chant to honor the "water warriors" in our midst. (Barlow 2000)

In a subsequent description of the trip, Chief Gary John explained his purpose as "solidar-ity with the indigenous protests that were taking place there" (Bonfanti and Wright 2001).

As a result of this visit, the delegation and the Coordinadora penned the "Cochabamba Declaration." The declaration was for the "right to life, for the respect of nature and the uses and traditions of our ancestors and our peoples." And it continues: "For all time the following shall be declared as inviolable rights with regard to the uses of water given us by the earth." This circuit also included the Latin American meeting of the Water Workshop in Tiquipaya, Bolivia, June 9–12, 2001.[16] In addition to Olivera, this meeting included participation of Caesar Pilataxi, an Ecuadorian indigenous leader, as well as Chilean Mapuche representatives. It culmin-ated with direct discussions with local "peas-ants," "Indian rituals" in "recognition to Mother Nature," and a "convivial lunch based on llama meat and potatoes" (Bou-guerra 2001). This was followed by an inter-national forum in British Columbia called "Water for People and Nature," July 5–8, 2001, part of the Blue Planet Project, attended by representatives of the Coordina-dora. This meeting featured a forum on "In-digenous Rights and Water," which produced an "Indigenous Declaration on Water," expli-citly recognizing the earlier Cochabamba Declaration. It begins: "As Indigenous Peoples, we recognize, honour and respect Water as a sacred and powerful gift from the Creator" (Council of Canadians 2001:10).

In such contexts, the metamorphosis of the regional Water War as an issue of inter-national indigenous solidarity is apparent. Reminiscent of the international indigenous congress held in 1992 to organize the anti-quincentenary campaign (see Brysk 2000, Hale 1994), a clear goal of these many meet-ings was the systematic coordination be-tween both the indigenous North and South around panindigenous issues like water. Oli-vera's own participation in this transnational social movement network has been charac-terized by the essentializing and primordialist strategies of testimonial accounts, the prece-dent of "customary law," a rhetoric of popular ecology, as well as the prominent authority of panindigenous rights activists in this network. Cochabamba's regional "populist" coalition is relevant only in terms of the "indigenous South." Here Olivera's own self-presentation, and the goals of the Coordinadora, are refracted through a global activist prism that disregards the plural iden-tity so crucial to the Water War's regional success. Its tendency to interpret the Water War as an indigenous movement unwittingly duplicates the tactics of the movement's local critics, though trading the specter of a leftist demagogue for an ecological noble savage. Taken together, these international strategies amount to the symbolic recovery of the "noble savage" as "global citizen." A question to consider, however, is whether such a politics of recognition – as an international solidarity strategy – distorts the local realities of the Water War in ways counterproductive to solving the original regional crisis.

Deep Citizenship and Democratic Utopia

Historically, interclass cultural engagements in Cochabamba have both masked class differences in business dealings and underwritten social inequalities with idioms of collusion (see Lagos 1994). But I have argued for the Water War as illustrating a new plural political subject in Bolivia. "Pluralism," though, has been an unpopular term. Critics of pluralism have suggested the idea is complicit in both elite and state efforts to make basic categories of differences – such as "race" or "class" – invisible. For critics, pluralism leaves unaddressed the social inequalities built into these differences, which then typically become the basis for collective social movements (see Gilroy 1987, Rivera 1993). Theories of democratic citizenship also view pluralism as a potential problem, since it might encourage people to retreat behind the boundaries of their own corporate (ethnic, racial, or class) identities (Beiner 1995:6). But there exists no necessary equation between "pluralism" and collective action in terms of "unitary identities," even though critics seem to assume one.

Breaking with any notion of a "unitary subject" for the Water War, I have explored conjunctural relations among different kinds of social networks that, taken together, compose the Coordinadora as a key "popular" subject. I have argued that we must instead specify the processes of network identification, and associated cultural contexts and codes, as one way to avoid the mystifying and uncritical reification of "the people" as a unitary collective subject. These networks in part depend on their shared orientation toward what I have called utopic recovery – what in another context Fernandez (1986:184) dubs a "return to

the whole," and Touraine (2000:195) likewise labels the "recomposition of the world." Breaking with the contemporary tendency to disqualify utopian thinking along with ideological thinking as simply an "authoritarian ruse" (Hopenhayn 1995:97), both Appadurai (2002) and Holston (1999) have explored the semantics of "deep democracy" and "substantive citizenship," respectively, as ways to build depth and durability into international rights movements. The diverse participating networks of the Water War added depth to the recovery of a utopian project temporarily lost in the myriad effects of neoliberal reform by collectively mining the plenipotentiary concept of "citizenship."

Susan Stokes's recent assessment of the limits to popular sovereignty in South America's new democracies suggests that the emergent "tension between popular sovereignty and political capital" (1995:77) creates a lack of effective political representation. In the case of Bolivia's neoliberal and multicultural reforms, this tension has effectively fragmented a more comprehensive set of rights as part of democratic citizenship. As Kohl (2000:6) has put the issue, "The 'reinvented' Bolivian government has extended civil citizenship to Bolivia's multi-ethnic citizens with one hand while awarding economic rights to national and multinational firms with the other." The Water War responds directly to the evident fissures in civil society exacerbated by this reinvention through "institutional engineering." It does so by appropriating the state's own multicultural language reformulating the grounds of citizenship,[17] and then using the state's discourse to criticize its own formal democracy as a "simulation of democracy," and to contrast it with a more participatory "true meaning of democracy" (Coordinadora 2000b). This is conceived as a collective and popular sovereignty that parallels, circumvents, and when necessary rejects the state's authority to define the limits of the rights of its own citizens, in favor of people's direct defense of their interests.

As a key term in this utopian project of popular sovereignty, I have emphasized the interplay of the different conceptualizations employed in the social construction of citizenship. But this raises some concerns. Most obvious is a potential contradiction between the citizen as "consumer" (with the further assumption of private, individual, rights) and citizenship as "ownership" (with the assumption of a collective and ancestral patrimony). But just as recent social movements in Latin America have demanded the recognition of "multiple types of citizenship" (Yashar 1998:39), the discourse of citizenship in the Water War is not a unitary claim, but a plural one. It includes the idea of ancestral patrimony (*usos y costumbres*) as popular sovereignty, where "water" is not a commodity but a natural right, and an attempt to reconstitute the lost collective rights of the labor movement. In turn, these conceptions find resonant echoes in the new US populist tradition of "active citizenship," as well as the idea of "global citizenship" forwarded by popular ecologists, anti-globalists, and pan-indianists. In this way, citizenship has quickly become a key common cause among the many local social movements in Latin America and global activism. Perhaps the utopian spirit of efforts like Bolivia's Water War is starting to have its effect. In December, 2002, for the first time the United Nations formally declared safe and secure drinking water a human right. As the UN committee stated, "Water should be treated as a social and cultural good, and not primarily as an economic commodity."

NOTES

1   Bolivia's recent national reforms have come in two primary waves: 1985 and 1993. The privatization of SEMAPA continues the precedents established in the first set of reforms, begun in 1985. Very generally, these include the closure of the state mines, devaluation of the exchange rate, removal of price controls and public subsidies, curtailment of public expenditures in such areas as health and education, major tax reforms, and trade legislation to promote exports.

2   See the World Bank's *Bolivia Public Expenditure Review*, Report No. 19232-BO, for June 14, 1999, the executive summary.

3   For discussions of the cosmological significance of water in Andean indigenous and peasant communities, as well as the diverse communal and ritualized forms of managing and distributing water within these communities, see the collection edited by Mitchell and Guillet (1994).

4   Such public accountability is highly reminiscent of the media-driven strategy of "populist" Carlos Palenque, and his TV "talk show democracy called the *Tribuna Libre del Pueblo*" (Sanjinés 1996:261), where normally invisible "clients" were given a forum to publicize their concerns.

5   Bolivia's Water War might be a watershed event in the growing disenchantment with privatization measures throughout Latin America. In 2002 Arequipa, Peru, was the site of a comparably successful uprising against government attempts to privatize two local electric companies.

6   The blurb about Shultz's work on the Water War, as it appears on the Democracy Center's own web site, reads: "Writing directly from the scene, the Democracy Center's executive director, Jim Shultz, captured the developments of this story as it broke, in a series of dispatches and articles that circulated to thousands around the world via the Internet and were also reprinted in newspapers and magazines across the US and Canada" (see http://www.democracyctr.org/waterwar.index.htm).

7   The Institute for Policy Studies is a think tank dedicated to progressive social change. As stated in its overview, "At a time when other think tanks celebrate the virtues of unrestrained greed, unlimited wealth, and unregulated markets, the IPS is striving to create a more responsible society – one built around the values of justice, nonviolence, sustainability, and decency." The Letelier–Moffit prize honors the memory of two colleagues of

the Institute for Policy Studies assassinated in Washington, DC in 1976 by agents of Pinochet's regime in Chile. For more information see http://ips-dc.org/lm-awards/index.htm).

8   The AFL–CIO has in fact provided funding for the Coordinadora (Zoll 2000).

9   The Water War was also recently profiled on PBS television, as a segment on Bill Moyer's "Frontline" in July 2002. "Frontline" produced the program in conjunction with the *New Yorker*, which sent a reporter, William Finnegan, to Cochabamba for an in-depth story. Finnegan's story, the plot for Moyer's program, appeared in the April 8, 2002 issue of the *New Yorker*. "Frontline" on the Web includes a timeline of events in the ongoing Water War and a description of the "key players," as well as links to other water conservation sites (See http://www.pbs.org/frontlineworld/stories.bolivia.html).

10 Khanna, who has a 3,000-name e-mail list, noted to me that this kind of activism was "unimaginable until the Web." For more on 1World, go to http://1worldcommunication.org.

11 Reminiscent of the Coordinadora itself, the following definition of the PGA provides more details: "It is hard to define exactly what the PGA is. In many ways it doesn't really exist. PGA is not an organization, it has no members or constituted legal identity, no central funds, leaders or spokespeople. Instead, it is more of a tool or a fluid network for communication and coordination between diverse social movements who share a loose set of principles" (see http://www.ainfos.co/01/dec/ainfos00120.html).

12 For more details on Barlow's efforts to combat water privatization see Barlow (1999).

13 For discussions of connections between the Water War and the ongoing anti-globalization effort, see Ainger (2001), Shapiro (2000), and Weiss (2000a, 2000b).

14 Thanks to Tom Kruse for allowing me to view a videocassette of the meeting.

15 This is not to suggest that the Coordinadora has steered clear of contemporary currents of indigenous activism and political mobilization in Bolivia. In fact, as the spokesperson for the Coordinadora, Olivera has made several well-publicized attempts to reach out to overtly indigenous organizations, including the CSUTCB and the coca growers led by Evo Morales.

16 The meeting was held in Cochabamba because of the "murderous confrontations to protest against the privatization of the city's water," making it "the symbol for the steps forward realized by its citizens and the civil society for the water appropriation and for its democratic management." Previous meetings had been held in Casablanca (1996), Penang (1997), Tehran (1999), and Alexandria (2000).

17 The Law of Popular Participation (1994) also grants legal recognition to traditional indigenous and popular forms of political organization according to a group's "uses, customs, and statutory dispositions."

REFERENCES

ELECTRONIC SOURCES

http://1worldcommunication.org
http://www.ainfos.co/01/dec/ainfos00120.html
http://www.americas.org
http://www.canadians.org
http://www.cedib.org/cedib/Index.html
http://www.cedla.org
http://www.citizen.org
http://www.democracyctr.org/waterwar.index.htm
http://www.goldmanprize.org
http://ips-dc.org/lm-awards/index.htm
http://www.nadir.org/nadir/initiativ/agp/en/

http://www.pbs.org/frontlineworld/stories.
  bolivia.html

http://www.projectcensored.org/stories/
  2001/1.html

PRIMARY SOURCES

Asamblea Permanente de los Derechos
  Humanos de Cochabamba
  2000a Violations of Human Rights
    During the Mobilizations of the 4th
    and 5th of February, 2000. Cocha-
    bamba, Bolivia.
  ——2000b State of Siege Still in Effect
    while Repressive Measures of Political
    Control are Heavily Implemented. Report,
    April 9. Cochabamba, Bolivia.
Carpio San Miguel, Edwin
  2001 Cochabamba vive el "boom" de las
    ferias. Los Tiempos de Cochabamba.
    July 29.
Coordinadora (Coordinator for Water and
  for Life)
  1999 Untitled communication, December.
  2000a "Los bolivianos jamás hemos
    tenido alma de esclavos." Communi-
    cation, January 15. Cochabamba,
    Bolivia.
  ——2000b "Y...El Agua sigue siendo
    nuestra!" Communication, February 6.
    Cochabamba, Bolivia.
  ——2000c "Denuncia de secuestro de
    dirigentes de la Coordinadora Departa-
    mental de Defensa del Agua y de la Vida."
    Communication, April 8. Cochabamba,
    Bolivia.
  ——2000d "Comunicado sobre el viaje de
    Oscar Olivera a EEUU." Communication,
    October 11. Cochabamba, Bolivia.
De Ugarte Lazcano, Jaime
  2001 El mal ejemplo de la Coordinadora.
    Los Tiempos de Cochabamba. June 15.
García Mérida, Wilson
  2002 La Coordinadora y las ansias de
    poder. Los Tiempos de Cochabamba.
    January 27.
Gonzáles Quintanilla, Luis
  2001 En espera de abril, con piedras,
    palos y macanas. Los Tiempos de
    Cochabamba. April 12.

Laserna, Roberto
  2001 A dos años de la guerra del agua, nada.
    Los Tiempos de Cochabamba. April 28.
Los Tiempos
  2001a La "Coordinadora," un año
    después. Los Tiempos de Cochabamba.
    February 7.
  ——2001b La Coordinadora y el fin de un
    engaño. Los Tiempos de Cochabamba.
    June 15.
  ——2001c El pueblo tomó justicia "por
    manos propias." Los Tiempos de Cocha-
    bamba. April 11.
Salinas, Cayo
  2002 El masoquismo de los cochabambi-
    nos. Los Tiempos de Cochabamba.
    June 18.
Varnaux Garay, Marcelo
  2001 La Coordinadora cochabambina:
    Un grotesco socio político. Los Tiempos
    de Cochabamba. June 26.
World Bank
  1999 Bolivia Public Expenditure Review,
    Report No. 19232-BO. The executive
    summary, June 14. Washington, DC.

SECONDARY SOURCES

Ainger, Katherine
  2001 A Culture of Life, A Culture of
    Death. New Internationalist 340:1–6.
Albó, Xavier
  1987 Por qúe el campesino qhochala es
    diferente? Cuarto Intermedio 2:43–59.
  ——1995 Our Identity Starting from Plur-
    alism in the Base. In The Postmodernism
    Debate in Latin America. J. Beverley, J.
    Oviedo, and M. Aronna, eds. Pp. 18–33.
    Durham, NC: Duke University Press.
  ——1996 Making the Leap from Local
    Mobilization to National Politics. NACLA
    Report on the Americas 29 (5):15–20.
Alvarez, Sonia, Evelina Dagnino, and Arturo
  Escobar
  1998 The Cultural and the Political in
    Latin American Social Movements. In
    Cultures of Politics and Politics of Cul-
    tures: Re-Visioning Latin American
    Social Movements. S. Alvarez, E. Dag-
    nino, and A. Escobar, eds. Pp. 1–29.
    Boulder, CO: Westview Press.

Anonymous
   2000 Profile: Maude Barlow – An Unre-
   pentant Canadian. Inter Press Service. May 1.
Appadurai, Arjun
   2002 Deep Democracy: Urban Governmentality and the Horizon of Politics.
   Public Culture 14(1):21–47.
Auyero, Javier
   2000 Poor People's Politics: Peronist Survival Networks and the Legacy of Evita.
   Durham, NC: Duke University Press.
Bailey, F. G.
   1988 Humbuggery and Manipulation:
   The Art of Leadership. Ithaca, NY: Cornell University Press.
Bailey, J., and T. Knutsen
   1987 Surgery Without Anesthesia: Bolivia's Response to Economic Chaos.
   World Today 43:47–51.
Barlow, Maude
   1999 Blue Gold: The Global Water
   Crisis and the Commodification of the
   World's Water Supply. Report. Inter-
   national Forum on Globalization.
   ——2000 Report on International Solidarity Trip to Cochabamba, Bolivia, December 6–11. International Forum on
   Globalization.
Beiner, Ronald, ed.
   1995 Theorizing Citizenship. Albany:
   State University of New York Press.
Bigenho, Michelle
   1996 Imaginando lo imaginado: Las nar-
   rativas de las nociones bolivianas.
   Revista Andina 14(2):471–507.
Bonfanti, Sabrina, and Gavin Wright
   2001 Stories of the Water Ways. Peak
   Features. July 16.
Bouguerra, Larbi
   2001 Report of the Latin American Meet-
   ing of the Water Workshop. Tiquipaya,
   June 9–12. Unpublished manuscript.
Boyte, Henry
   2001 On Silences and Civic Muscle, or
   Why Social Capital is a Useful but Insuf-
   ficient Concept. Paper presented at the
   Havens Center, University of Wisconsin
   a Madison. April 10.
Brysk, Alison
   1996 Turning Weakness into Strength: The
   Internationalization of Indian Rights.
   Latin American Perspectives 23 (2):
   38–57.

——2000 From Tribal Village to Global
   Village: Indian Rights and International
   Relations in Latin America. Palo Alto,
   CA: Stanford University Press.
Calderón Gutiérrez, Fernando
   2002 Oscar Olivera Foronda. In Política
   y sociedad en el espejo: 18 entrevistas a
   líderes. Fernando Calderón, ed. Pp.
   135–150. La Paz: PNUD.
Chanez Mendia, José Francisco
   n. d. The Water Issue in Cochabamba:
   The Dilemma Between Economical
   and Social Values. Unpublished manuscript.
Conklin, Beth and Laura Graham
   1995 The Shifting Middle Ground: Amazonian Indians and Eco-Politics. American Anthropologist 97 (4):695–710.
Conniff, Michael L.
   1999 Introduction. In Latin American
   Populism in Comparative Perspective.
   2nd edition. M. Conniff, ed. Pp. 1–21.
   Albuquerque: University of New
   Mexico Press.
Council of Canadians, ed.
   2001 Water for People and Nature:
   Final Report. An International Forum
   on Conservation and Human Rights.
   Quebec City: Council of Canadians.
Crespo, Carlos
   1999 "La Guerra de los pozos": El Con-
   flicto por la perforación de pozos pro-
   fundos en Vinto-Sipe Sipe. In Conflictos
   Ambientales. Pp. 23–83. Cochabamba:
   CERES.
   ——2000 Continuidad y ruptura: La
   "Guerra del Agua" y los nuevos movimientos sociales en Bolivia. Observatorio Social
   de América Latina 1 (2):21–28.
Dandler, Jorge
   1983 Sindicalismo campesino en Bolivia:
   Cambios estructurales en Ucureña,
   1935–1952. Cochabamba: CERES.
D'Emilio, Lucia
   1997 Processes of Change and Indigenous Participation. Cultural Survival
   Quarterly 21 (2):43–46.
de la Torre, Carlos
   2000 Populist Seduction in Latin America: The Ecuadorian Experience. Ohio
   University: Research in International
   Studies. Latin American Series,
   No. 32.

Dolinsky, Lewis
    2001 Cochabamba's Water Rebellion – and Beyond. San Francisco Chronicle. February 11.
Fernandez, James W.
    1986 Returning to the Whole. *In* Persuasions and Performances: The Play of Tropes in Culture. Pp. 188–213. Bloomington: Indiana University Press.
Finnegan, William
    2002 Leasing the Rain. New Yorker. April 8: 43–53.
Flórez, Margarita, and Pablo Solón
    2001 The Water War: Hydraulic Resources Strategy and Citizen Participation at the IDB in the Case of Bolivia. Cochabamba: Fundación Solón.
Franklin, Sheila
    2000 The Water is Ours, Damn It! Documentary Film. Ravi Khanna, producer. World Productions.
Gamarra, Eduardo
    1994 Market-Oriented Reforms and Democratization in Latin America: Challenges of the 1990's. *In* Latin American Political Economy in tbe Age of Neoliberal Reform. W. Smith, C. Acuña, and E. Gamarra, eds. Pp. 1–15. Miami, FL: Transaction.
Geertz, Clifford
    1963 The Integrative Revolution: Primordial Sentiments and Civil Politics in the New States. *In* Old Societies and New States. Pp. 105–157. New York: Free Press.
Gilroy, Paul
    1987 There Ain't No Black in the Union Jack: The Cultural Politics of Race and Nation. Chicago: University of Chicago Press.
Goldstein, Daniel
    1998 Performing National Culture in a Bolivian Migrant Community. Ethnology 36 (2):117–132.
Gugelberger, Georg, and Michael Kearney
    1991 Voices for the Voiceless: Testimonial Literature in Latin America. Latin American Perspectives 18(3):3–14.
Gutiérrez, Raquel, Alvaro García, and Luis Tapia
    2000 La forma multitud de la política de las necesidades vitales. *In* El Retorno de la Bolivia plebeya. A. García, R. Gutiérrez, R. Prada, and L. Tapia, eds. Pp. 133–184. La Paz: Muela del Diablo.

Gutiérrez Aguilar, Raquel
    2001 La Coordinadora de Defensa del Agua y de la Vida: A un año de la guerra del agua. *In* Tiempos de rebelión. A. García, R. Gutiérrez, R. Prada, F. Quispe, L. Tapia, eds. Pp. 193–211. La Paz: Muela del Diablo.
Hale, Charles
    1994 Between Che Guevara and the Pachamama: Mestizos, Indians and Identity Politics in the Anti-Quincentenary Campaign. Critique of Anthropology 14(1): 9–40.
——1997 Cultural Politics of Identity in Latin America. Annual Review of Anthropology 26:567–590.
Hall, Stuart
    1981 Notes on Deconstructing "the Popular." *In* People's History and Socialist Theory. R. Samuel, ed. Pp. 227–240. London: Routledge.
Healy, Kevin
    1989 Sindicatos campesinos y desarrollo rural, 1978–1985. La Paz: HISBOL.
——1991 The Political Ascent of Bolivia's Coca Leaf Growers. Journal of Inter-American Studies and World Affairs 33(1):87–133.
——2001 Llamas, Weavings, and Organic Chocolate: Multicultural Grassroots Development in the Andes and Amazon of Bolivia. South Bend, IN: University of Notre Dame Press.
Healy, Kevin, and Susan Paulson
    2000 Political Economies of Identity in Bolivia, 1952–1998. Journal of Latin American Anthropology 5(2):2–29.
Holston, James
    1999 Spaces of Insurgent Citizenship. *In* Cities and Citizenship. J. Holston and A. Appadurai, eds. Pp. 155–176. Durham, NC: Duke University Press.
Hopenhayn, Martin
    1995 Postmodernism and Neoliberalism in Latin America. *In* The Postmodernism Debate in Latin America. J. Beverley, M. Aronna, and J. Oviedo, eds. Pp. 93–109. Durham: Duke University Press.
Institute for Policy Studies
    2000 IPS Announces Winners of 2000 Letelier-Moffitt Human Rights Awards. Institute for Policy Studies News 4:1.

Juhasz, Antonia
  2002 Bechtel V. Bolivia. San Francisco
       Bay Guardian. April 17.
Kearney, Michael
  1996 Reconceptualizing the Peasantry:
       Anthropology in Global Perspective.
       Boulder, CO: Westview Press.
Keck, M., and K. Sikkink
  1998 Activists Beyond Borders. Ithaca,
       NY: Cornell University Press.
Kohl, Benjamin
  2000 Restructuring Citizenship in Bolivia
       at the End of the Twentieth Century.
       Paper presented at the Latin American
       Studies Association Meeting, Tampa,
       FL.
Korten, Fran
  2000 From DC: A New Global Solidar-
       ity. Yes! A Journal of Positive Futures.
Kruse, Tom
  2002 Las victories de abril: Un historia
       breve y balance de la "Guerra del Agua."
       Unpublished manuscript.
Laclau, Ernesto
  1977 Politics and Ideology in Marxist
       Theory. London.
Laclau, Ernesto, and Chantal Mouffe
  1985 Hegemony and Socialist Strategy:
       Towards a Radical Democratic Politics.
       London: Verso.
Lagos, Maria
  1994 Autonomy and Power: The Dynam-
       ics of Class and Culture in Rural Bolivia.
       Philadelphia: University of Pennsylvania
       Press.
  ——1997 "Bolivia La Nueva": Construct-
       ing New Citizens. Paper presented at the
       meeting of the Latin American Studies As-
       sociation. Guadalajara, Mexico.
Langman, Jimmy
  2002 Bechtel Battles Against Dirt-Poor
       Bolivians. San Francisco Chronicle.
       February 2.
Larson, Brooke
  1998 Cochabamba (Re)Constructing a
       History. In Cochabamba, 1550–1900.
       2nd edition. Pp. 322–390. Durham,
       NC: Duke University Press.
Lienhard, Martin
  2000 Of Mestizajes, Heterogeneities,
       Hybridisms and Other Chimeras. Jour-

nal of Latin American Cultural Studies
       6(2):183–200.
Lins Ribeiro, Gustavo
  1998 Cybercultural Politics: Political
       Activism at a Distance in a Trans-
       national World. In Cultures of Politics
       and Politics of Cultures. S. Alvarez,
       E. Dagnino, and A. Escobar, eds. Pp.
       325–352. Boulder, CO: Westview Press.
Mallon, Florencia
  1996 Constructing mestizaje in Latin
       America: Authenticity, Marginality, and
       Gender in the Claiming of Ethnic Iden-
       tities. Journal of Latin American An-
       thropology 2(1): 170–181.
Martínez-Echazábal, Lourdes
  1998 Mestizaje and the Discourse of
       National/Cultural Identity in Latin
       America, 1845–1959. Latin American
       Perspectives 25(3):21–42.
Marvin, Simon, and Nina Laurie
  1999 An Emerging Logic of Urban Water
       Management, Cochabamba, Bolivia.
       Urban Studies 36(2):341–357.
Mayorga, Fernando
  1991 Max Fernandez: La política del si-
       lencio. La Paz: ILDIS.
McLennan, Gregor
  1995 Pluralism. Minneapolis: University
       of Minnesota Press.
Melucci, Alberto
  1996 Challenging Codes: Collective
       Action in the Information Age. Cam-
       bridge: Cambridge University Press.
Menchú, Rigoberta
  1984 I...Rigoberta Menchú: An Indian
       Woman in Guatemala. E. Burgos-Deb-
       ray, ed. London: Verso.
Mitchell, William P. and David Guillet, eds.
  1994 Irrigation at High Altitudes:
       The Social Organization of Water Con-
       trol Systems in the Andes. Society for
       Latin American Anthropology Publica-
       tion Series: Vol. 12. United States:
       American Anthropological Association.
Neary, Dyan M.
  2001 Bolivia: The Fight for Public Water.
       Earth Times News Service. December 18.
Nickson, Andrew, and Claudia Vargas
  2002 The Limitations of Water Regula-
       tion: The Failure of the Cochabamba

Concession in Bolivia. Bulletin of Latin American Research 21(1): 99–120.

Public Citizen
2002 Profit Streams: The World Bank and Greedy Global Water Companies. Critical Mass Energy and Environment Program. http://www.citizen.org.

Ribeiro, Darcy
1971 The Americas and Civilization. New York: Dutton.

Rivera, Silvia
1984 Oprimidos pero no vencidos. La Paz: HISBOL.
——1990 Liberal Democracy and Ayllu Democracy in Bolivia: The Case of Norte de Potosí. The Journal of Development Studies 26(4):97–121.
——1993 La raíz: Colonizadores y colonizados. In Violencias encubiertas en Bolivia. Pp. 27–139. La Paz: CIPCA.

Sanjinés, Javier
1996 Beyond Testimonial Discourse: New Popular Trends in Bolivia. In The Real Thing: Testimonial Discourse in Latin America. G. Gugelberger, ed. Pp. 254–265. Durham, NC: Duke University Press.
——2001 Outside in and Inside out: Visualizing Society in Bolivia. The Latin American Subaltern Studies Reader. I. Rodríguez, ed. Durham, NC: Duke University Press.

Shapiro, Bruce
2000 Not Just a Seattle Sequel. The Salon. April 15.

Shultz, Jim
2000 Behind the New Globalization Protests Lies an Old Demand, Democracy. Pacific News Service, May 4.

Stephenson, Marcia
2003 Forging an Indigenous Counterpublic Sphere: The Taller de Historia Oral Andina in Bolivia. Latin American Research Review 37(2):99–118.

Sterling, Robert
2000 Let Them Sip Champagne: The Battle of Bolivia. http://www.disinfo.com/pages/dossier/id428/pg1.html/

Stokes, Susan
1995 Democracy and the Limits of Popular Sovereignty in South America. In The Consolidation of Democracy in Latin America. Joseph Tulchin and Bernice

Romero, eds. Pp. 59–81. Boulder, CO: Lynne Rienner.

Taylor, Charles
1994 The Politics of Recognition. In Multiculturalism: A Critical Reader. David Theo Goldberg, ed. Pp. 25–73. Oxford: Basil Blackwell.

Toranzo Roca, Carlos
1991 Burguesía chola y señorialismo conflictuado. In Max Fernández: La política del silencio. N.p. La Paz: ILDIS.

Touraine, Alain
2000 Can We Live Together? Equality and Difference. Palo Alto, CA: Stanford University Press.

Van Cott, Donna Lee
2000 The Friendly Liquidation of the Past: The Politics of Diversity in Latin America. Pittsburgh, PA: University of Pittsburgh Press.

Vargas, Humberto, and Thomas Kruse
2000 Las Victorias de Abril: Una historia que aún no concluye. Observatorio Social de América Latina 1(2):7–14.

Weiss, Larry
2000a A Breakthrough in D. C. Resource Center of the Americas. May.
——2000b Here's What the World Bank Protests Are All About. Minneapolis Star Tribune. April 29.

Weyland, Kurt
2000 Clarifying a Contested Concept: Populism in the Study of Latin American Politics Comparative Politics 34(1): 1–23.

Yashar, Deborah
1998 Contesting Citizenship: Indigenous Movements and Democracy in Latin America. Comparative Politics 31(1): 23–42.

Zavaleta, René
1986 Lo nacional-popular en Bolivia. Mexico City: Siglo XXI.

Zoll, Daniel
2000 Soaking the Poor: S. F.'s Bechtel Wants the Bolivian People to Pay for its Bad Water Investment. San Francisco Bay Guardian. December 13.

15

From the Cosmopolitan to the Personal: Women's Mobilization to Combat HIV/AIDS

Ida Susser

HIV/AIDS forces those of us working in anthropology to confront the biological with the social and the political, and perhaps allows us to integrate these approaches in new ways. Geeta Rao Gupta, as plenary speaker at the groundbreaking Durban International HIV/AIDS conference in July 2000, noted that to adequately address women's issues we must start with the construction of gender, historically and culturally (Gupta 2000). But gender is a sociological concept: with respect to infection with HIV/AIDS and the development of strategies for prevention, it is the interaction between social and biological difference that can determine life and death.

Let us highlight the "simple" biological contrasts. Only women contract HIV/AIDS through vaginal intercourse and, in fact, in heterosexual relations, women are more easily infected than men. Secondly, invisible, internal vaginal infections may be one of the most common early and continuing manifestations of the opportunistic diseases of HIV/AIDS for women. Thirdly, only women can become pregnant and in this way transmit the HIV virus to their children. Only

women can transmit the virus to children through their breast milk. As a corollary, only pregnant or breastfeeding women can transmit possibly harmful medications through their bloodstream to infants. Thus, before we even begin to outline the historical, social, and economic discrimination women have suffered, combined with the lack of access to equal inheritance, and educational and employment opportunities today, we have to recognize that biology has also condemned women in this epidemic.

Obviously, in the poorer countries where heterosexual transmission is dominant, women are in a central and, therefore, powerful position with respect to the HIV epidemic. They run the terrible risk of being blamed and victimized for their positive status as well as being considered to hold the potential key to limiting the devastation. Clearly, approaches to treatment and prevention within existing patterns of inequality and discrimination by gender may increase or erase the impact of such crucial biological difference. Nevertheless, what is known biologically is also determined culturally and historically. Our priorities for biological research, funding, and even our initial questions are framed within a social context that can have consequences for survival and mortality (Haraway 1991, Martin 1987, Parker 2001, Rapp 1999, Scott 1999). This becomes all too clear in the history of HIV diagnosis and treatment.

First, initial research with respect to HIV/AIDS in the Western medical academy focused on middle-class gay men. Most women in the United States who were HIV positive were poor and did not become the focus of the bulk of US research and funding on AIDS (Farmer et al. 1996, Heise and Elias 1995). Thus, diagnosis did not originally include the opportunistic diseases that were most frequently found in women. This lack of diagnostic criteria made it difficult for women and medical professionals to recognize HIV/AIDS in women and for many years limited the access of women to medical benefits, treatment, and disability assistance from the US government. Since increasingly in the United States women who contracted HIV were poor, this dearth of diagnostic criteria was doubly significant for them as they were denied the label which made them eligible for financial assistance.

In areas in the poorer countries and specifically in central and southern Africa, where testing was not widely available, the diagnostic criteria for women (which were based on the experience of gay white men in the United States) limited the possibility that women could recognize that they had the virus. These diagnostic criteria were also, of course, problematic for African men, since they did not recognize local differences in the diagnosis of a disease that, while caused by the same virus, had distinct regional opportunities for transmission and specific regional manifestations according to the local opportunistic diseases.

Secondly, for the first decade after HIV was identified, US women were not included in the experimental drug trials that allowed many US middle-class men early access to treatment. This exclusion from early access to experimental drugs had ongoing implications as the US Food and Drug Administration (FDA) regularly insists that new medications be licensed only to the age and sex groups included in the trials.

Both men and women in poor countries were excluded from access to these new and expensive medications. Currently, this is being contested. Affordable treatment may become available in poor countries as a result of powerful social demands. However, the way in which the availability and types of treatment will be distributed by gender is still open to debate and in poor countries, women are disadvantaged in relation to men in their access to both treatment and care (Susser and Schneider 2004).

Adding further to the saga of unequal treatment, both doctors and women were initially concerned that anti-retroviral treatments would harm the fetus. It was not until about fifteen years into the epidemic that physicians were permitted to try such treatments for pregnant women. Only then was it discovered that, in fact, drug treatments during pregnancy and labor reduced the number of children who would test positive for HIV after the first year. Drug treatment during labor and early infancy has now become one of the leading tools of prevention for children in the battle against the virus. In the United States and Western Europe, the problem of infants who develop HIV/AIDS has almost disappeared. However, in sub-Saharan Africa, anti-retroviral programs for mothers and infants have not yet been extensively implemented. Typically, in those clinics in which there is a program to protect the newborn child, the mother herself is not treated. As a result, the infants may be saved but not the mothers. In a welcome contrast, in some new programs infants, mothers, and other positive members of the household will receive anti-retroviral treatment (Bassett 2001). So far, this innovative policy initiative is still at the planning stage in many areas.

In fact, children have suffered inordinately as the result of the neglect of women's health concerns. For example, it was documented early in the 1980s that breast milk transmit-ted the HIV virus to HIV negative babies. Nevertheless, following the general pattern of neglect of issues significant to women, systematic research on this issue did not emerge for another ten years. In addition, data on orphans has documented extensively the miserable fate of children without mothers, often growing up as servants in extended family households or left to wander the streets and possibly forced to prostitute themselves owing to the lack of parental sup-port. Even foster-care providers for orphaned children are usually female relatives, who are forced to take on extra responsibility in the face of the epidemic and are themselves at greater risk for infection (Kalipeni et al. 2004, UNDP/Government of Botswana 2000). Because women have been dying at younger ages and more quickly than men, the failure to address women's concerns with respect to HIV has also dramatically increased the tragedy for children.

There are currently only two known methods to help people prevent the spread of the virus through sex: the man's condom and the woman's condom. In conventional terms, "condom" usually refers only to the man's condom, but in fact, a woman's condom has existed for over ten years. Both the male and the female condom, if used correctly, have been shown to prevent the spread of the HIV virus almost 99 percent of the time. In addition, the woman's condom is made of an extremely strong form of polyurethane and is less likely to break than the male condom.

A man's condom, whether provided by the man or the woman, is clearly under the con-trol of the man. It has to be put on at the moment of intercourse and requires that the man have an erection. A woman's condom, larger than a man's and designed to fit into the vagina, can be inserted by the woman at any point before sex, even several hours earlier. Although, once inserted, the edges of the female condom can be seen by the man, it is under the control of the woman and can be perceived, like the diaphragm, as part of the woman's effort for reproductive health.

In southern Africa today, most of the women becoming infected with HIV/AIDS are in fact married and many of them have already become accustomed to taking re-sponsibility for family planning (Piot 2001). At the moment, family planning measures, such as, for example, depo-prevera, provide no protection against HIV/AIDS. It is in this context that the woman's condom may prove most useful to HIV prevention.

However, there has been a worldwide dis-parity in the provision of the woman's condom as opposed to the man's. The man's condom was made available practically as soon as sexual transmission was understood. It was provided in great quantities, free of charge, by the US government and inter-national agencies both in the United States and in many other countries around the world.

No requirement was instituted for testing the man's condom to see if it prevented HIV infection before it was distributed universally in the campaign to halt the AIDS epidemic. When men did not like it and did not use it, it was not withdrawn from the market. Exten-sive education and social marketing cam-paigns were introduced using film and rock stars on education videos, and music, colors, smells, and tastes were used to sell the prod-uct and make it more fashionable and appealing to sexual partners.

The fate of strategies for women to protect themselves from the virus has been different. At least three styles of women's condom were developed in the 1980s in response to the epidemic. They were all subjected to exten-sive testing and bureaucratic regulation. Only one style survived financially. In 1992, after seven years of trials and legislative hurdles, the Reality Female Condom was ap-proved by the US FDA. In 1993, the woman's condom was also approved by the US Medic-aid system to be available at reduced costs to women eligible for Medicaid.

However, another seven years later, in 2000, 880 million men's condoms were used per year worldwide and only 5 million women's. Little effort or funding from either US or African governments or international agencies have been used to promote this strategy – it is said that women will not use it, or that they already have the man's condom. Why spend money on promoting a condom for women? There is a voluminous literature to answer this question. My own collection of articles documenting the usefulness, feasibility, and cost-effectiveness of the woman's condom stands several feet high on my desk (Aggleton et al. 1999, Gollub 2000).

To cite some of the most convincing and thorough studies. In Brazil it was found that when the woman's condom was introduced by knowledgeable and supportive providers, many couples used it and the prevalence of sexually transmitted diseases decreased considerably more than when only the man's condom was made available to women (Barbosa 2000). In Senegal and Mexico UNAIDS experimental programs demonstrated that some women preferred the woman's condom and were more likely to use it than to be able to persuade their husbands to use a man's condom (Mane and Aggleton 2000). In South Africa, when UNAIDS made women's condoms available free to women sex workers in Mpumulanga Province, the workers reported that men offered to pay more for the woman's condom as they preferred it to the man's condom. In Zimbabwe, 30,000 women signed a petition requesting that the woman's condom be made available (for a review of the studies of the female condom in the United States and elsewhere see Aggleton et. al. 1999 and Gollub 2000).

There has been extensive testing of vaginal microbicides that would not be seen or felt in sexual interactions but would kill the virus. Clearly this would be preferred by men and women around the world, but it was announced in July 2000 in Durban that none of these has yet been successful. Current projections suggest that such a method may become available by 2007, at the earliest. The idea that women worldwide should wait for this option has to do with the prob-

lematic representation of women's sexuality, at least among a professional elite. It would appear that many national governments, funding agencies, and global nongovernmental organizations (NGOs) prefer to wait for an invisible method, possibly more conducive to "beauty" and sexual fantasy, rather than to promote access to any other method, even if more clumsy and awkward, that will save women's lives *now* (Susser 2001).

The search for the invisible vaginal microbicide that would kill the virus but allow pregnancy is a powerful and important goal. However, women are currently dying for lack of the immediate options such as the female condom in sexual negotiations.

We must therefore ask why this option has not been made available to women on a national or an international level. It is, in fact, sometimes the elision of biological difference, and at other times the stress on the difference that contributes to the unequal access for women to strategies for HIV diagnosis, treatment, and prevention.

For example, women were denied access to experimental drug trials because the medical community feared the impact of the drugs on pregnancy. In this case, denial was based on the biological differences between men and women. In contrast, in the distribution of the male condom it was assumed that women were somehow equivalent to men. If women had access to male condoms, that was the same as if men had them. In the case of access to condoms, inequality was justified by ignoring biological difference.

The consequences of the patterns of gender and sexual inequality outlined here are apparent in the shifting demographics of HIV/AIDS worldwide (Barnett and Whiteside 2002). In the early 1980s in sub-Saharan Africa, HIV was found in a ratio of one man to one woman. In the same region in 2000 more women than men are infected, and while men are dying between the ages of 25 and 45, women are dying of HIV/AIDS between the ages of 15 and 25 (Piot 2001, UNDP/Government of Botswana 2000). In fact, twice as many young girls as young boys, age 15–24, in Namibia, Botswana, and throughout southern Africa are living with AIDS. In Namibia, 20 percent of young girls age 15–24 are living with AIDS and 9 percent of young boys. In Botswana, 34 percent of young girls, 15–24, are living with AIDS, as compared to 16 percent of young boys (UNICEF 2000). One community sero-prevalence study in Ndola, Zambia found four sero-positive girls age 14 for every one seropositive boy of the same age (UNDP/ Government of Botswana 2000). Clearly, if the growing gender disparity among youth is any indication, the epidemic of the future bodes worse for women. In southern Africa, it is powerfully driven by the search of older men for younger women, perhaps in the ill-fated effort to find sexual partners who will not infect them with HIV/AIDS.

Similar trends toward the greater infection of young women can be traced in the United States. Here, in the 1980s, more men were HIV positive than women, around 10:1. In 2000, 15 years later, young minority women were the fastest growing sector of the popula-tion contracting HIV/AIDS. In the United States, HIV has even shifted regionally, following worldwide trends, and poor young black women in the rural South are one of the fastest growing populations for HIV positiv-ity. Clearly we are watching the interplay of race, class, and gender inequality reflected in the medical and health experience.

In the next section, I outline the ways in which women in Namibia have begun to fight this trend by demanding preventive methods women can use.

The strategies available to women to deal with the HIV/AIDS epidemic can be represented by a contemporary case study which allows us to begin to disentangle the complexities of sexual/gender discrimin-ation as it emerges at the global level, among international organizations and in the international media, and as it links with national, local, and interpersonal events and perceptions.

Global links are ever intensifying in terms of funding, media networks, and the world-wide impact of the decisions of professional experts. Nevertheless, women and men still find work, get married, and inherit property according to local and national social and political organization and regulation. Histor-ically created community relations, class div-isions and social movements, alliances and hierarchies, determine much of what happens on the ground and in the case of women's strategies for HIV prevention, may both con-strain possibilities and allow unrecognized political agency.

In addition, our research led us to recog-nize the significance of a fourth level: the personal territory of the body and the nego-tiation and control of the boundaries of the body. The variability in the definitions of power and sexual rights in the territory of the body needs to be underscored particu-larly, although certainly not exclusively, in relation to HIV/AIDS and the strategies women can use in sexual negotiation.

The Introduction of the Woman's Condom in Namibia: Political Effects from the Personal to the Global

Over the last few years Richard Lee and I have been conducting intermittent fieldwork in Namibia and Botswana with respect to the strategies available to women to negotiate safe sex (Lee and Susser 2002, Susser 2003). In addition, we have been conducting a training program on the social context of AIDS at the University of Namibia in which we discussed our ethnographic findings and worked with graduates and undergraduates in fields such as sociology and nursing to develop local research projects. As Namibian students from the first year (1996) returned each year to work on their own projects, they became supervisors of research projects, and several were recruited to work in national HIV prevention programs, to supervise vol-unteers and to represent issues concerning HIV/AIDS with respect to women (Iipinge et al. 2000).

A major focus of our research had concerned the woman's condom (Iipinge et al. 2000, Susser 2001, Susser and Stein 2000). When we began the research, the woman's condom was not available to Namibians at an affordable price, if at all. Some people had seen it in drugstores, but although we inquired we never actually found any. We introduced the female condom to students in all our seminars. In addition we interviewed men and women in Northern Namibia as well as in the Kalahari desert region about whether they would use such a device (Susser and Stein 2000).

As noted in previous publications, both men and women were enthusiastic about the potential use of the female condom although they had never had access to it as an option. In June, 1999, UNAIDS in cooperation with the Reality Company offered 10,000 free female condoms to Namibia. But the Ministry of Health did not make female condoms available. According to the UNAIDS representative and the World Health Representative in Namibia at that time, there was a concern that the demand would be greater than the affordable supply and they did not want to be subjected to women's demands for more.

At a meeting in Mahenene in the Omusati region of northern Namibia on July 20, 1999, Veronica De Klerk, the leader of Women's Action for Development (WAD), began to demand publicly that the female condom be made available to Namibian women. According to De Klerk, "in the presence of Health Authorities, Decision-makers, Community Leaders, Traditional Authorities etc.... [WAD] boldly pioneered the introduction of the female condom and opened the debate on the free distribution of free female condoms by the Ministry of Health" (De Klerk, keynote address, April 20, 2001:2).

WAD, a Namibian NGO focused on women's social and economic self-help, is funded by the Konrad Adenauer-Stiftung Foundation in Germany. This foundation has funded similar projects in Zimbabwe and other parts of the world and formed WAD in Namibia in 1994. Veronica De Klerk was born in Namibia and has worked through WAD to develop economic status and political voices for rural women in that country. WAD has initiated a number of successful sewing cooperatives and agrarian training projects and is particularly committed to helping women form savings clubs to finance their future activities. Relevant to this case study is the emphasis in WAD on training women to lobby for political influence. WAD elects women as "Women's Voices" in each region to lobby for the needs of women in that area. When the cause of the female condom was adopted by WAD, these "Women's Voices" led the public outcry in each region.

Also significant are the close links between WAD and the Namibian government. President Sam Nujoma contributed a preface to the 1999 edition of the WAD booklet and, as will be discussed below, when the female condom was finally launched by the Namibian government, Veronica de Klerk was invited to speak.

In August, 1999, a few days before an official "National Condom Use Day" scheduled by the Ministry of Health, De Klerk was quoted in the daily newspaper, *The Namibian*, under the headline "'Where are our condoms?' asks women's group: Women's Action for Development says the National Condom Use Day declared by the Ministry of Health and Social Services violates women's rights by making only male condoms available" (Christof Maletsky, August 19, 1999, p. 5).

WAD, using its regional links in the northern rural areas, followed its announcements with a march and demonstrations among its member groups. WAD demanded the government provide "female condoms available to women, free of charge, as was the case with male condoms" (De Klerk, April 20, 2001).

On September 15, 1999, the Permanent Secretary of Health and Social Services, Dr. Kalumbi Shangula, announced that a second National Condom Use Day was being planned and that it would include the woman's condom. The Ministry of Health then assigned the problem of the woman's condom to the Ministry of Women Affairs and Child Welfare.

By July, 2000 the Namibian government had formed a Technical Working Group, under the administration of the Ministry of Women Affairs and Child Welfare, and the female condom had been placed under its jurisdiction. The Technical Working Group included representatives of the Ministries of Health as well as Women Affairs, UNAIDS, WAD, the Okutumbatumba Hawkers and Shebeen Associations, the AIDS Care Trust, the Namibia Planned Parenthood Association, National Social Marketing (NaSoMa), and others, a number of whom had been participants in the Fogarty Program. The group conducted a pilot study (funded by UNAIDS) to see if couples would use the woman's condom and to document their reactions. They held public meetings to educate people in general about HIV/AIDS, to demonstrate the use of the female condom, to answer questions from the audience and to recruit volunteers, both men and women, to try the condoms and to train others to use them.

The report on the trials is informative and useful in understanding the significant role for the female condom in Namibia (Ministry of Women Affairs and Child Welfare 2001). Although there is no claim that the respondents formed a random or necessarily a representative sample, the volunteers did come from a number of different regions and the findings give important insight into people's concerns. The majority of people who volunteered to try the condom were women, although about a third were men. The volunteers ranged in age from 18 to 52 and came from a variety of occupations, including a policeman, several clerks, house cleaners, and two women construction workers. At training sessions, following the initial public demonstrations, volunteers were given female condoms. A major complaint at this point was that there were too

few samples for the large number of people willing to volunteer. Eight female condoms were distributed to each volunteer: two for demonstration, three for use, and three to give away.

Each person who volunteered to try the female condom was asked to fill out an initial questionnaire and then contacted a few weeks later to ask how they fared. Many of those who received the female condoms did not respond to the follow-up questions. Some responded that they had given the condoms away to a friend or neighbor, or had not used them because they had no partner, or their partner refused to try them. One volunteer even said, "lost all condoms or may be stolen"! However, the comments of the 88 volunteers who actually completed the training process and answered questions about their use of the free condoms were on the whole positive.

Frequently, people simply said, "no difficulties experienced" or "fine, no problems." Some were negative, such as the following: "My partner complained all the way through, saying he was having sex in plastic" or "My partner's attitude puts me off, he was complaining too much," "My partner was talking too much." Some were positive after some difficulty, as one woman noted: "Partner objected at first but said it was fine after sex," or "difficult to insert at first," "first insertion was painful," or a woman who was later successful said, "I tried to insert the condom the first time with no success, maybe because I was under the influence of alcohol." One man reiterated a common problem among partners when he said, about the first use, "It was very difficult explaining to the girlfriend how to insert the condom," but on the third use he reported "used, easy to insert and comfortable." In fact, in spite of numerous complaints, including the slipperiness of the condom, the noise it made, and difficulty with the initial insertion, of the 88 volunteers who reported back on their use of three free female condoms each, an astonishing 65 said that by the third try, the female condom was easy to insert and comfortable! This was an encouraging and surprising result partly because, as the report on the trials notes, the training sessions were much criticized for the lack of training provided and the unevenness of the educational programs.

Following the female condom meetings and trials, the Ministry of Women Affairs began to receive letters and petitions requesting that the government provide the woman's condom as one of the options for HIV prevention in Namibia. In addition, the internationally funded NGO, Sister Namibia (which, like WAD, receives much funding from Germany, a significant contemporary manifestation or perhaps reversal of colonial history as Namibia was a German colony prior to World War I), which focuses specifically on sexual rights and has championed the rights of lesbian and gay people in Namibia, published articles describing the female condom both in English and in Oshiwambo (the language of the Ovambo people of northern Namibia), and joined the general outcry calling for free female condoms. In fact, Sister Namibia is quoted in the opening pages of the Ministry of Women Affairs and Child Welfare Report on the female condom:

> Many of us have heard about the female condom. Some lucky ones might have seen it and even luckier ones might have used it once or twice. Despite widespread curiosity about the female condom, as it is also known, most of us are, to say the least, still in the dark about it. Are there any plans to introduce the female condom in Namibia? (*Sister Namibia* 12 (2001): 3,4)

Interestingly enough, just to complete the analysis of global–local links, the researcher for Sister Namibia was a student in our training program in Windhoek in July, 2000 and had even e-mailed me in New York City asking for information about a shipment of about 100 female condoms I had tried to bring to Namibia the previous July. At that time the shipment, was, for some mysterious reason, stopped by customs and, in spite of

assistance from UNAIDS and other groups, we were not able to get them released in time for a demonstration seminar at the training program.

In April, 2001, the female condom was approved for widespread distribution by the Namibian government. In fact, the female condom was "launched" at a much publicized event organized with UNAIDS by the Ministry of Women Affairs and Child Welfare and attended by a number of other cabinet ministers and government officials. Veronica De Klerk was invited to give the keynote speech.

Throughout the process, the female condoms had been supplied and paid for by a number of donors, coordinated by UNAIDS in cooperation with the Female Health Company. In 1999, the Female Health Company had worked with UNAIDS to develop a subsidized rate for the female condom in poor countries such as Namibia. Initially, during the pilot project and the launch, more than 20,000 female condoms were distributed by the Ministry of Women Affairs and Child Welfare. A further 100,000 are expected to be distributed through the regional centers, possibly at youth centers. Nevertheless, as of yet, no free female condoms are available at clinics, hospitals, or other venues.

However, since the launch, female condoms have been on sale at subsidized rates in most of the local pharmacies. NaSoMa (National Social Marketing) sells them to pharmacies and other outlets for N\$5.22 (about US75c) and they are sold by the stores for N\$8 (approximately US \$1) for three. Male condoms are also subsidized by NaSoMa and are much cheaper: the man's condom, Cool Ryder, cost N87c for six wholesale and the store price is N\$1.50 (approximately US25c) for six.

Thus, women's condoms, even at subsidized prices, are selling for ten times as much as men's. Nevertheless, after the public launch, NaSoMa estimated that they would sell 1,000 female condoms per month. In fact, in the first three months, 18,000 were sold in Namibian stores. Certainly, female condoms were finally available at an affordable price, and people were buying them in unprecedented numbers.

In July, 2001, we saw female condoms for sale for the first time at the truck stop on the new trans-Kalahari highway on the Namibian side of the border with Botswana. This was a particularly significant location. The long straight two-lane highway that connects three countries as it stretches from Johannesburg, South Africa to Gaborone in Botswana as well as to Windhoek, Namibia and points north was opened in 1998 as part of the much-awaited economic development of southern Africa. Clearly, as the trucks race by, they open the door to both new trade and HIV, and the question is whether the development is possible or whether the gains will be canceled out by the devastation of HIV.

Nevertheless, although female condoms are now available for a reasonable price in stores in Namibia, this case also illustrates the unevenness of access for all methods. They are not yet available free for all Namibian women. Most Namibian women are, in fact, too poor to buy such protection consistently even at these subsidized prices and will not have access to them until the female condoms are distributed free of charge by the Namibian government. This has not yet happened. There is much hope that the Ministry of Women Affairs will distribute the free condoms as they are shipped from the international donors. One shipment of 100,000 may save many lives, but to stem the epidemic, a consistent predictable process of free distribution to poor women in both the urban and rural areas needs to be worked out. This is the next challenge for Namibia.

I present this case as a clear illustration of the crucial ongoing interaction between the local, the national, and the global in the implementation of strategies women can use to protect themselves from HIV/AIDS.

On the personal level, our research documented the active agency of Namibian women. In semi-rural northern Namibia women were knowledgeable about the het-erosexual transmission of HIV/AIDS and discussed the issue openly. In 1996, an Ovambo woman said: "Women are very open. They talk to each other about AIDS.... Yes, they acknowledge it is possible that they have it. They are very afraid." In addition, women saw themselves as having the right to protect their own bodies and their own home and were willing to use a female barrier method in sex if it were available. To quote another Ovambo woman, "A woman can make her own decision," and another, "This will be protective from the woman's side."

Next, at the local community level, women were not sure how to address the problem but ready to take action and make political demands for methods women could use. To quote a group of Kavango women in a sewing cooperative in Rundu, a small country town, "Go to the ministry [of health] and tell them to order female condoms ... maybe it's better if ... we write them a letter."

At the national level, members of the Ministry of Women Affairs and Child Welfare, of the Ministry of Higher Education and the Ministry of Health and Social Services, as well as several of the women and men from the Fogarty Training Program, from the University of Namibia and employed in civil service positions in the Namibian capital of Windhoek, initiated discussions of methods women can use. However, they could not have proceeded without the strong advocacy by national and international NGOs for women's rights, sexual rights, and human rights, or without the petitions signed by local women (such as the letter referred to above) asking for the female condom. As a result of research, petitions, and community initiatives, in addition to the support of UNAIDS and WHO, national women's representatives were able to add the female condom to the list of options available to Namibian women and men in the negotiation of safer sex.

At the international level, without the support of women's interests and alternative options for women by the UNAIDS and WHO representatives in Windhoek and the funding, expertise, research, and policy analysis these international agencies provided, without the stimulus of the Durban 2000 International Conference on HIV/AIDS which inspired work to proceed in southern Africa, as well as the initial stimulus provided by the Fogarty Program, funded from the United States, the local and national initiatives to develop methods women could use might not have been able to proceed.

Conclusions

Sexual discrimination may be one of the most powerful killers as it is refracted through HIV/AIDS. Obviously, first, because of women's lack of employment and education and sexual subordination to men. But secondly, because of this pervasive discrimination, women have been systematically denied methods they can use.

As noted above, only five million women's condoms have been made available per year, in contrast to the almost one billion men's condoms used worldwide. Epidemiologists have pointed out that in sub-Saharan Africa, the epidemic has long passed beyond any specific "target" or "risk" groups. We have to work not only with sex workers but focus as well on the millions of women with long-term partners and husbands at risk in the general population (Piot 2001). Both women sex workers and women in long-term relationships have demonstrated a willingness to use the woman's condom, and take responsibility for this as they do for birth control. While men have been given the male condom, whether or not they chose to use it in most countries, women have not yet been given the option of the female condom.

As the case of the woman's condom demonstrates, while we stress the multiple constructions of gender and sexuality, we also have to understand how these manifest themselves within pervasive institutional sexual discrimination – from the global to the state to the local to the personal – they are different at each level.

At the personal level, men and women continuously negotiate boundaries and control over the body (Susser and Stein 2000). Thus, we have to present people with a variety of options which take women's biological and social situation into account and also present the options in ways acceptable to both men and women. The female condom is one such important option which is still not available and affordable for most women who could use it.

We also have to consider gendered perceptions and strategies of prevention and caring with respect to HIV/AIDS at the local level (Susser and Schneider 2004). In what ways are women able to mobilize locally, in terms of voluntary associations, the church, and such groups as the women's cooperatives described earlier, and in what ways are they excluded? In southern Africa, many of the local organizations that now represent "tradition" also maintain men's control over resources and political representation. In addition, while church groups mobilize women, they frequently carry oppressive moral codes weighted in favor of the freedom of men and the restraint of women. Nevertheless, as the case of WAD described here demonstrates, women's groups have been some of the most effective in combating HIV/AIDS on a community level.

At the national level, governments such as the Museveni administration in Uganda have worked hard to address the issue of HIV. Since 1986, President Yoweri Museveni has been outspoken about HIV, and encourages research and public statements. His policies were partly inspired and certainly supported by women's mobilization around AIDS in the form of TASO (The AIDS Support Organization), and other NGOs in Uganda. The Ministry of Health distributes over sixty million male condoms annually and nearly one million female condoms each year (Rosenfield et al. 2001). As a result of Uganda's open and supportive policies for research and prevention, the prevalence of HIV has actually declined in the country, from an estimated 14 percent in the early 1990s to an estimated

8.3 percent by the end of 1999 (ibid.). Significantly, some decline has been noted among young women, although it was more significant among young men (ibid.: 62). The country has become an international example of successful HIV prevention.

In contrast, in South Africa Thabo Mbeki has suggested that the HIV virus may not cause AIDS, and has recruited from the United States the unrepresentative researcher, Peter Duesberg, whose work he found on the internet, and who ignores other scientists. This has confused many South Africans trying to address the HIV virus and has precipitated gendered dissension, as women ask men to use condoms and their partners reply that Mbeki has said there is no virus. The government of South Africa has now begun to implement treatments for preventing mother-to-child transmission and, after some politically costly false starts, the female condom is slowly being made available by the Ministry of Health.

At the global level, organizations such as WHO and UNAIDS are predominantly staffed by the cosmopolitan educated professionals described in much of the literature (Appadurai 1996) and subject to the gendered and racial perspectives generated at this level and specifically in the United States. Professional global elites may perpetuate sexual discrimination but, as noted in the Namibian case, they also have an important role in supporting effective change.

In recognizing the overall issue of sexual discrimination, on global, state, local, and personal levels, we must also recognize the power of social movements as they emerge and interact across the levels or scales. Gender may be defined and negotiated differently at various levels (Susser 2002). Nevertheless, as exemplified by Sister Namibia, WAD, and a number of other NGOs, a social movement for women's health rights or sexual rights can shift national priorities. Funding channeled from an international foundation to a national one with local community links, such as WAD, can also help to reorient the options for people at the local level.

Grassroots protest, national support and state commitment are crucial to the implementation of effective social change. However, European, US and other social movements can and do affect the availability of resources in the Third World. In the United States or other wealthy countries, mobilization around issues of sexual discrimination specifically with respect to strategies women can use to prevent HIV infection can have long-term international implications.

As researchers and by necessity, in the field of HIV, activists, we need to carefully unravel the important differences and needs at each level (personal, local, state, international), as well as the common threads of the struggles for women's rights as part of the general battle for human rights worldwide.

NOTES

I would like to acknowledge the University of Namibia, the Columbia University HIV Center for Behavioral and Clinical Sciences, and the MacArthur Foundation for support for the research undertaken while compiling this chapter.

The lack of recognition for women, and particularly poor women and women in poor countries, with respect to all aspects of HIV has been extensively documented (Farmer et al. 1993, Heise and Elias 1995, Schoepf 2004, Susser and Schneider 2004). In this chapter I briefly outline these issues in order to begin to analyze the continuing global, national, and local impact of the long-term historical discrimination as it reverberates in contemporary policies.

REFERENCES

Aggleton, P., K. Rivers, and S. Scott
  1999 Use of the Female Condom: Gender Relations and Sexual Negotiation. *In* Sex and Youth: Contextual

Factors Affecting Risk for HIV/AIDS: A Comparative Analysis of Multi-Site Studies in Developing Countries. Geneva: UNAIDS.

Appadurai, A.
1996 Modernity at Large. Minneapolis: University of Minnesota Press.

Barbosa, R.
2000 The Female Condom in Brazil. 13th International Conference on AIDS, Breaking the Silence, Durban, South Africa, July.

Barnett, T., and A. Whiteside
2002 AIDS in the Twenty-First Century: Disease and Globalization. New York: Palgrave Macmillan.

Bassett, M.
2001 Keeping the M in MTCT: Women, Mothers and HIV Prevention. American Journal of Public Health 91:701–703.

De Klerk, V.
2001 Speech to Launch the Female Condom. Women And Development Report, April.

Elias, C., L. Heise, and E. Gollub
1996 Women-Controlled HIV Prevention Methods. *In* AIDS in the World II. Jonathan Mann and Daniel Tarantola, eds. Pp. 196–201. New York, Oxford University Press.

Farmer, P., M. Connors, and J. Simmons, eds.
1996 Women, Poverty and AIDS: Sex, Drugs and Structural Violence. Monroe, ME: Common Courage Press.

Farmer, P., M. J. Good, and S. Lindenbaum
1993 Women, Poverty and AIDS: An Introduction. Culture, Medicine and Psychiatry 17(4):387–398.

Gollub, E.
2000 The Female Condom: Tool for Women's Empowerment. American Journal of Public Health 90:1377–1381.

Gupta, G.
2000 Plenary Presentation: Women and AIDS. 13th International Conference on AIDS, Breaking the Silence, Durban, South Africa, July.

Gupta, G., E. Weiss, and D. Whelan
1996 Women and AIDS: Building a New HIV Prevention Strategy. *In* Aids in the World II. Jonathan Mann and Daniel Tarantola, eds. pp. 215–229. New York, Oxford University Press.

Haraway, D.
1991 Simians, Cyborgs and Women: The Reinvention of Nature. New York: Routledge.

Heise, L. L., and C. Elias
1995 Transforming AIDS Prevention to Meet Women's Needs: A Focus on Developing Countries. Social Science and Medicine 40: 931–943.

Iipinge, S., P. Ipinge, R. Lee, and I. Susser
2000 Capacity Building in Social Research on AIDS Case Studies in Namibia. 13th International AIDS Conference, Breaking the Silence, Durban, South Africa, July.

Kalipeni, E., S. Craddock, J. Oppong, and J. Ghosh, eds.
2004 HIV & AIDS in Africa: Beyond Epidemiology. Malden, MA: Blackwell.

Lee, R., and I. Susser
2002 Confounding Conventional Wisdom: Women's Power and Low HIV/AIDS Among the Ju/'Hoansi of Namibia and Botswana. In Session WePeE63671, 14th International AIDS Conference, Barcelona, July.

Mane, P., and P. Aggleton
2000 Cross-National Perspectives on Gender and Power. *In* Framing the Sexual Subject. R. Parker, R. Barbosa, and P. Aggleton, eds. Pp. 104–116. Berkeley: University of California Press.

Martin, E.
1987 The Woman in the Body. Boston: Beacon Press.

Ministry of Women Affairs and Child Welfare
2001 The Female Condom. Republic of Namibia, funded by UNAIDS and the National Social Marketing Program.

Parker, R.
2001 Sexuality, Culture and Power in HIV/AIDS Research. Annual Reviews in Anthropology 30:163–179.

Piot, P.
2001 A Gendered Epidemic: Women and the Risks and Burdens of HIV. Journal of the American Medical Women's Association 56:90–91.

Rapp, R.
  1999 Amniocentesis: Moral Pioneers. Berkeley: University of California Press.
Rosenfield, A., L. Myer, and M. Merson
  2001 The HIV/AIDS Pandemic: The Case for Prevention. Report prepared for the Henry J. Kaiser Family Foundation, June.
Schoepf, B.
  2004 AIDS in Africa: Structure, Agency and Risk in HIV & AIDS in Africa: In Beyond Epidemiology. E. Kalipeni, S. Craddock, J. Oppong and J. Ghosh, eds. Pp. 121–133. Malden, MA: Blackwell.
Scott, Joan
  1999 Gender as a Useful Category of Historical Analysis. In Culture, Society and Sexuality: A Reader. Richard Parker and Peter Aggleton, eds. Pp. 57–76. London: UCL Press.
Susser, I.
  2001 Sexual Negotiations in Relation to Political Mobilization: The Prevention of HIV in Comparative Context. Journal of AIDS and Behavior 5(2):163–172.

——2002 Women's Health Rights in the Age of AIDS. International Journal of Epidemiology 31:45–48.
——2003 Ju/'Hoansi Survival in the Face of HIV: Questions of Poverty and Gender. Anthropologica 45: 121–128.
Susser, I., and H. Schneider
  2004 The Political Economy of Gender and Care: HIV/AIDS in South Africa. United Nations Research Institute for Development (UNRISD) Report.
Susser, I., and Z. Stein
  2000 Culture, Sexuality and Women's Agency in the Prevention of HIV/AIDS in Southern Africa. American Journal of Public Health 90(7):1042–1048.
UNDP/Government of Botswana
  2000 Botswana Human Development Report: Towards an AIDS-Free Generation.
UNICEF
  2000. Aid for AIDS Unequal to the Challenge. Data Briefs: Progress and Disparity. The Progress of Nations. Geneva: UNICEF Publications, July, p. 9.

16

Political Organization among Indigenous Women of the Brazilian State of Roraima: Constraints and Prospects

Ligia T. L. Simonian

Introduction

The participation of indigenous women in the political life of Amazonian villages dates from the earliest records that have marked their presence both in day-to-day struggles as well as in critical conflict situations (Detén 1990, Hughins 1990, Simonian 1997a, b). Their political importance can be drawn from archaeological, ethno-historical and anthropological evidence (Etienne and Leacock 1980, Forline 1995, Roosevelt 1991, Velthem 1996). However, problems persist concerning the exercise and recognition of these women's leadership and representation in formal organizations, whether they stem from local, pan-indigenous or inter-ethnic sources.

Indigenous women's political struggles are inspired by the limitations imposed on them by the state and national governments, and even churches of different denominations. Their actions are further constrained by their husbands, fathers and brothers who combine to restrict the possibility of women organizing (Abbott 1993, Detén 1990, Peixoto 1997, 1998, p.c., Simonian 1997a, b).

Stordhal (1990), when analyzing the organizational processes of Suami women, queried "Why are they so few?," a question that pertains to most of the Amazonian area: Despite the history of restrictions imposed on women, their situation has changed in recent years.

In fact, more and more women are demanding their rights, presenting proposals, and organizing their own political agenda (Adamson 1997, Armstrong 1995). During this process of organization, which is often referred to as a "movement", women in many indigenous societies have found support for their efforts within their own society or from other non-indigenous institutions. In the Brazilian Amazon, the women's formal organization, especially in pan-indigenous organizations, is much more recent, beginning in the middle of the last decade. Recent studies have shown that many indigenous women have advanced in terms of how they see their roles within their societies and in pan-indigenous and interethnic political context (Detén 1990, *Equal Means* 1991, Peixoto 1997, Sérgio 1997, Simonian 1997a, b, 200la). It is important to stress that, until a short time ago, the indigenous peoples in question were divided as a result of fragmented indigenous politics as well as external interference and pressure. According to N. Frank (1999, p.c.), it was only recently at a meeting on the 27th and 28th of November, 1999 in the Amajari region, that these indigenous women created OMIR – the Indigenous Women's Organization of the Roraima State.

I witnessed important moments of this organizing process when working on research in the Serra and Lavrado in Roraima in 1997, 1998 and 1999. I participated in two state meetings of indigenous women and a meeting of the regional council of CIR – Indigenous Council of Roraima, as well as a state assembly of the "tuxauas" – political caciques or local main leaders[1] – linked to this council. I have also participated in a workshop of arts and craft production held in the Maturuca village – indigenous women from neighboring villages also participated – as well as attending meetings with indigenous leaders from Brazil, Guyana and Venezuela and an indigenous delegation's trip to a women's meeting outside of the state of Roraima. I accepted an invitation to perform as an *ad hoc* adviser during the second Meeting of the Roraima State's Indigenous Women Movement "Maria de Guadalupe", and took part in a delegation that attended the Meeting of Women of the Forest (*sic*), held in the state of Acre in December 1998. In the course of my observations and interviews undertaken with eloquent female leaders and their assistants, I became thoroughly acquainted with the problems and progress.

The purpose of this chapter is to promote understanding of the potential, the present-day conditions, and the limits to the process of organization among indigenous women of the Amazonian area. My discussion will focus on the Movimento de Mulheres Indígenas do Estado de Roraima "Maria de Guadalupe". My impression, based on extensive fieldwork, underscores the persistence of these women from Roraima's Lavrado and Serra, especially that of a group of Macuxi

women from Serra, Surumu and Raposa, despite innumerable difficulties.

Women and Gender Relations

Historically there is evidence that women's political organizing among the Macuxi and the Wapixana from the Lavrado, and the Serra and other indigenous women of Roraima, date from a very distant past. Like many other indigenous peoples such as New Zealand's Maoris (Ofner 1993) and the Parakanã of the Brazilian state of Pará (Magalhães 1996), the women of Roraima may have participated in the indigenous resistance to the process of conquest, although no specific reference to this has yet been found.

Among the new directions in studies of women's political action in society, is that which demonstrates the structural conditions that promote women as social agents. Women's struggles in Third World countries begin when the subsistence base of their communities is threatened (Evers 1993, Nash 1994, Shiva 1993, Vargas 1995). Feminist studies indicate that women's empowerment through engagement in political action has promoted structural changes that improve subsistence levels (Mies 1993). Educated middle-class women have played an important role in demanding services that should be the responsibility of the government while also creating non-profit-making organizations to offer services to women who were poor or victims of violence. Also, many women from the lower classes took part in revolutionary movements that have influenced the processes of organization of indigenous women of the Amazon in recent decades (Hernández Castillo 1995, *Marie Claire* 1996). Nevertheless, the majority of women from newly assimilated indigenous populations, many of whom belong to Pentecostal Christian religions, as well as those who have migrated to the cities, do not benefit from or feel the effect of such changes.

The idea of empowerment is enlightening since the organizing process involves indigenous women who have historically been sub-ordinated. Some authors debate that women's subordination is a universal condition, asserting that this is a result of the impact of colonization and the introduction of patriarchy into aboriginal society (Etienne and Leacock 1980, Lea 1994, Leacock 1981). Indigenous women face intensification of domestic violence in the new conditions in which they find themselves (Azevedo 1985, Green 1992, Simonian 1994). Despite this history, many of these women have shown an extraordinary capacity to resist domination as they open new political spaces (Detén 1990, Green 1992, Hughins 1990). However, as Rowlands (1997) warns, it is fundamental to identify persisting tensions, conflicts, and the many forms of violence in gender relations in order to avoid a mythic view of women's participation in the political organizing processes.

Currently the questions that have priority in these organizing processes are mainly related to promoting support through national and international connections (Adamson 1997, Barrientos 1993, Chilangwa-N'gambi 1993, Rajamma 1993, Simonian 1997c, 2001a). It is necessary to go beyond these immediate issues affecting the survival of women's organizations to probe the potential growth, given the structural obstacles on the one hand, and the women's ability to establish connections and advancements on the other. I shall follow this line of thought in analyzing the process of organization of the indigenous women's movement from Lavrado and Serra's regions of Roraima analyzed here.

The evidence from our studies indicates a wide range of levels of organization that vary from those in which the indigenous women are well organized to those in which the women take part only on a local level. I shall attempt to identify the historical and cultural dynamics of this process that account for differentiation in the scale of organization.

Violence has spread since colonial times in Roraima, especially towards indigenous peoples, but in recent times it has intensified against the Yanomami and the Macuxi and Wapixana from the Lavrado and Serra regions. As the expulsions and violence spread in the Lavrado and Serra region, the political role of women emerged and became recognized. As the women consolidated their position in the local and domestic economy, from the 1970s onward, they took on a rear-guard action in defence of the land, while the men took the lead in resisting non-Indian farmers, gold prospectors, etc. (Macuxi 1997, p.c., Simonian 1997, f.n.). Women often became the victims of the conflict as shown in a story based on eyewitness accounts (Montanha 1994:68–70) of the rape of "Viviana" by a non-Indian bandit who humiliated her by forcing her husband and brother to witness the hideous act (see also Simonian 1994:102). The women's constant confrontation with violence and the drunkenness of family members contributed to building a conscious awareness of their need for collective action, particularly because of the many restrictions weighing down on them (Peixoto 1997, Simonian 1997a). This consciousness is cultivated in the activities in which these women have been involved in recent decades, such as catechism, teaching, and community activism. Most important, however, is the women's own effort and that of few allies, both Indian and/or non-Indian.

The Catholic Church has given its support for indigenous women to form a women-only group, albeit at a much later date than the support given to male leadership. According to a CIDR publication (1990:42–43), the "tuxauas" met for the first time in 1968.[2] From then until 1995, the few indigenous women who were present in those "tuxaua" assemblies were not allowed to speak or to vote, while other women were called but only to provide support by cooking and cleaning (Simonian 1997b, 1997–8, f.n.). Only long after that first assembly of male leaders held in 1977 was it possible for the women to have their own meeting (Peixoto 1997). The Indigenous Women of the State of Roraima "Maria de Guadalupe" movement held three state meetings between 1996 and 1998 (Peix-oto 1997, Raposo 1997, Sérgio 1997, Simo-nian 1997c, 1997–8, f.n.). At the end of 1999, as already mentioned, they met once with indigenous women from other move-ments, in order to create OMIR. As a conse-quence of this process, the importance of the indigenous women as political agents began to be publicly recognized.

The process by which these women have organized themselves into a movement in-volves four trends showing distinct levels of political participation from 1996 on, with a fifth tendency to appear in 1999. In the first trend, starting in 1996, indigenous women connected with the Catholic Church and the CIR formed a council in which they repre-sented the Women's Bureau. They consider themselves to be a part of CIR, although they mainly identify themselves with the "Maria de Guadalupe" movement. The second tendency began in 1997, as indigen-ous women from the Association for the De-velopment of Indigenous Women of Roraima (ADMIR) became linked to other indigenous organizations and associations, as well as to conservative non-indigenous political forces in Roraima. In the third tendency women took a distinct turn as they became involved primarily in their private interests and did not involve themselves with any sort of women's organization. The fourth tendency includes indigenous women who live in com-munities with little contact with non-Indian society and belong to Christian Pentecostal religions, or who, living in cities, find them-selves estranged from any process of political organization. These third and fourth trends cannot be identified through specific dates, as such indigenous women simply follow their everyday life without any interest in organ-izational processes. The fifth and most recent tendency appearing in 1999, incorporates both the organized Indian women in the "Maria de Guadalupe" movement with those linked to ADMIR and even those who live in indigenous territories, but find themselves distanced from any organized political process. Together, all these Indian

women are in the process of integrating within OMIR.

A complex mixture of factors has influ-enced this process. For example, not only do these indigenous women share in common in their individual and social conditions (Peixoto 1997, p.c., Simonian 1997–8, f.n.), but also in the changes forced by the action of the state and by non-indigenous societies. Among these forced changes are the democ-ratization of the state in underdeveloped countries, greater involvement from national and international institutions in those coun-tries, and in the politics of those nation-states; the democratization in contexts of more general indigenous politics, and the dis-semination of feminist and ecological thought (Brasileiro 1996, Simonian 1997c, Women's Studies Quarterly 1996). But, as a contradiction, the anti-indigenous politics and actions, in particular those concerning land and natural resources, have also influ-enced the political process of organization by these women. In this sense, Roraima is exem-plary, as the growth of a fifth tendency clearly demonstrates. This trend grew stronger with the fight in defence of Raposa/Serra do Sol "One Land" movement and the repossession of their land in I. L./ Indigenous Land São Marcos. What follows is an attempt to characterize the process of organization of the Indian women of Ror-aima in all their internal diversity and their conflict.

The Problems, the Connections and the Proposals

In their process of organization, Indian women of Roraima have highlighted a series of problems that moved them to search for contacts that could help them make their projects viable. These issues relate to their individual and communal identities, as well as to non-indigenous societies and to a state that practically ignores their existence. Amongst such questions are those concerning violence, the basis of subsistence, the prejudices faced and the difficulties in participating in decision-making processes (Peixoto 1998, p.c., 1997, Simonian 1997a, b, 1999). In searching for contacts to promote their cause, their possibilities have been limited, mainly due to the lack of financial and political backing on the part of their own societies, of the State, and of non-Indian society. Nevertheless, the recent creation of the Women's Bureau (CIR) and OMIR, has increased the chances of greater independence for women in their search for funding. The fight against alcoholism, the search for alternative ways to sustain the individual and the community, and the valorization and/or rescue of the indigenous language and culture are the movement's specific proposals.

The "Maria de Guadalupe" Movement of Indigenous Women of the State of Roraima

In January 1996, indigenous women who belong to the movement "Maria de Guadalupe" held their first state meeting in Roraima, in the Maturuca indigenous village or *maloca*, in the Serra region. At that time many women struggled to understand the significance of the experience they were living (Peixoto 1997), even though some, catechists and teachers in particular, already had participated in larger meetings. Previously the indigenous women only had one kind of organization, a type of "mothers' club", which was created in the 1980s and linked to schools with sewing and seamstress projects provided by the Catholic Church, by CIR, or by the state government (Peixoto 1997:1). Given the limited pan-indigenous organizational experience of these women, this external incentive was the only possible beginning.

From the beginning the process of organization was permeated with tension since the men, whether they were leaders or otherwise, questioned the women's organization and even feared the women could supplant them in positions of power (Peixoto 1997). No

agreement was reached in the "tuxauas" general assembly, held in January 1996, but a separatist movement by the women was underway within the communities, and the women who belonged to it wanted to form part of the CIR (Peixoto 1997–1998, p.c.). Backed by members of the Catholic Church, this movement managed to make its presence felt. Despite the kind of control discussed below, many tensions still exist in relations between this movement and CIR.[3]

An important moment for the consolidation of a more formal and systematic organization took place in 1995, with the annual meeting of the catechists linked to the Indigenous Pastoral section of the Catholic Church in the diocese of Roraima. According to Peixoto (1997) and Sérgio (1997), in that meeting, on the day for the discussion of the problems faced by the women five questions were posed to the group, namely: "How did indigenous women live in the past? How do the indigenous women live nowadays? What makes the indigenous women from the community unhappy? What do we expect the indigenous women of the future to be like? How can the indigenous women contribute, together with the men, to transform the indigenous society?" (Peixoto 1997:1, Sérgio 1997). In response, the women presented a drama with role-play based on those questions and answers, which they refer to as a starting point to the collective organization that ensued, when they began to think as a group. Therefore, that play came to symbolize the emotion and consciousness-raising experienced by these women.

Following this, the indigenous women linked with CIR and the Catholic Church also held three state meetings: the first one in Maturuca in 1996, the second in Taxi in 1997, and the third in Canuanin, in 1998 (Simonian 1997–8, f.n.). In these meetings, the women laid out the objectives and guidelines for the organization. During the first meeting in the Maturuca *maloca* three women received support from the communities and from CIR and the Catholic Church to attend with transportation and food provided. Apart from choosing a general co-ordinator and regional co-ordinators, these women made a work plan for the next twelve months. The plan included the following proposals: to spread and make more widely known the campaign "No to alcoholic beverages";[4] to restart and/or organize the sewing and seamstress groups; to undertake works to rescue the indigenous culture and language, and to search for self-sufficiency (Peixoto 1997). As trends, these proposals not only reflect an interest in the rescue and preservation of the indigenous culture but also in creating an opening for new experiences. To develop these proposals, the indigenous women would count on the moral and political support of their communities;[5] furthermore, especially CIR and the Catholic Church would back the women.

Despite the difficulties encountered by the women during the year that followed – resistance from the men, a lack of financial resources and transport, the women held a second meeting in January 1997, in the Taxi *maloca*, of the region of Surumu, attended by 107 women. As stressed in Fotonorte II (1998:165) and by Simonian (1997, f.n.), the words "We are responsible for the life of the people" announcing the Second Meeting sums up the influence that "Teologia da Libertação" (Liberation Theology) has on the theoretical basis for their organizing process.

During this meeting, the women were able to raise and analyse many issues that were occurring in the "malocas":

> "Many men do not want us to participate in the meetings, because if we go, we expose the problems we have with them, but we need to have courage to confront these men";

> "The majority of our leaders [for leaders, read male leaders] are involved in heavy drinking sessions";

> "Lack of respect is everywhere; yesterday, there was a man here criticizing the women for using feathers and dancing "Alelula." For example:

> "We have to go with our men, to take part with them"

> "There are men that only go to the fields when women force them to go";

> "We have to encourage the community to take the lead";

> "We have to have the courage to face the evil [men's alcohol problem], not allowing it to grow";

> "We are able to help our men and our youngsters";

> "Women have to respect themselves, the family, the community, and not do as many do when they betray their children and husbands by going to town seeking white men";

> "There are male and female Indians that do not want to assume their identity";

> " We have our rights, we cannot allow them [husbands and leaders] to humiliate us."

The list reveals the prevalence of gender relations problems with men of their own communities.

At the same meeting, the women also spoke of their accomplishments from the proposals made at the first meeting and explained why they had not been able to do more. For instance, the women from Cotingo Lower River stressed the problems they faced, especially the resistance from the men to their work. They said the men had been happy in the past, but with the arrival of non-Indians, Indian men started to drink more and more. All they want now is strong beverages made by women from fruits that they cultivate and collect, and after drinking they argue with the family, beat the women, and in some cases even abandon their wives and children. These women also mention that men's resistance increased after the women decided not to make strong beverages anymore.

In another *maloca*, the spread of alcoholism was considered alarming. At the same meeting, one of the women emphasized that alcoholic beverages were forbidden, but the traditional strong beverages were still produced, and that both the leaders and the catechists continued to drink, with alcoholism becoming rife. She also said that she did not agree with the situation, but felt she could not do much. Another woman reported that a "Tuxaua" himself brought crates of alcoholic drinks. On one of last occasions, when he brought alcohol, one of the woman's sons-in-law got drunk, had an argument at home, and when she went to tell the "tuxaua", he told her off, resulting in a fiery argument. "How can you, as an authority here, bring alcohol and even use the CIR's car to do it?" was the answer the woman gave to the abusive "tuxaua".

As a side note, according to what the indigenous women revealed at the Second Meeting, this kind of behavior on the part of the leaders and the ensuing arguments are commonplace in the *malocas*. Another example of the problems provoked by alcohol was when a "tuxaua" authorized the sale of a locally produced *cachaça* – aguardiente, or white rum – in the communal canteen. As a result, for a whole month the indigenous men kept drinking, missed work and got involved in all sorts of disturbances. Tension reached such a point that, in this *maloca*, the men asked the women to brew the beverages as they had decided to go hunting. Nevertheless, the men ended up not going and continued to disturb the whole community. The same "tuxaua" also wanted to reprimand the women. One of the women faced him saying: "You are drunk. Get sober before telling us off!" Thus, despite all the effort, the consumption of alcoholic drinks continues and is a disturbing factor for the families and communities.

Control of the consumption of alcohol has improved only in a few "malocas". In Camará, people commented that Christmas 1996 was a much happier time as non-Indian alcoholic beverages were not allowed, and many women do not brew the traditional drink any more. At the meeting, the women's co-ordinator gathered all the women together to discuss strategies to end the brewing of this kind of drink. But, according to her, it has not been easy as many men criticize the women and accuse them of being "gossips".

Some men argue that they do not want this sweet drink, as it is brewed on the same day

or the day before and it "gives you a belly-ache and diarrhoea." What the women want, according to their own statement, is more than just to forbid drinking, but to have "good fruit" [meaning to promote well-being, development] for the "malocas." The women want to prevent the men getting drunk because they "stop digging the ten or fifteen banana holes a day" (Simonian 1997, f.n.). In this sense, it can be said that the objectives of these women go beyond strict feminist objectives, as they are concerned not only with women's interests, but also with those of the community.

In general terms, at the end of the Second Meeting, the same commitments proposed in Maturuca in the previous year were maintained, which shows little progress as a result of difficulties faced by the women in carrying on their work. More precisely, the following proposals were ratified: No to alcoholic drinks; an increase in the sewing and seamstress works and indigenous art and crafts production; rescue of the language; work that leads to sustainability. Two of the women were chosen to accompany the CIR entourage to other states, which would be financed by the PPG7, in order to observe sustainable development projects (Simonian 1997a, c). And, according to what was shown during this indigenous women's Third Meeting, which took place in Canauanin, in the region of Serra da Lua (Pauta 1997, Simonian 1998, f.n.), the process of their organization has been very slow in their homes and *malocas*.

Among the reasons for the slowness of this process are relations with CIR, which continue to be very tense. At the "tuxauas'" assembly, which took place in Bismark in February 1997, the women publicly stood up against the interference of this Council (Simonian 1997b, 1997–8, f.n.). One of the CIR members, in an unauthorised interview to a newspaper from Boa Vista, gave inexact information concerning the "Maria de Guadalupe" movement. Taking this opportunity, the women reasserted their wish to be respected and heard, saying that they did not wish to create a separate association from CIR headquarters, as the newspaper had published. It was their intention to integrate into the Council and work side by side with the "tuxauas." However, due to the more recent setting up of OMIR, this perspective changed.

Despite their determination to carry on the fight, many indigenous women expressed discouragement in 1998. As it was then discussed, the women had little chance to carry out the plans elaborated in 1997. According to many of the women, they lacked resources and sensed a political willingness on the part of CIR and other institutions that backed them. Also, many of them lacked motivation (Simonian 1997–8, f.n.). Many of the problems raised at the Second Meeting were taken up again at the Third Meeting: alcoholism; a lack of support from husbands and "tuxauas"; economic and transport difficulties to carry out the proposals and to organize the work projects; persistence of tense relations with CIR, etc. (Pauta 1997; Simonian 1997b, 1997–8, f.n.). At the time of the meeting itself, a lack of transport resulted in the delay of some committee members with some even cancelling their journey. Asked about the possible advances in this process of political organization, a female church representative who had provided advice to the indigenous women said that advances had been made but only in the area of political connections. Yet, independent of such impasses, some of the meeting's achievements can be considered notable.

The advances that were possible occurred in very localized areas. In the Contão *maloca* for example, with the backing of the male leaders, the women succeeded in blocking the sale of alcoholic beverages in the bars and markets. In Uiramutã, the Macuxi of the Serra, with the support of many "tuxauas," held a public demonstration with the same object in mind. In this region, the indigenous women carried out a program of workshops of indigenous arts and crafts, and the sale of ceramic pots has been a success in the market fairs of Maturuca (Simonian 1997, f.n.). Two indigenous women also undertook journeys planned from the Second Meeting to visit projects involved with the sustainable extraction of natural resources. However, a point that again caused a bitter debate in the Third Meeting was the centralism of CIR, particularly in the face of the "Maria de Guadalupe" movement.

When asked to adapt their projects to gender questions in order to have them financed by international agencies, the Council's directory introduced a proposal for sewing and seamstress work in projects sent to three international agencies. However, the directory did not consult the leaders from the movement (Simonian 1997–1998, f.n.). So, the directory argued that the deadline to hand the projects over did not allow time for consultation, and since the women's meetings always proposed sewing and seamstress projects, the CIR did not feel there was "so much need for new consultation." Ultimately, points raised recently were taken up again by CIR, not allowing the indigenous women to be involved in the planning of these projects.

This incident allowed antagonistic positions to come about once more in the context of the organization of the indigenous populations. Some raised voices in the Third Meeting, even proposing the withdrawal of the project from the institutions that were financing it, in order to allow for more detailed debate. One of the indigenous women raised deeper issues, suggesting that the movement and CIR should promote work that took the indigenous culture into consideration, and not adopt projects from other cultures (Simonian 1997–1998, f.n.). She said: "... we don't need to look for techniques from the white people, we have our own techniques to work and advance." Whether this is a romantic or a utopian idea should be discussed in more detail; however, the group that considered that it was not possible to go back – despite opinions to the contrary – won the argument. At the time, CIR's finances depended on the granting of some resources, with the risk that these grants may not be approved, so there was little to be done except to remain silent.

In any case, greater participation with CIR was achieved, as the women's representative began to take part in the "bigger meetings" of the Council Body, which allowed for the presentation of proposals for changes in the Statute (Propostas 1997). A fundamental change happened with the creation of a Women's Bureau in this Council, which demanded the presence of a representative from the indigenous women in Roraima's capital itself. Although it was delayed until 1999 (Potiguara 1998, p.c.), even before the change came about, CIR again proposed the creation of an independent woman's organization. Consequently, the setting up of the Women's Bureau represented a strategy to guarantee further funding. Although the indigenous women of Roraima, in particular those that had links with CIR, had initially resisted the creation of an independent organization, the OMIR was created incorporating indigenous women who come from organizations other than the "Maria de Guadalupe" movement.

The Association for the Development of Indigenous Women of Roraima (ADMIR)

In addition to those indigenous women who have advanced to a more formal and systematic political organization belonging to the "Maria de Guadalupe" movement, a number of groups linked with organizations throughout the state were formed by the Wapixana, Macuxi and Capon tribes created ADMIR.[6] These groups are linked to the Roraima State government and the conservative political forces that sustain it (Simonian 1997b, 1997-8, f.n.), even though they have been participating in OMIR since 1999. With the federal government, which theoretically assumed a progressive trend as the PT–Workers' Party led the coalition that took power in January, 2003, changes may occur in Roraima's indigenous political milieu.

Anyway, women in these organizations also emphasize problems of alcoholism and the need to fight for the "development" of indigenous women. Among the proposals was a survey of the materials necessary to begin works such as arts and crafts, ceramics, indigenous medicine, sewing and dressmaking, native crochet, rescuing the language, and other cultural work. The mothers' clubs were to be organized and or restarted, so as to provide a base to carry out these works (Raposo 1997:1–3). This association moved closer to the "Maria de Guadalupe" movement as they looked forward to unifying their proposals. From a formal point of view a significant advance occurred, once a consensus was agreed to create OMIR.

The presence of indigenous teachers in the process of political organization plays an important role in leadership training. Although the number of indigenous teachers is fewer than a third of all 362 indigenous teachers (Sarmento 1998, p.c.), they play a role in OPIR – Indigenous Teachers' Organization of Roraima, which came into existence in 1991 and is currently directed by an indigenous woman teacher (Simonian 1997, f.n.) and in the catechist group of the "Pastoral Indigenista" of the Catholic Church. The recent coordinator of the "Maria de Guadalupe" movement is a retired national teacher, and belongs to the group of catechists just mentioned. Another teacher, Maria Lúcia da Silva Marculino, who is from the Contão *maloca*, was elected in the 1996 municipal election as the vice-mayor of Pacaraima, one of the municipalities of Roraima, which inclusively is located in the I. L. Raposa/Serra do Sol. Also in the same year, the male indigenous teacher Orlando Oliveira Justino, from the Raposa *maloca*, was elected to the same political position.

The indigenous women who take part in the group of catechists from the Catholic Church are active in local politics. With the church's support, these women have met annually to retrain and elaborate the yearly work plans in the villages (Simonian 1997–8, f.n.). At these meetings, the women get involved in art production and discuss politics in terms of their problems as women (Peixoto 1997; Sérgio 1997). Consequently, the women return to their *malocas* after the meetings with new ideas, including ideas about women's rights and their role in society. Clearly the establishment of the "Maria de Guadalupe" movement owes a lot to the catechists.

More noticeable still is the growing interest of indigenous women in the party organization, although resistance still exists. For example, in 1997 the majority of women from the "Maria de Guadalupe" movement who met at the Second Meeting proposed a boycott of the politicians and parties. Faced with possible intervention from CIR, which had encouraged indigenous people to stand as candidates for the elections, the movement's co-ordinating committee backed down from its threatened boycott. Despite this, few women are effectively affiliated with the political parties and no women were chosen as candidates in the last elections (Simonian 1997–1998, f.n., 2003, f.n.) Lately, the indigenous women of Roraima have also taken part in sporadic events or acted on an individual basis. Women connected to CIR and to the OMIR have taken part in business trips abroad and within Brazil.

Indigenous Women, Local Power and Disenfranchisement

Indigenous women who live in cities often find themselves equally distanced from any process remotely connected with organization, whether one that is linked to the general organization of the indigenous people or more specific to the indigenous women. The attempts of the Women's Nucleus of Roraima to get such indigenous women involved has not yet been successful (Frank 1999, p.c.). In any case, the number of these women who live in cities is significant. According to Pereira, in Boa Vista, where the indigenous population is estimated at 10,000, females account for 50 per cent of this number (1997, p.c.). These women city dwellers

work as maids, while many get involved in prostitution and the number of young single mothers is quite significant. Many of these indigenous women emigrated from Guyana to come and work as domestic servants. As a result, their participation in more formal processes of organization is very difficult.

A clearer understanding of indigenous women's involvement in politics within the *maloca*, or even in the city, is still to be researched. As these women play a significant role in the productive activities within their *malocas* and because of their increasing interest in finding solutions for local public issues and in discussing women's needs, it can be supposed that, at the least, their political role is relevant. In the cities, at least within the family, these women have political importance, however minimal, due to their contribution to the family finances.

It is still too early to say is whether the women who have stayed on the margins of a more formal political organization will integrate themselves within the recently created OMIR. This probably will happen if a joint effort from all those already involved in politics and more formal organizations is made to integrate these indigenous women. However, all kinds of resistance still exist, even on the part of those bodies that advise these women, such as the Catholic Church, the state and municipal administrations.

The Indigenous Women's Organization of the State of Roraima

The recent unification of the Roraima's indigenous women's process of organization through the creation of OMIR is still being discussed, but this unification has already influenced strategies to mobilize the women, forming what was previously identified as a fifth organizing tendency. Among the factors influencing this process are threats made by non-Indians and by the State from federal, state and municipal administrations to stop the demarcation of land boundaries of the I. L. Raposa/Serra do Sol and to hinder the withdrawal of non-Indians from the indigenous land of Roraima. In addition, the proposal for legislation that allows mineral extraction from indigenous territories, presently being debated at the Brazilian National Congress, has had an impact on unification.

CIR was also important to OMIR's creation. For instance, during the First Indigenous Women Coordinators' State Meeting held from May 26th to June 2nd 1999, CIR not only suggested the creation of an organization such as OMIR to the indigenous women, but also succeeded in implementing its proposal. Incidentally, the discussion process to create OMIR was accelerated (Proposta 1999, Relatório 1999), especially with the suggestion to hold a "committee meeting for the elaboration of a statute proposal for the organization of indigenous women of the state [sic] of Roraima". This took place in July of the same year and according to what was previously mentioned in this chapter, these meetings gathered indigenous women from political orientations other than CIR.

Within a short period of their existence, a statute proposal and a change in the CIR Statute were elaborated, and a discussion at a meeting in the *malocas* and with all the women was planned for November of 1999. Due to the speed at which everything had been happening, lots of doubts still persisted (Relatório 1999:3). Anyway, during July's meeting, a debate concerning the proposal for a statute for OMIR was suggested. At that time, a proposal was elaborated to change some articles from the CIR Statute (Relatório 1999:4–5), especially regarding the role of the Women's Bureau, which constitutes a part of CIR. OMIR's process of regularization/formalization was completed in 1999.

Little can be said of the future of this organizing tendency, but CIR and the indigenous women in charge of this process are showing determination. This Council will be partly released from the direct responsibilities regarding the indigenous women's organization. On the other hand, these women will have to have their wits about

them in order to avoid becoming just a "helping hand" to CIR. Their success will partly depend on the funding and resources they obtain and the quality of the advisors they choose.

Discussion: Between Impasses, Work, and Dreams

There are many socio-economic and political implications of the recent experiences of the indigenous women from Roraima's Serra and Lavrado. Among these are limitations faced by these indigenous women, such as a lack of resources, as well as a lack of information and organizing experience, opposition from relatives, from the communities where they belong, from the State and from non-Indian society. However, the persistence of the women themselves deserves to be emphasized.

The limits faced by indigenous women can be understood either in the framework of their society or in the post-conquest culture in which they live. In fact, pan-indigenous organizing processes did exist in periods before and during the European conquest but these processes were restricted to some regions and situations (Marientras 1982, Simonian 1993). Many indigenous social systems were, or are, also oppressive to women, with even the women themselves often accepting this situation (Abbott 1993, Simonian 1994). And, in fact, in the Brazilian Amazon as well as in other areas and countries, it is only in the last decades that the indigenous women have started to take part in more formal organizing processes backed by other sectors of their society or by non-Indian institutions.

A lack of knowledge of the country's official language, and of the Western schooling system in addition to a lack of information, or even a lack of financial independence, have been pointed to as some of the main difficulties responsible for hindering a more effective and systematic participation in these processes. The indigenous women of Lavrado and Serra have raised these points. According to what Lindalva Peixoto noted in 1997, the difficulties that many of these women experienced in taking part in the First Meeting of the "Maria de Guadalupe" movement were an indication of such limitations. In recounting North American indigenous women's experiences (Okanagan and Sioux), Adamson (1997) and Armstrong (1995) have pointed out similar issues to those faced by the Roraima women. According to Adamson (1997:10), it has to be admitted that without financial independence political organization is not possible.

On the other hand, the indigenous women's lack of knowledge of their own culture can be a limiting factor. In one of the recent indigenous women's meetings of Roraima's Lavrado and Serra, a woman from the Wapixana tribe said that nothing had been done to "rescue the mother-tongue" in her *maloca*, as had been previously proposed, because "... there wasn't a mother-tongue [read indigenous mother-tongue]" (Simonian 1997, f.n.). Also, this woman, whom I met not long after, had nothing to show from the proposed work aimed at benefiting the indigenous culture, and said that she would not take part in the movement any more since this did not interest her community. Amstrong (1995) resolved a similar situation by returning to her Okanagan nation and community after finishing university in order to learn more about the indigenous culture and be able to act more effectively on behalf of her community. Although such an attitude can be very important in some situations, in general the indigenous women of Roraima and even those from other places have not had a similar chance.

In the internal social arena and particularly domestically, various tensions and conflicts have kept women from a deeper and more comprehensive commitment. Faced with problems such as alcoholism and abandonment, many women end up having to provide for the family, which is increasingly affecting families and women, be they indigenous or otherwise (Eber 1995, Simonian 1993, 1994, 1997a, 2001b). Consequently, these women

find themselves not having time for their own affairs, or time to take part in women's organization or deal with general matters related to their communities. The situation is worse in Roraima because (as has already been pointed out) women cannot count, most of the time, on the support of their husbands, relatives or on the support of the male leaders (Simonian 1997a). Even though the "Macuxi" and "Wapixana" women have resisted the constant male drunkenness, this problem has considerably affected their potential and their capacity for political action.

The limits imposed by the male leadership or by organizations managed by the women themselves are other obstacles that these indigenous women have tried to overcome. In the "Maria de Guadalupe" movement these limits have become a "tradition", as frequent clashes occur due to attempts by CIR to control women's process of organization from the center. Nevertheless, this centralism is not limited only to CIR, but is a part of the status quo. Incidentally, queries raised by Stordhal (1990) and by Detén (1990) regarding the Suami and Peruvian Amazon Indians' control of indigenous politics reflect some instances of this centralism. Some while ago, a Shuar told this author that his indigenous organization "... didn't want the women's movement ..." among them, and were determined to hinder any project related to that. He claimed that this was to avoid conflicts (*sic*) at a local level (Simonian 1997, f.n./Ecuador). According to the written report (1997) of ADMIR's first meeting, it is possible to note great control exercised by the male leaders (Raposo 1997). One of these male leaders even wrote the final report, despite the presence of indigenous women who could both read and write. This kind of control and centralism reflects more general forms of domination practiced by indigenous men over the indigenous women themselves and their interests.

In relation to the restrictions imposed by non-Indians, including those imposed by the State over indigenous women of Roraima, the main restrictions are political and economic. The impunity for acts of violence and crimes committed against the indigenous population (Pereira 1996) has intimidated many of these women. For example, a Macuxi woman of the I. L. São Marcos recently stated that she did not have the courage to take part in the meetings as she was forced to stay alone, controlled by non-Indian invaders or by their hired men (Simonian 1997–1998, f.n.). In Boa Vista, the situation is one of great tension and violence amongst the indigenous people (Wapixana 1998, p.c.), which also constitutes an intimidating factor for the women there.

The lack of financial support from the State or other non-indigenous institutions is also a predominant factor affecting the organization for the women. Despite their efforts, these indigenous women live in conditions well below those considered minimal for a healthy and dignified life. Therefore, except on rare cases, it is practically impossible for these women to invest the little they have in organizing processes. When FUNAI/ Brazil's Foundation for National Indigenous, the Canadian Embassy and Brazil's Bureau of the United Nations' Commission on Women supported the First National Meeting of Indigenous Women held in Brasilia, in 1995 (Simonian 1995, f.n.), indigenous Brazilian women experienced a moment of hope, but this hope was soon dashed and the women did not even manage to hold the planned regional meetings afterwards (Kaingang 1998, p.c.). The indigenous women of the equatorial Amazon are experiencing similar difficulties. In Roraima, except for important support (even if local and restricted) from bodies such as the Catholic Church, and occasionally from FUNAI, there is no prospect of obtaining funds for changes considered necessary by the indigenous women in order to widen their capacity of organization.

Even when such a possibility of funding exists,[7] these women have rarely taken part in defining, elaborating and setting-up of these proposals. A critical view must be taken concerning the fact that these women's opinions were not heard, as the proposal presented was quite out of date in comparison to what has been discussed by the indigenous women from the "Maria de Guadalupe" movement. Also, when faced with low prices of commonly worn clothes, to continue with a sewing and seamstress project seems a limited option. In response to a question addressed to me in my *ad hoc* advisory role at the meeting held in the Taxi *maloca* and during the Tuxauas' Assembly in Bismark, both in 1997, asking what the indigenous people in general and the women in particular proposed in the discussion groups, I responded that it was something more sophisticated and wide-reaching (Simonian 1997b, f.n.). Among those proposals were: the need to have access to transportation to make the work in the *malocas* feasible; new technologies to exploit the natural resources and to process the products; the need for a higher level of schooling and for resources to raise awareness of the indigenous culture and language. According to the resolutions reached in 1997–1998, not only the centralism exercised by CIR became evident, but also the advisory help was outdated. The indigenous women succeeded in getting some financial help for the meeting at which OMIR was created from contacts encountered when a group of representatives of the indigenous women went to a meeting held in Acre in 1998.

Apart from these impasses, deeper divisions resulting from different political orientations have also proved to be difficult barriers to overcome. These divisions can be exemplified by various groups of women: one group linked to the Catholic Church and to CIR; another group linked to other indigenous organizations which maintain strong links with Roraima's government; finally, a high number of women who are either individually linked to local political activities or organizations or are even removed from such processes. According to what was previously seen, the recent process towards a unification of the organization of indigenous women of Roraima could alter this diversity of political orientation. In fact, if OMIR manages to establish itself, it is possible that the differences in the internal process of organization of these indigenous women will disappear.

According to what was forecast in 1997, regardless of such differences and faced with pressure on all fronts, it was considered likely that these indigenous women would end up meeting at the door of other financial institutions, of other possible allies and or allying themselves to each other, which is what actually happened. The meeting in May, June and July 1999 made this alliance possible. It is also known that the Catholic Church itself has been passing on control of projects to CIR, and is considering the possibility of withdrawing financing of many of Roraima's indigenous population's activities (Simonian 1997b, f.n.), which will complicate such processes of organization. However, as a result of new facts which have emerged, new ways are becoming feasible, from direct contacts with other financial agencies or even as a consequence of these women's activities, carried out with the intention of obtaining funding for this organizing process.

The close correspondence among many of their proposals enabled diverse groups to unite around a program of joint action. This unification of diverse indigenous associations in Roraima overcomes the difficulty of determining who represented the indigenous population that public authorities once claimed as the major hurdle in implementing policies (Simonian 1997–8, f.n.). Just as the dissemination of organizational processes has proven feasible, so has the unification of interests among indigenous women overcome factionalism and segmentation that had dominated the political process in the region. In fact, if the indigenous women of Roraima have had difficulties in reaching agreement – something in which women are not the exception – material conditions of living have brought them closer together. For example, there are many dissenting voices when it comes to the definition and regularization of indigenous lands.

The discussion concerning some of the current impasses in the process of organization of the indigenous women of Roraima demonstrates simultaneously how much they have advanced in terms of organization. Despite little outside backing, many of these indigenous women have persevered in organizing statewide meetings despite divergent political beliefs. When compared with the political process in other Brazilian states, and even countries, this amounts to an exceptional achievement. Precisely, between 1996 and the end of 1999, five state meetings were held, three by the "Maria de Guadalupe" movement and two by ADMIR. Despite many internal problems, the performance of many of the Serra and Lavrado women has been exemplary, mainly in the organization of workshops, land clearing, campaigns against alcohol, etc.

Even though there still are many impasses, and in general terms the advances have come with the making of connections with other groups (according to a religious adviser, the determination of many of these women may alter this outlook in the near future). According to what can be learned from the description and analysis of Detén (1990) concerning the experience of indigenous women of the Peruvian Amazon and of Vargas (1995) concerning the Peruvian women's movement in general, it is possible to overcome the difficulties.

The women of the world have organized themselves in search of alternatives to overcome the impasses resulting from particular social and historical constructions concerning women's condition as well as from general conditions for the human condition (Mies 1993). Although the United Nations (United Nations 1992, *Women's Studies Quarterly* 1996) has worked in this direction, there are many who find themselves left out of the organizing processes. Experiences such as those of the indigenous women of Roraima, of the Peruvian Amazon (Detén 1990), and of women from the Brazilian Amazon in general (Almeida 1995, ASMU-BIP 1999, Maneschy, Alencar, and Nascimento 1995, Pinto 1998, Quebradeiras 1997, Simonian 1986, 1997–8, f.n., 1997a), are sources of inspiration for any political proposals and actions.

What should be clear from any discussion concerning women's processes of organization is the necessity to guarantee both a formal and informal project of education that democratizes information. At the Beijing meeting, held by the United Nations in 1995, this issue was amply discussed as a central point (Binh 1996, Bonder 1996, *Women's-Studies Quarterly* 1996). In Roraima there is a lack of programs that provide information (and service), particularly to the indigenous men and women concerning issues such as health in general, the health of women, particularly relating to cancer and sexually transmitted diseases.[8] From this viewpoint, it is not possible to consider a process of change that does not guarantee the minimum conditions of education and health. There is also a lack of basic information available to these indigenous women regarding the sustainability of productive activities, the use of technology and adequate knowledge, and the capacity to carry out diagnostics and elaborate proposals for work and to negotiate loans.

The number of women in the Brazilian Amazon who do not know their basic rights, or the possibilities to organize themselves and demand even the most elementary political and public action, is still great. In fact, from the talks held at the 1996 Beijing meeting I demonstrated that for the Brazilian Amazon area, the question of the lack of information is paramount since it affects the majority of women there. Lacking information, it is difficult to guarantee any rights (Simonian 2001a). Anti-indigenous politics persist, on the part of the state, and of the non-Indian society and even of the many indigenous people who act against their own interests. However, since these women are courageous, the indications are that they will not retreat; instead it is likely that they will create new spaces to participate in, which could consolidate their process of organization.

Conclusions

Until recent decades, indigenous women of the Amazon have played a rearguard position in the fight against invasions of their lands and against the practice of all kinds of violence on the part of the non-Indian population. With the recent creation of OMIR, this tendency has a great chance to change. They have suffered not only the violence from the State and non-indigenous societies but also that of their husbands and male relations. When women began to meet in the *malocas* around the middle of the 1980s to set up sewing and seamstress projects, mother's clubs and others of that type, their discussion of a series of common problems contributed to the development of a political consciousness. Working with indigenous people of Roraima, the Catholic Church has contributed to the formal education, especially in the training of teachers and catechists, many of whom are women.

Despite the obstacles, the women have demonstrated growing effectiveness in their organizing. Up to the end of 1999, the indigenous women from Serra and from Lavrado held five meetings, three connected to the "Maria de Guadalupe" movement and two for those integrated within ADMIR. Other events have occurred on a local or a regional level, like workshops, fairs, regional, national and international meetings of indigenous women, working trips, etc. Recently, women linked to ADMIR have taken part in meetings with women connected to the Women's department of CIR, which resulted in the formation of OMIR. Yet the participation of indigenous women in the grassroots of working politics, including those from cities, is still limited.

Internal divisions and tensions have permeated this process of organization. In fact, it is not just the ideological and pragmatic directions that differentiate them, but also resistance from their husbands and relatives and even from larger indigenous organizations. Men's involvement in the process of organization cannot be undervalued, especially if the success of OMIR is to be given priority. These women have also felt the impact of the State's anti-indigenous policies and of the non-Indian society whose effort has been to annul or disrespect the basic rights already recognized, such as those rights relating to education, health and access to the necessary resources for productive activities etc. As the issues that are the essence of the indigenous women's situation are of a structural nature and, therefore, far-reaching, OMIR will find it difficult not to integrate itself in interethnic and party political mobilizations.

Considering the persistence of these indigenous women in overcoming structural limitations, it is clear that they will be able to become financially independent, thus being capable of undertaking a more active role in all levels of politics. The unifying of indigenous women's struggles from Roraima's Serra and Lavrado was noticeable from the middle of the 1990s in many of their proposals but, except on rare occasions, their ability to join together to carry them out has been limited. Yet, there is hope for the future, as these women have already advanced in this direction. The very uncertainty over their territorial rights and the scarcity of resources, together with issues concerned with their identity as women and questions of gender have brought women closer together.

NOTES

1 A "tuxaua" is the indigenous chief of a "maloca," or village.
2 It was from 1997 that these meetings started to be held annually and became assemblies. It was also from then on that the *tuxauas* started to use the whole length of the meeting to raise issues, and discuss and approve common proposals.
3 The origin of this separatist movement of women is disputed. According to Peixoto (1997:1), the "Maria de Guadalupe" movement started on July 3, 1986, with the sewing and seamstress project, which

was created by the regional councils of CIR During the Third State Meeting of this movement, held in January, 1998, the general coordinator, Lindalva M. Peixoto, told another version of the movement's origin, but without giving more substantial details. She said, precisely and succinctly, that "this movement [was] much older," based on information she had received from the testimony of the missionary Jorge Dal Ben, a priest connected to Consolata mission who lived among the indigenous population of Serra of Roraima for more than twenty years (Simonian 1997–1998, f.n.). Thus, regardless of any contribution that this missionary gave to a more precise understanding of the beginning of the aforementioned movement, it is evident that the movement became more visible and politically consistent from 1996 onward, after the women's meeting held in Maturuca.
4 See Simonian (1997a) with regard to this campaign.
5 In respect to this, during a mass celebrated by the Catholic bishop Dom Aldo Mondiano, a woman asked people to pray so that "the women do not lose their fear of denouncing the abuses they suffer" or, in other words, do not lose the courage (Simonian 1997, f.n.).
6 Especially APIR/Association of the Indigenous People of Roraima, ARIKOM/Regional Association of Indians from the Kinôr, Cotingo and Monte Roraima rivers, SODIU/Society in Defense of the Indians from the North of Roraima, and the TWM/Society for the Communal Development and Environment Community of the Taurepang, Wapixana, Wai-Wai, Macuxi and Maiongong. It is important to note the recent creation of innumerable associations, such as ARIA/Regional Indigenous Association of Amajari, ARTID/Regional Association of the Indigenous Workers of Roraima, ARIAM/Indigenous Association of Maú Upper River, etc.
7 For example, the aforementioned proposal on the interests of the indigenous women presented to international agencies by the CIR.

8 I raised this question (Simonian 1997–1998, f.n.) at the Second Meeting of the "Maria de Guadalupe" Indigenous Women's Movement and suggested the presence of one specialized advisory service for the next meeting. This actually happened at the Third Meeting, but did not have the desired effect.

REFERENCES

Abbott, L.
  1993. Interview. *In* Local Heroes. H. Chryssides and Lana Abbott, eds. Pp. 141–169. North Blackburn: Collins Dove.

Adamson, R.
  1997. Interview with E. Cabral. Cover story: Rebecca Adamson. Ford Foundation Report. Spring. Pp. 10–13.

Almeida, A. W. B. De
  1995. Quebradeiras de coco-babaçu: identidade e mobilização. São Luis: III Encontro interestadual das Quebradeiras de Coco Babaçu.

Armstrong, J.
  1995. Interview with D. Thorpe. The spirit of the people has awakened and is enjoying creation through us. Native Americans (Fall):50–53.

ASMUBIP/Associação das Mulheres Quebradeiras de Coco do Bico do Papagaio
  1999. Dados coletados no arquivo da Associação. Sete Barracas.

Azevedo, M. A.
  1985. Mulheres espancadas. São Paulo: Cortez.

Barrientos, S.
  1993. The other side of economic success: Poverty, inequality, and women in Chile. *In*: Women and Economic Policy. B. Evers, ed. Pp. 38–40. Oxford: Oxfam.

Binh, N. T.
  1996. Invest in education of women. Women's Studies Quarterly 24(1–2): 110–111.

Bonder, G.
  1996. From quantity to quality: Women and education in the platform for action. Women's Studies Quarterly 24(1–2): 84–90.

Brasileiro, A. M. (ed.)
  1996. Building Democracy with Women. New York: UNIFEM.

Chilangwa-N'gambi, C.
  1993. Investment finance: Off limits for women. *In*: Women and Economic Policy. B. Evers, ed. Pp. 40–41. Oxford: Oxfam.

CIDR–Centro de Informação Diocese de Roraima
  1990. Índios e brancos em Roraima. Boa Vista: Col. Histórico-Antropológica, 2.

Detén, R.
  1990. Experiência de las mujeres nativas en la Amazonía peruana. *IWGIA*. Mujeres indígenas en movimiento. Copenhague, n.11. pp. 49–55.

Eber, C.
  1995. Women and Alcohol in a Highland Maya Town. Austin: Texas University Press.

Equal Means
  1991. Wilma Makiller wins her re-election. n.1. p. 13.

Etienne, M. and Leacock, E. B., eds.
  1980. Women and Colonization. New York: Praeger.

Evers, B., ed.
  1993. Women and Economic Policy. Oxford: Oxfam.

Forline, L. C.
  1995. A mulher do caçador: uma análise a partir do caso Guajá. *In*: A mulher existe? Estudos sobre a mulher e relações de gênero na Amazônia. L. M. M. Álvares and M. A. D'Incao, eds. Pp. 57–79. Belém: M. P. Emílio Goeldi.

Fotonorte II
  1998. Amazônia: o olhar sem fronteiras. Rio de Janeiro: FUNARTE. pp. 164–165.

Frank, N.
  1999. Personal communication. Boa Vista.

Green, R.
  1992. Women in American Indian Society. New York: Chelsea House.

Hernández Castillo, R. A.
  1995. De la comunidad a la convención estatal de las mujeres. *In*: International Work Group for Indigenous Affairs No. 19. La explosión de comunidades en Chiapas. Nash, J. et al., eds. Pp. 57–67. Copenhagen: IWGIA.

Hughins, J.
    1990.   La mujer aborigen australiana y el
    movimiento de liberación de la mujer.
    International Work Group for Indigen-
    ous Affairs No. 11. Mujeres indígenas
    en movimiento. Pp. 37–47. Copen-
    hagen: IWGIA.
Kaingang, R.
    1998.   Personal communication. Brasília.
Lea, V.
    1994.   Gênero feminino Mebengokre
    (kayapó). Cadernos Pagu 3:85–116.
Leacock, E. B.
    1981.   Myths of Male Dominance. New
    York: Monthly Review Press.
Macuxi, J. A.
    1997.   Personal communication. Taxi
    Indian village.
Magalhães, A. C.
    1996.   Mulheres e política entre os Para-
    kanã. Trabalho apresentado na Mesa
    Redonda "Mulheres Indígenas", do II
    Encontro Amazônico Sobre Mulher e
    Relações de Gênero, realizado em abril,
    em Belém, sob os auspícios de GEPEM-
    UFPA.
Maneschy, M. C., E. Alencar and I. H. Nas-
    cimento
    1995.   Pescadoras em busca de cidadania.
    In: A mulher existe? Estudos sobre mul-
    her e relações de gênero na Amazônia. L.
    M. M. Álvares, M. A. D'Incao, eds. Pp.
    81–96. Belém: MP Emílio Goeldi.
Marie Claire
    6.   Elas desafiam a morte para erguer um
    sonho na selva. n.16. pp. 39–44, 46, 48.
Marientras, É.
    1982.   La resisténcia india en los Estados
    Unidos. México: Siglo Vientuno.
Mies, M.
    1993.   The need for a new vision: The
    subsistence perspective. In: Ecofemin-
    ism. M. Mies and V. Shiva, eds. Halifax:
    Fernwood.
Montanha, V.
    1994.   Os bravos de Oixi: índios em luta
    pela vida. Uma estória baseada em fatos
    reais. Petrópolis: Vozes.
Nash, J.
    1994.   Global integration and subsistence
    insecurity. American Anthropologist
    96(2): l–31.

Ofner, S., ed.
    1993.   New Zealand Women in the 19th
    Century. Auckland: Macmillan.
Pauta do III Encontro Estadual das Mulheres
    Indígenas de Roraima/Maloca Canaua-
    nim/ Serra da Lua
    1997   Canta Galo. Novembro 9.
Peixoto, L. M.
    1997.   Memória sobre a fundação e
    desenvolvimento do movimento das
    mulheres indígenas de Roraima. Boletim
    Avulso. Boa Vista.
——1997–1998. Personal communication.
    Boa Vista.
Pereira, E.
    1996.   Roraima: um estado de violência
    institucionalizada. In: Povos indígenas
    do Brasil/1990–1995. Pp. 166–168. São
    Paulo: ISA.
——1997. Personal communication. Boa
    Vista.
Pinto, J. N. A.
    1998.   Novos atores em cena: organização
    e mobilização das mulheres dos rios Par-
    uru e Manoel Raimundo, PA. Monogra-
    fia de especialização. Belém: NAEA-
    UFPA (Curso de Especialização em Popu-
    lações Tradicionais na Pan-Amazônia).
Potiguara, P.
    1998.   Personal communication. Boa
    Vista.
Proposta de estatuto: Organização das Mul-
    heres Indígenas de Roraima/OMIR
    1999.   July. Roraima. Mimeo.
Propostas para reforma estatuária
    1997.   Boa Vista: CIR. 1 p.
Quebradeiras expõem em Belém
    1997.   Informe fax 5. Brasília: GTA. pp. 2.
Rajamma, G.
    1993.   Empowerment through income-
    generating projects. In: Women and
    Economic Policy. B. Evers, ed. Pp. 53–
    55. Oxford: Oxfam.
Raposo, C. A.
    1997.   Relatório das Mulheres Indígenas
    de Roraima, realizado na maloca do
    Milho (em 28 de Janeiro). Aldeia do
    Milho. Mimeo.
Relatório do Encontro da Comissão de Ela-
    boração da Proposta de Estatuto da orga-
    nização das Mulheres Indígenas do Estado
    de Roraima

1999. Boa Vista. Mimeo.

Roosevelt, A.
1991. Mountbuilders of the Amazon. San Diego, CA: Academic Press.

Rowlands, J.
1997. Questioning Empowerment. London: Oxfam.

Sarmento, Z.
1998. Personal communication. Boa Vista.

Sérgio, P.
1997 Mulheres indígenas: primeiros passos para uma organização estadual. Projeto experimental. Boa Vista-Roraima. Vídeo documentário.

Shiva, V.
1993 The Chipko women's concept of freedom. *In*: Ecofeminism. M. Mies and V. Shiva, eds. Pp. 65–82. Halifax: Fernwood.

Simonian, L. T. L.
1986 Babaçuais e trabalho feminino no PNRA: à guisa de uma proposta. Brasília: Mimeo.

——1993. "This bloodshed must stop": Land claims on the Guarita and Uru-Eu-Wau-Wau reservations, Brazil. Ph.D. Dissertation, City University of New York.

——1994. Mulheres indígenas vítimas de violência. *Cadernos do NAEA*. n.12. pp. 101–114.

——1995. Mulheres seringueiras na Amazônia brasileira: uma vida de trabalho silenciado. *In* A mulher existe? Uma contribuiçao ao estudo da mulher e gênero na Amazônia. Pp. 97–115. Belém: MPEG.

——1997. Field notes. Puyo, Ecuador.

——1997a. Mulheres indígenas de Roraima discutem alcoolismo. *Porantim*. Maio. Pp. 5.

——1997b. Mulheres indígenas de Roraima e seu II encontro. *Folha de Boa Vista*. 16 de janeiro. pp. 2.

——1997c. Mujeres y desarollo en la Amazonía brasileña: resistencias, contradicciones y avances. *In*: III Jornadas Internacionales Amazónicas (Puyo). G. M. Restrepo, ed. Pp. 55–73. Quito, Ecuador: CEDIME/UNICEF.

——1997–1998. Field notes. Roraima.

——1999. Terras indígenas no contexto do PPTAL: T. I. Mãe Maria, São Marcos e Ureu-wau-wau. *In*: Demarcando terras indígenas: experiências e desafios de um projeto de parceria. C. Kasburg and M. M. Gramkow eds. Pp. 65–82. Brasília: UNAI/PPTAL/GTZ.

——2001a *Mulheres da floresta amazônica*: entre o trabalho e a cultura. Belém: NAEA/UFPA. 270 pp. Il.

——2001b Familia en la frontera Amazonica: idealizaciones, contradicciones y tendencias actuales. Papers do NAEA, Belém, no. 158, Pp. 1–30.

——2003 1998–1997. Field notes. Roraima.

Stordhal, V.
1990 Por qué son tan pocas? International Work Group for Indigenous Affairs No. 11. Mujeres indígenas en movimiento. Pp. 57–76. Copenhagen: IWGIA.

United Nations
1992 Global action for women towards a sustainable and equitable development. Report of the UN's Conference on Environment and Development. Vol. 3. Rio de Janeiro. Pp. 5–10.

Vargas, V.
1995 Women's movement in Peru: Rebellion into action. *In*: Subversive Women. S. Wieringa ed. Pp. 89–100. London: Zed Books.

Velthem, L. H. Van
1996 A mulher indígena e o trabalho artesanal em São Gabriel da Cachoeira. "Paper" apresentado na Mesa Redonda Mulher Indígena, do Encontro Mulher e Modernidade na Amazônia, uma promoção do GEPEM-UFPA. Belém. Mimeo.

Wapixana, J.
1998 Personal communication. Boa Vista.

Women's Studies Quarterly
1996 Theme issue. Beijing and beyond: Toward the twenty-first century of women. 24(1–2):154–158.

17

At Home in the World: Women's Activism in Hyderabad, India

Deepa S. Reddy

The Indian women's movement has been shaped over time by several political and intellectual influences, from nineteenth-century social reform, to Maoist/Marxist revolution in the 1940s and 1950s, to the rise of identity politics and religious nationalism in the 1980s and 1990s. During the different periods of its evolution, what pre-Independence social reformers called the "women's question" has inevitably been posed in relation to several overlapping concerns. In the context of the struggle for Independence, for example, addressing the problem of the status of women was simultaneously a means of responding to the colonialist charge that Indian women were deified but downtrodden (Chatterjee 1989, Sinha 2000). Later generations of Indian women activists have, as we shall see, consistently read Western feminist and other writings, but have always tailored their praxis to the specific needs of local communities. In other words, gender-focused activism has always, albeit to varying degrees and in varied ways, straddled the boundaries between the internal and the external, the traditional and the modern, the local and the global.

It is hardly a coincidence, then, that Indian feminists responded as early as the 1970s – a full two decades prior to the formal liberalization of the Indian economy – to issues which are generally associated, in whole or in part, with the twin forces of industrialization and globalization: growing commercialization, the wholesale import of agency models of development, the rising prices of basic commodities, import and export policies, ecological devastation, and so on. At the time, feminists debated how much each of these were properly "women's issues," but through these very debates arrived at an understanding of what Susie Tharu would later describe as the centrality of gender to "our social architecture" (Tharu 1990:63). By the time of the Union Carbide leak in Bhopal, the pressing issue for Indian feminism was less one of definition and more one of organizing priorities: as critical as it was to lend support to groups representing the victims of the gas leak, the practical implications of becoming involved in all such people's agitations were so overwhelming that activists began to feel the need for a radically transformed praxis. No less critically toward the end of that decade, the dramatic decline of communism in Eastern Europe and the rise of Hindu religious nationalism in India together forced a rethinking of the ways in which the women's movement had conceptualized such categories as "class" and even "women." No longer, it seemed, was it possible to think of women as a unified group, nor even to understand social difference primarily in terms of economic disparity. The result of thus coming to terms with both the practical limitations of activism as well as significant challenges to its established theoretical models was a greater emphasis on Women's Studies research and writing, and a far less direct involvement in grassroots activism. From this point onward, the activist organization itself becomes more research-oriented, concerned with keeping in step with national and international academic programs in Women's Studies, and fashioning itself as a node that links grassroots organizations to the wider worlds of research, inter/national funds, intellectual exchanges and, indeed, global activist networks. In other words, the newly emergent activist non-governmental organization (NGO) begins to function within, and indeed to take advantage of, the very globalized terrain whose underside it continues to study, analyze, and sharply critique.

This critique, however, although no less stringent than in the past, now has a somewhat altered place in activist discourse. The changing fortunes of Marxist/class analysis in combination with the multiculturalist turn of Indian feminism makes it that much harder for activists to organize over specific *issues*: even questions regarding the most basic rights are sometimes complicated by groups who emphasize instead the right to cultural difference. Having grown themselves increasingly conscious of their privileged social positioning, activists now tend to leave the specific articulation of social issues and goals to the communities in question, be these rural, caste-based, or minority. One of the sharpest criticisms of globalization is that its impact is differential, enabling some while

greatly disenfranchising others. The emergent activist NGO certainly offers the established critiques, keeps a close watch on new encroachments and analyses their ramifications. In general, however, it is far more cautious about intervening, instead allowing local communities to define their needs, oftentimes facilitating their access to – but still advocating their rights within – rapidly expanding global marketplaces.

Using an example from Hyderabad, I trace the history of evolving praxis that has brought Indian feminist activism to this present juncture, and has led to the establishment of the modern, institutional activist NGO. Betty Wells's distinction between "globalization as the context in which organizing occurs and as the focus of organizing" (2002:142) is especially relevant to this discussion, for the organizations that I describe are among those that draw upon global resources and networks even as they focus on globalization as an object of critique. In this, they are also involved in establishing mechanisms to ensure women and local communities the access to information, funds, and support on various levels, thereby enabling their greater political participation as they enter – willingly or otherwise – increasingly global landscapes.

Pre-Emergency Activism: POW

Although nineteenth-century articulations of the "women's question" provided an initial model for social reform, it was predominantly Maoist/Marxist ideology that first gave the modern women's movement its motivation, ideology, and format. Nearly twenty years after Indian Independence, and despite sweeping land reforms, feudalism had still not been dismantled, and slackening economic growth was fueling the cynical view that the only ones to reap the rewards of *swaraj* (self-rule) were capitalists, landlords and, of course, politicians. At the same time, the volatile spirits of revolution seemed to infuse the Indian atmosphere. Hyderabad had already witnessed the Telangana Armed Struggle against feudal zamindars and the Razakars, the notorious old guard of the Nizam's army, between 1948 and 1951.[1] In West Bengal, an uprising of workers in the tea gardens of the northern countryside near Naxalbari would lend its name to several other communist uprisings in other parts of the country: to this day, "Naxalism" remains synonymous with communist revolution to some, and with terrorist activity to others. In eastern Andhra Pradesh, the Srikakulam Girijan (tribal) struggle of the late 1960s, organized by the (then undivided) Communist Party of India (CPI), demanded an end to practices of extortion and land-grabbing by landlords and forest officials, marking perhaps the beginnings of the Naxalite movement in the state. Young radicals in Maharashtra's Dhule district formed a group called the Sharamik Sangatana (or "Toilers' Union"), and organized tribals who had been dispossessed by Gujar landlords to recover their lands. Four thousand acres of land were returned to tribal control as a result of this agitation in the early 1970s. Again in Maharashtra, a rise in commodity prices brought on by conditions of drought and famine led to the formation of the United Women's Anti-Price-Rise Front under the auspices of the CPM (Communist Party–Marxist) and the Socialist Party. Eventually spreading to neighboring Gujarat, the agitation came to be known as the Nav Nirman movement, and was influenced greatly by Jai Prakash Narayan's concept of "total revolution": "fighting to reform as well as to limit State power, arguing that *rajniti* (State rule of law) had become corrupt...and the time for *lokniti* (people's rule of law) had come" (Kumar 1993:103). Narayan's ideas also had a huge impact on students and organizers elsewhere in the country: at a time when, almost routinely, the state seemed to respond to popular movements with force and violence, Narayan's own "Citizens for Democracy" movement strongly opposed what he saw as an increasingly dictatorial political system, by that time under Indira Gandhi.

Activist work in Hyderabad was centered around the campus of Osmania University, inspired to a great extent by perspectives and strategies developed elsewhere in the country. Some students had even left their colleges to participate in the Srikakulam Girijan struggle, just as their Bengali counterparts did to go to Naxalbari. The Progressive Democratic Students' Union (PDSU) – a group with connections to the CPI – was especially active on campus, for example, organizing students around the Anti-Price-Rise issue in 1973. Associated with the PDSU were a group of six women, who had their first experience of participating in a wider struggle in the Anti-Price-Rise agitation, and who were beginning to feel the need for a separate group to address women's issues. As women they "discovered they had to face different barriers to their participation from the [men] – families who tried to hold them back, the weight of socially inculcated femininity which made it difficult for them to have self-confidence, the complete lack of understanding of the men in the movement about all these problems" (Omvedt 1980:50, specifically of the group in Hyderabad). In 1974, these women activists began discussing the need for a separate women's organization. As K. Lalita, herself a member of that group, writes: "the principle response of male students was that it was anti-Marxist to have a separate women's organization; that women are not a class by themselves; that only an economic revolution would ultimately and automatically emancipate women" (Lalita 1988:58). In their classes these women students were reading everything from Marx and Marxist literature on the one hand to Kate Millett, Betty Friedan, Simone de Beauvoir, and Germaine Greer on the other.[2] Their approach was overwhelmingly leftist, but they saw no contradiction between the need for class revolution and the need to organize as women. The group that was formed in September, 1974, calling itself the Progressive Organization of Women (POW), in fact both separated and connected the oppressions of class and gender in its draft manifesto: "The majority of Indian women are slaves of slaves.... They are slaves to the men who are themselves slaves to this exploitative economic system. It is thus necessary that we women take a direct, leading role in organizing the masses of women in their struggles for a better life and a changed system" (quoted in Omvedt 1980:50).[3]

And so, out of the specific difficulties of being involved in a radical mass movement, emerged what was perhaps the first autonomous women's organization of the modern Indian women's movement. As a loosely defined adjunct to the PDSU, the group had already begun work on women's issues, and this continued with greater momentum for about a year after POW was formally established. The group organized against dowry and "eve-teasing" (the harassment of women in public places), and embarked on a militant anti-obscenity campaign. They again participated with the PDSU in a second series of Anti-Price-Rise protests, marching alongside women from Hyderabad slums, banging empty *thalis* (stainless-steel plates) with spoons as they went. Holding all along that a strong women's movement could not develop without a solid working-class base, the POW began a *Bastee* (slum) Services Committee to involve laboring women and address their specific needs. In several districts of the Telangana region, smaller POW organizing committees were soon formed, and at least one of these is still functioning (and was recently involved in the anti-arrack agitation that brought prohibition to Andhra Pradesh in 1992).

The Emergency

In the meantime, however, a crisis was slowly building at the center of Indira Gandhi's government. Student strikes and mass protests were rocking Gujarat and Bihar. Jai Prakash Narayan and Moraji Desai (Mrs. Gandhi's one-time colleague) had joined forces under the new Janata Morcha (People's Front), in protest at government corruption and Mrs. Gandhi's purported ineptitude. Then in June, 1975 the Congress lost a crucial by-election in Gujarat (Desai's State), and at around the same time the Allahabad High Court found Mrs. Gandhi guilty of electoral malpractice during her previous Lok Sabha campaign. Rather than be forced to resign, on the advice of her younger son Sanjay, Mrs. Gandhi persuaded President Fakhruddin Ali Ahmed to declare a national Emergency.

Politically, this meant that almost every opposition leader was either jailed or kept under house arrest, along with several prominent journalists, lawyers, and educators. The press was severely censored. To address the country's poor economy, Mrs. Gandhi then announced a "twenty-point program" directed at reducing inflation and punishing tax-evaders, smugglers, and other "real" criminals. Wages were frozen, and pressure applied in government enterprises to increase discipline and efficiency. Sanjay Gandhi – who held no public office at the time – was charged with the responsibility of monitoring newspaper leads and editorials, and he initiated a birth-control program that required sterilization for all families with two or more children.[4] On the economic front, things began to look up: prices came down, and production indexes were rising dramatically. Perhaps because of these economic gains, or perhaps because Mrs. Gandhi knew she would eventually be forced to seek electoral mandate for her policies, she called an election in 1977. Both she and her son Sanjay lost their bids for Lok Sabha seats, and a Janata Party government was formed with Desai once again at the helm.

In India today, most people seem to remember the Emergency as the period when all the trains ran on time. Some men remember getting ready to be sterilized, as per the requirements of Sanjay Gandhi's birth-control program, but few among the middle class recall fear, despair, or facing any more than the usual levels of difficulty. Even politicians in opposition regard their time in jail as a not-too-trying rite of passage that marks them now as veterans of sorts, linked by the experience of incarceration to other national-ist leaders jailed arbitrarily by the British. For student leaders, protestors, and other activists associated with leftist parties, however, the 20 months under Emergency rule were anything but normal. The CPI–M/L (Marxist–Leninist) was one of 26 political parties and groups banned by the government under Emergency policy. Since nearly all members of the POW were by that time card-holding members of the M/L Party, they too became the targets of police suspicion. Charged with being a front for a much larger underground organization, POW members were intimidated, and at least three had been arrested for no apparent reason by the beginning of 1976 under the MISA (Maintenance of Internal Security Act). Jumping bail or anticipating arrest, several POW and PDSU activists went underground with the support of the Party, leaving homes and families overnight and disappearing for nearly two years to safe-houses or traveling to the North, where they could not be easily recognized or found.

Post-Emergency Activism: Stree Shakti Sanghatana

It would be well-nigh impossible for me to describe here the impact of the Emergency arrests on the women activists involved without myself adding (perhaps unnecessary) flavor to the description. Suffice it to say, therefore, that the experiences of the Emergency changed lives and altered relationships to such an extent that the POW could never again come together as an organization. But the fact that the POW did in fact have a post-Emergency successor – a group called Stree Shakti Sanghatana, or Stree Shakti for short – brings me to a larger question that needs to be posed at this juncture: what was the impact of the Emergency on the future of social activism? There is a fair amount of literature on the Emergency itself: on the constitutional/legal aspects, the political repercussions, Sanjay Gandhi's birth-control program, and even on police tactics and

treatment of prisoners during that period, but nothing – quite surprisingly – on activism, even though activists as a group were among those most affected by Emergency crackdowns. Since I do not have room here to address such a question in detail, however, I offer only a few preliminary thoughts as a means of tracing the links between the pre-Emergency POW and the post-Emergency Stree Shakti.

The most substantial and significant fallout of the Emergency was a virtual burgeoning of civil liberties work all over the country. Most civil rights/civil liberties organizations functioning in India today have their origins during or around that period.[5] From the APCDRC[6] (a precursor of the APCLC[7]), formed in response to state repression of the Srikakulam struggle, to the PUCL/PUDR,[8] convened in Delhi at the height of the Emergency by Narayan and other members of the opposition; from people's groups from Assam to Kerala, the most stunning effect of the Emergency seemed to be a deepening consciousness of civil and democratic rights. In May 1977, the Janata government appointed Retired Chief Justice J. C. Shah as the head of a committee to investigate excesses and malpractice carried on during (or just prior to) the Emergency. In the previous month, Narayan (functioning as President of his "Citizens for Democracy" group) had already appointed a committee to investigate "encounter" deaths in Andhra Pradesh that occurred during the same time. The Tarkunde Committee, as it came to be known (after its chair, V. M. Tarkunde), comprised nine lawyers, journalists, and civil rights activists, four of whom were from Hyderabad.[9] Amongst these was K. G. Kannabiran, a lawyer with an interest in civil liberties, already well known at the time for his work on "extra-judicial" killings in the Srikakulam struggle, and poised to begin pleading a series of sedition and conspiracy cases lodged against revolutionary activists and writers of the Left. Above all else, and especially to the growing community of civil rights activists represented by such figures as Kannabiran, the Emergency provided irrefutable evidence of the repressive nature of the state apparatus. Although the PDSU/POW combine had directed some of its anger against the government and "ruling classes" – an approach very much in keeping with its leftist leanings – the events of the Emergency shifted the focus from corruption and government hypocrisy to outright repression. The context, in the months after elections were called, was one of concentrated civil liberties activism. And the focus of *all* activist attention was the state, now understood to be an inherently repressive body. So subversive were activist attitudes toward the state, that when a judge asked K. G. Kannabiran how Naxalites could lay claim to their civil rights when they rejected the Constitution, the lawyer replied: "in such circumstances it is not *their* beliefs which are on trial, but *ours*" (quoted in Kakarala 1993:301, my emphasis). Around the same time as the Tarkunde Committee began functioning, other activists who had been jailed or had gone underground were beginning work once again, and many of them with the APCLC. And so from this work and these associations, sometimes through husbands or through friends, another group of women came together in 1978 to form Stree Shakti Sanghatana.[10] The context of civil liberties activism from which the group emerged stamped Stree Shakti as a post-Emergency formation in this important sense. Its activism, although gender-based, would remain almost exclusively state-focused for some years to come.

The impact of the Emergency is evident also from the changed relationship of the women's organization to the M/L Party and to the broader left community. Activists seem to have been well aware that party connections were what landed the POW in so much trouble during the Emergency. As K. Lalita writes:

without taking into consideration the preparedness of the women [cadres] to partici-

pate in political struggle, [the POW] exposed itself to repression by regularly associating with left-wing student organizations, which gave [the agents of state power] an excuse to intimidate the POW members.... Ultimately by going underground and becoming "illegal," the main organizers of POW attracted even more repression... when the organization was still too weak to withstand this assault. This was the reason for its disintegration during and after the Emergency. (1988:67)

So if a break with party politics had not been crucial in pre-Emergency days, it was crucial now, for an activism based on women's issues could not function according to party dictates or under what had amounted before to party supervision. Members of Stree Shakti were clearly aware that the Party, in spite of its claims to the contrary, had not been internally democratic: it had marginalized women and gender-specific concerns, and privileged those occupying leadership positions over the general cadre. In an effort to distance itself from party work and party formations, then, Stree Shakti decided deliberately to avoid mass organization, which would inevitably "absorb and neutralize" the very concerns that the group sought to address. Members opted instead to keep the group small, with "a loose structure where all women could work according to their capacities": a necessary move equally because all members had their own jobs and careers (many as teachers and educators) to balance alongside activism (Kannabiran 1986:602). Further, to avoid any other form of external control, the group decided *not* to seek funds from outside sources. This meant that for the seven-odd years that Stree Shakti was active, funds for its upkeep came mostly from group members, with a small component coming from donations (on which also there was a cap of 100 rupees). Stree Shakti members then consciously attempted to ensure that the group functioned as democratically as possible, leaving no one out of the decision-making processes.[11] The group had two halves, as it were: one English-speaking, vocal, and articulate, and the other Telugu-speaking and somewhat less vociferous. Again, anxious not to allow language barriers to become either impediments to group participation or the implements of dominance, all conversations that took place in English were scrupulously translated into Telugu, and eventually discussions naturally took place in a mixture of both languages.[12]

Yet the break with the Party was not, and indeed could not have been, a clean one: party politics may have been rejected as exclusionary and undemocratic, but Marxist ideology remained *the* source of inspiration and sustenance for activism. As two Stree Shakti members would later write, "our proximity to the Left provided us with analytical tools and a broader political perspective that many of us felt was invaluable for our growth ... [we] looked towards the progressive Left sections for support, and were extremely anxious to emphasize the *Marxist* component in our Marxist-feminist approach..." (Kannabiran and Shatruguna 1986:25, 24). As a result, Stree Shakti activists eventually found themselves under considerable pressure to support any and all issues "publicly articulated in a manner with which we fully concur" – be these agrarian or environmental movements, or other people's struggles (such as those emerging in Bhopal after the Union Carbide leak), that may or may not have had anything specifically to do with women or gender issues (26). Refusing to become involved in such wider movements meant being branded anti-Marxist or bourgeois. "Attempts to co-opt us," the activists would complain, "have alternated with attempts to decry us" (26). The emancipatory potential of Leftist ideology in practice was clearly a limiting factor, and the tension between Marxism and feminism could only complicate other matters: "when women with rightist assumptions came into the group in its early stages, we were troubled not only by their disruptive influence on the group but also about the image we would present to the public – our public

being, of course, the Left" (25, Kannabiran 1986:602). For years after its formation, then, Stree Shakti would feel the twin pressures of its ambiguous relationship to the Left: on the one hand being watched, monitored, and urged at times to return to the "correct path" and on the other justifying itself, its actions, and its perspectives to friends and associates in leftist groups (cf. Kannabiran 1986: 601–2).[13]

Campaigns

Beyond its relationship to the intellectual and political Left, Stree Shakti saw its role fairly simply, "in the field of propaganda and conscientization," to publicize and politicize women's issues (Kannabiran and Shatruguna 1986:24).[14] As Sara Evans writes of incipient feminist activism in 1967 Chicago, "In typical new left style their first impulse was to get the word out, expose the situation – women's oppression – and call on women to mobilize" (1979:199). But which issues were women's issues? Clearly rape was one. In 1975 a verdict was handed down in the Mathura rape case: the two policemen accused of raping the 14-year-old Mathura were acquitted because the rape was determined to be "consensual intercourse." Stree Shakti did not come together specifically to rally around this case, as did several other groups: Vimochana (Bangalore), for example, and the Forum Against Rape (which would later call itself the Forum Against the Oppression of Women, Mumbai). But when the group began functioning in 1978, case upon case of police rape or other forms of custodial rape were coming to light, and the group almost naturally converged on those, in part because they were working with other groups to lobby for amendments in rape law,[15] but more I think because it enabled a critical focus on the state. In the group's own words,

> here the "battle lines" were already so clearly drawn. [In] other cases of rape and

gang rape, we found it difficult to articulate the question of rape and its implications publicly. *Our background and our political connections made it almost mandatory to focus on police violence*...Police or custodial rape was an issue that had already been articulated for us in a political context, whereas ordinary rape seemed an issue fraught with misunderstandings with which we were not yet ready to deal. (V. Kannabiran 1986: 605, emphasis added)

Other issues clearly identified as gender-based were family violence, dowry death,[16] and contraception. On family violence, Stree Shakti wrote and produced a film with director Deepa Dhanraj, entitled *Idi katha maatramena? (Is this only a story?)*, and around the same time also developed a play on the subject for street performance. The group's involvement in cases of dowry death led to the formation of the Dowry Death Investigation Committee, an adjunct group established largely in an attempt to allow other women not directly part of Stree Shakti or uncomfortable with the group's political perspectives to contribute their strengths and their energies to the effort. In reality, however, women not directly part of the Stree Shakti core group were always involved in one campaign or another; the group's functional looseness easily allowed such outside participation.

But if the inclusion of different perspectives within Stree Shakti allowed the group to adopt a wider range of strategies and tackle a wider range of issues, it did not ultimately alter the largely state-focused nature of the group's activism. This is not to say that Stree Shakti deliberately drew all its battle lines in opposition to the state; rather that the state invariably appeared among the final objects of feminist critique. In cases of dowry death, for example, much attention was focused to be sure on the family as the site of violence against women. But these were equally cases of murder dressed up to look like accidents or suicide, attracting therefore very little police attention and fore-

closing any real possibility of prosecuting the victim's family for the crime. If the state was not this time the direct perpetrator of violence, its personnel and machinery were certainly complicit with those responsible for the deaths of the women involved. To take up a case of dowry death, then, was to collide headlong with both the patriarchal family and the patriarchal state. Interestingly, a similar perspective emerged from the campaign against the use of the injectable contraceptive Net-Oen (Norethisterone Enanthate). What began as a journey to Patancheru (just outside Hyderabad) to stop a scheduled drug trial among rural women would end with an understanding of contraception and family planning as tools of state population-control programs. It became clear that government initiatives were driven less by a concern for women's rights, and more by dire predictions of exploding population in the Subcontinent (and, interestingly, in other select places in the world, such as China and even Puerto Rico); that they were less concerned with assisting in individual family planning decisions than with implementing aggressive population-control measures, at least partly in response to international pressures. As Susie Tharu would later comment, the campaign led the group to the argument that "there is *no* contraceptive that is a feminist contraceptive."[17] Assisted by the Delhi-based Saheli, Stree Shakti, five medical doctors and a freelance journalist with an interest in women's health joined forces to file a writ in the Supreme Court to prevent further Net-Oen testing in India. Their efforts yielded tangible results: further testing of Net-Oen and Depo Provera (both injectables) was banned.[18]

Such perspectives as I am describing may appear commonsensical to us now, but they were anything but self-evident at the time. And they would become indelible in feminist praxis. If the state was no longer easily identified as *the* enemy, it remained still one among many powerfully inimical forces with which women (and women's groups) had to contend. In the context of the continuing Naxalite movement in Andhra Pradesh, activist groups never really lost sight of the overtly repressive character of the Indian state that made its first appearance in Naxalbari, Srikakulam and then again in the Emergency. But they would additionally come to identify the state and state ideology with other, more covert, systems of oppression: patriarchy, religion, and caste. How did such perspectives develop? I would argue that this was part of a growing trend in feminist activism to see all issues as women's issues on one level or another, and each social concern as fundamentally linked to myriad others. Looking back at the 1978 Anti-Vegetable Export Campaign, for example, it becomes clear that such an integrative approach was not always part of feminist politics. Failed rains were driving food prices skywards, and yet vegetable exports to the Middle East were continuing unabated. A wider forum of activist groups and the women's wings of some political parties rallied immediately around the issue, but Stree Shakti – at first in any case – had reservations about joining this campaign. The central question for the group was this: *Were vegetable exports a women's issue at all?*[19] It is difficult to say what exactly may have resolved Stree Shakti's doubts at the time, but in retrospect, activists do not hesitate to name the vegetable export issue as *obviously* a concern for women. As vendors running businesses in competition with wealthier individuals or partnerships, *and* as consumers responsible for managing household budgets and buying vegetables for daily meals, women would have been among those most acutely affected or burdened by vegetable shortages in the country. There was no question that such apparently unrelated things as international exports, national economic policies, and women's daily lives were in reality intimately linked, nor any doubt that fortunes in the international market were made at women's expense.

In part, of course, the emergence of integrated approaches were products of Stree Shakti's Marxist heritage, that at the very least discerned the mutually constitutive nature of "economy" and "society." If Stree Shakti began with the assumption that the oppressions of gender could not be collapsed with those of class, the group moved eventually towards a greater understanding of gender oppression as the specific product of the collusions of power on multiple levels, both local and global, and not just as an incidental outcome of Indian tradition. In this emerging discourse, the "state" – increasingly now a conceptual category rather than a literal reference to the police – became a device that *enabled* an integrated approach, while itself remaining a primary object of critique. The character of state-focused activism was markedly different from what it had originally been, although its direction remained very much the same.

The Politics of Personal Struggle

Militant, radical, articulate, and visible, it was not long before the name Stree Shakti was synonymous with women's activism in Hyderabad. Stree Shakti members now remember with amused incredulity people arriving at their doorsteps in the early mornings with some concern or some new case, demanding immediate attention. Or dashing off for a few hours to pursue a case, and returning before the morning was over to classrooms and careers. The group would meet after work for a brief conference and then disperse, often to police stations, investigating or following up one case or another. When they finally reached home again at 10 P.M. or later, husbands would be pacing outside, young children waiting within.

Of course the development of a more integrated approach in feminist activism did not mean that Stree Shakti could – or would – get involved in every issue it came across on the logic that *somehow* it must have specific implications for women. By the group's own admission the area of women's oppression was gray and uncharted, and the directions of Stree Shakti's activist work were never entirely fixed. I make this last remark not to criticize, but to draw attention to a set of unresolved – and indeed perhaps irresolvable – questions that would eventually lead to the group's dissolution in the mid-1980s. Lines already quoted earlier in this chapter are worth repeating in this context: "How much longer can we keep on with wife-beating, dowry death, and rape? Should we set up crisis centers to help? Should we be a social service or a political organization?" Other questions about theorizing, reflecting, documenting, and deciding how much of a component each of these should be in political activism were also persistent concerns – naturally, for a group of women who were themselves college-level teachers with research interests of their own. The central question – *What kind of group should Stree Shakti be?* – was one that was never fully answered. To some extent, it could not have been: there were no precedents, after all, no tested and tried models to work with for Indian feminism at the time, and much uncertainty about the exact nature of work the group would be involved with. Activism just had to be devised and learned along the way. Each member was to contribute according to her capacity, in time, money, and effort, and the group was to remain a "loose" aggregate rather than a formal institution. But if organizational "looseness" enabled a much-needed flexibility, it also effectively was a rejection of any comprehensive attempt at group definition. And this factor would, in time, begin to pose some specific difficulties.

In the absence of formal decisions on agenda, which issues and which campaigns would Stree Shakti decide to take up? Would they get involved with movements as far removed from Hyderabad as the Narmada Bachao Andolan (a movement against the damming of the Narmada River in Maharashtra) and the incipient struggles in Bhopal, the site of the deadly Union Carbide gas leak? How, in any case, would they relate to those and other movements in the country, and indeed, in the world? In Hyderabad itself, on what basis would they choose one rape

victim or one case of dowry death over another? And then, once they became involved, how far would this involvement go – and what did they expect to come out of it? For all their energy and enthusiasm, the group was frequently left with little sense of achievement. In 1978, for example, the group got involved with Rameeza Bee's case – possibly one of Hyderabad's most publicized police-rape cases – but the constant media attention and virtual harassment eventually led Rameeza to withdraw the case and claim that the rape never took place. The case was eventually tried (and the accused policemen acquitted), but Rameeza Bee's modified stance came as a blow to the group. Who or what were they representing – and at what cost was their activism forged? There were also those families who merely wanted the group to get jewelry back from estranged in-laws, or parents who wanted their daughters kidnaped from husbands' homes. How was the group to limit the reach of its activism, and where was it to draw the lines? And then, after all was said and done, what would be left, what would be the outcome of all this ceaseless activity? "The challenge that any movement provides to the individual," Vasanth Kannabiran would write, "is measured perhaps in terms of personal growth. When one begins to feel that there is no longer any scope for growth in certain kinds of action, then where does one go? If we as a group continue to act without broadening our perspective, then what is the price?" (Kannabiran 1986:612).

Stree Shakti's approach to such questions as emerged from its work is reflected, I believe, in the phrase used to frame its discussions at the time: "the politics of personal struggle." Under this heading was placed everything from activists' individual accounts of struggle and growth with and within the group, to speculations on why some women may have felt uncomfortable, to broader theoretical understandings of what constitutes the realm of the "personal" and how it should be the primary locus of women's activism. This was the first time Stree Shakti as a group – deeply self-conscious in some ways from the very outset – sought to re-examine and recast itself in the context of the new questions and new difficulties it was increasingly having to face. As such, the discussions on the "politics of personal struggle" mark a turning point for the group, the start of a much longer process of articulating and rearticulating the need for a modified activism. Consider, for example, Susie Tharu's characteristically eloquent delineation of the "personal" as it figures in even the most mundane of social issues: water. I quote at some length from a talk she gave at the start of the Third World Women's Film Festival, held in Hyderabad in January, 1986:

> If we consider the women's question as it has been legitimated today, it has by and large been legitimated at levels which exclude the personal. Let me explain. Most people – politicians, planners, social workers – would agree that water is a women's issue. They would also agree that price and the availability of food is a women's issue. Or, let me put it another way, and there is a distinction – that water is an important issue for women since women are primarily responsible for the household economy. In fact I'd say that today to speak about women and water, to organize women to demand for water, would by and large be regarded a laudable thing. What the world would seem to be saying is please work on the issue of water, on the issue of price rise. If you do that, the chances are that you will stay within the *traditional articulation of the problem*. [W]hat you will *not* ask is what does a scarcity of water mean in terms of a woman's time, her work, her health, the amount of water she herself gets. Who is it who will wash her clothes less often, forgo a bath, and perhaps even a drink if there is less to go around? Who is the only one skilled enough to scour the pans when there's a shortage of water, who reorganizes her life to make sure she is at the communal tap on time, who keeps her ears constantly perked for the trickle that will start at night? Who is held responsible for the new tensions in the

> family? Whose are the friendships jeopardized in the long, tiring queues at the tap? What does an economy of water centered on her show us? How do we estimate the cost of all this and how does it change the way we pose the question of water, the way we estimate its value or the criteria for its allocation? How can this knowledge be built into the politics of water? And who does it? I have yet to see something written or said about water which reckons with the problem of what water is for women, and what its political dimensions become when women are included in an analysis of the question. (Tharu 1986:2)

Tharu's call for a radical, non-traditional articulation of women's issues comes at an interesting moment in the evolution of Indian feminist praxis. As I have suggested, this is a moment when Stree Shakti is discovering and confronting the boundaries of its activism, wondering perhaps about what has concretely emerged from all the years of frenetic activity. The group's dissatisfaction with its methods and approaches, however, was not in fact a reflection on its achievements. Quite the contrary, "[o]ne must acknowledge," writes Tharu,

> that in the last seven or eight years, as a result of a great deal of effort through campaigns about the Rape Bill, about dowry deaths, about family violence, about media depictions of women, and the subtle exclusion of women from development programs, *perceptions have altered*. The "suicides" so common among young wives, for instance, are no longer simply attributed to their inability to adjust or to their arrogance. No longer is this perceived as merely a *personal* problem. Considered in itself, or in terms of its immediate payoff, this is indeed a major achievement. (Tharu 1986:1–2, my emphasis)

The "major achievement" of which Tharu speaks, however, comes with a new problem. The very fact that "perceptions have altered" means that the "women's question" is now one that is legitimated by none other than "politicians, planners, and social workers": representatives of government and bureaucracy who have thus far been, in one form or another, *the* object of activist critique. The success of the women's movement in establishing the centrality of women's issues also throws activists into a deeply unsettling collusion with the powers that be, compelling them therefore – for the first of many times to come – to seek out new sites for an activism which must at all costs remain radical. A liberal state and a liberal society have accepted, broadly speaking, the brutal reality of dowry death and made it a crime, understood the horror of custodial rape and made it a crime, but have refused to look any farther: "you can do anything you like to a woman, this means, so long as you don't beat her – or burn her, of course" (fieldnotes 3). The liberal articulation of such issues is equally what Tharu calls "traditional" (fieldnotes 3); so activism undergoes a fundamental transformation when activist use of the language of liberalism has reaped some of its rewards and found some of its limits, and state use of the language of liberalism powerfully takes over. "The whole politics of the family in which questions of dowry deaths ought to be framed; the politics of sexuality and power from which the problematics of rape take on a rationality, the politics of marriage, which is different from the politics of the family, in the light of which we have to understand wife-beating" (fieldnotes 3) – these become the complex excluded realms of the "personal" in which a revived radical activism must locate itself.

It is at this juncture, then, that Stree Shakti ceases its ("traditional") activist work and becomes a Resource Center for Women's Studies called "Anveshi," which appropriately means "search" or "quest." It would be glamorous, of course, to think of this as a transition defined exclusively by ideological shifts and intellectual growth, but clearly it was also a time when personal life intervened as never before. On the one hand, were the interests of career, and professional growth

and advancement. In some sense, "Anveshi" had already begun functioning years before the idea for such a center was actually born, in the form of a research project on the life stories of the women who took part in the Telangana Armed Struggle between 1948 and 1951. The result was a book – "We Were Making History..." *Life Stories of Women in the Telangana People's Struggle* (1989) – Stree Shakti's best-known work, and an important contribution to the field of women's history.[20] For Stree Shakti, living and working in urban areas of the same Telangana region of Andhra Pradesh, this project was in no small measure genealogical. The group would write that the histories of those other women "constituted, as it were, the basis of our attempt to recover for ourselves a tradition of struggle"; that it represented a means to "reclaim a past and celebrate a lineage of resistance and growth, for to be deprived of a past is to inherit an impoverished present and a future sealed off from change" (Stree Shakti Sanghatana 1989:258, 19).

Somewhat ironically, however, working on the Telangana book – and a second project to "Indianize" and translate into Telugu *Our Bodies, Our Selves*, brought out years before by the Boston Women's Health Collective[21] – seems to have kindled more of an interest in writing *about* struggle than in shaping struggle from the ground, more of an interest in women's studies and the behind-the-scenes activism from the academy than in being part of a movement. So on the one hand were the changing interests of Stree Shakti members, a new kind of excitement derived from the success of the Telangana book, and on the other, that consuming exhaustion with activist work that demanded everything and returned disproportionately small dividends. Five women with careers of their own could not continue this running around, they said; Stree Shakti belongs to nobody, so other people should take over. But who would step in to take the reins? The looseness of the group had effectively blocked the emergence of an institution that could function even after its heads retired or withdrew. There were no predetermined processes for decision-making, no formal allocation of responsibilities, only the informal consensus of five women on which all activity had to turn. And so it was that the group which was supposed to belong to nobody or to everybody, actually belonged *only* to these women. Cases continued to come in, and since they could not in good conscience be turned away, work continued unabated. The sense of tiredness deepened.

Institutions

It is by now 1986. Punjab has long been the site of rebellion and terrorism, and in the aftermath of Indira Gandhi's assassination, anti-Sikh riots in New Delhi have awoken some among the intelligentsia to the stark realities of religious/ethnicist tension. Hindu–Muslim conflicts, too, have been escalating in several parts of the country since the start of the decade, but only sporadically, and it seems without the intensity of the Delhi riots. So it will be some months still before religion drops like a stone into the hands of the women's question, before the furious debates on minority rights and multiculturalism make it impossible to chart the "personal" as an area of oppression and radical feminist politics when it has so clearly become a protected area of identity and *not* a bastion that can be raided. So far there has only been gender, and class. But now feminists will have to face all the old questions in new light: How do you theorize the "personal" when it becomes the site of religious expression? How do you speak in the language of liberalism for women's rights when not just the state but the Hindu nationalist wings of government are talking the same talk? In sum: how do you understand the individual and the local when both are increasingly produced by the far less individualized, in some ways far more global, politics of community and cultural difference?

With such questions emerging gradually in the background, the processes of institu-tion-building begin in Hyderabad. Osmania University gives Anveshi a space from which to function: an old staff house, tucked into the western edge of the campus, surrounded by a large, lush garden.[22] Anveshi's library is in the process of building up a collection, the Telangana book is published in 1989, and no longer are people finding copies of old Stree Shakti fliers with phone numbers printed on top, calling for help. By 1990, Susie Tharu and K. Lalita, working with a team of regional language editors and several others, finish editing a two-volume anthology of women's writing in ten different Indian languages, translated into English. *Women Writing in India* (Volume I: *600 B.C. to the Early 20th Century*, 1991; Volume II: *The 20th Century*, 1993) is intended, like the Telangana book, *not* merely to add the contributions of women to the corpus of Indian literature, but more to "begin a reconceptualization of what it has meant for women to be writing at the margins of the complex histories of patriarchy and empire" (Tharu 1990:62). And then Susie Tharu formally introduces Anveshi to a wider Indian academic audience:

> Everyone in Anveshi is broadly speaking working in the field of education. Among us are writers, artists, journalists, people working in adult education, scientists, researchers and activists drawn from different institutions in Hyderabad.... Most of us have one foot in Anveshi and another in a mainstream educational organization. But when we came together to form this center, we came as people who had been involved in the everyday rough and tumble of the movement; as people who had experienced its tensions, its contradictions, its unexpected advances, and had many demands to make of scholarship, many questions to ask of knowledge, many problems to think through. We came as people who realized that the task of grounding feminist interventions in the soil of our particular history and our society required that we raid the academy." (Tharu 1990:60)

The period between the dispersal of Stree Shakti and the formation of Asmita appears to have been one of upheaval, both personal and professional, for many of the activists involved. Stree Shakti's absence inevitably created a vacuum that needed filling, at least for some of the women involved, but neither was there any nostalgia for Stree Shakti-style activism, nor apparently any predetermined idea of what alternative model would operated more effectively. Some of this indeterminacy is signaled by the fact that the activists soon became involved with other forms of activism, other activists, and other organizations: with the Deccan Development Society (DDS, a rural development organization working with village communities some distance from Hyderabad); the Confederation of Voluntary Associations (COVA, allied with the DDS, which works to empower the urban poor and promote communal harmony in Hyderabad's old city); Maithri, a women's organization, to name a few. None of these associations would prove permanent, however, for reasons which activists are often unwilling or hesitant to address, and although the DDS and DDS-COVA continue to function with somewhat distanced relationships to one-time Stree Shakti activists, Maithri no longer exists.[23]

Some six years later, however, even as associations with other organizations and models of activism were still evolving, another group of women would begin Asmita in Hyderabad's twin city, Secunderabad. Only two of this group – Vasanth Kannabiran and Kalpana Kannabiran – had any links to Stree Shakti.[24] They style this organization as a "Resource Center for Women" and so also distance it from Anveshi's exclusive women's studies research focus.[25] Asmita seeks to provide, among other things, the *resources* of an activist group (legal aid and legal counseling, for example, or research and documents) without limiting its focus on gender to the issues raised by individual cases. Both Anveshi and Asmita today claim to draw together women – several

hundred women – from diverse backgrounds, with different interests and different needs, and all with individual reasons to form associations with women's groups. Both are funded largely by foreign sources;[26] both fund research projects; both organize seminars at local and national levels, for both English and Telugu/Urdu-speaking audiences; and both conceive of themselves quite literally as "spaces" to which women may turn, whatever their reasons or their needs.

This styling of the women's organization as a broad and inclusive "space" could well be the hallmark of the modern Indian feminist NGO, in Hyderabad as indeed elsewhere in the country. As such, it also defines the modern Indian feminist NGO as a *public institution*: no longer is it assumed that all women will feel comfortable meeting in the private space of someone's house. Neither are such personal(ized) environments sufficient to accommodate larger numbers of women, nor are these spaces regarded as conducive to broader, possibly more uncomfortable, dialogue. As such, institutional "space" becomes a prerequisite for theorizing the complexities of gender in the modern world, and the means by which to connect local communities to the wider worlds of research and intellectual discourse, funding, global activist networks, and more. The differences lie perhaps in the qualitative nature of the spaces that institutions seek to create. On a day-to-day basis, Anveshi is part library, part academic department, functioning much like any other but without the control of any academic institution. Much of its work is conducted by subcommittees which discuss, write, and sometimes organize workshops on issues of interest or contemporary relevance.[27] Its members sometimes take on active roles in specific initiatives organized by other NGOs (although here again, their interests are frequently research-oriented), but the organization as a whole remains at some distance from these. Quite literally, Anveshi is a retreat from the turmoil of the city, from the burdens of university policy, and from the irrepressible pushes and pulls of the movement: a place to read, reflect, discuss, write. Asmita is somewhat more a place of business, an institutional node linking people and groups to each other and to sources of information: lawyers to women in need of legal counsel; students to mentors and reference material; women writers and artists to other women with similar interests, and in common facilities available for their use. Asmita also functions as an information base, most significantly for other NGOs or community groups working in the area, providing everything from booklets about the nuclear tests, liquor consumption, and the Women's Reservation Bill, to recorded cassettes of songs about the movement, and posters with catchy slogans on a variety of themes. It has worked with educational institutions to strengthen and de-link Women's Studies teaching from its associations with the "Home Sciences," in particular by conducting a Summer School in Women's Studies for research scholars. Both Asmita and Anveshi are women's "spaces," then, to varying degrees and at varying moments retaining the flavor of the movement or acquiring that of an academic department.

Predictably, if somewhat ironically, given Stree Shakti's organizational looseness, it is not Anveshi but Asmita that has become more obviously corporatized. In July, 1998 Asmita moved into its impressive new offices on the top floors of a residential building in Secunderabad. The new office had been carefully and meticulously designed to see to the needs of the various women involved in running Asmita on a day-to-day basis, including those of the women with disabilities hired to answer telephones. Somewhat more visible than this logic of design, however, are the trappings of the corporate office, including a designated reception area, multi-line phone system, the best in office furniture, and separate conference room and work areas for members of the Asmita Board. With corporate hierarchy built into its office floor plan, diversity built into its institutional ideology, "networking," "professionalism," "accountability," and "conflict management/reso-

lution" are increasingly terms that help describe Asmita's refashioned feminist praxis in the jet-set world of the modern institutional NGO. The realities of informal functioning, however, have not disappeared: sketches of small groups of women sitting on the floor in tight circles intently engaged in discussion, or of traditionally attired women holding hands or dancing in celebration of "sisterhood" continue to appear frequently on office bulletin boards. Combined with the corporatized appearance and functioning of the organization, then, these indicate the multiple levels at which the modern women's NGO operates: from *basti sangams* (community organizations) and Mahila Chaitanya Jatras ("festivals" organized to reach the Dalit – a movement of the lower castes for social justice and political representation – and other women in rural/agricultural communities on the one hand, to national women's studies research conferences and ranges of international congresses on gender, education, and NGO-related issues, on the other.

The institutionalization of activism notwithstanding, Asmita's apparently open embracing of corporatized structure has provoked critical comments. Asmita might have responded by saying that an open hierarchy, with clear channels for the expression of difference and predetermined processes of conflict management, is preferable to a set-up in which also authority operates, but does so invisibly and therefore far more harmfully.[28] The debate is not mine to settle, however, and I bring it up here only to note that the legacies of Stree Shakti's decisions live on in ongoing debates about what kind of institutional structure is best suited to activist work of the kind that is now necessary.

At Home in the World

What kind of activism *is* now necessary? It would be no exaggeration to say that events of the late 1980s and early 1990s – the Mandal-Masjid years, so-called after the anti-

Mandal agitations and the BJP's Babri Masjid campaign[29] – not only change the political landscape in New Delhi, but profoundly alter intellectual perspectives on such issues as multiculturalism, diversity, "secularism," and "communalism." In the process, each of these issues becomes a lens through which gender is refracted time and again in very specific ways. For activist groups, this means that all the old perspectives will have to be further broadened to include considerations of religion and caste, and that not merely by adding and mixing. If the Indian women's movement developed over the years a partial critique of Marxism – "Marxism does not have an analysis of women's oppression that anywhere near matches the sophistication or the scope of its analysis of economic exploitation," wrote Tharu in 1986 (4) – this critique did not at any time extend to the Marxist paradigm itself, or to assumptions about rationality and the primacy of class in conceptualizing social oppression. Groups like Stree Shakti clearly had the tools to connect the worlds of international finance to the daily lives of women, but even their delineations of the "personal" did not significantly include considerations of caste or religion. Class, and within it gender, were the social unifiers within this scheme; after all, religion and caste represented only such primeval affiliations as were bound to fade in modernity. The Mandal-Masjid years challenged just these assumptions with bewildering force, shaping modern Hindu ethnicism to a large degree and galvanizing what is known in India today as the Dalit movement. It became impossible after these "events" to deal with categories like gender *except* in relation to other markers of social difference. Since the early 1990s, then, feminists have grown increasingly concerned with describing how women's experiences, roles, access to justice, political participation, educational opportunities, and more are each modulated along religious and caste lines. In other words, caste and religion had joined gender – and complicated it – as fundamental cat-

egories of social analysis. As Tharu notes, "It has become increasingly clear to us...that women's studies or feminist research is not necessarily only about women. Its starting point is certainly women...[but] the question of women is not a separate issue. *Gender is central to our social architecture*" (Tharu 1990:63, my emphasis; see also Tharu and Niranjana 1996). So the focus shifts in the mid-1990s, not away from gender, of course, but to the "social architecture" within which gender is inscribed. "As a result of the work we have done," says Anveshi's most recent brochure, expressing a sentiment I believe most other academically oriented women's groups would equally endorse, "it has become clear to us that women's studies is about changing the situation of women by also challenging received notions of caste, class and community. This awareness, in particular, has had an important bearing on many of our ongoing projects."

I have explored the theoretical implications of this new awareness for Indian activism elsewhere; in closing, therefore I restrict myself to a few cursory remarks on the place of the feminist NGO in a globalizing world. For although it cannot be said that such approaches as this chapter has described are the direct outcomes of globalization, it is also true that this model of activism thrives in a global(izing) context. The recognition, for instance, that the activist approach to any given issue needs to be pitched at multiple levels – so education needs to be addressed as a social issue at the grassroots level, as a pedagogical issue within academic circles, as a policy issue for planners and politicians, and in some combination thereof at international meetings – enables and indeed requires activists to traverse both grassroots and global terrains, translating concepts or refocusing them as needed. The fact that activists are usually involved with local studies (on governance, health, and environmental issues, for instance), while being active members of the NAWO (National Association of Women's Organizations) and IAWS (Indian Association for Women's Studies),

and occasional travelers to foreign universities and UN-organized or other meetings,
bears testimony to the fluid, multidimensional character of Indian feminist activism,
its ability to function within a range of more-
or-less globalized frameworks. The further
recognition that activists cannot, if only because of their own upper-class/caste positioning, claim to represent the interests of Dalits
and minorities demands an activism that is
discussion-, dialogue-, and research-centered,
that provides organic intellectuals and local
groups the opportunities for interaction, ensures that their diverse perspectives are represented in the mainstream presses, academic
writings, international conferences, and so
on. As such, much contemporary Indian
feminist activism both helps create and pre-
supposes the existence of international networks of activists, writers, and scholars;
draws on the resources of international agencies in order to be able to make the case for
localized social change. Globalization does
not disappear as an object of activist critique,
far from it; as a range of cultural and economic processes that alter people's lives it is
better understood for the differential impact
it has on different groups of people. It is an
irony, then, or even more an indication of
globalization's varied potential that such critique should be sustained, indeed refined, by
an activist praxis that draws upon the many
exchanges of a globalizing world to conduct
its daily work.

NOTES

A version of this chapter appears in my book,
"Hindutva" in the Culture of Ethnicism
(Lanham, MD: Rowman & Littlefield, forth-
coming). My grateful thanks to Rowman &
Littlefield for allowing me to excerpt sections
of the book here.

1   The erstwhile state of Hyderabad was
    governed, in British times, by the Asaf
    Jah dynasty, of which the Nizam Osman

Ali Khan was the last ruler. When the
future of the princely state was thrown
into jeopardy by political developments
at the national level, a paramilitary wing
of the Majlis Ittehaad-ul-Muslimeen
(MIM), known as the Razakars, assumed
the responsibility of guarding the boundaries of the state. Though *razakar* means
"volunteer," the group gained notoriety in
border regions for creating mini-regimes
of terror. Hyderabad joined the Indian
Union only after Operation Polo brought
the Indian army into the state in 1948.
With the linguistic reorganization of
states in 1956, the State of Hyderabad
was trifurcated, and the Telangana region
(to which the present-day city of Hyderabad belongs) joined Andhra Pradesh. The
Telangana Armed Struggle that took
place between 1948 and 1951 was organized largely by the CPI, and saw the Razakars, the landlords, and later, the Indian
army, each in turn, as enemies of the
people, each representing the might and
power of a still essentially oppressive,
feudal state.

2   Also, as Lalita would later tell me, such
    titles as *Sandino's Daughters: Testimonies
    of Nicaraguan Women in Struggle, Let
    Me Speak! The Testimony of Domitila,
    a Woman of the Bolivian Mines*, and
    Charlotte Perkins Gilman's *The Yellow
    Wallpaper*.

3   The POW's complete draft manifesto is
    included in an Appendix to Omvedt's
    book. There are parallels here that we
    may note in passing: feminist conscious-
    ness in the United States of the 1960s also
    developed out of women's experiences
    participating in new left movements. As
    Sara Evans writes: "women from the
    new left explained the sources of their
    new awareness by pointing to the disc-
    repancy between the movement's ega-
    litarian ideology and the oppression
    they continued to experience within it"
    (1979:220). Evans points out, however,
    that "the new left did more than simply
    perpetuate the oppression of women,"
    but that "even more importantly, it
    created new arenas – social space – within

which women could develop a new sense of self-worth and independence; it provided new role models...and allowed [women] to claim the movement's ideology for themselves" (220). In the Indian context, the task for Hyderabad's activists became one of distancing women's issues from the paradigmatic control of Marxist thought – and so this kind of genealogical connection that Evans traces in the American context is also not often acknowledged as such, though it remains equally relevant.

4   Interestingly, Sanjay Gandhi's was a program that targeted men (requiring vasectomies for men with more than two children) rather than women. This fact is not often remembered, though virtually all population-control programs since that time have focused predictably on supplying birth control (hormonal contraceptives over devices) to women.

5   The first Indian Civil Rights Union was formed much earlier, of course, in 1936, in the context of anticolonial civil disobedience movements. The modern civil liberties movement, however, did not begin until around the time of the Emergency.

6   Andhra Pradesh Civil and Democratic Rights Convention.

7   Andhra Pradesh Civil Liberties Committee.

8   People's Union for Civil Liberties/People's Union for Democratic Rights.

9   V. M. Tarkunde (President); Nabakrishna Choudari (Orissa); M. V. Ramamurthy (Hyderabad); Kaloji Narayana Rao (Warangal, AP); Balwant Reddy (Hyderabad); K. Pratap Reddy (Hyderabad); K. G. Kannabiran (Hyderabad); B. G. Verghese (Delhi), and Arun Shourie (Delhi).

10 "Stree Shakti Sanghatana" does not lend itself well to translation. Literally, it means "Women – Power – Organization." The core group included K. Lalita, who had been President of the POW; Veena Shatruguna, a physician with the National Institute for Nutrition in Hyderabad; Susie J. Tharu, who taught (and still does) at the Central Institute for English and Foreign Languages; Rama Melkote, a lecturer in political science at Osmania University, and Lalita's one-time teacher; Vasanth Kannabiran, who taught English at Reddy College. Several others would join the group and participate in its activities until the dissolution of Stree Shakti: Uma Maheshwari, who approached the group first in need of help herself and now works on issues of women's health; D. Vasantha, a speech therapist at Osmania University; Vijayakumari, now an architect; Kalpana Kannabiran, then a student and now President of Asmita; Gita Ramaswamy, ex-POW member, who now runs the Hyderabad Book Trust; Ratnamala, who eventually became President of the APCLC; Kameshwari Jandhyala, who later initiated and headed the government's Andhra Pradesh Mahila Samata in Hyderabad; and scholars Ramarajyam, Sumati Nair, and Krishna Kumari. Still others would come and go over the years. Stree Shakti remained more an idea than an active organization until the second group of women joined in (my thanks to Asmita for this and other clarifications). All the original Stree Shakti members and several others associated with the group over its life continue to live and work (as activists, among other things) in Hyderabad.

11 Perhaps obviously, this attempt at egalitarianism was not built on the concept of "sisterhood" that once characterized North American white feminist discourse. Nor was it directly a reply to that notion, though other Indian activists also have lent their voices to that critique. Drawing on the Latino concept of *compañera* ("companionship," or "partnership"), María Lugones (1995) has suggested a notion of "pluralist friendship'" as an alternative model that I believe more closely approximates that on which Stree Shakti was formed, although not quite so self-consciously. The "company of women," to borrow Sara Suleri's (nostalgic) words describing an

characteristic feature of domestic life in the Subcontinent, gave Stree Shakti its twin rationales of looseness and of egalitarianism in the context of political struggle. "Compañera," continues Lugones, "can be and is used in hierarchies...although there is some tension there. The term is most at home in an egalitarian political companionship where everyone shares the rights and burdens of political struggle" (134). But as the "rights and burdens" could never entirely be evenly distributed in service to the egalitarian ideal, the feminist model of friendship would have to be modified too in Stree Shakti's case, as we shall soon see.

12   While this was true of discussions, however, the tension between languages has never entirely disappeared: there has always been, to lesser or greater extents, a palpable hierarchy of languages. Predictably, English has retained its position of dominance and privilege and giving English speakers – and later also those fluent in theoretical vocabularies of various kinds – an edge, a greater visibility, and an authority, all of which are often the sources of much discomfort and sometimes also of conflict. In an attempt to bridge these kinds of gulfs, Asmita regularly oversees the translation of English texts and essays into Telugu and Urdu (the two most widely spoken local languages), and Anveshi has formed the Telugu Materials Production Committee to undertake translations of important theoretical works from their original English into Telugu. Asmita also regularly oversees the translation of important texts and essays written in English into both Telugu and Urdu. Sometime before this, ex-POW member Gita Ramaswamy also established the Hyderabad Book Trust (HBT), explicitly for the purposes of translating important books on a variety of subjects from other Indian and foreign languages into Telugu. Although at the time of its formation, the HBT explicitly intended to

reach a wider (Communist) Party audience (as a means of educating the cadre to fight party oppressions), it continues its work today I believe with a broader purpose, complementing the work done by the Anveshi Committee and by Asmita, and often working in conjunction with these organizations.

13   In September, 1998, when a one-time Stree Shakti member was made President of the Andhra Pradesh Civil Liberties Committee – now a group with openly Naxalite sympathies and with clear M/L Party backing – some activists joked that they had always wondered who the "plant" from the Left was, and now they knew. Party connections are no longer of much importance to activist groups, although affiliations clearly still matter as indications of personal politics.

14   Kannabiran and Shatruguna (1986:24). Different members of Stree Shakti have written about the campaigns the group took up over the years (see Kannabiran 1986, Kannabiran and Kannabiran 1997, Kannabiran and Shatruguna 1986, Tharu and Melkote 1983). I do not therefore reproduce an exhaustive account of those here, but provide an overview with an eye to understanding the evolution of the group's ideological perspectives and strategies.

15   Specifically, the amendments being sought were as follows: "to include specified punishments for rape of a wife during separation, rape by a public servant, by a superintendent of a jail, and by hospital staff. The amendments would also hold all participants in a gang rape liable...shift the burden of proof to the accused in cases of custodial rape or rape of minors ... [disallow] the use of the victim's past sexual history, except where relating to the accused, in the trial" (Kannabiran 1986:605).

16   "Dowry death" refers to the killing of young married women when their natal families do not meet demands for more dowry. Husbands and parents-in-law

are often involved, and the murders usually made to look like kitchen accidents or suicides. Dowry deaths first came to the attention of women's groups in cities like Delhi, when it was noticed that a great many "accidental deaths" of young women were being reported, with no further explanation or investigation of the incidents.

17 Interview with Susie Tharu, August 12, 1998.

18 Years later, feminists would again become involved in a very similar campaign – similar arguments for the urgent need for contraceptives, and similar arguments opposing it – when Norplant devices were introduced in India. Clearly, the battle had to be fought one company or one device at a time.

19 And related to this question, also whether involvement in the campaign would only reinforce the popular view of women as consumers. It bears mentioning that these sorts of concerns were named at least once before, during the Maharashtrian Anti-Price-Rise campaigns of the early 1970s: why should food and food prices be specifically women's concerns, when both men and women have to eat? Should this be a women's agitation, or should it not involve men also? What kind of images of women would such movements be projecting, if only women were to get involved?

20 The book was also published in London by Zed Books, introducing Stree Shakti to an international audience.

21 The translated book is titled *Savaalaaksha Sandehaalu,* or *One Hundred Thousand Doubts: Women and Health Issues* (n.d.).

22 Shortly after I completed fieldwork in Hyderabad, Osmania's Chancellor told Anveshi it could no longer use this space, and the group soon moved into its new home, still not far from the university, in Barkatpura. Anveshi never wanted the control of the university, but clearly proximity to the space demarcated by the university campus was (both practically and ideologically) an advantage.

23 It is worth mentioning in this context that I was turned down for a few interviews with women who would have been able to talk about this period, for health-related or other reasons, but heard from friends that this may have been because of a reluctance to talk – least of all to an outsider – about the politics of the period. Others offered sketchy accounts or no information about these interim years. As a result, I have few resources to be able to adequately trace the many and complex processes that eventually led to the formation of Asmita after the dispersal of Stree Shakti.

24 The other members involved in establishing Asmita were: Volga (Feminist Study Circle); Rukmini Rao (DDS); Vijaya Kumari (Stree Shakti); Kishori Sharma (an architect, who first provided Asmita with free office space and later designed Asmita's new offices); Indira Jena (Stree Shakti, who would provide Asmita with funding); Leela Masilamoni (English Professor); V. Lalitha (Nava Vikas and Telugu Lecturer), Jamuna, Kalpana Alexander (obstetrician and gynecologist) and Vasanth Kannabiran (Stree Shakti and DDS); Kalpana Kannabiran (Stree Shakti, Maithri). My thanks to Asmita for sending me the complete list.

25 A note about the comparison of Asmita and Anveshi: activists associated with both organizations insist that they do not compare themselves or their work in any way; that they are by no means competitors in the field of women's activism. While I certainly concur that the two groups are not competitors (I would suggest their work and approaches are complementary), a comparison of these two models of activism is inevitable. In tracing a history of activist praxis in Hyderabad, I trace also the processes by which shared experiences of urban grassroots activism eventually produced a variety of groups, a variety of approaches, and indeed a variety of activisms. At the same time, and from

the point of view of an outsider such as myself, it is impossible to ignore the fact that Asmita and Anveshi are the only *urban* women's NGOs which function in local, national and, indeed, also international contexts, facilitate and produce women's studies research on a regular basis, and which are far more interested in conceptualizing women's, caste, and minority issues rather in engaging themselves in grassroots activism. Most other organizations that focus on women's issues in Hyderabad are directly involved in establishing or running educational institutions, micro-credit finance initiatives, and more. My interest in the kind of institution that produces a particular kind of analysis of women's issues leads, then, inevitably to Asmita and Anveshi and so also to a comparison of the models of their activisms: it defines both the scope and the limitations of the present undertaking.

26 At the time fieldwork for this project was conducted (1997–9), Asmita was funded largely by the Humanist Institute for Co-Operation with Developing Countries (HIVOS) in the Netherlands (with some of its initiatives being supported by other local and international organizations: for instance, its Summer School in Women's Studies by the Ford Foundation's Rights and Social Justice program), and Anveshi – for at least two years previously – by the Ford Foundation.

27 Some key examples of their work: on gender justice in the context of minority rights, Anveshi Law Committee (1997) and on the rustication of Dalit students from the University of Hyderabad, Anveshi Law Committee (2002).

28 I should point out that this is not my conjecture, but a response drawn from a conversation with Kalpana Kannabiran, President of Asmita, several weeks after the inauguration of Asmita's new office. Criticisms of Asmita's institutional glamor aside, the inaugural party clearly provided an opportunity

to meet and discuss funding with the Indian representative of HIVOS, who was present.

29 The late 1980s and early 1990s are commonly referred to in India as the Mandal-Masjid years, after two events that gripped the country, set several new movements in motion, and altered forever the way women's groups would look at the twin issues of religion and caste. The first was an unexpectedly dramatic and furious upper-caste response to the then Prime Minister V. P. Singh's decision to implement the recommendations of the Mandal Commission Report, which called for increased reservation quotas for certain lower-caste groups. Also around this time, riding a wave of Hindu (upper-caste?) anger after the fallout of the Shah Bano affair, the then BJP President L. K. Advani began his famous *Rath Yatra* (journey on a chariot) demanding the demolition of the Babri Masjid in Ayodhya, said to have been built on the ruins of a temple marking the birthplace of the Hindu diety Rama. Riots followed in the path of the *rath*, but the worst rioting happened after the mosque was demolished by *kar sevaks* (volunteers) of the Sangh Parivar in December 1992, shattering the cosmopolitan veneers of even cities like Bombay.

REFERENCES

Anveshi Law Committee
  1997 Is Gender Justice only a Legal Issue? Political Sstakes in the UCC Debate. Economic and Political Weekly (March 1–8): 453–458.
—— 2002. Caste and the Metropolitan University. Economic and Political Weekly (March 23): 1100–1102.
Chatterjee, Partha
  1989 Colonialism, Nationalism, and Colonized Women: The Contest in India. American Ethnologist 16(4):622–633.

Evans, Sara
  1979 Personal Politics: The Roots of Women's Liberation in the Civil Rights Movement and the New Left. New York: Knopf.
K. Lalita
  1988 Women in Revolt: A Historical Analysis of the POW. *In* Women's Struggles and Strategies. Saskia Wieringa, ed. Pp. 54–67. Brookfield, VT: Gower.
Kakarala, Sitharamam
  1993 Civil Rights Movement in India. Ph.D. dissertation, Center for Social Studies, Surat.
Kannabiran, Vasantha
  1986 Report from SSS, a Women's Group in Hyderabad. Feminist Studies 12(3):601–612.
Kannabiran, Vasantha, and Kalpana Kannabiran
  1997 Looking at Ourselves: The Women's Movement in Hyderabad. *In* Feminist Genealogies, Colonial Legacies, Democratic Futures. M. Jacqui Alexander and Chandra Talpade Mohanty, eds. Pp. 259–279. New York: Routledge.
Kannabiran, Vasantha, and Veena Shatruguna
  1986 The Relocation of Political Practice – The Stree Shakti Sanghatana Experience. Lokayan Bulletin 4(6):23–34.
Kumar, Radha
  1993 The History of Doing. London: Verso
Lugones, María C., in collaboration with Pat Alake Rosezelle
  1995 Sisterhood and friendship as feminist models. *In* Feminism and Community. Penny A. Weiss and Marilyn Friedman, eds. Pp. 135–145. Philadelphia, PA: Temple University Press.
Omvedt, Gail
  1980 We Will Smash This Prison: Indian Women in Struggle. London: Zed Books.

Sinha, Mrinalini.
  2000. Refashioning Mother India: Feminism and Nationalism in Late Colonial India. Feminist Studies 26(3):623–644.
Stree Shakti Sanghatana
  1989 "We Were Making History..." Life Stories of Women in the Telangana People's Struggle. New Delhi: Kali for Women.
Tharu, Susie
  1986 The Politics of Personal Struggle. *In* Women Take One: Beginning of a Dialogue in the Third World Women's Film Festival 1986. Abha Bhaiya and Sheba Chhachhi, eds. Pp. 1–5. New Delhi: Jagori.
—— 1990. "Introducing Anveshi." Lokayan Bulletin 8 (3): 59–63.
Tharu, Susie, and K. Lalita
  1991 Women Writing in India: 600 B.C. to the Present. Susie Tharu and K. Lalita, eds. Volume I. Delhi: Oxford University Press.
—— 1993. Women Writing in India: The 20th Century. Susie Tharu and K. Lalita, eds. Volume II. Delhi: Oxford University Press.
Tharu, Susie, and Rama Melkote
  1983 An Investigative Analysis of Working Women's Hostels in India. Signs 9(1):164–171.
Tharu, Susie, and Tejaswini Niranjana
  1996 Problems for a Contemporary Theory of Gender. Subaltern Studies IX. Shahid Amin and Dipesh Chakrabarty, eds. Pp. 232–260. New Delhi: Oxford University Press.
Wells, Betty L
  2002 Context, Strategy, Ground: Rural Women Organizing to Confront Local/Global Economic Issues. *In* Women's Activism and Globalization: Linking Local Struggles and Transnational Politics. Nancy A. Naples and Manisha Desai, eds. Pp. 142–155. New York: Routledge.

Index